The
Social Work
Dictionary

The Social Work Dictionary

5th Edition

by

Robert L. Barker

NASW PRESS

National Association of Social Workers
Washington, DC

Terry Mizrahi, PhD, MSW, *President*
Elizabeth J. Clark, PhD, ACSW, MPH, *Executive Director*

Cheryl Y. Bradley, *Publisher*
Paula L. Delo, *Executive Editor*
Stephen D. Pazdan, *Copy Editor and Project Coordinator*
Gail W. Martin, *Proofreader (Editorial Associates)*
Elizabeth Mitchell, *Proofreader*
Andre Barnett, *Staff Editor*
Christina Bromley, *Editorial Assistant*

Cover by Eye to Eye Design Studio, Bristow, VA

Interior design and typesetting by Cynthia Stock, Silver Spring, MD

Printed and bound by Port City Press, Baltimore, MD

Library of Congress Cataloging-in-Publication Data

Barker, Robert L.
   The social work dictionary / by Robert L. Barker.— 5th ed.
      p. cm.
   ISBN 0-87101-355-X (pbk.)
     1. Social service—Dictionaries. 2. Social service—United States—Dictionaries. I. Title.

HV12.B37 2003
361.3'03—dc21   2003054062

Printed in the United States of America

Contents

Editorial Review Board

Foreword

NASW is proud to publish the fifth edition of *The Social Work Dictionary*, reflecting the exciting evolution of the social work profession and signaling new opportunities for growth in the future.

The expansion of social work research in recent years has enhanced several methods of social work practice. In addition, the changing national landscape of health and mental health services has dramatically reshaped the way many social workers assist their clients.

As a result, the language of the profession has shifted to capture not only the development of social work practice over time, but also the increasing diversity of the people and communities we serve. Social work skills are in demand everywhere—in schools, hospitals, community agencies, and businesses of every type—and our language expands constantly to reflect the profession's impressive scope.

Dr. Robert L. Barker first applied his scholarship to the task of creating this important reference work in 1987, with the publication of the first edition of *The Social Work Dictionary*. The *Dictionary* has since become recognized as a key element of the social work profession's knowledge base.

Students consult *The Social Work Dictionary* during their orientation to the profession and then rely on it throughout their studies to obtain concise and accurate answers to specific practice questions. Essential to researchers and librarians alike, the *Dictionary* also sits on the desks of numerous social work practitioners and other human services professionals seeking information within and outside their own specialties.

For the fifth edition, Dr. Barker has added more than 1,000 new entries, updates for over 2,000 definitions from previous editions, and Web site addresses for many of the several hundred organizations described.

Thank you for making *The Social Work Dictionary* part of your resource collection. We are confident that you will turn to it regularly as a valued source of professional knowledge.

Elizabeth J. Clark, PhD, MPH, ACSW
Executive Director
National Association of Social Workers

Preface

The language of social work, like the profession itself, continues to grow and become more complex. This is the result of both increased social work knowledge and the profession's desire to communicate with greater precision. It is also the product of closer relationships with other professions and segments of society, each of which has its own jargon and terminology.

A dynamic vocabulary is healthy but represents a formidable challenge. To express themselves effectively and to comprehend the words of their colleagues and members of other professions, social workers must be familiar with an extensive body of complex terms. They also are expected to have ready access to a variety of resources, organizations, and services that can help meet the needs of their clients.

Another challenge to clear communication arises from the divergent specialties and conceptual orientations within the profession itself. For example, social workers who are policymakers or social advocates do not usually share identical vocabularies with their colleagues in clinical work. Even within a single social work practice specialty, there is risk of misunderstanding because of the variety of theoretical perspectives in current use. Clinical social workers with psychodynamic orientations, for example, may have different interpretations of terms used by their colleagues with behaviorist, psychosocial systems, existential, or cognitive perspectives, and vice versa.

Although these trends increase the potential for communication problems, social workers face mounting pressure to minimize such difficulties. Malpractice suits and other legal actions have become more frequent. So, too, are sanctions against professionals who misinterpret or improperly disseminate information. Society demands that professionals prove they are competent and current, usually through licensing and certification exams. To a great extent, passing these exams requires that the social worker understand the terms and concepts used in the profession.

The Social Work Dictionary was developed to address these challenges. The idea for it originated in the early 1980s when I participated on a panel to write questions for social work state licensing exams. All the panelists often debated about how the profession generally understood certain terms that it used. All the test writers bemoaned social work's lack of a glossary of its language to use in arbitrating these disputes. As a result, I decided to try to write *The Social Work Dictionary*.

I began by compiling a long list of entries that have appeared in the indexes of the major social work journals and textbooks of the past three decades. The journals and texts were those in most general use in graduate and undergraduate schools of social work and in the larger social agencies. I added to this list by going through the indexes of the journals, manuals, and textbooks of disciplines related to social work, especially in psychiatry, law, sociology, economics, anthropology, and psychology. Over time, I presented the list to hundreds of my colleagues in social work education and clinical practice as well as students and members of related professions. On the basis of their suggestions, hundreds of additional terms were added to this list.

In defining the terms, I found it necessary to review how they were used by different writers. All too frequently, I found slight differences in the interpretations various writers gave to certain terms. I tried to provide a definition that was closest to the majority view and to the mainstream of social work thinking. I also tried to make each definition original for this project, a policy I have maintained through all editions of the published work. No definitions are deliberately quoted from any known published sources.

Once I finished writing the definitions, they were critiqued, edited, and revised by several hundred colleagues and students. I began the evaluations by presenting two or three pages of definitions to my students at The Catholic University of America. Then I gave short glossaries to students, through their professors, at several other schools of social work in the Washington, DC, metropolitan area. Students and faculty at Howard University, Gallaudet University, and the University of Maryland, as well as Catholic, were the original participants. The definitions were thus subjected to heavy scrutiny for two years before I felt ready to consider publication of a dictionary of our profession's terminology.

After the National Association of Social Workers (NASW) and NASW Press agreed to publish the work, I assembled a panel of colleagues who were widely considered to be among the preeminent scholars and practitioners in their respective fields. The members of the editorial review board were chosen for their considerable expertise in at least one area of social work knowledge or a related field such as medicine, law, administration, or economics. To each member, I sent approximately 50 to 100 definitions that were understood to be within the panelist's realm of special expertise. I asked them to review their definitions as to accuracy, clarity, conciseness, and relevance of examples. Typically, three different experts reviewed each definition.

The experts did not always agree with one another on how a term should be defined or on what parts of it should be emphasized, so compromises had to be made. Some reviewers believed certain words were offensive or outdated and recommended their exclusion. However, I chose to retain most of those terms that are still in common, perhaps improper, use and to indicate why they are considered improper for use by competent professionals. This reflects my view that the purpose of a dictionary is to explain the meaning of terms, not judge whether people should use the terms or pretend they do not exist.

This process of reviewing my definitions has been followed throughout all five editions of *The Social Work Dictionary*. Every term and definition that I have written has been evaluated, edited, and sometimes modified by at least three experts and two editors. With each revision and updating of the *Dictionary*, I asked many new reviewers to join the editorial review board. Some members are new to this edition, whereas others have served on the board through all five editions. With each new edition, all the defined terms were re-reviewed and, when appropriate, updated or revised. Some definitions were deleted with each new edition. But mostly the *Dictionary* has grown. The first edition contained approximately 4,000 definitions; the current fifth edition contains well over 9,000 defined terms.

The first edition of *The Social Work Dictionary* was published in early 1987. Subsequent editions appeared in 1991, 1995, and 1999 and were all well received. Colleagues from around the world expressed approval and indicated where the *Dictionary* was being used—in schools of social work, in social agency libraries, in licensing exam preparation centers, and in the offices of experienced and novice social work practitioners.

The terms defined here are used in social work administration, research, policy development, and planning; community organization; human growth and development; health and mental health; macro and micro social work; and clinical theory and practice. They are the terms that relate to social work's values and ethics and to its historical development. The definitions include descriptions of some of the organizations, trends, people, philosophies, and legislation that have played major roles in the development of social work and social welfare.

The biographical entries are reminders of the rich lives of people who have made significant contributions to the profession and to social welfare. The criteria for including these small biographies are that the person is now deceased and is identified as a member of the social work profession or is primarily known for significant work in social welfare. The section entitled "Milestones in the Development of Social Work and Social Welfare" represents a chronology of the significant developments in the United States and the world toward social welfare policies and practices and the betterment of humanity.

The terms are those that have been developed within the profession as well as those that social workers have adopted for their own use from sociology, anthropology, medicine, law, psychology, and economics. The symptoms and diagnostic labels for various forms of mental disorders are defined as they are understood by social workers, psychiatrists, psychologists, and other mental health professionals. All the diagnostic terms and criteria found here are consistent with those in the *Diagnostic and Statistical Manual of Mental Disorders, Fourth Edition;* the *International Classification of Diseases, Tenth Edition;* and the *Person-in-Environment (PIE) System.* Many terms are derived from the theoretical orientations of psychodynamic, cognitive–behavioral, and existential, as well as systemic and linear, approaches. Also included are concepts in social work practice with individuals, groups, families, and communities.

As before, this fifth edition of *The Social Work Dictionary* for the most part uses the standard format for professional dictionaries and glossaries. The terms are listed in word order. Many terms are cross-referenced, and words that appear in italics within definitions are themselves defined elsewhere in the publication. This dictionary does not purport to present all the words a social worker could ever use, nor does it provide "official" definitions of terms. The development of new knowledge and changing perspectives will necessitate commensurate revisions of the publication. *The Social Work Dictionary* strives to give the social worker an abbreviated interpretation of the words, concepts, organizations, historical events, and values that are relevant to the profession. As such, it is designed to provide a concise overview of social work's terminology, not encyclopedic detail. Naturally, it is hoped that any omissions, discrepancies, and errors are minimal. But in a dynamic field populated by intelligent professionals with divergent views and experiences, it is inevitable that some discrepancies will occur. As the author of this work, I assume full responsibility for the terms that have been included and excluded as well as for the way they are defined.

The NASW Press and I plan to produce subsequent editions of *The Social Work Dictionary* every few years. I urge anyone who has suggestions, recommended changes, additions, deletions, or corrections to contact me by letter or e-mail in care of the NASW Press. I promise to give your suggestions close consideration and will reply personally to you. In this way, the *Dictionary* will remain a living, ever-improving document—the product of input from the widest possible range of social workers and members of related professions. I hope that this edition of *The Social Work Dictionary* will continue to be a useful tool for social workers in their efforts to communicate clearly and achieve professional understanding.

—*Robert L. Barker*
July 2003

Acknowledgments

Many people have made significant contributions to the development of *The Social Work Dictionary*. The members of the editorial review board have always been supportive, generous in sharing their ideas and expertise, and prompt in responding to specific questions. The many baccalaureate, master's, and doctoral students at several schools of social work and universities reviewed terms to ensure that the definitions were clear and relevant to their needs.

Most helpful were the staff members of the libraries at the National Institute of Mental Health, Bethesda, MD; the Library of Congress, Washington, DC; The Catholic University of America, Washington, DC; the University of Washington School of Social Work, Seattle; the University of Washington—Tacoma; the Pacific Lutheran University, Parkland, WA; the Tacoma, Washington, Public Library system; and especially the NASW National Social Work Library, Washington, DC.

Those who were especially resourceful with specific projects included John English, PhD (educational philosophy); Michael G. Donovan, PhD candidate (urban policy and planning); Robert Steiner, PhD (computer science); Cynthia Branson, MA (speech pathologies); Mary Loovis, MA (housing resources); Chris Webster, PhD (employment law); Francis D. Miller (neoconservative philosophy); John Eyler, PhD (philosophy of science and epidemiology); Florence Sandler, PhD (bibliotherapy); Wilmot Ragsdale, MA (New Deal history); Kirsten Swanson Barker (health care and child nutrition); Walter Lowrie, PhD (historical analysis); Greg Yuckert, JD (labor law); Carol Webster, PhD (state health and welfare programs); James Brown, PhD (social philosophy); Ronald Pinckney, LLB (tax law and policy); Kent Hooper, PhD (language studies); and Kenneth Witkoe (radio/TV/media communications).

Staff members at the National Association of Social Workers and at the NASW Press were always dedicated, efficient, and competent. NASW Executive Directors and NASW Press leadership lent their encouragement, guidance, and expertise to this project. The meticulous tasks of copyediting and fact checking were accomplished effectively by NASW staff throughout the first four editions. I also want to note that Steve Pazdan did an outstanding job as the copy editor for this fifth edition.

Finally, one person deserves considerable praise for her patience, support, and editorial suggestions throughout this project. Her knowledge, especially in the realm of educational technology, was invaluable. *The Social Work Dictionary* would not have been possible without the help of my wife, Dr. Mary Elizabeth Donovan.

—*R.L.B.*

Acronyms Frequently Used by Social Workers

AA	Alcoholics Anonymous
AAA	American Arbitration Association; Area Agencies on Aging
AADA	Association for Adult Development and Aging (of ACA)
AAFSD	American Association of Food Stamp Directors (of APHSA)
AAGW	American Association of Group Workers
AAHSW	American Association of Hospital Social Workers
AAIA	Association on American Indian Affairs
AAISW	American Association of Industrial Social Workers
AAMD	American Association on Mental Deficiency
AAMFT	American Association for Marital and Family Therapy
AAMHPC	American Association of Mental Health Professionals in Corrections
AAMR	American Association on Mental Retardation
AAMSW	American Association of Medical Social Workers
AAP	affirmative action program
AAPOR	American Association of Public Opinion Research
AAPSW	American Association of Psychiatric Social Workers
AAPWA	American Association of Public Welfare Attorneys (of APHSA)
AARP	American Association of Retired Persons
AAS	American Association of Suicidology
AASCIPSW	American Association of Spinal Cord Injury Psychologists and Social Workers
AASECT	American Association of Sex Educators, Counselors, and Therapists
AASSW	American Association of Schools of Social Work
AASW	Advanced Award in Social Work (in the United Kingdom); American Association of Social Workers; Asian American Social Workers; Australian Association of Social Workers
AASWG	Association for the Advancement of Social Work with Groups
AATA	American Art Therapy Association
AB	Aid to the Blind
ABA	American Bar Association
ABAWDs	able-bodied adults without dependents
ABD	all but dissertation
ABE	adult basic education; American Board of Examiners in Clinical Social Work
ABL	adaptive behavior level
ABPN	American Board of Psychiatry and Neurology
ABW	average body weight
AC	alternative care
ACA	American Counseling Association
ACBSW	Academy of Certified Baccalaureate Social Workers
ACCH	Association for the Care of Children's Health
ACF	Administration for Children and Families (of DHHS)
ACLU	American Civil Liberties Union
ACM	anticult movement

ACME	Association for Couples in Marriage Enrichment
ACOAs	adult children of alcoholics
ACORN	Association of Community Organizations for Reform Now
ACOSA	Association for Community Organization and Social Administration
ACOSS	Australian Council of Social Service
ACSW	Academy of Certified Social Workers
ACT-UP	AIDS Coalition to Unleash Power
ACYF	Administration on Children, Youth, and Families (of DHHS)
A&D	alcohol and drug
ADA	Americans for Democratic Action; Americans with Disabilities Act
ADAA	Anxiety Disorders Association of America
ADAM	American Divorce Association of Men, International
ADAMHA	Alcohol, Drug Abuse, and Mental Health Administration
ADD	Administration on Developmental Disabilities (of DHHS); attention deficit disorder
ADEA	Age Discrimination in Employment Act
ADF	alternative dispute resolution
ADHD	attention deficit hyperactivity disorder
ADL	activities of daily living; Anti-Defamation League
ADS	alternative delivery systems
ADTA	American Dance Therapy Association
AEA	Adult Education Association
AFC	adult foster care
AFDC	Aid to Families with Dependent Children
AFDC–EA	Aid to Families with Dependent Children—Emergency Assistance
AFDC–UP	Aid to Families with Dependent Children—Unemployed Parent Program
AFGE	American Federation of Government Employees
AFL–CIO	American Federation of Labor—Congress of Industrial Organizations
AFSCME	American Federation of State, County, and Municipal Employees
AFSW	Association of Federated Social Workers
AFTA	American Family Therapy Academy
AGE-SW	Association for Gerontology Education in Social Work
AGI	adjusted gross income
AGS	American Geriatrics Society
AHA	American Hospital Association
AHRQ	Agency for Health Care Research and Quality
AI	Amnesty International
AICF	American Immigration Control Foundation
AICP	Association for Improving the Condition of the Poor
AID	Agency for International Development
AIDS	acquired immune deficiency syndrome
AIM	American Indian Movement
AIME	average income monthly earnings
AIRS	Alliance of Information & Referral Systems
AIUSA	Amnesty International of the United States
AJLI	Association of Junior Leagues International
ALF	assisted living facility
ALI	American Law Institute
ALS	amyotrophic lateral sclerosis
ALSWE	Association of Latino Social Work Educators
AMA	American Medical Association

AMBER	Abducted Minor Broadcast Emergency Response
AMCD	Association for Multicultural Counseling and Development (of ACA)
AMHCA	American Mental Health Counselors Association
AMTA	American Music Therapy Association
ANA	Administration for Native Americans; American Nurses Association
ANOVA	analysis of variance
ANS	autonomic nervous system
ANSWER	Action Network for Social Work Education and Research
AoA	Administration on Aging (of DHHS)
AOSW	Association of Oncology Social Workers
APA	American Psychiatric Association
APHA	American Public Health Association
APHSA	American Public Human Services Association
API	Asian and Pacific Islanders
APM	annual program meeting
APS	adult protective services
APSAC	American Professional Society on the Abuse of Children
APTD	Aid to the Permanently and Totally Disabled
APWA	American Public Welfare Association (now APHSA)
ARA	American Relief Administration
ARC	AIDS-related complex; alien registration card (green card); American Red Cross; Association for Retarded Citizens
ARHP	Association of Reproductive Health Professionals
ART	assisted reproductive technology
ASCA	American School Counselors Association
ASCO	Association for the Study of Community Organizations
ASGW	Association for Specialists in Group Work (of ACA)
ASH	Action on Smoking and Health
ASHA	American Speech–Language–Hearing Association
ASL	American Sign Language
ASPA	American Society for Personnel Administrators
ASPCA	American Society for the Prevention of Cruelty to Animals
ASPCC	American Society for the Prevention of Cruelty to Children
ASW	Approved Social Worker (in England)
ASWB	Association of Social Work Boards
AT	appropriate technology
ATF	Bureau of Alcohol, Tobacco, Firearms and Explosives
ATOD	alcohol, tobacco, and other drugs
ATPD	Aid to the Totally and Permanently Disabled
ATR	Americans for Tax Reform
ATSDR	Agency for Toxic Substances and Disease Registry (of DHHS)
AVA	Association of Volunteer Administrators
AVSC	Association for Voluntary Surgical Contraception
AWO	Arbeiterwohlfahrt Bundesverband (of Germany)
AWSW	Association of Women in Social Work
AZT	azidothymidine
BAAF	British Adoption and Fostering
BAL	blood alcohol level
BASW	British Association of Social Workers

BB/BSA	Big Brothers/Big Sisters of America
BCD	Board Certified Diplomate in Clinical Social Work (of ABE)
BCRS	Bertha Capen Reynolds Society
BD	behavioral disorders
BEAM	brain electrical activity mapping
BEST	benefits eligibility screening tool
BFSA	Behaviorists for Social Action
BFT	behavioral family therapy
BGCA	Boys and Girls Clubs of America
BHP	Bureau of Health Professionals
BHRD	Bureau of Health Resources Development
BIA	Bureau of Immigration Appeals; Bureau of Indian Affairs
B.I.D.	take medication twice daily (from the Latin "bis in die")
BLM	Bureau of Land Management
BLS	Bureau of Labor Statistics
BMD	bone mineral density
BMR	basal metabolism rate
BOC	Bureau of the Census
BPD	Association of Baccalaureate Social Work Program Directors; bipolar disorder; borderline personality disorder
BRR	benefit reduction rate
BSA	Boy Scouts of America
BSW	bachelor of social work
BTS	Border and Transportation Security Directorate
CAB	Citizens Advice Bureau
CACFP	Child and Adult Care Food Program
CAI	Children's Aid International; computer-assisted instruction
CALC	Clergy and Laity Concerned
CAM	complementary and alternative medicine
CAN	child abuse and neglect
CAP	child access prevention; community action program
CAPI	computer-assisted personal interview
CAPTA	Child Abuse Prevention and Treatment Act
CARE	Community and Resource Exchange; Cooperative for Assistance and Relief Everywhere
CASA	court-appointed special advocate
CASS	computer-assisted social services
CASSP	Child and Adolescent Services System Program
CASSW	Canadian Association of Schools of Social Work
CASW	Canadian Association of Social Workers
C-ASWCM	Certified Advanced Social Work Case Manager
CAT	computerized axial tomography
CATI	computer-assisted telephone interviewing
CBP	Bureau of Customs and Border Protection
C-CATODSW	Certified Clinical Alcohol, Tobacco, and Other Drugs Social Worker
CCC	Civilian Conservation Corps; Commodity Credit Corporation
CCDBG	Child Care and Development Block Grant
CCETSW	Central Council for Education and Training in Social Work
CCF	Christian Children's Fund

CCMS	Child Care Management Service
CCR	Commission on Civil Rights
CCRC	continuing care retirement communities
CCSD	Canadian Council on Social Development
CCW	carrying concealed weapons
CDA	child development associate
CDC	Centers for Disease Control and Prevention
CDF	Chapter Development Fund; Children's Defense Fund
CD-ROM	compact disc—read-only memory
CEC	Council on Exceptional Children
CECs	continuing education credits
CEDAW	Convention on the Elimination of All Forms of Discrimination Against Women
CEIP	Carnegie Endowment for International Peace
CEN	U.S. Census Bureau
CEO	chief executive officer
CERCLA	Comprehensive Environmental Response, Compensation, and Liability Act
CES	current employment statistics
CETA	Comprehensive Employment and Training Act
CEUs	continuing education units
CFA	Child Find America
CFC	Combined Federal Campaign
CFS	chronic fatigue syndrome
CHAMPUS	Civilian Health and Medical Program of the Uniformed Services
CHAP	Children Have a Potential; Comprehensive Homeless Assistance Plan
CHEA	Council for Higher Education Accreditation
CHINS	children in need of supervision
CHIP	Children's Health Insurance Program; comprehensive health insurance plan
CHOICE	Concern for Health Options, Information, Care and Education
CHST	Canada Health and Social Transfer Program
CIA	Central Intelligence Agency
CID	crisis (or critical) incidence debriefing
CIDES	Inter-American Social Development Center
CIHRI	Committee for International Human Rights Inquiry
CIP	Cleveland International Program
CIRS	Certified Information and Referral Specialist
CIS	Bureau of Citizenship and Immigration Services; Cancer Information Service
CISD	critical incident stress debriefing
CLASP	Center for Law and Social Policy
CMHC	community mental health center
CMHS	Center for Mental Health Services
CMI	chronic mental illness
CMSA	Case Management Society of America
CNCS	Corporation for National and Community Service
CNPP	Center for Nutrition Policy and Promotion (of USDA)
CNS	central nervous system
COA	Commission on Accreditation
COAs	children of alcoholics
COBRA	Consolidated Omnibus Budget Reconciliation Act
COC	continuum of care
CODAs	children of deaf adults

COI	committee on inquiry
COLA	cost-of-living allowance (or adjustment)
COMPSYCH	Computer Software Services for Psychologists
CON	certificate of need
COPA	community-oriented primary care
COPD	chronic obstructive pulmonary disease
COPPA	Children's Online Privacy Protection Act
CORE	Congress of Racial Equality
CORF	comprehensive outpatient rehabilitation facility
CORPA	Council on Regulating Post-Secondary Education
COSs	Charity Organization Societies
COSAs	Children of Substance Abusers
COSSMHO	Coalition of Spanish-Speaking Mental Health Organizations
CP	cerebral palsy
CPA	Center for Policy Alternatives
CPI	Consumer Price Index
CPR	cardiopulmonary resuscitation; customary, prevailing, and reasonable
CPS	child protective services; curriculum policy statement
CPSC	Consumer Product Safety Commission
CPT	current procedural terminology
CPU	central processing unit
CQI	Child Quest International
CR	conditioned response
CRA	Community Reinvestment Act
CRC	Children's Rights Council
CROs	Children's Rights Officers (United Kingdom)
CRS	Catholic Relief Services; certified resource specialist
CS	conditioned stimulus
CSA	child support assurance
CSAP	Center for Substance Abuse Prevention
CSAT	Center for Substance Abuse Treatment
CSE	child support enforcement
CSHCN	children with special health care needs
CSOs	Community Service Organizations
CSP	Community Support Program
CSRS	Civil Service Retirement System
C-SSWS	Certified School Social Work Specialist
CST	child study team
C-SWCM	Certified Social Work Case Manager
CSWE	Council on Social Work Education
CSWF	Clinical Social Work Federation
CTCs	Community Technology Centers
CTS	carpal tunnel syndrome
CVA	cerebrovascular accident
CVS	chorionic villus sampling
CWEP	Community Work Experience Program
CWI	Child Welfare Institute
CWLA	Child Welfare League of America
CWS	Child Welfare Services; Church World Services
CYSED	children and youth with serious emotional disturbances

DALYs	disability adjusted life years
DARF	Depressives Anonymous—Recovery for Depression
DARS	Disciplinary Action Reporting System
dB	decibels
DBMS	database management system
DC	District of Columbia (Washington)
D&C	dilation and curettage
DCSW	Diplomate in Clinical Social Work
DD	developmental disability
DDS	Disability Determination Service
DEA	Drug Enforcement Administration
DF	dengue fever
DHEW	U.S. Department of Health, Education and Welfare
DHHHSW	Deaf, Hard of Hearing, and Hearing Social Workers
DHHS	U.S. Department of Health and Human Services
DHS	U.S. Department of Homeland Security
DHUD	U.S. Department of Housing and Urban Development
DI	Disability Insurance
DIALOG	online database for psychology, sociology, and related fields
DID	dissociative identity disorder
DipSW	Diploma in Social Work
DME	durable medical equipment
DMT	dimethyltryptamine
DNA	deoxyribonucleic acid
DNC	Democratic National Committee
DNR	do not resuscitate
DO	doctor of osteopathy
DOC	U.S. Department of Commerce
DOD	U.S. Department of Defense
DoE	U.S. Department of Education
DOE	U.S. Department of Energy
DOMA	Defense of Marriage Act
DOS	U.S. Department of State
DPD	dependent personality disorder
DPH	doctor of public health
DRGs	diagnosis-related groups
DSM	*Diagnosis and Statistical Manual of Mental Disorders*
DSM-III	*Diagnosis and Statistical Manual of Mental Disorders, Third Edition*
DSM-IV	*Diagnosis and Statistical Manual of Mental Disorders, Fourth Edition*
DSM-IV-TR	*Diagnosis and Statistical Manual of Mental Disorders, Fourth Edition, Text Revision*
DSS	decision support system; Department of Social Services
DSW	doctor of social work
DTs	delirium tremens
DUI	driving under the influence of alcohol or drugs
DWI	driving while intoxicated
DWP	Department for Work and Pensions (United Kingdom)
EAP	employee assistance program
EAPA	Employee Assistance Professionals Association
EBD	emotional or behavioral disorder

EBT	electron beam tomography; evidence-based practice
ECA	epidemiologic catchment area
ECF	extended care facility
ECHO	elder cottage housing opportunity
ECOA	Equal Credit Opportunity Act
ECOSOC	United Nations Economic and Social Council
ECP	empirical clinical practice
ECSWPR	European Centre for Social Welfare Policy and Research
ECT	electroconvulsive therapy
ED	U.S. Department of Education; emotional disorder; erectile dysfunction
EdD	doctor of education
EDL	equitable distribution law
EEG	electroencephalogram
EEO	Equal Employment Opportunity
EEOC	Equal Employment Opportunity Commission
EFAP	Emergency Food Assistance Program
EHA	Education for All Handicapped Children Act
EHCY	Education for Homeless Children and Youth Act
EIC	earned income credit
EITC	Earned Income Tax Credit
ELBW	extremely low birth weight
ELISA	enzyme-linked immunosorbent assay
EMSC	emergency medical services for children
EMTs	emergency medical technicians
ENP	Elderly Nutrition Program
ENT	ear, nose, and throat specialist
EOA	Economic Opportunity Act
EOS	episode of service
EPA	Environmental Protection Agency
EPO	exclusive provider organization
EPSDT	early and periodic screening, diagnosis and treatment (Medicaid)
EPSS	electronic performance support system
ERIC	Educational Resources Information Center
ERISA	Employment Retirement Income Security Act
ESL	English as a second language
ESOL	English for speakers of other languages
ESOPs	employee stock ownership plans
ESP	extrasensory perception
ESR	Educators for Social Responsibility
ESRD	end-stage renal disease
EST	electroshock therapy
ETA	Employment and Training Administration
ETRP	exposure therapy and response prevention
EVTs	empirically validated treatments
FAIR	Federation for American Immigration Reform
FAO	Food and Agriculture Organization
FAP	Family Assistance Program
FAPE	free appropriate public education

FAQ	frequently asked questions
FAS	Federation of American Scientists; fetal alcohol syndrome
FBCIs	Faith-Based and Community Initiatives
FBI	Federal Bureau of Investigation
FBOs	Faith-Based Organizations
FCIC	Federal Consumer Information Center
FDA	Food and Drug Administration
FDCPA	Fair Debt Collection Practices Act
FDIC	Federal Deposit Insurance Corporation
FDS	Friends Disaster Service
FEHBP	Federal Employees Health Benefits Program
FEMA	Federal Emergency Management Agency
FEPC	Fair Employment Practices Committee
FER	Fathers for Equal Rights
FERA	Federal Emergency Relief Administration
FERS	Federal Employee Retirement System
FFA	force field analysis
FFF	Freedom Fellowship Foundation
FFS	fee for service
FGM	female genital mutilation
FHA	Federal Housing Administration
FHEO	Fair Housing and Equal Opportunity Office (of DHUD)
FICA	Federal Insurance Contributions Act
FIDCR	Federal Interagency Day Care Requirements
FLE	family life education
FLSA	Fair Labor Standards Act
FMLA	Family and Medical Leave Act
FMR	fair market rent
FNS	Food and Nutrition Service
FOE	Friends of the Earth
FOIA	Freedom of Information Act
FPLS	Federal Parent Locator Service
FQHC	Federally Qualified Health Center
FRPA	Family Rights and Privacy Act
FSA	Family Service America; Family Support Act; Federal Security Administration
FSAA	Family Service Association of America
FSI	Family Service International
FSIS	Food Safety and Inspection Service (of USDA)
FTC	Federal Trade Commission; Feed the Children
FTE	full-time equivalent
FTPA	Family Therapy Practice Academy (of CSWF)
FWAA	Family Welfare Association of America
FY	fiscal year
FYSB	Family and Youth Services Bureau
GA	Gamblers Anonymous; General Assistance
GAD	generalized anxiety disorder
GADE	Group for the Advancement of Doctoral Education in Social Work
GAF	global assessment of functioning

GAI	guaranteed annual income
GAIN	Greater Avenues to Independence
GALS	guardians ad litem
GAO	General Accounting Office
GARF	Global Assessment of Relational Functioning
GBMI	guilty, but mentally ill
GDP	gross domestic product
GED	general equivalency diploma
GI	Armed Forces personnel; gastrointestinal; government issue
GIDAANT	gender identity disorder of adolescence or adulthood, nontransexual type
GLAAD	Gay and Lesbian Alliance Against Defamation
GLBT	gay, lesbian, bisexual, and transgendered
GLBTQ	gay, lesbian, bisexual, transgendered, and queer
GNMA	Government National Mortgage Association (Ginny Mae)
GNP	gross national product
GOP	"Grand Old Party" (Republican Party of the United States)
GPRA	Government Performance and Results Aid
GRAS	generally recognized as safe
GRE	Graduate Record Examination
GROWL	Grass Roots Organizing for Welfare Leadership
GSA	General Services Administration; Girl Scouts of America
GSCC	General Social Care Council of England
HALT	Americans for Legal Reform (formerly Help Abolish Legal Tyranny)
HCFA	Health Care Financing Administration
HDI	human development index
HELP	U.S. Senate Health, Education, Labor and Pensions Committee
HEOPs	higher education opportunity programs
HEW	U.S. Department of Health, Education and Welfare
HFH	Habitat for Humanity
4-H	Head, Heart, Hands, and Health
HHS	U.S. Department of Health and Human Services
HI	hospital insurance
HIAS	Hebrew Immigrant Aid Society
HIPAA	Health Insurance Portability and Accountability Act
HIPCs	heavily indebted poor countries
HIV	human immunodeficiency virus
HMO	health maintenance organization
HOPING	Helping Other Parents in Normal Grieving
HPV	human papillomavirus
HRA	Health Resources Administration
HRHSA	Health Resources and Health Services Administration (of DHHS)
HRR	Human Rights Report
HRT	hormone replacement therapy
HRW	Human Rights Watch
HSA	Health Services Administration; health system agency; human services agency
HSB	Head Start Bureau
HUD	U.S. Department of Housing and Urban Development
HUGO	Human Genome Organization

IADL	impairment in activities of daily living; instrumental activities of daily living
IAEWP	International Association of Educators for World Peace
IAMFC	International Association of Marriage and Family Counselors
IANLP	International Association for Neurolinguistic Programming
IAPSWP	Institute for the Advancement of Political Social Work Practice
IASSW	International Association of Schools of Social Work
IASWR	Institute for the Advancement of Social Work Research
I-CAPP	International Conference for the Advancement of Private Practice
ICD	International Classification of Diseases
ICE	Bureau of Immigration and Customs Enforcement
ICFs	immediate care facilities
ICIDH	International Classification of Impairments, Disabilities and Handicaps
ICSSW	International Committee of Schools of Social Work
ICSW	International Council on Social Welfare; International Council of Social Work
ICWA	Indian Child Welfare Act
IDAs	individual development accounts
IDEA	Individuals with Disabilities Education Act
IDPs	internally displaced persons
IECs	institutional ethics committees
IEP	individualized education program
IFA	International Federation on Aging
IFPS	intensive family preservation services
IFSW	International Federation of Social Workers
IHHS	In-Home Health Services
IHS	Indian Health Service
ILCs	Independent Living Centers
ILO	International Labour Organization
IMRAD	introduction, method, results, and discussion
INS	Immigration and Naturalization Service
INSSW	International Network for School Social Workers
IPA	International Phototherapy Association
IPAs	independent practice associations
IPEC	International Programme on the Elimination of Child Labour
IPO	independent practice organization
IPS	Institute for Policy Studies
IQ	intelligence quotient
I&R	information and referral
IRAs	individual retirement accounts
IRBs	institutional review boards
IRC	International Rescue Committee
IRCA	Immigration Reform and Control Act
IRET	Institute for Rational Emotive Therapy
IRS	Internal Revenue Service
ISH	Index of Social Health
ISS	International Social Service
ISSA	International Social Security Association
IST	incompetent to stand trial
IUCISD	Inter-University Consortium on International Social Development
IUCW	International Union for Child Welfare

IUD	intrauterine device
IUPAE	Independent Union of Public Aid Employees
IV	intravenous
IWL	Izaak Walton League
IWW	Industrial Workers of the World
JAPA	Jane Addams Peace Association
JASW	Japanese Association of Social Workers
JCA	Joint Custody Association
JCAHO	Joint Commission on Accreditation of Healthcare Organizations
JCIA	Joint Commission on Interprofessional Affairs
JCSA	Jewish Communal Service Association
JFS	Jewish Family Service
JINS	juveniles in need of supervision
JJDPA	Juvenile Justice and Delinquency Prevention Act
JOBS	Job Opportunities and Basic Skills
JTPA	Job Training and Partnership Act
KKK	Ku Klux Klan
KS	Kaposi's sarcoma
LAAM	L-alpha-acetylmethadol
LAN	local area network
LAWS	Lawyers Alliance for World Security
LBW	low birth weight
LCSW	Licensed Clinical Social Worker
LD	learning disability
LDC	least-developed countries; less-developing countries
LDS	Church of Jesus Christ of Latter Day Saints; Legal Defense Service
LEAA	Law Enforcement Assistance Administration
LEP	limited English proficiency
LFPR	labor-force participation rate
LGBT	lesbian, gay, bisexual, and transgendered
LICSW	Licensed Independent Clinical Social Worker
LICWAC	Local Indian Child Welfare Committee
LIFE	Love Is Feeding Everyone
LOC	Library of Congress
LPA	Little People of America
LPN	licensed practical nurse
LRCS	League of Red Cross Societies
LRE	least restricted environment
LRUP	La Raza Unida Party
LSC	Legal Services Corporation
LSD	lysergic acid diethylamine
LSS	Lutheran Social Services
LSWO	Latino Social Workers Organization
LTC	long-term care
LTLTC	long-term long-term care
LULAC	League of United Latin American Citizens

LWF	Lutheran World Federation
LWV	League of Women Voters
MADD	Mothers Against Drunk Driving
MAG	Mothers Against Gangs
MAGI	modified adjusted gross income
MALDEF	Mexican American Legal Defense and Education Fund
MAO	monoamine oxidase
MAP	member assistance program
MBD	minimal brain dysfunction
MBDA	Minority Business Development Agency
MBO	management by objectives
MCH	maternal and child health
MCHB	Maternal and Child Health Bureau
MCO	managed care organization
MDRC	Manpower Development Research Corporation
MEDLARS	Medical Analysis and Retrieval System (of the National Library of Medicine)
MEP	Migrant Education Program (of DoE)
MEPA	Multi-Ethnic Placement Act
MFB	Maximum Family Benefit
MHA	Mental Health Association
MIPRAs	mentally ill persons in recovery from addictions
MIS	management information system
MLPs	midlevel practitioners
M/MAP	Medicare/Medicaid Assistance Program
MMPI	Minnesota Multiphasic Personality Inventory
MOE	maintenance of effort
MORE	Member Organized Resource Exchange
MPB	Migrant Program Branch (of Head Start)
MPH	master of public health degree
MR	mental retardation
MRI	magnetic resonance imaging
MSA	metropolitan statistical area
MSD	multiple stressor debriefing
MSPA	Migrant and Seasonal Agricultural Worker Protection Act
MSS	Medical Social Service
MSSA	master of social service administration degree
MSSW	master of science in social work; master of social service work
MST	multisystemic therapy
MSW	master of social work degree
MUA	medically underserved area
MWC	Mothers Without Custody
NA	needs assessment; Narcotics Anonymous
NAACP	National Association for the Advancement of Colored People
NABSW	National Association of Black Social Workers
NACA	National Association of Child Advocates
NACCHO	National Association of City and County Health Officials
NACHS	National Association of County Human Services Administrators

NACSDC	North American Conference of Separated and Divorced Catholics
NACSW	North American Association of Christians in Social Work
NADD	National Association of Deans and Directors of Social Work Programs
NAEYC	National Association for the Education of Young Children
NAHHSO	National Association of Health and Human Service Organizations
NAIC	National Aging Information Center
NAILS	National Immigration Lookout System
NAMI	National Alliance for the Mentally Ill
NAP	National Academy of Practice
NAPCWA	National Association of Public Child Welfare Administrators
NAPRHSW	National Association of Puerto Rican/Hispanic Social Workers
NAPSW	National Association of Perinatal Social Workers
NAPWA	National Association of People with AIDS
NAS	National Audubon Society
NASI	National Academy of Social Insurance
NASPAA	National Association of Schools of Public Affairs and Administration
NASSA	National Association of Schools of Social Administration
NASSW	National Association of School Social Workers
NASUA	National Association of State Units on Aging
NASW	National Association of Social Workers
NAVS	National Anti-Vivisection Society
NBCC	National Board for Certified Counselors
NBD	neurobiological disorders
NCAI	National Congress of American Indians
NCATE	National Council for Accreditation of Teacher Education
NCCAN	National Center on Child Abuse and Neglect
NCCC	National Civilian Community Corps; National Conference on Charities and Corrections
NCCS	National Center on Charitable Statistics
NCDO	New Community Development Office
NCEH	National Center of Environmental Health
NCF	National Civic Federation
NCHSR	National Center for Health Statistics Research
NCI	National Cancer Institute
NCL	National Consumer League
NCLC	National Child Labor Committee
NCMEC	National Center for Missing and Exploited Children
NCN	NASW Communications Network
NCOA	National Council on Aging
NCOI	National Committee on Inquiry
NCOLGI	National Committee on Lesbian and Gay Issues
NCOMA	National Committee on Minority Affairs
NCORED	National Committee on Racial and Ethnic Diversity
NCOWI	National Conference on Women's Issues
NCPCA	National Committee for the Prevention of Child Abuse
NCPCR	National Center for the Prevention and Control of Rape
NCPSSM	National Committee to Preserve Social Security and Medicare
NCRP	National Committee for Responsive Philanthropy
NCSC	National Council of Senior Citizens

NCSPP	National Center for Social Policy and Practice
NCSW	National Conference of Social Work; National Conference on Social Welfare
NCSWE	National Council on Social Work Education
NCVS	National Crime Victimization Survey
NDMS	National Disaster Medical System
NEA	National Education Association
NEH	National Endowment for the Humanities
NEI	National Eye Institute
NES	non-English speaker
NFB	National Federation for the Blind
NFCSP	National Family Caregiver Support Program
NFSCSW	National Federation of Societies for Clinical Social Work (now CSWF)
NGO	nongovernment organization
NGRI	not guilty by reason of insanity
NGT	nominal group technique
NHIP	National Health Insurance Program
NHO	National Hospice Organization
NIAAA	National Institute on Alcohol Abuse and Alcoholism
NIADC	National Institute on Adult Day Care
NIAWR	National Institute on Aging, Work, and Retirement
NIBRS	National Incidence-Based Reporting System
NICCYD	National Information Center for Children and Youth with Disabilities
NICSWA	National Institute for Clinical Social Work Advancement
NIDA	National Institute on Drug Abuse
NIH	National Institutes of Health
NIMBY	not in my back yard
NIMH	National Institute of Mental Health
NIOSH	National Institute for Occupational Safety and Health
NISW	National Institute of Social Work (United Kingdom)
NISWA	National Indian Social Workers Association
NIT	negative income tax
NIV	nonimmigrant visa
NLC	National League of Cities
NLP	neurolinguistic programming
NLRA	National Labor Relations Act
NLRB	National Labor Relations Board
NLS	National Library Service
NMCOP	National Membership Committee on Psychoanalysis in Clinical Social Work
NMHA	National Mental Health Association
NMHCSHC	National Mental Health Consumer Self-Help Clearinghouse
NMHPA	Newborns' and Mothers' Health Protection Act
NNSWM	National Network for Social Work Managers
NOHSE	National Organization for Human Services Education
NORD	National Organization for Rare Diseases
NOS	not otherwise specified
NOW	National Organization for Women
NP	nurse practitioner
NPG	negative population growth
NPV	net present value

NRA	National Recovery Administration; National Rifle Association; normal retirement age
NRLC	National Right-to-Life Committee
NTU	National Taxpayers Union
NVOAD	National Voluntary Organizations Active in Disaster
NVRA	National Voter Registration Act
NWF	National Wildlife Federation
NWP	Neighborhood Watch Program
NWRO	National Welfare Rights Organization
NYA	National Youth Administration
OAA	Old Age Assistance
OAS	Organization of American States
OASDHI	Old Age, Survivors, Disability, and Health Insurance
OASI	Old Age and Survivors Insurance
OBE	outcome-based education
OBRA	Omnibus Budget Reconciliation Act
OC	oleoresin capsicum (pepper spray)
OCA	Obsessive–Compulsives Anonymous; Office of Consumer Affairs
OCD	obsessive–compulsive disorder
OCSE	Office of Child Support Enforcement
OD	organizational development
ODP	Office of Domestic Preparedness
OED	Office of Economic Development
OEO	Office of Economic Opportunity
OFA	Office of Family Assistance (of DHHS)
OHDS	Office of Human Development Services
OJJDP	Office of Juvenile Justice and Delinquency Prevention
OMB	Office of Management and Budget
ONDCP	Office of National Drug Control Policy
OPACs	online public-access catalogs
OPM	Office of Personnel Management
ORR	Office of Refugee Resettlement (of DHHS)
OSERS	Office of Special Education and Rehabilitation Services
OSHA	Occupational Safety and Health Administration
OT	occupational therapy
OTA	Office of Technology Assessment
OTC	over the counter
OVC	Office for Victims of Crime
OVR	Office of Vocational Rehabilitation
OWH	Office of Women's Health
OXFAM	Oxford Committee for Famine Relief
OYS	Office of Youth Services
PA	Parents Anonymous; physician's assistant; professional association
P&A	protection & advocacy
PAC	political action committee
PACE	Political Action for Candidate Election
PAM	Parents Against Molesters

PAR	population-attributed risk
PAS	postabortion syndrome
PASSO	Political Association of Spanish-Speaking Organizations
PC	personal computer; political correctness; professional corporation
PCI	Population Control International
PCP	phencyclidine hydrochloride
PDD	pervasive developmental disorder
PDPD	passive dependent personality disorder
PEBES	Personal Earnings and Benefits Estimates Statement
PERT	program evaluation review technique
PET	Parent Effectiveness Training; positron emission tomography
PETA	People for the Ethical Treatment of Animals
PFC	Partnership for Caring
PhD	doctor of philosophy degree
PHP	Parents Helping Parents
PHS	Public Health Service
PI	Population Institute
PIA	primary insurance amount
PID	pelvic inflammatory disease
PIE	person-in-environment
PINS	person in need of supervision
PIP	Parent Involvement Program
PIRG	public-interest research group
PKU	phenylketonuria
P.L.	Public Law
PMDD	premenstrual dysphoric disorder
PMS	premenstrual syndrome
PN	practical nurse
PNS	peripheral nervous system
POMC	Parents of Murdered Children
POR	problem-oriented record
POS	point of service; purchase of service
POSSLQ	partner of the opposite sex sharing living quarters
PPBS	Program Planning and Budgeting System
PPFA	Planned Parenthood Federation of America
PPI	Producer Price Index
PPOs	preferred provider organizations
PQSW	Post-Qualifying Award in Social Work
P.R.N.	take medication as needed (from the Latin "pro re nata")
PROs	peer review organizations; Professional Review Organizations
PRS	personal response systems
PRWORA	Personal Responsibility and Work Opportunity Reconciliation Act
PSA	pediatric sexual abuse; public service announcement
PSR	psychosocial rehabilitation
PSRO	professional standards review organization
PsySR	Psychologists for Social Responsibility
PT	physical therapy
PTP	Procedural Terminology for Psychiatrists
PTSD	posttraumatic stress disorder

PUSH	People United to Serve Humanity
PVOs	private voluntary organizations
PVS	persistent vegetative state
PWA	Public Works Administration
PWAs	people with AIDS
PWP	Parents Without Partners
QCs	quarterly credits
QCSW	Qualified Clinical Social Worker
QDRO	qualified domestic relations order
Q.I.D.	take medication four times per day (from the Latin "quater in die")
QITs	quality improvement teams
QMB	qualified medical beneficiary
QMCSO	Qualified Medical Child Support Order
QMRP	qualified mental retardation professional
QOL	quality of life
RAD	reactive attachment disorder
RAM	reverse annuity mortgage
RAP	recognize, anticipate, and problem-solve
RBRVS	resource-based relative value scale
RDA	recommended daily allowance; recommended dietary allowance
RDS	respiratory distress syndrome
REA	Retirement Equity Act
RFP	request for proposal
RICO	Racketeer Influences and Corrupt Organizations Act
RIF	reduction in force
RLIN	research libraries information network
RMD	repetitive motion disorder
RMP	regional medical program
RN	registered nurse
RNC	Republican National Committee
RR	risk ratio
R&R	resource and referral; rest and recuperation
RSVP	Retired Senior Volunteer Program
RSWC	Rural Social Work Caucus
RURESA	Revised Uniform Reciprocal Enforcement of Support Act
SAD	seasonal affective disorder
SAFAH	Supplemental Assistance for Facilities to Assist the Homeless
SAMHSA	Substance Abuse and Mental Health Services Administration
SASG	sexual assault survivor group
SAT	Scholastic Assessment Test; Standardized Achievement Test
SBHC	school-based health center
SCHIP	State Child Health Insurance Program
SCI	spinal cord injury
SCLC	Southern Christian Leadership Conference
SCMWA	State, County, and Municipal Workers of America
SCORE/ACE	Service Corps of Retired Executives/Active Corps of Executives

SD	standard deviation
SDAT	senile dementia of the Alzheimer's type
SDI	Strategic Defense Initiative
SE	supported employment
SECA	Self-Employment Contributions Act
SED	serious emotional disturbance
SEID	Self-Employment Investment Demonstration Program
SEIU	Service Employees International Union
SEM	standard error of measurement
SERVE	Service Employees Registration and Voter Education
SES	socioeconomic status
SGA	substantial gainful activity
SHIP	State Health Insurance Program
SI	service integration
SIDS	sudden infant death syndrome
SIECUS	Sex Information and Education Council of the United States
SIGs	special interest groups
SLMB	Specified Low-Income Medicare Beneficiary
SMI	Supplemental Medical Insurance
SNCC	Student Non-Violent Coordinating Committee
SNF	skilled nursing facility
SOAP	subjective, objective, assessment, and plan
SOFAS	Social and Occupational Functioning Assessment Scale
SOR	sex offender registry
SPCA	Society for the Prevention of Cruelty to Animals
SPCC	Society for the Prevention of Cruelty to Children
SPICES	Social, Physical, Intellectual, Cultural, Emotional, and Spiritual
SPMI	serious and persistent mental illness
SRO	single-room occupancy
SS	social services
SSA	Social Security Administration
SSD	single-subject design
SSDI	Social Security Disability Insurance
SSEU	Social Service Employees Union
SSI	Supplemental Security Income
SSWAA	School Social Work Association of America
SSWAHC	Society for Social Work Administrators in Health Care
SSWR	Society for Social Work Research
SSWS	School Social Work Specialist
STD	sexually transmitted disease
STEPA	Street Terrorism Enforcement Prevention Act
STLTC	short-term long-term care
SUDS	sudden unexplained death syndrome
SWAA	Social Welfare Action Alliance
SWAN	Social Work Access Network
SWAP	Social Workers Assistance Program
SWC	Simon Wiesenthal Center
SWRG	Social Work Research Group
SYMLOG	Systematic Multiple-Level Observation of Groups

TA	transactional analysis
TANF	Temporary Assistance to Needy Families
TB	tuberculosis
TCF	The Compassionate Friends
TD	tardive dyskinesia
TED	traumatic event debriefing
TFC	therapeutic foster care
TFP	Thrifty Food Plan
THC	tetrahydrocannabinol
TIA	transient ischemic attack
TIAC	Temporary Inter-Association Council of Social Work Membership
T.I.D.	take medication three times per day (from the Latin "ter in die")
TIPS	Terrorist Information and Prevention System
TIS	task implementation sequence
TLI	Tough Love International
TLP	Teen Living Program
TOEFL	Test of English as a Foreign Language
TQM	total quality management
TRO	temporary restraining order
TSA	Transportation Security Administration
TSS	toxic shock syndrome
TTB	Alcohol and Tobacco, Tax, and Trade Bureau
UAW	United Auto Workers
UCCJA	Uniform Child Custody Jurisdiction Act
UCR	Uniform Crime Reports
UFWA	United Federal Workers of America
UI	Urban Institute
UJA	United Jewish Appeal
UN	United Nations
UNAUSA	United Nations Association of the United States
UNCA	United Neighborhood Centers of America
UNDP	United Nations Development Program
UNDRO	United Nations Disaster Relief Organization
UNEP	United Nations Environmental Program
UNESCO	United Nations Educational, Scientific, and Cultural Organization
UNHCR	United Nations High Commissioner for Refugees
UNICEF	United Nations Children's Fund
UNOS	United Network for Organ Sharing
UNRRA	United Nations Relief and Works Agency for Palestine Refugees
UOPWA	United Office and Professional Workers of America
UPA	Unwed Parents Anonymous
UPWA	United Public Workers of America
UR	unconditioned response
UR/EM	unaccompanied refugee/entrant minor
URESA	Uniform Reciprocal Enforcement of Support Act
US	unconditioned stimulus
USCC	United States Catholic Conference
USCCHSO	U.S. Conference of City Human Service Officials

USCRA	United States Coordinator for Refugee Affairs
USDA	U.S. Department of Agriculture
USINS	U.S. Immigration and Naturalization Service
USIP	United States Institute of Peace
USO	United Service Organizations
USOCDC	U.S. Overseas Cooperative Development Council
USPC	U.S. Parole Commission
USSW	Uniformed Services Social Workers
UWA	United Way of America
VA	Veterans Administration; Veterans Affairs
VAT	value-added tax
VBA	Veterans Benefits Administration
VHA	Veterans Health Administration
VIPS	Volunteers in Police Service
VISTA	Volunteers in Service to America
VITA	Volunteers in Technical Assistance
VOLAGS	voluntary agencies
VR	vocational rehabilitation
VS	vital signs
VSC	voluntary surgical contraception
WAIS	Wechsler Adult Intelligence Scale
WAN	wide-area network
WASP	white Anglo-Saxon Protestant
WB	World Bank
WCTU	Women's Christian Temperance Union
WFTC	Working Families Tax Credit (United Kingdom)
WHO	World Health Organization
WIA	Workforce Investment Act
WIC	Women, Infants, and Children Program
WICS	Women in Community Service
WILPF	Women's International League for Peace and Freedom
WIN	Work Incentive Program
WISC	Wechsler Intelligence Scale for Children
WMD	weapons of mass destruction
WPA	Works Progress Administration
WSP	Women Strike for Peace
WTO	World Trade Organization
WTW	Welfare to Work
YMCA	Young Men's Christian Association
YM-YWHA	Young Men's and Young Women's Hebrew Association
YTD	year to date
YWCA	Young Women's Christian Association
ZDV	zidovudine
ZPG	Zero Population Growth

A

AASW credential In the United Kingdom, the "advanced award in social work" for professional social workers who have completed postqualifying work requirements, work-based learning experiences, or both. The credential is similar to the MSW degree. See also *DipSW* and *PQSW credential.*

abandonment Voluntarily giving up one's possessions, rights, or obligations with no intention of subsequently reclaiming them. For social workers the term usually refers to premature termination of services or being unavailable to a client when needed.

abatement The removal of a problem that endangers, inconveniences, or annoys others or that is against the public good.

ABAWDS Able-bodied adults without dependents, a designation used frequently in state and local welfare and human services programs for financially needy people who do not easily fit into welfare benefits categories, which are often geared toward families with dependent children, older people, or people with disabilities.

Abbott, Edith (1876–1957) A pioneer in social work education who was dean of the School of Social Service Administration at the University of Chicago from 1924 to 1942, a founder of *Social Service Review,* and author of several seminal social work texts. She also helped draft the original *Social Security Act* of 1935.

Abbott, Grace (1878–1939) An advocate for child labor laws and long-term director of the *Children's Bureau* who organized one of the first *White House conferences* on children and was an adviser to President Woodrow Wilson.

ABD All but dissertation. When social workers and other professionals complete all the requirements for their doctoral degrees (PhD, DSW, EdD, DPsy, and so forth) other than their dissertations, this designation is sometimes added to their résumés as a shorthand status report. Some social work educators believe adding this to one's list of "degrees" is misleading to the public and unethical.

abduct To transport someone against that person's will often by force or *coercion* or, if the person is a child, without the consent of the parent or legal guardian.

abet To encourage someone to commit a *crime.* To "aid and abet" means that an individual encourages and actively facilitates the commission of a crime.

able-ism Stereotyping and making negative generalizations about people with disabilities.

"abnormal" A term denoting atypical functioning that usually is seen as *maladaptive.* In social work, the term usually refers to *behavior* rather than a person. There is rarely a clear and consistent demarcation between "normal" and abnormal, but rather a continuum. In assessing whether a behavior is abnormal, social workers apply objective criteria such as those found in the *DSM* or the *Person-in-Environment (PIE) System.*

abolition movement Coordinated and independent efforts in all parts of the pre–Civil War United States to end the institution of slavery through protest activities, leading enslaved Africans to freedom through the *underground railroad,* political lobbying, boycotts, and educational efforts.

Aboriginal Peoples Descendants of the earliest known human inhabitants of a region; the Indigenous Peoples of a territory (for example, Native Americans). The term "aborigines" was/is often used as a term of contempt by the territory's more recent settlers or colonizers.

abortion Termination of *pregnancy* before the *fetus* has developed enough to survive outside the woman's body. The term usually refers to a deliberate procedure to end the pregnancy. However, many pregnancies are lost through natural or spontaneous abortions (miscarriages), in which the woman's body rejects the fetus. See also *Roe v. Wade, prochoice movement,* and *right-to-life movement.*

abscond An abrupt departure, usually to avoid some legal action.

absentee ownership An economic system in which a person, family, or corporation controls and derives income from property in a region away from the owner's home residence. Frequently this means the owner charges higher rents, provides less property maintenance, and has less incentive to develop or improve the conditions where the property is located.

absolute confidentiality A position held by some professionals that no information about a client shall be disclosed to others, regardless of circumstances. The social worker who practices this position would not put the information obtained from a client into any written form—for example, a *case record* or a computer file—or discuss it with colleagues or supervisors. Most social workers believe that absolute confidentiality is impractical and that *relative confidentiality* is ethical and more productive.

absolute poverty The possession of scant income and assets such that one cannot maintain a *subsistence level* of income. This is compared to *relative poverty,* in which one's standard of living is beneath the standard of the mainstream community but still higher than the subsistence level.

abstinence Voluntary avoidance of physical activities such as eating, drinking alcohol, taking drugs, or engaging in sexual intercourse.

abstinence policies Advocacy about sexual behavior in which governments, churches, educational organizations, and other institutions admonish people to avoid sexual intercourse until marriage. Some organizations advocate an "abstinence-only" policy for young people to encourage them to refrain from erotic contact until they marry. Others advocate an "abstinence-plus" policy in which people are given information about how to engage in meaningful and safe sexual practices at a later point in their lives.

abstinence syndrome A synonym for *withdrawal symptoms.*

abstracts Summaries of scholarly articles. They usually appear immediately before the text in published articles and are often included in indexing and abstracting services, such as *Social Work Abstracts.* Abstracts usually consist of a single paragraph of fewer than 200 words that outlines what the article is about, its key concepts, the method

used to study the problem, and the conclusion reached.

Abstracts for Social Workers See *Social Work Abstracts.*

abulia Apathy; lack of motivation, indifference to the consequences of any actions, and indecisiveness.

abuse Improper behavior intended to cause physical, psychological, or financial harm to an individual or group. See also *child abuse, drug abuse, elder abuse, spouse abuse,* and *substance abuse.*

academic freedom The opportunity, granted by some nations and jurisdictions to professors, teachers, and students to think, engage in research, write, express viewpoints, and engage in debate, free of control by government, institutions, or social norms.

academic skills disorder A term formerly used by professionals for *learning disorder.*

academic underachievement A long-standing pattern of poor performance in school, including substandard grades and minimal classroom participation relative to the student's intellectual and social skills. If the pattern is formally diagnosed, it is usually called *learning disorder.*

Academy of Certified Social Workers (ACSW) An NASW credential established in 1962 to evaluate and certify the practice *competence* of individual social workers with advanced degrees. Social workers are eligible for ACSW membership if they have obtained an *MSW* degree from an accredited school; have two years of full-time or 3,000 hours of part-time practice experience under the supervision of a social worker; provide references from a colleague and sign an agreement to adhere to the *NASW Code of Ethics* and the *NASW Standards for Continuing Professional Education;* and successfully pass the ACSW examination.

acceptance Recognition of a person's positive worth as a human being without necessarily condoning the person's actions. In social work, it is considered one of the fundamental elements in the helping *relationship.* See also *unconditional positive regard.*

access barriers Economic, psychological, cultural, educational, and physical obstacles between people and the services they need and to which they are entitled. These obstacles may include lack of knowledge about the existence of the resource, inability to understand how to apply for the service, family or ethnic taboos against the use of needed programs, language barriers, transportation limitations, overcrowded clinics, limited availability of appointment times in the agency, long waiting times, fear of legal problems, and stringent qualifications.

access provision The actions and procedures of a social program or service provider organization to ensure that its services are available to its target clientele. Three of these procedures are (1) educating the public about the existence of the service, its functions, and eligibility requirements; (2) establishing clear and convenient referral procedures; and (3) obtaining legal or *ombudsperson* services to overcome obstacles to getting the service. See also *information and referral service.*

accessibility of service The relative opportunity for people in need to obtain relevant services. For example, a social agency with greater accessibility is located near its natural clientele; is open at convenient hours; maintains shorter waiting lists; has affordable fees; and has personnel, resources, settings, and policies that make clients feel welcome. Also, appropriate ramps and doors to permit entrance by people with disabilities are essential to an agency's accessibility.

accessory to a crime One who assists, advises, or commands another to commit an offense. An "accessory after the fact" is one who conceals or otherwise helps an offender avoid arrest or trial. An "accessory before the fact" is one who aids in the commission of a *crime* but is not present at the time of the act. See also *accomplice.*

"accident prone" A term applied to individuals who tend to become injured because of supposedly chance occurrences. Being accident prone is thought to be the result of personality factors.

ACCION The *NGO* serving poor people throughout the Americas, primarily by providing *microcredit* (small loans) and training to individuals to establish small businesses.

acclimatization Biological and psychosocial adjustment to living in a new environment.

accommodation 1. In *community organization,* the ability of one group to modify aspects of its culture to deal better with other groups or aspects of the environment. 2. In *health care* and *geriatrics,* a property of visual perception in which the lens of the eye is able to change its shape to permit focusing on objects at different distances from the observer. 3. In developmental and *Piagetian theory,* a person's growing ability to modify current thought structure to deal with new or newly perceived features of the environment.

accomplice Someone who assists actively and directly in committing a crime. This is more serious than one who is an accessory (one who helps but is not directly involved). See also *accessory to a crime.*

accountability 1. The state of being answerable to the community, to consumers of a product or service, or to supervisory groups such as a *board of directors.* 2. An obligation of a profession to reveal clearly what its functions and methods are and to provide assurances to clients that its practitioners meet specific standards of competence. See also *quality assurance.*

accreditation The acknowledgment and verification that an organization (such as an educational institution, social agency, hospital, or skilled-nursing facility) fulfills explicit specified standards. For example, schools of social work in the United States are evaluated periodically by the *Council on Social Work Education (CSWE)* and accredited if they meet CSWE standards.

accrual accounting An accounting procedure in which each expenditure is recorded and considered a liability when the obligation is established rather than when the cash has been disbursed. Each item of revenue is recorded and considered an asset when the obligation has been incurred rather than when the actual cash has been received.

acculturation 1. The adoption by one cultural group or individual of the *culture* of another. 2. The process of *conditioning* an individual or group to the social patterns, *behavior, values,* and *mores* of others. See also *socialization.*

ACE Approval Program A service of the *Association of Social Work Boards (ASWB)* to evaluate a provider's ability to deliver relevant, high-quality social work continuing education. (ACE stands for Approved Continuing Education.) Approval from ASWB-ACE tells social workers that the provider has met standards for course relevance, content, currency, and instructor expertise. Many state licensing authorities that require continuing education of license holders use the ACE Approval Program as a tool in defining acceptable courses and programs.

acedia   Loss of interest in life.

acetylcholine   A biochemical that transmits information between nerve cells.

achievement age   A student's acquired level of academic proficiency as indicated on educational *achievement tests.* Thus, a 14-year-old eighth grader who scores well on all parts of an achievement test might have an achievement age of 16, which corresponds to the 10th grade.

achievement tests   Formal examinations that attempt to measure what one has learned. See also *aptitude tests.*

acid rain   Precipitation in which the water is fouled by noxious chemicals, primarily sulfur dioxide and nitrogen oxides, mostly from automobiles and factories that burn *fossil fuels.* This rain pollutes lakes and rivers and damages buildings, crops, and forests, often far from the source of the chemicals. Efforts to minimize the problem emphasize cleaner and more efficient fuel burning and chemically neutralizing the acid before and after it enters the lakes and soil.

ACORN   The Association of Community Organizations for Reform Now. A federation of community organization groups and individual families of low to moderate incomes to advocate for stronger voices in local government and other institutions. ACORN has focused especially on neighborhood problems such as real estate *blockbusting* and redlining, utility rate increases, tenant–landlord power imbalances, and electoral politics. Their Web site address is http://www.acorn.org

ACOSS   The Australian Council of Social Service, the national federation of community agencies, consumer and social services provider groups, religious and secular welfare agencies, and low-income groups to advocate for less affluent people and consumers and to facilitate the exchange of information about these issues. Each state and territory has a regional council of social services. ACOSS publishes the monthly magazine *Impact* and the *Australian Journal of Social Issues.* Their Web site address is http://www.acoss.org.au

acquaintance rape   Forced or coerced sexual intercourse by someone who is known to the victim. Typically, the victim is in some social encounter with the perpetrator such as a date or private meeting and is then manipulated into sexual intercourse through physical violence, restraint, threats, or power. The perpetrator ignores protests or interprets them as subtle encouragement. Often victims do not report the event, and frequently they or their assailants do not identify it as *rape.* See also *date rape.*

acquired citizenship   A designation by the *Bureau of Citizenship and Immigration Services* indicating that people born outside U.S. territory whose parents are U.S. citizens living abroad have U.S. citizenship automatically conferred on them.

acquired immune deficiency syndrome (AIDS)   A life-threatening, slowly progressing disease in which the human immunodeficiency virus (HIV) infects the body through contact with blood or tissues that line the vagina, anal area, eyes, and mouth or through breaks in the skin. At the first (primary) stage of infection, the patient's symptoms are flulike and may include fever, swollen lymph nodes, and night sweats. This is followed by a stage of chronic asymptomatic infection, which may last for many years depending on access to treatment programs. In the third stage, acquired immune deficiency syndrome (AIDS) symptoms appear when complications develop. These symptoms include one or more unusual infections or cancers (for example, *Kaposi's sarcoma*), excessive weight loss, dementia, and other symptoms. HIV grows by reproducing itself, and it can mutate its own structure, which enables the virus to become resistant to drugs that were previously effective. Combinations of drugs have been developed to decrease the growth of the virus to prevent or delay viral resistance to drugs. Drug treatment has significantly curtailed the death rate of AIDS in developed nations, but, in poor nations where people cannot afford or obtain these drugs, the AIDS epidemic has continued.

acquittal   Setting free or discharging from further legal prosecution for a charge of criminal misconduct. In a trial, the accused person is acquitted when the judge or jury renders a "not guilty" verdict.

acrasia The inability or limited ability to control one's own impulses.

acrophobia The pathological *fear* of high places or of being in the air.

acting out Expressing strong emotions through *overt behaviors* rather than words. When an individual's outward response to inner feelings is expressed in a disguised way to cover the emotion that cannot be revealed directly, the behavior is often destructive or *maladaptive*.

action research In *social planning* and *community organization*, the linking of the data-gathering process with the development of a program designed to alleviate the identified problem.

action sociogram In *social group work,* techniques used to illustrate and learn about a group member's roles and characteristic ways with others. These techniques include *sculpting, choreography, doubling,* and *mirroring*.

action system The people and resources in the community with whom the social worker deals to achieve desired changes. For example, the action system for a client who is being evicted might include the other residents of the apartment building, local housing officials, and the media contacted by a social worker in an effort to change a landlord's policies.

ACTION The U.S. volunteer program that included the *Peace Corps, Volunteers in Service to America (VISTA),* and the *Senior Corps.* In 1994, ACTION and its programs were merged into the *Corporation for National and Community Service (CNCS)*.

action theory Social science concepts to understand social and personality systems by analyzing "acts" and the individuals who perform them, that is, the "actors." In assessing an act, the investigator considers the actor's values and goals in carrying out the act, as well as *overt behaviors*. Action theory differs from classical *behaviorism* in that it emphasizes the value-motivated behavior of individuals and the subjective meanings attached to an action. *Behavior* is seen as occurring within culturally defined situations and relationships and includes the actor's internalized values and expectations of the reactions of others.

action therapy Treatment procedures and intervention strategies based on direct alterations of behaviors or of obstacles to change. Such therapies include *behavior modification,* some *cognitive therapy* methods, and *experiential therapy.* The term "action therapy" is often used to make a distinction from so-called *informational therapy,* which is oriented toward helping clients gain knowledge and insight and other forms of self-awareness that foster changes indirectly.

actionable The demonstrable existence of enough facts, circumstances, or other evidence to fulfill the legal requirements to file a lawsuit. If a complaint does not have the facts required to make a case, then an action may not be taken.

activism Planned behavior designed to achieve social or political objectives through activities such as *consciousness-raising,* developing a coalition, leading voter registration drives and political campaigns, producing *propaganda* and publicity, and taking other actions to influence social change. See also *political activism*.

activist An individual who works to bring about *social change*.

activist role In social work, a rejection of the so-called objective or neutral stance in favor of taking specific actions in behalf of the client system. These actions may include engaging in overt side-taking, making specific recommendations to clients, leading campaigns to change a social institution, or exerting an influence on client *values*.

activities of daily living (ADL) The performance of basic self- and family-care responsibilities necessary for *independent living*. Such activities include meal preparation, bathing, dressing, shopping, cleaning, handling financial matters, light home maintenance, and household chores. Social workers consider the degree of ADL performance when assessing the client's needs. See also *instrumental activities of daily living (IADL)*.

activity catharsis A psychotherapeutic procedure in which the client portrays *anxiety* and the effects of *unconscious* material through actions rather than words. The procedure is used primarily in *group psychotherapy*.

activity group A form of group involvement, which may or may not have a specifically designed therapeutic purpose, in which the participants work on programs of mutual interest. The members engage in activities as diverse as cooking, folk singing, carpentry, or crafts. Historically, activity groups were prevalent in early *social group work,* especially in *settlement houses* and *youth services organizations.* Their primary orientation was not therapeutic per se, but was a means for learning *social skills,* engaging in democratic decision making, and developing effective relationship capacities. More recently, activity groups are found in nursing homes, mental hospitals, and recreation centers.

acute 1. Intense conditions or disturbances of relatively short duration. For example, a *mental disorder* lasting fewer than six months often is considered to be acute, and one lasting more than six months is considered *chronic.* 2. The relatively sudden onset of a condition.

acute brain syndrome A state of confusion, known as *delirium,* often accompanied by *delusion, anxiety,* and *emotional lability.* The disorder lasts fewer than six months, usually is reversible, and is caused by changes in cerebral metabolism typically induced by *drug abuse, shock,* or fever. The term is now obsolete.

acute care A set of health, personal, or social services delivered to individuals who require short-term assistance. Such care usually is provided in the community in hospitals or social agencies in which the extended treatment that exists in *long-term care* is not expected.

acute paranoid disorder One of the types of *paranoid disorders* in which symptoms have occurred for fewer than six months. The condition is most common in people who suddenly encounter severe crises and usually subsides after a period of *adaptation.* See also *delusional (paranoid) disorder.*

acute stress disorder An *anxiety disorder* that occurs within a month of encountering a distressing situation and results in recurrent thoughts, dreams, flashbacks, and upset when reminded of the *stressor.* The person develops *anxiety symptoms* (such as sleeplessness, poor concentration, restlessness, exaggerated startle response) and *dissociative symptoms* (such as numbing and emotional detachment, feeling dazed, *depersonalization, derealization,* and inability to remember aspects of the trauma). If the symptoms persist, the diagnosis becomes *posttraumatic stress disorder (PTSD).*

ad hoc coalition An alliance of individuals and ideological groups to achieve a specific goal or address a single issue or social problem. The group is expected to disband once the goals are reached.

adaptation The active efforts of individuals and species over their life spans to survive, develop, and reproduce by achieving *goodness of fit* with their environments. Adaptation is also a reciprocal process between the individual and the environment, often involving changing the *environment* or being changed by it. Social workers oriented to *systems theories* consider that helping people move through stressful life transitions by strengthening or supporting their adaptive capacities is a central part of their *intervention* strategies. See also *environmental treatment, direct treatment,* and *indirect treatment.*

adaptedness A relationship between an organism and its environment in which the *goodness of fit* supports the needs of both. Adaptedness is a state, and *adaptation* is a process by which adaptedness is achieved.

adaptive capacity The ability to change behavior, lifestyle, worldview, values, and cultural orientations to live more effectively in a different environment. Adaptive capacity also includes psychological flexibility that allows a person greater ability to adjust intrapsychically to challenges such as new parenthood, loss, and poor health. See also *rigidity.*

adaptive spiral In *social group work* and *group psychotherapy,* the successfully integrated, healthy progression of the client from interpersonal distortions and their resulting anxiety and social inhibition to the formation of rewarding relationships within the group and then outside. As the client's interpersonal relationships on the outside become healthier, the relationships within the group become healthier, too.

Addams, Jane (1860–1935) One of the founders of social work, she was a community organizer, peace activist, and leader of the *settlement house* movement. With *Ellen Gates Starr,* she founded *Hull-House* in Chicago, which became a prototype for other such facilities. She advocated for honest government, world peace, and U.S. membership in the League of Nations and the World Court and was corecipient of the Nobel Peace Prize in 1931.

addiction Physiological and psychological dependence on a behavior or substance. Behavioral addictions (sex, gambling, spending, obsessive internet use) and consumptive addictions (alcohol, drugs, food) often have similar etiologies, prognoses, and treatment procedures. Most professionals now use the term *"substance dependence"* for consumptive addictions.

additive effect The impact on a substance abuser of two or more drugs that, taken simultaneously, result in greater or different responses than if taken separately.

additive empathy The interviewer's process of drawing out the inner and more-hidden feelings of the client with *interpretation* and questions about underlying emotions and experiences (for example, "Perhaps you're feeling this way because. . . ."). Additive empathy is used sparingly until a sound social worker–client *relationship* is established, and only when clients are engaged in self-exploration. Additive empathy responses are made only in relation to the client's current awareness and experience and presented tentatively rather than authoritatively. To minimize client *resistance,* the social work interviewer avoids making several additive empathic responses in succession and retreats or acknowledges error if the client indicates a need to avoid the information.

adhesion Physiologically, the attachment or growth together of body tissues or other substances, sometimes causing organs to be abnormally connected.

adhocracy A type of administrative organization characterized by minimization of personnel hierarchies, theoretically designed to achieve greater program flexibility; in social agencies, an alternative to *bureaucracy.*

adiadochokinesia Limited ability to perform rapid alternating movements of the limbs. During physical exams, neurologists or other physicians may ask patients to perform movements of their extremities to help determine the existence of neurological disorders.

adjudication 1. In law, a court decision and the process of reaching that decision through a trial or legal hearing. 2. In a professional organization, the process of determining whether a professional action is in violation of the *code of ethics* or *personnel standards.*

adjusted average per capita cost The estimate used by administrators of government, insurance, or other social agency programs as to how much the program will spend in a year for each beneficiary.

adjustment The activities exerted by an individual to satisfy a need or overcome an obstacle to return to a harmonious fit with the environment. These activities may become habitual responses. Successful adjustment results in *adaptation;* unsuccessful adaptation is called *maladjustment.*

adjuvant therapy A supplementary intervention to improve or extend the effect of the primary therapy. The term is often used in conjunction with cancer therapy, but also applies to psychosocial treatment.

Adlerian theory The concepts about human personality and psychosocial therapy developed by Austrian psychiatrist Alfred Adler (1870–1937). He hypothesized that humans have an inherent drive for power and strive from feeling inferior toward superiority and perfection. The individual does this through one's lifestyle. People achieve goals by developing their social interests, and healthy people ultimately learn to place the good of society over immediate personal gain.

Administration for Children and Families (ACF) A major unit of the *U.S. Department of Health and Human Services* established in 1991 through a consolidation of various programs and agencies. ACF is the lead agency in providing for the welfare of the nation's children and families, through funding, policy direction, and providing information to public and private state and local organizations. ACF components include the *Administration on Children and Families (ACF),* the *Office of Family Assistance (OFA),* the Administration on Developmental Disabilities (ADD), the *Administration for Native Americans (ANA),* the *Office of Child Support Enforcement (OCSE),* the *Office of Community Services (OCS),* and the *Office of Refugee Resettlement (ORR).*

Administration for Native Americans (ANA) The *HHS* organization to ensure that *American Indians* and *Alaska Natives* have the same access to the nation's health care and welfare provisions as do all other Americans and that their unique needs are addressed. The functions of the administration complement those of the *Bureau of Indian Affairs (BIA)* within the *U.S. Department of the Interior.*

administration in social work   Methods used by those who have administrative responsibility to determine organizational goals for a *social agency* or other unit; acquire resources and allocate them to carry out a program; coordinate activities toward achieving selected goals; and monitor, assess, and make necessary changes in processes and structure to improve effectiveness and efficiency. In social work, the term is often used synonymously with management. For social work administrators, implementation of administrative methods is informed by professional values and ethics with the expectation that these methods will enable social workers to provide effective and humane services to clients. The term also applies to the activities performed in a *social agency* that contribute to transforming *social policy* into *social services.* See also *management tasks.*

Administration on Aging (AoA)   The organization within the *Administration for Children and Families (ACF)* of the *U.S. Department of Health and Human Services (HHS)* that oversees and facilitates the nation's programs for older people. The organization monitors the overall condition of older Americans, facilitates research, helps develop legislation, disseminates relevant information, and coordinates programs designed to foster the well-being of older Americans. Their Web site address is http://www.aoa.dhhs.gov. See also *Older Americans Act.*

Administration on Children, Youth, and Families (ACYF)   The HHS organization within the *Administration for Children and Families (ACF)* to facilitate social services to families, including *day care, adoption,* and *foster care* for children, particularly young *special-needs clients.* Through grants the ACYF helps state and other organizations provide child welfare services, Head Start, and services for runaway children. Their Web site address is http://www.acf.dhhs.gov/programs/acyf

administrative hearing   An official presentation of an argument or case to a governmental agency or administrative law judge that results in a legal decision.

administrative tribunal   Courtlike agency set up to hear cases and issue rulings. Located sometimes in established courthouses and other government buildings, it is often presided over by "referees" rather than judges and may or may not use attorneys in adversarial proceedings. Tribunals were established primarily because the high number of cases has overwhelmed traditional courts of law and because some kinds of cases seem better suited to less-formal arrangements. Tribunals have dealt mostly with cases involving minor offenses, juvenile and family issues, landlord–tenant disputes, and traffic offenses. This term also refers to panels established by organizations to hear disputes, for example, a professional association or professional licensing board panel to determine whether sanctions and licensing revocations are appropriate.

admissions   The department or unit of a health, mental health, or social services agency responsible for administering the procedures by which patients or clients enter the program.

admissions procedures   The explicit rules and modes of action for bringing an individual under the care of an organization, social agency, or health care facility. Such procedures often include obtaining consent from the client (or those responsible for the client) to provide the appropriate care; obtaining pertinent background information about the client from a variety of sources (that is, interviews with the client or client's family, medical records, social histories, and medical and psychological tests); contracting with the client or third parties to provide financing for the care; advising the client about when to go to the appropriate place; and coordinating the initial information exchanges between the client and those concerned about the client. Admissions procedures often include criteria for screening applicants for service.

adolescence   The *life cycle* period between *childhood* and *adulthood,* beginning at *puberty* and ending with young adulthood. Adolescents struggle to find self-identity, and this struggle is often accompanied by erratic behavior.

adoption   Taking a person, usually an infant or child, permanently into one's home and treating the child as though born into the *family.* A legal as well as a *child welfare* function and process, adoption includes changes in court records to show the legal transfer of the individual from the *biological parents* to the *adoptive parents.* Adoption usually gives the individual the same rights of inheritance as birth children, and the adoptive parents the same responsibilities and rights of control as biological parents. See also *subsidized adoption, independent adoption, gray-market adoption, black-market adoption, intercountry adoption, kinship adoption, stepparent adoption,* and *relinquishment adoption.*

Adoption and Safe Families Act   The 1997 federal legislation (P.L. 105-89) to facilitate the efforts of child welfare workers to remove children from dangerous situations and help states find adoptive or permanent homes for foster children, especially those with special needs. The law amends the 1980 *Adoption Assistance and Child Welfare Act* by placing limitations on the reasonable efforts to reunite families and make permanency decisions within 12 months.

Adoption Assistance and Child Welfare Act   The U.S. federal legislation (P.L. 96-272), known as the *permanency planning* law, to help facilitate and improve the *adoption* process and protect the rights of children, their parents, and others. The law requires making reasonable efforts to prevent unnecessary placement of children in out-of-home care and to facilitate reunification, periodic case reviews of all children in care, and increased efforts to achieve a permanent family for every child in a timely manner. The act also provides federal financial support for adoption subsidy, improving opportunities for children with special needs to achieve permanence through adoption. The act was amended in 1997 with the *Adoption and Safe Families Act.*

Adoption Information Clearinghouse, National   The U.S. resource administered by the *Children's Bureau* on all aspects of adoption, including facilitating the adoption process; educating adoptive and birth parents; facilitating access to adoption records; facilitating searches for birth relatives; and assisting professionals through publications, conferences, support for research, and program development. Their Web site address is http://www.calib.com/naic

adoptive parents   Couples and individuals who build a family through *adoption* rather than procreation. Adoptive parents include those who are single, married with children, or those who have already parented children biologically; they come from all social, educational, and economic levels.

adrenaline   A hormone secreted by the adrenal glands that mobilizes the body to meet perceived emergency or stressful situations. Adrenaline acts to release sugars from the liver and increase blood volume in the muscles to increase strength, stimulate the heart beat, increase mental alertness, and generally prepare the body for extraordinary activity.

adult   An individual who has reached the legal age of maturity; in most nations and states this age is 18.

adult antisocial behavior   An enduring pattern of criminal conduct and other acts that are counterproductive to social *norms* in a person whose behavior cannot be attributed to a specific and diagnosable *mental disorder.* This label is often applied to professional thieves, drug dealers, organized crime figures, and white-collar criminals.

adult children of alcoholics (ACOAs)   People who have been raised in the stressful environments created by parents who abused alcohol or other substances. Many ACOAs share similar emotional disorders, including *anxiety, depression,* low *self-esteem, anger,* and their own predisposition toward *alcohol abuse* and *substance abuse.* A national 12-step organization called "Adult Children of Alcoholics" began forming in the 1970s and was formally established in 1985. The organization also serves incest victims and other dysfunctional families. Its Web site address is http://www.adultchildren.org. See also *support system* and *codependency.*

adult day care   Programs that provide personal, social, and homemaker services to adults who are unable to care for themselves when their primary guardians are unavailable. Those most likely to require such care are people with physical and mental disabilities whose caregivers must be away every day for extended periods. Such care may be provided in private homes, nursing homes, and other facilities.

adult day center   Publicly or sometimes privately funded facilities in which seniors or other adults gather to participate in recreational, social, educational, and developmental programs. Such facilities often are used by independently functioning seniors as well as by the clients of *adult day care.*

adult development   Normal changes that occur in the individual from maturity to death. These include the physical, cognitive, social, emotional, and personality changes that occur after adolescence.

adult education   The process—with people who are beyond the age of general public education—

of acquiring and imparting knowledge, skills, and values. Adult education programs have been used to eliminate *illiteracy,* improve vocational and economic opportunities, and enhance human potential. The Adult Education Association of the United States sponsors research, issues publications, and maintains standards for those who provide such services.

adult foster care Residential care programs in the private homes of nonrelatives provided for adults who cannot live independently, including some people with a mental disorder, or mental retardation, and *frail elderly* people. Caregivers usually provide room and board and assistance in *activities of daily living (ADL)* in family-like environments, in exchange for a monthly payment, under the supervision of human services professionals. The professionals, who are employed by social services agencies, find these homes, match them with appropriate adults in need, and provide ongoing counseling and needed health and community resources.

adult learner model An educational ideology that recognizes students as being responsible, self-directing, and motivated to learn and share from their accumulated life experiences. This model views adult learning as being more effective when students experience direct and relevant application of their developing problem-solving skills. This is the model of education in professional schools of social work. See also *andragogy.*

adult protective services (APS) *Human services* often including social, medical, legal, residential, and *custodial care* that may be provided for adults who are unable to provide such care for themselves or who have no others to provide it. Such people often are incapable of acting judiciously on their own behalf and, thus, are vulnerable to being harmed by or to inflicting harm on others. In such situations, and typically after a legal decision has been made, the *social agency* or other care facility provides the relevant service until it is no longer deemed necessary. The 1975 *Title XX* legislation mandated that APS be provided without regard to a person's financial or residency eligibility.

adulthood The life cycle stage in human development that begins at maturity and ends at death. Social scientists often divide adulthood into several periods, such as early adulthood (18 to 44 years), middle adulthood (45 to 64 years), and late

adulthood (65 years to death). In legal terms, in many jurisdictions, adulthood is generally considered to begin at age 18.

adultified child A youth who, because of the family's relationship patterns, psychopathology, or socioeconomic circumstances, is compelled to assume roles and responsibilities normally reserved for older people. An example is a child who is a primary caregiver for younger siblings as well as meal preparer, housekeeper, and major emotional source of support for a single, working parent.

adultolescent People, usually in their 20s and 30s, who stay in or return to their parents' homes and resume a somewhat dependent role. Frequently they remain unemployed or underemployed and supported by their parents. Their behavior is not age appropriate, that is, it seems younger than that of an adult and older than that of an adolescent.

advance directive A properly witnessed and documented statement that describes in detail the medical options a person would or would not want used to prolong life when one is no longer able to make such choices known. The document may also name someone who could make such decisions for the individual. See also *living will* and *Patient Self-Determination Act* and *death with dignity.*

adventitious disability A condition acquired later in life, such as those caused by accident or disease rather than *congenital abnormalities* or *developmental disabilities.* A major cause of adventitious disabilities is child abuse, and hearing impairment is one of the more-common permanent disabilities resulting from child abuse.

adventure training A self-development and training program typically conducted in wilderness settings to help participants develop confidence in themselves and their associates, build trust and teamwork skills, and improve problem-solving skills. Typically participants learn by performing seemingly frightening and challenging tasks, such as scaling trees and running obstacle courses.

adversarial process A procedure for reaching decisions by hearing and evaluating the presentation of opposing viewpoints. The adversarial process is most notably seen in courts of law, in which opposing attorneys present evidence and arguments in support of their respective views or clients. See also *arbitration* and *mediation*.

adverse impact   In personnel management, the discriminatory effect of the organization's selection procedures on one's opportunity for employment or promotion. See also *disparate impact* and *four-fifths rule*.

advice giving   An *intervention* in social work in which the social worker helps the client to recognize and understand the existence of a problem or goal and to consider the various responses that might be made to deal with it. The social worker then recommends the best strategies to accomplish the objectives.

advisory board   A committee that provides needed information, *expert opinion*, and recommendations about how to achieve an organization's goals, often according to predetermined criteria. Members of the advisory board are consulted for their expertise as a group or as individuals. Members may be elected, hired, or recruited as volunteers and may or may not include the organization's *board of directors*.

advocacy   1. The act of directly representing or defending others. 2. In social work, championing the rights of individuals or communities through direct intervention or through *empowerment*. According to the *NASW Code of Ethics*, it is a basic obligation of the profession and its members.

advocacy research   Systematic investigation of specific social problems and objective measurement of their extent, progression, and response to corrective actions. This type of research also heightens public awareness of the social problems and recommends possible solutions.

advocate role   Speaking out on behalf of the client to achieve changes in the conditions that contribute to the client's problems and securing and protecting a client's existing right or entitlement. See also *enabler role, broker role, mediator role,* and *educator role*.

AFDC–EA programs   The emergency assistance provision of the former *Aid to Families with Dependent Children (AFDC)* program, which had been designed to help such families meet their costs of temporary, unexpected needs such as natural disasters, extraordinary home-heating costs, and utility cutoffs. The programs were eliminated or significantly modified by the *Personal Responsibility and Work Opportunity Reconciliation Act* of 1996.

affect   An individual's expression of *mood, temperament,* and feelings; an individual's overt emotional state.

affective congruency   Feelings that are consistent with those of most other people about the same thing. For example, a social worker who is distressed at seeing an abused child has affective congruency with most other people.

affective disorder   Emotional disturbances characterized primarily by chronic or episodic changes of *mood,* such as *depression, euphoria,* or *mania.* This term has been replaced by the term *mood disorder*.

affiliation   1. An ongoing explicit relationship or association. 2. A coping strategy of dealing with emotional conflict or stress by turning to others for help and support and mutual problem solving.

affirmative action   Steps taken by an organization to remedy imbalances in the employment of people of color and women, promotions, and other opportunities. Many opponents of affirmative action now refer to it as "racial preferences." See also *protected class*.

affirmative action groups   Those segments of the society identified by federal, state, and local jurisdictions as meriting protection from employment *discrimination* on the basis of race, color, age, disability, religion, gender, or national origin. Employment discrimination refers to people who are currently discriminated against (for example, are not hired, promoted, or retained as often as members of other groups or whose group is underrepresented because of past discrimination). See also *protected class*.

African American   Black people who are residents of the United States who came from, or whose ancestors came from, Africa. This term is generally preferred over the term "Afro American."

Afrocentricity   An orientation, social philosophy, or *worldview* that uses the cultural values, history, and shared experiences of people of black African descent as a framework to explain social phenomena and to solve human problems. Many social workers prefer the term "Africentricity."

aftercare   The continuing treatment, physical maintenance, and social support of formerly hospitalized or institutionalized clients during extended convalescence or social transition back to the community. See also *halfway houses* and *quarterway houses.*

aftercare, juvenile   In judicial terminology, the status of a juvenile who has been conditionally released from incarceration as a result of delinquency and placed in a supervised treatment or rehabilitation program while living at home, in foster placement, or in a transitional living facility. The system is also known as *juvenile parole.*

age at onset   The point in one's life when a specific disorder or problem started.

age discrimination   Unfair treatment of people on the basis of their ages. If these people are discriminated against as employees, the employer is breaking U.S. federal law (the *Age Discrimination in Employment Act [ADEA] of 1967*).

Age Discrimination in Employment Act (ADEA) of 1967   A U.S. federal law that prohibits employers with 20 or more employees from discriminating against people older than age 40. The law is enforced by the *Equal Employment Opportunity Commission (EEOC)* and explicitly forbids *age discrimination* in hiring, discharge, pay, promotions, and other aspects of employment. See also *mandatory retirement.*

age integration   Bringing together people of different generations. The current trend is toward de facto *age segregation,* manifested in communities— for example, residential buildings, neighborhoods, and even cities that are restricted to people older than a certain age. There have been many negative consequences of this, for young as well as older people. Thus, some programs, facilities, and social causes are designed to combine the needs of people of all ages to encourage their interaction and mutual benefit.

age of consent   The legal age, established by statute in the relevant jurisdiction, at which time an individual is permitted to marry without parental approval, enter into business contracts, or engage in sexual relations of his or her own volition. Engaging in sexual relations with one who is younger than the age of consent can result in criminal charges and conviction of the older person for *statutory rape.* An erroneous belief that the younger person was of the age of consent usually is not a sustainable defense against these charges.

age segregation   Isolating people from one another based on their ages. This may occur as a result of *ageism,* personal preferences, social convenience, or the necessity of providing different services to people with different needs and lifestyles. Examples occur in *gray ghettos,* in public elementary schools, and in retirement communities. When a community or society discourages this type of segregation, it is seeking a high degree of *age integration.*

"aged"   One term for older people. In the United States, this term is generally applied to people who have reached at least age 65. Developmental psychologists identify three groups of the aged population: (1) the "young old" (ages 60 to 64), (2) the "middle old" (ages 65 to 74), and (3) the "oldest old" (older than age 74).

ageism   Stereotyping and generalizing about people on the basis of their ages; commonly, a form of *discrimination* against older people. This term is also spelled "agism." See also *gerontophobia.*

agency adoption   See *relinquishment adoption.*

Agency for Healthcare Research and Quality (AHRQ)   The U.S. government's lead organization for research on the national health care system, including its effectiveness, costs, access, utilization, and outcomes. The AHRQ is a *HHS* organization, formerly known as the Agency for Health Care Policy and Research.

Agency for International Development (AID)   The U.S. State Department program, created in 1961 by a consolidation of other international relief organizations, that administers and coordinates economic and social welfare assistance to other nations. Their Web site address is http://www.usaid.gov

agency   See *social agency.*

Agent Orange   A herbicide used most notably in the Vietnam War to defoliate areas where enemy troops were thought to be hiding. Some veterans have claimed that their exposure to this dioxin resulted in their subsequent contracting of various diseases, including cancer.

age-related cognitive decline Diminished capacities in thought processes, such as memory and problem solving, within the normal limits of aging.

AGE-SW The Association for Gerontology Education in Social Work, an organization primarily made up of social work faculty and gerontology social work practitioners, established in 1981, to facilitate the integration of content about aging in graduate and undergraduate schools of social work. AGE-SW provides social work educators in this field with mentoring, linkages, information exchanges, conferences, and the regular newsletter *AGEnda*. Their Web site address is http://www.agesocialwork.org

aggravated assault A severe or intensified form of *assault* involving an attack or threat with a dangerous weapon. The Federal Bureau of Investigation (FBI) classifies this as a violent crime.

aggression Behavior characterized by forceful contact and communication with other people. Human aggression is expressed directly as verbal or physical attacks and indirectly through competition, athletic endeavors, and similar activities. Aggression may be appropriate and used for self-defense or self-enhancement, or it may be destructive to oneself and others. Some social scientists use the term "aggression" to refer only to harmful behaviors and the term *assertiveness* for behavior that is not intended to harm others.

"aging out" The informal term used for status changes among young people who outgrow their qualification as dependents while in the responsibility of the health care and welfare system, such as foster care, juvenile detention facilities, or educational facilities. Often when such youngsters are runaway children or kidnap victims or are moving from one foster care facility to another, they "age out" and get lost. They still exist but are no longer counted, sought, or served when located and are extremely vulnerable to exploitation.

agitation 1. Extreme restlessness or gestures of nervousness. 2. The organized effort to produce discomfort with the status quo to win popular support for some *social change.*

agitator In *community organization,* a role in which an individual or group challenges existing social structures by means such as publicity, public debate, and voter registration drives and by or-

ganizing active and *passive resistance* campaigns. The goal is to create new institutions or to change the ways in which established ones operate.

agitprop *Propaganda* intended to agitate.

agnosia The inability to comprehend familiar objects that are being perceived by the sense organs. This may be a partial or total inability to attach meaning to the input from one or more of the five senses. For example, in visual agnosia, the individual takes in all the normal light sensations in the visual field but cannot decipher or process this information to recognize or interpret what is being seen. This condition is often the result of brain damage, especially to the cortex, often the result of *stroke.*

agoraphobia An irrational and persistent *fear* of being in unfamiliar places or of leaving one's home. Most people with this condition make special efforts to avoid crowded rooms, public transportation facilities, tunnels, and other environments from which escape seems difficult and where help is unavailable.

agraphia See *dysgraphia.*

agrarian society Those nations or peoples whose means of subsistence is primarily based on growing crops.

Agriculture, U.S. Department of (USDA) The federal agency created in 1862 to administer the nation's farm programs, meat and dairy inspection, food production and distribution; to conserve farmland; and to provide education and information to farmers. The USDA also administers the *Food and Nutrition Service* (which includes the *Food Stamp program,* the *School Lunch program,* and the *WIC program.* Its Web site address is http://www.usda.gov

Aid to Dependent Children (ADC) A program that originated with the *Social Security Act* of 1935 to provide financial and social assistance to needy children. In 1950, ADC was modified to help provide for the needy caregivers of these children and was later renamed *Aid to Families with Dependent Children (AFDC).*

Aid to Families with Dependent Children (AFDC) A former *public assistance* program that originated in the 1935 *Social Security Act* as *Aid to*

Dependent Children. It was funded by the federal and state governments to provide financial aid for needy children who were deprived of parental support because of death, incapacitation, or absence. AFDC was administered on the state and local levels, usually through county departments of public welfare (or human or social services). At the national level, it was administered by the *Administration for Children and Families (ACF)* of the *U.S. Department of Health and Human Services (HHS)*. Eligibility was determined by a *means test.* The program was replaced in 1996 by *Temporary Assistance to Needy Families (TANF)*. See also *Personal Responsibility and Work Opportunity Reconciliation Act* of 1996.

Aid to the Blind (AB) A *categorical program* for needy blind people, originating in the *Social Security Act.* The program was administered at the state and local levels before 1972, when it was consolidated with *Old Age Assistance (OAA)* and *Aid to the Permanently and Totally Disabled (APTD)* programs into the *Supplemental Security Income (SSI)* program.

Aid to the Permanently and Totally Disabled (APTD) A program that was established by a 1950 amendment to the *Social Security Act* to provide financial assistance to needy people with serious and permanent physical or mental *disabilities.* In 1972, with passage of the federal *Supplemental Security Income (SSI)* program, the program was consolidated with the *Old Age Assistance (OAA)* and *Aid to the Blind (AB)* programs.

AIDS See *acquired immune deficiency syndrome.*

AIDS dementia complex Impairment of cognitive functioning due to infections of the *central nervous system (CNS)* related to the *human immunodeficiency virus (HIV)*. As with other CNS disorders, the symptoms vary from day to day but at worst include grandiosity, poor impulse control, aimless wandering, memory loss, and disorientation.

AIDS-related complex (ARC) An imprecise term referring to the signs and symptoms that occur during the progression from *human immunodeficiency virus (HIV)* infection to *acquired immune deficiency syndrome (AIDS)*. These symptoms include diarrhea, weight loss, fever, headaches, bruising, bleeding, oral thrush, stomachache, fatigue, disease of the lymph glands, and neurological changes. The progression from infection to the final stages of AIDS may take from a few months to

many years, and the symptoms attributed to ARC appear during that time. Thus, although ARC once was thought to be a discrete stage in the progression of AIDS, researchers now think that it is not a useful concept and one that may even interfere with the accurate understanding of AIDS and HIV.

AIDS-related stigma Negative and hostile attitudes directed toward and about people with *HIV disease.* The stigma originated in the belief that the disease is contagious and incurable and that AIDS has been associated with people already stigmatized, that is, gay men and intravenous drug abusers.

akathisia A sustained pattern of fidgety movements, such as swinging of the legs, rocking, tapping the feet or hands, pacing, and being unable to remain in a position for long. This pattern can be a symptom of *anxiety, psychosis, substance abuse,* or a *medication-induced movement disorder.* The term is also properly spelled "akathesia."

akinesia Reduced or minimal motor movement.

Al-Anon A voluntary *self-help organization* comprising primarily the relatives of alcoholics who meet regularly to provide *mutual help* and to discuss how to help solve common problems. Al-Anon, founded in 1951, has chapters in most communities in the United States and many other nations. Its Web site address is http://www.al-anon.org. To serve Al-Anon members who were teenagers, Alateen was founded in 1957. See also *support system.*

alarmist One who excites popular fear; often this is a term of derision made by political or administrative leaders against people seeking social change. See also *agitator.*

Alaska Natives The *ethnic group* of American citizens, many of whom are commonly known as Eskimos and Aleuts, whose ancestors lived in the area now known as Alaska before Europeans explored and settled the Western Hemisphere.

alcohol abuse Consumption of alcohol in such a way as to harm or endanger the well-being of the user or those with whom the user comes in contact. Such consumption often leads the abuser to cause accidents, to become physically assaultive and less productive, or to deteriorate physically.

alcohol dependence A pattern of alcohol use that results in *impaired social functioning.* The behavior pattern typically includes a daily need or wish for alcohol, inconsistent attempts to control drinking, physical disorders aggravated by use of alcohol, occasional binges, absences or ineffectiveness at work, violence, and social relationship problems. Because it is rare for people with alcohol dependency to have all these symptoms, they sometimes rationalize that they do not suffer from *alcoholism*.

alcohol hallucinosis   Imaginary perceptions that occur after a person with an *alcohol dependence* problem has stopped or reduced the consumption of alcohol. The most common type of *hallucination* is auditory. The disorder most frequently lasts a few hours or days and rarely more than a week.

Alcohol, Tobacco, Firearms and Explosives, Bureau of (ATF)   The federal law enforcement organization within the *U.S. Department of Justice* that regulates the use, sale, and distribution of alcohol, tobacco, firearms, and explosives. This bureau was created in 2002 when the *Homeland Security Act* divided the functions of the former Bureau of Alcohol, Tobacco and Firearms. The U.S. Department of Justice took over the enforcement functions and the U.S. Department of the Treasury took over the tax collection system as part of the new Alcohol and Tobacco Tax and Trade Bureau (TTB).

alcohol withdrawal   Symptoms in one who suffers *alcohol dependence* following cessation or reduction in drinking, including some, but not necessarily all of the following: *tremor* ("the shakes"), nausea, *depression* and *anxiety*, irritability, hypersensitivity to environmental stimuli, weakness, *tachycardia*, sweating, agitated behavior, *delusion*, and *withdrawal delirium* (*delirium tremens [DTs]*). See also *withdrawal symptoms*.

Alcoholics Anonymous (AA)   A voluntary *self-help organization* of people who have experienced problems related to *alcohol dependence*. Founded in 1935 by two men who had experienced long-term alcohol problems, AA functions through thousands of local groups throughout the world. Its Web site address is http://www.alcoholics-anonymous.org. None of these groups has formal officers, constitutions, or dues, and all groups are open to anyone with a drinking problem. See also *12-step programs* and *Al-Anon*.

alcoholism   Physical or psychological dependence on alcohol consumption. Alcoholism can lead to social, mental, or physical impairment. See also *primary alcoholism, secondary alcoholism,* and *reactive alcoholism*.

alexia   A reading disability that begins during adulthood and is usually brought about by head injury, *stroke,* or some other abnormality in the *central nervous system (CNS)*.

alexithymia   Inability to recognize or describe one's own emotions, often associated with mental disorders that impede healthy cognitive functioning.

algophobia   The pathological *fear* of pain.

alias   A name one uses other than his or her legal or given name, usually to conceal an identity.

Alien Labor Certification Division   A division of the *U.S. Department of Labor* that authorizes workers from foreign nations to remain in the United States for a specified time to help meet labor demand. See also *green card* and *mica*.

alien   One who resides in a country but is not a citizen or national of that country. See also *undocumented alien*.

Alien Registration Recipient   U.S. Government Form I-551, which is issued to citizens of other nations who become permanent U.S. residents. The form is more commonly known as the *green card*.

alienation   The feeling of apartness or strangeness experienced in cultural or social settings that seem unfamiliar, unacceptable, or unpredictable.

alimony   Money paid by one former spouse to the other to provide for separate *maintenance* according to domestic law. Alimony is distinct from the obligation of child support payments. The term now preferred is maintenance. See also *palimony* and *spousal support*.

alimony pendente   A pretrial order for *spousal support*.

Alinksy, Saul (1909–1972)   A community organizer based in Chicago, he developed methods for effectively mobilizing a community such as realistic goal setting and personalizing social problems by identifying scapegoats or "villains."

All Work Test   See *personal capability assessment.*

allergen   Small particles of material, such as pollen, dust, mold, and animal dander, that can cause allergic reactions in some people.

allergy   A reaction of the immune system after exposure to specific substances (antigens). Nearly anything in the environment can be an antigen, but the most common ones include tree pollen, household dust mites, pet dander, and certain foods and drugs. The intensity of reaction varies greatly from person to person, from mild or barely perceptible discomfort with some sneezing and tears to life-threatening shock reactions with symptoms of low blood pressure, labored breathing, swollen tongue, constricted breathing tubes, and suffocation.

Alliance for Progress   The program established in the Kennedy administration in 1961 to aid Latin American nations that agreed to begin democratic reforms.

Alliance of Information and Referral Systems   The association of information and referral (I&R) specialists, established in 1973, to develop the field, sponsor testing and certification for I&R providers, and maintain standards. Credentials for specialists include Certified Information and Referral Specialist (CIRS), Certified Resource Specialist (CRS), and Certified Resource Specialist–Aged (CRS–A). Their Web site address is http://www.airs.org

allied health professionals   The generic name for the professional personnel of hospitals and other health care facilities other than physicians and nurses. Social workers, including those specializing in *medical social work,* are usually included in this designation. Others include audiologists, optometrists, physical and occupational therapists, pharmacists, psychologists, registered dietitians, speech pathologists, radiology technicians, and respiratory therapists.

allocentric   An orientation to the thoughts, feelings, values, and customs of others rather than oneself (the opposite of egocentric).

alloplasty   In *psychoanalytic theory,* the psychic process in which the *libido* is directed away from the *self* and onto other people or objects in the environment. See also *autoplasty.*

allotment   A financial grant or portion of a budget set aside to accomplish some purpose or manage some program. For example, the United Way has an annual allotment for local family services agencies.

almoner   One who distributes money or needed goods to poor people. Many social workers were called "almoners" before the 20th century. In contemporary Great Britain the term sometimes refers to medical social workers who determine whether hospital patients are entitled to benefits.

alms   Money or goods to be given charitably by individuals to poor people. This term has been rarely used since 1900. See also *philanthropy.*

almshouse   A home for poor people; a form of *indoor relief* prevalent before the 20th century, in which shelters funded by *philanthropy* were provided for destitute families and individuals. In recent decades, almshouses have largely been replaced by *outdoor relief* programs in which needy people are provided with money, goods, and services while living in their own homes. See also *relief* and *workhouse.*

alogia   Poverty of thinking as manifested by restricted speech consisting mostly of short, concrete, repetitive, and stereotyped replies lacking in spontaneity or information.

alopecia   Hair loss that frequently occurs in patients undergoing chemotherapy for cancer or suffering from other diseases in which cell-killing, or cytotoxic, drugs are used.

alphabet agencies   Government bureaus and organizations that are as well or better known by their initials, such as the FBI, NIMH, FDA, and OSHA. The term was once used in derision to apply to President Franklin Roosevelt's *New Deal* agencies, such as WPA, CCC, and FERA.

alternative delivery systems (ADS)   A combined *health care* and financing program. Unlike the traditional method of paying the physician or hospital directly or through *third-party payment* arrangements, the ADS consumer pays a fixed premium in advance and receives services at nominal or no charge. ADS programs include the *health maintenance organization (HMO), independent practice associations (IPAs),* health care alliances, *preferred provider organizations (PPOs),* and primary-care networks. See also *managed health care program.*

alternative dispute resolution (ADR) Systematic procedures in which disagreements are settled out of court, including *arbitration, mediation,* and *negotiation.* Courts sometimes order disputants to seek an ADR mechanism before agreeing to hear the case.

alternative medicine See *complementary and alternative medicine (CAP).*

Altmeyer, Arthur J. (1891–1972) A principal designer of the legislation that became the *Social Security Act* in 1935. As a federal administrator he helped design the merit system for the *U.S. Civil Service* and state personnel programs.

altruism Unselfish regard for the well-being of others, accompanied by motivation to give money, goods, services, or companionship. See also *philanthropy* and *charity.*

Alzheimer's disease An organic *mental disorder* occurring most often in older people. The condition is also known as "SDAT" (senile dementia, Alzheimer's type). Alzheimer's disease is characterized by confusion, forgetfulness, *mood swings,* impaired *cognition* to learn, disorientation, and *dementia.* It is thought to be the result of diffuse brain *atrophy,* especially in the frontal lobes.

AMBER Alert A national emergency notification procedure in the United States for ongoing child abduction situations. When a child has been recently abducted, the public is notified about the perpetrator through electronic highway billboards, radio news announcements, and TV news "crawls." The system originated in 1996 and is named for Amber Hagerman, a 9-year-old Texas girl who was abducted and murdered. AMBER is also an acronym for Abducted Minor: Broadcast Emergency Response.

ambiguous mandate Expectations and requirements made of a social welfare administrator or other official by the relevant constituency that are unclear and not sufficiently specific. Effective administrators often see ambiguous mandates not as frustrating obstacles but as opportunity for creative leadership and innovation.

ambisexual The possession of male and female sexual traits or role behaviors in approximately equal degrees such that neither sex seems predominant in the individual. The term is similar to *androgyny,* but emphasizes physical more than established *role behavior* characteristics.

ambivalence Contradictory emotions, such as love and hate, that occur simultaneously within an individual. In its extreme form, the term is related to indecisiveness and rapidly shifting emotional attitudes toward someone or some idea.

ambivert In the psychoanalytic theories of Carl Jung (1875–1961), an individual whose personality contains nearly equal characteristics of an *introvert* and an *extrovert.*

ambulantes People in Spanish-speaking cultures who make their living selling goods and providing minor services on street corners.

ambulatory care Medical treatment and health care in outpatient clinics, dispensaries, and in offices of physicians—that is, noninstitutional health care.

Amerasian One who has one parent from the United States and the other parent from an Asian nation. Often these people are the offspring of American military men and women of Vietnamese, Hmong, Kampuchean (Cambodian), Korean, Japanese, or Philippine origins.

American Arbitration Association (AAA) The nonprofit public service organization founded in 1926 to help resolve disputes through *mediation, arbitration,* elections, and other voluntary procedures. The AAA does not itself arbitrate but helps disputants find qualified, impartial arbiters from among those it certifies. Their Web site address is http://www.adr.org

American Association for Marriage and Family Therapy (AAMFT) An interdisciplinary professional association founded in 1942 (as the American Association of Marriage Counselors). Its functions and goals include the enhancement of the well-being of families and couples in the United States and professional development of its members through conferences, accredited educational and training programs, and publications. AAMFT publishes the *Journal of Marital and Family Therapy* and the magazine *Family Therapy*. Its Web site address is http://www.aamft.org

American Association of Food Stamp Directors (AAFSD) The professional organization composed of state and local administrators of the *Food Stamp program* to provide a forum for mutual efforts and concern about efficient delivery of the food stamp service. AAFSD was founded in 1975 and is affiliated with the *American Public Human Services Association (APHSA)*.

American Association of Group Workers (AAGW) An organization of professional social workers who specialized in working with small groups. AAGW was formed in 1936. In 1955 it merged into the *National Association of Social Workers (NASW)*.

American Association of Hospital Social Workers (AAHSW) The organization, established in 1918, comprising social workers employed in medical facilities and hospital social work departments. In 1934 it was renamed the American Association of Medical Social Workers (AAMSW). In 1955 it merged with six other professional groups to form the *National Association of Social Workers (NASW)*.

American Association of Industrial Social Workers (AAISW) The organization of professional social workers, founded in 1982, who provide occupational social work services through employment with business organizations or through *employee assistance programs (EAPs)*. It develops and maintains standards of *quality assurance* and encourages the effective use of industrial social workers. See also *industrial social work*.

American Association of Mental Health Professionals in Corrections (AAMHPC) The multidisciplinary professional association of social workers, psychologists, nurses, physicians, and other professionals employed in prisons, juvenile detention facilities, and other carceral institutions to treat, rehabilitate, conduct research, advocate for, and provide information to the community about inmates with *mental disorder* and *mental retardation*. The organization was founded in 1940, sponsors annual conferences, and publishes the scholarly journal *Corrective and Social Psychiatry*.

American Association of Psychiatric Social Workers (AAPSW) The membership associa-

tion, founded in 1926, of social workers who specialized in clinical work with people with mental disorders or who worked with *mental health teams*. AAPSW merged with six other social work organizations in 1955 to form the *National Association of Social Workers (NASW)*.

American Association of Public Opinion Research (AAPOR) The organization of pollsters and public opinion research professionals, established in 1947, to promote, facilitate, and ensure ethical and quality practices in public opinion research.

American Association of Public Welfare Attorneys (AAPWA) The professional association, founded in 1967, composed of lawyers who work for or with public assistance organizations. AAPWA is affiliated with the *American Public Human Services Association (APHSA)* and provides a forum for considering legal issues in the administration of public welfare programs.

American Association of Retired Persons (AARP) The largest senior citizens' group in the United States, founded in 1958 to influence legislation and provide social, economic, and recreational services to people older than 50 (retired or not). The AARP Web site address is www.aarp.org

American Association of Schools of Social Work (AASSW) The organization founded in 1985 to enhance the quality and focus of social work education and the educational institutions that provide it. Formerly an organization of deans of social work schools, the association comprises deans, faculty, and other concerned professionals. An earlier organization by the same name, established in 1919, was a forerunner of the *Council on Social Work Education (CSWE)*.

American Association of Sex Educators, Counselors, and Therapists (AASECT) The multidisciplinary professional organization founded in 1967 that advocates for greater public knowledge about and healthy expressions of human sexuality. The association, which publishes the *Journal of Sex Education and Therapy*, educates the general public and professionals about aspects of sexuality and treatment of its problems. Its Web site address is http://www.aasect.org

American Association of Social Workers (AASW) A membership organization of professional social workers founded in 1921 and merged into the *National Association of Social Workers (NASW)* in 1955.

American Association on Mental Retardation (AAMR)   The interdisciplinary professional organization, established in 1876, comprising professionals who study and work with those affected by *mental retardation*. Its Web site address is http://www.aamr.org

American Board of Examiners in Clinical Social Work (ABE)   An independent credentialing organization created in 1987 to assure the public and third parties that qualified practitioners are competent, current, ethical, and effective. ABE awards the Board Certified Diplomate in Clinical Social Work credential for qualified applicants who have 7,500 hours of clinical practice experience (3,000 hours under supervision); an MSW degree or above with appropriate clinical training from an accredited school of social work; relevant licensing; and completion of the ABE evaluation process, in which three peers complete a rating form. Their Web site address is http://www.abecsw.org

American Board of Psychiatry and Neurology (ABPN)   An organization of physicians established in 1934 that examines and certifies diplomates in psychiatry, neurology, and related fields of medical practice. A "board-certified" *psychiatrist* or *neurologist* is credentialed by this group.

American Civil Liberties Union (ACLU)   A *civil rights group* formed in 1920 and dedicated to the restraint of governmental interference with individuals' personal freedom. Its Web site address is http://www.aclu.org

American Competitiveness and Workforce Improvement Act   U.S. federal law (P.L. 105-277) enacted in 1998 primarily to facilitate the immigration of highly skilled workers from foreign countries when U.S. employers cannot find such workers from within the nation.

American Counseling Association (ACA)   The professional association founded in 1952 (as the American Personnel and Guidance Association) to promote the professional development of its members, maintain standards of practice, facilitate research and information dissemination, and advocate for its members and their clients. Its Web site address is http://www.counseling.org

American Federation of Government Employees (AFGE)   An AFL–CIO affiliated labor organization, founded in 1932, whose members are employed by the government of the United States. Many AFGE members are social workers employed as administrators, researchers, supervisors, and providers of direct social services. Their Web site address is http://www.afge.org

American Federation of Labor–Congress of Industrial Organizations (AFL–CIO)   The oldest and largest *labor union* in the United States. AFL was founded in 1886 to help assure workers of fairer and more stable working conditions. In 1935 several AFL unions—unhappy with the emphasis on skilled craftspeople—broke away and formed the CIO to give greater voice to industrial workers. The two groups merged in 1955 and now include nearly 100 distinct unions, including the *American Federation of Government Employees (AFGE)* and the *American Federation of State, County, and Municipal Employees (AFSCME)*, with which many social workers are affiliated.

American Federation of State, County, and Municipal Employees (AFSCME)   An AFL–CIO affiliated labor organization founded in 1936, whose members are employed by nonfederal governments. Many of its members include state and county public assistance workers, child welfare workers, and other social services personnel as well as police personnel, firefighters, and public agency administrators. Its Web site address is http://www.afscme.org

American Geriatrics Society (AGS)   The nonprofit organization, established in 1942, composed of physicians, scientists, and health care professionals to promote and direct research in the field of aging; to develop geriatric training centers throughout the nation; and to disseminate information on the diagnosis, treatment, and prevention of diseases in elderly people. AGS publishes the influential *Journal of the American Geriatrics Society*. Their Web site address is http://www.americangeriatrics.org

American Hospital Association (AHA)   An organization founded in 1899 comprising more than 5,500 hospitals and other patient care institutions in the United States. AHA establishes and sanctions standards and guidelines to maintain *quality assurance*. Its Web site address is http://www.aha.org. One of its many affiliated membership groups is the *Society for Social Work Administrators in Health Care (SSWAHC).*

American Indian Movement (AIM) A *civil rights group,* founded in 1968 to encourage self-determination among *American Indians* and gain recognition of their treaty rights. AIM also conducts research, maintains historical archives, and sponsors educational programs.

American Indians Also known as *Native Americans,* the ethnic–racial–cultural groups of American citizens whose ancestors lived in the Western Hemisphere before its exploration and settlement by the Europeans.

American Law Institute Formulation See *Brawner rule.*

American Public Health Association (APHA) An organization founded in 1872 to advocate for societal rather than individual responses to disease and health care. Members of APHA led the movement to prevent epidemics and to enhance the nation's sanitation, nutrition, health education, and government health programs. Its Web site address is http://www.apha.org

American Public Human Services Association (APHSA) The nonprofit national organization of people employed in and concerned about the human services and public welfare, and members of more than 1200 national, state, territorial, and local human services agencies. Founded in 1930 as the American Public Welfare Association, the APHSA develops, promotes, and implements public policies that improve the well-being of families and individuals. APHSA sponsors conferences, lobbies lawmakers, publishes books and journals, and mobilizes client groups in behalf of the nation's economically disadvantaged. Their Web site address is http://www.aphsa.org

American Relief Administration (ARA) The U.S. organization to provide emergency food and medicine to Europeans suffering through the aftermath of World War I. Its leader, Herbert Hoover, soon changed it from a government to a private relief organization, and during its existence, from 1919 to 1924, it saved millions of lives from famine, especially people in the former Soviet Union.

American School Counselor Association (ASCA) The professional association founded in 1953 for counselors employed in school systems. ASCA members provide guidance to students with academic, vocational, and personal problems. Their Web site address is http://www.schoolcounselor.org

American Sign Language (ASL) Also known as "AmesLan," a language with a unique grammatical structure, vocabulary, and system of communication. Communication takes place not by vocalization, but by specific movements and shapes of hands, arms, eyes, face, head, and body that correspond to the words of spoken language. It is used primarily by people with hearing impairments.

Americans with Disabilities Act of 1990 (ADA) U.S. federal legislation (P.L.101-336) to combat discrimination by employers, and extend to people with disabilities (including people with visual or hearing impairments, alcohol or drug problems, and HIV disease) the same protections and guarantees as given to nondisabled persons. See also *disability rights movement.*

Americares Foundation A private, nonprofit organization located in more than 80 countries that obtains medical supplies and services for people around the world in need of health care and disaster relief and solves food shortages and refugee problems. Their Web site address is www.americares.org

America's Charities A coalition of philanthropic organizations, established in 1980, to consolidate fundraising, especially in the workplace, and assure donors that member agencies are responsible and honest.

America's Job Bank A database of more than one million jobs nationwide maintained by the U.S. Department of Labor. Employers and job seekers can post resumes and requirements and conduct automated job searches. Their Web site address is http://www.ajb.dni.us. See also *O*NET.*

AmeriCorps The U.S. national service organization to recruit, administer and coordinate volunteers in various programs. AmeriCorps was established in 1994 to help the nation solve some of its social problems by offering volunteers training, college education and money for education in exchange for specific lengths of full-time service (usually from 10 months to two years). AmeriCorps also provides grants to localities to fund community-based programs including tutoring, mentoring teenage parents, providing crime victim assistance, restoring parks, helping homebound and disabled people, and assisting in homeland security programs. Their Web site address is http://www.americorps.org. AmeriCorps is part of the U.S. *Corporation for National and Community Service.* Major components include *AmeriCorps*VISTA, AmeriCorps*NCCC,* and *AmeriCorps Promise Fellows.*

AmeriCorps*NCCC   A national volunteer service program (the National Civilian Community Corps) in which men and women between the ages of 18 and 24 reside for 10 months in one of five regional campuses (near Denver, Colorado; Charleston, South Carolina; Sacramento, California; Perry Point, Maryland; and Washington, DC) to take part in projects in those areas. The major projects involve public safety, disaster relief, the environment, education, and other community-based needs. Volunteers receive a living allowance; room and board; training; and other benefits, including an educational award upon successful completion.

AmeriCorps Promise Fellows   See *Promise Fellows.*

AmeriCorps*VISTA   See *Volunteers in Service to America (VISTA).*

AmesLan   See *American Sign Language (ASL).*

***amicus curiae* brief**   A suit filed by a third party, generally a professional individual or organization, who is not a party to the litigation. Professionals in human services have used *amicus curiae* briefs to advocate for clients or for social causes. The term literally means "friend of the court."

amimia   A communication disorder characterized by limited ability to make or understand gestures.

amnesia   Inability to recall some or all past experience as a result of emotional or organic factors, or combinations of both. See *retrograde amnesia* and *anterograde amnesia.*

amnestic disorder   Impaired memory resulting from some specific organic impairment within an individual who otherwise has a clear consciousness (that is, no conditions such as *delirium* or *intoxication*) and no loss of major intellectual ability. If memory loss occurs where no organic

impairment is known to exist, the condition is known as *psychogenic amnesia.*

amnesty   An excuse granted to individuals or groups to free them from being tried or punished for alleged criminal offenses. Amnesty is usually granted by a nation's chief executive or ruler in response to political pressure or public demand, rather than for legal reasons. Amnesty is usually granted to groups or classes of people, whereas the term *pardon* applies to individuals. See also *clemency.*

Amnesty International   The worldwide movement of people concerned with human rights and opposed to actions taken by governments and groups to deprive people of these rights. Established in London in 1961, Amnesty International (AI) won the Nobel Peace Prize in 1977. AI seeks to free political prisoners detained solely for their beliefs or status, to ensure fair and prompt trials for political prisoners, to abolish the death penalty for and torture and cruel treatment of prisoners, and to end political killings and "disappearances." AI is independent of any government or ideology, is funded by its members and donors, and is impartial about any government or political system. Their Web site address is http://www.amnesty.org

amniocentesis   A test to determine the presence of some specific defect in a developing *fetus* by extracting and examining a sample of the amniotic fluid. See also *chorionic villus sampling (CVS).*

amok   A *culture-bound syndrome,* identified originally in Malaysia, characterized by a person's period of brooding, followed by violent or homicidal outbursts.

amotivational syndrome   A pattern of behavior often found in patients who have exhibited extensive *substance dependence* in which there seems to be cooperation and little resistance to the intervention process but also little effort or interest expended toward resolution of either *substance abuse* or other social and emotional problems.

amphetamine   A drug that stimulates the cerebral cortex, tends to increase one's mental alertness temporarily, produces a sense of *euphoria* and well-being, and reduces fatigue. Commonly known as "bennies," "uppers," and "speed," amphetamines are addictive and usually require increasingly large doses as *tolerance* develops.

amygdala   The almond-shaped part of the brain of which the central nucleus is thought to contain the circuitry that mediates specific signs of fear and anxiety. It is also thought to play an important role in motivation and emotional behavior, especially phobic or anxiety responses.

amyotrophic lateral sclerosis (ALS)   "Lou Gehrig's disease," a degenerative disease of the nervous system involving muscle *atrophy.*

anabolic steroids   See *steroids.*

anaclitic   A form of dependency, such as that experienced by an infant for its *caregiver.* A typical characteristic of young children, it indicates *pathology* when excessive in adults. It is most commonly seen as a form of *depression* that one experiences when fearing the possible loss of an important source of *nurturance.*

anal character   See *"anal personality."*

"anal personality"   A descriptive term from *psychoanalytic theory,* referring to an individual who is excessively fastidious, miserly, rigid, and compulsively obsessed with orderliness; also known as "anal character."

anal phase   The second stage of personality development in *psychosexual development theory,* which occurs between the ages of two and three. During this stage, the child becomes oriented to the functions of the anus and learns to have more control over the environment by giving or withholding feces.

analysand   One who is being psychoanalyzed.

analysis   A systematic consideration of anything in its respective parts and their relationship to one another. The term is commonly used to indicate *psychoanalysis.*

analysis of variance (ANOVA)   A statistical procedure commonly used in social work *research* for determining the extent to which two or more groups differ significantly when one is exposed to a *dependent variable.*

analyst   See *psychoanalyst.*

anancastic   A behavior pattern in which the individual is compulsive—that is, obsessed with rules, is emotionally constricted and intolerant, and perfectionistic. See also *compulsive personality disorder* or *obsessive–compulsive disorder.*

anarchism   A doctrine and *social movement* that espouses the abolition of formal government and freedom from controls on individual actions.

ancillary care   Nonprimary services. For example, in hospitals, ancillary care may include social services, the clergy, occupational therapy, the laboratory, and the pharmacy.

Anderson, Joseph (1910–1979)   A founder of NASW and its executive director from 1955 to 1969, he also helped create the Council on Social Work Education and other social work organizations. He was head of the American Association of Social Workers from 1943 to 1955 and helped establish social work as a unified profession.

andragogy   The practice of helping adults to learn.

androcentrism   An orientation or set of beliefs that views culture, history, and social relationships from the male perspective only and tends to discount or ignore the perspective, experience, and relationships of women.

androgyny   A *sexual orientation* in which mannerisms, appearance, and behaviors that are usually considered either male or female are both incorporated into one's behavioral repertoire. The term is similar to *ambisexual* but emphasizes *sex role* behavior more than physical characteristics.

anecdotal evidence   The use of single examples, stories, or isolated cases in an attempt to demonstrate the existence of some general phenomenon. For example, a client says "I made more progress with a social worker than with a psychiatrist." The statement is anecdotal rather than based on systematic research; whether it is generally true or not remains unproved by the single subjective experience.

anemia   A disorder in which the blood is deficient in red cells or hemoglobin. The most apparent initial symptom is a feeling of tiredness resulting from the blood's inability to transport enough oxygen through the body.

aneurysm   A permanent dilation of a weakened artery. Major causes of the weakening are infection, injury, *hypertension, arteriosclerosis,* or *congenital abnormalities.* The most serious and life threatening of these are the aortic aneurysm, which can result in loss of blood from the heart to the body cavities, or brain aneurysm, in which the blood flow to parts of the brain can be interrupted.

"angel dust"   Slang for the psychedelic or hallucinogenic drug *PCP* (phencyclidine). It has a high incidence of psychological *dependency.*

anger   A common and usually normal *emotion* that occurs in response to an individual's perception of being threatened or harmed. Its manifestations often include irritability, physical or verbal attacks, increased heart rate and respiratory activity, and rage and negativism. Anger may be continuous or intermittent, directed inward or outward, intense or mild, and according to some psychologists, conscious or unconscious. It is considered *maladaptive* or pathological when it is relatively continuous or occurs even when there is no immediate catalyst.

angina pectoris   Sharp pains in the chest that occur when the heart muscle receives insufficient blood. Caused by sudden closure of the coronary arteries, often brought on by excitement or physical exertion, angina often is treated with drugs that dilate the blood vessels as well as with surgical procedures to remove obstructions.

angkan   In Philippine communities and groups, the gang or clan.

"Anglos"   U.S. citizens of European ancestry, as designated by people of Latin American or other non–European American backgrounds.

anhedonia   An emotional state in which the individual lacks the full capacity to experience pleasure in situations that seem pleasurable to most others. It is a symptom frequently seen in clients with *depression.*

anima   In the *psychoanalytic theory* of Carl Jung (1875–1961), the feminine aspect of a male's personality. The male inherits this feminine *archetype* from the accumulated experiences of men as they have related to women through the ages.

animal welfare acts   U.S. laws to control the way animals of all species, dead or alive, are to be handled, treated, or used, for any purposes, including research, education, exhibition, food, work, recreation, breeding, selling, and as pets. These laws began with the 1966 Laboratory Animal Welfare Act (P.L. 89-544) to control animals used in research. Subsequent laws and revisions in 1970 (P.L. 91-579), 1976 (P.L. 94-279), and 1985 (P.L. 99-198) have addressed different aspects of the humane treatment of animals.

animal welfare organizations   Groups seeking to protect animals from mistreatment or needless exploitation. Many groups are oriented to specific causes (such as advocacy against *vivisection*), to certain animals (such as baby seals), or to habitat issues. Others generally seek to protect all animals, to educate people to treat animals better, and to protect species through environmental advocacy. The organizations include the American Society for the Prevention of Cruelty to Animals (ASPCA) founded in 1866, the Humane Societies, Friends of Animals, People for the Ethical Treatment of Animals (PETA), and National Anti-Vivisection Society (NAVA).

animus   In the *psychoanalytic theory* of Carl Jung (1875–1961), the masculine aspect of a female's personality. The female inherits this masculine *archetype* from the accumulated experiences of women as they have related to men through the ages.

annona civica   An institutionalized tradition in ancient Rome, established before 100 B.C.E., requiring patrician families to donate and distribute free or low-cost grain and other food to needy people.

annulment   A religious or legal declaration that an agreement, contract, covenant, or relationship such as marriage does not and never has existed.

anomie   Normlessness, or the elimination or reduction of social and personal *values, mores, norms,* and codes of conduct; also, the inability of an individual or group to recognize the values, mores, or codes of conduct of another group with whom it must relate. Anomie frequently occurs in rapidly changing societies and communities or groups subject to catastrophic stress. In such circumstances, individuals often become alienated, apathetic, and devoid of previously valued goals.

anorexia nervosa   An *eating disorder* most often encountered in girls and young women whose extended refusal to eat leads to severe weight loss, *malnutrition,* and cessation of menstruation. The usual medical criteria for this diagnosis include the loss of 15 percent or more of one's body weight. This life-threatening condition is related to a disturbed body image and an exaggerated fear of becoming obese. The word "anorexia" literally means loss of appetite, although the person in this condition has not lost appetite. See also *bulimia nervosa.*

anosmia   The partial or complete absence of the sense of smell that is the result of injury, illness, or genetic problem. Because the sense of smell is crucial to the sense of taste, this condition is also considered to be applicable to the absence or limitation of the sense of taste. There are several terms related to this disorder. Osme refers to all smell and taste disorders. Dysosmia refers to impairment or defect in the sense of smell. Phantosmia is the term for perceiving odors that do not actually exist. Parosmia refers to distortions in the sense of smell.

anosognosia   Unawareness of one's own mental or physical illness.

anoxia   Absence of oxygen supply to body tissues; when there is an insufficient supply it is called *hypoxia.*

ANSWER   Action Network for Social Work Research and Education, a coalition of the following organizations: Association of Baccalaureate Program Directors (BPD), the Institute for the Advancement of Social Work Research (IASWR), the Council on Social Work Education (CSWE), the Group for the Advancement of Doctoral Education (GADE), the Society for Social Work and Research (SSWR), the National Association of Deans and Directors (NADD), and the National Association of Social Workers (NASW). The coalition's mission is to increase legislative and executive branch advocacy on behalf of social work education, training, and research. This is accomplished through collaboration among researchers, practice organizations, social work education programs, and other groups. ANSWER has recently focused on the development of a National Center for Social Work Research.

Antabuse   Trade name for disulfiram, a drug that induces nausea when in the bloodstream of an individual who ingests alcohol. It is used to facilitate *aversion therapy* in the treatment of *alcoholism.*

antecedent   In *behavior modification* and *social learning theory,* an event *(stimulus)* that precedes a behavior *(response)* and is thought to influence it.

antenuptial agreement   See *prenuptial agreement.*

anterograde amnesia   The inability to recall experiences that have occurred after a certain time, usually after some physical injury or psychic stress. See also *retrograde amnesia.*

anthropocentrism   The view that the environment centers around and exists primarily for humans.

antianxiety drugs   See *tranquilizer.*

anticathexis   In *Freudian theory,* the psychic energy the individual uses to keep repressed material in the *unconscious.* This term is not synonymous with *decathexis.*

anticult organizations   Coordinated efforts and groups, often led by traditional church organizations and parents of young *cult* members, to counter the perceived destructive influences of cults and *new religious movements (NRMs).* Such efforts include monitoring and exposing the activities of cults, *counseling* and *deprogramming* cult members, and providing therapeutic mutual-help groups for families of cult members. The most influential anticult organizations include the Cult Awareness Network, the American Family Foundation, and the Citizens Freedom Foundation.

Anti-Defamation League (ADL)   A *civil rights group* founded in 1913 by Sigmund Livingston to combat *anti-Semitism,* improve *intergroup relations,* and promote the democratic process. Their Web site address is http://www.adl.org. See also *Jewish communal agencies.*

antidepressant medication   *Psychotropic drugs* used by psychiatrists and other physicians to help patients achieve relief from the symptoms of *depression.* Some of the major drugs of this type are known by the trade names Prozac, Elavil, Vivactil, Tofranil, Pertofrane, Sinequan, Marplan, Parnate, and Nardil. Relief through antidepressant medication is not usually apparent until several days after it has been taken in compliance with prescription.

antigen test   A medical test to determine the presence of antibodies in the blood, particularly HIV antibodies. When test chemicals react with proteins on the coating of the virus, the presence of the antibody is shown.

antiglobalization movement   Organized and spontaneous efforts to reduce the power and influence of international corporations and organizations such as the World Bank, economic and political alliances of nations, and trade practices that affect nations, people, and the environment. The movement involves diverse groups, including environmental advocates, labor unions, and people opposed to the increasing power of multinational corporations. The movement is motivated by concerns that exporting jobs to low-wage areas exploits workers in countries with few collective rights, that the environment is at risk from unregulated activities of multinational corporations, and that increasing competition among rich and poor nations creates pressure to curtail the social welfare benefits offered by advanced industrial nations. The movement sometimes calls for sufficient protection, which may include trade barriers and quotas.

antimanic medication   *Psychotropic drugs* prescribed by physicians to counter the symptoms of *mood disorder, manic episode,* and some forms of *bipolar disorder.* The most popular of these drugs, *lithium carbonate,* is sold under trade names such as Eskalith and Lithane. See also *major affective disorder.*

antinuclear movement   Worldwide efforts to ban nuclear technology, especially weapons of mass destruction and their delivery systems. Many individuals, groups, and formal organizations and some nations sponsor programs to educate the public and legislators against the development and proliferation of such devices.

antipoverty programs   Public and private associations and activities devoted to the eradication of *poverty.* Such activities include research into the causes and consequences of poverty and actions that may eliminate economic inequality and instability, as well as direct aid to poor individuals.

antipsychiatry movement   A view that most of the theories of mental illness and the practice of psychiatry are not valid and are used by the establishment as a vehicle for social control. Proponents of this view cite the work of R.D. Laing, Thomas Szasz, Erving Goffman, Michel Foucault, and many others who have written that nonorganic "mental illnesses" are actually problems in living and that the practice of psychiatric labeling and mental hospital commitments should be discontinued.

antipsychotic medication   The group of *psychotropic drugs* prescribed by physicians to control certain symptoms seen in *schizophrenia* and other psychoses. These drugs include those sold under the trade names Compazine, Haldol, Mellaril, Navane, Prolixin, Serentil, Stelazine, Thorazine, and Trilafon.

anti-Semitism   Negative attitudes and behaviors about Jewish people manifested in *discrimination, bias,* and the attempt to prejudicially attribute to them some of the problems of society. The term "Semitic" actually refers to a group of languages of the Middle East, including Arabic and Hebrew. Thus, technically, anti-Semitism also suggests bias against Arabic speakers. See also *Anti-Defamation League (ADL).*

antisocial behavior   A pattern of actions that results in an individual's isolation from other people or frequent conflict with others and social institutions.

antisocial personality disorder   One of the 11 types of *personality disorders* characterized by irresponsibility, inability to feel guilt or remorse for actions that harm others, frequent conflicts with people and social institutions, the tendency to blame others and not to learn from mistakes, low frustration tolerance, and other behaviors that indicate a deficiency in *socialization.* The less precise labels *psychopathic personality, psychopath,* and *sociopath* are often used as synonyms.

antitrust laws   Legislation to prevent or restrict the development of business monopolies. The major premise of a capitalist free economy is that competition will keep prices lower and keep the quality of goods and services higher; but when one corporation becomes a monopoly, competition no longer exists. Antitrust laws to preclude such events include keeping corporations from merging; breaking up companies that become dominant; and legally preventing companies from conspiring on pricing, marketing unfairly, or selling below costs to drive out competing businesses. The Sherman Anti-Trust Act of 1890 and the Clayton Act of 1914 were major antitrust laws in the United States.

anxiety   A feeling of uneasiness, tension, and sense of imminent danger. When such a feeling occurs within a person with no specific cause in the environment, it is known as *free-floating anxiety*. When it recurs frequently and interferes with effective living or a sense of well-being or is otherwise *maladaptive*, it is known as *anxiety disorder*.

anxiety disorder   A chronic or recurring state of tension, worry, fear, and uneasiness arising from unknown or unrecognized perceptions of danger or conflict. The major types of anxiety disorders include *generalized anxiety disorder; acute stress disorder; obsessive–compulsive disorder; posttraumatic stress disorder (PTSD); panic disorder,* with and without *agoraphobia; social phobia; specific phobia;* and *substance-induced anxiety disorder.*

anxiety disorder of childhood   An emotional or mental disturbance found in youngsters from infancy through adolescence characterized by excessive fear; apprehension; nervousness; and often symptoms such as trembling, fainting, nausea, choking, headaches, and overall tension. These symptoms occur even though there is no directly related cause or threat in the environment. Specific types of anxiety disorders in childhood or adolescence include *separation anxiety disorder of childhood, avoidant disorder of childhood,* and *overanxious disorder of childhood.* This term is no longer used as an official psychiatric diagnosis.

Anxiety Disorders Association of America (ADAA)   A national nonprofit organization to promote the welfare of individuals with anxiety disorders. ADAA facilitates research, provides information, sponsors publications, and hosts conferences. Its members are researchers, clinicians, educators, and people affected by anxiety disorders in themselves or their loved ones. ADAA was established in 1980 as the Phobia Society of America and took its present name in 1990 to encompass all anxiety disorders. Their Web site address is http://www.adaa.org

anxiety hysteria   A psychoanalytic term referring to *psychoneurosis* that includes intense anxiety-induced dramatic behavior, *free-floating anxiety,* and *phobia.* Analytically oriented therapists consider this condition to be the result of repressed sexual conflict.

anxiety neurosis   See *generalized anxiety disorder* and *panic disorder.*

anxiety symptoms   The psychophysiological responses one experiences as a result of *anxiety.* The most common of these include nervousness, sweating, irritability, sleeplessness, motor agitation, fidgetiness, muscular tension, fear, uneasiness, compulsive behavior, obsessive thoughts, trembling, pain, apprehension, forgetfulness, poor concentration, depression, confusion, and general discomfort.

anxiolytic   Pertaining to substances or procedures for reducing *anxiety.* Antianxiety drugs are called anxiolytics.

APA citation system   The format and style by which references are indicated in the texts of academic books and scholarly journal articles as developed by the American Psychological Association. The system is now preferred by most social science publications, including the social work literature. In this style the references are "cited in the text using the author's last name and date of publication" (Barker, 2003, p. 33) with the full reference at the end of the article, with all the other articles referred to and placed in alphabetical order by author's last name [for example, Barker, R. L. (2003). *Social Work Dictionary* (5th ed.). Washington, DC: NASW Press].

apartheid   A term in the Afrikaans language meaning "separate development" that refers to the policy of racial separation once maintained by the white-controlled South African government. The policy ended with South Africa's 1994 national elections giving people of all races the right to vote. However, apartheid has left an institutional legacy of different opportunities for education, sanitation, health services, housing, employment, and land distribution.

apathy   Indifference; lack of interest in or desire for anything. Apathy is often a symptom of mental disorders such as *depression* or a response to social conditions such as oppression, restricted opportunities, or limited education.

Apgar rating   A score, devised by Dr. Virginia Apgar (1909–1974), in 1954, to indicate the relative health of a baby at birth. This measure is now commonly used in neonatal care facilities. Five factors are each assigned the values 0, 1, or 2, so that a baby in ideal health would achieve an Apgar rating of 10. The criteria are heart rate (absent = 0, slow or irregular = 1, rapid = 2), respiratory effort (absent = 0; slow or irregular = 1; good, crying =

2), reflex irritability (absent = 0; grimace = 1; cough, sneeze = 2), color (blue = 0; body pink, extremities blue = 1; completely pink = 2), and muscle tone (flaccid = 0, weak = 1, strong = 2).

aphasia The inability to use previously possessed language skills. Specific types of aphasia may include loss of ability to utter words, loss of ability to understand written or spoken words, inability to put words and phrases together properly, or various combinations of these. See also *developmental expressive language disorder.*

aphephobia The abnormal *fear* of being touched.

aphonia Loss of ability to speak normally as a result of physiological or emotional disorders.

aplastic anemia Failure of the bone marrow to produce sufficient blood elements, especially red cells, often occurring as a result of overexposure to antibiotic drugs, X-rays, or toxic substances.

APM Annual Program Meeting, the name social work educators use to refer to the *Council on Social Work Education (CSWE)*–sponsored conference that meets in a different U.S. city every March.

apnea A disturbance in the respiratory mechanism, usually resulting in temporary cessation of breathing. In some infants, the disturbance may be related to *crib death.* See also *sudden infant death syndrome (SIDS)* and *sleep disorder.* Some clinicians use the term *breathing-related sleep disorder.*

apparatchik An administrative functionary. The term is the Russian for "bureaucrat" but, as used in English, implies a public official who mindlessly follows rules even if those rules keep the official and others from reaching the organization's goal. See also *technocrat.*

appeal In legal terms, a request of a higher court to review and reverse a lower court decision or grant a new trial.

appeasement Any action or inaction considered overly accommodating to those with whom one disagrees, for example, when the actions of an aggressor nation are tolerated to avoid armed conflict.

appellate court A judicial institution and procedure that determines if the judgments made in

lower courts were in accordance with law. Appellate courts only scrutinize previously adjudicated cases, not by reviewing new testimony or evidence, but by reviewing written briefs and oral arguments about how the previous judgment was made.

applied research Systematic investigations to acquire facts that can be used to solve or prevent problems, enhance lifestyles, advance technologies, or increase income. This is contrasted to *basic research.* Most social work research is applied research because it pertains mostly to the interactions between people and their environment, social problems, and methods for helping.

apportioned tax A tax collected by one level of government whose proceeds are shared with other governmental entities. For example, a city or county government distributes some of the funds collected from property taxes to the state or to school and park districts. See also *revenue sharing.*

apprenticing Putting one person under the care and tutelage of another, ostensibly for the purpose of learning certain skills. This process was widely practiced in the United States in the 18th and 19th centuries as a way to care for homeless youths.

appropriate technology (AT) Methods for handling environmental problems or developing resources that are suitable and efficient for people of the area given their stage of economic and social progression. For example, building a small windmill to pump water in a primitive village might be a more appropriate technology than installing a hydroelectric dam or irrigation system.

appropriation An allocation of funds, usually made by a government legislative body, to an organization or program empowered by that body to accomplish a specific goal.

Approved Social Worker (ASW) In England and Wales a social worker qualified to perform a range of statutory duties in mental health care. ASWs were established in the 1980s to ensure mental health specialization continued with the introduction of generic training for social workers. In Scotland the equivalents are Mental Health Officers.

apraxia The inability to perform purposeful movements, which usually is related to lesions in the motor area of the cortex rather than paralysis or dysfunctioning senses.

aptitude tests Formal examinations that attempt to determine an individual's innate ability and potential for a future undertaking, such as success in an educational or workplace setting. See also *achievement tests.*

aquaphobia The pathological *fear* of water.

Arab American The ethnic group of U.S. residents whose ancestry originated in an Arabic-speaking region or nation in the Middle East, including Egypt, Saudi Arabia, Syria, Iraq, Jordan, Lebanon, Yemen, Oman, Palestine, nation–states around the Gulf of Arabia, and the nations of the African Sahara.

Arbeiterwohlfahrt Bundesverband (AWO) The German national organization of professionals, citizens, agencies, and groups concerned with social welfare. Founded in 1919, the AWO conducts professional and public education programs; sponsors assistance programs for children, youths, and elderly people; coordinates the operation of many charitable programs; and publishes the monthly *AWO Magazine.*

arbitration A decision-making mechanism used when two or more opposing factions cannot reach agreement or continue working toward complementary goals. The disputing parties agree to appoint a neutral person and to abide by that person's decision following a hearing on the issues at which the parties have had an opportunity to present their case. See also *mediation* and *alternative dispute resolution (ADR).*

archaic ego state The psychoanalytic concept pertaining to feelings that originated in early stages of *ego* development that have persisted into adult life.

archetype In the theories of Carl Jung (1875–1961), the inherited structural component of the *collective unconscious.* It is a deep, unconscious representation of a group of experiences that have been accumulating within each new generation of humans. This collection of experiences remains part of the individual's personality in the *unconscious* and influences the thought and behavior patterns of each individual to varying degrees. Archetypes are also referred to as primordial images or *imagos,* and the major archetypes are the *anima* and the *animus.* See also *nativism.*

Area Agencies on Aging (AAA) A national network of federally funded agencies established in 1965 to advocate and provide human services for older people.

area sampling A procedure in *social research* involving the selection of a representative segment of a population based on geographic location.

Armenverbände In Germany, public agencies partly responsible for the care of poor people during the 19th century until the end of World War I.

aromatherapy A form of holistic intervention said to promote good physical, mental, and spiritual health through the controlled use of essential oils. The National Association of Holistic Aromatherapy (NAHA) coordinates efforts to educate the public about the benefits of aromatherapy and to maintain standards among qualified aromatherapists. NAHA has annual conferences and sponsors the quarterly *Aromatherapy Journal* (formerly called *Scentsitivity*).

arousal 1. A state of becoming excited into action. Social workers involved in community organization sometimes seek to provoke arousal in client groups by making them aware of a relevant problem and its potential solution. 2. In human sexuality, the term refers to physiological and psychological changes in response to stimulation and leading to preparation for sexual intercourse. Sexologists William Masters and Virginia Johnson described arousal as occurring primarily in the first of the four stages of sexual response (excitement, plateau, orgasm, and resolution). They indicated that arousal begins in the excitement phase, in which vasocongestion (swelling of the blood vessels) commences, the heart and pulse rates increase, and the skin becomes flushed.

arraignment Legal procedure in which an individual who is accused of a crime hears information or formal charges before a judge, before any guilty or not guilty plea is made.

arrearage The amount of money that is still owed after part of a debt has been paid. For example, when a divorced father has paid half the amount of support, the remaining half is the arrearage.

arrears A debt not paid, usually the sum of a series of unpaid amounts, as in rent, child support payments, and restitution.

arrhythmia Heartbeat outside the normal range of 60 to 90 beats per minute in adults. When the heartbeat exceeds 90 beats per minute, the condition is known as *tachycardia;* when it is below 60 beats, it is *bradycardia.*

art therapy The use of painting, sculpture, and other creative expressions in the treatment of people with emotional problems. Art therapy is often used in *social group work* and in *group psychotherapy.* Often used with institutionalized people or inpatients, it is also considered to be effective with healthy people who wish to share art as a means of enhancing personal growth and development. In some forms of art therapy, clients create their own works and discuss the results with the therapist or with other members of an art therapy group. In other forms, the clients are exposed to works of art by a variety of artists and asked to assess how the works affect their own feelings and understandings. The American Art Therapy Association (AATA), founded in 1969, is the professional association that establishes and maintains standards for the training and practice of art therapists, monitors programs, and publishes the quarterly journal *Art Therapy.* Their Web site is www.arttherapy.org

arteriosclerosis Hardening of the arteries or loss of elasticity of arterial wall, a condition that makes it difficult for the blood to circulate. This can result in *hypertension, stroke, aneurysm,* and brain cell destruction, with consequent loss of memory, confusion, and inattention.

arthritis Painful inflammation of the joints of the body. Causes include dysfunction of the endocrine glands, nerve impairment, or degeneration as a result of infections and old age. The major types include rheumatoid arthritis, osteoarthritis, and gout.

articulation disorder A speech problem characterized by the inability to pronounce certain sounds clearly. The individual may have difficulty pronouncing one or more sounds or sound blends such as r, sh, th, f, z, l, or ch, often making substitutions for these sounds and giving the impression of "baby talk." Most professionals now prefer the term *phonological disorder.*

artificial insemination The joining of sperm and ovum for the purpose of reproduction by

means other than sexual intercourse or natural *conception.* Using surgical instruments, the physician implants semen taken from the woman's husband, or sometimes from an anonymous donor, into a fallopian tube or into the uterus, where sperm can form a union with the ovum. See also *in vitro fertilization, reproductive technology,* and *surrogacy.*

asbestos A construction material found widely in homes, schools, and other buildings erected before 1970, linked to respiratory diseases and lung cancer. Asbestos may release harmful fiber particles into the air when it becomes worn, damaged, or punctured. It may be safe when properly coated, but because of the risk, many jurisdictions now require its removal by licensed contractors in most schools and public buildings.

asceticism A lifestyle involving rigid self-discipline and self-denial, abandonment of worldly goods, and social isolation, usually to improve one's spiritual or moral state.

ashram A retreat or dwelling house occupied by a teacher or wise leader and students who are devoted to the study of some philosophy or religion. The term comes from Hindu philosophies but is commonly used in other movements, cults, and religions.

Asian American Social Workers (AASW) The national professional association established in California in 1968 by social workers of Pacific–Asian background. The purpose of AASW is to develop and promote social welfare programs that benefit and protect the rights of *Asian Americans* as well as to enhance its members' professional development.

Asian Americans Residents or citizens of the United States whose racial background and sometimes ethnic identification is with the peoples of Pacific–Asian areas, including Chinese, Japanese, Vietnamese, Koreans, Filipinos, Thais, Hmong, Laotians, migrants from the Indian subcontinent, and others.

as-if assumptions A psychotherapy technique to help the client understand the reasons for resisting or fearing change. The therapist suggests the client is behaving "as-if" change would lead to specified problems. The client and group then look more objectively at the anticipated consequences and come to fear them less.

Asociación Nacional por Personas Mayores   The U.S. organization for Hispanic senior citizens that provides information to its members (individuals and organizations) about the opportunities, benefits, and problems of older people of Spanish-speaking heritage and represents these people to lawmakers, policy makers, and other organizations.

asocial behavior   Behavior characterized by indifference to people or social norms.

Asperger's disorder   One of the *pervasive developmental disorders* characterized by severe and sustained impairment in social interaction and the development of restricted, repetitive patterns of behavior, interests, and activities, causing impairment in most areas of functioning. Similar to *autistic disorder* but with a later onset, the individual with the disorder usually has difficulties in social interactions throughout life.

assault   An attempt or threat to harm physically or intimidate an individual through the use of unlawful force. Assault may be found even where no physical injury occurs if the victim has been subjected to a reasonable fear of harm.

assertiveness   Behavior characterized by self-confident communication of one's rights and values.

assertiveness training   A program designed to teach individuals to express their feelings, needs, and demands directly and effectively.

assessment   The process of determining the nature, cause, progression, and prognosis of a problem and the personalities and situations involved therein; the social work function of acquiring an understanding of a problem, what causes it, and what can be changed to minimize or resolve it. See also *diagnosis.*

assimilation   1. The social integration or adoption of one group's *values, norms,* and *folkways* by another group. For example, a group of immigrants may eventually integrate with or adopt many aspects of the culture of their new society. 2. In *Piagetian theory,* the individual's act of incorporating an aspect of his or her environment into an existing thought structure. See also *culture shock.*

assimilationism   An idealistic view that members of diverse ethnic and racial groups will or should meld and become culturally indistinguishable. The contrasting view is *cultural pluralism,* in which members of diverse ethnic and racial groups maintain distinctive identities and orientations while integrating in the predominant culture.

assisted living facility (ALF)   A residential setting for people who need some help with *activities of daily living,* such as dressing, bathing, preparing food, and housekeeping, but do not require extensive health care, as in *skilled nursing facilities.*

assisted suicide   Intentionally providing someone with the means and information needed to commit *suicide.* See also *physician-assisted suicide* and *right to die.*

Association for Community Organization and Social Administration (ACOSA)   An international *professional association* established in 1987 and composed mainly of social work educators and practitioners interested in macro practice including community organization and administration. It provides communication, resources and advocacy related to the advancement of macro practice. It sponsors the *Journal of Community Practice.* Their Web site address is http://www.acosa.org

Association for Improving the Condition of the Poor (AICP)   An organization founded in New York by *Robert M. Hartley* in 1843 to combat poverty primarily through "character-building" activities.

Association for Retarded Citizens (ARC)   An organization, founded in 1950, primarily of the parents of people with intellectual limitations. ARC provides mutual support, information, and access to services, and has been an effective lobbying organization for the equal rights of people with *retardation.* Their Web site address is http://www.thearc.org

Association for the Advancement of Social Work with Groups (AASWG)   An international professional association established in 1985 to facilitate the exchange of knowledge, maintain standards, and advance the goals and values of social workers employed in group settings. AASWG sponsors conferences, publications, symposia, and research about social work with groups, and works with social work educators to strengthen the teaching of group work skills in the foundation and advanced curricula. Their Web site address is http://www.aaswg.org

Association for the Study of Community Organization (ASCO) An organization established in 1946 by social workers specializing in or interested in *community organization*. In 1955 it was merged into the newly established *National Association of Social Workers (NASW)*.

Association of American Indian Social Workers (AAISW) See *National Indian Social Workers Association (NISWA)*.

Association of Baccalaureate Social Work Program Directors (BPD) The national organization of social work educators who lead undergraduate degree programs accredited by the *Council on Social Work Education (CSWE)*. Founded in 1975, BPD sponsors an annual conference, provides programmatic and professional development resources, and publishes the *Journal of Baccalaureate Social Work*. See also *baccalaureate social work*.

Association of Oncology Social Workers (AOSW) The association of psychosocial professionals who provide direct services to cancer patients and their families. Established in 1984 as the National Association of Oncology Social Workers, AOSW holds an annual meeting and sponsors the quarterly *Journal of Psychosocial Oncology*. Its Web site address is http://www.aosw.org

Association of Pediatric Oncology Social Workers The professional association of social work clinicians, educators, advocates, and researchers involved in the psychosocial and physical problems of children with cancer and their families. Established in 1977, the association sponsors conferences, workshops, publications, and workshops. Their Web site address is http://www.aposw.org

Association of Social Work Boards (ASWB) The national organization of jurisdictional state licensing boards that regulates professional social work. Formed in 1979 as the American Association of State Social Work Boards, the ASWB develops and maintains the social work *licensing examinations* used by its member boards and enables boards to communicate with their counterparts on professional regulatory issues. ASWB also maintains the *Disciplinary Action Reporting System (DARS)*, a database containing listings of all disciplinary actions taken against social workers by licensing boards, including license suspensions, revocations, and voluntary surrenders. Their Web site address is http://www.aswb.org

Association of Women in Social Work (AWSW) A professional association founded in 1984 that advocates equal opportunities, rights, and benefits for female social workers. The association also brings together social workers to consider the special needs and concerns of women social workers and their clients.

asthenia Lack of strength or musculature.

asthma One of the *pulmonary disorders,* in which the muscles in the walls of the bronchi contract, causing the individual to have difficulty breathing.

asylee One who is granted *asylum* (protection and some services). To the Bureau of Citizenship and Immigration Services, an asylee is the same as a *refugee,* except the asylee comes from a U.S. territory, and the refugee comes from another country. Both terms represent people who fear persecution because of race, religion, allegiances, membership in particular social groups, or political opinion.

asylum 1. A refuge or sanctuary. 2. An institution for the care of people suffering from mental disorders, certain physical illnesses, or economic destitution.

asynchronous development Growth of a child's physical, mental, and emotional maturity at varying rates of progress so that, for example, the individual may be chronologically age 11, emotionally age eight, physically age 14, and intellectually age 18. This term is also known as dyssynchronous development.

ataque de nervios A *culture-bound syndrome* found most commonly among Latin American and Latin Mediterranean groups in which individuals experience a wide range of panic and anxiety symptoms, including fainting, attacks of crying, shouting, aggressive behavior, suicide gestures, and dissociative experiences, usually following a stressful life event.

ataxia Loss of ability to control all or some voluntary muscle movement.

atherosclerosis   Artery wall congestion caused by accumulation of fats, cholesterol, and calcium salts and resulting in increased risk of *hypertension,* impaired circulation, and *stroke.*

ATOD   An acronym for alcohol, tobacco, and other drugs (for example, ATOD abuse).

at-risk population   Those members of a group who are vulnerable to, or likely to be harmed by, a specific medical, social, political, or environmental circumstance. For example, overweight people or smokers are an at-risk population because they are more likely to have heart attacks or cardiovascular problems. This term is roughly synonymous with *vulnerable populations.*

atrophy   Wasting away of body tissues.

attachment   1. An emotional bond between individuals, based on attraction and dependence, that develops during critical periods of life and may disappear when one individual has no further opportunity to relate to the other. 2. In legal terms, the seizure of property by legal processes while a court action is pending.

attachment disorder   A developmental condition in which the individual is unable to form normal and needed emotional bonds with caregivers and others. This has been shown to result in serious, negative, long-term effects on social and emotional development. If the disorder is the result of certain early childhood experiences, such as trauma, abuse, inconsistent caregiving, or similar factors, the condition is known as *reactive attachment disorder (RAD).*

attachment theory   Concepts developed in the 1970s by developmental researchers C. Ainsworth, N. Bowlby, and others about the stages through which young children progress in their development of social relationships and the influence of this development on personality characteristics in later life. In four sequential stages toward social attachment, the healthy young child exhibits characteristic behaviors: At birth to age three months, the infant maintains closeness with the *caregiver* through sucking, grasping, visual tracking, and cuddling. From age three to six months, the infant becomes more responsive to familiar people and discomforted by others *(stranger anxiety).* At age six months to toddler age, the infant seeks contact and closeness with the object of *attachment* and

experiences discomfort *(separation anxiety disorder of childhood)* when the object is missing. Beyond toddler age, the child uses a wide variety of behaviors to influence the actions of the object of attachment to meet the child's needs for closeness. In this development, three general patterns of attachment occur: *secure attachment, avoidant attachment,* and *resistant attachment.*

attendance allowance   A benefit in the British social security system in which people who need home care receive a monthly stipend to help pay for the help. The amount varies depending on whether the help needed is night, day, or around the clock.

attendant care   A home health care service in which individuals trained in nontechnical nursing, home care, and other activities make regular visits to assist homebound people. Attendants often help in light housekeeping, meal preparation, hygiene, and health care monitoring.

attending   In social work and other professional *interviews,* maintaining attentiveness expressed through appropriate verbal following, eye contact, mindful but relaxed posture, and disciplined attention. A nonattending interviewer might be staring out a window or glancing at a clock, yawning, or generally showing lack of focus on the *relationship* process. See also *following responses.*

attention span   The duration of time one can continuously focus on a given task. Usually this time is highly related to one's age, level of emotional health, anxiety, physical comfort, and environmental stimuli.

attention-deficit hyperactivity disorder (ADHD)   A neurobehavioral disorder that starts in infancy, childhood, or adolescence, characterized by impulsive behavior, inattentiveness, excessive motor activity, and short *attention span.* Subtypes of this disorder include "predominantly inattentive type," "predominantly hyperactive–impulsive type," and the "combined type." The term "ADHD" is now used in place of several less-accurate and less-precise terms, including *hyperactive child syndrome, minimal brain dysfunction, hyperkinetic reaction of childhood,* and "attention deficit disorder, hyperactive type." Apparently, in most cases, it is the result of one or more factors, including *anxiety, stress,* physiological disorder, *neurological disorder,* and some *organic mental disorders.* See also *"504 student."*

attitude   A mental predisposition or inclination to act or react in a certain way. It is often used as a synonym for *mood* or opinion, and in a current slang usage, it is a synonym for "defiance."

audio feedback   A procedure in social work and other professional interventions to show clients how they sound to others, by playing back tape recordings and systematically analyzing the results. See also *video feedback*.

audiologist   A professional who specializes in the evaluation and treatment of hearing loss and disorders related to functions of the ear, including balance disorders and *tinnitus*. The audiologist also fits and dispenses hearing aids and other devices designed to help the patient achieve better auditory function.

audit   An inspection of the accounting records or procedures of an individual or organization to verify their accuracy and completeness. For example, the records of a social agency might be audited annually by representatives of funding sources. Auditing also can involve inspecting the work done by staff, determining compliance with regulations, and completing inventories.

auditory hallucination   An imagined perception of a sound; hearing something that does not exist outside subjective experience.

austerity measures   Economic cutbacks designed to limit inflation or reduce debt. Often this is a code term for reducing benefits to the least powerful and poorest citizens.

Australian Association of Social Workers (AASW)   The professional association of social workers in Australia, formed in 1946 when several social work organizations merged. The AASW helps promote the profession and social welfare policies in the nation, sponsors conferences and publications to enhance the knowledge base of Australian social workers, and reviews graduate and undergraduate social work education programs. AASW publishes the quarterly journal *Australian Social Work*. Their Web site address is http://www.aasw.asn.au

authentic assessment   Testing under actual or more natural conditions rather than in clinical settings or artificial environments. In education this term refers to evaluating students based on their demonstration of learning rather than answering traditional test questions.

authoritarian   Pertaining to a system in social organizations and administration characterized by the relative absence of democratic decision making and implementation processes and the requirement of submitting to higher-ranking members of the organization. Punishments or sanctions are often imposed on those members of the organization who do not comply, and rewards are given to those who do.

authoritarian management   An administrative style sometimes used in social welfare organizations by leaders who tend to make most of the decisions unilaterally and to use their power to demand that the members of the organization accept and support these decisions.

authority   Expertise or power.

authority figure   One who is recognized by others in the role relationship as having power, knowledge, influence, or the ability to control.

authorization bill   Legislation that provides authority to create a program or agency and outline its policy. In the U.S. Congress, authorization bills are to be in place before final budgets are made. Authorizations may be annual, multiyear, or permanent and may require reauthorization.

autistic disorder   A *pervasive developmental disorder* in which the individual appears to have little interest in the external world or capacity to relate effectively to people or objects and is presumed to be devoting full attention to inner wishes and sensations. Other symptoms may include deficient communication and social skills, abnormal interpersonal skills, and unusual responses to stimuli. This condition is most commonly seen in young children and infants.

autoimmune disorder   A physical condition in which the body's immune system functions improperly, impairing its capacity to respond to threats, and also turns the body's defenses against itself when there is no external source of harm. These disorders include rheumatoid *arthritis, lupus, multiple sclerosis,* and *myasthenia gravis*.

automation   Methods of producing goods that rely on technology, machines, assembly lines, and information distribution techniques as a replacement for human labor. Some say that automation results in unemployment of underskilled workers. Others believe that automation leads to increased productivity and improvement in overall standard of living.

autonomic Functioning automatically and without willful or conscious intent. See *autonomic nervous system (ANS)*.

autonomic conversion symptoms Psychogenic physical symptoms that suggest *autonomic nervous system (ANS)* responses, such as *tachycardia* and vomiting.

autonomic nervous system (ANS) That part of the nervous system that regulates the nonvolitional bodily responses such as digestion, breathing, and the rate of heartbeat and glandular secretions. See also *central nervous system (CNS)* and *peripheral nervous system (PNS)*.

autonomous practice Professional activity and decision making that occur in relative independence of social agency auspices, supervision, and organizational requirements. The practitioner sets the standards of performance and self-monitors the work done. This is a relative concept, in that all professions and professional activities are regulated and influenced to some extent by social, ethical, legal, political, and economic forces. Some social workers use this term to indicate *private practice*.

autonomy 1. An individual's sense of being capable of independent action; the ability to provide for one's own needs. 2. Independence from the control of others.

autonomy versus shame and doubt The basic conflict found in the second stage of the *psychosocial development theory* of Erik Erikson (1902–1994), occurring approximately between ages two and four. During this stage, the toddler may come to feel more in control of the environment and exhibit growing independence of actions or may be overcome with feelings of guilt if independent actions are inconsistently tolerated by others.

autoplasty In *psychoanalytic theory*, the psychic process in which the *libido* is directed toward the *self* and away from other people or objects in the environment. See also *alloplasty*.

Average Income Monthly Earnings (AIME) A measure used by the *Social Security Administration (SSA)* in determining *Old Age, Survivors, Disability, and Health Insurance (OASDHI)* benefits. AIME is calculated on the basis of earnings made in covered employment during the worker's lifetime, minus five years of low earnings. Earnings are indexed to account for changes in average wages over the years. See also *social insurance*.

aversion stimulus In *behavior modification*, an object or situation that the subject identifies as being painful or unpleasant and attempts to avoid whenever possible. See also *aversion therapy* and *social learning theory*.

aversion therapy A procedure commonly used in *behavior therapy* designed to eliminate a maladaptive behavior, such as overeating or *substance abuse*, by associating the behavior with some real or imagined *aversion stimulus*.

avoidance 1. In *behavior modification* procedures, an individual's response that postpones or averts presentation of an aversive event. 2. In *psychodynamic theory*, an ego *defense mechanism* resembling *denial*, involving refusal to face certain situations or objects because they present unconscious impulses or punishments for those impulses.

avoidant attachment A form of *insecure attachment* first observed in children who show less distress than other children when left alone but seem as anxious when in the presence of their *caregiver* as with others. Such children avoid contact with parents and other caregivers or ignore their efforts to interact. See also *attachment theory, secure attachment,* and *resistant attachment*.

avoidant disorder of childhood A childhood disorder characterized by intense efforts to avoid strangers. The child with this disorder wants relationships with familiar people but has difficulty in peer relationships and new contacts. The child may act embarrassed, relatively immature, self-conscious, and inarticulate when compelled to confront strangers. These symptoms are similar to the normal developmental behavior known as *stranger anxiety*, which disappears in healthy children younger than age two to three. This is no longer an official psychiatric diagnosis. See also *social phobia*.

avoidant personality disorder One of the *personality disorders* in which the individual is hypersensitive to potential rejection, has low self-esteem, is socially withdrawn, and is generally unwilling to enter social relationships unless there is assurance of uncritical acceptance.

avolition   Loss of willingness or ability to pursue goals.

axon   A nerve fiber attached to the *neuron*, through which signals are transmitted to adjacent neurons.

ayurveda   An alternative medical system, originating in India around 3000 B.C.E., focusing on balancing the body's energy points and vital force ("prana") through diet, natural medicines, bloodletting, enemas, and purification.

AZT   An FDA-approved drug used in the treatment of people with HIV disease, usually in combination with other drugs. AZT is an abbreviation for azidothymidine (now called zidovudine) and helps by suppressing the replication of HIV by terminating DNA synthesis. AZT use is well established for some high-risk HIV conditions, especially in reducing the risk of mother-to-child transmission of the virus. AZT is very expensive and thus not accessible to all who might benefit from it.

B

BAAF Adoption and Fostering   The British association that facilitates the child placement process by providing educational tools, publications, and research to adoption and foster care agencies throughout Great Britain. BAAF also trains, coordinates, and raises funds for these programs and helps to educate the people of the nation as to the needs of these children. Their Web site address is http://www.baaf.org.uk

Babinski reflex   An automatic response in infants in which the toes extend and spread out when the sole of the foot is gently stroked. As the infant's nervous system matures, the same type of stroke tends to result in the toes curling downward.

baby boom generation   The men and women in the United States who were born in the two decades immediately following World War II. Demographers indicate that many more than the usual number of births occurred during these years because many people had postponed having children during the war. This "bulge" in the population necessitates many adjustments in social and economic planning as the baby boomers move through the *life cycle*. When this group reaches retirement age in the years 2010 to 2020, it is anticipated that the *social security* system will be severely strained. See also *Generation X* and *senior boomers.*

baccalaureate social work   The entry level of professional social work practice. Baccalaureate social workers hold undergraduate degrees from programs accredited by the *Council on Social Work Education (CSWE).* Accredited programs award *BSW* degrees or BA or BS degrees in social work.

background investigation   A systematic process of verifying the accuracy of a subject's biography, claims, and information provided in questionnaires and application forms and sometimes to evaluate the subject's character. Such investigations are conducted by potential employers, government organizations, law enforcement authorities, and financial agencies and range in thoroughness from simple calls to previous employers to extensive interviews with all the subject's previous contacts. Increasingly, background investigations are also requiring fingerprinting, criminal record checks, and testing for drug use.

backlash   A group reaction of anger, obstructionism, activism, and sometimes violence when members of that group come to believe that another group is receiving more favorable advantages. The term is usually used with an adjective that identifies the group with the reaction, as in "white backlash," "conservative backlash," or "smokers' backlash." For example, white backlash was said to have begun shortly after civil rights and affirmative action legislation was passed when, for the first time, white workers had to compete with African Americans for jobs.

backloading   Legislation designed to minimize the negative consequences of budget cuts by putting them into effect gradually, with the most severe cuts coming automatically but in the distant future.

backsheesh   In Middle East cultures, a customary payment made for performing some informal services, such as giving directions, carrying loads, or easing some transactions.

bad debt   Money that is owed but uncollectable, as evidenced by actions of the debtor, such as disappearing, declaring bankruptcy, or concealing collateral security. Federal income tax policy allows the amount owed to be deductible from ordinary income or capital gains taxes. However, a bad debt for services rendered, such as social work psychotherapy, cannot be deducted because there is no income on which to be taxed.

"bag lady"   A term often applied to impoverished, homeless women, many of whom are mentally ill and carry their possessions in shopping bags.

bail   A monetary or other form of security posted by or for someone accused of a *crime.* The purpose is to enable the accused to avoid imprisonment while awaiting trial, to ensure that the accused person will appear at subsequent legal proceedings, and to relieve the authorities of the cost of incarcerating the accused during this period. See also *"jump bail"* and *own recognizance.*

bailout Granting massive subsidies or loans to private organizations or governments to keep them fiscally solvent. See also *corporate welfare.*

bait and switch The business practice of attracting customers with a bargain offer and then claiming the offer is unavailable or undesirable before offering something similar that is not a bargain. In most jurisdictions the practice is illegal.

balance of payments The money value of all economic transactions between a nation and all other nations during a stated time. A balance-of-trade deficit occurs when a nation buys more goods and services from other countries than it sells to them. This situation causes the nation to borrow, devalue its currency compared with other nations, or pay back debts from its stock of gold and foreign currencies.

balance of power Relative equality in strength between two or more rival nations, groups, political parties, or officeholders that helps ensure stability or continuation of the status quo.

Balch, Emily Greene (1867–1961) A social work and economics educator, social reformer, and antiwar activist, she founded the *Women's International Peace Congress* in 1915 and was a winner of the 1946 Nobel Peace Prize.

balkanization Division of a nation or organization into smaller units in which members are often at odds. The term derives from the Balkan peninsula in Eastern Europe, which was divided into several small countries.

bancarrota In Spanish-speaking cultures and neighborhoods, the state of being without funds; bankruptcy.

bankruptcy Financial insolvency resulting in the legal process of fairly distributing the remaining property among the creditors, except for those properties that the debtor is permitted to retain to meet *basic needs* and to achieve fiscal rehabilitation. See also *Chapter 7 bankruptcy,* and *Chapter 11 bankruptcy.*

baohu zu A care group in China; these teams are primarily composed of volunteers who provide short-term home-based nursing and social services for people in need in the local neighborhood.

bar graph A depiction of data in which parallel strips are drawn from a common base. Each strip represents a quantity of something being studied, and the strips' respective lengths illustrate their comparative values. For example, a state public assistance office wants to show that all its white client–families receive twice as much money as black families and four times as much as Hispanic families. A graph with three strips of appropriately varying lengths represents the three groups.

barbiturates Drugs that act as *central nervous system (CNS)* depressants. Physicians often use them clinically to facilitate their patients' sleep and to control convulsive disorders. In slang, they are known as *"downers."*

Barclay Report The 1980 British government–sponsored study about the need for and delivery of social services. The report also evaluated and delineated the role of social workers in providing social services. The report recommended increased involvement in *counseling, social planning,* promoting *community decision networks, negotiation,* and social *advocacy.*

bargaining Negotiating of agreements between various factions so that the parties can compromise and make equitable exchanges. A plan to bring together the parties in such a *negotiation* is called a "bargaining strategy." Bargaining is an important component of labor–management relations and in *community organization* and *planning.*

Barnardo, Thomas John (1845–1905) Irish-born physician who came to London to help during a cholera epidemic, discovered thousands of destitute children, and set up ragged schools for children to get protection, nutrition, and basic education. Later he set up schools and orphanages for poor boys and girls, care systems for unwed mothers and their babies, and the first national foster care system in England as well as an emigration program for children with no families. His movement led to the creation of Dr. Barnardo's Homes (orphanages), which were all replaced by the 1970s with family-oriented residential placement programs for children with physical and emotional disabilities. Today, the Barnardo organization is one of the largest providers of social services for children and families outside the public system of services in the United Kingdom, Ireland, Australia, and New Zealand. Their publications have influenced the movement in those nations toward more *evidence-based practice.*

Barnett, Samuel A. (1844–1913) A founder of the original *settlement houses,* he worked with *Octavia Hill* in the development of the original *Charity Organization Societies (COSs)* in England. He used his church for a type of discussion group that became a model for many *social group work* methods. A community organizer and activist for improved housing and treatment of mental illness, in 1884 he founded *Toynbee Hall,* the first settlement house, and named it after one of his recently deceased volunteer workers. Later he came to the United States and worked with *Jane Addams* and *Ellen Gates Starr* in establishing *Hull-House.*

barnvernspedagog In Scandinavian nations, a social worker who specializes in work with children and their families, primarily in *child welfare* offices and institutions.

barratry The illegal practice of stirring up disputes to charge fees for settling the matter.

Barrett, Janie Porter (1865–1948) Leader in the *settlement houses* movement and proponent of education for African American women. She founded one of the first settlement houses for African Americans (the Locust Street Social Settlement) and the influential rehabilitation facility, the Virginia Industrial School for Colored Girls.

barriadas In Spanish-speaking cultures, poor neighborhoods located near urban centers. Many residents are newer immigrants from rural areas who seek better opportunities. Many earn incomes through street-corner selling (*ambulantes*), employment as household servants, and recycling of discarded goods. Few government services are available in barriadas, forcing residents to develop informal programs for *mutual help.* In Brazil, these neighborhoods are called *favelas.*

barrio In Spanish, a neighborhood. In the United States, the term often connotes a residential area inhabited primarily by people of Spanish-speaking backgrounds of low or moderate incomes. See also *barriadas.*

barter The direct exchange of goods or services for other goods or services.

Bartlett, Harriett M. (1897–1987) A founder and early developer of the field of *medical social work,* she later devoted her attention to conceptualizing about all social work practice. She led in the development of NASW's first Commission on Practice, which developed the "working definition of social work practice" and the classic text *The Common Base of Social Work Practice.*

Barton, Clara (1821–1912) A founder of the American Red Cross and its longtime leader, she supervised *relief* work for *disaster* victims of war, famine, and epidemics in various nations. She also led the movement of the International Red Cross to provide relief in disaster situations other than war.

basal metabolism rate (BMR) The amount of energy used by an individual at rest.

baseline The frequency with which a specific behavior or event occurs in a natural state, measured before any attempts are made to influence it.

basic eight curriculum The core courses recommended in *social work education* before the 1952 *Council on Social Work Education (CSWE)* policy statement permitted more flexibility. The eight courses were *social casework, social group work, community organization, administration in social work, research, public welfare,* psychiatric information, and medical information.

basic needs Those items considered to be essential for the maintenance of human well-being, including adequate food, shelter, clothing, heating fuel, clean water, and security from bodily harm.

basic research A systematic knowledge-building inquiry for which the product has no known practical or commercial use (that is, seeking "truths" for their intrinsic worth).

basic skills training Structured educational programs to help students acquire rudimentary proficiency in reading, writing, and arithmetic; also, sometimes improving attention span, memory, and the ability to transfer and generalize recently acquired knowledge.

battered child A youngster who has been physically abused or injured. The injury is usually inflicted on the child by a parent, other adult *caregiver,* or older sibling and may occur intentionally or impulsively in episodes of uncontrolled *anger*. See also *child abuse*.

battered spouse A wife, or sometimes a husband, who has been physically injured by the other. Battering is a physically violent form of *spouse abuse*.

battered spouse syndrome A pattern of behavior observed in some women, or on rare occasions men, who have been subjected to physical and psychological abuse over a long period during which they seem unable to take actions to improve their situations. Some manifestations of this behavior include having a love/hate relationship with the abuser, feeling forced to remain in the situation despite its dangers, failing to seek help as needed, or acting violently. The condition is largely the result of the victim having lived in constant fear and uncertainty, experiencing a loss of self-esteem, and having no confidence in judgments. See also *learned helplessness*.

Batterers Anonymous A national *self-help organization*, with chapters in most larger communities, in which members (most of whom have been wife abusers) help one another to end abusive behavior. Also known as Batterers Anonymous/Beyond Abuse, they work with all persons over 18 in domestic partnerships, sponsor regular meetings to provide support and encouragement, and maintain a "buddy system" and telephone hot lines.

battery 1. A form of illegal *abuse* that involves physical force or injury. 2. A group of tests that have been validated on the same sample population so that results on several parts of the battery are comparable.

bayanihan The Philippine tradition of working together to achieve mutual goals.

"bean counter" A term of derision applied to accountants, financial planners, and budget officers who seem focused only on the economic aspects of the organization rather than its goals and positive visions.

Beck, Bert (1918–2000) The creator and original administrator of the *Academy of Certified Social Workers (ACSW)* and longtime leader of the Henry Street Settlement in New York, he directed the Mobilization for Youth research demonstration project and was an influential social policy theoretician and practitioner.

bed-wetting *Enuresis*, the involuntary discharge of urine, usually by a child who had formerly achieved bladder control, during sleep or bed rest.

bedlam Chaotic behavior of a group that seems to be acting irrationally and without reference to one another. The term derives from the London asylum for people with mental disabilities, officially named Priory of St. Mary of Bethlehem (Bedlam) when it opened in 1247. Bedlam became a synonym for *mental hospitals* for several centuries.

Beers, Clifford W. (1876–1943) Leader of the *mental hygiene* movement in the United States. After spending three years in a mental hospital, in 1908 he wrote the influential book *A Mind That Found Itself* and told the world about the inhumane conditions in the treatment of people with mental disorders.

behavior Any action or response by an individual, including observable activity, measurable physiological changes, cognitive images, fantasies, and emotions.

behavior modification A method of assessing and altering *behavior* based on the methods of applied behavior analysis, the principles of *operant conditioning, classical conditioning,* and *social learning theory* (for example, *positive reinforcement, extinction,* and *modeling*).

behavior therapy Application of *behavior modification* principles in clinical settings to assess and alter undesired behaviors such as *fear, anxiety, depression, sexual disorder,* and other problems using techniques based on empirical research.

behavioral assessment In *social learning theory* and *behavior therapy,* the attempt to establish the antecedent stimuli and consequences that shaped and/or maintain a given discrete behavior or more complex behavioral repertoire. The psychosocial origins of behavior are sought in terms of environmental events, not in mental ones. Behavior is described in quantifiable dimensions such as how much, how often, and how long. See also *psychosocial assessment*.

behavioral family therapy (BFT) The use of *social learning theory* and the therapeutic techniques of *behavior modification* to help families achieve specific goals. In behaviorally oriented *family therapy,* family members are helped to define their problems clearly in terms of *overt behaviors* and develop problem-solving behaviors to which all agree. Homework assignments, quantifying specific actions, and maintaining certain communications activities are frequently part of this form of *intervention.*

behavioral rehearsal   The technique used by helping professionals, especially those with behaviorist orientations, to suggest or demonstrate desired behavior to a client and then encourage the client, through description, *role playing,* and other demonstrations, to behave similarly. With practice, feedback, and repetition of the behavior in the relatively "safe" environment of the professional's office, the client is more likely to be successful in achieving the desired behavior at the appropriate time.

behavioral sciences   The academic disciplines that gather and evaluate data about human and animal behavior, especially through systematic experimental research, including psychology, sociology, and anthropology.

behaviorism   The school of psychology and related sciences established by Ivan Pavlov (1849–1936), J. B. Watson (1878–1958), B. F. Skinner (1904–1990), and others to explain behavior in terms of events (antecedent stimuli) that occur before a behavior and consequences (reinforcing and punishing ones) that occur following behavior. Behaviorism contends that many maladaptive behaviors are, at least in part, acquired through learning processes and can potentially be unlearned. Behaviorism has led to the development of *social learning theory* and of behavior analysis and therapy as models of practice.

Bell's palsy   Muscle paralysis on one side of the face, resulting from temporary damage to the facial nerve. Most patients recover completely, many without treatment.

Belmont Report   A study and statement of the fundamental principles, ethical considerations, and legal constraints involved in conducting research involving human subjects. The report was issued in 1978 by the National Commission for the Protection of Human Subjects.

Beltway   A metaphor referring to the way federal government bureaucrats and Washington, DC, newspaper writers and political operatives think and act, which has great interest to them but little to people outside Washington, DC. The term refers to the Capital Beltway (I-495), a multilane highway that surrounds the nation's capital and many Maryland and Virginia suburbs.

benchmark   A reference point or standard of excellence against which similar or subsequent marks are compared.

Bender gestalt test   A test used in diagnosing certain psychological and neurological disorders. After the subject has copied several designs, the results are analyzed, usually by a trained psychologist or neurologist, for spatial errors that help locate and determine the type of disturbance.

benefactor   One who provides financial or other support for some aspect of the public good.

beneficence   Actions motivated by the wish to enhance the welfare of others. Some suggest that this leads to *paternalism* and to minimizing client *self-determination* and *empowerment.* Thus, many social workers espouse *limited beneficence,* which seeks to enhance the client's well-being without interfering with basic liberties. *Selective beneficence* is designed to protect a client's interest in specific areas. This term also applies to the obligation to protect persons by doing no harm, by maximizing possible benefits, and by minimizing possible risks of harm.

benefit reduction rate (BRR)   In social welfare programs, the amount of money that is withheld from a *public assistance* payment for each additional dollar of household income beyond a specified amount. For example, in the *Temporary Assistance to Needy Families (TANF)* program, the *Food Stamp program,* and *housing programs,* benefits vary depending on the other sources of client income. Thus, when a client becomes employed, the benefits may be reduced by 100 percent of the amount earned. However, the major practical alternative leads to the *cliff effect,* which is also a *disincentive.*

benefits   1. Cash benefits are payments in the form of money or redeemable vouchers. 2. In-kind benefits are services or goods rather than money (for example, food baskets, agricultural surpluses, housing, and personal counseling).

Benefits Eligibility Screening Tool (BEST)   A Web-based questionnaire provided by the U.S. *Social Security Administration* to help people determine if they, or people they are helping, are eligible for the benefits offered in the Social Security system, including Medicare, Old-Age Insurance, Disability Insurance, Survivors Insurance, and Supplemental Security Income. BEST is not an application procedure itself but informs possible beneficiaries if and how they should proceed with their applications. Their Web site address is http://best.ssa.gov

benefits specialist   An employee of a county or other local jurisdiction who helps residents, particularly older persons, learn about, obtain, and remain compliant with Medicare and other social services programs and benefits.

benevolence   Motivation to do good for others, especially those in need.

benign neglect   The purposeful withholding of assistance, usually with the understanding that the help that has been given may be ultimately more harmful than worthwhile. The term was popularized by Daniel Patrick Moynihan (1927–2003). See also *limited beneficence.*

benzodiazepines   A group of *psychoactive drugs* that act as *central nervous system (CNS)* depressants. Popularly referred to as tranquilizers, benzodiazepines are prescribed by physicians to help patients reduce *anxiety* and pain and to help them sleep. Trade names include Valium and Librium. Some substance abusers use these drugs nonmedically to produce a state of alcohol-like *intoxication.*

bereavement   The emotional and physical reaction to loss of a loved one. See also *grief* and *uncomplicated bereavement.*

Bereavement Benefit   A social security payment plan used by various governments, including Great Britain, Australia, and New Zealand, in which survivors of deceased spouses are granted a tax-free lump-sum payment soon after the spouse's death and a weekly stipend thereafter, the amount depending on previous insurance contributions, the beneficiary's age, and eligibility for other benefits.

bereavement counseling   A therapeutic intervention to help clients cope with the death of loved ones. Such treatment is usually focused and relatively short-term and often includes support by *mutual-aid groups,* neonatal death support

groups, compassionate friends, and widow-to-widow programs.

beriberi   A nutritional disease caused by an insufficiency of vitamin B.

Bertha Capen Reynolds Society (BCRS)   The national organization for those interested in *progressive social work,* founded in 1985 and named after the Smith College social work educator (whose so-called "radical" and Marxist views caused her to be fired and blacklisted). The society changed its name to the *Social Welfare Action Alliance* in 2000.

Besant, Annie (1847–1933)   An English community organizer, she helped organize unions for poor working women and published and distributed information about *birth control* to poor families. She helped found and lead the British Malthusian Society to promote *contraception.*

Bethune, Mary McLeod (1875–1955)   A leader in the movement for the education and social development of African Americans, she founded what is now Bethune–Cookman College in Daytona, Florida, and organized and led several *civil rights* groups. She was also influential in the administration of Franklin D. Roosevelt, especially in ensuring that *New Deal* programs included African Americans.

Better Business Bureau   A voluntary association found in most cities and towns consisting of business owners and managers who define fair and ethical practices in the conduct of business. These bureaus often accept complaints from the public about businesses that violate their standards and exercise persuasion to encourage their compliance. The national Web site address is http://www.bbb.org

Beveridge Report   A 1942 report, by economist *William Henry Beveridge* (1879–1963), that proposed a plan providing for *"cradle-to-grave"* economic and social protection. The report formed the basis for development of the postwar British welfare state, including education, health care, and the social security system. This system remained in effect until the 1980s, when political changes resulted in an erosion of support for public welfare and free public services.

Beveridge, William Henry (1879–1963)   Founder of the British welfare state. Before World

War II, he planned and wrote major social legislation to help poor people, laborers, and children. An early *settlement house* leader and social worker, Beveridge served as director of *Toynbee Hall*. His 1942 *Beveridge Report* was implemented after the war and is the basis for Great Britain's current social security and health care system. It has also been used as a model by many other nations, especially former British colonies.

bias 1. An *attitude* that can influence feelings, usually resulting in an individual's having positive or negative predispositions about a particular group, individual, idea, or object. 2. In research, a tendency for the results to lean in one or another direction because of improper *sampling*, misuse of statistical or research tools, or other improper methods.

biased sample In social research, a *sample* that has been produced through methods that yield a sample that is systematically different from the population. For example, if a survey sought to determine the general public's attitude toward welfare programs and drew its sample entirely from applicants at a welfare office, the sample would not represent the general population.

biased writing See *unbiased writing*.

bibliotherapy The use of literature and poetry in the treatment of people with emotional problems or *mental illness*. Bibliotherapy is often used in *social group work* and *group therapy* and is reported to be effective with people of all ages, with people in institutions as well as outpatients, and with healthy people who wish to share literature as a means of personal growth and development. See also *art therapy* and *poetry therapy*.

biculturalism The efforts of people belonging to two different sociocultural groups, whose homes and workplaces are in close proximity, to adapt to the ways of the other. Their efforts may include learning and being accommodating to the other group's language, values, customs, and patterns of behavior. In actuality the smaller and weaker culture usually has the greater burden of accommodation to the dominant cultural group.

Big Brothers/Big Sisters of America *Voluntary associations* in which work under professional supervision, usually by social workers, provides individual guidance and companionship to boys and girls deprived of a parent. Big Brothers was founded in 1946, especially to provide role models for fatherless boys. Big Sisters was formed in 1971, primarily to provide role models and positive female images for girls and boys. The two groups were merged in 1977. Their Web site address is http://www.bbbsa.org

bigamy The illegal offense of having more than one wife or husband at the same time. In the United States, bigamous marriages have no legal validity in any state. See also *polygamy*.

Bilingual Education Act U.S. federal legislation (P.L. 100-297) first enacted in 1968 to fund public education programs that accommodate to the language needs of all students. Bilingual education was upheld by the U.S. Supreme Court (*Lau v. Nichols*), which unanimously ruled in 1974 that public schools must provide for students who speak little or no English. See also *English-Only Movement*.

bilingual special education An educational alternative for Limited English Proficiency students with disabilities. Several laws specify that children with disabilities must be given the same educational opportunities as other children and that these opportunities are not precluded by poor command of English.

bilis A *culture-bound syndrome* found especially among Latino groups in which the individual experiences nervous tension, trembling, and various *somatic complaints,* said to be the result of feeling intense anger or rage. This syndrome is also known as *muina*.

bimodal In frequency distributions, two categories in which values occur most frequently. For example, in a city where the delinquency rate peaked every January and July, there would be a bimodal distribution of delinquency.

binding out The practice in Colonial America of indenturing children of poor families into the care of more affluent families; often the process was not to provide more secure homes for the children but to provide inexpensive labor for the "caregivers."

binge eating disorder The rapid consumption of unusually large amounts of food in a short time without necessarily being hungry. Individuals often feel embarrassed, guilty, or depressed about the lack of control over it.

biodegradability   The capability of decaying (being broken down into component elements, usually including water; carbon dioxide; and other simple, small molecular substances), caused by the actions of living things such as bacteria and molds. Biodegradability is an important environmental concern because it is a natural recycling process; all new life and the substances necessary to sustain life use the products of biodegradation. Because synthetic materials are not biodegradable, their disposition after use is not a resource but an environmental problem.

biodiversity   A wide variety of plant and animal species living within an environment in which components have considerable interdependence. Reductions in biodiversity occur primarily by human activity such as deforestation, agriculture, urban expansion, mining, pollution, and global warming. Reduced biodiversity is thought to have serious but still not completely known consequences.

bioethical decision making   The system and procedures for establishing the type and degree to which medical services will be provided to a patient. These patients are most frequently newborns with birth defects or very old people suffering from serious mental or physical dysfunctions. Although modern medical technology can maintain at least a diminished quality of life for people with extremely debilitating health problems, health care professionals must use carefully specified criteria in deciding whether to use these procedures. Moreover, their work must be overseen by representatives from the public.

bioethics   Also known as biomedical ethics, the analysis and study of legal, moral, social, and ethical considerations involving the biological and medical sciences. Issues of particular interest include *genetic engineering, reproductive technology, surrogacy,* organ transplantation, use and withdrawal of medical and mental health treatment, *suicide,* and *patients' rights.*

biofeedback   A method of training people to modify their own internal physiological processes, such as heart rate, muscle tension, blood pressure, and brain wave activity, through self-monitoring. Usually, this is done by using mechanical instruments to provide information about variations in one or more of a subject's physiological processes. The resulting information is displayed to the subject *(feedback)*, which helps the individual control these processes even though he or she may be unable to articulate how the learning was achieved.

biogenic   Originating physiologically or biologically rather than psychologically.

biological parent   A male or female whose sperm or egg provided part of the genetic makeup of the child. This term is replacing the term "birth parent," which was often used to differentiate adoptive parents from those who conceived the baby. The term biological parent is more appropriate than birth parent because of advances in reproductive technology.

biomedical ethics   See *bioethics.*

biometry   The study of all the factors that determine an individual's probable life span.

Bion group   See *Tavistock group.*

biopsy   Removal and examination of body tissue samples to detect the presence of *cancer* and other diseases.

biopsychosocial   Phenomena that consist of biological, psychological, and social elements, such as *stress.*

biorhythms   Cyclical variations in one's level of activity, alertness, mood, and general effectiveness.

biosocial   The interaction of environmental, biological, social, cultural, and physical factors.

bioterrorism   The malicious introduction of biological or chemical agents into the air, water, or food supply to cause death, debilitation, intimidation, or social disruption. Anthrax, botulism, plague, smallpox, and other diseases are the agents currently favored by bioterrorists. The perpetrators' motivation is usually to harm a perceived enemy, gain publicity, make political statements, or assert a sense of power.

bipartisan   Cooperation between two or more groups, such as political parties, to achieve a mutually desired objective, such as passage of a law.

bipolar disorder   A category of mental illnesses in which *mood* and *affect* are *maladaptive.* Formerly known as *manic–depressive illness,* the category may be subcategorized as *manic* type (symptoms often include *hyperactivity, euphoria,* distractibility, pressured speech, and *grandiosity*), depressed type (symptoms often include deep sadness, *apathy,* sleep disturbance, poor appetite, low *self-esteem,* and slowed thinking), and mixed type (frequently alternating patterns of manic and then depressed traits). The diagnosis of this condition distinguishes between *bipolar I disorder* (predominantly manic) and *bipolar II disorder* (predominantly depressive).

bipolar I disorder The bipolar *mood disorder* characterized by a single *manic episode* or much more commonly by recurrent *manic episodes* or *hypomanic episodes* often immediately preceded or followed by a major depressive episode. In formal diagnoses the clinician also indicates the type of most recent episode, as in "bipolar I disorder, most recent episode hypomanic" (or manic, depressed, mixed, or *NOS*).

bipolar II disorder The bipolar *mood disorder* characterized by one or more major depressive episodes and at least one *hypomanic episode.* By definition there has never been a manic or mixed episode (in which case the diagnosis becomes *bipolar I disorder*). In formal diagnoses the clinician also indicates the type of episode, as in "bipolar II disorder, most recent episode hypomanic" (or depressed).

birth cohort All the people who were born within a specific year or other time frame.

birth control Limiting or preventing reproduction by various means. These include contraceptive (antipregnancy) devices such as *condoms,* contraceptive pills, diaphragms, intrauterine devices (IUDs), and spermicides. Another type of birth control occurs through the more-or-less permanent surgical *sterilization* of men (as in *vasectomy*) or women (as in *tubal ligation*). Among the more common efforts to control *conception* is "natural *family planning,*" in which there is awareness of the *fertility* cycle, and sexual intercourse occurs only during those times in the cycle believed to be less likely to result in *pregnancy. Abstinence* from sexual intercourse and *abortion* are other methods used in birth control. See also *contraception* and *reproductive technology.*

birth defects See *congenital abnormalities.*

birth-order theories Hypotheses to explain apparent differences among *siblings* depending on whether they are oldest, middle, or youngest children. Some theorists suggest that the personalities of the first born are influenced by the fact that more is usually expected of them, so they tend to become achievers but also tend to have more feelings of insecurity and failure. Middle children are often made to feel inferior to their older siblings, so they may try harder to catch up or display traits of inadequacy feelings or anger. Youngest children, according to many of these theorists, may refine attention-getting skills and narcissistic traits. The research on such hypotheses is still inconclusive and somewhat contradictory.

birth parents An individual's genetic mother and father. Adopted children and adoptions workers prefer this term to words such as "real parents." However, surrogate parentage has complicated use of "birth parent;" as a result the preferred term is *biological parent.*

birthrate The ratio of the number of births in a given population and period of time to the total *population,* usually expressed in terms of the number of births per 1,000 or 100,000 of the population.

birthright Anything to which one is entitled by birth. These rights vary greatly in different cultures but generally include citizenship of the country of birth (or parents' citizenship), inheritance of parental-owned properties, freedom from slavery, and in many cultures opportunities for education and good health care.

bisexuality 1. Erotic attraction to males and females. 2. The coexistence in an individual of *homosexuality* and *heterosexuality.*

bivariate analysis Statistical analysis focusing on the simultaneous relationship between two variables. One example is *cross-tabulation.*

Black Lung program A federally regulated *workers' compensation* program for coal miners disabled by a tubercular-type illness associated with working in underground mines. The program is financed primarily through a tax on mine owners.

black-market adoption The *adoption* of children by couples or individuals who are unable to adopt through legitimate public or *private adoption agencies.* Typically, the party who wants a child contracts with an intermediary to obtain a child and makes monetary payments to the intermediary and indirectly to the child's legal guardian. See also *gray-market adoption* and *independent adoption.*

Black Muslims   See *Nation of Islam.*

"black people"   The term often used for people of color who come from, or whose ancestors came from, middle and southern Africa. Some people prefer the term *African American;* however, this designation excludes black people who are not Americans.

black power   The *social movement* in which the goal is the achievement of greater racial *equity* in economic, political, and social influence. A basic premise of the movement is that black influence will grow as more black people gain positions of leadership in elective office, government, and business and acquire enough money to use in seeking legal rights and educational opportunities. The movement seeks to get black people who achieve these positions to work together in pursuit of these goals rather than dilute such efforts by working in disparate directions.

Blackey, Eileen (1902–1979)   A social work educator and theoretician, she helped develop schools of social work in Hawaii, Israel, and the United States and established in-service training programs in many government relief agencies. She also served as director of the United Nations Child Search and Repatriation Program in Germany after World War II.

blacklist   A file containing the names of those people deemed ineligible to participate in some activity or privilege because of their alleged behaviors or adherence to certain ideologies. For example, a group of business leaders might share the names of people who are considered potential union organizers and agree not to hire them. See also *security risk.*

blackmail   The *crime* of unlawfully taking money or property from a person or forcing that person to commit a crime by using fear, *coercion,* or threats. Typically, the coercion involves disclosing information the victim wants to keep concealed. See also *extortion.*

"blackout"   Lay term for the loss from memory of experiences, thoughts, or perceptions that occur during the state of alcohol or other substance *intoxication.*

blamer role   A recurrent pattern of interpersonal communication characterized by acting superior, finding fault, behaving dictatorially, and attributing one's problems to others. The role was delineated by *Virginia Satir,* who described the blamer as a person who conceals inner feelings of loneliness and failure by making persistent accusations. Other roles are the *computer role,* the *distracter role,* and the *placater role.*

blaming the victim   Attributing self-responsibility to individuals who are poor, socially or educationally deficient, victims of rape or other crimes, mentally or physically ill, or in some other ways casualties of unforeseen circumstances. This practice (for example, "if they had worked harder or saved their money, they wouldn't be poor"; "if she hadn't worn those clothes, she wouldn't have been raped or harassed") is often used by opponents of programs to prevent victimization or to help victims.

blanket group   In *social group work* or *group psychotherapy,* the type of group that has no criterion for membership or orderly procedures. It is the opposite of *structured group.* Groups that are totally unstructured are rare, because group leaders usually have some plan for the composition of its membership.

"bleeding heart"   A pejorative expression, often applied to social workers and others who compassionately show concern for those who are disadvantaged or who attempt the *consciousness-raising* of more advantaged people about disadvantaged people.

blended family   1. A family that is formed when separate families are united by marriage or other circumstance; a *stepfamily.* 2. Various kinship or nonkinship groups whose members reside together and assume traditional family roles. See also *reconstituted family.*

Blenkner, Margaret (1909–1973)   Social work researcher who helped establish research as a principle method in the field and facilitated social work's integration of research into its educational curriculum.

blighted area   A land area, region, or urban center damaged by economic depression, toxic chemicals, or social changes.

bloc   A *group* or *coalition* of groups with a common interest in advocating, promoting, or obstructing an ideology, cause, or legislation. Such groups often achieve power far above their individual numbers by voting uniformly.

block grant   A system of disbursing funds to meet a locality's health, education, and social welfare needs while permitting the recipient organizations to determine how best to distribute the money. Used mostly by the federal and sometimes state governments, the system is designed to consolidate budget itemization and eliminate the necessity of earmarking funds for every individual and *categorical program.* Proponents say it increases efficiency and local control, and opponents suggest that it is a covert way of reducing expenditures for social welfare needs.

block organizations   Formal or informal social groups who live in physical proximity to one another (as in a city block); have shared values, problems, and vulnerabilities; and meet to achieve their mutual goals.

block placement   In *social work education,* an alternative to the traditional *concurrent placement* in *field instruction.* In the traditional model of *field placement,* the student alternates classroom experiences with work in a *social agency* on different days of each week. In block placements, the student attends classes only for several months and then works virtually full-time in a social agency under academic and professional supervision for several months. The amount of time spent in the agency during a block placement is the same as in concurrent placement, and students must meet the same academic requirements.

blockbusting   The practice of inciting residents of a neighborhood to sell out precipitously. Often initiated by realtors and investors, the homeowners are told their property values will soon drop because members of different racial or ethnic groups are about to move in. This generates business for the realtors and opportunities for investors to gain property at favorable prices. In the United States, the practice was made illegal with Title VIII of the Civil Rights Act of 1968 but continues today in more subtle and covert ways.

blocking   A temporary failure of memory, interrupting one's flow of speech or thought.

blood alcohol level (BAL)   The amount of alcohol in a person's bloodstream expressed as a percentage of the total blood volume. For example, if the level is 0.05 percent, then five parts alcohol per 10,000 parts of blood exist. The amount may be determined by direct chemical analysis of the extracted blood or by a *Breathalyzer.* After alcohol is consumed, much of it enters the bloodstream until it is processed (that is, oxidized). The liver oxidizes alcohol at the rate of about one-half ounce per hour.

blood poisoning   See *septicemia.*

Bloods and Crips   See *Crips and Bloods.*

Bloom's Taxonomy   A systematic classification of educational objectives developed in 1956 by psychologist Benjamin S. Bloom. The taxonomy divides learning into three domains: cognitive, affective, and psychomotor (skills), with each domain subdivided by educational level. The taxonomy has influenced curricular development from elementary through graduate and professional education, including *social work education.*

Blue Book   Common name used by the U.S. Social Security Administration for the *Disability Evaluation Under Social Security* book, which delineates the medical criteria used by physicians, social workers, and other health professionals for evaluating disability claims. The Blue Book defines and lists all qualified impairments in children and adults, the evidence needed to assert a claim, and procedures for qualifying or appealing.

blue collar   Members of a wage-earning *socioeconomic class.* The term originally applied to people who worked in factories or manual labor settings in which blue or dark clothes were worn and were used to distinguish these workers from those employed in offices or retail stores (white-collar workers).

blunted affect   A dulling or deintensifying of the expression of *mood* or *emotion,* often noted as an important symptom in *schizophrenia.*

board of directors   A group of people empowered to establish an organization's objectives and policies and to oversee the activities of the personnel responsible for day-to-day implementation of those policies. The boards of social agencies often consist of volunteers who are influential in the community and reflect the views prevalent in the community.

boarder babies Infants born of drug-addicted parents who, because they are also addicted, must remain hospitalized until healthy enough to be released into the care of natural or foster parents. The term is also used for infants kept in any institution or care facility while awaiting more permanent homes.

"boarding school era" Term used by many Native American groups to refer to the period of 1880 to 1950, when U.S. policy was to "help" tribal children assimilate into the predominant culture by placing them in government boarding schools or Christian mission schools. The schools were typified by harsh disciplinary methods, English-only speaking, and Anglo-oriented history lessons. The schools began closing in the 1930s, but many survived into the 1950s as facilities for neglected Native American children.

boat people Refugees who flee their homelands in barely seaworthy vessels to find more hospitable environments in other nations. Many of these people have faced great risks, including capture by their governments, piracy, malnutrition, and possible exploitation at the sites of their new locations. People from Southeast Asia, Haiti, and Cuba are recent examples.

body dysmorphic disorder A type of *somatoform disorder* characterized by excessive preoccupation about some imagined defect in appearance by someone who is of normal appearance. See also *dysmorphophobia* and *anorexia nervosa*.

body language See *kinesics*.

bonding The development by one person of *attachment* for another. The process begins when the individual has needs that are regularly fulfilled by the other and his or her identity is partially shaped by the interrelationship.

bone marrow transplantation A cancer treatment in which marrow destroyed in radiation or chemotherapy is replaced; the replacement marrow is donated by another person or taken from the patient before treatment begins.

bone mineral density (BMD) A measure of the relative strength and durability of bones. Low BMD is an important risk factor in osteoporosis and has also been linked to depression in some people.

boomerang children Young adults who return to live in their parent's homes after a period of adult independence.

"boondoggle" A negative term applied to allegedly wasteful or seemingly unproductive public works projects. The term first became prominent during the 1930s *New Deal* programs, which seemed to some to be more concerned with putting people back to work than with producing any goods or services of value.

boot camp A justice system program, primarily for younger adult law offenders, that resembles military basic training and focuses on discipline, physical conditioning, and authoritarian controls.

Booth, Charles (1840–1916) A British pioneer in methods of surveying social problems, he wrote one of the first treatises on the conditions and causes of poverty and the working classes. He developed a classification of the types of poor people, used in early social work literature, and advocated many of the old-age and survivors insurance programs that were implemented in Great Britain.

bootleg To make, carry, or sell alcohol or other illegal products unlawfully.

borantia In Japan, public service voluntary work.

Border and Transportation Security Directorate (BTS) An organization within the *U.S. Department of Homeland Security (DHS)* formed in 2003 to help secure the nation's borders, airports, and transportation systems. Its major components include the *Bureau of Customs and Border Protection (CBP)*, the *Bureau of Citizenship and Immigration Services (CIS)*, and the *Transportation Security Administration (TSA)*.

borderline A descriptive term applied to a premorbid condition or any phenomenon located between two categories. Social workers and mental health workers often use the term informally in describing individuals who are at or near the dividing line between psychosis and nonpsychosis or normalcy and mental illness; not to be confused with *borderline personality disorder*.

borderline intellectual functioning *Intelligence* abilities that measure on *intelligence quotient (IQ)* tests at the 71 to 84 range (just below what psychologists refer to as *dull-normal* and just above the highest level of *mental retardation*).

borderline personality disorder   One of the 11 *personality disorders* characterized by some of the following symptoms and traits: deeply ingrained and maladaptive patterns of relating to others, impulsive and unpredictable behavior that is often self-destructive, lack of control of anger, intense mood shifts, identity disturbance and inconsistent self-concept, manipulation of others for short-term gain, and chronic feelings of boredom and emptiness.

"borderline schizophrenia"   A descriptive term applied to individuals who, to some clinicians, seem to be at or near a conceptualized line between *schizophrenia* and a *normal* state. In such people, some of the symptoms seen in schizophrenia are observed or inferred, but the severity, duration, and progression of those symptoms are inconsistent or do not meet all the diagnostic criteria. The term has been confused with or considered synonymous with *latent schizophrenia* or *simple schizophrenia*. Because it is so imprecise, the term is now rarely used by skilled diagnosticians. Many who were once diagnosed as people with "borderline schizophrenia" are now given the diagnosis of *schizotypal personality disorder*.

Borstal system   The former corrections program for young offenders (ages 15 to 23) in the United Kingdom that attempted to emphasize education, training, and rehabilitation in closed or open prisons. The system was established in 1895 and abolished in 1982. See also *reformatory*.

botanica   A botanical shop or commercial establishment selling herbs, natural foods, medical compounds, and healing paraphernalia. More typically found in Latin American and Asian communities, botanicas are cultural versions of pharmacies, and the proprietors also provide counseling, ombudsman services, neighborhood socializing, and the maintenance of cultural traditions.

botulism   A serious type of food poisoning caused by a bacteria found in improperly canned or refrigerated foods. The toxin attacks the *central nervous system (CNS)* causing headaches, weakness, constipation, and paralysis.

boufee delirante   A *culture-bound syndrome* found mostly in West Africa and Haiti in which the individual experiences a sudden outburst of excitement, aggressive behavior, confusion, and sometimes paranoid thoughts and hallucinations.

boundaries   Regions separating two psychological or social systems. A central concept in *family system theories* pertaining to the implicit rules that determine how the family members or subsystems are expected to relate to one another and to nonfamily members. Analogous to the membranes of living cells, a function of boundaries is to differentiate systems and their subsystems and to permit the development of *identity*. Healthy family functioning largely entails clear boundaries; less-healthy functioning is seen where boundary subsystems are either inappropriately rigid or not consistently clear (that is, in a *disengaged family* or an *enmeshed family*). See also *family rules*.

bounded rationality   In *social planning* theory, the recognition that rationality (specifying all the alternative strategies toward goal achievement, determining all their consequences, and evaluating these consequences) is the most efficient means toward action but that such complete listings and evaluations are ultimately impractical. Given that the obtainable information will be incomplete and somewhat inconsistent, the social planner instead decides on an action that is good enough to meet minimal criteria. See also *satisficing*.

bovine spongiform encephalopathy (BSE)   Popularly called "mad cow disease," a progressive neurological disorder of cattle resulting from contact with other infected animals but probably originating from feeding them meat and bone meal with their food. The fears of a widespread epidemic, mostly in Europe, and that a form of the disease may spread to humans (*Creutzfeldt–Jakob disease*) has led to closer scrutiny of the way animals are fed and treated.

Boy Scouts   The international organization to help boys develop as healthy and productive citizens. The Boy Scout movement was established in Great Britain in 1907 by Robert Baden-Powell. The Boy Scouts of America was formed in 1910 by William Boyce. The Boy Scouts have three levels: Cub Scouts (ages seven to 10), Boy Scouts (ages 11 to 18), and Explorers (ages 15 to 20, also open to girls). Their Web site address is http://www.bsa.scouting.org

boycott   An organized refusal to maintain certain relationships with a person, organization, or government body. For example, a community organizer might convince all residents of a neighborhood to stop patronizing a store that discriminates against people from certain racial or ethnic groups.

Boys and Girls Clubs of America   The U.S. national organization for children, founded in 1906, with local facilities in nearly every larger community in the United States. The clubs offer recreational and educational facilities, arts and crafts, community and civic work, free meals for needy youngsters, tutoring, nurturing, and role-modeling opportunities for young people. Funding is through individual voluntary contributions, philanthropies, and community fundraising organizations and from the nominal membership fees paid by the young people who are members. The organization originated as the Boys Clubs of America and gradually included girls in individual facilities. Their Web site address is http://www.bgca.org

Boys Town   A privately funded child care organization originally located near Omaha, Nebraska, founded in 1917 by Father Edward Flanagan (1886–1948) as an orphanage for parentless boys. Now called Girls and Boys Town, it has locations throughout the nation to serve boys and girls without caregivers and those who are victims of abuse or are addicted to alcohol or drugs. Their Web site address is http://www.girlsandboystown.org

Brace, Charles Loring (1826–1890)   Founder of the *Children's Aid Society* in 1853, the private organization that provided shelter, education, and family *placing out* for homeless children, more than 50,000 of whom were sent on *orphan trains* to be adopted by Western farmers. His work influenced modern *child welfare* programs and the *foster care* system.

bracero program   The transportation of Mexican farm laborers (braceros) to and from U.S. farms for seasonal work. This federal program was created during World War II to alleviate shortages of farm workers, and it ended in 1964 because of opposition by organized labor. An informal and unlawful bracero program still exists on many U.S. farms with illegal aliens from Mexico.

Brady Bill   Gun control legislation signed into law (P.L. 103-159) in 1993 that requires a five-day waiting period before certain handguns can be purchased and requires gun sellers to check appli-

cants to ensure they comply with laws. The law was named after President Ronald Reagan's Press Secretary James S. Brady, who was shot during an assassination attempt against the president. See also *gun lobby* and *CAP laws.*

bradycardia   Abnormally low heartbeat (usually below 60 beats per minute in adults).

brain damage   A lay term referring to extragenetic influences that impair or stop the normal growth, development, or function of brain tissue. A damaged brain does not necessarily impair learning, and impaired learning is not always caused by brain damage.

brain drain   A nation's or institution's loss of scientific, technical, or leadership talent when these people relocate. This is a problem in *developing countries,* which use their limited resources to educate citizens only to see them migrate to nations that offer higher salaries or other desirable conditions.

Brain Electrical Activity Mapping (BEAM)   A computerized diagnostic tool for assessing *central nervous system (CNS)* functioning by turning signals from an electroencephalograph into colored maps depicting blood flow and other electrochemical processes in the brain.

brain fag   Short for "brain fatigue," a *culture-bound syndrome* most frequently identified among people of West Africa in which the individual feels anxious, depressed, and tired and has a headache attributed to intense mental exercise.

brain trust   A group of expert advisers to a public official, political candidate, or planning organization.

brainstorming   1. A method used in organizations to encourage members to produce rapidly as many ideas as possible. Groups, often with five to 12 members and a leader, generate the ideas in a freewheeling and noncritical atmosphere, record the results, and present them to the organization for further consideration. 2. In social work administration, a method of stimulating the development of ideas by assembling certain staff and board members and encouraging open discussion, while postponing criticism or analysis of the ideas proposed. See also *electronic brainstorming.*

brainwash The use of propaganda, persuasion, and sometimes coercion to influence people to accept new and different beliefs unquestioningly.

Brawner **rule** The legal standard in many jurisdictions for determining that a person is to be found not guilty by reason of insanity, formulated by the American Law Institute (ALI). The ALI formulation states that "a person is not responsible for criminal conduct if at the time of such conduct as a result of mental disease or defect he lacks the substantial capacity either to appreciate the wrongfulness of his conduct or to conform his conduct to the requirements of the law." See also *McNaughten rule.*

breach of promise Failure to wed after both parties have made a serious and specific agreement to marry and then one party unilaterally decides not to go through with it. In legal terms, "breach" refers to any failure to fulfill an agreed-on act or duty owed to an individual or to society, as in "breach of contract" or "breach of the peace."

bread line A procedure for distributing to assembled, needy people those bakery products, groceries, agricultural commodities, and surplus items that typically cannot be sold on the open market because they usually do not meet optimal quality or freshness standards. See also *soup kitchen.*

Breathalyzer Trademark for a test device used to determine if a person is intoxicated. Most commonly administered by a trained police officer on those people operating motor vehicles, the test chemically analyzes the *blood alcohol level (BAL)* as indicated by a breath test. Most states require that applicants for driver's licenses consent in advance to taking the test when requested, and failure to take or pass the test is admissible in court.

breathing-related sleep disorder A synonym for *apnea,* a *sleep disorder* involving disruption of sleep patterns caused by abnormalities of ventilation. This usually results in sleepiness, irritability, and less effectiveness in carrying out activities of daily living (ADL). Typically it results in loud snoring, gasps, and body movements likely to disturb the individual or bed partner.

Breckinridge, Sophonisba (1866–1948) A developer of *social work education* within universities, she was a founder of the School of Social Work at the University of Chicago, where she established

much of the graduate school curriculum for social workers. She introduced the *case method system* of teaching and was a founder of the *American Association of Schools of Social Work (AASSW),* now known as the *Council on Social Work Education (CSWE).*

bribery The *crime* of offering or giving to a person, especially an official such as a police officer or legislator, money or something of value to influence that person's actions.

bridge housing 1. A *transitional living facility* for people who move from institutional settings to relatively autonomous homes, as in *halfway houses* or *quarterway houses.* 2. Temporary shelters for those people who have left their homes because of natural disasters, war, or economic problems but who lack the resources, opportunity, or replacement shelters for more permanent residence.

brief psychotic disorder The sudden onset of psychotic symptoms such as *delusion, hallucination,* disorganized speech or behavior, or *catatonia,* lasting at least one day and less than one month. This condition is not caused by medical conditions, substance abuse, or other mental disorders. The disorder may be the result of a marked stressor (such as loss of a loved one or other psychological trauma) or occur without marked stressors or within four weeks postpartum. This disorder, when the result of marked stressors, was formerly known as *brief reactive psychosis.*

brief reactive psychosis A term formerly used for *brief psychotic disorder* caused by marked stressors.

brief therapy *Psychotherapy* or *clinical social work* intervention in which specific goals and the number of sessions are predetermined. Brief therapy is usually goal oriented, circumscribed, active, focused, and directed toward specific problems or symptoms.

Briquet's syndrome A rarely used diagnostic term for *somatization disorder.*

British Association of Social Workers (BASW) The largest professional association of social workers in the United Kingdom, established in 1970, to facilitate the growth of the profession and the exchange of knowledge between professionals, and to assure the public of the high and ethical standards of membership. BASW hosts workshops and annual conferences and sponsors many publications including the magazine *Professional Social Work* and the *British Journal of Social Work*. Their Web site address is http://www.basw.co.uk

British Department for Work and Pensions (DWP) The government organization in the United Kingdom responsible for implementing its welfare, employment, and education systems. Established in 2001 by a merger of the Department of Social Security and parts of the Department for Education and Employment, the DWP assists working-age people to obtain work benefits and jobs through its Jobcentre Plus program. It administers the Pension Service for retired workers and the Child Support Agency. DWP's Web address is http://www.dwp.gov.uk

British National Insurance Act The 1911 *social security* legislation in Great Britain devised by Lloyd George that provided old-age insurance; *unemployment compensation;* sickness insurance; and, in 1925, survivors insurance for most workers. Many of the features of the National Insurance Act were emulated in the U.S. *Social Security Act.* The National Insurance Act was replaced by the post–World War II social security system recommended in the *Beveridge Report.*

British Youth Council (BYC) The United Kingdom's organization for youths, established in 1948, with local councils in hundreds of communities throughout the nation. The BYC, the leadership of which includes young people at all levels, represents its views to central and local government, political parties, pressure groups, and the media. The BYC advocates for issues of special concern to young people, including lowering the voting age to 16, increasing minimum wages, children's rights, and educational improvements. Their Web site address is http://www.byc.org.uk

brittle bone disease See *osteogenesis imperfecta.*

Brockway, Zebulon Reed (1827–1902) A prison reformer and administrator, he began his career as an *almshouse* worker and eventually became superintendent of various prisons. He led many successful campaigns to bring about more humane and effective circumstances for prisoners.

broken home A family in which at least one parent is absent because of *divorce, death,* or *desertion.*

Social workers now generally prefer the term *single-parent family.*

"broken-window theory" The premise that crime and urban decay increase in city neighborhoods in which buildings remain in dilapidated condition (that is, windows remain broken). Those prone to antisocial behavior gravitate to such areas, claims this theory, leading to an increase in crime. Conversely, if a community encourages or forces landlords to make repairs promptly, the area becomes more attractive, populated, and scrutinized, and crime is reduced. The theory was developed by James Q. Wilson and George Kelling in 1982.

broker role A function of social workers and community organizers in which clients (individuals, groups, organizations, or communities) are helped to identify, locate, and link available community resources; and various segments of the community are put in touch with one another to enhance their mutual interests. See also *advocate role, educator role, enabler role,* and *mediator role.*

brown lung disease Environmentally induced damage to the respiratory system, often from inhalation of materials in the air such as cotton dust. The formal name is byssinosis.

Brown v. Board of Education The 1954 U.S. Supreme Court ruling that the "separate but equal" interpretation of the 14th Amendment was unconstitutional and that racial *segregation* of public schools was illegal. See also *Plessy v. Ferguson.*

brownfield Land in cities or beyond that is abandoned or unused because it may contain environmental contaminants left there by previous industrial or commercial occupants.

Bruno, Frank J. (1874–1955) One of the first developers of a theory base in the new field of social work, he led the George Warren Brown School of Social Work at Washington University in St. Louis for many years. A *civil rights* activist, he worked to achieve opportunities for minorities in *social work education.* He wrote some of the most influential early social work texts, including *The Theory of Social Work* in 1936.

bruxism The habit of gnashing, grinding, and clenching one's teeth, often resulting in dental injury.

BSW A bachelor's degree awarded to qualified students who major in social work in an undergraduate college accredited by the *Council on Social Work Education (CSWE)*.

buccal swab A genetic-testing procedure used primarily to help determine paternity by examining the saliva, collected voluntarily from the *putative father's* mouth with a Q-tip.

bucket-and-broom brigade A labor movement in the 1890–1920 era in which wives and daughters of miners and other industrial workers would carry household instruments as they marched on employer's facilities to call public attention to the laborers' plight and to assist in carrying out strikes. The movement was led by *Mary Harris Jones* (Mother Jones).

budget An itemized list of the amount of all estimated revenues a social agency or organization anticipates receiving and the delineation of the amount of all estimated costs and expenses necessary to operate the organization; a statement of probable revenues and expenditures during a specified period.

Buell, Bradley (1893–1976) A developer of the *community organization* and *social planning* fields in social work, he helped found the *American Association of Social Workers (AASW)* and published numerous books, including the influential *Community Planning for Human Services* in 1952.

bulimarexic One who has *bulimia nervosa.*

bulimia nervosa An *eating disorder* in which a pathologically excessive appetite with episodic eating binges is sometimes followed by purging. The purging may occur through means such as self-induced vomiting or the abuse of laxatives, diet pills, or diuretics. Bulimia usually starts as a means of dieting. Its subtypes include the purging and nonpurging type (using other inappropriate compensatory behaviors such as fasting or excessive exercise).

bullying Abusive, insulting, or intimidating behavior that is persistent and offensive and makes the victim feel threatened and vulnerable. The bully uses some form of real or imagined power over the victim and opportunistically seeks weakness in the victim to exploit. The motivation for bullying behavior is often related to the bully's poor self-image, poor anger management skills, ignorance, prejudice, and envy. See also *relational aggression.*

bumping In bureaucratic organizations, the practice under which a senior employee, whose job has been eliminated, is allowed to take over the job of a junior employee. Some organizations refer to this as *decruitment.*

Bureau of Citizenship and Immigration Services See *Citizenship and Immigration Services, Bureau of (CIS).*

Bureau of Health Professions (BHPr) The bureau within the U.S. *Health Resources and Services Administration* to facilitate the training and coordinate the distribution of people in the health care professions. Their Web site address is http://www.hrsa.dhhs.gov/bhpr

Bureau of Immigration and Customs Enforcement See *Immigration and Customs Enforcement, Bureau of (ICE).*

Bureau of Indian Affairs (BIA) A federal organization within the U.S. *Department of the Interior* to provide social services, health care, and educational programs; agricultural and economic assistance; and *civil rights* protections to *American Indians* and *Alaska Natives.* Established by Congress in 1824 as the Office of Indian Affairs within the War Department, it took its present name in 1947. Their Web site address is http://www.doi.gov/bia. See also *Indian Self-Determination Act.*

Bureau of Labor Statistics (BLS) A research agency of the *U.S. Department of Labor* that compiles and publishes statistics about many variables of interest to social workers and social planners, including employment and unemployment rates, consumer prices, and wage rates. Their Web site address is http://www.bls.gov

Bureau of Primary Health Care (BPHC) The bureau within the U.S. *Health Resources and Services Administration* (of HHS) that ensures greater access to, and more equitable distribution of, health care providers in the nation. The BPHC maintains databases of underserved areas and people and facilitates better staffing in these areas. Their Web site address is http://www.bphc.hrsa.dhhs.gov

Bureau of the Census, U.S. The bureau functioning within the *U.S. Department of Commerce*

that carries out the constitutional requirement that all the people in the nation be counted every decade. The bureau, centered in Suitland, Maryland, conducts surveys and analyzes and disseminates resulting data about individuals, population groups, and social trends. Their Web site address is http://www.census.gov

bureaucracy A form of social organization in which distinctive characteristics include a task-specific division of labor; a vertical hierarchy with power centered at the top; clearly defined rules; formalized channels of communication; and selection, promotion, compensation, and retention based on technical competence. See also *technocrat, apparatchik,* and *adhocracy.*

bureaucratization The trend in social institutions and organizations toward more centralized control and enforced conformity to rigidly prescribed rules and channels of communication.

bureaus of public assistance State and county organizations that administer programs to provide economic and social services to needy families; funded from local, state, and federal revenues, these bureaus often help administer programs such as *Temporary Assistance to Needy Families (TANF)* and the *Personal Responsibility and Work Opportunity Reconciliation Act* of 1996 (P.L. 104-193). In some jurisdictions, these bureaus are known as the department of welfare, the department of social services, or the bureau of health and human services.

burglary The *crime* of breaking and entering into someone's home, office, or other place with the intention of stealing property therein.

burnout A nontechnical term to describe workers who feel apathy or anger as a result of on-the-job stress and frustration. Burnout is found among social workers and other workers who have more responsibility than control.

Burns, Eveline M. (1900–1985) A social work educator and consultant to government planners on economic security programs, she helped write the *Social Security Act* and drafted plans for public assistance and work programs. She wrote the influential text *Social Security and Public Policy* (1956).

business improvement districts (BIDS) An urban strategy in which private corporations and public agencies redevelop areas that have succumbed to inner-city decay. The focus is primarily on infrastructure development, including restoring and using abandoned buildings, filling empty lots, and cleaning up streets. See also *broken-window theory, enterprise zones,* and *gentrification.*

busing The transporting of students across school district boundaries, usually court ordered, to facilitate more equitable racial balance.

busti In India, poor neighborhoods or ghettos.

buying pool A group practice in which people join to purchase larger quantities of a given commodity than they could buy separately, thus benefiting from lower costs. Buying pools have often been organized by or on behalf of poor people's groups or homeless organizations.

buzz grouping A procedure to encourage participation by all the individuals in a large group by breaking the gathering into smaller groups (about six to eight people). These small groups then appoint one of their members to report their comments when the larger group reconvenes. Some refer to this as "huddle groups."

bylaws The formal written rules of an organization, which usually include procedures for electing officers and directors, duties of officers and committees, decision-making processes, scope of responsibility, and other related matters.

bystander apathy The tendency of witnesses to an accident, crime, or other emergency not to provide assistance to the victim. Research has shown that the more onlookers there are the less likely anyone will help.

Cabot, Richard C. (1865–1939) A physician and medical educator who worked with the *Children's Aid Society.* Cabot established the nation's first *medical social work* department at Massachusetts General Hospital in 1905.

cachexia A weakened, emaciated, run-down (cachectic) condition usually associated with malnutrition or serious disease.

caffeine withdrawal Symptoms of *withdrawal* (headache, marked fatigue, drowsiness, anxiety, depression, nausea, or vomiting) caused by abrupt cessation or reduction in use of caffeine (in products such as coffee, tea, cocoa, cola, and chocolate).

CAI program Computer-assisted instructional program. See also *IVD program.*

calumny An intentional, false accusation of a crime to injure a person's reputation.

campaign Organized, intensive efforts to achieve a goal, such as raise funds, win an election, gain publicity, or increase membership of an organization. See also *negative campaigning.*

Canada Assistance Plan The Canadian welfare program from 1966 to 1996, when it was replaced by the current *Canada Health and Social Transfer Program.* In the program, half the social assistance costs were from the federal treasury and half from the provincial governments, fostering more uniform standards for social programs in all regions.

Canada Health and Social Transfer Program The foundational Canadian welfare program, established in 1996 to replace the Canada Assistance Plan of 1966. The newer program combines funding for health, postsecondary education, and welfare and transfers from the national treasury a specific amount of money to each province, based on the size and affluence of its population and some other considerations. The earlier program contributed a percentage (50 percent) of the province's actual costs, in exchange for compliance with certain national standards. The effect is to reduce expenditures for social programs and place standard setting more at the local level.

Canadian Association of Schools of Social Work (CASSW) The nation's association of university faculties and departments offering professional education in social work at the undergraduate, graduate, and postgraduate levels, established in 1967. The Board of Accreditation, a semiautonomous body within CASSW, is responsible for the assessment of educational programs and for their period reviews. Their Web site address is http://www.cassw-acess.ca

Canadian Association of Social Workers (CASW) The *professional association* of qualified Canadian social workers, founded in 1926 and headquartered in Ottawa. CASW, a federation of ten provincial and one territorial social work organizations, enhances professional development of its membership through educational programs, conferences, and publications, and the development and enforcement of ethical standards. CASW produces various publications including the quarterly journal *Canadian Social Work* in English and French. Their Web site address is http://www.casw-acts.ca

Canadian Council on Social Development (CCSD) A Canadian national federation of social agencies, along with organizations representing education, health, business, labor, and churches, to promote social justice and the quality of life for all citizens. Founded in 1920 as the Canadian Council on Child Welfare, CCSD is based in Ottawa and sponsors research and training programs, conventions, and publications and informs the public and legislators about such social issues. Their Web site address is http://www.ccsd.ca

Canadian system See *single payer health care plan.*

cancer A malignant tumor; uncontrolled growth of abnormal cells. Unlike normal body cells, cancer cells do not stop growing when in contact with other cells and thus may spread in the body. The cells spread either by invading surrounding tissue or by *metastasis.* Cancer cells compete with normal tissue for nutrients and eventually kill normal cells by depriving them of needed nutrition. See also *carcinoma, sarcoma, leukemia,* and *lymphoma.*

cannabis See *marijuana.*

cannabis abuse   Continued use of psychoactive substances derived from or based on the cannabis plant such as *marijuana, hashish,* or purified tetrahydrocannabinol *(THC),* despite the related health, socioeconomic, or vocational difficulties. Except when cannabis is used legally for medical purposes, all other use is considered abusive.

cannabis organic mental disorder   Intoxication, delusion, or both, occurring after *marijuana, hashish,* or tetrahydrocannabinol *(THC)* use. Symptoms of cannabis intoxication include euphoria, *tachycardia,* the feeling of intensified perceptions, increased appetite, paranoid ideation, panic attack, depression, and impaired social functioning. When these symptoms occur with severe persecutory delusions, marked anxiety, depersonalization, and amnesia, it is called "cannabis delusion disorder." The usual duration of cannabis intoxication and delusional disorder is less than several hours.

Cannon, Ida M. (1877–1960)   A founder of medical social work, conceptualizer, and developer. She advocated for the establishment of social work departments in the nation's hospitals and published influential works for the field, including *Social Work in Hospitals* in 1923. She was a founder of the American Association of Hospital Social Workers, which was renamed the *American Association of Medical Social Workers (AAMSW).*

Cannon, Mary A. (1884–1962)   An early systematizer of knowledge about medical social work and psychiatric social work, she was also an influential social work educator and an organizer of the Social Services Employees Union. She coauthored the 1933 social work text *Social Casework: An Outline for Teaching.*

canvass   To make a systematic inquiry of specified groups of people (such as potential consumers, registered voters of a city, or members of a legislature) to determine their intentions or to influence their actions.

capital intensive   Pertaining to business organizations that require considerable financial commitment and technology but relatively few workers. See also *labor intensive.*

capital offense   A crime punishable by death.

capital punishment   Government-sanctioned implementation of the death penalty, imposed on some criminals convicted of a *capital offense,* which may include murder, *rape,* or treason.

capitalism   An economic system in which the production and distribution of goods and services for consumers are controlled through private ownership and open competition.

capitation   A set amount of money per person. Managed care companies generally express capitation in terms of revenue or cost per member per month.

CAP laws   CAP, or child access prevention, laws are statutes in many states that require people who own guns to store them in places inaccessible to children or to place locking devices on the guns. The adult may be held criminally liable if the child obtains an improperly stored and loaded gun. See also *Brady Bill* and *gun lobby.*

carceral organization   A facility in which individuals are isolated from the rest of society, such as a prison, jail, psychiatric hospital, boarding school, or military barracks.

carcinogen   A substance that causes or aggravates *cancer.*

carcinogenic   *Cancer* causing.

carcinoma   One of the four major types of *cancer* (including *sarcoma, leukemia,* and *lymphoma*), characterized by the "clawlike" spread of the disease over the skin and membranes of internal organs.

cardiopulmonary resuscitation (CPR)   Emergency efforts to make the heart resume pumping and the victim to get oxygen during a heart attack. CPR may include compressing and releasing the chest to make the heart resume its action and forcing oxygen by mouth-to-mouth ventilation. Such actions can improve the chances of surviving a heart attack until medications, electric shock of the heart, and other medical measures can be administered.

cardiovascular disease   Disease of the heart or blood vessels, responsible for nearly 50 percent of all deaths in the United States. Those at greatest risk are smokers and men with elevated blood pressure and serum cholesterol levels. Other risk factors are heredity, obesity, stress, and physical inactivity.

care management   A synonym for *case management*.

care-and-protection proceedings   The legal intervention on behalf of a dependent whose parents or guardians no longer seem willing or able to provide for the dependent's needs.

career counseling   The procedure used by social workers, personnel, and guidance advisers, educational specialists, and other professionals to provide information, advice, support, and linkage of resources to people who are deciding about future vocations or to workers who seek to maximize their vocational potential.

caregiver   One who provides for the physical, emotional, and social needs of another person, who often is dependent and cannot provide for his or her own needs. The term most often applies to parents or parent surrogates, day care and nursery workers, health care specialists, and relatives caring for older people. The term is also applied to all people who provide nurturance and emotional support to others, including spouses, clergy, and social workers.

caregiver support group   A support group comprising individuals who have in common the responsibility of managing the lives and providing for the needs of those unable to do so independently. Typically, such groups are made up of people who care for frail elderly parents, children with a disease or disability, special-needs clients, or family members with a mental disorder. The stress of caregiving is often relieved through the mutual support the members provide one another. The groups may be led by social workers, other professionals, or the members themselves; the degree of structure varies widely.

Caregiver Support Program, National Family (NFCSP)   A program established in 2000 and maintained by the U.S. *Administration on Aging* to assist in developing support programs for those who provide care for older persons. Their Web site address is http://www.aoa.dhhs.gov

Careplanner   An Internet tool established in 2001 by the U.S. *Centers for Medicare and Medicaid Services* to help people who need care, including seniors or others with physical disabilities and chronic illnesses, to make informed decisions about their care options. It is used by the person in need as well as by caregivers, families, and professionals to understand, evaluate, and have access to living and care options. *Careplanner* poses an extensive series of questions about the senior, the type of health or social problem, treatments required, finances, daily living needs, and caregivers. On the basis of the respondent's answers, *Careplanner* offers extensive information about options in home care, retirement communities, continuing care communities, assisted living arrangements, personal care at home, nursing homes, and hospice care. A care plan is then proposed along with procedures for implementation. The *Careplanner* Web site address is http://www2.careplanner.org

carers   In the United Kingdom and other nations, those people who provide individualized care for those who cannot care for themselves, either as paid employees, volunteers, or loved ones. Carers UK is an organization that gives voice to the needs, concerns, and issues of carers. It provides carers with information about the needs of their patients and especially a unified voice to communicating with professionals who often do not respect, listen to, or consider their advice sufficiently. A major goal of Carers UK is to ensure that carers' views are considered in National Health Service policymaking. In Australia, a carer allowance, or carer payment, is made to people who care for persons with disabilities to ensure that a carer has a basic income. The Carers UK Web site address is http://www.carers.gov.uk. See also *young carers*.

caries   Decay of the bones or teeth.

carnal knowledge   A legal term for sexual intercourse.

carpal tunnel syndrome (CTS)   Inflammation of the tendons in the wrist. Symptoms include numbness, weakened grip, and excruciating pain that may radiate to the shoulder. CTS occurs when repetitive arm and hand movements over time thicken the membranes covering the nerves and tendons that control finger movements, forcing them against inflexible bones and ligaments. Treatments may include medication, splints, immobilization, or surgery. CTS is a widespread disorder in modern times, especially affecting typists, computer operators, and assembly-line workers. See also *ergonomics*.

Carpenter, Mary (1807–1877)   English advocate for poor children, women's education, and girl's reformatories, she founded the Working and

Visiting Society, a movement to reach out in poor communities to provide those in need with better nutrition, health care, and opportunities.

carrier screening A *genetic counseling* service, primarily for people making reproductive decisions, using blood samples to determine the existence of defective genes. Candidates for this screening include members of ethnic groups known to have greater predisposition for certain inherited disorders and people whose ancestors had known histories of inherited genetic conditions. Carrier screening exists as well for newborns and in prenatal diagnosis that tests amniotic fluid.

cartel An association of businesses in the same or related industries that seeks to stabilize the supplies or conditions of production and thus influence prices.

case aide In social work, a *paraprofessional* who helps the social worker, as a member of a *social work team,* to provide specified services for the client. Most case aides are paid employees of the social worker's agency, but some are volunteers or part of the *natural helping network.* See also *social work associates.*

case conference A procedure used in social agencies and other organizations to bring together members of a professional staff and others to discuss a client's problem, objectives, intervention plans, and prognoses. The participants in the conference may include the social workers who are providing the direct service to the client or client system and the professional supervisor of these social workers. Additional participants might include other agency workers who have special expertise or experience with similar problems or populations, members of other professional groups or disciplines who can provide more information and recommendations, and sometimes personal associates or relatives of the client who may be asked to provide information or helping resources. Some agencies schedule conferences on all ongoing cases; others review cases of special interest or concern. Case conferences are intended to improve communication, generate new ideas, and improve services.

case finding Searching out and identifying those individuals or groups who are vulnerable to or experiencing problems for which the social worker or social agency has responsibility to provide needed help and service. See also *child find* and *outreach.*

case integration Coordination of the activities of social workers and service providers from other relevant auspices who are simultaneously serving the needs of a client. This coordination means that the respective providers' services are consistent, additive, nonduplicative, and directed purposefully toward achieving the same goals. Case integration occurs both within and between organizations. See also *case management.*

case management A procedure to plan, seek, and monitor services from different social agencies and staff on behalf of a client. Usually one agency takes primary responsibility for the client and assigns a case manager, who coordinates services, advocates for the client, and sometimes controls resources and purchases services for the client. The procedure makes it possible for many social workers in the agency, or different agencies, to coordinate their efforts to serve a given client through professional teamwork, thus expanding the range of needed services offered. It limits problems arising from fragmentation of services, staff turnover, and inadequate coordination among providers. Case management may involve monitoring the progress of a client whose needs require the services of several professionals, agencies, health care facilities, and human services programs. It typically involves *case finding,* comprehensive multidimensional *assessment,* and frequent reassessment. Case management can occur within a single, large organization or within a community program that coordinates services among agencies. See also *case integration* and *Certified Social Work Case Manager (C-SWCM).*

Case Management Society of America (CMSA) The international organization of social workers, nurses, case managers, and allied health professionals whose mission is to provide education, standards, and networks for case management. CMSA sponsors the professional journal *The Case Manager* and other publications as well as regional and national conferences. Their Web site address is http://www.cmsa.org

case method system In professional education, the procedure in which students review, discuss, and propose solutions to detailed descriptions of a representative hypothetical or actual problem. Social work education has made extensive use of this procedure since it was first advocated by *Sophonisba Breckenridge.*

case record Information about the client situation and the service transaction that is documented by the social worker during the intervention process and retained in the files of the social agency or social worker. Case records are an important source of information about clients, services, goals, intervention strategies, and outcomes. They are used in *case management* and interprofessional communication on *quality assurance.* Case records also exist to demonstrate *accountability,* justify funding, and support supervision and research. See also *problem-oriented record (POR)* and *SOAP charting method.*

case study A method of evaluation by examining systematically many characteristics of one individual, group, family, or community, usually over an extended period.

caseload All the clients for whom a given social worker is responsible.

case-mix reimbursement A system in which government or third-party organizations pay an institution, such as a nursing home or hospital, for its expected services to a group over a specified period. Typically, the amount paid to the institution depends not on the individual's specific health care requirements but on the variety of services likely to be required for the group for which care is provided. The system of *diagnosis-related groups (DRGs)* is one form of case-mix reimbursement.

casework See *social casework.*

cash benefits See *benefits.*

cash out Providing a welfare benefit in money rather than coupons, vouchers, or in-kind service. For example, some states provide food stamp benefits in cash rather than coupons with cost reductions and greater convenience to clients, social workers, and storekeepers.

cash vouchers A certificate permitting the recipient to purchase up to a specified amount from a designated supplier. Such vouchers are offered in various government programs to provide for needy individuals and stimulate the business of the supplier.

Cassidy, Harry (1900–1951) A Canadian social worker and reformer, he helped organize Canada's social welfare system and helped develop schools of social work at the University of Toronto and the University of California, Berkeley.

caste A highly restrictive *social class.* In some societies people are born into their castes, which thereafter limits their choices of level and type of education, occupations, associations, and marital partners.

castration anxiety A theory held by some psychoanalysts and others that boys fear harm to their genitals usually by their fathers once the boys become sexually attracted to their mothers. According to this theory, girls fear they already have been castrated. See also *penis envy theory.*

casual laborer An individual who seeks employment and works periodically, often based on current economic need or availability of desired jobs.

CAT scan Computerized axial tomography, a medical diagnostic tool for taking pictures of the interior of the head and body of the patient. See also *EBT scan.*

Catalog of Federal Domestic Assistance An online and printed publication of the U.S. General Services Administration, describing the programs that provide financial, technical, and in-kind assistance for all service groups in the United States. It describes procedures for obtaining grant funding and the organizations that issue the grants. Its Web site address is http://www.cfda.gov

catalyst role The intervention process whereby the social worker creates a climate of introspection and self-assessment for the client or community and facilitates communication, stimulates awareness of problems, and encourages belief in the possibility of change.

cataract Cloudiness in the lens of an eye resulting in impaired vision. Surgical treatment for cataracts, by removing the lens and replacing it with an intraocular plastic lens, has become relatively convenient and inexpensive.

Catastrophic Care Coverage A *social insurance* plan to reimburse eligible people for expenses incurred as a result of *catastrophic illness.* In 1988 the U.S. Congress passed a catastrophic care coverage legislation to protect Medicare recipients against these costs, but the bill was repealed in less than a year because of public dissatisfaction with its funding provisions.

catastrophic illness   A physical or mental disorder that represents a sudden and very serious change in an individual's lifestyle. The term is defined more narrowly by the *Social Security Administration (SSA)* and *Medicare* as prolonged and disruptive illness requiring long hospital stays and expensive treatment.

catatonia   The state of a person with a *mental disorder* who seems detached from reality and oblivious to environmental stimuli. Typically, catatonic people move very slowly and rigidly or may be stiff and statuelike. On some occasions and with no apparent provocation, their movements may become active and uncontrolled, and their moods may become excited. This is usually followed by a return to the more characteristic state of stupor. See also *waxy flexibility.*

catatonic schizophrenia   Technically known as "schizophrenia, catatonic type," one of the five major subtypes (also including *paranoid, disorganized, undifferentiated,* and residual) of *schizophrenia,* characterized by marked psychomotor disturbance that may involve immovability or excessive movement, *echolalia, echopraxia,* inappropriate postures, extreme negativism, and *mutism.*

catchment area   The geographic region in which all potential clients are served by a given *social agency.*

catecholamines   Biochemicals that transmit information between nerve cells. Some researchers hypothesize that deviations in these *neurotransmitters* may sometimes lead to depression, mood disorder, and schizophrenia. See also *dopamine hypothesis.*

categorical assistance   Welfare programs for specific groups of people identified in the *Social Security Act.* Originally, the programs were *Old Age Assistance (OAA), Aid to the Blind (AB), Aid to Dependent Children (ADC),* and *Aid to the Totally and Permanently Disabled (ATPD).* Needy people in these categories could receive financial assistance from their respective states, supplemented by federal grants. In 1974 responsibility for the three adult categories was assumed by the federal *Supplemental Security Income (SSI)* program.

categorical grant   Payment of funds or transfer of goods made by an organization, social agency, or individual (grantor) to a recipient (grantee) for agreeing to accomplish some specified objective. For example, public assistance programs such as *Temporary Assistance to Needy Families (TANF)* are funded in part by categorical grants made by the federal government to state governments, which distribute funds to needy families in a prescribed way. See also *grant* and *block grant.*

categorical imperative   The philosophic principle, attributed to Immanuel Kant, that holds, among other things, that some moral laws are unconditional; one version of that imperative is that people are to be treated as ends in themselves, rather than as means to ends.

categorical program   The provision of social services and other benefits to people who belong to specifically designated groups that are particularly at risk, such as older people, children without parents, and people who are blind or physically disabled.

categorically needy   People who are automatically eligible for certain welfare benefits, without a *means test,* because they fit some predetermined criteria. For example, some needy categories of people eligible for *Medicaid* include recipients of *Supplemental Security Income (SSI).* See also *joint processing.*

catharsis   Verbalization and other expression of ideas, fears, past significant events, and associations, the expected result of which is a release of anxiety or tension, resulting in improved functioning; also called *ventilation.*

cathexis   The concentration of emotional energy and feelings onto a person, idea, object, or oneself. See also *decathexis.*

Catholic Charities USA   The organization founded in 1910 to coordinate the 3,000 Roman Catholic Church–related local organizations and individuals who provide voluntary social services such as family therapy, child welfare, vocational and financial counseling, and recreational and educational services. The organization was formerly known as the National Conference of Catholic Charities. Their Web site address is http://www.catholiccharities.org

Catholic Relief Services (CRS)   The international organization founded and sponsored by the

Roman Catholic Church to raise funds and distribute needed resources and provisions to those populations victimized by poverty and disasters, including famine, epidemics, floods, hurricanes, droughts, earthquakes, war, and civil disorder. CRS coordinates many of its activities with the *United Nations Disaster Relief Organization (UNDRO)* and through the *Steering Committee for International Relief,* other church organizations, and *private relief groups.* Their Web site address is http://www.catholicrelief.org

Catholic Worker Movement   The sociopolitical movement that began in 1933 under the leadership of *Dorothy Day* (1897–1980) to promote social justice and social welfare for all, particularly immigrants to the United States, unemployed and marginally employed breadwinners, and people from various racial and ethnic groups. The movement has been influential in advocacy for *pacifism, equal rights* for women and African Americans, and organized *labor unions.* The organization publishes *The Catholic Worker,* which has always been sold for one penny per copy.

caucus   A meeting, usually closed or semiprivate, comprising the leaders of an organization, to establish its agenda or platform or to nominate candidates.

cause-oriented organization   A formal or informal group comprising individuals who are united by shared values and goals and devoted to achieving specific social change or solving certain problems.

cause-versus-function issue   The controversial historical dichotomy in social work between *social reform* activities and *social casework.* Some early social workers, such as *Jane Addams* (1860–1935), advocated a cause orientation, emphasizing social change through political action and community organization. Others, such as *Mary E. Richmond* (1861–1928), stressed the function of individual betterment through the technical skills of the social worker, such as interviewing and advice giving. The current view among most social workers is that the field must include both cause and function orientations.

cease-and-desist order   A statement issued by a judicial authority and court of law prohibiting a person or organization from commencing or continuing a specified activity, such as tearing down a historic building, clearing a forest, or removing a child from one city to another. These orders are generally issued after the court is shown that the activity will likely be found to be unlawful.

CEDAW   The United Nation's Convention on the Elimination of All Forms of Discrimination Against Women, enacted in 1979.

Center for Health Statistics   See *Department of Health and Human Services, U.S. (HHS).*

Center for Nutrition Policy and Promotion (CNPP)   The USDA organization established in 1994 to coordinate research about the nutritional needs of the public, coordinate nutrition policy with the USDA, and educate the public about nutrition. It publishes *Dietary Guidelines for Americans* and maintains the *Thrifty Food Plan.* Their Web site address is http://www.usda.cnpp.gov

Center for Social Development and Humanitarian Affairs (CSDHA)   The United Nations organization oriented to the world's development of social welfare and cultural development programs. The organization provides member nations with technical assistance, research, and information in their efforts to enhance their human services programs.

Centers for Disease Control and Prevention (CDC)   The Atlanta-based *HHS* organization that coordinates efforts throughout the nation to prevent and minimize the spread of *disease.* The center acquires, analyzes, and disseminates data about the incidence of disease and its etiology, progression, and elimination. Their Web site address is http://www.cdc.gov

centers for independent living   See *independent living, centers for.*

Centers for Medicare and Medicaid Services (CMS)   The *HHS* organization that administers the nation's health care financing program for the aged *(Medicare)* and poor *(Medicaid).* It also coordinates with states the *State Children's Health Insurance Program (SCHIP).* Prior to 2001 the organization was the Health Care Financing Administration. Their Web site address is http://www.cms.hhs.gov

Central Council for Education and Training in Social Work (CCETSW)   The educational organization in the United Kingdom to establish and maintain standards for the education of British social workers and accredit its schools. CCETSW ended in 2001, and its functions were assumed by the *General Social Care Council* in England.

central nervous system (CNS)   The brain and spinal cord. The CNS supervises and coordinates the activity of the entire nervous system. See also *autonomic nervous system (ANS)* and *peripheral nervous system.*

centralization   The concentration of administrative power within a group, organization, or political entity. For example, public assistance programs that had been managed primarily at the state and local levels became more centralized with the passage of the *Social Security Act* and later the *Supplemental Security Income (SSI)* program.

centration   A tendency to focus attention on one part of an object, situation, or aspect of a relationship while ignoring others that may be equally significant. See also *decenter.*

Centrelink   The Australian government organization that helps all Australians go to one place for needed social assistance payments and that links to all government agencies. Australians in need begin at Centrelink for access to programs such as the Disability Support Pension (for people with disabilities who are unable to work), the Mobility Allowance (for persons with disabilities to meet the costs of transportation), the Carer Allowance (income support for people who are taking care of those who have disabilities), Job Seeker benefits (for unemployed persons looking for work), Newstart (for people who have lost jobs), and Return to Work, Mature Age, and Youth Allowances. Centrelink replaced the old Department of Social Security in 1997. Their Web site address is http://www.centrelink.gov.au

centrifugal family structure   In *family systems theory,* the pattern of relationship among family members in which there is little cohesiveness or attachment, and each member feels compelled to seek emotional support from outside the family.

centripetal family structure   In *family systems theory,* the pattern of relationship among family members in which each person is bound into the family and relatively isolated from outsiders. For example, the children remain at home even after reaching adulthood, and all family members encourage each other to remain highly interdependent.

centrist   One who holds an ideological position between the extremes; a moderate or "middle of the roader." See also *leftist* and *right wing.*

CERCLA   The Comprehensive Environmental Response, Compensation and Liability Act (P.L. 96-510), the formal name for the *Superfund,* that assists individuals and communities affected by toxic waste sites.

cerebral palsy   A disability of muscle control and coordination caused by brain damage that occurred before or during birth. The degree of severity depends on the extent of the brain damage. Although no cure exists, appliances such as braces and treatment involving physical, occupational, speech, and psychosocial therapy are often effective in minimizing disability. Detailed information is available at the United Cerebral Palsy organization's Web site address: http://www.ucpa.org

cerebrovascular   Pertaining to the brain or the blood vessels that supply it.

cerebrovascular accident (CVA)   See *stroke.*

certificate of need (CON)   A permission grant to developers permitting them to build new hospitals or health facilities only when properly justified. The purpose of CON legislation is to distribute and control the number of hospitals and medical resources equitably to help keep down health care costs. The national network of health systems agencies reviews, plans, and recommends certification.

certification   An official assurance that someone or something possesses the attributes he, she, or it claims to have. Legal certification of a profession is the warranting by a state that the people certified have attained a specified level of knowledge and skill. *Professional certification* is such warranting by a *professional association.* Certification typically does not prohibit uncertified people from engaging in the specified activity (as does a license), but it prevents their use of the title "certified." Certification is usually considered to be a stronger form of regulation than *registration* but weaker than the license.

Certified Advanced Social Work Case Manager (C-ASWCM)   The specialty credential sponsored by NASW for advanced-level case managers. Requirements are an MSW from a CSWE-accredited school of social work; one year of paid, post-master's-level MSW-supervised social work case management experience in an agency or institutional setting; and a passing score on NASW's ACSW or DCSW examination or a state licensing exam at the intermediate, advanced, or clinical level. The holder of this credential also must present a knowledge and skills evaluation from his or her supervisor, a reference from a social work colleague, and a signed agreement to practice according to the *NASW Code of Ethics* and *NASW Standards for Continuing Professional Education.*

Certified Clinical Alcohol, Tobacco and Other Drugs Social Worker (C-CATODSW)   The specialty credential sponsored by NASW for social work experts with clients who have substance abuse problems. Requirements are an MSW from a CSWE-accredited school of social work plus 180 hours of additional ATOD-specific education; two years of paid, postmaster's ATOD-specific counseling experience in an agency or institutional setting under a qualified ATOD supervisor; and a current highest state clinical social work license (including passing the clinical or advanced exam). The holder of this credential also must present a knowledge and skills evaluation from his or her ATOD supervisor, a reference from a social work colleague, and a signed agreement to practice according to the *NASW Code of Ethics* and *NASW Standards for Continuing Professional Education.*

certified nursing assistant (CNA)   A paraprofessional who provides qualified nursing care services. Most CNAs are employed in nursing homes and institutional settings.

Certified School Social Work Specialist (C-SSWS)   The specialty credential sponsored by NASW for advanced school social workers. Minimum requirements are an MSW from a CSWE-accredited school of social work; two academic years of paid postmaster's MSW-supervised social work in a school setting employed by a school system; and successfully passing a recognized state licensing or NASW credentialing examination. The holder of this credential also must present a knowledge and skills evaluation from his or her MSW supervisor, a reference from a social work colleague, and a signed agreement to practice according to the *NASW Code of Ethics* and *NASW Standards for Continuing Professional Education.*

Certified Social Work Case Manager (C-SWCM)   The specialty credential sponsored by NASW for qualified case managers. Requirements are a bachelor's degree in social work from a CSWE-

accredited program; one year of paid, supervised post-BSW work in an agency or institutional setting; and successfully passing the ACBSW test and other requirements or a basic-level state exam or BSW-level license. The holder of this credential also must present a knowledge and skills evaluation from his or her supervisor, a reference from a social work colleague, and a signed agreement to practice according to the *NASW Code of Ethics* and *NASW Standards for Continuing Professional Education.*

certified social worker   A social work practitioner who is warranted by a professional association or legal body to have attained a specified level of education, knowledge, and skills; the title "certified social worker" is protected by statute in some jurisdictions and by professional associations in others, so that its use is restricted to those who qualify. Social work certification in the United States includes the *Academy of Certified Social Workers (ACSW)* and specialty certifications such as *Certified Social Work Case Manager (C-SWCM), Certified Advanced Social Work Case Manager (C-ASWCM), Certified School Social Work Specialist (C-SSWS),* and the *Certified Clinical Alcohol, Tobacco, and Other Drugs Social Worker (C-CATODSW).*

CETA   The Comprehensive Employment and Training Act (P.L. 93-203), a federal program begun in 1973 to retrain and place long-term unemployed, underemployed, or disadvantaged people in more suitable jobs and jobs with future potential. In 1982 most of its functions were acquired by the *Job Training Partnership Act,* which encouraged more private-sector, local, and state involvement in training programs.

CEUs   Continuing education units; a specific amount and type of formal education required by certain professional associations, state licensing authorities, and employers to demonstrate that the professional is keeping current in relevant knowledge. For example, attending a three-hour workshop at a professional conference that is recognized or accredited by the authority might "earn" a social worker three CEUs to be counted toward continuing education requirements.

"CFSers"   People with *chronic fatigue syndrome.*

Chadwick, Edwin (1800–1890)   Controversial social reformer and newspaper writer who was a pioneer in methods of inquiry about social problems. His writings about the sanitary conditions in London slums led to cleanup, renewal, and public health programs. Oriented to *blaming the victim,* he was the major author of the *Poor Law of 1834.*

chain picket   A continuous line of people united to espouse some social cause or protest some condition; they move or stand in close proximity to one another to prevent others from crossing their line.

chaining   In *behavior modification,* a specific and complex series of connected or associated stimulus–response units that terminate with the delivery of a reinforcer. Social workers using behavioral techniques also use "backward chaining" in which the last stimulus–response unit of a chain is established first, and the other units are then added in reverse order until the desired chain is complete.

Chalmers, Thomas (1780–1847)   Scottish theologian who developed a system of private philanthropies to help Glasgow's poor population. He organized volunteer workers and contributors to meet regularly with disadvantaged people to give them encouragement and training as well as material aid. Many of his writings were used as guides for later efforts to help the poor. See also *Joseph Tuckerman.*

Chamorros   People in the United States who are natives of Guam and other Mariana Islands.

CHAMPUS   The Civilian Health and Medical Program of the Uniformed Services, a federally funded health insurance program for the dependents of active-duty and retired U.S. military personnel. Most of its functions were incorporated into the military's *Tri-Care* program in 2001. See also *military social work.*

chance score   A concept in statistics in which a test result is significantly likely to occur on the basis of random selection of answers.

chancroid   Sexually transmitted disease caused by the *Hemophilus ducreyi* bacteria. Lesions appearing as pimples, chancre sores, or ulcers on the skin of the genitals appear after an incubation period of three to five days. Chancroid is highly contagious and may be a factor in the transmission of HIV.

change agent   A social worker or other helping professional or a group of helpers whose purpose is to facilitate improvement.

change agent system   The organizations, social agencies, and community institutions that provide the auspices and additional resources through which the social worker *(change agent)* provides service.

change of venue   A change in the location of an upcoming trial or a change of judges because the site is not conducive to a fair trial or the judge may not be able to be impartial.

change residue   In the planned changes that community organizers help to bring about, the side effects that occur after the newly implemented structures are in place. The residue may be intended or unintended, desired or not, tangible or elusive. Because side effects are inevitable, organizers find it necessary to build ways of dealing with them into the plan.

channeling   In social work, an administrative procedure in *case management* in which social agency workers are aware of resources in the community and often direct their clients to relevant programs for additional or supplementary service during the ongoing helping process. See also *linkage.*

Chapter 7 Bankruptcy   A legal process to discharge debts through liquidation of one's remaining assets. After the debtor files public notice of an inability to pay debts and lists all assets and debts, a trustee assigned by the court sells all nonexempt assets and distributes the proceeds to creditors according to priority of debt. The debtor may keep only exempt property (a small amount of clothing and personal items, some equity in home and vehicle). Remaining debts are then discharged. Some debts are nondischargeable, including child support, student loans, DWI (driving while intoxicated) fines, and taxes. See also *Chapter 13 Bankruptcy.*

Chapter 13 Bankruptcy   A legal process to reorganize the way debts will be discharged or paid over a three- to five-year period. The debtor, who has certain income and assets but has fallen behind on payments, files a plan to repay creditors (especially mortgage holders and vehicle loan organizations) without threat of foreclosure or repossession. In certain circumstances the debtor may repay as little as 10 percent of some debts in the three- to five-year period, after which the remaining obligations are discharged. Taxes, child support, student loans, and legal fines are nondischargeable. See also *Chapter 7 Bankruptcy.*

character   The most deeply ingrained aspects of personality and the resulting habitual modes of response.

character building   Efforts to improve one's behavior, habits, and effectiveness in dealing with the biopsychosocial and physical environment, particularly through study and education, hard work, experience in relevant activities, and moral and spiritual training. Sometimes this term is used by unsympathetic authority figures to justify imposing difficult conditions such as excessive work demands or deprivation on others.

character disorder   A *maladaptive* personality pattern involving inflexibility in thinking, perceiving, and reacting; also known as "character neurosis." Individuals with this dysfunction are often obsessively meticulous, pedantic, and cruel in an intellectual way. Psychoanalytically oriented professionals also describe certain specific maladaptive character traits such as the *oral character, anal character,* and *genital character.*

charette   A technique used by community organizers and disaster relief planners to stimulate *citizen participation* during *crisis planning.* Professionals and community members (especially those most likely to be affected by the crisis) work together intensively to plan a means of coping with the situation. See also *community reorganization.*

charismatic leader   An individual whose influence is derived primarily from force of personality rather than legal authority or official title. Often the leader or founder of a social movement is charismatic (such as Martin Luther King, Jr., Mohandas K. Gandhi, and *Jane Addams*), but their successors often base their leadership on legal or official sanction.

Charitable Choice   A U.S. government rule that permits *faith-based social services* providers to apply for public funding for the work they do on behalf of the general public.

charitable contribution   A donation to an organization that serves the public good, such as a religious, cultural, scientific, or charitable program. Donors can deduct the amount of their gift from their annual gross income to pay less taxes.

charitable gambling   Organized legal playing of games of chance to raise money for educational, religious, or public services uses. The games are usually conducted by churches, service clubs, civic associations, and similar organizations and include activities such as bingo, raffles, card games, and casino games.

charitable trust   A legal and financial arrangement in which someone designates a significant gift to a charity to obtain income and estate tax savings but retains some rights to the gift until death.

charity   1. Literally, love for one's fellow humans. 2. The donation of goods and services to those in need.

Charity Organization Societies (COSs)   Privately administered and philanthropically funded organizations that were the essential forerunners of modern social services agencies. The first COS was established in London in 1869. The first American COS was in Buffalo, New York, in 1877 and was duplicated in most larger eastern cities soon thereafter. COSs were staffed by volunteer workers who provided direct services to clients and coordinated community efforts to deal with social problems. As more COS workers, sometimes known as *friendly visitors,* gradually became professionalized, they were called *social workers.* By the 1930s, as government assumed more responsibility for people's economic and social security, the original COS goal was reached; thus, most of the organizations suspended their operations or became or merged with other social agencies.

charter school   A tax-supported public school that is granted permission to operate (chartered) outside the public school bureaucracy as long as it complies with specified regulations and guidelines.

Chartist Movement   The reform campaign conducted by English workers (1838–1848) demanding universal male suffrage, voting by secret ballot, proportionally divided electoral districts, and the abolition of property qualifications for members of the House of Commons. The people were reacting to a period of low wages, high prices, and the recently enacted *Poor Law of 1834.*

checkbook activism   Donation of funds to public-interest organizations because the contributor lacks the time, opportunity, or inclination for personal involvement.

check-in   A structure exercise often used in social work with groups or families in which each of the members is asked, at the beginning of the session, to indicate what they are specifically concerned about or would like to discuss. Check-ins are used to ensure that all members of the session are heard from and become the focus of some attention. When the procedure occurs at the end of a group session, it is known as the "check-out." Check-in is the most common of the group procedures known as *go-round.*

checklist An information gathering tool consisting of sets of specific statements or questions that is prepared in advance to remind the interviewer about the range of information needed from the subject. Each item may be checked off when that information has been obtained or that task has been achieved.

checkpoint A site near a national border from which vehicles and individuals seeking entry are inspected to determine if they have the legal right to do so. Checkpoints are managed by immigration, military, or other law authorities. In the United States the *Bureau of Immigration and Customs Enforcement (ICE)* maintains these sites, located within 100 miles of the border.

"cheeking" A practice used by some supervised patients to avoid taking their prescribed medications by concealing the pills inside their cheeks rather than swallowing them. The patients save the pills for later inappropriate use, or they discard the pills when unobserved. The practice is widespread because many patients dislike the effect or side effects of medications or wish to create their own side effects.

chemical castration A medical treatment in which a man's male sex hormones are suppressed by administration of opposing hormones, temporarily reducing or eliminating sex drive. This treatment is one current approach to treating some chronic sexual offenders and sometimes used in the treatment of some cancers of the male reproductive system. Physically, a drug such as Depo-Provena suppresses production of testosterone. The treatment is not effective with many sex offenders because psychosocial factors as well as physical factors influence their actions.

chemotherapy The treatment of a disease, such as *cancer,* with chemicals.

"cherry picking" The practice of accepting or enrolling those clients deemed least likely to require costly services and avoiding those who may have more expensive needs. The practice exists among some insurance companies, managed health care plans, and private social services agencies, among others. See also creaming.

chi square (χ^2) The statistical symbol representing the technique of estimating whether the observed values in a distribution differ from the expected values in the distributions, thus suggesting that the outcome is not due to chance alone.

"Chicano" A term sometimes used to describe American citizens of Mexican birth or ethnic heritage. Some Mexican Americans dislike the term because of its identification with political agitation and civil rights activism.

chicken pox The common name for *varicella.*

Child Abuse Prevention and Treatment Act (CAPTA) The U.S. federal legislation (P.L. 93-247), enacted in 1974, to assist states and localities in the prevention, identification, and treatment of *child abuse* and *child neglect* by funding effective programs, research, and dissemination of information and a state grant program for community-based efforts to prevent child maltreatment. CAPTA was expanded in 1992 as the Child Abuse Prevention, Adoption, and Family Service Act (P.L. 102-295). The 1996 reauthorization eliminated the National Center on Child Abuse and Neglect and authorized the *U.S. Department of Health and Human Services (HHS)* discretion to establish a new Office of Child Abuse and Neglect to implement CAPTA.

child abuse The recurrent infliction of physical or emotional injury on a dependent minor, through intentional beatings, uncontrolled *corporal punishment,* persistent ridicule and degradation, or *sexual abuse.* Most child abuse is committed by parents, guardians, or caretakers. State laws require social workers and other professionals to report instances of suspected child abuse to the appropriate authorities. See also *child neglect.*

child advocacy Championing the rights of children to be free from abuse or exploitation by others and to have opportunities to develop toward their full potential. Social workers have led in this effort by fighting for *child labor* laws; calling public attention to inadequate care facilities and *orphanages;* and working to set up juvenile justice programs, to expand *foster care* and *adoption* care, and to eradicate *child snatching, kidnapping,* and *child abuse.*

child advocacy organizations   Privately funded groups located and administered locally, nationally, and internationally to lobby the public and lawmakers about children's needs and problems and to facilitate programs that will enhance children's development. Such organizations include the *Child Welfare League of America (CWLA),* the *Children's Defense Fund (CDF),* the Child Welfare Institute, and the National Association of Child Advocates (NACA).

Child and Adult Care Food Program (CACFP)   The U.S. federal program that ensures that needy children and adults in day care facilities have access to nutritious food. Established by law (P.L. 95-627) in 1977 after years of informal and pilot programs, it is part of the USDA's Food and Nutrition Service. Their Web site address is http://www.fns.usda.gov/cnd/care/CACFP

child bondage   Compulsory obligation of a child to an employer, most commonly the result of a debt owed by the child's parent. Bonded child labor is widespread in resource-poor countries and third world and fourth world nations and is a mainstay of the brothels of Southeast Asia and carpet factories of the Indian subcontinent.

child care   Nurturance and management of the day-to-day requirements to sustain the successful development of children. Although the term can apply to any activity in which a youngster's needs are provided for by a parent or guardian, it is specifically applied to children in institutions or 24-hour group-living situations. In this context, child care activities include physical care (such as feeding and clothing), habit development (such as personal hygiene and socialization), self-management (discipline), therapeutic care (counseling), tutoring, and first aid. These activities also include running the living group as a cohesive unit and managing the institutional program.

child care worker   A professional or paraprofessional who is responsible for the daily care and nurturance of a group of youngsters who reside in an institution. Such workers are often known as house parents, residential workers, or group-living counselors. They fulfill the activities of institutional *child care* and are employed primarily in residential-care facilities for emotionally disturbed and dependent children and for people who are men-

tally retarded, in corrections facilities, in institutions for people with disabilities, and in homes for unwed mothers.

child custody   See *custody of children.*

child find   Diagnostic programs in many public schools in which children between the ages of three and five are screened to determine the existence of any physical or *developmental disorder* and when appropriate, then placed in early-intervention preschool programs.

child find organizations   Social agencies and programs oriented to locating *runaways* or *thrownaway children* and changing the conditions that contribute to such problems. These programs often are staffed by volunteers and funded by voluntary contributions and sometimes supported by public monies. The organizations work closely with local law enforcement organizations, child find organizations in other regions, and the *National Center for Missing and Exploited Children (NCMEC).* Among the larger organizations of this type are Child Find America (CFA), Find the Children, the Commission on Missing and Exploited Children, the Polly Klaas Foundation, and Child Quest International.

child guidance   The process of helping youths make optimal life decisions, develop decision-making skills, channel behaviors appropriately, and solve their problems. The guidance counselor, usually a person with a specialized background in education, provides youths with necessary information or access to that information. Special focus is on educational planning, academic and relationship problems, scholarships, and family problems. Counseling and testing (especially in terms of aptitude and vocational and personality factors) are major activities. See also *achievement tests.*

Child Health and Human Development, National Institute of (NICHD)   The organization within the *National Institutes of Health,* established in 1962, to support and conduct research about children, including the problems of birth defects and mental retardation, reproductive health, reducing infant deaths, improving the health of women and men, understanding growth and development, and enhancing function across the life span. The institute also provides information and expertise on factors such as sudden infant death syndrome, congenital abnormalities, and developmental disabilities. Their Web site address is http://www.nichd.nih.gov

child labor Paid or forced employment of children who are younger than a legally defined age. The minimum age for employment may vary from ages 14 to 18 depending on the nature of the work and the child labor standards of the country in which it takes place. The *International Labor Organization (ILO)* and the U.N. Convention on the Rights of the Child consider child labor to be exploitative when the work or conditions are harmful to the child's health or physical, mental, spiritual, moral, and social development. In the United States, child labor standards were established in 1938 by the *Fair Labor Standards Act.* See also *apprenticing, child bondage, Rights of the Child Convention,* and *work permit.*

child molestation 1. Forcing a child to participate in some sexual acts that can include *rape, incest,* and erotic fondling. 2. Compelling a child to behave in a way that erotically stimulates the perpetrator. Two major types of child molesters are identified, those who are fixated and those who are regressed. A fixated child molester always prefers a child over an adult for erotic gratification; a regressed molester's usual sexual orientation is with adult partners, but in certain stressful situations he or she regresses emotionally and acts out sexually with children.

child neglect The failure of those responsible for the care of a minor to provide the resources needed for healthy physical, emotional, and social development. Examples of neglect include inadequate nutrition, improper supervision, or no provisions for educational or health care requirements. This includes the lack of adequate clothing, school supplies or protection from the elements. Child neglect is seen as an act of omission by caregivers because of limited abilities or resources or other circumstances; it is differentiated from *child abuse,* which is seen as more willful.

Child Nutrition Programs Organizations within the U.S. Department of Agriculture's *Nutrition Assistance Program* that ensure that all the nation's children have regular access to nutritious food. These programs include the *School Lunch Program,* the *School Breakfast Program,* the *Special Milk Program,* the *Summer Food Service Program,* the *Child and Adult Care Food Program,* and *Team Nutrition.* These food purchases also subsidize farmers.

child protective services (CPS) Human services, often including social, medical, legal, residential, and custodial care, which are provided to children whose *caregiver* is not providing for their needs. Social workers who work in units of government agencies often help legal authorities with investigations to determine if children are in need of such services, help children obtain services when needed, and may provide such services themselves. Social workers investigate alleged abuse and neglect and make assessments and recommendations to legal or social welfare authorities. CPS also includes the related shelter services and community supervisor services. See also *adult protective services (APS).*

child psychoanalysis The use of *psychoanalytic theory* and methods in helping children overcome psychic conflicts and emotional disturbances that impede their healthy development. Practitioners of this discipline, which also is known as "child analysis," are psychiatrists, psychologists, and social workers with education in *psychoanalysis* and added training for work with children.

child psychotherapy Treatment by trained professionals of youngsters for mental illness, emotional conflict, impaired psychological development, or behavioral maladaptations. *Psychotherapy* with children includes all the theory and method applied to other psychotherapies but may emphasize *play therapy, small-group therapy,* and supportive and re-educative therapies. Professionals who provide child psychotherapy services include specially trained psychiatrists, social workers, psychologists, educational specialists, mental health nurses, and other mental health professionals.

child sexual abuse A form of *child abuse* in which a dependent child is compelled, by manipulation or force, to fulfill the sexual demands of an older person, often a family member. See also *child molestation.*

child snatching The illegal act of removing a dependent child from the legal care and authority of the parent or guardian, usually by another of the child's relatives. Most typically, child snatching occurs among families that are dissolving, as in divorces or foster care placements, and one of the former caregivers does not accept the legal ruling granting custody to another person or group. The unauthorized person takes the child and often conceals the child's whereabouts or otherwise keeps moving so that the authorities have difficulty returning the child to the rightful custodian. See also *custody of children* and *stolen children.*

Child Support Enforcement, Office of   The organization within the *Administration for Children and Families (ACF)* of the *U.S. Department of Health and Human Services (HHS)* that helps states and local jurisdictions compel parents to meet their obligations to their children. The office helps plan and manage programs to locate absent parents, establish paternity, coordinate activities among states, and bring to justice parents who do not fulfill their obligations. Their Web site address is http://www.acf.hhs.gov/programs/cse

child welfare   Programs and policies oriented toward the protection, care, and healthy development of children. Within a national, state, and local policy and funding framework, child welfare services are provided to vulnerable children and their families by public and nonprofit agencies with the goals of ameliorating conditions that put children and families at risk; strengthening and supporting families so that they can successfully care for their children; protecting children from future abuse and neglect; addressing the emotional, behavioral, or health problems of children; and when necessary, providing permanent families for children through adoption or guardianship.

Child Welfare League of America (CWLA)   The national voluntary organization for promoting the interest of children. Founded in 1920, the association of nearly 1,000 public and private child welfare agencies and organizations sets standards for the child welfare field; publishes books, journals, and training materials; provides information, training, and consultation; provides technical leadership to state and local governments; and advocates for public policies and programs that ensure that needed services are available to protect and support vulnerable children and strengthen families. Their Web site address is http://www.cwla.org

Child Welfare Waivers   A U.S. federal demonstration program, established by law in 1995 (P.L. 103-432), to permit state child welfare offices to develop more flexible measures on behalf of needy children as long as they demonstrate that the new initiatives would continue to fulfill basic child welfare needs and be cost neutral.

childhood   The early stage in the human *life cycle* characterized by rapid physical growth and efforts to model adult roles and responsibilities, mostly through play and formal education. Many developmental psychologists say this stage occurs after infancy and lasts until *puberty* (that is, from about 18 to 24 months to 12 to 14 years) or until *adulthood* (18 to 21 years). This stage is sometimes divided into early childhood (from the end of infancy to about age six) and middle or late childhood (from age six to, or through, *adolescence*).

childhood disintegrative disorder   A *developmental disorder* characterized by a marked regression in the child's development after more than two years of apparently normal development. After age two and before age 10, the child loses previously acquired communication skills, social relationships, and adaptive behavior and exhibits behavior generally observed in autistic disorders. The loss of skills eventually reaches a plateau and minimal improvement may occur; however, the difficulties remain relatively constant throughout life.

childhood schizophrenia   A chronic psychosis involving disturbances in thought, perception, affect, and behavior that appear in an individual before puberty. A youngster typically shows extreme withdrawal, gross immaturity, and failure to develop much autonomy or identity separate from parents or surrogate parents. Because this term is imprecise, professionals now rarely use it.

childhood vaccination   Immunization at an early age against certain diseases that can especially attack children. The U.S. Public Health Service recommends that every child (except those whose doctor specifically advises against) should be immunized at as young an age as possible against the following: hepatitis B, diphtheria, tetanus, pertussis, haemophilus influenzae type B (HIB), poliovirus, measles, mumps, rubella, and varicella zoster virus (chickenpox).

childminders   In England and Wales, people who care for children in their own homes for more than two hours each day and are paid directly by parents. Childminders have been registered and annually inspected under English law since 1989.

children   Youngsters who are under the legal age of responsibility or emancipation; in most states and nations, this age is 18 years.

Children Act of 1989, U.K.   The comprehensive reform of child care law and programs in the United Kingdom. The act emphasizes parental responsibility to the child, rather than only parental rights, and takes account of the child's wishes in some types of family disputes.

Children with Special Health Care Needs (CSHCN) program The combined federal–state program to provide and promote family-centered and community-based coordinated care for children with special health care needs. The program was originally funded through federal Maternal and Child Health block grants and other federal and state funding sources.

Children's Aid Society The private organization founded by *Charles Loring Brace* (1826–1890) in 1853 in New York to provide shelter, education, care, and family placement for homeless and destitute children. The society's methods greatly influenced modern *child welfare* programs and the *foster care* system.

children's allowances See *family allowance.*

children's antiabuse organizations Private and volunteer groups organized to help society end child molestation, deprivation, or other forms of abuse and to facilitate programs that prevent abuse or treat abuse victims and their victimizers. Some of these organizations are traditional advocacy groups and professional organizations, and others consist of parents concerned about the well-being of their children or about their own roles in the problem. Organizations include the Child Abuse Prevention Association, Childhelp USA, Parents Anonymous (PA), and Parents Against Molesters (PAM).

Children's Bureau The U.S. government organization, created in 1912 and now part of HHS's *Administration on Children, Youth, and Families (ACYF),* that plans, integrates, and advocates national programs on behalf of children. In its earliest decades, under the leadership of *Julia Lathrop* and *Grace Abbott,* the bureau was an independent federal agency with enormous influence; most of the legislation to protect children was initiated by the bureau. The best-selling book *Infant Care* and the widely read periodical *Children Today* originated in the bureau. In recent decades many of its programs have been terminated or placed within other government administrations. The medical services component of the bureau was placed within the *U.S. Public Health Service* in 1969.

Children's Defense Fund (CDF) A Washington, DC–based advocacy and lobbying organization, established in 1973, to scrutinize regulations and legislation affecting the nation's children and propose new and modified programs. The CDF strives to create and enforce *child welfare* laws and to support organizations that serve the special needs of children. Their Web site address is http://www. childrensdefense.org

Children's Health Insurance Program See *State Children's Health Insurance Program (SCHIP).*

children's international charity organizations Secular and church-related charitable organizations that obtain contributions from citizens of more affluent nations and distribute the money to needy children and their families in underdeveloped nations. Some organizations subsidize individual children, but most also engage in community development programs to help all the children in the area. Among these organizations are the Christian Children's Fund (CCF), Childreach, Compassion International, Action for Child Protection, Childhelp, Save the Children Fund, and Children's Aid International (CAI).

Children's Online Privacy Protection Act (COPPA) A U.S. federal law (P.L.105-277) enacted in 1998 to help shield children younger than age 13 from online predators, pedophiles, and others who would use the Internet to exploit youngsters. The law requires that those who collect personal information from children online obtain informed parental consent first.

children's rights officers (CROs) In Great Britain, specialists in providing children with support, advice, and advocacy, especially when they come in contact with legal and social services agencies. These positions were established in 1984 partly because of the feeling that children's rights and needs were not being respected enough when they get into the social services system.

chilling effect The intentional creation of a social climate that inhibits an individual's exercise of some right or action, usually by employers, government policies, legislation, or judicial decisions. For example, a legislature votes to curtail food stamps for those who protest welfare cutbacks.

CHINS Children in need of supervision; a designation used in some states for young people and for those who habitually are truant, use drugs or alcohol, runaway, or are antisocially aggressive. In most instances those designated as CHINS are children who have committed offenses that would not be considered illegal if they were adults. See also *status offender.*

chiropractic   A treatment method that relies especially on adjusting the spine, manipulating the joints, and massaging the muscles to relieve pain, prevent disease, and reduce symptoms such as backaches, tension, and fatigue. Many chiropractors also use nutritional programs, herbal supplements, diets, exercise, counseling, and holistic and alternative therapies.

"chiseler"   A slang expression referring to one who gets money and goods by cheating, begging, or "sponging off" others. The term often has been applied disparagingly to welfare recipients who are said to have misrepresented their needs and resources to increase benefits.

Chisholm, Carolina (1808–1877)   A community organizer in Australia who established homes and programs for poor immigrant women and facilitated family colonization programs for people moving from England to Australia.

chlamydia   One of the *sexually transmitted diseases (STDs)* caused by nongonococcal (not gonorrhea) organisms. Symptoms are similar to those of *gonorrhea* and are equally severe in women but usually less severe in men. In women, symptoms include inflammation in the pelvic region, scarring of tissue, and sometimes sterility; in men, they include inflammation in the urethra and prostate gland. Babies born to infected women can develop pneumonia and eye infections. Often no symptoms are evident until the disease has advanced to more serious levels. Early treatment of the infected person and partner with antibiotics is usually successful.

chlorpromazine   See *antipsychotic medication.*

Choice in Dying   See *Partnership for Caring.*

cholecystectomy   Surgical procedure to remove the gallbladder.

cholera   An epidemic disease spread through polluted water resulting in symptoms such as diarrhea, vomiting, thirst, and cramps.

choleric   Historical term indicating a personality that is irritable, hot-tempered, and overly sensitive.

chore service   A home maintenance program, in which unskilled or semiskilled tasks that would usually be done by family members, such as washing walls and windows and removing trash, are provided by public departments of human services and social agencies for needy, homebound people. These services exclude skilled housing repairs or regular cleaning that is necessary if the person is to be able to remain at home. See also *homemaker services.*

choreiform movements   Irregular, nonrepetitive, dancelike movements, often symptomatic of mental or physical disorders.

chorionic villus sampling (CVS)   A medical procedure for detecting chromosomal abnormalities and inherited metabolic disease in the *fetus* by removing and examining a small amount of placental tissue. See also *amniocentesis.*

Christian Democracy   A political movement and philosophy that espouses traditional Judeo–Christian religious values in combination with the social values of *capitalism.* The philosophy is the foundation of the Christian Democrat parties that are particularly influential in Germany and Italy.

chromosomal disorders   A type of *genetic disorder* resulting from faulty structure or incorrect numbers of chromosomes. These chromosome aberrations can cause miscarriage, stillbirths, neonatal death, *congenital abnormalities,* and *Down syndrome.* Women younger than 15 and older than 35 have greater chances of giving birth to children with chromosomal disorders.

chronic   Pertaining to problems, abnormal behaviors, and medical conditions that have developed and persisted over a long period. Many helping professionals consider problems that have lasted more than six months to be chronic and those that last fewer than six months to be *acute.*

chronic fatigue immune dysfunction syndrome (CFIDS)   The name preferred by patient advocacy groups for what has been called *chronic fatigue syndrome,* to emphasize the organic nature of the disease.

chronic fatigue syndrome   A physical disorder characterized by excessive and prolonged lethargy, low energy, sleepiness, and apathy, often accompanied by psychosocial problems such as depression, anxiety, vocational difficulties, and family conflict. See also *chronic fatigue immune dysfunction syndrome (CFIDS)*.

chronic motor or vocal tic disorder   A persistent pattern of involuntary rapid muscle movements and vocalizations that have lasted for more than one year. A condition of this type that has lasted less than one year is known as a *transient tic disorder.*

chronic pain   Physical pain in any or all parts of the body that lasts longer than six months; it usually leads also to depression, disturbed social functioning, job and family problems, excessive health concerns, and withdrawal from social activities. The etiology varies from psychosomatic factors to nerve disorders, bone and joint inflammation, vascular reactivity, and other diseases. See also *fibromyalgia.*

Chrysostom, St. John (347–407)   Clergyman and early advocate for poor people and those who care for them. Using biblical scripture he argued that care of poor people was a Christian duty and that wealth was not one's inviolable possession but a loan from God to use in service to those in need. His views were opposed by other church leaders such as St. Augustine of Hippo (354–430) and St. Ambrose (340–397).

church social work   The practice of social work under the auspices of a church organization. Workers are employed by the congregation or church organization often in carrying the church's *social ministry.* Other workers are employed in denominationally sponsored social services agencies, such as those sponsored by *Catholic Charities, Lutheran Social Services,* and *LDS Social Services* or *interdenominational agencies* representing communities. Church social work also occurs in mission programs in other nations or regions. See also *spirituality* and *faith-based social services.*

circadian rhythm sleep disorder   A *dysomnia* type of *sleep disorder,* formerly called *sleep–wake schedule disorder,* in which the individual's routine sleep pattern is mismatched with daily demands regarding the timing and duration of sleep. This disorder occurs often in nightshift workers, people on watches in which sleep is taken at short intervals, and those experiencing "jet lag."

circuit-breaker tax relief   State or local tax laws that reduce the property tax rates on the homes of needy residents. The provision occurs when the home escalates in value to a point at which the homeowner can no longer afford to pay all the property taxes.

circular causality   The concept, particularly in *systems theories,* that describes the cause of an event, behavior, problem, or pattern as being part of a complex sequence of reciprocally influential interactions. Behavior in one component of an organized system affects behavior in another component, which affects behavior in the first, and so on, in a recurring circular fashion. In this view, the *linear causality* concept is an error in *epistemology.*

circumflex model   A model for viewing and understanding human relationships that assumes a curvilinear relationship between variables. For example, community representatives sit around a circular table, with those most similar to one another sitting on either side and others who are progressively less similar sitting farther removed, until those with no similarities sit opposite.

cirrhosis   The scarring of body tissue, most commonly the liver. Those most susceptible to cirrhosis are middle-age men with a nutritional (protein) deficiency brought about by *alcoholism.* The damage to the liver may result in symptoms such as *emaciation,* jaundice, gastrointestinal disturbances, *hepatitis,* enlargement of the liver and spleen, and distension of the veins. Treatment usually includes a diet with adequate protein, vitamin supplements, and sometimes blood transfusions and excess fluid removal.

cisvestism   Dressing inappropriately in the clothes of one's own gender (for example, adult as a child, civilian as a firefighter). See also *transvestism.*

Citizen Corps   A U.S. *Freedom Corps* program established in 2002 to organize volunteers to help in cases of national emergency, terrorism, and other threats to homeland security. The Citizen Corps relies on local Citizen Corps Councils to establish local systems for recruiting, bringing together, and organizing emergency first responders, social agencies, houses of worship, hospitals, and community-serving institutions. The Citizen Corps operates several programs, including the *Community Emergency Response Team (CERT), Neighborhood Watch Program (NWP), Volunteers in Police Service (VIPS),* and the *Medical Reserve Corps (MRC).* Their Web site address is http://www.citizencorps.gov

citizen participation   Involvement of members of the general public who are likely to be affected by a changed social policy, law, or circumstance in the process of planning and implementing that change. Community organizers usually attempt to facilitate citizen participation in change efforts.

citizen's advice bureaus (CABs)   Organizations to provide *information and referral services* and *counseling* in an informal setting. Staffed by social workers and other professionals, as well as volunteers, and funded by governments, private donations, and user contributions, CABs have different goals and methods in different countries. In Great Britain, where the CAB movement began in 1939 to meet emergency wartime conditions, CABs are now found in nearly every community and provide client advocacy, follow-up, legal aid, and housing services.

citizens committee   A supposedly nonpartisan organization established to bring about social change or elect a candidate. Often such committees develop in response to a specific problem, stay focused only on that problem, and disband when that problem is solved. See also *voter registration drives, Common Cause,* and *rainbow coalition.*

citizenship   The sense of loyalty and duty to one's nation or community, along with the rights, obligations, and privileges that accrue from membership in that community; also, an official status granted by a nation to some of its people, which entitles them to specified rights and obligations. The status is most often acquired through birth, citizenship of parents, *naturalization,* or other entitlement.

Citizenship and Immigration Services, Bureau of (CIS)   The organization within the *U.S. Department of Homeland Security (DHS)* established in 2003 to take over service functions of the former *Immigration and Naturalization Service.* The bureau focuses on assisting people who seek to live in the United States and become citizens. The bureau processes immigration applications, evaluates documentation and eligibility issues, and processes asylum and refugee applications and family-based petitions. It also maintains the toll-free National Customer Service Call Center at 1-800-375-5283 (for those who are hearing impaired, 1-800-767-1833). Their Web site address is http://www.immigration.gov

city planning   Systematic efforts to order urban development; establish priorities; and implement goals pertaining to the overall well-being of a city, town, neighborhood, or metropolitan region. City planners were originally oriented toward the physical development of a city, including development of its infrastructure and aesthetic amenities. Later, their objectives expanded to include developing sound land-use patterns, improving governmental procedures, and enhancing the quality of life and welfare of citizens.

civic associations   Private *voluntary associations* in which members meet regularly to socialize and to plan and implement activities for the benefit of the community. Some of these associations, which have chapters in most communities, include the Rotary, Lions, Jaycees, Junior League and Soroptomists.

civil contempt   A form of *contempt of court* that occurs when an individual fails to follow a court order, such as not making regular child support payments or not appearing for scheduled meetings with a social worker for court-ordered therapy.

civil defense   Procedures, structures, plans, and systems designed to protect the people and infrastructure from enemy attack, natural disaster, or other community emergency.

civil disobedience   Noncompliance with a government's laws or demands, usually to call attention to those laws that are considered unfair and to bring about changes or concessions in them. Civil disobedience often takes the form of group actions such as marches and assemblies, deliberate nonpayment of taxes, and the obstruction of the free movement of others. See also *passive resistance* and *freedom riders.*

civil disorder   A public disturbance in which a group is involved in violent activity causing danger, injury, or property damage to others.

civil liberties   Certain freedoms that may not arbitrarily be taken away or denied by society or external authority. The freedom to act according to one's own conscience; to worship, speak, and travel without restriction; and to choose one's own profession or associates are examples of civil liberties.

civil rights   Rights of citizens to be protected against *discrimination* or arbitrary treatment by government or individuals and to engage in certain behaviors as long as they do not infringe on the rights of others. In the United States, these rights include those guaranteed in the Constitution's Bill of Rights (such as freedom of speech, religion, and the press) and others instituted since the adoption of the Bill of Rights (such as due process and equal protection under the law). Several civil rights acts and constitutional amendments have sought to bestow specific protections on African Americans and other racial and ethnic groups. This legislation includes acts such as the *Civil Rights Act of 1964,* the Voting Rights Act of 1965, and the 1968 housing acts designed to eliminate discrimination in housing and real estate. See also *civil liberties.*

Civil Rights Act of 1964 The comprehensive federal legislation (P.L. 88-352) prohibiting *discrimination* for reasons of race, gender, religion, or national origin in schools, employment, and places of public accommodation including restaurants, theaters, and hotels.

civil rights group A *cause-oriented organization* in which members share the goal of achieving equal opportunity for all people including racial and ethnic groups, people with a disability, and women. Civil rights groups seek changes in the sociopolitical system that fosters *discrimination, ethnic stereotyping,* and inequitable treatment in legal institutions. Some of the major national civil rights groups include the *National Association for the Advancement of Colored People (NAACP), National Urban League, American Civil Liberties Union (ACLU), American Indian Movement (AIM), Anti-Defamation League of B'nai-B'rith, National Organization for Women (NOW), Congress of Racial Equality (CORE), Southern Christian Leadership Conference (SCLC),* the *National Abortion Rights Action League (NARAL),* and the *National Right-to-Life Committee (NRLC).* Many state and federal organizations, including the *U.S. Commission on Civil Rights,* are concerned with the enforcement of *civil rights* laws.

Civil Rights, U.S. Commission on An independent U.S. federal agency established in 1957 to discourage discrimination or denial of equal rights protections. The Civil Rights Commission investigates complaints alleging discrimination, collects and disseminates information about the problem, reviews relevant federal laws, issues public service announcements, and makes recommendations to the president and Congress. Their Web site address is http://usccr.gov

civil servants Government employees below elected or policymaking ranks whose employment is based on the specified and needed skills and performance of certain duties.

Civil Service Retirement System (CSRS) The U.S. federal program for its employees who were hired before 1984. Those hired after 1984 are covered under the *Federal Employees Retirement System.*

Civil Service, U.S. The federal organization responsible for managing most of the nonelected, nonappointed civilian employees of the U.S. government. Civil servants were regulated by the U.S. Civil Service Commission beginning in 1883. The agency is not part of the U.S. Office of Personnel Management.

Civil Works Administration (CWA) A federal program established in 1933 to provide employment for millions of citizens in public works projects and to stimulate depressed industries such as construction. The program was abolished at the beginning of World War II. See also *Public Works Administration (PWA).*

Civilian Conservation Corps (CCC) A federal program established in 1933 to conserve and develop U.S. *natural resources* and create jobs for unemployed young men. The program was abolished in 1942.

civilian review board A panel of citizens set up to oversee and investigate public bodies, such as police departments and firefighters.

civility Politeness, courtesy, and adherence to certain implicit rules of conduct and norms that are conducive to the development of effective interpersonal relationships; the opposite of *incivility.*

clang association A mental process in which the sound of one word reminds an individual of a similar-sounding expression. Often this process leads the person to think of the meaning in the new expression or to other similar-sounding words. Frequent fixation on clang associations is sometimes symptomatic of mental disorders such as *schizophrenia* and *obsessive–compulsive disorder.*

CLASP Center for Law and Social Policy (CLASP) A nongovernment membership organization composed of legal and social policy professionals, established in 1968, to focus on the economic problems of low-income families and to ensure their access to civil legal assistance. Their Web site address is http://www.clasp.org

class action social work   Collaborative litigation with the goal of obtaining a favorable court ruling that will benefit the social welfare of a group of socioeconomically disadvantaged people.

class action suit   A civil legal action taken by or on behalf of a group, community, or members of a social entity against an alleged perpetrator of harm to that group or some of its members.

class consciousness   Awareness of one's own set of values, lifestyles, mores, level of education, family background, race, and ethnic heritage, stemming from one's socioeconomic status, and awareness of having those same qualities in common with a large group of other people. This awareness can become a vehicle by which one chooses to separate from those who do not share the same class.

class crystallization   The reduction and cessation of social mobility. In societies with a high degree of class crystallization there is little or no chance for individuals to move from one socioeconomic class to another through their own behaviors.

class polarization   The tendency in some societies for the socioeconomic gap to widen between the wealthy and the poor populations with a corresponding decrease in the number of people who belong in the middle class.

classical conditioning   See *respondent conditioning.*

classical conservatism   The sociopolitical *ideology* that tends to prefer the status quo or only minimal, incremental changes in social institutions. The British philosopher Edmund Burke (1729–1797) advocated that society should conserve the best institutions of the past and slowly blend them into the needs of the present, rather than destroy and replace them with untested social innovations. This ideology is not synonymous with *neoconservatism.*

classical liberalism   The sociopolitical *ideology* that originally promoted personal freedom and limited government control, a *free-enterprise system,* and a belief in *human rights* that are inherent and independent of the state. This philosophy was developing during the time of the Magna Carta in 1215 and was further delineated by political philosophers such as John Locke (1632–1704) and Thomas Jefferson (1743–1826). Classical liberalism influenced many national revolutions, especially during the period 1688 to 1789, and the establishment of many governments that had detailed bills of rights. The liberal view that "government that governs least governs best" began to change at the beginning of the 20th century. The emerging view, now most commonly called *neoliberalism,* was that individual freedom is mitigated by poverty and unequal opportunity and that government is the suitable vehicle to overcome these wrongs.

classification   The process of organizing information into categories or classes so that the data can be more readily analyzed and understood. For example, a social worker might plan for the needs of potential clients in the agency's *catchment area* by categorizing the area's population by age, gender, economic well-being, recent hospital intakes, and incidence and type of mental illness.

classism   Stereotyping and generalizing about people, usually negatively, because of the socioeconomic class to which they are thought to belong. Classism may also be institutionalized by policies that systematically lead to unequal opportunities for advancement based on socioeconomic status. For example, the unequal distribution of educational funding in public schools leads to unequal educational opportunities for poor children living in poor school districts.

claustrophilia   The irrational desire to be confined or to remain in a small space.

claustrophobia   The pathological *fear* of closed spaces.

clearing house   A central site used by people and organizations with mutual interests to store, process, analyze, and retrieve information. For example, in the United States the *National Institutes of Health (NIH)* maintains many clearing houses, each for designated diseases, for the use of health care providers and patients.

cleft palate   A congenital abnormality in which a groove in the roof of the mouth occurs because the palate bones fail to fuse. Often accompanying this birth defect is the cleft lip, a split between the nostril to the margin of the lip.

clemency   An official grant issued by a nation's chief executive that forgives an individual for any liability or punishment for specified criminal acts. Clemency differs from *amnesty* in that it applies to specific crimes and people rather than classes of people. See also *pardon*.

client   The individual, group, family, or community that seeks or is provided with professional services.

"client dumping"   A term used to depict the unethical practice by some social workers and other professionals of discontinuing services to clients who are still in need. *Premature termination* of service occurs most commonly because the client's financial resources or insurance benefits have diminished. The three principal ways professionals terminate services without revealing to the client or others their motivation for termination include (1) telling the client that goals have been reached; (2) referring the client to another service provider on the premise that only the other has the skills necessary to meet the client's need; or (3) making unreasonable demands, changes, or recommendations and then ending treatment when the client does not comply.

client self-monitoring   A procedure used by social workers in direct practice and research to measure *client behavior* and behavioral changes by having clients note their own behaviors outside the interviews using systematic procedures and assessment tools. Typically, the social worker has the client maintain a diary, checklist, or log to check the frequency of specified behaviors. Client self-monitoring seems most effective when used in conjunction with *collateral monitoring*.

client system   The *client* and those in the client's environment who are potentially influential in contributing to a resolution of the client's problems. For example, a social worker may see a *nuclear family* as the client and the *extended family* and neighbors, teachers, and employers as making up part of the client system.

client-centered therapy   A form of *psychotherapy* originated by psychologist Carl Rogers in the 1940s. Its central hypothesis is that clients are inherently

motivated to develop and maximize their capacities (that is, to self-actualize) and can resolve their own problems provided that the therapist establishes a caring, warm, empathic, permissive, and nonjudgmental atmosphere. The client-centered therapist assumes a nondirective stance and usually does not advise, interpret, or challenge, except to encourage the client or to restate the client's remarks to clarify them. See also *nondirective therapy*.

cliff effect   The abrupt termination of eligibility of some social *benefits* once the client's earnings have reached a certain point. Making one more dollar causes loss of all benefits. This often results in clients striving to keep any income below that point. Many public assistance administrators point out that people become trapped in the public assistance cycle by fear of losing all their economic and medical benefits under this system and thus recommend more gradual reductions. However, other administrators claim the alternative is the *benefit rate reduction (BRR)*, which also has *disincentives*.

clinical gerontology   The professional practice of helping older people with psychosocial, physical, and lifestyle problems and with the coping tasks unique to them.

clinical picture   The overall impression of a client or case based on the observed symptoms, *presenting problems*, test results, data input from all available sources, and client self-assessment.

clinical social work   The professional application of social work theory and methods to the treatment and prevention of psychosocial dysfunction, disability, or impairment, including emotional and mental disorders. The term is considered a synonym for *social casework* or *psychiatric social work*. Most professional social workers agree that clinical social work practice includes emphasis on the *person-in-environment perspective*. See also *methods in social work*.

Clinical Social Work Federation (CSWF)   A *professional association*, established in 1971 as the National Federation of Societies for Clinical Social Work (NFSCW). The federation, which took its present name in 1997, includes qualified social workers who engage in clinical practice in agencies or private practice. CSWF maintains a legislative advocacy program in Washington, DC, and represents clinical social workers' interests on national peer review and agency regulatory committees. The federation offers a malpractice insurance program; provides access to licensing and vendorship assistance in all state societies; and produces many publications, including the *Clinical Social Work* journal. The CSWF sponsors the *Family Therapy Practice Academy (FTPA)* and the National Membership Committee on Psychoanalysis in Clinical Social Work (NMCOP). The CSWF Web site address is http://www.cswf.org

clinical trial In research a controlled study to evaluate the potential safety and effectiveness of new treatment techniques, drugs, or devices.

clinician A professional, working directly with clients, whose practice occurs primarily in an office, hospital, clinic, or other controlled environment. In such settings, the practitioner studies the problem, assesses and diagnoses the client situation, and directly treats or helps the client to achieve prescribed goals. The social work clinician is generally one who provides direct treatment to the client (individual, family, or group), usually in the social worker's office.

clique A small group of associates who try to maintain some prestige by being exclusionary.

clitoridectomy A form of "female circumcision" or *female genital mutilation* involving the severing of the suspensory ligament of the clitoris or the removal of the tip of the clitoris. This has been a common procedure on young girls in some developing nations.

cloning The procedure of reproducing an organism from the nucleus of a single cell, resulting in a new organism with the same genetic makeup as the single "parent."

closed adoption The form of adoption in which biological parents and the adoptive children have no contact with one another and possess little if any information about the other. This form of adoption is gradually giving way to other forms, particularly *open adoption* or *cooperative adoption*.

closed-ended questions Questioning designed to encourage the client to reveal specific information concisely and factually, without opinion, embellishment, or detail. Such questions are usually posed by the social worker to keep the client from digressing, evading, or providing irrelevant information when interview time is limited. Such ques-tions are frequently answered "yes" or "no" or with one-word responses. Examples of closed-ended questions are "Did you go to school every day this week?" and "When did you lose your job?" See also *open-ended questions.*

closed family A family structure in which members maintain highly interdependent relationships, providing little opportunity for relationships with nonfamily members. See also *centripetal family structure.*

closed group In *social group work* or *group psychotherapy,* a group in which no new members are added once it has begun. Usually in such groups, all the members remain with the group until a predetermined time has been reached, at which time all the members terminate. The more common group intervention model is the *open group.*

closed shop An employment setting in which only union members may be hired.

closed system In *systems theories,* a self-contained system with rigid *boundaries* that is organized to resist change and maintain the status quo. For example, a closed family system is relatively uninvolved with nonfamily members, less tolerant of ideas that differ from the *family myths,* and structured to maintain its interrelationships with minimal outside interference. See also *open system.*

clouding A symptom in which the conscious awareness of the client seems disoriented, ill-focused, inattentive, or confused.

Cloward, Richard (1926–2000) Social work scholar, theoretician, and activist who helped lead the nation's antipoverty and welfare rights movements and electoral inclusion movement. He was cofounder with his wife, Frances Fox Piven, of HumanServe, an organization that helped poor people have access to voter registration. He was author and coauthor of several influential books, including *Regulating the Poor, Social Perspectives on Behavior,* and *Delinquency and Opportunity.*

clozapine An *antipsychotic medication* (trade name Clozaril) found effective in treating many people diagnosed with *schizophrenia.* It has fewer side effects than many other antipsychotic drugs (for example, chlorpromazine), but is much more expensive and, in some patients, may cause a decrease in white blood cells.

cluttering A speech disorder involving an abnormally rapid rate or erratic rhythm of speech that impedes the listener's ability to comprehend what is being communicated. See also *stuttering*.

coaching An intervention procedure in which the social worker tells the client how to do something and follows with suggestions for improving the activity until optimal performance is reached. This procedure is used primarily with people who are poorly functioning, undersocialized, and lacking in currently needed social skills, or with people who have not responded to nondirective interventions.

coalition An alliance of various factions or ideological groups in a society brought together to achieve a goal. Social workers in community organization attempt to form such alliances among influential groups or among less-powerful groups to increase their influence. Coalitions may be ad hoc (organized to address a specific goal or single issue and expected to disband when it is achieved), semipermanent (more formally organized around broader and longer-range goals), or permanent (such as political parties). See *ad hoc coalition*.

Coalition of Spanish-Speaking Mental Health Organizations (COSSMHO) A U.S. national consortium of groups and individuals who treat people with mental disorders. Founded in 1973 and headquartered in Washington DC, COSSMHO works with Hispanic communities to strengthen social infrastructures, conduct and disseminate research, promote health and mental health and substance abuse programs, and prevent delinquency. The organization is affiliated with the National Alliance for Hispanic Health. Their Web site address is http://www.hispanichealth.org

Cobbe, Frances Power (1822–1904) An Irish philanthropist and activist, she campaigned throughout her life for social justice in Ireland, especially the education of poor people, the treatment of girls in workhouses, women's suffrage, and antivivisectionism.

COBRA The Comprehensive Omnibus Budget Reconciliation Act (P. L. 99-272), which was passed in 1985 and changed some health care funding systems. One feature was to extend health insurance coverage to workers for a specified time after they leave their employment. Another feature was to require all hospitals participating in *Medicare* in the United States to provide appropriate medical screening examinations and treatment to all individuals in their care who had medical conditions, regardless of their economic status or insurance benefits.

cocaine A *drug of abuse* derived from the leaves of the coca plant that gives the user feelings of euphoria, energy, alertness, confidence, and heightened sensitivity. Sometimes known as "coke" or "snow," the drug is usually taken through the nostrils ("snorting") and sometimes injected in combination with other drugs such as *heroin* ("speedballing") or chemically converted and smoked ("freebasing"). Cocaine has a particularly strong reinforcing capability. For example, when allowed to freely self-administer cocaine rapidly, animals escalate their dosage and prefer taking it to meeting their biological and psychological needs. Repeated use can produce marked deterioration of the nervous system and general physical deterioration, destruction of the mucous membranes, paranoia, depression, and hallucination. See also *"crack."*

code of ethics An explicit statement of the values, principles, and rules of a profession, regulating the conduct of its members. See also *NASW Code of Ethics*.

Code of Federal Regulations The online and printed compilation of all the rules that apply to specific legislation and programs. Their Web site address is http://www.access.gpo.gov/nara/cfr

code words Phrases or expressions made primarily by political office seekers and others under public scrutiny to reveal adherence to an ideology without addressing it directly. For example, a political candidate might espouse "equal rights for the unborn" as a code for opposition to *abortion*.

codeine A narcotic analgesic (pain-relieving drug) found in some prescription medications and, in certain states, in over-the-counter medications such as some cough syrups. Like all *narcotics,* codeine is addictive when used with some degree of frequency.

codependency A relationship between two or more people who rely on each other to meet and provide for reciprocal needs, particularly unhealthy emotional ones. For example, a widow and her adult daughter both lack self-esteem and are consequently fearful about contacts with others, so they meet most of their social needs by being virtually inseparable. This pattern is considered similar to but not as seriously pathological as *conjugal paranoia, shared paranoid disorder, folie à deux,* or *induced psychotic disorder.* See also *adult children of alcoholics (ACOAs).*

Codetermination Principle   The German economic policy and law mandating that workers participate in their employer's management decisions. Employees elect delegates from their ranks every three years to participate in all meetings with management and stockholders to ensure that the interests of the workers are always considered.

coding   The *social research* procedure in which numbers or other symbols are assigned for each *variable* or category of answer in a survey or other study. For example, a "1" may be assigned for every "yes" response and a "0" for every "no."

coercion   Forcing or compelling an individual or group to perform (or stop performing) some activity. This may occur through legal actions, government interventions, social influence, or political pressure, as well as through threats of violent harm. An important role of social workers, especially those in community organization, is to bring people together so that they can resist the attempts of others to coerce them into actions they do not want to take.

coexistence   An *ideology* that advocates and seeks to enable nations and organizations of different values and interests to maintain their territorial integrity, *self-determination,* and sovereignty.

cognition   The mental process of recognizing, understanding, remembering, and evaluating relevant information.

cognitive–behavioral therapies   Approaches to treatment using selected concepts and techniques from *behaviorism, social learning theory, action therapy, functional school in social work, task-centered treatment,* and therapies based on *cognitive models.* These forms of therapy are contrasted with those known as *insight therapies* and tend to be comparatively short term, focused on the present, and fairly limited and specific in goals. The therapist with a cognitive–behavioral orientation tends to be fairly directive and focused on the client's *presenting problem.*

cognitive development   The process by which individuals acquire the intellectual capacity to perceive, evaluate, and understand information. Jean Piaget (1896–1980) formulated one of the most complete cognitive development theories to date. He divided *human development* into four typical stages: (1) the *sensorimotor stage* (birth to age two); (2) the *preoperational stage* (ages two to seven); (3) the *concrete operations stage* (ages seven to 11); and (4) the *formal operations stage* (age 11 to adulthood). See also *Piagetian theory.*

cognitive dissonance   The mental state in which a person experiences two or more incompatible beliefs or cognitions simultaneously. In the healthy individual, this state usually leads to psychological discomfort that remains until the person acts to clarify the discrepancy.

cognitive dysfunction   Any temporary or permanent decrease in the ability to think, remember, comprehend, or process information.

cognitive impairment   Significantly diminished capacity for judgment and reasoning due to mental illness, developmental disorder, degenerative diseases affecting the brain, and sometimes substance abuse.

cognitive map   An individual's image or perceptual picture of the environment.

cognitive models   Representations of the ways by which people come to know, perceive, or understand phenomena. Such models can be used to envision or describe how humans develop their abilities to organize knowledge and understand their worlds, as in *Piagetian theory.* Such models can also be used to describe certain treatment approaches, such as *rational–emotive therapy* (Albert Ellis), *reality therapy* (William Glasser), *individual psychology* (Alfred Adler), and *rational casework* (Robert Sunley and Harold D. Werner).

cognitive restructuring   Psychotherapy techniques designed to reveal faulty logic in the client's pattern of thinking and to help the client replace those patterns with rational and logical thinking. Cognitive restructuring is the major endeavor of *rational–emotive therapy.*

cognitive style   An individual's preferred way of organizing and processing information. There are individual differences in how people perceive, remember, understand, and solve problems that influence the way information is organized and processed. For example, some people are more analytical and others have more global approaches to their environments.

cognitive theory A group of concepts pertaining to the way individuals develop the intellectual capacity for receiving, processing, and acting on information. Cognitive concepts emphasize that behavior is determined by thinking and goal determination, rather than primarily resulting from instinctive drives or unconscious motivations.

cognitive therapy Clinical intervention using *cognitive theory* concepts that focus on the client's conscious thinking processes, motivations, and reasons for certain behaviors. Alfred Adler (1870–1937) is said to have been a major originator of cognitive therapy. Current forms of this approach include *rational–emotive therapy, reality therapy, existential social work,* and *rational casework.* The psychosocial orientation of early, pre-Freudian social workers was considered to have much in common with the cognitive approach.

cohabitation The term that is commonly applied to a man and woman residing together in husband–wife roles without formal marriage; however, it also applies to others such as *gay* men and lesbians and to more than two people living together. See also *POSSLQ.*

Cohen, Nathan (1910–2001) The first president and a founder of NASW, he enhanced the role of professionalism in social work. He influenced the development of social work doctoral education and wrote several classic texts, especially in social welfare history.

Cohen, Wilbur (1913–1987) Social work educator and administrator who became Secretary of the *U.S. Department of Health, Education and Welfare (HEW)* during the Johnson administration and implemented many of the programs of the *Great Society.*

cohort In *demography* research studies, a group of subjects who were born during a specific time or who share another characteristic that is related to the subject being investigated. For example, when life expectancies are being calculated, one

cohort might be a group of 100,000 people who were born in the same month.

cohort sequential analysis A *research* method that systematically evaluates selected age groups of people over a staggered period. This method helps correct any bias inherent in a *longitudinal study.*

coinsurance The requirement of some health care payment plans that the beneficiary pay a percentage of the eligible medical expenses, in excess of the *deductible.*

Coit, Stanton (1857–1944) Founder of the *settlement house* movement in the United States and leader in the Ethical Culture movement. Using his former experience at *Toynbee Hall* in London as his model, he developed settlements for poor New Yorkers and others. He also advocated for public works jobs for unemployed people, developed the "mutual-aid" model, and in 1891 published *Neighborhood Guilds.*

coitus Sexual intercourse.

Cold War The nonmilitary conflict and political competition for world power and influence over other nations waged between the United States and its allies and the former Soviet Union and its allies from 1945 to 1990.

coleadership In *group psychotherapy* and *social group work,* the use of two or more professionals, each fulfilling distinct roles, to facilitate group processes. Although the procedure is generally more costly and complex, the use of coleaders for groups has four advantages: (1) they may observe different aspects of the group processes, (2) together they might bring out behaviors in members that would not occur with a single leader, (3) they can play different roles and provide *role modeling* opportunities for members, and (4) they can expand the range of knowledge and values available to the group.

colic 1. A behavior pattern in infants manifested by continual crying for as long as 14 hours daily. Causes are unknown but usually not symptomatic of life-threatening diseases. For most, the worst consequence is distress to the parents. Usually the behavior resolves itself within a few months. 2. Pain in the stomach or intestines.

colitis Inflammation of the large intestine.

collaboration   The procedure in which two or more professionals work together to serve a given *client* (individual, family, group, community, or population). The professionals may work relatively independently of one another but communicate and coordinate their respective efforts to avoid duplication of services, or they may work as members of a single helping team. Collaboration also takes place among social agencies and other organizations on a variety of projects. See also *interdisciplinary teaming, interprofessional team, linkage,* and *interorganizational collaboration.*

collaborative avoidance   In *social group work* and *group psychotherapy,* the phenomenon in which group members consciously or unconsciously agree not to discuss certain topics.

collaborative learning   An educational process that emphasizes group or cooperative efforts between students and educators to achieve learning objectives. The format involves mutual interaction, dialogues aimed at information sharing, and generating ideas together.

collaborative therapy   A treatment format in which two or more social workers or other professionals each treat a single member of a family and, to some extent, coordinate their efforts. For example, a husband might be seen by one social worker and the wife by another, or a disturbed child might be seen by a child psychoanalyst and the parents treated conjointly by a social worker.

collateral   Property and other assets used to secure debt obligations. The bank or other lender may acquire the identified asset if the money is not repaid as agreed.

collateral damage   Military term for the deaths of civilians and destruction of their property because of their location near battle zones.

collateral monitoring   A procedure social workers in direct practice and research use to measure client behavior and behavioral changes by having others observe and record the client's actions. Typically, the social worker has the client's spouse or other family members, friend, coworker, or teacher do this monitoring using checklists, diaries, and logs in which the frequency of some behavior is counted. Collateral monitoring is usually used in conjunction with *client self-monitoring,* and it may be done overtly or unobtrusively, but it should be done only with the client's *informed consent.*

collective action   A *social movement* to seek political, economic, or cultural changes. Many people prefer this term to "protest" or "rebellion" because the use of such words often prejudices uncommitted people toward the side of those in power.

collective bargaining   A coordinated activity undertaken by a group of people who share a common interest or objective to influence change in some policy, law, or business arrangement. The term most commonly applies to the efforts of an organized *labor union* in negotiating a contract.

collective preconscious   Simultaneous or similar responses to a *stimulus* perceived on a *preconscious* psychological level among members of a group or society. Preconscious refers to thoughts that are *unconscious* at a particular moment but are not repressed or unacceptable impulses or ideas rendered unconscious. The collective preconscious is based on beliefs, *norms, mores,* and *values* acquired through the *acculturation* process of informal and formal education.

collective responsibility   Assignment of obligation, trust, or blame to more than one person or organization. For example, all the "smokestack industries" of a region may be considered responsible for *acid rain,* and special taxes might be levied on them to be used for cleaning up the problem.

collective unconscious   In *Jungian theory,* that part of the *unconscious* that contains the inherited psychic functions or brain structure of the human species. In this theory, some information, value orientations, and behavioral patterns for meeting needs are shared by all humans through genetic transmission. In the Jungian theory, the other part of the unconscious is the *personal unconscious.*

Collier, John (1884–1968)   An advocate for Native Americans, he began his social work career working with immigrants from Europe. He became head of various government organizations for Indians, helped pass significant legislation for Indian organizations, and wrote influential articles and books about the needs and promises made to Native Americans.

colloquy A panel discussion in which two or more teams, each representing different interests or views, compare their ideas.

Colonial Development and Welfare Acts A body of legislation enacted by the British Parliament, primarily in the first half of the 20th century, to establish, organize, finance, and administer the *social welfare* and economic programs of the British colonies. As most of the colonies became independent nations, they have tended to continue using the structure of these programs as the basis of their current social welfare systems.

colonialism Control by one nation over the lands of another people. Typically the political and economic decisions of the colonized land are made by the colonizing power.

colonias Unincorporated settlements of migrant workers on the Mexico–United States border, typically located near *maquiladoras* plants.

colostomy Surgery in which part of the colon goes through an artificial opening in the abdominal wall to allow body wastes to discharge into a bag.

colostrum The first milk produced by the mammary glands during late pregnancy and for several days after childbirth to provide the nursing infant with essential nutrients and infection-resistant antibodies.

coma A medical condition characterized by unconsciousness with complete absence of all voluntary activity.

comarital affair Mate swapping, or extramarital sexual relations in which both spouses participate voluntarily. This is contrasted with extramarital affair, which typically occurs when one spouse has sexual relations with someone without the knowledge or consent of the other spouse.

combined therapy A model of intervention in which a client participates in group therapy concurrently with individual therapy.

"coming out" The process of self-identification as a *lesbian* or a *gay* man, followed by revelation of one's *sexual orientation* to others. See also *outing* and *"passing."*

Commerce, U.S. Department of (DOC) The U.S. Cabinet-level organization that facilitates the nation's economic growth, sustainable development, and job creation and safeguards the nation's economic infrastructure. Among DOC's organizations are the *Bureau of the Census, International Trade Administration, Minority Business Development Agency, Patent and Trademark Office,* and the *Bureau of Economic Analysis.* Their Web site address is http://www.doc.gov

commitment 1. The act of consigning an individual to a hospital or prison, usually after undergoing *due process of law.* 2. A pledge or obligation. For example, social work students, to fund their education, sometimes accept "commitment scholarships," in which a social agency or organization provides financial support in exchange for agreement to work for that organization for a predetermined period after graduation.

Committee for the Advancement of Social Work with Groups See *Association for the Advancement of Social Work with Groups (AASWG).*

committee on inquiry Permanent and ad hoc groups of professionals and others brought together to determine if any wrongdoing has been committed by or to a peer. Of particular interest to such committees are alleged violations of professional *codes of ethics,* illegal activities, or other disputes among professionals or between professionals and clients. These committees also exist to raise the public consciousness about mistreatment of peers by governments or political organizations. Such groups are often sponsored by professional associations, third-party organizations, or alliances of consumers. For example *NASW* has a national committee for dealing with violations of the *NASW Code of Ethics* and personnel standards, and association standards require that each chapter maintain a committee on inquiry. See also *peer review organization (PRO), alternative dispute resolution (ADR),* and *accountability.*

Commodity Credit Corporation (CCC) A U.S. agency that loans money to farmers, using crops as collateral. At harvest time, if the market price falls below the previously established *price supports,* the farmer may turn the crop over to the CCC and keep the loaned money. If the market price is higher than the price supports, the farmer may sell the crop and repay the loan. Over the years this system stabilizes farm prices and farmer incomes and builds huge crop stockpiles. Critics say this system artificially inflates farm prices, discourages foreign buyers, and runs counter to tariff and trade agreements with other nations.

commodity food programs Various U.S. federal programs designed to make surplus supplies of food available to those in need through local organizations. The Emergency Food Assistance Program, established in 1981, provides existing stores of food to soup kitchens, food banks, and homeless shelters. The Food Distribution Program for Charitable Institutions offers food to churches and other organizations that feed the needy population. The Food Distribution Program on Indian Reservations makes food available to Native Americans living on or near reservations. The Commodity Supplemental Food Program also provides monthly food packages to low-income women who have children younger than age six.

Common Cause A voluntary association founded in 1970 and known as the "citizens' lobby." Its primary goal is to represent the interests of the public and to counterbalance special-interest lobbies. Its role is to inform the public about legislation and act as a *watchdog group* over the lawmaking process and its implementation. Their Web site address is http://www.commoncause.org

common-law marriage *Cohabitation* by a man and a woman who consider themselves, and are generally considered by others, to be married but who have not had a civil or religious marriage ceremony. In some jurisdictions, this marriage is recognized by law for some purposes.

common procedural terminology (CPT) Codes used by physicians and other health care providers to communicate with health insurance companies about the medical interventions used with a patient. Each procedure has its own code number, which enables the insurer to use computers in determining reimbursement.

communicable disease A disease that is transmissible from one person to another.

communication The verbal and nonverbal exchange of information, including all the ways in which knowledge is transmitted and received.

communication disorders Disorders usually first diagnosed in infancy, childhood, or adolescence pertaining to limitations in the ability to impart information to others. These disorders include *expressive language disorder, mixed receptive–expressive language disorder, phonological disorder,* and *stuttering.*

communication leakage The transmission of information that the sender did not intend to convey. For example, a social worker blushes when asking about the client's sexuality, or the client looks contemptuous when referring to a "loved one."

communication theory The body of concepts and hypotheses that pertains to the way people exchange information. Some major elements of communication theory are *content analysis, cybernetics, decoding, feedback, kinesics, metamessage, paralinguistics,* and *proxemics.*

Communications Workers of America (CWA) A labor organization founded in 1938 in which members are employed in telecommunications, printing and news media, public service, health care, electronics, construction, utilities, and social workers. Their Web site address is http://www.cwa-union.org

communism 1. An *ideology* that advocates a classless society based on need rather than productivity. 2. Theoretically, a society in which workers are not exploited by employers. When most people casually use the term "communism," they actually are referring to *Marxism.*

communitarianism The philosophy or belief system that says individual liberty is only possible within the context of a strong and unified community and that the governing structures of that community can only ensure individualism when the *polity* is committed and responsive to social values.

community A group of individuals or families that share certain values, services, institutions, interests, or geographic proximity.

Community Action Program (CAP) The neighborhood organizations established in 1965 under the *Office of Economic Opportunity (OEO).* The goal of the program and its agencies was to develop the social and economic resources in poor communities and to help find alternative ways to attack the forces that perpetuate poverty. CAP originally was responsible for the *Head Start* program, the *Legal Services Corporation (LSC),* and other programs that have since been transferred to other government agencies or have disbanded.

community-based corrections The public effort to change and improve the behaviors of convicted lawbreakers by programs that do not involve *incarceration.* Instead of being placed in jails or prisons, convicted adults and adjudicated juveniles remain in their homes, neighborhoods, and jobs (or sometimes in group homes and nonsecure residential treatment centers), but under specified conditions and supervised activities. These include *parole, probation, fines, community service sentences, suspended sentences, victim–offender mediation, restitution,* and *house arrest.*

community-based practice The integration of direct social work services with the skills traditionally associated with community organization and community development. For example, a social worker who provides some individual counseling or social group work in a neighborhood center might also facilitate efforts by community members to help improve their neighborhood, establish grassroots campaigns, and develop a community leadership group.

Community Chest An organization working for or on behalf of private social agencies in various geographic areas to raise and distribute funds through unified campaigns. The name originated in 1918, changed in 1956 to the United Community Funds and Councils, and in 1970 took its present name, the *United Way.* See also *Frances W. Jacobs.*

community decision network The aggregate of key organizations and individuals who have the formal or informal power to determine courses of action to be taken by a community. The decision network may include political leaders and legislative bodies, industrial leaders, religious groups, and civic associations. Its composition varies depending on the specific issue or community.

community development (CD) Efforts made by professionals and community residents to enhance the social bonds among members of the community, motivate the citizens for self-help, develop

responsible local leadership, and create or revitalize local institutions. Community development workers have been active in Third World nations at least since the 1920s, especially in *consciousness-raising,* helping community residents achieve greater collective participation, and developing local leadership. In the United States, CD workers have worked especially in underdeveloped rural settings and poor urban neighborhoods to facilitate residents' collaboration in increasing influence, self-sufficiency, and economic and educational opportunities.

Community Emergency Response Team (CERT) A program to train people who volunteer to assist during large disasters that would overwhelm the personnel and resources of professional first responders. CERT started in California in 1985 by training teams for responding in earthquake and fire situations. It has expanded to a national program coordinated by the Federal Emergency Management Agency (FEMA). Volunteers receive training in triage, life-saving, fire safety, and management of spontaneous volunteers in courses that typically are 2 ½ hours long, once a week, for seven weeks.

community mental health center A local organization, partly funded and regulated by the federal government, that provides a range of psychiatric and social services to people residing in the area. These include inpatient, outpatient, partial hospitalization, emergency, and transitional services; programs for older people and for children; screening and follow-up care; and programs that deal with *alcohol abuse* and *substance abuse.*

community notification Alerting the residents of a neighborhood or city, along with police, school officials, and others, that a sex offender has moved into the area.

community organization An intervention process used by social workers and other professionals to help individuals, groups, and collectives of people with common interests or from the same geographic areas to deal with social problems and to enhance social well-being through planned *collective action.* Methods include identifying problem areas, analyzing causes, formulating plans, developing strategies, mobilizing necessary resources, identifying and recruiting community leaders, and encouraging interrelationships among them to facilitate their efforts.

Community Organization and Social Administration, Association for (ACOSA) The professional membership organization for community organizers, activists, social work educators, planners, and administrators, established in 1987, to facilitate communication, research, and networking and to influence the public about its goals and values. ACOSA sponsors the *Journal of Community Practice* and other publications and hosts annual conferences, workshops, and other events. Their Web site address is http://www.acosa.org

community organizers Facilitators of planned efforts to achieve specified goals in the development of a group, neighborhood, constituency, or other community. Community organizers may be indigenous community leaders, political office holders, or government bureaucrats, but more often they are professionals with backgrounds in social work, political science, planning, interpersonal relations, public relations, sociology, or community development. They work as consultants, planners, grant developers, or active leaders; and they usually seek to help community members achieve social justice, economic or social development, or other improvements.

community-oriented primary care *Primary care* in which the community is seen as the patient, and the health needs and treatment programs are developed for this entire population.

Community Planning and Development Office The federal organization within the *U.S. Department of Housing and Urban Development (HUD)* responsible for stimulating growth, rehabilitation, and new development in urban areas, especially those that are economically distressed. The office seeks to provide adequate housing and suitable environments, especially for people of low or moderate incomes. Grants and loans are provided through state agencies. Their Web site address is http://www.hud.gov/cpd

community property The material possessions acquired by a husband and wife during the years of their marriage. Community property usually excludes all property owned by each party before the marriage or property acquired after the marriage through inheritance or gifts but includes salaries, investments, and unearned income that each partner has received while married.

community psychology The specialty within psychology that emphasizes prevention of mental illness, education about good mental health practices, and early diagnosis and treatment of mental disorders.

Community Reinvestment Act of 1977 A U.S. law (P.L. 95-128) forbidding the practice of *redlining.* The act obliges banks and other insured mortgage lenders to meet the reasonable credit needs of people in low-income communities.

community self-help The process of involving volunteers and other citizens in a community in decision making, social services planning, and coordination with professionals and agency employees. This process includes decentralization of responsibility and control from national, state, or local agencies to individuals and community groups.

community service Efforts by volunteers, paid indigenous workers, and professionals to meet the educational, recreational, health, legal, political, vocational, and social welfare needs of people at the local level. This term is used widely to refer to activities for neighborhood improvements made by *civic associations,* churches, social groups, and fraternal organizations. Typical community service activities include drug prevention education, recreation for people with disabilities, physical fitness programs for older people, and neighborhood cleanup drives.

community service sentence A punishment ordered by a court that requires some specified work to improve a relevant community by an individual convicted of a *crime.* The convict is obliged to perform the service for a specified amount of time in lieu of incarceration for an equal amount of time. Such work includes serving food in homeless shelters, taking parentless children on outings, giving antidrug talks at schools, and doing volunteer work in hospitals. See also *work release program.*

Community Services Block Grant Program A program of HHS's *Administration for Children and Families (ACF)* to help fund and operate a wide variety of antipoverty activities. These include the coordinating of local programs and providing nutrition services, emergency services, and employment services. Grantees of the block grant also seek funds from other sources to help operate programs such as *Head Start,* weatherization and low-income energy assistance, emergency food and shelter programs, employment and training, and legal services. This program was originally part of the *Office of Economic Opportunity (OEO)*. When OEO was dismantled in 1969, this program was transferred to ACF.

community standards   The norms and values of most of the people in a city, region, or neighborhood, established by custom and thought to be applicable to nearly everyone. However, because different groups even within one area may not have the same standards, there may be varying degrees of agreement and compliance with these norms, as seen in variations in the enforcement of laws from one community to the next.

commutation   In legal terms, a change from a greater to a lesser sentence or punishment, as in changing a death sentence to life imprisonment.

comorbidity   The simultaneous existence of two or more diseases or dysfunctions within an individual. Each disease may or may not exacerbate the severity, duration, or prognosis of the other but frequently leads the diagnostician to overlook one or the other disease.

compadrazgo   In Spanish-speaking cultures, those people who are tied to a family not through a kinship network, but through historical ties. They are considered companion parents who help with the raising of the family's children. See also *padrino* and *hijos de crianza*.

comparable worth   The concept that payment or salary is to be based solely on the value of the work performed instead of on considerations such as the employee's gender, minority status, or need; also known as *pay equity*.

comparative social welfare   Analysis of the alternatives for providing the social services, economic, educational, and health care needs of a nation or social group by reviewing how different societies have addressed the same objectives. See also *international social work*.

compassion   A feeling of sympathy leading to a desire to help others who experience suffering or hardship.

compassionate leave   Permission granted by an employer, such as a military organization, to take time away from the job for urgent or compelling family reasons.

compensation   1. A mental mechanism in which one tries to make up for imaginary or real characteristics that are considered undesirable. When this occurs unconsciously, it is considered a *defense mechanism*. 2. Payment for services rendered.

compensatory education   Special school programs for children or adults who previously have been deprived of educational opportunities. These programs often are used for children in poor neighborhoods to raise their levels of educational readiness. The most prominent of these programs is *Head Start*.

competence   1. The ability to fulfill the requirements of a job or other obligation. Competence in social work includes possession of all relevant educational and experiential requirements, demonstrated ability through passing licensing and certification exams, and the ability to carry out work assignments and achieve social work goals while adhering to the *values* and the *code of ethics* of the profession. 2. In the legal system, the capacity to understand and act reasonably. See also *social competence*.

Competence Certification Commission   A quasi-independent organization established in 1989 to define the standards for credentialing NASW's *Qualified Clinical Social Worker (QCSW)* and the *Diplomate in Clinical Social Work* and to identify those who meet the standards. Those so identified may be listed in the *NASW Register of Clinical Social Workers*.

competency-based practice   In social work, the demonstrated ability to fulfill the professional obligations to the client, the community, the society, and the profession. This demonstration occurs through acquisition of *certification* and *licensing*, keeping up with the *knowledge base* by fulfilling *continuing education* requirements, and participating in agency *supervision* and *in-service training*.

competent evidence   In the legal justice system, the facts about a case that are admissible in courts of law, as well as convincing, reliable, and valid. Such information is to be distinguished from the opinions, guesses, or secondhand data offered by a professional *expert witness*. For example, an assessment by a social worker that an infant's bruises were probably the result of child abuse owing to a past history of similar events in the family would not be considered competent evidence. Eyewitness testimony by a competent observer of an act of child abuse would be considered competent evidence.

competing mandate The legitimate requirements made of an organization to fulfill two or more functions even though no clear priorities are set and resources permit support for only one. For example, in combating the drug problem, various public constituencies have competing demands for better law enforcement and imprisonment, more effective controls against smuggling, preventative education, and treatment for drug abuse. However, public monies cannot fund all these programs; thus, choices must be made. Effective administrators cope with competing mandates by finding ways to increase resources and by establishing better systems for ordering priorities and long-range planning. See also *conflicting mandate* and *ambiguous mandate*.

complementarity 1. The fit of two or more roles within an individual. 2. The way certain roles of one individual fit with the roles of a *relevant other*. For example, the social worker–client roles are usually complementary because the behaviors expected of each are compatible. See also *role discomplementarity*.

complementary and alternative medicine (CAP) Health care practices, medications, healing philosophies, and therapies that generally are not used in the traditional Western medical establishment. Traditionalists argue that these interventions have not been scientifically evaluated as to their safety and effectiveness. Complementary medicines are used in addition to, whereas alternative medicines are used instead of, traditional approaches. See also *holistic medicine*.

complementary therapy An additional type of intervention that the social worker or other psychotherapist provides for certain clients, occurring along with individual therapy. Most commonly this is group therapy or family therapy. It is important that the two forms of therapy are well integrated so that the goals of the different procedures are consistent.

complex An interrelated group of ideas and experiences that are partially or entirely repressed but that compel the client to think, feel, and behave in a pattern. Carl Jung (1875–1961) said complexes were fundamental psychic conflicts that were dealt with by habitual types of attitude, responses, or acts. Some of the better known of these are *Oedipus complex, Electra complex,* authority complex, castration complex, femininity complex, and *inferiority complex*.

Comprehensive Employment and Training Act See *CETA*.

comprehensive planning Efforts by policymakers to coordinate knowledge, influence, and resources on a broad (rather than piecemeal) scale to achieve overall goals. This includes looking for the underlying causes rather than the overt symptoms of human problems. Comprehensive planning also considers and seeks to facilitate the reaching of human potential rather than confining itself to eliminating problems. To achieve this, comprehensive planning seeks to coordinate program resources not according to the specialized functions of existing social agencies and professions, but across organizational lines of responsibility.

compulsion 1. A strong and repetitive urge to act in a certain way. It is frequently a means of relieving anxiety that results from conflicting ideas and wishes that cannot be directly expressed. 2. Forcing a person to act according to the wishes of another.

compulsive personality disorder A type of *personality disorder* that has all or many of the following characteristics: perfectionist behavior, insistence on having others submit to a certain way of doing things, limited ability to express warm feelings or tenderness, preoccupation with trivial details and rules, stinginess, stiff formality in relationships, and poor ability to prioritize and make decisions. This disorder is also known as *obsessive–compulsive disorder*.

compulsory sterilization Forced prevention of pregnancy, through surgery, chemicals, or implanting contraceptive devices. This has been done in some nations to prevent certain people, such as those with mental deficiency or disorder, genetic defects, or disease, from conception. It is also imposed by some nations or regions confronted by problems of overpopulation to sterilize fertile adults who have already given birth to the number of children permitted to them.

compulsory volunteering   See *mandatory community service*.

computer addiction   See *Internet addiction*.

computer-assisted personal interview (CAPI) A data collection procedure in which the interviewer asks a participant the questions that appear on a laptop computer screen and then enters the responses into the computer. The specific responses lead to other questions.

computer-assisted telephone interviewing (CATI)   A method of obtaining and processing information from telephone interviews directly into a computer. CATI software automatically prompts the interviewer for appropriate questions based on previous answers and enters the responses into a usable format. The technique is widely used by social workers and other human services providers.

computer-assisted therapy   The use of computer programs in the treatment of those with emotional disorders. The primary use of these forms of *expert systems* has been to assist professionals in fact gathering and the facilitation of testing procedures, as well as in client self-treatment procedures. Studies suggest that some programs may be effective in helping to treat for *agoraphobia, depression,* and family relationship conflicts. Computerized therapy (unlike *computer-mediated intervention*) remains experimental and controversial.

computer literacy training   Programs of instruction to introduce people to the use of computers, to alleviate anxieties about automation, to teach people how to communicate with one another electronically, and to retrieve and interpret information through computers and the Internet.

computer role   A recurrent pattern of communication in relating to others, characterized by muted affect. This role was delineated by *Virginia Satir,* who described the person playing this role as one who feels vulnerable and responds to the perceived threat by pretending it is harmless and by hiding inadequacy feelings through intellectualizations. See also *blamer role, distracter role,* and *placater role.*

computerized databases   Electronic storage of information, especially from the academic, scientific, legal, medical, and business professional literature. NASW's Abstracts for Social Workers covers social work journal literature abstracts from 1977. The American Psychological Association's PsycINFO covers psychology, psychiatry, and social work literature since 1967. The National Library of Medicine covers the medical literature since 1966. Hundreds of other databases can be found in public and academic libraries. Online links to databases of interest to social workers include *SWAN, the Social Work Access Network* (http://www.sc.edu/swan) and World Wide Web Resources for Social Workers (http://webdb.nyu.edu/sociallinks).

computer-mediated intervention   The use of computers to assist professionals in fact-gathering, assessment, and service delivery to clients, as well as in client self-treatment procedures. Computers are used to help convene and conduct group sessions, determine client eligibility, and record and analyze client change in segments of single-subject designs.

con artist   One who skillfully but unlawfully takes money or property from others by winning their confidences and promising that their "contributions" will be rewarded. See also *confidence crimes* and *extortion.*

conation   That part of the mental function involving will or volition.

concentrations   The term used by social work educators for clusters of courses, parts of courses, or other formal learning experiences that provide the social work student with deeper and more-focused knowledge and skill in certain areas of professional concern. After students have acquired formal education in basic areas of social work knowledge, they are often required, as part of their education, to select one or more concentrations that reflect their own interests and professional directions. Schools of social work have different concentrations and ways of defining their concentrations. In most schools of social work, concentrations are defined according to specific methods in social work, fields of practice, special populations, and special problems. Methods concentrations may include clinical practice, community organization, administration–policy–planning combination, family–marital treatment, research, and a generalist practice combining a *macro orientation* and a *micro orientation.* Fields-of-practice concentrations include child welfare, mental health, health care, school social work, criminal justice, gerontology, rural social work, industrial social work, family and child welfare services, and various combinations. Special-problems concentrations include substance abuse and poverty, and special-populations concentrations include groups such as people of various racial and ethnic groups and women.

concentric zone theory An urban land use hypothesis in which cities are said to develop in rings around an inner downtown business core, with each successive ring representing different land use patterns. These might include a ring of low-rent and public housing apartments, a high-rise residential ring, heavy industrial and light industrial rings, a ring of working class homes, a suburb of affluent upper-class homes, lower-class rural areas, and exurban estates. No city fits this model precisely.

conception The uniting of a sperm cell and an egg, resulting in an embryo.

Concern for the Dying (CFD) See *death with dignity.*

conciliation A mediation process in which two or more parties seek to minimize or eliminate their differences. The role of the social worker in such instances is usually to advise, referee, and arbitrate. See also *mediator role, mediation,* and *divorce.*

concrete operations stage The phase of *cognitive development* that, according to *Piagetian theory,* occurs between ages seven and 11, in which the individual learns to apply logic to observable and manipulable physical relationships.

concrete services The type of direct social services in which clients are provided with tangible resources needed to resolve specific problems or attain a normative standard of well-being, such as food, housing, transportation, clothing, or access thereto. These social services are compared with those in which the social worker provides important but intangible services, such as reassurance, knowledge, psychotherapy, and relationship-building skills.

concretization A thought pattern that overemphasizes "hard data," detail, immediate experience, and objective phenomena and avoids locus on subtleties and subjective experience. Concretization is often symptomatic of mental disorders such

as *paranoia, personality disorders,* and some types of *schizophrenia.*

concubinato Spanish term for *common-law marriage* or concubine.

concurrent placement In *social work education,* the format for *field placement* in which the student alternates classroom experiences with work in a social agency on different days of each week. This provides the student with opportunities for discussion and questions in the classroom about field experiences as well as opportunities in the agency to apply what is learned in class. See also *block placement.*

concurrent therapy The treatment format in which the social worker or other helping professional sees different members of a family or client system separately in individual sessions. This format has been used most commonly in marital therapy to maintain confidentiality and to encourage the participants to reveal their thoughts and behaviors when they might not feel able to do so in the presence of their spouses. This format is the opposite of *conjoint therapy.*

concurrent utilization reviews A managed care procedure to determine if a medical treatment is necessary and effective, conducted while the intervention is underway. See also *prospective utilization reviews* and *retrospective utilization reviews.*

condemnation A legal process of acquiring privately held property for more public use through the power of *eminent domain.* For a condemnation to be successful, the purpose must clearly be to benefit the public and the owner must be given just compensation.

conditioned inhibition In *behavior modification,* the pattern in which the subject is taught not to respond to a *stimulus* that previously elicited a *response.*

conditioned response (CR) In *behaviorism,* a classically conditioned response that has been learned after being associated repeatedly with a *conditioned stimulus (CS).* For example, an abused child develops anxiety (CR) whenever in the presence of the abuser (CS).

conditioned stimulus (CS) A previously neutral event in the environment that begins to elicit a learned or *conditioned response (CR)* when paired with an *unconditioned stimulus (US)*. For example, seeing a dog does not elicit fear in all individuals, but if an individual associates dogs with being bitten, the sight of a dog can elicit fear.

conditioning A process through which behavior is learned. The two major types of conditioning, *respondent conditioning* (also known as classical) and *operant conditioning*, are differentiated by the sequence in which the *stimulus* is presented. See also *conditioned stimulus (CS)*, *unconditioned stimulus (US)*, and *respondent behavior*.

condom A thin sheath of rubber, latex, polyurethane, or similar material that fits tightly over the penis and is used for *contraception* and the prevention of *sexually transmitted diseases (STDs)* such as *HIV disease, syphilis, gonorrhea*, and genital *herpes*. Condoms for females are also available.

conduct disorder A repetitive and persistent pattern of behavior in which age-appropriate norms and social rules are violated. This condition, which is noted primarily in children and youths, is of four types: (1) aggressive conduct (causes or threatens physical harm to others), (2) nonaggressive conduct (causes property loss), (3) deceitfulness or theft, and (4) serious violations of rules. The disorder is classified as "childhood onset type" if it seems to begin before age 10 and "adolescent-onset type" if it occurs after age 10. See also *oppositional defiant disorder*.

confabulation The act of making up for gaps in memory by fabricating stories or details.

confianza In Spanish-speaking cultures, the establishment of trust, which is achieved only after lengthy interactions, but once achieved is intense and durable. Social workers seeking to establish relationships with Latino clients often find this more difficult but necessary to establish, but after it is achieved, the working relationship can be a strong source for effective work.

confidence crimes Unlawfully cheating people out of their money or property by winning their trust and falsely claiming that their money will be put to some beneficial use. Such an act is also referred to as a "con game." See also *con artist*.

confidence level A research term referring to the degree to which an inference is reliable. This is expressed quantitatively as a percentage. Thus, when

a conclusion is stated as being at the .05 level of confidence, the statement is likely to be wrong only 5 percent of the time. The lower the percentage (for example, .01 or .001), the higher the degree of confidence in the statement.

confidentiality A principle of *ethics* according to which the social worker or other professional may not disclose information about a client without the client's consent. This information includes the identity of the client, content of verbalizations, professional opinions about the client, and material from records. Confidentiality does not preclude the communication of pertinent information about the client to relevant colleagues in the worker's agency. In specific circumstances, social workers and other professionals may be compelled by law to reveal to designated authorities some information (such as threats of violence, commission of crimes, and suspected child abuse) that would be relevant to legal judgments. See also *Tarasoff, Jaffee v. Redmond decision, absolute confidentiality*, and *relative confidentiality*.

confiscation 1. Legal seizing of private property, often as a penalty or restitution for criminal conduct. 2. The taking of private property during times of military takeover or disaster emergencies.

conflict 1. In groups or communities, the striving by two or more parties to achieve opposing or mutually exclusive goals. 2. In psychological terms, the mental struggle of two or more mutually exclusive impulses, motives, drives, or social demands.

conflict-habituated relationship A pattern of behavior in some marriages or domestic partnerships, characterized by considerable tension, distrust, quarrelsome behavior, and fights over an extended period. See also *devitalized relationship* and *passive–congenial relationship*.

conflict induction The technique in which divergent issues and values are introduced to force members of the group into active confrontation, debate, and new coalition building. This is effective with those who habitually avoid conflict and social discomfort, thus maintaining a stalemate that is unhealthy for some or all of their members.

conflict management The ongoing and constructive process of dealing with *conflict* between members of an organization. Conflict is inevitable and serves positive functions such as identifying important problems and providing an impetus for change. It involves four basic steps: (1) recognizing the conflict or potential conflict, (2) assessing the conflict situation, (3) selecting appropriate strategy, and (4) intervening.

conflict of interest   A situation in which one's obligations to others or to the public can be subordinated to one's private interest. For example an office holder may authorize funding that benefits a relative more than the taxpayers. Or a social worker influences a client to name the worker in a will.

conflict resolution   The process of eliminating or minimizing the problems that result when different parties or groups compete with one another for the same limited objectives. This process most commonly occurs by facilitating compromises, achieving *accommodation,* or sometimes by the total surrender of one group to the other.

conflict theories   Explanations about the nature, progress, and consequences of social conflict. The most prominent theories have been developed by Karl Marx, George Simmel, Lewis Coser, and others. Marx hypothesized that conflict would eventually lead to an overthrow of the power group, leading to a classless, conflict-free society. Simmel and Coser suggested that conflict is not inherently bad and that it serves important functions such as solidifying the in-group, increasing group cohesiveness, and mobilizing the energies of group members.

conflicting mandate   The legitimate requirements made of an organization to fulfill a variety of functions that are inherently contradictory or opposed to one another. For example, the citizens of one city want the administration to get its homeless population off the streets but also to end overcrowding in its homeless shelters. See also *competing mandate* and *ambiguous mandate.*

conformity   Behavior that is consistent with the *norms* and expectations of the relevant social group.

confrontation   The act of bringing together opposing ideas, impulses, or groups for the purpose of systematic examination or comparison.

congenital   Existing since *conception.* The term is applied to a disorder or condition that originated before birth.

congenital abnormalities   Diseases or disorders present at birth, such as *cleft palate, hemophilia,* and *spina bifida.*

conglomerate   A business organization in which different enterprises keep separate legal and bureaucratic structures but are owned by a corporate holding company. When several different companies in different nations are owned by another company in a different nation, it is often difficult to subject the organization to any one nation's laws, taxes, and employment and environmental policies.

congregate housing   Residential facilities for those who benefit from group living but do not require institutional care such as in a nursing home.

Congress of Racial Equality (CORE)   The *civil rights* organization founded in 1942 to ensure fair application of the law to all races and to promote opportunities for people of various racial and ethnic groups. Their Web site address is http://www.core-online.org

Congressional Budget Office (CBO)   The organization within the legislative branch of the U.S. government that provides Congress with basic budget data and analysis of alternative fiscal and policy issues. CBO prepares an annual budget report to Congress that includes a discussion of alternative spending and revenue levels and allocations. CBO monitors the results of congressional action on individual authorizations and appropriations and provides five-year projections of the costs of continuing current policies on taxes and expenditures. See also *Office of Management and Budget (OMB).*

conjoint therapy   A type of intervention in which a therapist or team of therapists treats a family by meeting with the members together for regular sessions; also, a type of intervention in which a husband and wife are treated as a unit and seen together by the marital therapist or therapy team. See also *family therapy* and *marital therapy.*

conjugal paranoia   A form of *jealousy* in which one spouse suspects the other of infidelity without good reason.

conjugal rights   A legal term for the obligations and opportunities of husbands and wives to be together socially, sexually, spiritually, and regularly.

conjugal visitation   Private meetings in prisons and jails between inmates and their spouses or significant others to engage in sexual intercourse.

conscience   A person's system of moral values, standards of behavior, and sense of right and wrong. See also *superego.*

conscientious objector   One who is opposed to participation in war and military activity because of religious beliefs. A conscientious objector may be exempted from a combat role but not from public service duties such as military or civilian hospital work. One need not be a member of an established religious organization to become a conscientious objector, but the objection to war must be based on religious rather than social or political beliefs.

conscientization   The process of helping clients and others become aware of and feel concern about a problem, objective, or value. The term was coined by educator Paulo Freire.

conscious   Mental awareness; that part of the mind that is aware of the immediate environment and of feelings and thoughts.

consciousness raising   The process of helping an individual or group become aware of and more sensitive to a social condition, cause, or idea that had been of little prior interest.

consensual crime   An illegal action in which the victim is supposedly a willing participant, as in drug use, prostitution, and certain forms of gambling.

consensual validation   The use of mutual agreement as the criterion for the truth or reality of a phenomenon; often used in *community organization* and in *clinical social work* as the objective or goal and to demonstrate progress toward that goal.

consensus   The process by which individuals and groups achieve general agreement about goals of mutual interest and the means to achieve them. Consensus is often facilitated by the community organizer by focusing first on goals and methods of high acceptability, by emphasizing common values, and by mediating and circumventing conflicts.

consent decree   A court approval to put an agreement between disputing parties into the form of a binding judgment. For example, a judge would allow an employer or official to not admit to an alleged wrongdoing but agree to more effort to correct the situation.

consequence   In *behaviorism,* an event that follows a behavior and that may increase or decrease the probability of that behavior's recurrence. A consequence also may have no effect on the behavior.

conservation   1. The planned use, preservation, and protection of the natural environment. 2. In *cognitive theory,* the ability to remember or retain relevant information and also to ignore irrelevant cues. For example, conservation was seen in Jean Piaget's experiments when young children began to retain the idea that water does not change when it is poured into pitchers of different shapes.

conservation movement   Organized efforts by individuals, groups, nations, and societies to preserve and protect the natural environment. The effort is led by organizations such as the Sierra Club; American Forests; Center for Marine Conservation; Conservation International; Friends of the Earth; Izaak Walton League; National Audubon Society; National Wildlife Federation; The Nature Conservancy; The Wilderness Society; and hundreds of organizations that focus on a particular geographic area, ecosystem, river, or type of land.

conservatism   The sociopolitical orientation that currently emphasizes the maintenance of traditional values, mores, and social structures and the reduction of funding for government programs, especially in social welfare, health care, and public school education. The orientation inclines toward developing stronger military forces and stricter law enforcement programs. Use of this term, as well as that of *liberalism,* has accurate meaning only in the context and time frame in which it is used. This is because the orientation and goals of conservatism have changed through the centuries (see *classical conservatism* and *neoconservatism*).

conservator   A court-appointed guardian or custodian of the assets or property belonging to someone who is judged unable to manage them properly. The conservator may be an individual or, in some jurisdictions, a public or private agency.

conspiracy   Collaborative activities by two or more persons to commit a crime.

conspiracy theories　An elaborate system of beliefs, held by individuals and groups, that secret organizations are actively working to control society, suppress certain groups, or eliminate individuals who have opposing viewpoints or values. Many social movements seek to gain support by identifying and describing alleged conspirators. Such theories tend to flourish when people feel excluded from the economic, social, and political gains of their larger society. As a result, many social movements gain support by identifying and describing conspirators and preparing to combat them.

constellation　An arrangement or grouping of ideas, symptoms, or causes of problems.

constituency　A group of supporters, customers, voters, or clients whose interests are served by someone with the authority to represent them in seeking to meet their collective needs and interests. If the individual is an elected officeholder, the constituents are the voters, supporters from the relevant jurisdiction. See also *interest groups.*

constraint　In *social planning* and policy development, any general limitation on the level of rights. For example, zoning laws accompanied by fines, jail terms, and other penalties limit the rights of landowners.

constricted affect　Diminished variability and intensity with which emotions are expressed.

construct validity　In social research, a complex method for assessing the *validity* of an instrument. The instrument is regarded as valid to the extent that it is correlated with relevant variables in the theoretical framework.

constructive eviction　Actions or inactions by landlords that make their tenants so uncomfortable they feel compelled to move, even though no forced removal is taking place. For example, the landlord raises rents exorbitantly, or withholds services such as trash pickup or hallway maintenance.

constructive intelligence　Intelligence as indicated by one's ability to function effectively in society, including the ability to form healthy relationships, succeed vocationally and economically, and solve problems. Many social workers believe constructive intelligence is more meaningful than *intelligence quotient (IQ).*

constructivism　A theoretical model about the process by which knowledge is created, acquired, and processed. This model holds that knowledge is not necessarily a representation of "truth" or "reality" but of viability. The model holds that, although facts and information may be communicated, knowledge is not transmitted, because every knower has to build it for himself or herself. Therefore, it never claims objectivity; all knowledge is relative.

consultant　One with a special expertise or access to those with the needed expertise whose skills are sought by professionals or organizations. Consultants advise or educate about the nature of the problem or possible solutions or find better ways to achieve the organization's goals. Social workers are often sought as consultants to social agencies, law courts, political groups, activist organizations, and clinicians or to clients who need to know how to deal with specific social institutions.

consultation　An interpersonal relationship between an individual or organization possessing special expertise and someone who needs that expertise to solve a specific problem. Social work consultation is a problem-solving process in which advice and other helping activity from the consultant is offered to an individual, group, organization, or community that is faced with a job-related problem. Unlike *supervision,* which is relatively continuous and encompasses many areas of concern, consultation occurs more on an ad hoc, or temporary, basis and has a specific goal and focus. Unlike the supervisor, the consultant has no special administrative authority over those to whom advice is given.

consumer boycott　An organized refusal by a group to purchase goods or services from a firm or industry to change its methods of doing business. The goal is usually to lower prices, recognize a labor union, or put economic pressure on government to change its policies.

consumer-centered social work　An orientation by social work practitioners that places a high value on the self-determination of the client and emphasizes those intervention strategies that encourage client independence, self-advocacy, and self-judgment in negotiating the social services or welfare system. Thinking of the client as a consumer and one who is capable of deciding what is best helps move away from paternalism.

Consumer Price Index (CPI)   A measure of the *cost of living* issued monthly by the *Bureau of Labor Statistics (BLS)*. It shows changes in the expenses for goods and services purchased by moderate-income families. See also *Producer Price Index.*

consumerism   A social movement and orientation designed to advocate for and protect the interests of people in their roles as users of services or commodities and to scrutinize the activities, skills, training, effectiveness, outcomes, and products of those who provide these goods or services.

Consumers League, National   See *National Consumers League (NCL).*

consumption-versus-investment concept   See *investment-versus-consumption concept.*

Contact Family Program   In Sweden and other nations, a national program to recruit and modestly reimburse families who agree to provide specified supports for other families in need. Most recipient families consist of single mothers with younger children and minimal economic or social resources. The contact family often gives weekend respite care for the children, additional family supports and structure (for example, playing the "grandparent" role), helping in chore services, and providing transportation. The contact families are not especially trained and may see members of the recipient family once a month or more often if they all desire.

contact hours   The amount of time a professional spends directly with clients or students during a specified period, such as a week or month. For example, managed care companies reimburse social workers only for the specific amount of pre-approved time spent with a client; private practitioners bill clients only for the hours in face-to-face contact.

contagion   Transmission of disease, usually rapidly, by direct or indirect contact with one who carries a certain virus or bacteria. This term also applies to the rapid spread of an attitude, behavior, ideology, or rumor.

containment   Efforts to maintain boundaries and reduce movement beyond them; a method of *social control* in which a group of people separated from their peers is given special benefits so that the people have less incentive to challenge their separation.

contempt of court   Behavior that interferes with the administration of justice or shows disrespect for the dignity and authority of the court. Such behavior may occur within the courtroom during a trial ("direct contempt") or outside ("constructive contempt"). See also *civil contempt.*

content analysis   The systematic study of some group interaction, written document, or other exchange of information primarily by evaluating the frequency with which certain ideas, reactions, or expressions occur.

content-and-process issue   A historic debate in social work about the degree of emphasis the profession places on its knowledge versus skill components. Social work content is the "what" of professional practice and includes substantive knowledge about entities such as diagnostic criteria, resources, special populations, the nature of social problems, and the like. Social work process is the "how" of professional practice and includes interviewing skills, evaluation research, relationship-building qualities, and effective intervention techniques.

content validity   In social research, a method for assessing the *validity* of an instrument or a scale. Items that actually exist on a scale are compared with items that could have been used.

contextual theory   The *family systems* concept, originated by Ivan Boszormenyi-Nagy in the 1970s, that seeks to understand family interactions, conflicts, and loyalties in terms of the legacy of accumulated obligations, debts, and hurts that occur in a family system through several generations.

contextual variable   A fact, situation, or condition that may influence the *validity* of a test.

contingency   1. In social research and statistics, a term connoting an association or correlation between variables, as in contingency tables. 2. In *behaviorism*, the consequences that are expected to follow behaviors.

contingency analysis   An approach to social work practice based on principles of *behaviorism*, including four propositions that (1) individuals, families, groups, communities, and societies behave; (2) all behavior is followed by consequences; (3) the consequences of a given behavior largely influence the future occurrence of that behavior; and (4) empirical analysis of these contingencies can be used effectively in understanding and treating all strata of social work clients.

contingency contracting In *behavior therapy,* a technique in which an agreement is made specifying the behaviors to be performed for a certain consequence to follow. The technique is used particularly in behavioral family therapy to help family members carry out "if–then statements."

continuing care retirement communities (CCRC) Villages usually designed for about 300–500 older people, most of whom enter when older than age 75 and relatively healthy. CCRCs are usually for-profit real estate ventures and cater to affluent older people.

Continuing Disability Review (CDR) The legally required periodic evaluation of one who receives social security disability benefits to determine if that person continues to be disabled. The time between reviews depends on the beneficiary's age, type and severity of disability, and the chances of improvement. CDR requires a full medical review by the *Disability Determination Service (DDS)* and possibly a consultative medical exam.

continuing education Training taken by social workers and other professionals who have already completed the formal education required to enter their field. Most professions require their members to keep up with the current knowledge base by participating in specified additional training within certain time limits. For example, state licensing boards for social workers may require them to obtain a specific number of *CEUs* (continuing education units) by successfully completing qualified academic or professional courses. Some consider *staff development* to be a part of continuing education.

continuity of care Coordination of the efforts made by different organizations or divisions within one organization to provide for the needs of a client with a minimum of duplication or gaps in service; also, the continuous provision of services for clients moving from one provider to another or to follow-up after discharge.

continuous reinforcement In *behavior modification,* a *schedule of reinforcement* in which a *target behavior* is reinforced each time it occurs (compared with the less-frequent *intermittent reinforcement*). See also *reinforcement.*

continuum A phenomenon that has variability even though no discrete gaps or separate parts are evident.

continuum of care A range of specialized health, social services, rehabilitative, and in-home services that a seriously or chronically ill or frail elderly person might need. This continuum indicates that a person's well-being depends not only on medical care, but also on other services as well.

"contra non valentum" doctrine See *statute of limitations.*

contraception Any action or device used to prevent pregnancy. This includes abstaining; limiting coitus to nonfertile periods in the woman's cycle; or using a condom, intrauterine device (IUD), diaphragm, contraceptive pills, and sterilization.

contract A written, oral, or implied agreement between the client and the social worker as to the goals, methods, timetables, and mutual obligations to be fulfilled during the intervention process.

contract model An orientation in social work practice in which the social worker and client identify goals at the beginning of the relationship and formally establish a working agreement about how to reach them. The agreement includes a specification of terms, the timetables, and other procedures. The contract may be written or oral, and unlike a legal contract, may easily be renegotiated during the course of the intervention process. See also *covenant model.*

Contract with America A set of political and legislative objectives sponsored by Republican Congressmen in the 1994–1996 term to shift many federal government programs and responsibilities to state and local governments or to the private sector. See also *devolution.*

contracting The therapeutic procedure of discussing with the client the goals, methods, and mutual obligations of treatment to obtain a clear verbal understanding or to establish a formal agreement about them.

contracting out Employing individuals or organizations on a temporary basis to accomplish specific tasks for a set fee that usually does not include fringe benefits. Contracting out is also known as *outsourcing.*

contraindication A symptom, condition, or circumstance that warns against taking some course of action. For example, bruises and cuts found on a hospitalized foster child would be a contraindication for returning the child to that foster home.

contributing to the delinquency of a minor A criminal action by parents or guardians who through *neglect, coercion,* example, or outright encouragement foster unlawful behavior by their children. These actions may include permitting the child to avoid school, to stay out late at night, to consume alcohol and other drugs, and to be exposed to unlawful activities by the parents. This crime also occurs when adults influence children into some antisocial activity.

contributory benefit Income transfer payments to individuals based on their participation in a program through regular contributions. Examples are Social Security (OASDHI), unemployment compensation, and Medicare. Noncontributory benefits are entitlements and categorical benefits for which no contributions were necessary.

control 1. To regulate. 2. To exercise direction or restraint over another. 3. In social research, a standard for comparison. 4. In social welfare management, a procedure for regulating the flow of information and activity so that efforts to achieve goals are coordinated.

control group In research, a group of subjects who are equivalent in every possible respect with an *experimental group*, except that they are not exposed to the variable being tested.

control variable A variable introduced by a researcher to check the apparent relationship between an *independent variable* and a *dependent variable*.

controlled emotional involvement An ethical principle in social work in which feelings, support, and empathy for the client are felt and expressed but only to the extent that such reactions are effective, helpful, and part of the intervention plan. The skilled practitioner learns to show and conceal emotional reactions to the client, finding the optimal response somewhere between apathy and overidentification. Controlled emotional involvement is one of the major factors in the helping relationship.

controlled substances Drugs that, because of their potential for abuse or addiction, have limited availability and are strictly regulated or outlawed. These substances include *marijuana, narcotics* (*opiates* such as *opium, heroin, morphine,* and *codeine* and nonopiates such as *methadone*), *stimulants* (such as *cocaine* and *amphetamines*), *depressants* (such as *barbiturates* and *tranquilizers*), and *hallucinogens* (such as *LSD,* mescaline, and peyote).

controlled-substances categories The delineation in the U.S. Controlled Substances Act (P.L. 91-513) of five schedules or types of *psychoactive drugs,* rated according to their perceived degree of potential harmfulness, abuse potential, and accepted medical use. The higher categories have greater potential for medical use and less abuse potential. Category 1 includes *heroin, LSD, marijuana,* and most addictive drugs of abuse. Category 2 substances include *morphine, methadone, amphetamines,* and other drugs that have accepted medical use but high potential for abuse.

convalescent home A private or public health care facility for patients who no longer need to be hospitalized but who require greater care than would be available in their homes.

conventional morality The second of the three stages delineated in *Kohlberg moral development theory* that usually occurs in young people between ages nine and 20. In this phase, the youth obeys rules to gain approval and avoid rejection and later begins to appreciate the need for social rules and feel guilty in wrongdoing. See also *preconventional morality* and *postconventional morality.*

conversion A *defense mechanism* in which anxiety or emotional conflict is transformed into overt physical manifestations or symptoms such as pain, loss of feeling, or paralysis.

conversion disorder One of the *somatoform disorders.* The condition generally includes symptoms suggesting neurological disease, such as paralysis, coordination disturbance, anesthesia, blindness, or seizures. The psychological purpose of the disorder is primarily to achieve some *primary gain* or *secondary gain.* See also *hysteria* and *anxiety hysteria.*

conversion symptoms *Somatic complaints* that are *psychogenic.* The term derives from psychodynamic theories that hypothesized that unconscious and intolerable thoughts or drives are converted into physical manifestations, most commonly involving the nervous system (for example, paralysis and blindness).

cooling off rule A U.S. regulation enforced by the Federal Trade Commission that enables people who purchase some product or service to cancel the obligation and get a refund, under certain conditions. The rule applies to purchases over $25 that are made in the consumer's own residence. The right to a full refund must be exercised before midnight of the third day after the sale.

cooperative adoption A legal adoption arrangement in which biological and adoptive parents and the children maintain open contact through various forms, from contact through intermediaries to occasional communications (pictures, letters, telephoning) to active participation in the children's lives. This is considered by many to be a synonym for *open adoption*. See also *closed adoption.*

Cooperative for Assistance and Relief Everywhere (CARE) A *nongovernment organization (NGO)* founded in 1945 through which gift parcels are sent from the United States to needy people in other nations. Its original name was Cooperative for American Remittances to Europe. Their Web site address is http://www.care.org

co-optation A strategy for minimizing anticipated opposition by absorbing or including the opponent in the group's membership. Once a member of the group, the opponent has less ability to criticize the program in public. Opposition within the organization is also less effective because the person is in the minority. The term is also used to indicate any election of a person or group into another group's membership.

"cop a plea" An expression used by some people charged with crime as well as by their lawyers, when requesting an arrangement involving *plea bargaining.*

copayment A provision in some insurance programs that requires the policyholder to share the cost of any loss or claim. In many health insurance programs, the beneficiary is required to pay a percentage of the provider's bill before reimbursement is made for the rest. The major purpose of this arrangement is to discourage inappropriate use of resources and to encourage

responsible participation. See also *third party* and *third-party payment.*

coping index One of several rating systems that social workers and other professionals use to consistently rank and describe the degree of *coping skills* or resources a client can call on to address the problem. Several indexes are in current use. A typical coping index is found in the *Person-in-Environment (PIE) System;* rating scores range from no coping skills through outstanding coping skills.

coping mechanisms The behavioral and personality patterns used to adjust or adapt to environmental pressures without altering goals or purposes.

coping skills Effective behavior an individual uses in responding to or avoiding sources of stress. Typical coping skills include obtaining new needed information, preplanning, maintaining control over one's emotions and impulses, delaying gratification, and seeking more appropriate alternative ways to achieve goals.

copractice In *social group work,* the format in which two equally ranked professionals or leaders share responsibilities for the group.

coprolalia The frequent use of obscene or otherwise offensive language, often in an impulsive way.

Coram, Thomas (1668–1751) English philanthropist and colonist who assisted poor people and artists to live in the New World. He established England's first *foundling hospital* for abandoned babies in 1739 and developed it into a model for such facilities and for early *indoor relief* programs.

corespondent The person identified as the partner in an adulterous relationship.

coronary artery disease (CAD) A serious and potentially life-threatening disease that occurs when the walls of the coronary arteries (those adjacent to and circling the heart) accumulate plaques of hard cholesterol substances to restrict the flow of blood to the heart muscle. Restricted blood flow may lead to severe chest pains (angina pectoris), and blockage caused by clots may lead to a heart attack (myocardial infarction).

corporal punishment Inflicting physical pain for the purpose of punishment, as in spanking a misbehaving child.

corporate eldercare   The provision of facilities and caregivers in the workplace for older relatives of employees. This program, which is currently offered by few employers, is equivalent to child day care or nurseries in business and government organizations. The eldercare program is usually a short-term arrangement to enable employees to continue working while responsible for seniors who cannot be left alone.

corporate welfare   Providing services, financial assistance, subsidies, or other benefits to organizations to help them maintain their viability or profitability. For example, a national government might reduce the tax rates or subsidize part of the expenses of a labor-intensive industry because it supposedly provides many jobs. To enhance the local economy, a municipal government might offer to give land at low or no cost to companies that relocate to the area. Some who are most strongly opposed to governmental welfare benefits for individuals favor corporate welfare programs for businesses. See also *fiscal welfare* and *upper class welfare*.

Corporation for National and Community Service (CNCS)   The U.S. program that, in cooperation with local governments, private voluntary agencies, and business corporations, coordinates the major volunteer programs of the nation. Established in 1993, the CNCS's primary programs include *AmeriCorps* (including *Vista, National Civilian Community Corps,* and *Promise Fellows*), the *Senior Corps* (including *RSVP, Foster Grandparents,* and *Senior Companion* programs), and *Learn and Serve America*. Their Web site address is http://www.nationalservice.org

corrections   The specialty that seeks to change and improve the behaviors of convicted law offenders through *incarceration, parole, probation,* and ideally educational programs and social services. See also *penology* and *community-based corrections*.

corrective feedback   In social work administration and supervision, the communication of a discrepancy between existing and desired goals and behaviors. This feedback may be positive as well as negative and should occur privately, without blame, and with emphasis on desired behaviors. See also *supportive feedback*.

correlation   In research, a mutual relation; a pattern of variation between two phenomena in which change in one is associated with change in the other. High correlations are not necessarily indicative of causality.

correlation coefficient   A numerical index of the extent to which two variables are related. When the score is positive (+0.1 to +1.0), it indicates that the frequency of one phenomenon is associated with the frequency of the other. When the score is negative (–0.1 to –1.0), it indicates that a high frequency of one phenomenon is associated with a low frequency of the other. Perfect agreement between two variables is expressed as +1.0. Perfect inverse relationships are expressed as –1.0. A correlation coefficient of 0.0 indicates no apparent relationship.

corruption   In political and public service administration, the abuse of office for personal gain, usually through *bribery, extortion, influence peddling,* and special treatment given to some citizens and not to others.

cortisol   A hormone that helps regulate human stress reactions. In emergencies cortisol and other stress hormones help make energy available, sharpen attention, and temporarily suppress the immune response. Excess cortisol released over a long period may be related to depression, memory loss, and posttraumatic stress disorder.

corvée   A system of enforced, mandatory labor, often required to pay taxes.

COSH Groups   Committees on Occupational Health and Safety Groups; private, nonprofit organizations, located in most of the larger states in the nation, in which the goal is to help prevent worker injury, disease, and death. The groups maintain hot lines and provide information about things such as identifying and controlling toxic substances, and they refer callers to emergency health care providers and attorneys. See also *Occupational Safety and Health Administration (OSHA)*.

cosigning a loan   The act of pledging to repay a loan if the original borrower defaults. The cosigner guarantees that the debt will be repaid and is subject to the same liabilities, credit rating risks, credit collection agencies, and repossessions as the borrower.

cosmetic pharmacology   The use of medications, usually but not always prescribed by physicians, supposedly to enhance desired physical and personality characteristics.

cost–benefit analysis An administration and management procedure in which various goals of the organization are evaluated systematically along with the expenses and resources required to achieve them.

cost of living The amount of money required to purchase the goods and services needed to live adequately in a given society.

cost-of-living adjustment (COLA) An increase or decrease in benefits based on changes in the relative purchasing power of money (*inflation* or *deflation*).

cost-of-living allowance Increased cash or *in-kind benefits* based on the amount of money deemed necessary to live according to a specified economic standard. For example, social security recipients are paid in excess of their originally contracted income to take into account the increased amount of money required to maintain their living standard.

cost-of-living index A measure to determine the relative purchasing power of money at a given time in a given society. In the United States, the index is calculated by weighting the average prices of the major commodities that are considered important or representative of people's overall needs.

cost sharing A budgeting and administrative procedure that occurs when two or more governments or other organizations divide certain financial obligations. Each participating organization agrees to pay a portion of the total outlay—the amount usually depending on its own needs, resources, and expected benefits from the expenditure. For example, the federal government and a state government agree to share the costs of public assistance payments to eligible recipients in that state. In another example, two social agencies that provide similar services in the same area agree to employ one consulting firm to provide both agencies with information about the area's demographic characteristics. See also *revenue sharing*.

costing Estimating the total expenditure of a program or plan that would be necessary to reach a specified goal. Costing is also referred to as "costing out."

cotherapy Psychosocial intervention on behalf of a client conducted by two or more professionals working in *collaboration*.

Council of Economic Advisers An agency within the executive branch of the U.S. government established in 1946 to inform the president about its analysis of the economy; to evaluate the effect of proposed and existing government programs on the economy; and to help formulate national economic policies, including those pertaining to health care and welfare.

Council of Governments (COG) Comprehensive planning organizations comprising representatives of several local governments that are usually in geographic proximity (that is, several towns, cities, and counties in an area). COG members meet periodically to consider the mutual needs of the people in the area and ways of combining resources to meet those needs. Their purposes include planning, coordinating, and integrating their respective efforts and achieving more influence with their state governments and at the national level than could be achieved through their isolated efforts. Typical service-planning activities include transportation, water and sewage treatment, and services to older people.

Council of Nephrology Social Workers (CNSW) The professional association of social workers who assist those affected by the psychosocial stresses and lifestyle readjustments of kidney disease, urinary system disorders, diabetes, collagen disease, transplants, and related problems. An integral part of the National Kidney Foundation since 1973, CNSW sponsors conferences, standard setting, research, and publications such as the *Journal of Nephrology Social Work* and the *Renalink* newsletter. Their Web site address is http://www.kidney.org/professionals/cnsw/

Council on Accreditation of Services for Families and Children (COA) The U.S. and Canadian accrediting organization to ensure quality standards among direct-service social agencies and mental health clinics, which may be public, private, nonprofit, or for-profit. COA is sponsored by its affiliated membership organizations such as the *Child Welfare League of America (CWLA)*, *Family Service America (FSA)*, *Lutheran Social Services (LSS)*, and the *National Alliance for the Mentally Ill (NAMI)*. The organization sets standards, evaluates agency resources to meet those standards, and publicly recognizes outstanding contributions.

Council on Post-Secondary Accreditation (COPA)   An accrediting body for university and graduate school education in the United States, including social work, that was established in 1949. After it suspended operations in 1993, many of its functions were taken over by the *Council for Higher Education Accreditation (CHEA)*.

Council on Social Work Education (CSWE)   An independent organization comprising social work educators, professional organizations, social agencies, and academic institutions for the purpose of establishing and maintaining standards in *social work education*. A predecessor organization of CSWE was established in 1919 and later became known as the *American Association of Schools of Social Work (AASSW)*. Another group, the *National Association of Schools of Social Administration (NASSA)*, was founded in 1942. In 1952, AASSW merged with NASSA to form CSWE. The organization is the primary body for accrediting schools of social work in the United States. CSWE also sponsors an annual program meeting every March in different cities and publishes books, pamphlets, and the *Journal of Social Work Education*. Their Web site address is http://www.cswe.org. See also *curriculum policy statement*.

counseling   A procedure often used in clinical social work and other professions to guide individuals, families, groups, and communities by activities such as giving advice, delineating alternatives, helping articulate goals, and providing needed information.

counselor   Anyone who provides counseling. The term is often applied to highly trained mental health, education, or legal professionals, but it is also used for volunteers with minimal training and for paid workers who provide guidance and structure in group settings (as in camp and dorm hall counselors).

counterculture   A lifestyle chosen by a group because its values, norms, manner of dress, and choice of recreational activities are at variance with the predominant social order.

counterdependents   In *group psychotherapy,* a name given to those members who persistently communicate disagreement with and disparage-ment for the group leader's advice, suggestions, or efforts to facilitate the group process. These members are so designated because of their opposite counterpart, "dependents" who unquestioningly follow the leader's every word or suggestion.

counterinsurgency   Measures taken by a government to defeat revolutionary groups; this is typically done by seeking to infiltrate revolutionary cells and kill or capture opposition leaders and by motivating the populace to expose or fight the revolutionaries.

countertransference   A set of *conscious* or *unconscious* emotional reactions to a client experienced by the social worker or other professional, usually in a clinical setting. According to psychodynamic theory, these feelings originate in the professional's own developmental conflicts and are projected onto the client. Countertransference is identical to *transference* except that it applies to the feelings, wishes, and defensive operations of the therapist toward the client. Like transference, it must be constantly monitored and understood.

couples group therapy   A *family therapy* strategy and *group psychotherapy* format in which several couples meet on a regular basis with a therapist to work systematically on resolving marital and family problems.

Court-Appointed Special Advocates (CASA)   A program in many state court systems in which qualified volunteer citizens are appointed to advocate in behalf of individuals, usually young people. CASA volunteers have helped youths by scrutinizing the work of child welfare workers, lawyers, guardians ad litem, and others who are involved in the case. They also help by advocating solely for the child rather than other interest groups and by providing case continuity when many others involved tend not to stay with any given case to its resolution.

covenant marriage   A formal and solemn agreement made by some marrying couples in which there are supposedly greater obligations and binding commitments than are found in traditional legal marriages. Those who choose this form of marriage often engaged in extensive premarital (and often religious) counseling and then make legal contracts (and vows to God and each other) that make divorce more difficult and costly to obtain. Although covenant marriages have achieved some legal sanction and enforcement provisions in a few jurisdictions, most exist as matters of conscience between the partners and sometimes their spiritual advisers.

covenant model   An orientation in the social work relationship in which the social worker implicitly or explicitly promises a commitment to empathetically serve the whole client inclusively and to work toward meeting the client's maximum needs, whether or not the needs are known or specified in advance. This model emphasizes the social worker's role as teacher and companion to the client and commitment to a life of service to society and is in contrast to the *contract model,* which limits the goals, more narrowly defines client needs, and explicates the procedures for meeting them.

covert reinforcement   1. In *behavior therapy,* the strengthening of the likelihood of desirable behavior by remembering a pleasant event when a given act occurs. 2. The surreptitious presentation of a reward when the subject has acted in the desired way.

Cowan, Edith (1861–1932)   Australian social worker and political leader who advocated for and led the Children's Court movement. As Australia's first female member of Parliament she introduced the Women's Legal Status Act, which gave many rights to Australian women. A major university in Perth, Australia, bears her name.

Coyle, Grace L. (1892–1962)   A developer of the scientific approach to *social group work.* She wrote many textbooks and articles on the subject and, as president of various social work organizations, ensured that group work would be an integral part of the profession.

CPT Health and Behavior Assessment Codes   A component of the *Current Procedural Terminology (CPT) Codes* that pertains to the biopsychosocial aspects of patients. The assessment may include the patient's family background and social supports, the patient's adherence to medical treatments, health-related risk-taking behavior, behavioral observations, psychophysiological monitoring, and data interpretation. It is used, for example, with patients who do not have diagnosed mental illnesses but whose behavior might be relevant in their treatment and treatment prognosis for physical illness or symptoms. The assessment was added to the *CPT Codes* in 2002.

"crack"   A highly addictive form of *cocaine* made by mixing small amounts of it with baking soda and water. When dry, the substance is broken or cracked into small pebbles and usually smoked in special pipes. Crack is relatively inexpensive, highly potent, and can be lethal. Users tend to become obsessed about getting additional supplies. Effects may include agitation; confusion; anxiety; and sometimes convulsion, tremor, and heart attack.

crackdown   Efforts by governments and other organizations to be more rigorous in monitoring and enforcing administrative policy and in applying the rules and penalties for failure to comply. The term is frequently used in connection with public welfare programs to reduce the number of beneficiaries and their benefits.

"cradle to grave"   The phrase used, often pejoratively, in describing the socioeconomic security available to people in an idealized *welfare state.* The expression "womb to tomb" has the same connotation.

"crank"   A highly addictive methamphetamine that is injected to produce a period of intense euphoria that lasts up to 24 hours. Cheaply made and far less expensive than other drugs of abuse, crank often produces symptoms of acute depression and psychosis after the euphoria ends. When this substance is smoked, it is known as *"ice."*

creaming   Selection of clients, not based on their need, but on their likelihood of benefitting from the intervention. The effect is for the agency to appear to have more success than if all clients had equal access. See also "cherry picking."

creationism   Belief that the Biblical version of the origins of the universe, earth, and humans is literally true as it appears in the Book of Genesis.

creativity   The mental processes and skills that result in an original product of value or quality, which includes thinking that goes beyond what is already known and results in original ideas and novel solutions to existing problems.

credentialism   The placing of greater value and prestige on titles, licenses, academic degrees, and other symbols of learning than on demonstrated skills for doing the job.

credentials   In the social work profession, documentation indicating that the practitioner has fulfilled specified requirements and is recognized by the credentialing authority as having achieved advanced levels of professional experience and proficiency. NASW sponsors several credentials, including the *Diplomate in Clinical Social Work (DCSW)*, the *Qualified Clinical Social Worker (QCSW)*, and the *Academy of Certified Social Workers (ACSW)*. It also sponsors specialty certifications such as the *Certified Advanced Social Work Case Manager (C-ASWCM)*, the *Certified Social Work Case Manager (C-SWCM)*, the *Certified Clinical Alcohol, Tobacco, and Other Drugs Social Worker (C-CATODSW)*, and the *Certified School Social Work Specialist (C-SSWS)*. Other social work organizations also provide credentials. For example, the *American Board of Examiners in Clinical Social work (ABE)* has the *Diplomate in Clinical Social Work (DCSW)*, and the *Clinical Social Work Federation (CSWF)* has the *Family Therapy Practice Academy (FTPA)*. The *Association of Social Work Boards (ASWB)* coordinates the examinations and procedures of licensing boards. A U.K. credential for qualified social workers is the *DipSW*. In Germany the qualified professional social worker is awarded the Staatlliche Anerkennung (state recognition).

credit file segregation   An illegal procedure used by *credit repair services* supposedly to help people hide unfavorable credit information by establishing new or alternative credit identities. Often these services get clients to establish new credit accounts and employer identification numbers (that resemble social security numbers) to imply or fraudulently establish a new "identity" and conceal past bankruptcies and similar negative credit information.

credit repair services   Business establishments that promise to improve their clients' credit ratings, lower their interest rates, remove past bankruptcy files, and lower monthly repayment obligations. Advocates for economically disadvantaged people find that some of these services use deceptive and illegal practices such as *credit file segregation, predatory lending,* and excessively high repayment interest rates and operate mostly in poor neighborhoods where loans are difficult to obtain. Some reputable nonprofit organizations also provide similar financial services to low-income clients at much less cost.

"creeping socialism"   A derisive term, uttered mostly by people who espouse minimal government, referring to the gradual increase of health and welfare programs funded and maintained by government.

Creutzfeldt–Jakob disease   A *central nervous system (CNS)* viral disease, resulting in dementia and involuntary jerky movements. See also *bovine spongiform encephalopathy.*

crib death   See *sudden infant death syndrome (SIDS).*

crime   Any behavior that violates a law. Some social scientists extend this definition to include any behavior that is contrary to the society's moral codes for which there are formalized group sanctions, whether or not they are institutionalized as laws.

Crime Identification Technology Act   The 1998 U.S. law (P.L. 105-251) that provides states and local law enforcement organizations with funding and advice to upgrade crime detection capabilities using high-tech tools, including DNA identification, video surveillance, and effective nonlethal weapons.

Crime Stoppers   An effort by police and law officials to educate the public about crime problems in the local community and apprehend lawbreakers. Television shows are produced in which actors reenact recent local crimes, and rewards are offered for information leading to the perpetrator's conviction. Most of the operating funds come from private contributions.

criminal justice policy   Society's guidelines and established procedures to be considered when deciding how to cope with illegal conduct. Elements of current U.S. criminal justice policy include the right to trial by jury, the right to competent counsel, rights of appeal and *habeas corpus,* determinant sentencing, *probation* rather than *incarceration* for less-serious crimes with no prior conviction, and *parole* for appropriate conduct during incarceration.

criminal justice system   The programs, policies, sociopolitical and legal institutions, and physical infrastructure designed to help prevent and control crime and to adjudicate, incarcerate, and rehabilitate people engaged in illegal behavior.

criminally insane   A legal term referring to one who has committed a crime while under the influence of a *psychosis* or other *mental disorder* that inhibits the knowledge that such an act was wrong or the ability to refrain from doing it. An institution for the criminally insane would ideally combine the confinement of a prison with the therapy of a mental hospital.

criminogenic   Conditions and social structures out of which crime is much more likely to occur. The term is similar to "carcinogenic," for conditions leading to cancer, or "psychogenic," for physical symptoms that seem to come out of psychological conflict. Prisons and large public housing compounds are often cited as criminogenic facilities.

Crips and Bloods   Two of the larger American *street gangs*, both composed of predominately young African American males who use distinctive styles and colors of dress, symbols, and hand signals and try to control certain neighborhoods of larger cities, especially in the western United States.

crisis   A term used by social workers in two ways: (1) an internal experience of emotional change and distress and (2) a social event in which a disastrous event disrupts some essential functions of existing social institutions. When seen as a period of emotional distress, a crisis is considered to be precipitated by a perceived life problem or to pose an obstacle to an important goal resulting in internal discord because the individual's typical coping strategies are inadequate. The outcome of the crisis can be positive if the individual eventually finds new *coping mechanisms* to deal with the unfamiliar event, thus adding to the repertoire of effective adaptive responses.

crisis bargaining   Actions taken by people during times of upset or duress to improve the situation or minimize the conflict. The concept is delineated in the *Kübler-Ross death stages* theory. In this theory, bargaining is the third crisis stage in responses to impending death. After the individual typically goes through a period of denial and then anger, he or she attempts to avoid or delay death by making promises or "deals" or by conforming to different standards.

crisis care centers   Facilities in social agencies and health care organizations oriented toward providing short-term emergency assistance and helping individuals and groups return to precrisis functioning. These centers provide services such as disaster relief, suicide prevention, emergency food and shelter, counseling for victims of rape or other crimes, shelter to victims of spouse abuse or child abuse, detoxification for substance abusers, and many other activities. See also *emergency financial assistance*.

crisis counseling   Short-term intervention with people who have lived through a traumatic event to assist them cope better with the resulting psychosocial reactions. This type of work helps them to better understand their reactions, obtain needed emotional support and other resources, and resume their normal lives as much as possible thereafter. Crisis counseling does not include treatment for problems the person might have prior to the disaster, such as mental illness, but might also include connecting those people with professionals who might treat their mental illness.

crisis hot line   See *hot line*.

crisis intervention   The therapeutic practice used in helping clients in *crisis* to promote effective coping that can lead to positive growth and change by acknowledging the problem, recognizing its impact, and learning new or more effective behaviors for coping with similar predictable experiences.

crisis planning   Systematic preparation for the inevitable changes that will occur at unpredictable times in the life of an individual or community. Crisis planning ranges from *disaster relief* planning for communities to helping individuals prepare for deaths or disabilities of family members.

crisis sequence   A series of five predictable changes experienced by the person in *crisis*: (1) hazardous event (a stressor that may be a single catastrophic event or a series of mishaps that have a cumulative effect); (2) vulnerable state (heightened tension and anxiety caused by the hazardous event, intensified as the individual uses the entire repertoire of coping techniques before seeing that they do not work in this new situation); (3) precipitating factor (the "last straw," often seen as the *presenting problem* or event that brings tension to a peak); (4) active crisis state (disequilibrium has set in and is manifested by psychological and physical turmoil, aimless activity, disturbances in mood and intellectual functioning, and painful preoccupation with events leading to the crisis event); and (5) reintegration (the individual adjusts or accepts and learns new and effective coping techniques, a phase that may be adaptive or maladaptive). See also *coping index*.

crisis theory   Concepts pertaining to people's reactions when confronted with new and unfamiliar experiences. These experiences may come in the form of natural disasters, significant loss, changes in social status, and life-cycle changes. This theory suggests that when people experience crises, they tend to follow predictable patterns of response. See also *crisis sequence* and *crisis intervention*.

critical incident stress debriefing (CISD) A form of *debriefing* designed to occur within 48 hours of a *disaster*. The professional interviewer encourages the survivors and relief workers to tell their stories, ventilate their emotions, and review their own coping skills. The interviewer offers support and information and determines if subsequent mutual support activity or therapy is indicated. CISD usually helps clients return to their precrisis lives and to work as soon as possible.

cross-dressing Wearing clothing that is considered more appropriate to members of the opposite sex. See also *transvestism* and *cisvestism*.

cross-gender behavior Recurrently acting in a manner that some might consider appropriate for members of the opposite sex. In children the behavior is commonly referred to as "tomboyishness" in girls and "effeminancy" in boys. This behavior in children is usually normal and healthy.

cross-racial treatment Intervention by a professional who is of a different racial background than the client. Social workers debate whether this can be as effective as interventions within racial and ethnic boundaries.

cross-sectional research 1. A research design whereby the researcher collects data on the phenomenon under investigation at one point in time, as in a one-time survey. 2. A comparison of subjects who represent different aspects of a single variable, such as "upper class," "middle class," and "lower class."

cross tabulation In research reporting, a depiction of two or more frequency tables arranged so that each cell represents combinations of categories on more than one variable. For example, in the simplest two-way table, outcomes of an experimental social work program could be illustrated. Experimental and control programs could be depicted in columns and positive or negative outcomes in rows generating the four cells.

cross tolerance The condition in which use of one drug leads to *tolerance* in the use of one or more other drugs.

crystallized intelligence The mental skills and abilities accumulated through *socialization,* cultural contact, and other acquired information, and the ability to use these skills appropriately and ef-

fectively. Unlike *fluid intelligence,* which is thought to decline in later adulthood, crystallized intelligence continues to increase with age as experience and exposure to new knowledge accumulates. See also *multiple intelligences.*

CSHCN patients Children with special health care needs, including those who have or are at risk of chronic physical, developmental, behavioral, or emotional conditions.

CSWE Curriculum Policy Statement See *curriculum policy statement.*

cue Any signal that seeks to communicate information, including words or vocalizations, facial expressions, posture, manner of attire, or gestures.

cult 1. A group in which members hold strong beliefs associated with the teachings of a leader. 2. A body of beliefs and rites practiced by a group that usually attributes religious, mystical, or magical powers to its leader. See also *new religious movements (NRMs).*

cultural bias A belief about the supposed superiority or inferiority of individuals, groups, or nations based on their cultural or ethnic affiliations.

cultural care The transmission of values and traditions, especially to people who have been isolated from the sociocultural group of their heritage. This can take the form of educational programs, returning to groups to participate in the traditions, or efforts by the group to reach out and reengage those who have become isolated.

cultural competence Possession of the knowledge, attitudes, understanding, self-awareness, and practice skills that enable a professional person to serve clients from diverse socioethnic backgrounds. In the *NASW Code of Ethics* (section 1.05), cultural competence and social diversity have three components: (a) that social workers should understand culture and its functions and the strengths that exist in all cultures, (b) that they should have knowledge about their clients' cultures and differences among cultural groups, and (c) that they should seek education and understanding about the nature of social diversity and oppression for all cultural groups.

cultural deprivation The absence of certain *socialization* experiences that an individual may need to cope effectively in new social situations. One who has been deprived in this way often lacks the social skills, values, or motivations necessary to deal with the relevant environment. See also *anomie.*

cultural diversity   The existence within a society of various racial, religious, and ethnic groups, as well as other distinct groups, each of which has different values and lifestyles. An appreciation of those variations, rather than efforts to facilitate assimilation, has been the goal of social workers in ethnic-sensitive practice. Cultural diversity is also known as "cultural pluralism."

cultural imperialism   The intentional or unintentional spread of influence by one culture over others, often through international media outlets, economic hegemony, people exchanges, and tourism. The United States is often accused of this through its entertainment and communications programs, which are so widespread and dominant that the cultures of other lands are becoming increasingly subordinate.

cultural lag   The retention of customs, habits, and technologies even though they have become obsolete or irrelevant to the new standards set by the prevailing culture.

cultural literacy   The accumulation of information and knowledge that members of a culture must have to be considered able to function effectively. The term also refers to one's knowledge about and use of the arts, philosophies, values, language, and history of a society.

cultural marginality   Belonging to two or more cultural groups while being fully accepted by neither. This often occurs with people from racially mixed or interfaith marriages or with individuals who immigrate.

cultural pluralism   The existence within a society of various racial, religious, ethnic, and other distinct social groups and the recognition of and accommodation for their different values and lifestyles.

cultural racism   The belief in the inherent inferiority of a particular cultural group's language, music, art, interests, lifestyles, and values.

cultural relativism   The view that specific norms or rituals can be understood accurately only in the context of a culture's goals, social history, and environmental demands.

culturally biased tests   Examinations designed to determine an individual's intelligence, aptitude, or anticipated success in a given endeavor but that are inherently disadvantageous to members of some groups. For example, a test item asks something about European history, a disadvantage to children from Asian backgrounds. An effect of such tests is to justify placement of culturally disadvantaged people into limited opportunity situations.

culturally disadvantaged   Individuals, families, groups, or communities who do not have full access to the society in which they live because of factors such as poor education, geographic isolation, discrimination, poverty, and political or ethnic conflicts.

culturally sensitive practice   In social work, the process of professional intervention while being knowledgeable, perceptive, empathic, and skillful about the unique as well as common characteristics of clients who possess racial, ethnic, religious, gender, age, sexual orientation, or socioeconomic differences. Theoretically, all professional social work practice is culturally sensitive practice. The term is synonymous with *ethnic-sensitive practice.*

culture   The customs, habits, skills, technology, arts, values, ideology, science, and religious and political behavior of a group of people in a specific time period.

culture-bound syndrome   A pattern of nonnormative (aberrant) behavior for which unique symptoms and progression tend to be specific to a particular geographic, ethnic, or cultural group. Examples include *ataque de nervios, mal de ojo, spells,* and *zar.*

culture-free test   An examination of one's knowledge that is written to avoid cultural influences; if it is properly prepared and administered, the participants' scores will not be affected by their socioeconomic backgrounds, ethnicity, gender, or other demographic characteristics.

culture of poverty   A premise according to which poor people are impoverished because their values, norms, and motivations prevent them from taking advantage of widespread opportunities to achieve economic independence.

culture shock   The experience of temporary confusion, depression, and anxiety when an individual enters another cultural or subculture group environment and is uncertain about the expected roles and norms. When these symptoms become chronic, the problems are called *disorders of change.* See also *anomie.*

culture war   The clash between different sociocultural groups when one group tries to impose its values, knowledge, and ways of doing things on another group, which responds in kind.

curandero   In the cultures of some Hispanic groups, a person without formal medical training who is consulted about cures for various physical, emotional, or spiritual problems.

curfew   A time deadline after which certain groups of people (such as children in some jurisdictions or racial groups in some countries) are not permitted to be outside designated areas.

Current Procedural Terminology (CPT) Codes
A system used by physicians and other health and mental health care providers to quantify the procedures and resource allocations needed to meet patients' specific health care needs. The *CPT Codes* were first published in 1966 as a way insurance companies would know how much physicians should be reimbursed for each service performed. The original *CPT Codes* also included a *Procedural Terminology for Psychiatrists Code* for treatment of various mental illnesses. In 2002 the *CPT* was expanded to include *CPT Health and Behavior Assessment Codes,* which can be used by clinical social workers and other nonphysician providers in billing insurance companies.

curriculum   The defined program of study in an educational institution. In schools of social work, the curriculum includes a prescribed number and variety of required and elective courses, field placement, and other educational experiences.

curriculum development   The process of planning, designing, validating, and implementing an educational program.

curriculum policy statement   A document that formally and officially describes the educational objectives, standards, and required outcomes of education programs. Beginning in 1932, curriculum policy statements in social work have been produced at approximately 10-year intervals, first by the *American Association of Schools of Social Work (AASSW)* and, after 1952, by the *Council on Social Work Education (CSWE).* The current document delineates the official criteria for accrediting master's and baccalaureate social work programs. The statement does not prescribe any particular curriculum but does specify certain content areas to be covered and how they are to be related to each other; the purpose and values of social work; and the mission, resources, and educational content of each professional program. See also *Hollis–Taylor Report.*

custodial care   The provision of shelter, food, and basic physical needs without amenities. Social workers also use this term to refer to assistance that does not require specialized medical training—that is, help with *activities of daily living (ADL).* Most health care insurance programs, including *Medicare,* do not cover these services.

custodial parent   A mother or father who, after divorce, is granted by legal authority the responsibility for care and control of minors. This parent is considered by the court to be the most likely one to promote the child's best interests. See also *joint custody* and *Mothers Without Custody.*

custody   A legal right and obligation of a person or group to possess, control, protect, or maintain guardianship over some designated property or over another person who is unable to function autonomously (for example, children and certain adults with disabilities). See also *guardian.*

custody of children   A legal determination in divorce cases specifying which parent or other *guardian* will be in charge of the children. This determination is based on what is considered to be in the best interests of the children. In some circumstances, *joint custody* is awarded so that responsibility is shared between both parents. See also *custodial parent.*

customary charge   The amount of money that is to be paid for each professional service, based on the amount that most others in the area with the same qualifications require for the same services. Insurance companies usually look at the customary charge that prevails in a community to determine how much they will reimburse. The term used by *Medicare* is "customary, prevailing, and reasonable."

Customs and Border Protection, Bureau of (BCBP)   An organization within the *U.S. Department of Homeland Security,* formed in 2003 primarily to monitor the movement of goods and people into the United States. The Bureau includes the Border Patrol, the Customs Service (including canine enforcement), and Agricultural Quarantine Inspection.

cutback   Reduction in service, funding, budget, or allocation of resources usually related to a decline in demand, cessation or reduction of former sources of revenue, inaccessibility of personnel, or discontinued support.

cutback strategies   The planned activities for reducing or eliminating programs, which are necessitated by financial constraints, new priorities, ineffectiveness of programs, or achievement of goals. These activities include instituting administrative and labor efficiencies (through increased workloads, reduced support services, contracting out services, and hiring lower paid workers), reducing services (by eliminating programs and reducing the *accessibility of service*), and *cost sharing* and mergers with other organizations.

cybercounseling   The use of technology, including audio and video conferencing, e-mail feedback, two-way television systems, telephone and Internet communication, and other tools to provide information, support, focus, and direction to students, professionals, distance learners, and other clients. See also *Internet therapy.*

cybercrime   The use of the Internet to commit illegal activities. The most prevalent illegal uses on online services include fraud, identity theft, child exploitation and pornography, illegal intrusion (hackers), trafficking in illegal goods, and intellectual property crimes (copyright infringement, plagiarism, software piracy, movie and recording piracy, and trademark counterfeiting).

cybernetics   The study of the processes that regulate or control systems, especially the flow of information. See also *communication theory.*

cyberterrorism   The intentional attack and destruction of computer/Internet information systems and the data contained therein by introducing viruses, reprogramming critical systems, flooding or overloading networks, and physically destroying computer hardware. Cyberterrorism may be accomplished by malicious individual hackers or by terrorist groups or nations intent on weakening their enemies.

cycle of abuse   The perpetuation of abusive behavior patterns that occur when an individual who has been abused acts similarly toward others. Studies confirm that people who commit *child abuse, spouse abuse,* or *elder abuse* are far more likely to have been abused themselves. The cycle is likely to continue in the succeeding generation when the abused children of such parents become parents and spouses themselves.

cycle of poverty   The condition of *poverty* that exists within one family from one generation to the next. Because the children of impoverished parents are more likely to be deprived of quality education, healthy lifestyles, vocational opportunities, self-esteem, financial backing to pursue opportunities, and nurturing family support, they are more likely to remain poor and to raise their own children to be poor.

cyclical unemployment   Loss of jobs caused by periodic downward trends in the business cycle. Usually this type of *unemployment* affects more workers for longer periods than the other types of unemployment (*frictional unemployment, seasonal unemployment,* and *structural unemployment*).

cyclothymia   See *cyclothymic disorder.*

cyclothymic disorder   A chronic fluctuating mood disturbance that has lasted more than two years (one year in children or adolescents) and includes numerous depressive symptoms and *hypomanic episodes.* The condition is similar to *bipolar disorder* except that the symptoms are not as severe (that is, no major depressive, manic, or mixed episodes). The symptoms are not due to physiological or medical problems but cause clinically significant distress or *impaired social functioning.* This disorder was formerly called "cyclothymia."

cystic fibrosis   A hereditary disease of the endocrine glands that leads to obstructions in the pancreas, liver, and lungs. Symptoms most often include nutritional deficiency, diarrhea-distended abdomen, and respiratory infections. The Cystic Fibrosis Foundation provides information and access to resources and sponsors research. Their Web site address is http://www.cff.org

D

D&C Dilation and curettage, a procedure in which the woman's cervix is widened and the lining of the uterus (endometrium) is scraped. This is often done after miscarriage, to treat disorders or potential disorders of the uterus, or to effect an early-stage abortion.

dance therapy The therapeutic intervention process of using stylized and controlled movement with music. This form of treatment often accompanies more verbally and cognitively oriented therapies to help clients express themselves, give vent to emotions, and acquire or maintain physical capacities and self-control. Organizations such as the American Dance Therapy Association (founded in 1966) facilitate professional development with this form of treatment. See also *music therapy* and *movement therapy*.

database A large pool of organized information available to users of computer systems and the Internet. Because each user seeks only portions of the data, the computer program extracts only that data sought. For example, a social agency might request from the NASW online system information about all the articles published on the topic of AIDS in the past three years.

database management system A computer software program used to obtain access to specific information found in the *database*. The management system organizes the data in the database so that it becomes most useful and accessible to its users, unifies data files, eliminates redundancies and useless information, and permits multiple users simultaneously.

date rape Coerced sexual intercourse by someone with whom the victim has a social relationship. The coercion may be through physical violence, power, or threats, but more commonly occurs through manipulation, seduction, and nonconsensual enticement. Sometimes the perpetrator spikes drinks using sedative-type drugs, including Rohypnol (called "roofies" or "rope" by users) and GHB ("liquid ecstasy") to cause compliance, blackout, amnesia, or confusion.

Davis, Katherine Bement (1860–1935) A penologist and prison reform leader who began her social work career by operating a settlement house in Philadelphia. After earning her PhD in political economy from the University of Chicago, she became superintendent of a women's prison and a pioneer in the progressive treatment of prisoners. Later, as New York state commissioner of corrections, she led many additional prison reform initiatives. She was a prolific writer of texts on corrections and various social causes.

Dawes Act The 1887 U.S. federal legislation, also known as the Indian General Allotment Act, that replaced the Indian system of communal land tenure by allocating 160 acres each to individual Indians who conformed to U.S. practices. The ultimate effect was that most of the nation's tribal lands passed out of Indian hands.

day care Facilities and programs that care for children or other dependents when their parents or guardians are unavailable for their care. The term also applies to physical and health care programs for people of all ages who return to their homes each evening. These facilities include *adult day care, day hospitals,* medical day care, mental health day care, and social adult day care.

day hospitals Facilities primarily for older people and people with disabilities who sleep in their own homes but receive medical and social services in hospital-like settings during the day.

Day, Dorothy (1897–1980) Founder of the *Catholic Worker Movement* and social activist, especially for immigrants to the United States and unemployed people of color.

Deaf, Hard of Hearing, and Hearing Social Workers (DHHHSW) The professional association for social workers who have hearing problems and for those interested in the problems of clients with hearing disorders. Established in 1979, the group took its present name in 1999. Their Web site address is http://www.gallaudet.edu/prof/dhhhswweb.nsf

de facto In actual fact, regardless of legal or normative standards. For example, de facto *segregation* occurs when a neighborhood is underrepresented by people of color even though it has no legal provision to exclude them. See also *de jure.*

de jure According to law or by statute. For example, de jure *segregation* refers to the legally enforced separation of groups of people (by race, gender, age, and so on). See also *de facto.*

de Paul, Vincent (1581–1660) Catholic priest and advocate for the poor people of France, he established seminaries and poor relief organizations, including the Daughters of Charity, to provide relief and assistance to needy people. He was canonized in 1737. See also *Ozanum, Antoine Frederic,* and *deMarillac, Louise.*

death The total and permanent cessation of vital functions; currently, in humans, the determining factor is the absence of measurable brain waves.

death control Actions taken by a nation, society, or organization to decrease the *death rate,* usually through programs in hygiene, nutrition, safety, disease prevention, environmental initiatives, and avoidance of war.

death rate The ratio of the number of deaths in a specific period to the total population or to an identified segment of that population; it is usually expressed in terms of the number of deaths per 1,000 or 100,000 people. It is also known as *mortality rate.*

"death tax" Inheritance tax; the tax that an estate must pay the government before any bequeaths to heirs. Government tax laws usually include exemptions so that taxes are collected only if the value of the estate exceeds a certain amount. If current laws are not revoked in the United States, the amount exempted from taxes will increase. Currently, after 2006 no taxes will be owed on estates worth less than $2 million, and after 2010 all inheritance taxes will be abolished.

death wish A person's behavior or thought patterns that become self-destructive, physically harmful, and oriented toward one's own death. According to some psychoanalytic theories, every individual has a certain degree of unconscious desire to die that may be consciously manifested in *masochism,* masochistic tendencies, or *self-defeating personality disorder.*

death with dignity End-of-life measures in keeping with a person's wishes (that is, a do-not-resuscitate order, or *DNR order*) that his or her life not be prolonged under artificially invasive or expensive circumstances but that maintain procedures of pain management, *palliative care, hospice,* and the patient's right to refuse medical treatment when faced with inevitable death. It also includes concern for the subsequent well-being of loved ones through estate planning, grief management, and funeral and memorial arrangements. Death with dignity proponents and some patients' rights groups also advocate the possibilities, under very specific circumstances, of the withdrawal of life support systems, *euthanasia,* and *physician-assisted suicide.* See also *Patient Self-Determination Act* and *advance directive.*

debt bondage A condition of involuntary servitude in which one pledges work or other personal services as a security for some debt obligation. Typically the nature of the service is not well defined nor limited and the debtor has little or no chance to clear the obligation through the service. Debt bondage has become a primary form of slavery in the world as well as the major method for trafficking in persons for sexual labor. See also *Trafficking Victims Protection Act.*

Debt for Nature Swap The practice of removing a debt obligation by a developing nation in exchange for conserving some of the nation's dwindling environmental resources, such as rain forests. Typically, some private environmental or conservation groups negotiate with banks to pay off or forgive the debt if the nation agrees to turn the threatened land or other resource into a nature preserve.

decathexis The mental process of reducing and eliminating emotional energy and feelings an individual has held for another person, idea, object, or oneself. Thus, a client might decathect from a social worker as part of the *termination* process. See also *cathexis* and *anticathexis.*

decenter Getting clients to focus their attention on aspects of their situation other than the one of most immediate concern. See also *centration.*

decentralization Diffusion of responsibility, planning, and implementation of change from the highest levels of an organization's authority toward those closer to the problem or area of action. An example is the federal government's *revenue sharing* with states and municipalities.

decertification The process of removing the title and commensurate responsibility and privileges from an identified individual or group because they have not complied with predetermined qualifications or criteria or because they no longer want the designation.

decile In presenting statistical data, any one of nine scores or points that divide a distribution into 10 equal parts, each consisting of 10 percent of all the cases. See also *quartile* and *percentile.*

decision support systems (DSS) In management and administration, the use of computer systems to gather and categorize data and to help administrators decide from among specified choices. The computer program uses a predefined set of facts in conjunction with decision rules to recommend optimal choices. The administrator can then concur with or reject the recommendation.

decision theory A mathematical approach to decision making using devices such as *gaming, modeling,* and simulation.

decision tree A procedure used in organizational management to systematically arrive at decisions. It is used by giving yes or no answers to a series of sequenced questions; a "yes" answer leads to one series of questions, and a "no" answer leads to a different series of questions.

declassification A personnel policy used by public and private employers, often as a means of reducing personnel expenditures, to eliminate educational and experience requirements for holding a job and performing its functions. For example, some professional social work positions were declassified when agencies no longer required that specific jobs had to be done only by social workers with MSW degrees.

decoding In *communication theory,* the process of translating verbal and nonverbal cues, body gestures, and other signals into messages that are comprehensible to the recipient.

decompensation The progressive loss of normal mental functioning, *defense mechanisms,* or coherent thought processes, often culminating in a form of *psychosis.*

deconstructionism A method of analysis in which the underlying assumptions and perceptions of phenomena are taken apart and reexamined,

especially as to each component and its relation to all other relevant components. Objective meanings are not assumed, only subjective interpretations. The analysis often considers the values and special interests that exist within the way a phenomenon is described and reveals possible contradictions and limiting dimensions of language.

decriminalization The repeal or adoption of legislation, the result of which is that an action formerly considered to be a crime is no longer so regarded and legal punishments can no longer be imposed.

decruitment Removal of older employers, usually middle to top managers, into lower-level jobs at lower pay. Some organizations refer to this as "bumping."

deductible A provision in health and other insurance coverage in which a beneficiary is required to contribute a specified sum for each claim in a given period before the insurer pays the remaining amount of the claim. See also *coinsurance.*

deductive reasoning The process by which particular conclusions are reached by starting with general principles believed or shown to be true. For example, a social worker believes that all rape victims subsequently suffer some degree of emotional distress. The social worker sees a client who was raped and deduces that she is experiencing some distress even without her saying so. See also *inductive reasoning.*

defamation Untrue or misleading statements made with malicious intent about another person that results in injury to reputation. See also *slander* and *libel.*

default Failure to comply with any legally enforced contract, agreement, lawsuit, or promise.

default judgment In the judicial system, a decision made against a defendant who fails to appear for a court hearing after due notice has been given and the statutory delays have elapsed.

defense levels Related groups of *defense mechanisms* and coping styles that may indicate the degree to which one is adapting to stressors. Individuals functioning at optimal adaptive levels use coping styles such as anticipation, affiliation, altruism, humor, self-assertion, self-observation, sublimation, and suppression. At lower levels the client relies more on disavowal (denial, projection, rationalization). The poorest level of defensive functioning is defensive dysregulation.

defense mechanism A mental process that protects the personality from anxiety, feelings of guilt, or unacceptable thoughts. Psychoanalytic theories consider such mechanisms to be *unconscious*. Some of the best-known defense mechanisms include *denial, displacement, idealization, substitution, compensation, overcompensation, conversion, sublimation, reaction formation, projection, rationalization,* and *intellectualization.*

Defense of Marriage Act (DOMA) Federal law enacted in 1996 (P.L. 104-199) that declares "marriage is between one man and one woman" to ban federal recognition of *same-sex marriage.* Often referred to as the "anti-gay law," DOMA also allows states to determine what is considered marriage under their own state statutes.

defensive dysregulation The poorest level of defensive functioning and a coping style in which the individual cannot deal with stressors, which leads to psychosis or other breaks with objective reality.

defensiveness 1. Excessive sensitivity to actual or potential criticism or disapproval. 2. Behavior that attempts to avert criticism or embarrassment.

deferred giving program A plan to encourage donations at some specified later time. Often donors are encouraged to make such bequests in their wills.

defibrillation Application of a mild and controlled electric shock to the chest, or directly to the exposed heart, to start the heart beating or to normalize its rhythms.

defibrillator An electronic device that determines the presence of irregular heart rhythms and sends electric shock to restore normal heartbeat action. Used commonly as a life-saving tool against sudden cardiac arrest, the devices are now located in many ambulances, air-evacuation helicopters and planes, and settings where large crowds gather. With proper training in their use, they are also being made available for purchase by places such as schools, offices, and even individual homes. See also *pacemaker.*

deficit The excess of expenditures and liabilities over income and assets during a budgetary period.

deficit spending The government economic action of spending more than it receives in taxes and other revenues. When this happens, the government must print new money, which leads to inflation, or borrow the difference, which further increases the national debt. To balance the budget would require raising taxes to pay for the desired expenditures or reducing the level of spending commensurate with revenues.

deflation A reduction in the *cost of living* and general price levels of an economy.

DeForest, Robert Weeks (1848–1931) Philanthropist and social reformer who helped develop the nation's first school of social work, the New York School of Philanthropy (now Columbia University School of Social Work), as well as the *Russell Sage Foundation* and many of the early programs for improving the conditions of poor people.

deforestation Permanent clearing of woodlands to make room for settlements, shifting cultivation, or permanent farmlands. Deforestation does not include selective logging. Ultimately the environmental consequences may be serious, leading to desertification, soil erosion, air pollution, and the removal of habitat for endangered species.

defrauding Criminally depriving a person of his or her rightful property through deception or misrepresentation.

dehiring Encouraging a marginal or unqualified employee to resign as an alternative to being fired.

deindividuation The subordination or loss of one's unique and distinctive values, personality, and lifestyle to adopt the behaviors and values of one's group.

deinstitutionalization The process of releasing patients, inmates, or people who are dependent for their physical and mental care from residential care facilities, presumably with the understanding that they no longer need such care or can receive it through community-based services.

delay of gratification An ability to postpone receiving pleasure or reward. This is an important factor in maturity and in accomplishments that take time to achieve, such as academic degrees or success in helping multiproblem families. Lack of ability to delay gratification is seen in young children, narcissistic adults, immature people, and some people with chronic mental disorders.

Delegate Assembly, NASW   The government body of the *National Association of Social Workers (NASW),* composed of 300 delegates elected by the membership to meet every three years and determine the association's basic positions on social and professional policy issues. Each NASW chapter is authorized to send its president, executive director, and at least one other member. The number of remaining delegates is determined by the number of voting members in each chapter.

delinquency   1. The failure to fulfill one's duties or obligations. 2. The actions of youngsters who violate laws or fail to conform to the reasonable demands of caregivers and other authorities.

delinquent   1. In the criminal justice system, an offender who is considered to be a minor (in most states, younger than age 18; in some, up to age 22) by the jurisdiction of residence or where the offense is committed. Some acts, which are not crimes for adults, are forbidden by law for children (such as curfew violations, drinking alcohol, smoking, and truancy). 2. A debt that has not been paid when due or an agreement that has not been fulfilled.

delirium   A state of confusion, often accompanied by *hallucination, delusion, emotional lability,* and *anxiety.* It is usually the result of changes in cerebral metabolism typically induced by alcohol or drug intoxication, shock or fever, general medical conditions, or multiple etiologies. See also *substance intoxication delirium* and *withdrawal delirium.*

delirium tremens (DTs)   A form of *delirium* resulting from withdrawal from excessive consumption of alcohol. The victim often develops symptoms such as fever, convulsions, tremor, and hallucination, generally occurring between one and four days after the drinking has stopped. The preferred professional term is *withdrawal delirium.*

Delphi method   A procedure, especially in social planning and community organization, that uses a highly structured, multistage questionnaire with a group of experts or panelists so that they can make focused assessments about the desirability, value, and feasibility of a proposed plan or policy, including feedback about results.

delusion   An inaccurate but strongly held belief retained despite objective evidence to the contrary and despite cultural norms that do not support such beliefs. It is often a characteristic of *psychosis* or *paranoid ideation.* Major types include *delusions of grandeur* and *delusions of persecution.*

delusional disorder   A mental disorder characterized by the existence of certain nonbizarre delusions (those involving situations that occur in life such as being followed, being deceived by a spouse or lover, or having a disease). The delusions persist more than one month and, apart from the impact of the delusions, psychosocial functioning is not severely impaired. Specific subtypes of delusional disorder include *erotomanic type, grandiose type, jealous type, persecutory type, somatic type,* and mixed delusions. This disorder was once known as "delusional (paranoid) disorder" and *paranoid disorder.*

delusional (paranoid) disorder   See *delusional disorder.*

delusions of grandeur   An exaggerated sense of self-importance. This may be symptomatic of *psychosis, narcissistic personality disorder, paranoid ideation,* or *overcompensation* for excessive *inadequacy feelings.*

delusions of persecution   The inaccurate but strongly held and persistent belief that one is being threatened or harmed by others. It is often a symptom of *psychosis, delusional disorder, paranoid ideation,* or excessive *inadequacy feelings.*

demagogue   One who uses oratorical skills to appeal to the audience's fears, hatred, greed, or paranoia. See also *charismatic leader.*

demand subsidy   The concept of providing *cash vouchers* or *tax incentives* so that consumers can purchase needed services or products through the existing marketplace. The *Food Stamp program* and *Medicaid* use this principle, which is in contrast to the concept of *supply subsidy.*

deMarillac, Louise (1591–1660)   Cofounder, with St. Vincent de Paul, of the Daughters of Charity to care for foundlings, slaves, and poor and elderly people. She also established training centers for poor women. In 1934 she was canonized by the Roman Catholic Church and named the church's patron saint of social workers.

dementia Deterioration of the mental processes, usually characterized by memory loss, personality change, and impaired judgment and ability to think abstractly or systematically. Dementia may be caused by physiological changes, the result of *stroke, Alzheimer's disease, substance abuse,* medical conditions, or multiple etiologies. Some of the medical conditions related to dementia include *head injury, HIV disease, Parkinson's disease, Huntington's disease, Pick's disease,* and *Creutzfeld–Jakob disease.*

dementia of the Alzheimer's type See *Alzheimer's disease.*

democratic socialism *Socialism* in a nation in which citizens have freely elected to have that form of political and socioeconomic system.

demogrant A benefit provided to those in specified population categories (for example, children, mothers, older people, or citizens) without regard to need. See also *income distribution, maternity benefits,* and *Medicare.*

demographics A depiction of the frequencies with which specified social characteristics occur within a designated population. These characteristics may include factors such as gender, race, ethnic group, educational level, socioeconomic class, and religious affiliation.

demography The systematic study of population variables and characteristics. See also *psychographics.*

demonstration 1. In social change efforts, a group action designed to call public or political attention to a problem or issue of interest to the participants. This typically takes the form of massing or marching together in highly visible settings or picketing the entrances of buildings where the behavior that the demonstrators find objectionable is believed to be taking place. 2. In direct practice, behaviors intended to show how something can be done effectively, such as when a social worker shows a client how to communicate better with others by *role playing.*

demonstration programs Service delivery programs that are usually limited by time and geographic range but are designed to test whether measures proposed for solving specific problems are desirable and effective. When these programs use rigorous controlled research, they are also known as experimental programs. In theory, programs that are demonstrated as effective can then be made permanent and expanded for a larger population.

demonstrative Behavior that is outwardly expressive of emotions and to people who exhibit such behavior.

demosclerosis A government's decreasing ability to adapt or respond to social conditions or the needs of its people. Its causes include public opposition to increased taxation, distrust of government, indifference by political leaders, disagreement about goals, bureaucratic entrenchment and unresponsiveness, and the power and effort of interest groups and their political action committees to prevent change.

dendrites The branched fibers of the *neuron* cell that carry impulses from other nerve cells into the cell body.

dengue fever (DF) A serious and often fatal infectious disease caused by viruses carried by mosquitoes in warm, humid climates. Symptoms include severe headaches, fever, shock, and hemorrhage.

denial The *defense mechanism* that protects the personality from anxiety or guilt by disavowing or ignoring unacceptable thoughts, emotions, or wishes.

deontology The philosophy of moral duty and obligation. The term is particularly associated with the view that certain kinds of actions are intrinsically right or wrong.

Department of Agriculture, U.S. (USDA) The federal agency created in 1862 to administer the nation's farm programs, meat and dairy inspection, and food production and distribution; to conserve farmland and related resources; and to provide education and information to farmers. This department also administers many food assistance programs, including the *Food Stamp program,* the *School Lunch program,* and the *WIC program.* Their Web site address is http://www.usda.gov

Department of Education, U.S. See *Education, U.S. Department of.*

Department of Health and Human Services, U.S. (HHS) See *Health and Human Services, U.S. Department of.*

Department of Health, Education and Welfare, U.S. (HEW) See *Health, Education and Welfare, U.S. Department of.*

Department of Homeland Security, U.S. (DHS) See *Homeland Security, U.S. Department of.*

Department of Housing and Urban Development, U.S. (HUD) See *Housing and Urban Development, U.S. Department of.*

Department of Justice, U.S. See *Justice, U.S. Department of.*

Department of Labor, U.S. See *Labor, U.S. Department of.*

Department of Social Services (DSS) The name used by many states and municipalities for their agencies that provide human services, public assistance, and other welfare services. See also *Human Resources Administration (HRA).*

Department of the Interior, U.S. See *Interior, U.S. Department of the.*

dependency A state of reliance on other people or things for existence or support; a tendency to rely on others to provide nurturance; to make decisions; and to provide protection, security, and shelter. When reliance becomes excessive, it is a symptom of *neurosis, regression,* or emotional *insecurity.*

dependent personality disorder One of the 11 *personality disorders,* in which the individual is generally passive in most relationships, allows others to assume responsibilities, lacks self-confidence, feels helpless, and tends to tolerate abusiveness from others. See also *passive–dependent.*

dependent variable In systematic research, the phenomenon or reaction to be tested or measured when a new stimulus, condition, or treatment is introduced. The factor that is introduced is the *independent variable.*

depersonalization A feeling of being in an unreal situation or a sense that one's self or body is detached from the immediate environment. This experience is often found in individuals who are subjected to inordinate stress or are in crisis, as well as individuals with specific mental disorders such as *neurosis* and *psychosis.*

depersonalization disorder A type of *dissociative disorder* in which the individual copes with internal conflict and anxiety through psychological detachment or by experiencing the feeling of being in an unreal situation. *Depersonalization* and *derealization* are the major symptoms, and some individuals also concurrently experience *depression* and *hypochondriasis.*

depopulation The rapid decline in the numbers of people in a society, within one or a few generations, sometimes leading to extinction. The phenomenon is brought about by cataclysmic changes in the environment, war, genocide, economic downturns, and disease.

deportation Eviction of persons from their country of residence usually to their country of nationality. In the United States, deportation refers to legal procedures to remove a noncitizen from the United States, usually for violating immigration laws (such as entry by misrepresentation or violating terms of nonimmigrant classification or status). This legal process begins by issuing the individual an order to show cause why the deportation should not occur.

deposition Legal testimony of a witness under oath taken outside a courtroom.

deprecated character Feelings of powerlessness and low self-esteem that an individual acquires by growing up in an environment that lacks nurturing, denies legal and civil rights, and maintains inconsistency between what the dominant culture says and what it does. Applied to some African Americans, the term was coined by Leon Chestang. The majority of people who encounter this environment are able to rise above the effects of the deprecated character. See *transcendent character.*

depressants A group of drugs that induce in their users a state of deep relaxation, apathy, lethargy, and emotional depression by inhibiting the responses and actions of the *central nervous system (CNS).* The drugs most common within this class are *barbiturates* and *tranquilizers.* See also *"downers."*

depression An emotional reaction frequently characterized by sadness, discouragement, despair, pessimism about the future, reduced activity and productivity, sleep disturbance or excessive fatigue, and feelings of inadequacy, self-effacement, and hopelessness. In some individuals, such traits may be mild, intermittent, and undetectable by observers, but in others they may be constant and intense. In its more severe forms, pathology may be a manifestation of a *major affective disorder, bipolar disorder,* or *cyclothymic disorder.* See also *exogenous depression* and *endogenous depression.*

depression, economic   A socioeconomic condition in which business activity is reduced for a prolonged time, unemployment rates are high, and purchasing power is greatly diminished. See also *stagflation* and *recession.*

depressive neurosis   See *dysthymic disorder.*

depressive reaction   A term indicating sadness, pessimism, and lowered activity often precipitated by an actual or perceived severe loss. The term is now replaced by *bipolar disorder, major depression, dysthymic disorder,* or *cyclothymic disorder,* depending on other symptoms.

deprivation   A state of unfulfilled, unmet, or incompletely met physical, social, or emotional needs.

deprogramming   An intense and systematic form of *direct influence* and *counseling* that focuses on changing a client's deeply held beliefs about something that is considered troublesome and harmful. These interventions are often conducted by social workers, clergy, and other experts and have been initiated most commonly by family members in behalf of people who belong to cults, hate groups, and associations with antisocial orientations.

derailment   A speech pattern in which the individual repeatedly changes the subject and moves from topic to topic, even within the same sentence.

derealization   A *dissociative symptom* in which one experiences the external world as strange or unreal. The individual may see others as being unfamiliar or robotlike and perceive alterations in the size or shape of viewed objects. Derealization is often a symptom of *panic attack* and *depersonalization disorder.*

deregulation   The reduction or cessation of government control over the operations of various industrial, governmental, professional, or other organizations. The policy of deregulation in the 1980s led to significant changes in the airline industry, railroads and trucking, and financial institutions.

derelict   1. A person who is experiencing homelessness and unemployment. 2. Property, such as a car, that has been abandoned by its owner.

derepression   Therapy designed to bring back to conscious awareness the thoughts and feelings that the client had unconsciously pushed to the unconsciousness. Much of psychoanalysis may be said to engage primarily in this activity. See also *psychodynamic.*

derivative citizenship   Citizenship conveyed to children through the naturalization of parents or, under certain circumstances, to foreign-born children adopted by parents of that country.

derived score   In social research, a *raw score* that has been statistically manipulated.

desaparecido   A Spanish term for "disappeared," the name given to people who are secretly arrested and detained by representatives of a repressive government. Many of these people have never returned and are presumed dead.

descriptive study   A research effort in which subjects or situations are observed and reported on without seeking to determine cause-and-effect relationships. The purpose is to accurately determine what the situation is. Descriptive studies, which include case studies, opinion and attitude surveys, polls, written records, and critical incident reports, may be quantitative or qualitative reports. These studies are usually contrasted with *experimental studies* or *quasi-experimental studies.*

desegregation   The act of abolishing *segregation,* whether *de facto* or *de jure,* that has been imposed on certain minority groups.

desensitization   The elimination or minimization of physical or psychological reactions to stimuli. Behaviorally oriented social workers use a form of this, known as *systematic desensitization,* especially to help some clients overcome certain fears or ineffective behavior patterns.

desertion   1. The act of abandoning a person or position to whom or to which one has certain obligations. 2. In marriage, desertion occurs when one spouse leaves the other without the other's consent and has no intention of returning. Desertion may or may not be accompanied by *nonsupport*. Desertion is usually grounds for divorce.

***DeShaney* decision**   The 1988 U.S. Supreme Court ruling (*DeShaney v. Winnebago County Department of Social Services*) that the social workers and their social agency could not be held liable for damages for failure to protect a child who had been abused by the father. The ruling does not, however, mean that social workers employed in *child protective services (CPS)* are free from the risk of lawsuits at the state court level; moreover, they may still be at risk at the federal level.

designer drugs   Compounds that differ slightly from the chemical structures of illegal drugs, usually made by "street chemists." Until recently, these drugs were technically legal but still had all the properties of their illegal counterparts. Now they are illegal.

destitution   A state of poverty in which one lacks sufficient resources even for food or shelter.

detention   The act of restraining a person, usually in an institution (a jail or other holding facility), for some legal purpose. This term usually implies a short-term holding while awaiting trial. See also *incarceration*.

determinism   The philosophy that all behaviors, social problems, and patterns of thought have preceding causes.

deterrence   A policy that uses fear of restraint and punishment to attempt to discourage a behavior considered undesirable. For example, prison sentences and the death penalty are imposed to deter crime; massive retaliation powers exist supposedly to deter wars or terrorist attacks.

"detox center"   Informal term for a health care facility specializing in *detoxification*. Such centers are licensed or certified by the state to treat patients with alcohol or drug dependence problems.

detoxification   The process of removing drugs or other harmful substances from the body for a sufficient length of time to restore adequate physiological and psychological functioning. This is achieved by withholding the substance from the individual while providing rest, proper diet, health care, medication, psychological support, and social services.

Deutscher Verein für Öffentliche und Private Fürsorge   The German Association for Public and Private Relief, an organization to represent the nation's public social welfare agencies and major welfare associations. Established in the 1850s as the Deutscher Verein für Armenpflege und Wohltätigkeit (German Association for Poor Relief and Charity), the organization provided a forum for discussion, study, and welfare planning. In the 1850s the Deutscher Verein surveyed the nation to determine needs and the way relief to poor people, and its *Elberfeld system,* was working. Many of its plans and recommendations were incorporated into Germany's national social insurance laws of the 1890s. It assumed its current name after the end of World War I.

devaluation   1. Attributing exaggerated negative qualities to one's self or others, usually as a way to deal with emotional conflict, stressors, or inadequacy feelings. See also *idealization* and *halo effect*. 2. In economics, the lowering of the worth of some commodity, such as currency, bonds, or tangible goods.

developing countries   Nations with low per capita incomes and relatively small financial reserves that have worked to develop their natural resources, develop numbers of skilled and educated citizens, and aspire to economic and political parity with developed countries. Often called *Third World* countries, this category includes India, Egypt, Nigeria, and Indonesia; not usually included are *underdeveloped countries* such as Bangladesh, Ethiopia, and Chad. See also *Fourth World*.

developmental approach   In direct practice, an orientation toward or focus on the predictable changes that occur throughout the human life cycle, including physical, mental, social, and environmental changes.

developmental arithmetic disorder   The inability to acquire arithmetic skills that is not a result of poor education and socialization or intelligence deficits. The preferred term for this is *mathematics disorder*.

developmental coordination disorder   Inhibited motor skills development so that the child or adult seems poorly coordinated, clumsy, and awkward; the child falls behind peers in his or her ability to tie shoelaces, play ball, or write. This disorder is not due to physical disability or mental retardation. The preferred term for this is *motor skills disorder.*

developmental disabilities A condition that produces functional impairment as a result of disease, genetic disorder, or impaired growth pattern manifested before adulthood, likely to continue indefinitely, and requiring specific and lifelong or extended care. Some of the conditions classified as developmental disabilities include *cerebral palsy, Down syndrome, epilepsy, mental retardation,* and *autism.*

Developmental Disabilities, Administration on An agency within the *U.S. Department of Health and Human Services (HHS)* that provides information and coordinates expertise about the causes, prevention, and treatment of human *developmental disorders* such as *mental retardation, autism, seizure disorders,* and *cerebral palsy.* Their Web site address is http://www.acd.dhhs.gov/programs/add

developmental disorder A classification of physical and mental dysfunctions that appear before the individual reaches maturity. *Pervasive developmental disorders* include *autistic disorder, Rett's disorder, childhood disintegrative disorder,* and *Asperger's disorder.*

developmental research Analysis, design, development, and evaluation of human services innovations. Developmental research in social work studies assessment methods, intervention methods, service programs and systems, policy analysis and development, and the physical and infrastructure aspects of providing for human services needs.

developmental social welfare An approach to social welfare that encourages and plans for indigenous and culturally appropriate models of social services delivery, according to the unique demands and resources of the *Third World.*

developmental stages The progression of physical and mental changes occurring over time and that result in clusters of identifiable and predictable characteristics tending to occur during specific periods.

deviance The act of differing sharply from normal behavior or maintaining standards of conduct, norms, and values that are in marked contrast to

accepted standards. The term was formerly used to indicate sexual perversion. See also *maladaptive* and *maladjustment.*

Devine, Edward T. (1867–1948) A contributor to *social work education* who helped found the New York School of Philanthropy in 1898 and guided it toward its development as the Columbia University School of Social Work. He also founded the leading social work journal of the time, *The Survey,* and wrote several texts about the history of social work and social welfare, including *Misery and its Causes* (1909), *Social Work* (1928), and *When Social Work Was Young* (1939).

devitalized relationship A pattern in some marriages and domestic partnerships in which both parties are bored with and apathetic toward one another.

devolution The process of moving social programs from administration by federal agencies to state agencies and from states to localities. See also *home rule.*

dhat A *culture-bound syndrome,* found most commonly in India, in which the individual experiences anxiety and fear of bodily dysfunctions because of the discharge of semen or the discoloration of urine. See also *shenkui.*

DHHS See *Health and Human Services, U.S. Department of.*

diabetes A disease, caused by a disorder in the islet of Langerhans in the pancreas, in which an insufficient amount of insulin is produced or secreted so that the body cannot process sugars properly.

diabetes mellitus A serious, chronic deficiency in the body's ability to produce insulin, resulting in excessive sugar in the blood and urine.

diagnosis The process of identifying a problem (social and mental, as well as medical) and its underlying causes and formulating a solution. In early social work delineations, it was one of the three major processes, along with social study and treatment. Currently, many social workers prefer to call this process *assessment* because of the medical connotation that often accompanies the term "diagnosis." Other social workers think of diagnosis as the process of seeking underlying causes and assessment as having more to do with the analysis of relevant information.

diagnosis of convenience   A term used by some providers of mental health services to refer to an inaccurate description of the condition of the client on an insurance form. This is sometimes done by providers because most insurance companies will reimburse only for diagnosable conditions. For example, the professional provides marital therapy, which is not usually reimbursable, but indicates depression as the diagnosis of convenience. This is a fraudulent as well as unethical practice, and it is also detrimental to the therapeutic relationship because it fosters an improper collusion between the provider and client.

diagnosis-related groups (DRGs)   The name applied to a federally mandated prospective payment mechanism designed to control the costs of medical and hospital care for *Medicare* recipients. Payments made to the hospitals caring for Medicare patients are determined in advance, based on which one of 467 discrete categories of disorder—or DRG—the patient has at the time of admission, as well as on the patient's age; whether surgery is necessary; and in some cases, the presence of complications. Each category, with relevant additional factors, is equated with a flat sum. If costs for care exceed the predetermined amount, the hospital is expected to bear the excess; if they are lower than the predetermined amount, however, the hospital may keep the difference. This is supposed to encourage shorter hospital stays, a less-extensive mix of services during hospitalization, and the diminished likelihood of rehospitalization.

Diagnostic and Statistical Manual   See *DSM.*

diagnostic school in social work   The name given to the orientation in social work that emphasized *psychodynamic* and *social change* theories and *insight therapies.* The term was first used to distinguish this group of social workers from colleagues who were identified with the *functional school in social work.*

diagnostic test   An *interview schedule, standardized test,* or other tool designed to identify the existence, nature, or origin of the subject's disorder.

dialysis   Treatment for kidney disease. The various types of dialysis include *hemodialysis, perito-*

neal dialysis, and chronic ambulatory peritoneal dialysis.

diaspora   The dispersal or migration of a people and their descendents from their original location to various sites throughout the world. The people resettle from their homelands because of economic, political, military, or environmental circumstances and become minorities within their new communities. The term is often associated with the dispersion of the Jewish people after their exile in 528 B.C.E.

diathesis   Genetic predisposition toward certain diseases. For example, the *dopamine hypothesis* suggests that certain people are "diathetic" toward *schizophrenia.*

diathesis–stress theory   See *stress–diathesis theory.*

dichos   Proverbs or folk sayings commonly used in Spanish-speaking cultures. Dichos are usually brief and spoken spontaneously, often in rhymes, and are used as guidelines in the development of attitudes, moral values, and social behavior (an English equivalent is "haste makes waste").

Dictionary of Occupational Titles   See *O*NET.*

didactic analysis   *Psychoanalysis* for which the primary goal is instruction rather than therapy; otherwise, the procedure is identical with all other forms of psychoanalysis.

didactic teaching   The traditional teacher-centered educational process characterized by lectures, demonstrations, questioning of students, and directed study. See also *discovery learning.*

differential acculturation   The varying degrees and speed by which different people adapt to new cultures (that is, to language, lifestyle, and norms). The rate of acculturation is influenced by age and developmental stage, education level, prior experience or knowledge of the new culture, level of sophistication and self-esteem, and degree of available emotional support and nurturance.

differential diagnosis   The process of distinguishing between similar mental disorders or social problems on the basis of their compared and unique characteristics.

differential life expectancy   The probable life span of people based on distinct classifications such as gender, socioeconomic class, race, and current age. Life expectancy is influenced by the degree to which people have access to economic benefits.

differential response   In *behaviorism* and *social learning theory,* a response that is elicited by a particular *stimulus* among many possible different stimuli. For example, a child may learn to smile when a parent smiles and frown when the parent frowns.

differential validation   In *social research,* the finding that different classes of subjects may achieve different scores or results on the same test. For example, elementary school girls may score higher on verbal tests than boys.

differentiation   In *family systems theories,* the ability of family members to distinguish or separate their identities, thoughts, and emotions from those of other family members. See also *fusion.*

differentiation phase   The fourth of five *group development phases* in which group members develop a greater sense of their own unique problems and ability to solve them within themselves and among the other group members. See *intimacy phase, power-and-control phase, preaffiliation phase,* and *separation phase.*

diffusion of innovation   The transfer of ideas, technology, and more efficient practices from their originators to the masses.

diminished capacity   A condition of mental, emotional, or physical disorder that prevents a defendant in a criminal case from fully comprehending the nature of the criminal act. The person is not considered psychotic, or insane in the legal sense, but unable to have premeditated the crime. Usually the claim of diminished capacity is to get a reduced sentence if convicted.

dioxin   A chemical compound often used as a herbicide. These toxic substances are long lasting and often a *carcinogen.* See also *Agent Orange.*

diphtheria   A contagious disease transmitted by exhaled moisture from infected individuals, mostly preschool children. The bacteria that cause the disease lodge in the mucous membranes of the throat, producing tissue-destroying toxins. Diphtheria

deaths are caused by tissue damage, particularly in the heart. Inoculations routinely given to infants have minimized its incidence rate.

Diplomate in Clinical Social Work (DCSW)   A professional credential in social work that signifies the highest level of professional certification. The applicant for the NASW-sponsored Diplomate must present documentation for the following: a master's degree from a CSWE-accredited social work school; two years (3,000 hours) of postgraduate clinical experience in an agency or organized setting, supervised by an experienced clinical social worker; three years of advanced clinical practice (in addition to the two years of supervised practice), with at least two years of practice in the past 10 years; a completed colleague reference form; possession of the highest level of certification or licensing available in the relevant state; proof of passing an advanced or clinical examination that requires a PhD or DSW and a minimum of two years of experience and that demonstrates a body of knowledge that qualifies him or her to practice social work independently; and successful completion of the NASW Diplomate Clinical Assessment Examination. The Diplomate also agrees to practice according to the *NASW Code of Ethics, NASW Standards for the Practice of Clinical Social Work,* and the *NASW Standards for Continuing Professional Education.* A Board Certified Diplomate in Clinical Social Work credential is also issued by the *American Board of Examiners in Clinical Social Work.*

dipsomania   An abnormal or insatiable desire to drink alcohol. This has become a rarely used term.

DipSW   Diploma in Social Work, the credential used in the United Kingdom for social workers who meet the standards maintained by the *General Social Care Council.* The DipSW credential was established in 1989 to replace the *Certificate of Qualification in Social Work (CQSW)* credential. Those with DipSW credentials may practice social work at one of three levels: the nongraduate, the undergraduate, and the graduate levels. Graduate level social workers may earn advanced credentials, including the PQSW (Post-Qualifying Social Worker) award or the AASW (Advanced Award in Social Work).

direct cost   The amount paid by a recipient of any goods or services—a sum that may only partially cover the expense of producing them. See also *indirect cost.*

direct deposit   The system of wiring funds to one's bank account rather than sending checks through the mail. Direct deposit is widely used to dispense Social Security funds, welfare payments, payroll checks, and insurance reimbursement.

direct influence   A social work intervention in which the worker attempts to promote a specific type of behavior in the client. It is done systematically and cautiously, often by offering suggestions and advice about how best to reach the client's own goals.

direct-mail campaigns   A marketing technique designed to raise funds or educate people by mailing materials (usually including return address envelopes for checks) to specific target audiences. The key part of the campaign is obtaining or creating lists of organizations and individuals considered most likely to respond.

direct practice   The term used by social workers to indicate their range of professional activities on behalf of clients in which goals are reached through personal contact and immediate influence with those seeking social services. It is to be distinguished from *indirect practice*.

direct practice skills   The ability to put social work knowledge into effective intervention activities with individuals, families, groups, and communities. The skills are inner (perception and cognition), interactional (setting the stage, dealing with feelings and information), and strategic (dealing with behavior and coping with conflict). Additional skills for working with groups include building groups, facilitating the work of groups, working with groups that do not verbalize readily, and providing nontalking times with groups. See also *social work skills*.

direct treatment   A group of intervention procedures used in social casework or clinical social work in which the social worker seeks to implement specific changes or improvement through personal contact with the client. The term was used by *Mary E. Richmond* (1861–1928) to designate a social worker's face-to-face interactions with individual clients, as distinguished from *indirect treatment* or problem solving and from developmental work in the environment.

directive therapy   A clinical procedure in which the professional offers advice, suggestions, information about resources, and prescriptions for more effective behavior.

disability   Temporary or permanent reduction in function; the inability to perform some activities that most others can perform, usually as a result of a physical or mental condition or infirmity. See also *International Classification of Impairment, Disability, and Handicapped (ICIDH); impairment;* and *handicap*.

disability-adjusted life years (DALYs)   A measure used by demographers and health statisticians to allow comparison of the burden of many different diseases, including death. The number of people with the disability are enumerated and multiplied by the number of years it affected them. DALYs measure lost years of healthy life whether lost to premature death or disability.

disability benefit   The provision of cash, goods, or services to one who is not capable of performing certain activities because of a physical or mental condition; a form of *categorical assistance* based on incapacity. In the United States, the *Disability Insurance (DI)* program for people who are disabled and the *Supplemental Security Income (SSI)* program for people who are needy and disabled are currently the most extensive examples of this type of program. See also *temporary disability insurance*.

Disability Determination Service (DDS)   A program within the *Social Security Administration (SSA)* for applicants for disability or *Supplemental Security Income (SSI)*. When a claim is about to be denied, the applicant can request reconsideration by means of a face-to-face meeting with a DDS examiner.

Disability Insurance (DI)   The *Social Security Administration (SSA)* program to provide for the economic needs of those who can no longer earn an income because of chronic incapacity. Eligibility is limited to people who have contributed to the social security system and their dependents. To receive benefits clients must no longer be able to do the work for which they were trained and experienced, nor can they hold other suitable kinds of employment. The disability must be expected to last for at least a year or to result in death. People who are disabled and needy but have not contributed to the work-based social security programs seek benefits in the *Supplemental Security Income (SSI)* program.

121

disability rights laws U.S. federal civil rights laws enacted since the 1960s to protect people with disabilities. The most important of these include the Architectural Barriers Act of 1968 (P.L. 90-480) to make publicly funded buildings accessible; the Rehabilitation Act of 1973 (P.L. 93-112) to prohibit discrimination by federally funded employers; the *Education for All Handicapped Children Act of 1975* (P.L. 94-142) to require equal access to all public school education; the 1986 and 1990 amendments to this act (P.L. 99-457 and P.L. 101-476, respectively) to mandate a free, appropriate public education for all individuals (ages three to 21) with disabilities; the Air Carrier Access Act of 1986 (P.L. 99-435) to prohibit airlines from discriminating against people with disabilities; the *Americans with Disabilities Act of 1990* (P.L. 101-336) to prohibit most other kinds of discrimination on the basis of disability; and the 1990 *Individuals with Disabilities Education Act (IDEA)* (P.L. 101-476) to rename, consolidate, and advance the Education for All Handicapped Children laws and amendments.

disability rights movement Organized efforts to change laws and cultural norms that preclude the equal opportunities of persons with disabilities. These efforts are conducted primarily by various organizations, lobbyists, professional associations including NASW, and people with disabilities and their families who have worked together at least since the 1960s to change laws and educate the public about the social obligation to people with disabilities. The movement has fought to make the environment and institutional resources more accessible to all and has taught that people with disabilities are disadvantaged as much by discrimination as by their limitations and has sought to reverse this trend. The movement was instrumental in achieving passage of the *Americans with Disabilities Act (ADA) of 1990* and other *disability rights laws.*

"disabled" A term used to describe an individual whose specific physical or mental condition or infirmity limits his or her ability to carry out certain responsibilities. The condition may be temporary or permanent; it may be partial or total. In the United States, the *Social Security Administration (SSA)* considers a person disabled if he or she is unable to do any kind of appropriate work because of a disability that is expected to last for at least one year.

"disadvantaged" A term used to describe an individual who is deprived of needed material resources, mental capacities, emotional and social development, or opportunities to acquire them.

disallowance Denial of payment for all or part of an amount claimed by a beneficiary.

disarmament The intentional decisions and actions that bring about a reduction in or elimination of the weapons possessed by a nation or group. Many social workers have been active in the peace movement, in which nations are encouraged to lay down their arms or discontinue supplying arms to others. See also *peace dividend.*

disassociation See *dissociation.*

disaster An extraordinary event, either natural or human-made, concentrated in time and space, that often results in damage to property and harm to human life or health and that is disruptive of the ability of some social institutions to continue fulfilling their essential functions. See also *major disaster.*

disaster relief Efforts and activities to provide immediate refuge and security from the continuing physical and emotional risks encountered in a *disaster* and also work toward restoring the social and physical structures that had existed to meet essential needs. See also *emergency basic needs services.*

Disaster Relief and Emergency Assistance Act U.S. legislation (P.L. 93-288, amended by P.L. 100-707) to give assistance to those regions that the U.S. President officially declares as *major disaster* areas. Formally known as the Robert T. Stafford Disaster Relief and Emergency Assistance Act, the law provides federal funding, personnel, expertise, and other services to the states and localities involved, as well as provisions for crisis counseling programs for victims.

disaster relief planner One who predicts the probabilities, consequences, and locations of a potential *disaster;* organizes people and structures to provide *disaster relief;* and educates the populace about how to respond to and minimize a disaster's consequences. Many communities have offices of emergency management in which this function is performed. The U.S. *Federal Emergency Management Agency (FEMA)* fulfills some of these functions nationally. See also *emergency basic needs services.*

disaster syndrome   The psychological and social relationship problems typically experienced by victims of a crisis or calamity. Social workers who specialize in *disaster relief* identify several phases of the syndrome: preimpact (apprehension and anxiety accompanying the threat or warning), impact (the hazard strikes, and the community organizes its relief effort), postimpact (often characterized as a "honeymoon" phase of high energy for coping and mutual cooperation), and disillusionment (when people encounter the long-term obstacles brought about by the disaster).

disautonomia   Disorder of the *autonomic nervous system (ANS).*

discharge planning   A social service in hospitals and other institutions that is designed to help patients or clients make timely and healthy adjustments from care within the facility to alternative sources of care or to self-care when the need for service has passed. When practiced by skilled social workers, discharge planning helps clients and relevant others understand the nature of the problem and its impact, facilitates their adaptations to their new roles, and helps arrange for postdischarge care. See also *channeling* and *premature termination.*

Disciplinary Action Reporting System (DARS)   A national database service of the *Association of Social Work Boards (ASWB)* to prevent a social worker who has been sanctioned in one licensing jurisdiction to withhold that information from another licensing jurisdiction. Information about the disciplined social worker is reported electronically to ASWB by all its jurisdictions. Aggregate information on all disciplined licensees is then shared electronically with all licensing boards.

discouraged worker   People who want to work but are no longer actively seeking employment because they believe the effort would be futile. A nation's unemployment rate usually does not take this group into account. See also *marginally attached worker.*

discovery learning   An educational method in which the student's existing knowledge is used as a basis on which to discover new ideas and information, using techniques such as problem-solving

activities, trial-and-error systems, and small-group processes. See also *didactic teaching.*

discretionary funds   The money available after purchase of necessities; also referred to as "disposable income." In budgeting, the term also refers to funds allocated outside rigid *categorical grants.* The use of these funds is generally determined by those empowered to choose how to spend them.

discrimination   1. The prejudgment and negative treatment of people based on identifiable characteristics such as race, gender, religion, or ethnicity. 2. In general terms, also the process of distinguishing between two objects, ideas, situations, or stimuli.

disease   A condition in which a system (including all or part of a living organism) is not functioning properly; a *disorder.*

disease patterns   In epidemiology, the incidence of a *disease* in a community and the frequency from one population group to another. Rates of disease are calculated by dividing the number of people who have the disease by the number at risk. See also *morbidity rate.*

disease risk factors   Phenomena in the environment or within the individual that are known to be associated with increased chances of developing a particular *disease.* A risk factor may or may not be the cause of the disease, but identifying it is important for prevention.

disenfranchisement   Eliminating or preventing an individual's opportunity to exercise some right, such as the right to vote; also a sense of having too little influence to effect any social change.

disengaged family   A family whose individual members and subsystems have overly rigid boundaries that result in restricted interaction and psychological isolation from one another. Some disengaged families may also have diffuse boundaries. See also *enmeshed family.*

disengagement theory   The view that some older people withdraw from society. In this perspective some older people are said to slow down and gradually become more self-preoccupied, to lessen emotional ties with others, to have less interest in world affairs, and to slowly detach from society. The theory also holds that society disengages from the older individual. The resulting mutual disengagement results in a decrease in life satisfaction. This theory is controversial because so many older people maintain active and involved lives and show no decrease in life satisfaction.

disfigurement   The malformation, distortion, blemish, or other condition of a person's face or body. These include scars, birthmarks, cleft palate and cleft lip, and cranial and skeletal abnormalities.

disincentive   A factor that discourages an individual or group from doing something. For example, reducing social security payments when people earn more discourages them from finding jobs. See also *cliff effect.*

disorder   A *disease* or ailment; a condition in which a system (including all or part of a living organism) is not functioning properly.

disorder of written expression   A type of *learning disorder* in which a student is below the norm in writing skills and the understanding of numbers concepts as that expected of others of similar ages, intellectual levels, and educational levels without physical and neurological problems. For the condition to be diagnosable, it must significantly interfere with the student's academic achievement or activities that require writing. Many educators call this disorder *dysgraphia* or *agraphia.* The other major types of learning disorder are *reading disorder* and *mathematics disorder.*

disorderly conduct   The crime of violating the public peace or safety. Often those charged with this crime are homeless people, those intoxicated in public places, social activists or agitators, and labor picketers.

disorders of change   Psychosocial problems an individual develops as a consequence of having to adapt to unfamiliar social environments or developmental experiences. These disorders may be permanent but generally are overcome in healthy people with good *coping skills.* See also *culture shock.*

disorganized schizophrenia   Technically known as "schizophrenia, disorganized type" (formerly known as *hebephrenic schizophrenia*), this disease is distinguished from other forms of *schizophrenia* by symptoms such as wild excitement, giggling, silly behavior, and rapid mood shifts.

disparate impact   The negative effect that would be imposed on some individuals or groups but not others when a new policy, law, or procedure is instituted. For example, if an employer announced that only people above a certain height would be eligible for promotions, it could negatively affect women more than men. The practice is unlawful, according to Title VII of the *Civil Rights Act of 1964,* unless the employer shows that it is a business necessity. Federal agencies determine the existence of disparate impact when any racial, ethnic, or gender group is selected less than 80 percent of the rate for the highest selected group. See also *four-fifths rule.*

displaced homemaker   A person who becomes widowed or divorced after spending years as a family's caregiver and who usually has not developed other marketable skills to facilitate economic independence.

displaced populations   Groups of people who are uprooted from their established locations and lifestyles, including *refugees, immigrants, undocumented aliens, migrant laborers,* and *seasonal workers.* These groups tend to adapt to their new locations in one of four general ways: (1) assimilation (giving up one's former culture and its values to acquire those of the host society), (2) integration (maintaining a significant part of the cultural identity of the past while participating in the larger society), (3) separation (establishing a separate set of institutions or interactions), or (4) marginalization (loss of cultural identity resulting in confusion, alienation, and striking out against the larger society).

displaced worker   Adults who have lost their jobs when their work site or company closed or moved, or their position was terminated because there was no longer economic need for their services. Corporate downsizing and plant closings are the major factors in worker displacement.

displacement   A *defense mechanism* used to reduce anxiety that accompanies certain thoughts, feelings, or wishes by transferring them to another thought, feeling, or wish that is more acceptable or tolerable.

disposable income   Money available to spend after one has paid all necessary taxes and other fixed expenses.

disposition The arrangement made on behalf of a client or patient by the provider of health care or a social service to conclude the intervention. This may include referral to a more appropriate resource, follow-up care, or successful achievement of goals so that help is no longer needed. In many types of case record, professionals conclude entries by writing "Disposition" (or "Disp."), followed by the course of action recommended for the ongoing care of the client.

disproportionate share hospital (DSH) Medical care facilities that serve a higher than average number of low-income or elderly patients. When the facility is designated as a DSH, state and federal funds may be obtained to help keep the facility solvent.

disregards Federal and state welfare policies of not counting some proportion of earned income so that working poor people do not lose certain welfare benefits.

disruptive behavior disorder A group of *developmental disorders* in which the individual's behavior persistently interferes with the social activities of those nearby. The specific types of disruptive behavior disorder include *attention-deficit hyperactivity disorder (ADHD), oppositional defiant disorder,* and *conduct disorder.*

disruptive tactics Actions that interfere with the normal operations of social institutions to bring about changes in laws, norms, or social structures. These activities are undertaken and coordinated, especially by social activists and community organizers, to call public attention to problems and injustices and to put pressure for change on an organization. Examples include *sitdown strikes, sit-ins* in the offices of corporate executives, picket lines on roads leading to nuclear reactors, organized heckling of political candidates during their speeches, and *greenlining.*

dissident An individual who disagrees with the policy of a government or other organization and refuses to participate therein.

dissociation A *defense mechanism* in which the individual has thoughts or feelings that are inappropriate to the current situation. For example, a client attending a funeral has thoughts about being at a party and begins to laugh. The mechanism is also known as "disassociation."

dissociative amnesia A *dissociative disorder* characterized by an inability to remember important (usually stressful or traumatic) personal information. The condition is not the result of *general medical conditions, substance abuse,* or *age-related cognitive decline.* Several types of memory disturbance include localized amnesia (inability to remember anything occurring during a specific time), selective amnesia (inability to remember parts of an experience within a specific time), continuous amnesia (inability to recall personal experiences after a certain point in one's life), and generalized amnesia (inability to recall any personal life experience). This term replaces *psychogenic amnesia.*

dissociative disorder A type of *mental disorder* characterized by a sudden, temporary change in the normal functions of consciousness, identity, and memory. Specific forms of the disorder include *dissociative amnesia* (which may be selective or generalized, continuous or intermittent), *dissociative fugue, dissociative identity disorder,* and *depersonalization disorder.*

dissociative fugue A *dissociative disorder* characterized by an individual's sudden travel away from familiar places, inability to recall past events, and sometimes the assumption of a new identity. The condition is not the result of *general medical conditions, substance abuse, age-related cognitive decline,* or *malingering.* This term replaces *psychogenic fugue.*

dissociative identity disorder (DID) Formerly known as *multiple personality disorder,* a form of *dissociative disorder* in which an individual has two or more distinct personalities. The individual may not be aware of the existence of these other personalities; alternative identities are experienced as taking control, supplanting the previous identity, or being in conflict with one another. The change in identity usually happens within seconds but in some cases occurs more gradually. The number of identities ranges from two to 100, with women averaging 15 and men averaging eight. Laypersons sometimes incorrectly call this condition "schizophrenia" (which is a very different disorder).

dissociative symptoms Psychophysiological reactions to stress by voluntarily or involuntarily changing one's functions and focus of consciousness, memory, identity, or perception of the environment. These symptoms include numbing, detachment, absence of emotional responsiveness, reduced awareness of one's surroundings, *derealization, depersonalization, amnesia, fugue, identity disorders, poor concentration,* and *preoccupation.*

dissociative trance disorder Involuntary entry into an apparent state of trance or possession in a way that is outside one's sociocultural or religious norms and that causes distress and *impaired social functioning.*

dissonance Behavior that is inconsistent with one's attitude about that behavior.

dissonance theory of groups The view that some discomfort and tension among group therapy members are important motivators and catalysts for growth. Those who hold this view seek a state of imbalance or *heterogeneous group* membership.

distance learning Education provided for students at remote locations, predominantly through telephones and mail, interactive video, satellite-delivered training, e-mail and the Internet, and occasional travel.

distracter role A recurrent pattern of communication in relating to others, especially family members, characterized by being evasive, diverting attention, bringing in irrelevant statements, changing the subject, and moving in such a way that the focus of attention is changed. The role was delineated by *Virginia Satir,* who described the distracter as a person who fears the threat of close relationships and obstructs them through these diversionary tactics. Other roles are the *blamer role,* the *computer role,* and the *placater role.*

distribution In research, the frequency with which a given variable or demographic factor appears in an identified category, geographic area, map, or graph.

distributive justice See *economic justice.*

disulfiram A drug used since 1949 in the treatment of alcohol dependence (trade name is Antabuse) that causes intense nausea when alcohol is consumed. Newer drugs such as naltrexone and acamprosate (which prevent the highs associated with drinking) are now considered more effective, especially when used in conjunction with verbal and supportive psychotherapies and 12-step programs.

diversity Variety, or the opposite of homogeneity. In social organizations the term usually refers to the range of personnel who more accurately represent minority populations and people from varied backgrounds, cultures, ethnicities, and viewpoints. Environmentalists use the term to indicate a variety of plant and animal forms in an area rather than a system in which only one or few species exist.

Diversity Immigrant Visa Program The U.S. Department of State's program to grant immigrant visas to nationals of underrepresented countries. The program is informally known as the "lottery visa"; when the number of applicants from underrepresented nations exceeds the number of openings, a lottery is used.

diversion from custody In the legal justice system of Great Britain an alternative to incarceration, usually for juvenile offenders. Rather than sending some offenders to prison or residential care, this system provides a variety of opportunities for offenders to pay their debts to society through restitution, residence with trained officers, movement to different environments, controlled community service programs, and the like.

diverticulitis Inflammation of small outpouchings along the wall of the colon (the large intestine). The outpouchings (diverticula) develop in most older people over time as the walls of the colon weaken and increased pressure along these walls occurs, often because of constipation.

division of labor The assignment of specified types of work to be accomplished by occupants of specified statuses or categories of people. Occupations are differentiated most commonly by gender, age, educational level, type of training, credentials, and family background.

divorce The legal dissolution of a marriage. Each state establishes its own laws determining the criteria (grounds) for dissolution. Adultery, incompatibility, and living apart for specified periods are the grounds most commonly accepted. Many marriages are also dissolved through *no-fault divorce.*

divorce mediation See *mediation, divorce.*

divorce organizations Voluntary groups composed primarily of divorced people and their children to advocate for more equitable divorce laws, economic protections for divorced spouses, child support, visitation, and custody issues and to provide mutual help and emotional support. Such organizations include the American Divorce Association for Men (ADAM), Fathers for Equal Rights, Joint Custody Association, North American Conference of Separated and Divorced Catholics, and the Children's Rights Council.

divorce therapy   A type of clinical intervention designed to help couples who have decided to dissolve their unions. Divorce therapy includes helping the couple consider alternatives to divorce, minimize adjustment problems, consider the needs and best interests of any children, review fair property dissolution, and discuss rationally how to disengage in the healthiest way possible. This therapy also deals with practical and legal aspects of the dissolution, such as custody of children and property decisions; it also helps people learn to manage relationships with their former spouses and to adjust to new lifestyles.

Dix, Dorothea (1802–1887)   Social activist and advocate for the humane treatment of prisoners and especially for people with mental illness. Her lobbying activities led to the establishment of many public and private mental hospitals.

DNA   Deoxyribonucleic acid, a complex molecule found in living cells. Its components are arranged in particular sequences, the pattern of which determines the genetic information carried by the chromosomes.

DNR order   An official written statement by a patient, and sometimes loved ones and physicians, that indicates "do not resuscitate" in the event of specified medical emergencies and conditions. Such statements, after careful consideration and preparation, are usually placed in the patient's medical files and in places where hospital and emergency teams would see them. Nonhospital DNRs are usually signed physician's orders so that emergency medical personnel will be obliged to not provide life-prolonging treatment. See also *death with dignity* and *Patient Self-Determination Act.*

DO   Doctor of osteopathy, the name used by graduates of colleges of osteopathy. The DO, or *osteopath,* has training, leisure, and health care responsibilities that are equivalent to physicians with MD (medical doctor) degrees, but DOs are usually more oriented toward treatment that is natural and holistic.

doctoral programs   In social work education, the professional and academic training that culminates in the PhD or *DSW* degree. Doctoral education in social work has tended to emphasize development of the student's research and knowledge-building skills and advanced practice competence. The DSW and PhD degrees are equivalent and have virtually the same requirements. It was sometimes erroneously believed that DSWs would be for those seeking increased professional practice competence and PhDs for those more involved in research and the building of theory or the knowledge base. However, the differences are more related to the preferences of the particular degree-granting institution than to different requirements. See also *Group for the Advancement of Doctoral Education in Social Work (GADE).*

Doctors Without Borders   The international French-based NGO that sends physicians and other health care personnel to treat people, usually in regions of extreme poverty, famine, war, and social unrest. Members of the 1999 Nobel Peace Prize–winning group, known in French as "Medicins Sans Frontières," also engage in social activism to reveal the conditions, injustices, and developing crises they encounter.

"do-gooder"   A term of derision often applied to social workers and other people whose professions or consciences require them to do what is necessary to uphold the laws and ethics of a society and to protect disadvantaged people from exploitation by privileged people.

"dole"   A pejorative term once commonly applied to public assistance payments.

domestic partners   In some jurisdictions a legal designation for those who register as cohabitating unmarried adults who intend to maintain permanent relationships. The designation was established primarily for (but is not exclusively used by) gay and lesbian partners to provide them with the same legal supports and mutual obligations that exist for married couples (such as access to rent-controlled apartments, survivors' benefits, and family health insurance programs).

Domestic Peace Corps   See *AmeriCorps/VISTA.*

domestic relations court   A court of law that handles cases involving divorce, spouse abuse, child abuse, relatives' responsibility, and family disputes.

domestic violence   1. Abuse of children, older people, spouses, and others in the home, usually by other members of the family or other residents. 2. The social problem in which one's property, health, or life are endangered or harmed as a result of the intentional behavior of another family member.

domestic violence center   A facility to provide safety, security, emotional support, crisis intervention, social services, and/or temporary residential care for victims of domestic violence (including assault, battery, sexual assault, or other offenses resulting in physical injury) by a relationship partner.

domicile   A person's legal and permanent home, rather than residence (which may be temporary).

domiciliary care services   Programs usually conducted by local and state departments of human services designed to assist people to remain in their own homes even if they are having problems that preclude basic self-care. Such programs include *homemaker services,* home-delivered meals, *chore service, home health services, respite care,* and attendant care. This also is called *home care service.* Some human services agencies use "domiciliary care" to refer to programs that help needy people with the physical maintenance of their homes and "home care" to refer to homemaker services.

donation   A gift of money, property, or personal service, usually to a charitable organization. The value of the gift may be deducted from one's tax liability under certain circumstances. The individual who makes the gift is a "donor" and the recipient is a "donee."

donor constituency   The contributors of funds and resources to a social agency or other organization. These people and groups may exert an implicit or formal influence on the priorities, values, and programs of the organization.

"Don't ask, don't tell" policy   A strategy implemented by the *U.S. Department of Defense* in 1995 in which gay and lesbian military personnel would no longer be discharged solely because of their sexual orientation. The policy prevents military authorities from asking about the sexual preferences of all military personnel and mandates that personnel not disclose their sexual preferences gratuitously.

door knob communication   A client's disclosure of apparently significant information just as the time for the therapeutic interview is about to conclude. This may be an unconscious attempt to prolong the session or set up the worker for an accusation of indifference. On the other hand, according to Lawrence Shulman, who coined the term, these communications can be of great importance to the client who has been uncomfortable discussing the information earlier in the session; it also may be an offering that the client raised earlier in the session that was missed by the worker.

dopamine hypothesis   In research on the biochemistry of the *central nervous system (CNS),* the possibility that the excessive amount of dopamine (a neurotransmitting chemical) found in *schizophrenia* causes some of its symptoms. See also *catecholamines.*

double bind   1. In *communication theory,* a form of paradoxical communication in which one person expresses a message that can be interpreted in two or more contradictory or mutually exclusive ways, and the recipient of the message is prevented from escaping the consequences or commenting on the contradiction. 2. Competing demands to which a person must respond.

double blind   In research, a technique in which neither the subject nor the experimenter knows whether a real change was actually introduced. For example, in researching the effects of drugs, the experimenter and the subjects do not know whether inert drugs (*placebo*) or active drugs are being administered. This technique is also known as the "double-masked design."

double-entry bookkeeping   An accounting procedure used in most social agency budget records, in which every transaction is recorded twice and the resulting increase or decrease in one account is reflected by a decrease or increase in another account.

double jeopardy   Being subjected to prosecution and trial a second time for the same offense. Freedom from double jeopardy is guaranteed to people in the United States by the U.S. Constitution in its *Fifth Amendment rights.*

doubling In social group work and family group therapy, a technique in which a group member acts as an alter-ego or "inner voice" of the protagonist. The double is asked to speak in first person, saying "I think . . ." or "I feel . . . ," while the protagonist is speaking, to reveal or interpret information that the protagonist may otherwise conceal.

doubling up Temporary residence of families or individuals in the homes of others, even though the facility lacks sufficient space or accommodation. In the arrangement the guest stays only at the discretion of the leaseholder and otherwise would be homeless.

"downers" A slang term referring to *barbiturates, tranquilizers,* or other *depressants* of the *central nervous system (CNS)* often used by certain drug abusers to induce a state of deep relaxation. Some abusers become highly dependent on these substances, often leading to increased *tolerance.*

downgrading Reclassifying a job description so that the employee continues with the organization but usually with reduced pay and responsibilities. See also *recruitment* and *bumping.*

Down syndrome A congenital form of *mental retardation,* often characterized by a flattened face, widely spaced and slanted eyes, a smaller head, and lax joints. Genetically determined by the presence of an extra chromosome, the disorder was formerly known as "mongolism."

downsizing A reduction in workforce and program. In the mid- to late 1980s, social work management—like its counterpart in corporations—was faced with the need to manage declining resources. This reduction in staff and funding represents a dramatic change after nearly 50 years of uninterrupted growth in the human services.

downward mobility Socioeconomic declines by individuals, groups, or nations. In nations, this decline is due to poor economic conditions resulting in unemployment and underemployment, lower wages, inflation, diminution of natural resources, and political changes. In individuals, it is also common among *dropouts* and may be the result of health problems, poor planning, relocation, and other idiosyncratic factors. See also *upward mobility.*

dowry The assets and personal property that a bride presents to her husband upon marriage. The practice is rare in developed nations but much more common in Third World nations.

draconian Unduly harsh or punitive response. For example, the threat to eliminate all welfare payments to able-bodied recipients was called a draconian attempt to reduce taxes. The term comes from Draco, the Greek political leader of the 7th century B.C.E., who drafted harsh laws with heavy punishments.

dream analysis A technique used in *psychoanalysis* and some other forms of *psychotherapy* and *counseling* in which the analyst interprets the dream content of his or her clients. Many analysts, beginning in 1900 when Sigmund Freud (1856–1939) published *The Interpretation of Dreams,* believed that access to the *unconscious* was made possible by dream analysis. The people, situations, and context in the dreams are viewed as symbols for deeper, more underlying mental constructs. See also *psychoanalytic theory.*

dream anxiety disorder A *sleep disorder,* paraphilia type, characterized by repeated awakening from sleep with detailed recall of frightening dreams. Clinicians refer to this condition as *nightmare disorder.* See also *sleep terror disorder.*

Dred Scott decision The controversial 1857 ruling by the U.S. Supreme Court that a slave was considered property and not a U.S. citizen. Dred Scott was a slave who lived for a time with his master in a "free" state.

drive In *psychoanalytic theory,* a basic impulse or urge that motivates *overt behavior.*

drop house A building, usually near international borders, where illegal aliens are concealed by smugglers while awaiting transportation to safer locations.

dropout One who withdraws from and terminates continued participation in some social activity in which there is an implied or explicit responsibility to continue. Such activities include attending school until graduation, continuing in therapy until goals are reached, or contributing to society as a taxpaying citizen. See also *school leaver.*

drug abuse The inappropriate use of a chemical substance in ways that are detrimental to one's physical or mental well-being. See also *substance abuse.*

drug abuse detection Efforts, usually by those with certain types of authority over others (for example, parents and employers), to assess the possibility that illegal or *controlled substances* are being used. Such efforts include urine sampling, confinement to observe the presence of *withdrawal symptoms,* covert investigation, and many other activities. Experts suggest that the presence of several of the following indicators can be clues to *substance abuse* in youths: long- or short-term forgetfulness; aggressiveness and irritability; school tardiness, truancy, or declining grades; difficulty concentrating; reduced energy and self-discipline; uncaring or sullen behavior; constant disputes with family members; disappearance of money and valuables; unhealthy appearance, including bloodshot eyes; changes in and evasiveness about friendships; and trouble with the authorities.

drug addiction The abuse of chemical substances that results in a physiological dependence in which the body tissues require the substance to function comfortably. In the absence of the substance, the individual experiences *withdrawal symptoms.* See also *substance dependence.*

drug courts Courts of law in local jurisdictions to deal with the trials, sentencing, judicial supervision, court-ordered treatment, drug testing, and case management of drug offenders. The goal is to minimize drug crimes and offender problems by combining the coercive power of the criminal justice system with court-monitored incentives, sanctions, treatment, and rehabilitation in lieu of incarceration. The U.S. Department of Justice Drug Courts Program awards grants to jurisdictions to organize and improve drug courts.

drug czar Informal title for the executive officer appointed by the U.S. President to develop policy and educate the public about the nation's drug problems. The formal title is Director, Office of National Drug Control Policy.

drug dependence The misuse of and reliance on chemical substances, resulting in *drug addiction* or *drug habituation.*

Drug Enforcement Administration, U.S. (DEA) A unit of the *U.S. Department of Justice* charged with enforcing the regulations that apply to *controlled substances.* DEA is also responsible for overseeing and managing the legal production and use of *narcotics, amphetamines,* and *barbiturates*

handled by pharmacists, physicians, and hospitals. Their Web site address is http://www.usdoj.gov/dea

Drug-Free Workplace Act of 1988 The U.S. federal law that requires organizations receiving federal funds to keep drugs out of their workplaces; it requires organizations to publish and distribute information about drugs and treatment opportunities and prohibits their manufacture, purchase, sale, distribution, possession, or use.

drug-free zone An area designated by police, public officials, residents, or concerned citizens as being off limits for any drug use, sales, purchases, marketing, or recruiting of dealers.

drug habituation The pathological craving for or abuse of chemical substances that results in psychological rather than physical dependence. The abuser who is habituated experiences psychological discomfort that may or may not be as severe as in *withdrawal symptoms.*

drug interaction The changed beneficial or toxic effect of one drug when another drug is used at the same time. This dangerous situation can occur when patients see different doctors who do not coordinate their treatments, patients use over-the-counter drugs while taking prescription drugs, and patients are misinformed or ignorant about the consequences of drug interaction.

drug intoxication Maladaptive behavior and other symptoms specific to the particular psychoactive substance recently taken. These symptoms may include impaired judgment, belligerence, impaired social functioning, occupational problems, depression, euphoria, coma, and death.

drug of choice The specific type of drug or chemical that a substance abuser settles on and prefers to use over all the other drugs with which the individual has experimented.

drug paraphernalia Materials associated with the production, distribution, packaging, concealing, or use of substances of abuse, including hypodermic syringes, needles, spoons, bongs, scales, testing equipment, adulterants, separators, mixers, grow lights, chemicals, and small plastic bags.

drug testing The systematic procedure for determining an individual's abuse of *illicit drugs. Urinalysis* is the most common procedure used, although analyzing samples of hair, blood, and saliva can also reveal drug use. These tests can detect the use of *cocaine, PCP, amphetamines, barbiturates,* and *heroin* taken within the past two to seven days. *Marijuana* can be detected over longer periods, up to 21 days. Because the tests are often inaccurate, the standard procedure for most employers is to conduct a second test on those employees whose first tests are positive. The second test, using a more reliable procedure, is nearly always accurate. Drug testing is part of most drug treatment programs, designed to help motivate and strengthen the determination of the patient.

drug tolerance See *tolerance.*

drugs of abuse *Psychoactive substances* that typically are used to produce, in the user, some sense of immediate pleasure or gratification, followed by long-term deleterious consequences. Most of these drugs are illegal, and all of them lead to *habituation* and *withdrawal symptoms.* The illegal drugs of abuse include opioids (including *heroin), cocaine, amphetamines* or similarly acting sympathomimetics, phencyclidine hydrochloride *(PCP)* or similarly acting arylcyclohexylamines, *hallucinogens* such as *LSD,* and cannabis *(marijuana).* Other psychoactive substances that are not illegal but have led to widespread abuse include alcohol, sedatives, nicotine, caffeine, and gluelike substances that are inhaled. See also *opioid abuse.*

DSM The *Diagnostic and Statistical Manual* of the American Psychiatric Association, psychiatry's official classification of mental disorders and the symptoms and characteristics found in each. Published periodically about every 10 years, the *DSM-IV* was published in 1994 and revised, as the *DSM-IV-TR,* in 2000. The manual labels each disorder and provides a numerical code and systematic criteria for distinguishing it from other mental disorders. It calls for the subject to be evaluated on each of five levels or axes. Axis I disorders include clinical syndromes as well as certain conditions that are not caused by mental illness but are the focus of attention or treatment. Axis II disorders are the *personality disorders* and *mental retardation.* Axis III is used for the subject's relevant physical diseases and conditions. Axis IV is for the subject's psychosocial and environmental problems, and in Axis V the clinician uses a *Global Assessment of Functioning (GAF) Scale.* Definitions of mental disorders in this dictionary are consistent with those in the latest edition of the *DSM.*

DSW Doctor of social work (or doctor of social welfare), an advanced professional degree in *social work education.* The DSW degree requirements typically include several years of previous experience in social work practice, acquisition of required preliminary degrees such as the *MSW,* successful completion of prescribed doctoral-level course work in a qualified school of social work, the passing of written and oral comprehensive examinations, and successful completion and defense of a dissertation. Most DSW programs are affiliated with professional schools of social work that are part of accredited colleges and universities. See also *doctoral programs* and *Group for the Advancement of Doctoral Education in Social Work (GADE).*

dual diagnosis The identification of coexistent diseases within an individual. Often the disease or its treatment influences the other disease or its treatment, especially if not identified. The use of this term is most commonly associated with a problem with drugs or alcohol and another, usually psychiatric, disorder.

dual economy Coexistence within one economy of two different economic sectors. Typically these two sectors have different patterns of trade, technologies, credit systems, and levels of labor intensity. For example, there are urban–rural, rich–poor, and colonial–underdeveloped dualities. This term is also called "dualistic economy."

dual eligible The term used by the *Social Security Administration (SSA)* for people who are eligible for both *Medicaid* and *Medicare.* Many *Departments of Social Services (DSS)* also apply the term to people who meet the criteria to benefit from two or more assistance programs simultaneously.

dual relationships In clinical social work, the unethical practice of assuming a second role with the client, in addition to professional helper, such as friend, business associate, family member, or sex partner. Dual relationships tend to exploit clients or have long-term negative consequences for them. Workers who engage in these relationships are liable to legal as well as professional sanctions and probably should seek help. The *NASW Code of Ethics* has explicitly forbidden sexual relationships since the 1979 revisions; the explicit prohibition against other dual relationships was included in the 1994 code revisions. The prohibition against dual relationships has been in the *code of* *ethics* of the *Clinical Social Work Federation (CSWF)* since 1988.

DuBois, W.E.B. (1868–1963) African American scholar, sociologist, and activist who led the early civil rights movement, helped establish the NAACP, and helped establish schools of social work in various universities.

due process of law Adherence to all the rules, procedures, protections, and opportunities legally available when a person accused of a crime is brought to trial and risks possible deprivation of life, liberty, or property.

dull-normal A term sometimes used by educators and educational psychologists in describing an individual whose *intelligence quotient (IQ)* scores are between 70 and 90 or an individual with slightly limited intellectual capacity but not of such deficiency as to require extensive care and protection by others.

Dunham, Arthur (1893–1980) Social work educator who developed the profession's systematic conception of *community organization*. He wrote the influential texts *Community Welfare Organization* (1958) and *Community Organization in Action* (1959).

durable medical equipment (DME) Health care devices and equipment, such as hospital beds, wheelchairs, and prosthetics, that can be used at home. Medicaid and Medicare and private health insurance may reimburse for part of the expense of renting and purchasing such equipment.

durable power of attorney A legal document authorizing another person to take action and make decisions on one's behalf, within certain conditions and guidelines, even when one suffers from *incapacitation* or is *incompetent*. The one given power of attorney may make all decisions or be limited only to things such as selling one's house. Whereas an ordinary power of attorney becomes nullified if the signer becomes incapacitated or incompetent, durable power keeps it in effect in such circumstances. See also *living will*.

durable power of attorney for health care A legal document by which an individual appoints someone trusted to make decisions about the individual's medical care in case he or she should

be unable to make them. Also known as a "health care proxy" or "appointment of a health care agent," this document becomes effective when an individual is temporarily incapacitated or irreversibly ill. State-specific documents are available through the *Partnership for Caring* organization.

duration index A rating scale used in the *Person-in-Environment (PIE) System* to indicate how long or how recently the problem of the client has persisted. The scale ranges from two weeks or less to more than five years.

***Durham* rule** The 1954 court decision declaring that if a person's unlawful act was the product of mental disease or defect, then the accused is not criminally responsible. This is a modification of the *McNaughten rule*, but is not in effect in many jurisdictions.

duty-to-warn laws Legislation and court judgments obliging social workers and other professionals to disclose their clients' future intentions to do harm to a specific person or specified organization. Beginning with the *Tarasoff* ruling in 1976, various states have passed laws and courts have issued decrees defining the conditions under which these warnings should be made. Many of these rulings are said to be inconsistent from state to state and even within the same jurisdictions (see, for example, *Jaffee v. Redmond decision*). The laws have raised many ethical issues for social workers, especially concerning *confidentiality*.

dyad Two people or objects in a relationship or interacting system.

Dybwad, Rosemary (1910–1992) Founder of the international movement for the rights and care of people with intellectual limitations and the International League of Societies for Persons with Mental Retardation. She also developed the *International Directory of Mental Retardation Resources* and wrote numerous articles on caring for people with mental disabilities.

dynamic 1. In theories of human personality, an orientation that emphasizes intrapsychic influences, conscious and unconscious thought processes, and nonobservable mental phenomena such as *drive, conflict, motivation,* and *defense mechanisms.* 2. In field theory, the forces that act on a psychological field. 3. In *systems theories* and in *general systems theory,* the process of striving for and maintaining *homeostasis.*

dysarthria   Speech and articulation problems caused by disturbances of muscular control.

dyscalculia   A *learning disorder* in which the student demonstrates mathematics skills significantly below average. The term more commonly used by social workers is *mathematics disorder.*

dysentery   An intestinal disease the symptoms of which include inflammation, pain, and diarrhea. The disease is caused by bacteria or viruses and is most commonly transmitted by contact with water or food that has been contaminated by human waste.

dysfunction   A deficiency in a system that precludes its optimal performance; synonymous with "malfunction."

dysgeusia   Impaired sense of taste.

dysgraphia   A *communication disorder* involving the partial or total inability to write letters, words, or phrases by a person who once possessed such abilities. This condition is also known less commonly as *agraphia.* See also *disorder of written expression.*

dyskinesia   A dysfunction of the involuntary muscle activities resulting in tics, spasms, and stereotyped movements. See also *tardive dyskinesia (TD).*

dyslexia   An impairment of reading and writing skills, often with the tendency to reverse letters or words while reading or writing them or not noticing certain letters or words.

dyslogia   Difficulty in speaking or communicating ideas because of mental disorder or mental deficiency. This is not synonymous with developmental *expressive language disorder.*

dysmenorrhea   Pain or discomfort during or just before a menstrual period.

dysmnesia   Any impairment of memory.

dysmorphophobia   Excessive preoccupation and fear of appearing to be ugly or defective. This term is outdated and is replaced by the term *body dysmorphic disorder.*

dysnomia   Difficulty in remembering names or words needed for verbal or written communication.

dyspareunia   The experience of pain during the act of sexual intercourse, which occurs more commonly in women. See also *vaginismus.*

dysphagia   Impaired ability to swallow resulting from nonorganic causes such as anxiety-related spasms of the throat muscles.

dysphoria   A condition of general unhappiness, dissatisfaction, pessimism, restlessness, and pervasive discomfort.

dyspnea   Breathing difficulty.

dyspraxia   Inability to perform skilled or specific movements; impaired coordination.

dyssocial   A term pertaining to an individual who behaves according to the norms of the immediate peer group or subculture but contrary to the norms of the larger society, or to one who engages repeatedly in criminal and destructive activities. This term is now used by professionals to replace the term "sociopath."

dyssomnia   A primary *sleep disorder* of the amount, timing, and quality of sleep, including *insomnia, hypersomnia, narcolepsy, breathing-related sleep disorder (apnea),* and *circadian rhythm sleep disorder.*

dyssynchronous development   See *asynchronous development.*

dysthymia   A synonym for *dysthmic disorder.*

dysthymic disorder   A *mood disorder* characterized by sadness, pessimism, *dyssomnia,* poor appetite or overeating, irritability, fatigue, low self-esteem, and indecisiveness. These symptoms occur most of each day, most days, for at least two years. The symptoms may be less severe than in *major depressive disorder* but may exist almost continuously for years.

dystonia   Sustained abnormal postures or muscle spasms, symptomatic of mental disorders (such as *catatonic schizophrenia*), *neurological disorders,* or a *medication-induced movement disorder.*

E

Early and Periodic Screening, Diagnosis, and Treatment Program (EPSDT) A *Medicaid* program that requires all states to evaluate, treat, and ameliorate any physical or mental conditions found in eligible children under age 21. The state programs are also required to inform all eligible persons and their families of the benefits available to them and help them obtain appropriate treatment.

early childhood program A program serving children up to age eight.

Early Head Start The U.S. federal program administered by the *Head Start Bureau* within the *U.S. Department of Health and Human Services* to serve low-income pregnant women, infants, and toddlers from birth to age three. The objective is to provide a healthy foundation for young children so they can benefit from the Head Start program. Early Head Start awards grant funding to new or existing community-based social agencies and monitors their progress. Early Head Start uses professionals with preschool training and experience as well as volunteers and other staff.

earmarked taxes Funds received by a government body from citizens and corporations, the purpose for which has been designated in advance. For example, gasoline sales taxes are usually designated for highway maintenance and construction, and a *payroll tax* is often earmarked for unemployment compensation.

earned income The amount of money one receives from work in the form of wages, salaries, and net proceeds from self-employed businesses. All other sources of income (from interest, gains on capital investments, rent, dividends, and inherited money) are *unearned income*. Social security revenues come from earned income collected from employees, their employers, and people who are self-employed.

Earned Income Tax Credit (EITC) A U.S. government *work-oriented antipoverty program* for qualified low-income workers to get refunds when they file their annual tax returns even if they owed no taxes. If their *adjusted gross earnings* fall below a specified amount (a modified "poverty line"), the payment helps to make up that difference. In effect EITC is an income supplement to encourage low-income workers, especially those with children, to remain in the workforce. EITC legislation (P.L. 94-164) began in 1975 and has undergone many revisions since. Some states that have income taxes also have programs similar to the federal EITC program.

earnings limitation The *Social Security Administration (SSA)* provision that the amount a beneficiary earns after retirement reduces the amount of social security commensurately.

Earth Day An annual observance by people in many nations to celebrate the natural environment and to raise the public consciousness through parades, teach-ins, demonstrations, and intensified lobbying activities about the need to protect and conserve the environment. Social workers have been among the leaders of the movement since its initial celebration on April 22, 1970.

Earthwatch A private, nonprofit organization with offices around the world established to provide funds and field research for scientists and volunteers investigating environmental problems.

Easter Seal Society The organization, founded in 1919, that coordinates fund-raising and disbursements made in the United States on behalf of children and adults with disabilities. Their Web site address is http://www.easterseal.org

eating disorders Maladaptive or unhealthy patterns of eating and ingestion. Major types include *anorexia nervosa* and *bulimia nervosa*. Eating disorders first diagnosed during infancy or early childhood include *pica* and *rumination disorder.*

Ebola A deadly disease caused by a virus that is transmitted by contact with blood, feces, or bodily fluids. Epidemics of Ebola, which kills as many as 90 percent of those infected, have occurred primarily in central African nations. Victims show signs of high fever and then suffer massive internal bleeding.

Ebonics A language form of *nonstandard American English* used in some African American communities. Ebonics has its roots in the linguistic and cultural African heritage of African Americans and has its own linguistic structure as well as unique patterns of pronunciation, grammar, and idiomatic use. Some educators have advocated recognizing ebonics as a second language.

EBT scan The use of an electron beam tomography (EBT) scanner to take computerized high-resolution X rays of internal organs and processes. EBT is particularly effective in scanning coronary arteries to detect the buildup of calcium and the resulting *atherosclerosis* and to predict the risk of heart attack. See also *CAT scan*.

ECHO housing Elder cottage housing opportunity, also known as a *granny flat,* that is a self-contained mobile-system home built for temporary use on the property of an existing residence, usually the older person's relatives. The utilities hookups are connected to the main house. This provides low-cost private housing for senior citizens with convenient access to their offspring but requires approval by local zoning laws.

echolalia Repetitive imitation of the speech of another. This is a normal phase of language development in the nine- to 12-month-old infant. Later, it is seen as maladaptive. It is often seen in adults with certain types of *schizophrenia.*

echopraxia Repetitive imitation of the movements or behavior of others, often a symptom of *schizophrenia* or other mental disorder.

eclampsia Recurrent convulsions occurring primarily during pregnancy or childbirth.

eclectic A collection of certain aspects of various theories or practice methods that appear to be most useful for practice interventions.

ecological overstress The application of more demands on an environment than it can meet, ultimately reducing its restorative functions and making it permanently unproductive or less productive. This phenomenon is notable in sub-Saharan Africa, the flood plains of the Indian subcontinent, and the areas adjacent to the South American rain forests. It is the consequence of the combined effects of population growth, overgrazing, deforestation, air and water pollution, soil erosion, and possibly the *greenhouse effect.*

ecological perspective An orientation in social work and other professions that emphasizes understanding people and their environment and the nature of their transactions. Important concepts include *adaptation, transactions, goodness of fit* between people and their environments, *reciprocity,* and *mutuality.* In professional interventions, the *unit of attention* is considered to be the interface between the individual (or group, family, or community) and the relevant environment. See also *life model.*

ecology The study of relationships between environment and organisms.

ecomap A diagram of family relationships created by Ann Hartman and used by social workers, family therapists, and other professionals to depict a variety of reciprocal influences between the client and those people related to the client, relevant social institutions, and environmental influences.

ecomunicipality movement A coalition of citizens groups allied with larger corporations to promote environmentally friendly economic development. The movement began in Sweden and has spread to other European nations.

econometrics Statistical analysis of economic trends and problems.

Economic and Social Council, U.N. (ECOSOC) The United Nation's administration to promote, among the peoples of the world, higher standards of living, full employment, and conditions of economic and social progress and development; solutions of international economic, social, health, and related problems; international cultural and educational cooperation; and universal respect for, and observance of, human rights and fundamental freedoms for all without distinction as to race, gender, language, or religion. ECOSOC elects representatives from 54 nations to serve for three-year terms and determine policy initiatives. International organizations, governments, and over 1,500 nongovernment organizations that deal with social and economic issues report to ECOSOC, including the U.N. Children's Fund, High Commissioner for Refugees, World Food Programme, U.N. Environment Program, International Drug Control Program, and U.N. Centre for Human Settlements. Their Web site address is http://www.un.org/esa/coordination/ecosoc

economic justice An ideal condition in which all members of society have the same opportunities to obtain material resources necessary to survive and fulfill their human potentials. For social workers the term embodies a principle in which governments and other social institutions ensure that all people receive adequate incomes above an agreed upon poverty threshold. Some social workers prefer the term "distributive justice." See also *justice* and *social justice.*

Economic Opportunity Act of 1964 The major legislation (P.L. 88-452) of President Lyndon B. Johnson's *War on Poverty.* Enacted in 1964, it established the *Office of Economic Opportunity (OEO)* and helped create programs such as *Volunteers in Service to America (VISTA),* the *Job Corps, Head Start, Upward Bound,* the *Neighborhood Youth Corps,* and the *Community Action Program (CAP).* Many of these programs were later dismantled.

economies of scale A tendency for some costs of providing services to increase less than proportionately with increased output. For example, in certain circumstances, a social agency might be able to triple its service output while only doubling its budget.

ecosphere The biological bubble in which life can survive around, on, and within Earth, including its land mass, surface waters, oceans, and atmosphere.

ecosystem A concept in the biological science of ecology pertaining to the physical and biological environment and the interaction between every component thereof.

ecosystems perspective A conceptual lens through which the social worker can note the systemic relatedness of case variables. The ecosystems perspective offers no prescription for intervention but as a meta-theory attempts to depict phenomena in their connectedness and complexity. This perspective permits multiple practice theories, approaches, and practitioner roles.

ecotage Ecological sabotage; planned action that obstructs, damages, or destroys facilities and equipment thought to be harmful to the environment.

ECP practitioner A social worker or other helping professional oriented to an empirical clinical practice that is said to use scientific methods of inquiry for data gathering and interpreting.

"ecstasy" Street name for an illicit *designer drug* that combines methamphetamine and hallucinogenic chemicals to make the compound MDMA (methylenedioxymethamphetamine). The combination of a stimulant and *hallucinogen* has a powerful effect, with many negative side effects that sometimes include depression, severe anxiety, sleeplessness, paranoia, blurred vision, faintness, chills or sweating, increases in heart rate and blood pressure, and possible long-term brain damage.

ECT Electroconvulsive therapy. See *electroshock therapy (EST).*

-ectomy The surgical removal of an organ, tissue, or something found in the body. For example, an appendectomy is the removal of the appendix, a hysterectomy is removal of the uterus, and a tonsillectomy is removal of the tonsils.

ectopic pregnancy Pregnancy in which the fertilized egg develops outside the uterus, usually in the fallopian tubes.

eczema A common skin condition in which the skin becomes inflamed, reddens, swells, itches, burns, and thickens to form scales that flake off.

edema Accumulation of fluid in the body tissues and cavities leading to swelling. Edema may be a symptom of a variety of disorders, including heart failure, kidney disease, pneumonia, and infection.

educable Having potential for learning, especially for formal education and basic survival skills. Professionals often use the term in referring to individuals with mental retardation whose retardation does not preclude learning certain social or academic skills.

Education for All Handicapped Children Act The federal law (P.L. 94-142) enacted originally in 1975 to provide funds for public school programs to ensure equal educational opportunities and free special services for all children with learning and other disabilities. Services include special testing, remedial lessons, counseling, and tutoring. The act was amended in 1986 to provide early intervention for children from birth to three who are at risk of developmental delay. The act was replaced in 1990 with the *Individuals with Disabilities Education Act (IDEA).*

Education for Homeless Children and Youth (EHCY) Program The national program to help homeless children gain full access to free, comprehensive, and appropriate public education and to eliminate school barriers to their enrollment, attendance, and success in school. The program was established in 1987 with the *McKinney Homeless Act* (P.L. 100-77).

Education, U.S. Department of (DoE) The federal agency, created in 1979 by separation from the *U.S. Department of Health, Education and Welfare (HEW)*, that administers programs to provide and promote the nation's educational opportunities and to supplement state and local educational efforts. It sponsors research on teaching methods and educational programs; provides financial aid for elementary through college education; provides educational programs for disabled, disadvantaged, and gifted students; and supervises numerous educational functions, including school social work programs. The Web site address is http://www.ed.gov

Educational Resources Information Center (ERIC) *U.S. Department of Education* centers in more than 500 locations across the United States that provide hard-copy and Internet data about the nation's educational programs and facilities. Information covers topics such as resources for exceptional children, disabled people, people unable to speak English, and people seeking to become teachers. Their Web site address is http://www.eric.ed.gov

"educationally deprived child" A term used by the *U.S. Department of Education* for those children who, because of some condition (such as neglect, poverty, delinquency, disability, or cultural or linguistic isolation from the community at large), require special assistance to raise their educational level to that appropriate for children of the same age.

educationally disadvantaged Children whose educational attainments are below age-appropriate levels not because of intellectual deficits but because of factors such as growing up in a home in which education is not valued.

educator role In social work, the responsibility to teach clients necessary adaptive skills. This is done by providing relevant information in a way that is understandable to the client, offering advice and suggestions, identifying alternatives and their probable consequences, modeling behaviors,

teaching problem-solving techniques, and clarifying perceptions. Other social work roles are identified as the *facilitator role*, the *enabler role*, and the *mobilizer role*.

efficacy 1. The degree to which desired goals or projected outcomes are achieved. 2. In social work, the capacity to help the client achieve, in a reasonable period, the goals of a given intervention.

egalitarianism A social value; a belief in human equality leading one to treat others as peers or equals and to espouse equal access to goods and resources.

ego The self; the part of the mind that mediates between the demands of the body and the realities of the environment, consisting of *cognition, perception, defense mechanism*, memory, and motor control. In psychodynamic theory, one of the three major spheres of the *psyche*, along with the *id* and the *superego*. The healthy ego finds ways to compromise among these competing pressures and enables the person to cope with the demands of the environment.

ego alien A synonym for *ego dystonic*.

ego boundary Limits set by the *ego* between the self and the environment.

ego defense See *defense mechanism*.

ego disintegration 1. Breakdown of the ability of the *ego* to carry out its functions, such as defending against stressors, distinguishing between reality and fantasy, delaying gratification, and mediating between the demands of the body and the environment. 2. In *psychoanalytic theory*, the ego's loss of ability to continue in its function of mediating between the competing demands of the *id* and the *superego*.

ego dystonic Traits of personality, behavior, thought, or orientation considered to be unacceptable, repugnant, or inconsistent with the individual's perceptions—conscious or unconscious—of himself or herself; a synonym for *ego alien*. The term "ego dystonic homosexual" is no longer considered a diagnosable category. See also *ego syntonic*.

ego functioning The manner in which the *ego* deals with the demands of society and mediates between internal psychological conflicts and psychosocial realities.

ego ideal 1. An individual's goals, positive standards, and highest aspirations. 2. One or more *significant others* in a person's life who are emulated.

ego integration Achievement of inner harmony and compatibility of the various aspects of one's personality as a unified whole.

ego-oriented social work Clinical social work that incorporates the principles of *ego psychology* into professional practice.

ego psychology Psychosocially oriented concepts that build on *Freudian theory* but emphasize the individual's adult development and ability to solve problems and deal with social realities. See also *defense mechanism.*

ego strengths 1. In psychodynamic theory, the degree of *psychic energy* available to the individual for solving problems, resolving internal conflicts, and defending against mental and environmental distress. 2. The individual's capacity for logical thinking, intelligence, perceptiveness, and self-control over impulses to achieve immediate gratification.

ego syntonic Traits of personality, thought, behavior, and values that are incorporated by the individual, who considers them acceptable and consistent with his or her overall "true" self. See also *ego dystonic.*

egocentrism 1. Excessive preoccupation with oneself. 2. An exaggerated view of one's importance. 3. In *Piagetian theory,* the normal state of a child younger than age six who has not yet learned to take into account another person's perspective.

Egypt, Ophelia Settle (1903–1984) An influential advocate for and pioneer of planned parent programs and sex education in public schools, she helped develop the curriculum at Howard University School of Social Work and authored historical accounts of former slaves.

ehrenamtliche arbeit Volunteer work in Germany, an activity that involves nearly one-fifth of that nation's population.

eidetic memory The ability to bring to consciousness a mental picture of such clarity and vividness that most of the details therein are retained; a "photographic memory."

ejaculatory inhibition A *sexual disorder* in which a man can become sexually aroused and erect but has difficulty ejaculating intravaginally.

Elberfeld system The German poverty relief program that originated in the town of Elberfeld in the 1850s. The highly organized program was designed especially to supervise those who were unemployed or had low-paying jobs, to ensure counseling and some living minimum wage. The Elberfeld system was emulated in most other German communities and existed until the nation's social insurance program was adopted in the early 1890s. The Japanese welfare system—*minsei i'in*—is based on this model. See also *Deutscher Verein für Öffentliche und Private Fürsorge.*

ELBW baby An infant with extremely low birthweight. These babies are usually born very prematurely and weigh less than 35 ounces, and they are at great risk of death, neurological damage, impaired sensory organs, and developmental delay. See also *low-birthweight (LBW) baby.*

elder abuse Mistreatment of older people and relatively dependent people, including physical battering, neglect, financial or other exploitation, and psychological harm. Abuse may be inflicted by the older person's adult children or other relatives, legal custodians, or other care providers.

Eldercare Locator A resource of the U.S. *Administration on Aging* to help older persons and their caregivers find local services at no cost. Nearly 5,000 such services are in the database. These are found by calling toll-free 1-800-677-1166 or by going to http://www.eldercare.gov

elderly Advanced in age. This term is commonly used to designate people older than age 65. Most social workers prefer the adjective "older" instead of "elderly." See also *pre-elderly* and *frail elderly.*

Elderly Nutrition Program A food program for people older than 60 (and their spouses of any age) administered by the U.S. Department of Health and Human Services' *Administration on Aging* and the *U.S. Department of Agriculture.* The program also facilitated the delivery of meals to homebound older and disabled people and provided shopping assistance and nutrition education. In 2000, with amendments to the Older Americans Act, the program was modified and renamed the *Nutrition Services Incentive Program (NSIP).*

elective mutism   The refusal to talk in almost all social situations even though the ability to speak and comprehend language exists and there is no organic or physical cause for the refusal. This condition is most commonly found in younger children during the time they are compelled to participate in social situations such as school.

elective surgery   Surgery considered nonessential because the related condition is not life-threatening, urgent, or physically incapacitating.

Electra complex   The term used in early *Freudian theory* for the unconscious sexual attraction that girls, especially from ages three to seven, have for their fathers. The term is roughly analogous to the *Oedipus complex* for boys.

electronic benefit transfer (EBT) system   The use of an encoded card, similar to an automated teller machine card, to facilitate receiving benefits such as the *Food Stamp program.* The client runs the card through the terminal at a store's checkout counter after entering the identification number. The value of the food purchases is deducted from the client's monthly allotment. This system helps remove the stigma of using food stamps and makes it more difficult for anyone to misuse them.

electroshock therapy (EST)   Treatments administered by physicians, primarily neurologists and psychiatrists, in which convulsions are induced in patients by applying small amounts of electrical currents to the brain. Its purpose is to treat patients who suffer from certain types of mental disorder, including some severe *depression, mood disorder,* and *psychosis,* when medications and other treatments have not been helpful.

"eleemosynary"   An obsolete term referring to charity and charitable donations or to the condition of being dependent on charity.

Elementary and Secondary School Improvement Amendments of 1988   See *Hawkins–Stafford Amendments.*

eligibility   1. The meeting of specific qualifications to receive certain benefits. 2. The criteria used in welfare and social services systems to determine

which people may receive help. For example, to be eligible for the *Food Stamp program,* a person must meet certain income requirements, and to be eligible for *Medicare* a person must be older than a certain age.

eligibility workers   Employees in *public welfare* offices who determine whether an applicant meets the criteria for *public assistance.* This function once was served by social workers until state and federal laws separated the provision of *social services* from *income maintenance.* Thus, eligibility workers have freed social workers to do more technical and professional work with clients on public assistance.

elimination disorder   Inability to control elimination of body waste, not as a result of a specific physiological disorder. The two types of elimination disorder are *encopresis* and *enuresis.* See also *functional encopresis* and *functional enuresis.*

ELISA   Enzyme-linked immunosorbent assay, a medical test for detecting the antibodies in the blood in response to AIDS infection. If these antibodies are present, the patient is *HIV-positive.*

Elizabethan Poor Laws   The statutes, codified in England in 1601 during the reign of Queen Elizabeth I, that established many of the principles that are still influential in dealing with economically disadvantaged people. Among their provisions were local rather than national responsibility for the care of poor people, the distinction between the *"worthy poor"* and the *"unworthy poor,"* punitive measures for those refusing to work, standards of responsibility for relatives, and the *means test* to determine need for assistance.

elopement   1. Running away. The term is often applied to patients in mental hospitals or other institutions who leave precipitously without authority. 2. The act of couples going away suddenly to marry.

emaciation   Extreme thinness as a result of starvation or disease.

emancipation   Freeing an individual or members of a social group from the control of another or others. For example, a minor child may become emancipated from parental control (and from the right to parental support or *maintenance*) after getting married.

emasculate 1. To castrate, literally or symbolically. 2. To act toward a man in such a way that his male *sexual identity* is supposedly diminished.

embezzlement The crime of willfully appropriating money or property that is in one's control but belongs to another. The embezzler has possession of the property by virtue of a business relationship or through some office, employment, or position of trust with the owner.

embolism A blood clot or other object blocking the vessel.

emergency basic needs services Programs often found in state and local departments of public welfare or human services designed to provide immediate food, shelter, clothing, and fuel for individuals and families in crisis. These programs are thought of as "one-time" services, in effect only until needy people can obtain a more permanent means of providing for their *basic needs.*

emergency financial assistance Programs often found in state and local departments of public welfare or human services designed to immediately provide cash or credit for individuals and families in crisis. These funds usually are granted on a "one-time" basis to prevent evictions, hunger, or deprivation of some *basic needs* until more permanent means of income provision occur.

Emergency Food Assistance Program See *commodity food programs.*

emergency medical technicians (EMTs) Health care workers who assist the more highly trained *paramedics* and physicians in administering critical and life-saving treatment.

Emergency Relief Administration See *Federal Emergency Relief Administration (FERA).*

emetic An agent used to cause vomiting, often as an immediate antidote to the ingestion of toxic substances.

emigrant One who permanently leaves a country.

eminent domain The legal right of a government, under certain conditions, to take ownership of private property to be used for public purposes. The procedure is to pay the owner fairly after a *condemnation* of the property.

emit To respond or behave. See *operant conditioning.*

emotion 1. A feeling, mood, or affect. 2. A state of mind usually accompanied by concurrent physiological and behavioral changes and based on the perception of some internal or external object.

emotional divorce A distancing between members of a *dyad,* usually a married couple, because they have experienced considerable pain, anxiety, anger, or other similar reactions in their previous encounters. Typically, the resulting behavior includes avoidance of one another's physical presence, avoidance of discussions about certain emotionally charged events, or refusal to provide needed emotional support.

emotional lability A tendency to change moods rapidly and frequently. This is a commonly encountered symptom of *affective disorder* and of immaturity.

empathy The act of perceiving, understanding, experiencing, and responding to the emotional state and ideas of another person.

emphysema A chronic disease of the lungs, characterized by extreme shortness of breath as a result of stretching or rupturing of the lung's air sacs. In many instances, emphysema is a *lifestyle-associated disorder,* often occurring among heavy smokers, coal miners, and people who live in air-polluted environments.

empirical Based on direct observation or experience.

empirically based practice A type of intervention in which the professional social worker uses research as a practice and problem-solving tool; collects data systematically to monitor the intervention; specifies problems, techniques, and outcomes in measurable terms; and systematically evaluates the effectiveness of the intervention used.

employable A term applied to those in the population who are potentially able to work. Economic planners sometimes identify this group as being within certain age parameters and without incapacitating infirmities.

employee assistance programs (EAPs) Services offered by employers to their employees to help them overcome problems that may negatively affect job satisfaction or productivity. Services may be provided on-site or contracted through outside providers. They include counseling for alcohol dependence and drug dependence, marital therapy or family therapy, career counseling, and referrals for dependent care services. See also *industrial social work.*

employer subsidization   Providing funds, benefits, and tax credits to private or public sector employers who hire welfare recipients. U.S. laws and policies encourage private sector job creation through programs that help pay all or part of the salary of the welfare recipient. Public sector jobs are created, often by TANF grants to employers that would have gone directly to welfare recipients, in the form of paid community service jobs.

employment   The state of working in exchange for money.

Employment and Training Administration (ETA)   A branch of the *U.S. Department of Labor* that focuses on programs to increase employment, help unemployed workers, facilitate access to jobs, enhance the quality and opportunity for vocational and on-the-job training, and encourage employers to hire workers. It includes the *Job Corps, Welfare to Work,* Migrant and Seasonal Farm Workers, Apprenticeship Training, and Adult Training Programs.

employment equity   Fairness in the workplace so that job performance is the only relevant consideration. When equity exists, pay and benefits, promotions, and influence are not based on one's gender, race, or membership in some social status.

Employment on Trial   A program in the British labor system in which a job seeker can try out a new position and leave it after a time between four and 12 weeks without losing the right to resume unemployment benefits.

employment policy   The principles, guidelines, goals, and regulations pertaining to the way a nation or an organization deals with its actual and potential workforce. Aspects of an employment policy include hiring and firing rules and procedures, salary and benefits structure, occupational safety and health provisions, and economic programs to stimulate the creation of more jobs. In the United States, organizations affiliated with the *U.S. Department of Labor* that shape employment policy include the *Occupational Safety and Health Administration (OSHA),* the National Commission for Employment Policy, the National Occupational Information Coordinating Committee, and the President's Committee on Employment of People with Disabilities.

employment programs   Programs at the federal, state, and local government levels and in private industry designed to secure more jobs for more people and to ensure that those jobs include decent wages and benefits and equal opportunities. In the United States, in addition to the *Unemployment Insurance* program, these programs have included the provisions of the *Job Training Partnership Act,* the *Job Corps,* and the *Neighborhood Youth Corps.* See also *Equal Employment Opportunity Commission (EEOC).*

Employment Retirement Income Security Act   See *ERISA.*

empowerment   In social work practice, the process of helping individuals, families, groups, and communities increase their personal, interpersonal, socioeconomic, and political strength and develop influence toward improving their circumstances.

empowerment zones and enterprise communities (EZ/EC)   The *U.S. Department of Housing and Urban Development* program established in 1993 to revitalize low-income American neighborhoods for economic improvement by providing tax incentives, performance grants, and loans to business organizations that locate therein and create jobs, help people find work, and expand business opportunities.

"empty nest"   A term applied to the *nuclear family* after the children have matured and left the home.

enabler   1. An individual who makes something possible. 2. In social work, the orientation of the social worker toward enhancing the ability of the client to solve problems and achieve goals by providing information and access to resources, strengthening coping skills, and changing socioenvironmental conditions that impede progress. 3. The term is used increasingly to indicate the actions of one who facilitates the dysfunctional behavior of another. An example is a spouse who keeps alcohol around while the partner is trying to deal with alcohol addiction.

enabler role In social work, the responsibility to help the client become capable of coping with situational or transitional stress. Specific skills used in achieving this objective include conveying hope, reducing resistance and ambivalence, recognizing and managing feelings, identifying and supporting personal strengths and social assets, breaking down problems into parts that can be solved more readily, and maintaining a focus on goals and the means of achieving them. Other primary social work roles are identified as the *facilitator role*, the *educator role*, and the *mobilizer role.*

enabling state A version of the modern *welfare state* that emphasizes the private production of welfare benefits. The enabling state also emphasizes *transfer payments* in the form of cash rather than *in-kind benefits* through tax expenditures, regulatory measures, and credit subsidies as well as direct public expenditures.

enactment 1. The process of institutionalizing an action that has great impact or influence on individuals or groups, as in the establishment of law. 2. In *psychoanalytic theory,* the symbolic interactions between the client and psychoanalyst that have unconscious meanings to both.

encephalitis Inflammation of the brain or its covering. Usually this is an acute condition but may lead to personality or organic changes that continue after the inflammation has occurred.

encopresis The repeated passage of feces into inappropriate places at least once per month over a period of three consecutive months. By definition the condition is not due to constipation and overflow or *incontinence.*

encounter group Intense, short-term *group therapy*—often using principles and techniques that include *gestalt therapy, group psychotherapy,* and *humanistic orientation* principles and techniques—designed to promote the personal growth of the participants. The emphasis is not on correcting disorders, but rather on increasing the emotional and sensory aspects of being and on increasing open communication and self-awareness.

enculturation Socialization; the process in which individuals learn and use a culture's patterns of behavior, thought, values, and knowledge.

Encyclopedia of Social Work The periodic publication of the *National Association of Social Workers (NASW)* that contains the general knowledge of the profession. Originally published in 1929 by the Russell Sage Foundation as the one-volume *Social Work Yearbook,* it became the two-volume *Encyclopedia of Social Work* with its 15th edition, published by NASW in 1965. Its 19th edition, in three volumes, was published by NASW in 1995.

endangered species Living organisms, including animals, plants, or other living beings, threatened with extinction. The U.S. Endangered Species Act specifies in detail the requirements for declaring a species endangered and mandates actions and protections to save them.

endemic A term applied to a phenomenon, social problem, or disease that is peculiar to a given population, group, culture, or geographical area. See also *pandemic.*

endogamy The practice of confining marriage to members of one's own social class or ethnic group. See also *exogamy.*

endogenous Something that originates in the body. See also *exogenous.*

endogenous depression Depression apparently resulting from internal mental or physical processes. This term often is used to describe depression that arises without any particular stressor or unhappy event in the person's life.

endometriosis A common condition in some women of childbearing age in which cells that grow inside the uterus instead grow outside the uterus, most often on the fallopian tubes and ovaries and anywhere on the surface of the pelvic cavity. Symptoms vary greatly, from no sign of the condition except through laparoscopy or surgery to pelvic pain during menstruation, the intensity of which may vary from month to month. Infertility is sometimes a result.

endowment 1. A permanent fund held by an educational institution, social agency, or other organization. Usually the fund comes from special donations rather than regular sources of revenue, and usually only the fund's interest proceeds are spent. 2. The inherited or inherent qualities of a person, nation, or people.

end-stage renal disease (ESRD)   Irreversible loss of kidney function, caused by genetic or metabolic factors or by external factors such as trauma or infection. ESRD patients require artificial *dialysis* treatment or kidney transplants to survive.

energy assistance   Programs to provide winter heating and weatherization to low-income households. The Low-Income Home Energy Assistance Program provides funds to the states based on the number of days the population requires heating because of cold weather; the states allocate these funds, or sometimes fuel, to people who are poor. Some funds are used for home cooling during especially hot summers. In some communities, public utility companies and voluntary organizations also provide such assistance.

enfranchisement   Obtaining the right to vote. Losing that right is to be disenfranchised.

English-Only Movement   A group of social activist individuals and organizations, located primarily in U.S. regions with high concentrations of Spanish-speaking residents, who want stronger laws and social sanctions to eliminate bilingualism in public institutions. The movement seeks a constitutional amendment stating that English is the nation's official language and also the elimination of the *Bilingual Education Act.*

enjoin   An order from a court requiring a particular individual to refrain from performing a specified act.

enmeshed family   A concept used in the *structural family therapy* orientation to designate an unhealthy family relationship pattern in which the *role boundaries* between various family members are so vague or diffuse that there is little opportunity for independent functioning. This condition is contrasted with the *disengaged family.*

enneagram   A star-shaped diagram in which personality types are depicted on a nine-point scale ("ennea" is nine in Greek). The personality types are perfectionist, giver, performer, romantic, observer, questioner, epicure, boss, and mediator.

ENT specialist   Physician for ear, nose, and throat disorders, formally called an otorhinolaryngologist.

enterprise zones   See *free-trade zones.*

entitlement   Services, goods, or money due to an individual by virtue of a specific status. Also, a legal obligation of the government to provide payments or benefits to one who meets certain criteria.

entitlement programs   Government-sponsored benefits of cash, goods, or services that are due all people who belong to a specified class. Examples include the social security programs such as *Old Age, Survivors, Disability, and Health Insurance (OASDHI)* and *Medicare* in the United States and *family allowance* in many European nations.

entrapment   A legal authority's act of inducing an individual to commit a crime not previously contemplated, usually to prosecute that person.

entrepreneurial social work   The activities involved in the provision of human services and social services for profit. Such activities include private clinical social work; providing consultations to social agencies and community organizations for fees; and establishing for-profit social services facilities such as private schools for children with emotional disturbances, employment agencies for unemployed social workers, training facilities for business organizations, and homes for at-risk populations such as frail elderly people, unwed mothers-to-be, and children requiring foster care.

entropy   A concept used in *systems theories* pertaining to the winding down, dissolution, or deorganization of a system. It is hypothesized that without intervention, systems are always going through this process in their movement toward and away from *equilibrium.*

enuresis   The involuntary discharge of urine. In the diagnosis "enuresis (not due to a general medical condition)," the discharge must occur at least twice weekly for more than three consecutive months. Three subtypes are nocturnal only, diurnal only, and both.

environment   All the influences, conditions, and natural surroundings that affect the growth and development of living things.

environmental modification   See *environmental treatment.*

environmental movement   Social activism by concerned citizens and groups directed toward protecting the natural world from civilization's destructive effects. Actions of environmentalist individuals and groups range from lobbying, public education, and financing research to litigation, protesting, and sometimes sabotaging enterprises that are considered environmentally harmful. See also *ecosystems, ecotage, social activist, ozone layer, Environmental Protection Agency (EPA), toxic waste sites, greenhouse effect, Earth Day,* and *Earthwatch.*

Environmental Protection Agency (EPA) The federal organization established in 1970 to develop and enforce standards for controlling water, air, and noise pollution and to promote those activities that result in a healthy habitat for wildlife and human well-being.

environmental racism The practice of operating hazardous businesses or storing toxic waste products in or near areas inhabited primarily by racial and ethnic minority groups.

environmental treatment The *social casework* concept that recognizes the effect of forces outside the individual and strives to modify these effects through techniques such as providing or locating specific resources, interpreting the needs of the client to others, *advocacy,* and *mediation.* Some social workers call this activity *indirect treatment* or "environmental modification."

environmentalist One who works toward resolving the problems of the *environment,* especially the *ecosystem,* pollution, wildlife habitats, and the natural world. Many social workers have been leaders among environmentalist movements.

envy Uncomfortable emotion pertaining to the wish to have something that others possess. See also *jealousy.*

ephebophilia A form of *pedophilia* in which the erotic attraction for children is limited to boys or girls past puberty age. Most professionals do acknowledge this distinction; sexually abusing any child (whether pre- or postpubescent) is a serious crime and symptomatic of a serious emotional disorder.

epidemic The occurrence of a disease, disorder, or social problem that spreads rapidly and affects many people in a community within a relatively short period. See also *disease patterns.*

epidemiology The study of the frequency and distribution of a specified phenomenon, such as a disease, that occurs in a population group during a given period. Usually this is expressed in terms of an *incidence rate* and *prevalence rate.* Other commonly used terms in epidemiology are *point prevalence, period prevalence,* and *morbidity risk.* See also *morbidity rate.*

epidermis The outer layer of the skin.

epigenesis 1. Emergence. 2. The perceived original occurrence of a phenomenon.

epilepsy A brain disorder characterized by recurrent, involuntary episodes of altered states of consciousness, frequently but not always accompanied by convulsive body movements. Most professionals now refer to this condition as *seizure disorders.*

episiotomy Surgical incision in the vaginal wall to prevent its tearing during childbirth.

episode of service (EOS) A specific social services goal and all the alternative means used by a social work team and their client to achieve it. The team members first assess the client's need and then, often with the client, translate this into specific and realistic goals. The team then discusses the variety of techniques and resources that might be used and selects those that are most feasible.

epistaxis Nosebleed.

epistemology 1. The study of the nature, methods, and limits of knowledge. 2. For many social workers and family therapists, the term means how we know what we know.

Epstein, Abraham (1892–1942) A leader in the movement for social security legislation, and one of the planners for the *Social Security Act* of 1935. He also taught about issues concerning retirement, the aging process, and financing social security.

Epstein, Laura (1914–1996) A social work educator, clinical practitioner, and theoretician, she was influential in the development of brief treatment models and *task-centered treatment.*

Equal Credit Opportunity Act (ECOA) The federal legislation (P.L. 93-495) enacted in 1974 that requires retail firms and lending institutions to use the same criteria for everyone in deciding whether to grant credit, regardless of gender, marital status, or racial or ethnic group.

Equal Employment Opportunity Commission (EEOC) The five-member federal panel that administers Title VII of the *Civil Rights Act of 1964* and the *Equal Opportunity Act of 1972,* prohibiting *discrimination* by employers, labor unions, or employment agencies and striving to promote fair practices in the workplace. Their Web site address is http://www.eeoc.gov

equal rights The obligations of a society or organization to provide the same opportunities and access to all, regardless of status.

equality The principle that individuals should have equal access to services, resources, and opportunities and be treated the same by all social, educational, and welfare institutions; a fundamental social work value.

equifinality 1. The property of living systems that permits them to reach identical points, although by different routes. 2. A concept in *systems theories* stating that different behaviors by living organisms can lead to the same or "equal final" results. The opposite of equifinality is *equipotentiality* or *multifinality.*

equilibrium A concept in *systems theories* in which opposing forces and elements achieve balance. See also *goodness of fit.*

equipotentiality The property of living systems in which subsystems may have identical origins or beginnings but achieve different outcomes. This is the opposite and corollary principle to *equifinality.*

equitable distribution law (EDL) Distribution of real and personal property between interested parties in a way that is fair and just. In divorce cases, this law requires that all the property acquired during the marriage be divided equally or according to criteria that ensure fairness.

equity The state of fairness or impartiality, including any systems (for example, the criminal justice system and the social welfare system) that determine how one's rights and claims are fulfilled.

equity planning An orientation in *social planning* that gives the most attention to problem solving for populations that are most in need with the fewest resources.

erectile dysfunction A *sexual disorder* in which a man is unable to achieve or maintain penis rigidity sufficient for completion of sexual intercourse. Clinicians use the diagnostic term *male erectile disorder.*

erethism A state of abnormal mental excitement or irritability; a rapid response to a stimulus.

ergonomics The study of human interface with work environments. Ergonomic engineers design equipment, furniture, and spaces to fit people, taking into account human posture and movements, the pace and repetitiveness of work activity, the width and height of work surfaces, lighting and noise, clarity and visibility of instrument panels, and the arrangement of controls. Disorders such as *carpal tunnel syndrome (CTS)* are minimized by effective ergonomic planning.

Eriksonian theory In human *psychosocial development theory,* the eight stages of life as proposed by German-born psychologist Erik Erikson (1902–1994). The stages are *trust versus mistrust* (occurring at about ages one to two), *autonomy versus shame and doubt* (about ages two to four), *initiative versus guilt* (ages three to six), *industry versus inferiority* (ages six to 12), *identity versus role confusion* (ages 12 to 18), *intimacy versus isolation* (ages 18 to 24), *generativity versus stagnation* (ages 24 to 54), and *integrity versus despair* (older than age 54).

ERISA The Employee Retirement Income Security Act of 1974 (P.L. 93-406), a federal program administered by the *U.S. Department of Labor* and other agencies that protects the interests of workers who participate in private pension plans.

erogenous zone Any area of the body for which stimulation leads to sexual arousal.

erotic orientation The orientation individuals have as to their objects of sexual desires. For example, an individual may be oriented for sexual gratification to a member of the opposite or the same sex, groups, objects, children, or various combinations. An individual's erotic orientation may change over time and in different circumstances.

erotomania Obsession with objects that lead to sexual arousal.

erotomanic delusion A *delusional disorder* in which the individual develops a sense of idealized love or sexual attraction for another who is not reciprocating. Usually, the object of this *delusion* is an unapproachable person, for example, a movie or athletic star or political leader.

erotomanic-type delusional disorder A disorder characterized by nonbizarre delusions, particularly the intense belief that one is the object of another person's secret or overt desires and love.

ESL/ESOL English as a Second Language/English for Speakers of Other Languages. These terms are often used interchangeably to describe programs of instruction designed to help individuals of limited English proficiency.

espiritistas In Puerto Rican cultural groups, healers or those who claim supernatural inspiration as they help clients overcome health and social problems. In other Hispanic cultural groups, the nearly equivalent term is *curandero.*

essential hypertension Chronic high blood pressure, not resulting from immediate reactions to threat, vigorous physical activity, or a temporary stress or crisis situation.

EST 1. See *electroshock therapy (EST).* 2. The initials are also used, often not capitalized, for the psychoeducational group experience founded by Werner Erhardt and originally called Erhardt Seminar Training.

estate recovery The legal process of acquiring funds from certain deceased *Medicaid* recipients' estates. When it is determined that the deceased beneficiary actually had enough assets to be disqualified from receiving this assistance, Medicaid's administrators may recover the amount spent by the state for all Medicaid services (for example, nursing facility, home- and community-based services, hospital, and prescription costs).

esteem The worth or value one attributes to another or to one's own self. See also *self-esteem.*

esteem needs One's normal desire for feelings of self-worth and self-acceptance and the ability to receive appropriate appreciation, respect, and acceptance from others.

estoppel A legal obstacle that is put into effect to prevent someone from making a claim or taking an action that is contrary to what had been previously established. For example, if a developer begins building on land long considered a wildlife habitat, an estoppel prevents the activity until the lawsuit is resolved.

estrangement The loss of contact with or antagonism toward one's relatives or associates because of apathy or active disagreement.

estuary Coastal, marshy area where saltwater and freshwater meet, providing important breeding and feeding grounds for a wide variety of wildlife. These areas are highly sensitive to chemical agents and changes in salinity as a result of humans changing the quality and quantity of the freshwater flow.

ET programs Employment training (ET) programs, used in many states to help recipients of *public assistance* become economically independent by training them to get and keep jobs and to help them learn marketable skills. In most states in which ET programs exist, the children of the recipients are provided with health care and day care services while the parent is in the training program. See also *GAIN programs.*

ethical conduct Behavior that meets a community's positive moral standards—distinguishing right from wrong and adhering to the right. For professional social workers, ethical conduct is also following the profession's *code of ethics;* providing the highest and most skillful level of service to clients as possible; and relating to colleagues, other professionals, all people, and society in an honorable manner.

ethical dilemma A situation that occurs when two or more moral values seem to be equally valid but contradictory and the individual is required to make the best possible choice from among them.

ethical will A spiritual document prepared by one to be read after death that expresses wishes and advice for loved ones and attempts to summarize what has been learned in life. This information is usually comforting to survivors and helps minimize controversy when such thoughts are not included in a last will and testament.

ethics A system of moral principles and perceptions about right versus wrong and the resulting philosophy of conduct that is practiced by an individual, group, profession, or culture. See also *code of ethics.*

ethics audit   A risk management strategy, used by social workers, social agencies, and other professional groups, to review, assess, modify, and monitor the ethical practices, policies, and procedures inherent in the professional helping relationship. The evaluation can be conducted by individual practitioners and social services organizations by examining all documents, policies, decision-making procedures, practitioner's credentials, and other factors relating to ethics. The reviewer considers the degree to which each factor meets established ethical principles. These factors include procedures for ensuring proper informed consent, confidentiality and privacy, client rights, documentation, boundaries, termination of services, procedures for practitioner impairment, and many others.

ethics committees   Formal panels established by a service organization to provide practitioners opportunities to consult with one another about ethical issues. *Institutional ethics committees (IECs)* and *institutional review boards (IRBs)* are located in hospitals, universities, federal agencies, and many public and private organizations. Their functions include educating practitioners and their clients, formulating agency policies on ethical issues, providing case consultation, and reviewing existing cases involving possible ethical dilemmas. The composition of the committees depends on the nature of the host agency but often includes interdisciplinary staffs or staff members from only one discipline and sometimes outside representatives such as clients, community leaders, lawyers, and independent experts on ethics. See also *committee on inquiry.*

"ethnic cleansing"   The term used for achieving racial, religious, or cultural homogeneity in a nation or area through policies that eliminate or force the permanent evacuation of minority group members and their sympathizers. See also *holocaust* and *genocide.*

ethnic enclave   Concentrations of people of an ethnic or racial group who reside in one neighborhood within a larger community. Often there is relatively little contact between these residents and the larger community. Many people who settle in these enclaves do so to be near others of their kind, with the same value orientation, and they try to re-create many of the familiar cultural symbols, institutions, and traditions. Others settle in these enclaves because of social pressures (such as poverty, discrimination, housing opportunities, and

availability of employment) that delimit the choices available to them.

ethnic group   A distinct group of people who share a common language, set of customs, history, culture, race, religion, or origin.

ethnic intimidation   A *hate crime* in which an individual or group threatens other individuals or groups who belong to racial or ethnic groups with words, gestures, or actions.

ethnic-sensitive practice   Professional social work that emphasizes and values the special capabilities, distinctive cultural histories, and unique needs of people of various *ethnic groups.* Social work *values* and *ethics* emphasize ethnic-sensitive practice.

ethnic stereotyping   Preconceived, usually negative, ideas about the behaviors of a racial, religious, or geographic group.

ethnicity   1. An orientation toward the shared national origin, religion, race, or language of a people. 2. A person's ethnic affiliation, by virtue of one or more of these characteristics and traditions. Ethnicity is a powerful determinant of an individual's patterns of feeling, thinking, and behaving.

ethnocentrism   An orientation or set of beliefs that holds that one's own *culture,* racial or *ethnic group,* or nation is inherently superior to others.

ethnography   The study and description of the behavior patterns of specific cultures or groups of people.

ethnology   The scientific study of humanity's division into *races* and the history, characteristics, and *culture* of these racial groups.

ethnomedicine   See *folk medicine.*

ethnomethodology   The scientific study of the way people of different ethnic orientations learn to understand things, especially society's structure and organization. The field considers the individual's culture, stages in the life cycle, ideology, social status, and unique experiences.

ethnoviolence   A purposeful act to harm someone or some organization identified with an *ethnic* *group.* Such activities include assaults, property destruction, harassment, firebombings, and distribution of hate propaganda. See also *hate crime.*

ethology The scientific study of the formation of human character and animal behavior by assessing the genetic, physiological, and evolutionary development and adaptation to the environment of living organisms.

ethos The moral beliefs or ethical character of a people or *culture.*

etiology 1. The underlying causes of a problem or disorder. 2. The study of such causes.

eugenics The science of "improving" human qualities genetically or minimizing genetic disorders. The practice may be negative (discouraging or preventing parenthood among those who are considered biologically deficient) or positive (encouraging reproduction among healthy people).

euphoria A perception of extreme well-being, excessive optimism, and increased motor activity. It is often pathological and indicative of conditions such as *bipolar disorder, mania, organic mental disorders,* and *drug intoxication.* See also *dysphoria.*

Eurocentrism An orientation in education, history, politics, and cultural development that emphasizes the contributions of Europeans to the relative neglect of contributions from other peoples.

Eurolink Age The London-based organization, founded in 1981 to work on behalf of older people who live in the nations of the European Union (EU). Its membership includes geriatricians and gerontologists, social workers specializing in older persons, NGOs, EU government agencies on aging, public and private social welfare organizations, unions, and older individuals and their advocates.

European Centre for Social Welfare Policy and Research An international organization of professional social workers (primarily faculty members at European schools of social work). Affiliated with the United Nations and headquartered in Vienna since its founding in 1974, the European Centre facilitates cross-national research on social problems and social welfare issues.

European Court of Human Rights A judicial body under the aegis of the Council of Europe,

established in 1959 to review and decide cases arising out of the European Rights Convention of 1950. The convention defined a wide range of rights for European workers, families, citizens, and organizations; when a party believes a member nation has failed to comply, the case may be heard. Judgments are not enforceable, but nations have honored its findings to avoid unfavorable publicity.

euthanasia 1. Elective *death.* 2. Putting to death or permitting the death of a person with terminal illness. See also *mercy killing, assisted suicide,* and *passive euthanasia.*

euthenics The study and movement oriented to improving lifestyles and environments to improve humans and other species.

euthymic state A condition of general well-being, positive mood, and emotional stability and the absence of mood disturbance that would impair effective social functioning.

evaluation research Systematic investigation to determine the success of a specific program. For example, a social work researcher might conduct a study of the incidence rate of nutritional deficiency in an Appalachian town before and after its citizens are made eligible for an antipoverty program.

eviction Forcing an individual, family, or business to discontinue its occupancy of housing, land, or other real property, usually by *due process of law.* See also *constructive eviction.*

evidence-based practice (EBP) The use of the best available scientific knowledge derived from randomized controlled outcome studies, and meta-analyses of existing outcome studies, as one basis for guiding professional interventions and effective therapies, combined with professional ethical standards, clinical judgment, and practice wisdom.

"ex-con" Slang for a person who once served time in a penal institution, that is, a former convict.

ex officio member Someone who belongs to a group or board by virtue of holding another office or status. For example, an ex officio member of the board of a sectarian social agency might be the highest-ranking local clergy of that denomination.

ex parte Legal term in which communication with the court or proceeding in the court occurs without the opposing side being present or being given notice.

ex post facto experiment   In research, an experiment conducted after the event being tested has already occurred. Thus, the experimenter cannot introduce the experimental stimulus but attempts to control, sometimes statistically, all extraneous factors.

exceptional children   A designation applied to dependent youths who, because of unusual mental, physical, or social abilities or limitations, require extraordinary forms of education, social experience, or treatment. These children include young people with mental retardation who can benefit from educational training facilities designed to help them reach their potential. Other children include those with physical disabilities, mental disorders, special talents, very high intelligence, or unusual physical abilities. See also *gifted child.*

exceptional eligibility   A policy in which services or benefits are established for people who constitute a special group even though they may not have unique or special needs and although others outside the group may have the same needs or be in the same circumstances. Such programs are often developed because of strong political pressure or public sympathy for the group. Some veterans' programs are a notable example.

exchange model   In social work administration, the concept of interorganizational linkages whereby similar agencies (for example, those agencies with the same mandates, constituencies, supervising organizations, or sources of funds) sometimes transfer or trade their resources (such as personnel, clients, or information) according to specified criteria.

exclusion allowance   A portion of some benefit that may not be counted as taxable income. Examples include certain tax-deferred retirement annuity plans and some *social security* benefits.

exclusive provider organizations (EPO)   A type of managed health care system, similar to the *preferred provider organization (PPO)* plan, in which beneficiaries are required to receive their care only from providers who belong to the EPO. Costs are usually lower, but services are limited.

exhibitionism   1. The tendency to show off one's real or imagined traits and talents to gain the attention of others. 2. Frequently, the display of one's genitals or sexual characteristics in socially unacceptable circumstances. See also *"flasher."*

existential social work   A philosophical perspective in social work that accepts and emphasizes the individual's fundamental autonomy, freedom of choice, disillusionment with prevailing social mores, sense of meaning derived from suffering, need for dialogue, and the social worker's commitment to the concept of client self-determination.

exit interview   In social research, a questionnaire procedure to investigate subjects as they leave a voting booth, workplace, job action, or similar activity to help determine how and why they acted as they did.

exogamy   The practice of restricting marriage to persons outside one's own locality, social class, or ethnic group. See also *endogamy.*

exogenous   Something that affects an individual emotionally or physically but originates outside the body or self.

exogenous depression   *Depression* apparently due to some external life event that is stressful or unhappy. The term is often used to imply acute depression in an individual who has healthy *affect* but who is currently experiencing sorrow or dejection, as in *bereavement* or failure to achieve an important goal.

expatriation   The process of leaving one's native country and living elsewhere, usually permanently.

expenditure   A payment, or obligation to pay, for some goods or services received.

experience rating   1. A measure of a corporation's employee retention–layoff rate. Employers with high ratings—that is, those who lay off fewer employees than their competitors in similar industries—may be rewarded with payroll tax benefits. 2. In the insurance industry, a measure used to indicate the probability of risk to a specified group.

experiential therapy   A form of psychosocial intervention or clinical treatment that emphasizes activity, acting out of conflicts and situations, *role playing, confrontation,* and the simulation of situations that are similar to the frequent life experiences of the client. Experiential therapies focus on the "here and now" and discourage the client from relying solely on a description of past circumstances. Experiential therapies often occur in *group therapy* or *family therapy* settings.

experiment   A systematic project to test a *hypothesis.*

experimental group   In research, a collection of subjects who are matched and compared with a *control group* in all relevant respects, except that they are also subject to a specific *variable* being tested.

experimental programs   See *demonstration programs.*

experimental study   Research conducted under carefully controlled conditions, in which the subjects being investigated are randomly selected and systematically compared with control groups, with treatment variables being introduced to the *experimental group* but not the *control group,* and the use of statistical analysis to determine if significant differences occur between the groups observed. See also *descriptive study* and *quasi-experimental study.*

expert opinion   The presentation of pertinent knowledge, thoughtful speculation, or demonstration of needed skills by a professional or an authority to a committee or organization that needs the information to make a decision with an effective means of implementing a plan it has developed. This information tends toward "educated guesses" and the provision of reasonable prognoses about the future consequences of an act the group is thinking about implementing. For example, a social worker may be asked by a court of law to provide information about the possible long-term harm and emotional consequence to a victim of child abuse.

expert systems   Interactive computer programs that permit users to answer specific and hypothetical questions that eventually result in obtaining detailed information that is relevant and specific. For example, programs help individuals prepare their own income taxes, assess their own health symptoms, and perform *computerized therapy.* At higher levels, such systems can plan budgets for nations, conduct war games, anticipate environmental problems, and redevelop infrastructures. Because there are many limitations with expert systems, they are still used primarily as "assistants" for human experts.

expert witness   One who testifies before a lawmaking group or in a court of law, based on special knowledge of the subject in question, enabling the decision makers to better assess the evidence or merits of the issue. Social work expert witnesses are often used in court hearings in disputes over *custody of children, child neglect, welfare rights, divorce,* landlord–tenant controversies, and care for people with mental and physical disabilities. See also *forensic social work.*

explosive disorder   An *impulse control disorder* characterized by an individual's loss of control of aggressive impulses and fits of rage out of proportion to any stressor. The individual may have numerous repeated episodes of this aggressivity *(intermittent explosive disorder)* or have a single discrete episode (isolated explosive disorder).

exponential growth   Expansion of a system in which the amount being added is proportional to the amount already present, so that the bigger the system the faster it increases. This term is often applied to uncontrolled growth in social phenomena such as urban sprawl, population, taxes, and waste products.

expressed need   An indication of the degree to which needs exist and the number of people who perceive themselves to have the need as revealed by specific factors. These factors might include the number of people who wait in lines to ask for a service, the amount of money most people seem willing to pay for the service, or the obstacles clients need to overcome to acquire the services.

expressive language disorder   A *communication disorder* characterized by markedly limited vocabulary and amount of speech, difficulty producing sentences of appropriate length and complexity, errors in tense, and general difficulty expressing ideas. The language difficulties interfere with academic or occupational achievement or with social communication. This disorder may be developmental or acquired (as a result of medical conditions such as head trauma). See also *mixed receptive–expressive language disorder, phonological disorder,* and *stuttering.*

expropriation   A government representative confiscating someone's property or rights to be used for the public need. The individual is entitled to just compensation, although some governments fail to honor that obligation.

expunge A legal procedure in which certain records about an individual are destroyed. In many jurisdictions, some juveniles may have records pertaining to delinquent acts expunged on reaching adulthood; also, people who have been arrested unlawfully or not convicted may apply to have their arrest records expunged.

extended-care facilities (ECF) Nursing homes for patients who need to remain in a *residential care facility* for extended periods, up to 100 days. To receive the ECF designation and thus be eligible for Medicare reimbursement, the facility must meet special federal and state certification standards. It must have staffs that usually include a medical director; registered nurse, nursing director, nursing supervisor, and skilled-nursing staff; dietician; physical therapist; occupational therapist; and a director of social services. ECFs are subject to *utilization review* by government bodies and *third parties*. See also *skilled-nursing facility*.

extended family A kinship group comprising relatives of a *nuclear family*, such as grandparents, uncles, aunts, and second cousins.

externality The concept in *social group work* in which the members apply what they have learned from their experiences in the group to their worlds outside the group and use their newly acquired skills to relate more effectively with their families and their communities.

externalization 1. The projecting of one's own thoughts or values onto some aspect of the environment. 2. The distinction young children make between themselves and their environments.

extinction In *behavior modification*, the elimination or weakening of a *conditioned response (CR)* by discontinuing *reinforcement* after the response occurs *(operant conditioning)*. In *respondent conditioning*, this occurs through repeated presentations of a *conditioned stimulus (CS)* without the *unconditioned stimulus (US)*.

extortion The crime of illegally taking money or other property from another person by using fear, coercion, or threats. Extortion is generally synonymous with *blackmail;* it differs from *robbery* in that the immediate personal and physical safety of the victim is not at risk.

extradition The legal process of bringing a person accused or convicted of a crime from one nation, state, or jurisdiction to another.

extrapolation Making inferential estimations based on, but beyond the scope of, available data. For example, a social worker might conclude that a client is not as ill as claimed because the case record indicates a tendency toward hypochondriasis.

extrinsic anxiety The client's unnecessary anxiety that occurs in the therapy situation and derives primarily from the uncertainty about the goals of the therapy and the methods by which the therapist will seek to reach them. This is contrasted with *intrinsic anxiety*.

extrovert An individual who tends to be outgoing and directs attention to others. Carl Jung (1875–1961) spelled this "extravert." The opposite is an *introvert*.

Fabian Society A group of British intellectuals formed in 1884 to advance progressive ideas. The Fabians, whose members included George Bernard Shaw, H. G. Wells, *Beatrice Webb*, and *Sydney Webb*, influenced British opinion toward evolutionary socialism and helped create the Labour Party.

face sheet A page, usually in the front of a client's *case record* or in front of a *questionnaire*, on which specific identifying data about the subject are recorded, such as age, gender, income, family members, and prior contacts with the agency.

face validity A simple method for assessing the *validity* of a scale or instrument, in which the researcher, using his or her professional judgment alone, accepts the instrument as valid if it looks or sounds valid.

facilitation An approach to social work intervention in which the social worker stimulates and mediates linkages between client systems, helps develop new systems, or helps strengthen existing ones. The social worker acts as an *enabler,* supporter, mediator, and broker for the client, paving the way for the client to reach desired goals. Facilitation activities include eliciting information and opinions, encouraging the expression of feelings, interpreting behavior, discussing alternative courses of action, clarifying situations, providing encouragement and reassurance, practicing logical reasoning, and recruiting members, usually within the context of a collaborative or bargaining relationship.

facilitator One who serves as a leader or catalyst for some group experience, usually to improve working relationships between members of the group. The facilitator seeks to help individuals and groups determine their own goals, develop their own solutions to problems, and coordinate their efforts to resolve conflicts. This typically occurs without imposing solutions or using formal authority, but through persuasion and nurturing. Social workers are often called on to act in this role.

facilitator role In social work, the responsibility to expedite the change effort by bringing together people and lines of communication, channeling

their activities and resources, and providing them with access to expertise. Other primary social work roles are identified as the *enabler role,* the *educator role,* and the *mobilizer role.*

fact-gathering interview An interview in which the social worker seeks predetermined and specific data from the client. The social worker asks specific questions and records relevant answers, often on a *face sheet* or forms. Its purpose is not primarily therapeutic and thus gives relatively little opportunity for the client to ventilate feelings or work through problems.

factions Coalitions of people who unite around an ideology, an issue, or an individual, usually to challenge other ideologies or individuals. Factions usually compete for the control of finite resources or the imposition of a specific position or policy.

factitious disorder Behavior that appears to be abnormal or a symptom of mental illness but is probably under the subject's voluntary control. It is similar to *malingering,* except that in factitious disorder there is no apparent benefit to be gained from the problem.

factitious disorder by proxy The condition of *factitious disorder,* in which it is not the individual with the apparent symptoms who reports them to helping professionals but that person's caregiver. This most commonly occurs when a parent or guardian of a child reports and induces the child's symptomatic behavior. Motivation is not for economic or other external gain but for the caregiver to assume a role in the illness or its treatment.

factor analysis A method in social statistics for identifying and interpreting the intercorrelations among variables or test scores.

failure to thrive See *marasmus.*

Fair Credit Billing Act (FCBA) Federal legislation passed in 1975 (P.L. 93-149) that protects consumers against errors in their credit card statements. Consumers are given 60 days to report any errors in their monthly bills, and the creditor must correct the mistake within 30 days.

Fair Debt Collection Practices Act   Federal legislation, passed in 1977 (P.L. 95-109), to control abusive behavior made by debt collectors such as late-evening telephoning, warnings about loss of reputation, and threats of job loss.

Fair Employment Practices Committee (FEPC)   The first federal program to monitor and eliminate *discrimination* in the U.S. labor force, created in 1941 by executive order of President Franklin D. Roosevelt. The program was opposed by Congress and finally abolished in 1945.

Fair Housing and Equal Opportunity Office   An organization within the *U.S. Department of Housing and Urban Development (HUD)* responsible for enforcing the laws that require home sellers and landlords to give all potential tenants or purchasers equal access.

Fair Labor Standards Act   Federal legislation originally enacted in 1938 (52 Stat. 1060) and amended periodically—and administered by the *U.S. Department of Labor*—that sets minimum wages, payment of time-and-a-half for work beyond 40 hours in a week, provisions of equal pay for equal work, and *child labor* standards.

fair market rents (FMR)   The maximum amount of rent a landlord can require of a *Section 8* tenant under the rules of *HUD*.

faith healing   The use of prayer and belief in divine intervention to alleviate symptoms of physical or mental disorders.

Faith-Based and Community Initiatives, U.S. Office of   The federal program to encourage and promote the use of religious and community groups for that part of their nonsectarian work that serves the general public by making them eligible for government grants and contracts. Established in 2001, the program includes a White House Office and five Centers for Faith-Based and Community Initiatives within the Departments of Housing and Urban Development, Labor, Justice, Education, and Health and Human Services. Religious organizations may apply for funding through these centers. All of the money awarded must go for community and social services projects that meet specified criteria and are to benefit all people regardless of their religious or spiritual ideologies. The White House Web site is http://www.whitehouse.gov/government/fbci/

faith-based social services   The provision of social services by people and organizations as part of their affiliation with religious groups. The services themselves may contain elements that are guided by the faith assumptions of the group or some form of spirituality.

falling out   A *culture-bound syndrome* occurring primarily among people in the southern United States and Caribbean islands in which the individual suddenly collapses; "blacks out"; feels dizzy; and even though he or she usually hears and understands what is going on nearby, feels powerless to move or respond.

false-negative/false-positive test result   An inaccurate conclusion based on some test, examination, or statistical analysis. When the conclusion is a false-negative, the test wrongly shows an effect or condition to be absent. For example, the false-negative test would show that the subject is free of drugs, when in fact the subject has been regularly taking drugs. When the result is a false-positive, the test incorrectly shows an effect or condition to be present. For example, a false-positive test would show that a woman is pregnant when she is not.

false-memory syndrome   *Confabulation*, the act of filling gaps in memory by fabricating and reporting these thoughts. Some clients with this syndrome come to believe they remember an event that did not happen. Others who have used *repression* or *suppression* to help avoid the distress of painful experiences eventually remember but distort all or parts of the experiences. The many others who eventually remember and accurately report what truly happened are not, of course, experiencing a false-memory syndrome. This is often used as a legal defense by accused child molesters. See also *memory recovery therapy*.

familial   Characteristics or traits that seem prevalent among closely related people.

familismo   The personal value in which the importance of family is paramount. This priority is widely held among Hispanic and other population groups and often extends beyond the immediate family to include the wider ethnic or geographic community of which one is a part.

family   A *primary group* whose members assume certain obligations for each other and generally share common residences. The NASW Commission on

Families (*Promoting Family Supports Statement,* 1990) defined a *family* as two or more people who consider themselves family and who assume obligations, functions, and responsibilities generally essential to healthy family life. Child care and child socialization, income support, *long-term care (LTC),* and other caregiving are among the functions of family life.

family allowance   A *demogrant* form of benefit in many nations, not including the United States, in which every eligible family, regardless of financial need, is allocated a specified sum of money. There are many variations to this system depending on the nation's social policy goals. These variations include making higher payments for families with more children, reducing payments if families have more than a prescribed number of children, and requiring families whose income exceeds a certain amount to pay back the family allowance at tax time. In some nations, these programs are known as *children's allowances* or *maternity benefits.*

Family and Medical Leave Act (FMLA)   The federal law (P.L. 103-3) enacted in 1993 that requires U.S. companies with more than 50 employees to offer employees up to 12 weeks each year of job-protected, unpaid leave with their health care coverage intact so they can care for any sick family member, newborn, or newly adopted or foster child.

Family Assistance, Office of (OFA)   The HHS organization within the *Administration for Children and Families (ACF)* that provides the department with guidance and technical assistance in administering its public welfare programs, including *Temporary Assistance to Needy Families (TANF).* The office provides information to states and territories, assesses their performance in administering the welfare programs, and recommends actions to improve effectiveness. Their Web site address is http://www.acf.dhhs.gov/programs/ofa

Family Assistance Plan (FAP)   A proposal to reform part of the U.S. *social welfare* system by providing every employed American family a *guaranteed annual income* above a specified low amount. The proposed legislation was developed in 1969 by the Nixon administration but was not passed by Congress.

family cap   A provision in some social welfare laws that allows jurisdictions to deny benefits after a specified amount of time or change in some status. For example, no additional funds may be granted to a welfare-recipient mother whose new baby exceeds the prescribed number of children allowed. Many nations have used the family cap to help limit population growth. In the United States, the family cap has been used in the *Temporary Assistance to Needy Families (TANF)* program; states may limit the number of recipients in a TANF family.

family care   The placement of institutionalized people into the homes of relatives or unrelated *guardians,* where they are permitted to participate as family members. Family care is often recommended for patients in mental hospitals, incarcerated juveniles, and frail elderly residents of nursing homes.

family cohesion   The tendency of members of a kinship group to stick together; spend time together; and rely on one another for companionship, support, recreation, and education. Families with less cohesion derive less companionship in their family relationships, spend more time with peers outside the family, and are more vulnerable to family breakdown such as divorce.

family court   A court of law that hears cases pertaining to conflicts among family members, such as *divorce, domestic violence, custody,* and *maintenance.* In many jurisdictions, family courts also include *juvenile court* functions.

family-driven support system   A program usually sponsored by state and local departments of public welfare and human services to help families provide at-home care for their members who have mental retardation. The system provides funds to the family to be used for purchasing services or goods.

Family Educational Rights and Privacy Act (FERPA)   The U.S. law enacted in 1975 (P.L. 93-380) that requires all schools that receive federal funds to protect the privacy of student education records. Parents and students may have access to the records and may contest any information they consider inaccurate or misleading. The records may be seen by others only with the written permission of the parent or student, except for school officials, juvenile law authorities, and very few others under carefully prescribed circumstances.

family, extended   See *extended family*.

family leave   An employee benefit in which workers are granted unpaid time off to provide care for family members, such as newborns, seriously ill relatives, and newly adopted children. See also *Family and Medical Leave Act (FMLA)*.

family life education (FLE)   A group-learning service designed to help family members of all ages develop knowledge and skills about strengthening relationships through transitions and crises. The format typically consists of a social worker or other professional leading a group of six to 12 members in weekly 90-minute to two-hour meetings. These sessions may be long term or closed ended (six to eight weeks), or sometimes single sessions. FLE services have been used especially by groups such as parents of newborns, parents of children about to enter school, groups preparing for marriage, empty-nest groups, and those entering retirement.

family map   A pictorial representation of the way a family is structured around a specific problem or concern. Each member of the family is represented by circles or squares, and the type of relationship that tends to exist between them is illustrated by drawing various types of lines.

family myths   A *family therapy* concept pertaining to a set of beliefs, based on distortions of facts or history, shared by members of a family. These beliefs serve to enforce the *family rules* that influence the way the members interact and ensure cohesiveness and stability in the family. (For example, one family might believe and communicate the view that its male members are less assertive than its female members.) The family members may be aware that these ideologies are inaccurate, but they are allowed to go unchallenged to preserve the existing family structure.

family, nuclear   See *nuclear family*.

family of orientation   A kinship group united not necessarily by blood but by factors such as common residence, shared experiences and backgrounds, mutual affection, and economic dependency.

family of origin   A kinship group united by blood or genetic similarity.

family of procreation   A kinship group created by an adult couple.

family planning   Making deliberate and voluntary decisions about reproduction. A couple practicing family planning decides on the number and timing of pregnancies after considering economic circumstances, life goals, the nature of the reproductive process, and *contraception* methods. See also *reproductive technology* and *birth control*.

family planning organizations   Privately funded voluntary associations that advocate *family planning* programs, laws, and social changes and that provide education, contraceptive opportunities, and national population policy changes. Major groups of this type include *Planned Parenthood Federation of America (PPFA)*, Alan Guttmacher Institute, Association of Reproductive Health Professionals, AVSC International (formerly the Association for Voluntary Sterilization or Surgical Contraception), Pathfinder International, and CHOICE (Concern for Health Options, Information, Care and Education). Some organizations of this type are more oriented to changing national and international population policies, research, and education. These include Zero Population Growth, Negative Population Growth, the Population Institute, and Population Communications International.

family policy   A nation's principles and planned procedures that are intended to influence or alter existing patterns of family life. Technically, all of a nation's *social policy* concerns (such as income maintenance, housing, education, and defense) affect families. Thus, the term "family policy" generally focuses more on issues such as fertility rates and family size, child care for working parents, care of older people, foster care programs, and income maintenance programs for families, as in *family allowance*. A nation's family policy may be explicit or implicit.

family preservation   Planned efforts to provide the knowledge, resources, supports, health care, relationship skills, and structures that help families stay intact and maintain their mutual roles and responsibilities. Government family preservation programs have been developed in many nations to help keep families from losing their children, especially through foster placement, abandonment, runaway, and juvenile incarceration. Some of these programs also help empower fathers and mothers so they can maintain traditional roles.

family projection process   A *family therapy* concept developed by Murray Bowen (1914–1990) that refers to the way some members of a family, especially parents, attribute sources of conflict to other members of the family, especially children. This process frequently results in one or more of the children in a family becoming the bearers of the symptoms of the family's ills.

family rules   A *family therapy* term that refers to repetitious patterns of behavior and mutual expectations regulating that behavior in a family. One family, for example, might maintain a mutual expectation that none of its members is to express outwardly any feelings of affection for one another. Another family might have a rule that every dispute is to result in threatened or actual physical violence.

family sculpting   An evaluation and intervention technique in some forms of *family therapy* in which family members are asked to position and choreograph the movements of other family members and to create a living tableau of people that reflects the communication and relationship patterns in the family unit.

family secrets   A *family therapy* concept pertaining to shared but concealed beliefs and perceptions that some or all of the family members may hold but hide from one another to achieve certain family interactions.

Family Service America (FSA)   The organization composed of privately funded, local family services organizations plus professionals and private citizens interested in social services for families. Its member agencies provide *family therapy* and *marital therapy*, guidance and educational programs, and social services to the community. The organization sets standards for member agencies; provides public relations and educational programs; and sponsors research and publications, including the journal *Families in Society* (formerly *Social Casework*). Its board helps set policy and advise lawmakers about family needs. Formerly known as the Family Service Association of America, the organization was established as an outgrowth of the National Association of Societies for Organizing Charities in 1911.

family services organizations   Social agencies that provide a variety of human services, especially to couples, families, and extended-family units. These organizations are most often funded through grants and private donations and follow policies

established by independently elected or appointed boards of directors. Services include *family therapy* and *marital therapy*, family life education, and community activities to enhance healthy family development. Many of these agencies are affiliated with national organizations.

family systems theories   The application of *systems theories* (those that emphasize reciprocal relationships and mutual influences between the individual components and the whole and vice versa). Virtually all current *family therapy* approaches and theoretical orientations that focus on understanding or treating families use a systems theory; however, there are many variations and differences in emphases in these theories.

family therapy   Intervention by a professional social worker or other family therapist with a group of family members who are considered to be a single *unit of attention*. Typically, the approach focuses on the whole system of individuals and interpersonal and communication patterns. It seeks to clarify roles and reciprocal obligations and to encourage more adaptable behaviors among the family members. The therapist concentrates on verbal and nonverbal communications and on the "here and now" rather than on family history. Variations in family therapy techniques are practiced by proponents of psychosocial, behavioral, systems, and other orientations. Some of the more influential family therapy "schools" have been influenced by Salvador Minuchin *(structural family therapy)*, Jay Haley *(strategic family therapy)*, *Virginia Satir* and the Palo Alto Group, Murray Bowen, Carl Whittaker, Henry V. Dicks, Mara Selvini-Palazzoli, and Peggy Papp.

Family Therapy Practice Academy (FTPA)   The professional association affiliated with the *Clinical Social Work Federation (CSWF)* to facilitate social work's role in *family therapy*. FTPA sponsors workshops and publications on social work in family therapy; raises the public consciousness about social workers in this field; and advocates for this social work specialty with legislators, other family therapy groups, and insurance companies.

Family Unification Program   A *HUD* program established in 1992 to provide rental housing assistance to families whose children are at risk of being placed in foster care because of the family's potential for homelessness.

"family values" A euphemism commonly used to suggest that there is a single ideal relationship between members of a traditional kinship group. The term often implies lifestyles in which children are raised in their homes with both parents (usually with the father as the leader and breadwinner) in nurturing environments that encourage hard work, economic affluence, emotional security, basic education, and adherence to religious and law-abiding traditions. As a political term, "family values" is sometimes used as code for policies that seek to discourage unwed parenthood, homosexuality, abortion, birth control, sex education, and public assistance.

family violence Aggressive and hostile behaviors between members of a family that result in injury, harm, humiliation, and sometimes death. These behaviors may include physical abuse, rape, destruction of property, and deprivation of basic needs.

family welfare One of professional social work's first designated *fields of practice*. The activities include *marriage counseling, parent training,* and *child protective services (CPS),* as well as helping clients obtain access to financial assistance, health care, educational provisions, and employment. Family welfare work takes place in public and private agencies such as departments of *public assistance* and *family services organizations.*

Family Welfare Association (of the United Kingdom) The British national federation of social agencies, including charities, adoption societies, almshouses, centers for people with disabilities, community councils, and citizen's advice bureaus. The association, established in 1869, coordinates efforts to improve social services in the United Kingdom and publishes the annual *Charities Digest.*

famine A widespread and severe scarcity of vital needs, especially food.

fantasy The mental picturing of events, objects, or other forms of symbolic thought in daydreams or while sleeping. Normally, fantasy is a healthy outlet for an individual's adjustment and creative needs but when excessive can be a symptom of *mental disorder.*

faqir In Arabic cultures, an impoverished or destitute person. The term also applies in some cultures to Islamic religious mendicants, or to people who are deemed mentally, morally, or religiously weak.

fascism A political ideology and party that advocates a totalitarian structure of governance, extreme nationalism under a charismatic dictator, high favor for private capitalism, a regimented populace devoted to social productivity, and sanctions against individuals who are considered less economically productive or responsible for economic problems. Benito Mussolini and Adolf Hitler espoused this ideology.

Fatherhood Initiative The program within the *U.S. Department of Health and Human Services* to support and strengthen the role of fathers in families through education, the facilitation of access to needed resources, enforcement, and encouragement.

Fauri, Fedele F. (1909–1981) A public welfare expert and social work educator, Fauri was longtime dean at the University of Michigan School of Social Work after serving as the state's director of social welfare. He helped develop doctoral programs for social work and presided over many national social welfare organizations.

favelas *Shantytowns* in some Latin American nations. See also *barriadas.*

fear The emotional and physical reaction to an identifiable or perceived source of danger.

feasibility study A systematic assessment of the resources needed to accomplish a specified objective and concurrent evaluation of an organization's existing and anticipated capabilities for providing those resources.

featherbedding Requiring an employer to hire workers who are not needed. For example, a union contract might require that 10 workers are hired even though the job needs only five. The Labor–Management Relations Act (Taft–Hartley Act) of 1947 forbids the practice, but it is easily circumvented.

fecundity A given *population* group's potential for reproduction, determined by counting the number of fertile women of childbearing age.

Federal Bureau of Investigation (FBI) The principal investigative arm of the U.S. Justice Department that investigates federal crimes and assists other law enforcement agencies with training, laboratory examinations, and procedures of scientific identification. It investigates issues such as civil rights, terrorism, foreign counterintelligence, organized crime and drugs, financial crimes, major offenders, kidnappings, and crimes that cross state boundaries. The FBI conducts background investigations on more senior-level employees of the federal government and collaborates with local investigative agencies. Founded in 1908 with a small force of special agents, the FBI now has more than 400 resident agencies, 56 field offices, and 40 foreign liaison posts with more than 25,000 agents and other employees. The FBI manages the "Ten Most Wanted List" and the Uniform Crime Reporting (UCR) Program. Their Web site address is http://www.fbi.gov

Federal Consumer Information Center (FCIC) The Pueblo, Colorado–based federal program established in 1970 to provide people with assistance and information about government services, consumer issues, safe and worthwhile products and services, and unscrupulous practices in the marketplace. FCIC distributes pamphlets on all consumer-related topics and assists other government departments to get their consumer information to the public. The public can reach the FCIC by telephone toll-free (in English and Spanish) at 1-800-686-9889; on the Internet at http://www.pueblo.gsa.gov; or by U.S. mail at FCIC, Pueblo, CO 81009.

Federal Crime Insurance Program A program established in 1971 and administered by the *U.S. Department of Housing and Urban Development (HUD)* that underwrites insurance against the risks of crime when it is unavailable from commercial insurance companies. It is used primarily by small businesses located in high-crime neighborhoods.

Federal Deposit Insurance Corporation (FDIC) A government corporation that insures people's deposits in national and some state banks that are members of the Federal Reserve System. Depositors are assured that their funds, up to an amount specified in advance, will be returned to them in the event that the bank fails or has insufficient resources to meet all its obligations.

Federal Emergency Management Agency (FEMA) An agency within the U.S. Department of Homeland Security designed to organize and coordinate the nation's emergency preparedness. It oversees

civil defense programs, urban riot response, and *disaster relief.* Their Web site address is http://www.fema.gov

Federal Emergency Relief Administration (FERA) The government organization established during the Roosevelt administration in 1933 and directed by *Harry Hopkins* (1890–1946), a social worker. The program distributed federal funds to the states for emergency unemployment relief and required every local administration to have at least one experienced social worker on its staff. FERA and other *New Deal* programs were terminated as World War II began.

Federal Employee Health Benefits Program (FEHBP) A program that provides health benefits for employees of the federal government. In 1986, the program was amended by the Federal Employees Benefits Improvement Act (P.L. 99-251); one of the provisions eliminated the requirement for physician supervision as a condition for reimbursing clinical social workers.

Federal Employee Retirement System (FERS) The insurance program for retired employees of the U.S. federal government who were hired after 1984; those hired before 1984 are covered in the *Civil Service Retirement System (CSRS).* FERS includes social security, a pension plan, and a thrift savings plan.

Federal Housing Administration (FHA) The national program implemented in 1938 to encourage home ownership. Its most important feature has been to guarantee loans to finance individual homes, permitting homeowners to make lower down payments (5 percent and 10 percent) and to take longer to pay the balance (30 and sometimes 40 years). Their Web site address is http://www.hud.gov/offices/hsg

Federal Insurance Contributions Act (FICA) The federal law that authorizes the government to levy payroll taxes on employers and employees. The revenues are earmarked to finance *Old Age, Survivors, Disability, and Health Insurance (OASDHI).* See also *Self-Employment Contributions Act (SECA) of 1954.*

Federal Parent Locator Service (FPLS) A U.S. program to help states and local jurisdictions enforce child support obligations. FPLS acquires information about parents through sources such as the *Internal Revenue Service* and *Social Security Administration* and provides it to local jurisdictions. The program was expanded in 1996 to help maintain registries of all hires in each state and any child support orders. FPLS also helps in establishing paternity as well as in establishing, modifying, and enforcing child support obligations. Their Web site address is http://www.acf.hhs.gov/programs/cse/newhire

Federal Register   The U.S. government online and print publication in which all executive orders, proclamations, proposed rules and legislation, and notices of all government agencies are made available to the public. Their Web site address is http://www.archives.gov/federal-register

federally qualified health center (FQHC)   A health care facility partly funded by the U.S. government to provide low-cost health care, often including preventive care. FQHCs include many community health centers, tribal health clinics, migrant health services, and health centers for homeless people.

Federations of Social Agencies   Organizations composed of private welfare agencies in a given community that combine some of their resources and efforts for fundraising, public relations, lobbying, and educational activities.

Federico, Ronald (1941–1992)   Social work educator who helped synthesize undergraduate social work education curricula and author of numerous books, including the influential 1982 textbook *Human Behavior: A Perspective for the Helping Professions.*

fee for service   A charge made to clients or their *fiscal intermediaries* for a specified service (such as an hour of psychotherapy).

fee schedule   A listing of the maximum fee that a health plan will pay for any service based on *Current Procedural Terminology (CPT)* codes.

"feeble minded"   The obsolete term laypersons and professionals alike once used in referring to people who are intellectually challenged. For example, the *American Association on Mental Retardation (AAMR)* originated in 1876 as the American Association for the Study of the Feeble-Minded.

feedback   Transmitting information about the results of an action to the individual who per-

formed that action. This permits a more objective evaluation of the action's effectiveness. It also permits modifications in the ongoing action to increase the likelihood of success. In social work administration, feedback is often used in supervision, personnel evaluations, client reports, and objective *outcome evaluations* to help social workers achieve desired improvements or to give them positive indicators when they are performing well.

feeding disorder of infancy or early childhood   Persistent failure to eat adequately, resulting in weight loss or failure to gain weight. The onset of this disorder is in the first year but occasionally occurs after ages two or three. The disorder is not the result of gastrointestinal, endocrinological, or neurological conditions or lack of food. See also *eating disorders, rumination disorder,* and *pica.*

Feingold diet   A treatment modality designed for children who have *attention-deficit hyperactivity disorder (ADHD)*. B. F. Feingold claimed that children with behavioral and learning problems have a natural toxic reaction to flavorings, preservatives, and coloring in food, and he proposed a nutritious diet free of such additives. The hypothesis is empirically unsubstantiated but has a wide following.

felony   A crime that is more serious than a *misdemeanor.* Felonies include *burglary* and some categories of *larceny, homicide, rape,* and *assault.*

female genital mutilation (FGM)   Surgical removal of all or part of the external female genitalia. The practice ranges from "milder" forms such as clitoridectomy, in which part of the clitoris is removed, to severe forms, such as infibulation, in which the clitoris, labia, urethra, and vaginal openings are cut away and the vagina is then stitched closed. The practice, which has affected from 80 million to 135 million girls (usually from four to 12 years old) is most common in parts of Africa, the Middle East, and Central Asia. See also *clitoridectomy.*

female orgasmic disorder   A *sexual disorder* in women characterized by the persistent or recurrent delay or absence of orgasm following a normal sexual excitement phase. This condition has also been known as "inhibited female orgasm" or as "orgasmic impairment." See also *male orgasmic disorder.*

female sexual arousal disorder   A *sexual disorder* in women characterized by a persistent or recurrent inability to attain or maintain a satisfactory lubrication and swelling in response to sexual excitement (when sexual stimulation is adequate in focus, intensity, and duration), leading to distress or interpersonal difficulties. When using this term as a diagnosis, therapists specify whether the condition is lifelong or acquired, generalized or situational, and due to psychological or combined factors. See also *male erectile disorder*.

feminism   The social movement and doctrine advocating legal and socioeconomic equality for women. The movement originated in Great Britain in the 18th century. See also *women's liberation movement*.

feminist group work   In social work with groups the professional practice of attaching the values, ideas, and sensitivities of *feminism* to female, and sometimes male, clients. Most clients are women who faced barriers to achieving their potential because of cultural norms that perpetuate those barriers. Many feminist groups serve women who have been victimized by rape, exploitation, prejudice, and other factors, and a major focus is to help them understand the societal and structural barriers underlying their problems.

feminist social work   The integration of the values, skills, and knowledge of social work with a feminist orientation to help individuals and society overcome the emotional and social problems that result from *gender discrimination*.

feminist therapy   A psychosocial treatment orientation in which the professional (usually a woman) helps the client (usually a woman) in individual or group settings overcome the psychological and social problems largely encountered as a result of *gender discrimination* and *gender role stereotyping*. Feminist therapists help clients maximize their potential, especially through raising their consciousness, eliminating gender stereotyping, and helping them become aware of the commonalities shared by all women.

feminization of poverty concept   The fact that women, especially those raising children without husbands or significant others, are far more vulnerable to being poor. The high rates of divorce, unwed motherhood, and family breakdowns and the burden of child care tending to fall on the mothers, many of whom have not had good employment experience, result in gender-skewed poverty rates.

"fence"   In criminal justice terms, one who receives stolen property and sells it for a profit.

Fernandis, Sarah (1863–1951)   Founder of the first black social *settlement house* in the United States and organizer for improved health and sanitation in black neighborhoods.

fertility   The biological capacity to reproduce.

fertility rate   A demographic characteristic indicating the number of live births that occur in a population group during a specific time span.

fertilization in vitro   See *in vitro fertilization*.

fetal alcohol syndrome (FAS)   Damage to a *fetus* as a result of heavy maternal alcohol consumption. Potential problems include slow growth, mental retardation, and sometimes craniofacial and limb abnormalities.

fetal protection policy   An employment policy in some industries and jurisdictions that excludes pregnant, and sometimes fertile, women from jobs considered hazardous to the unborn or to reproductive capacities.

fetishism   A *sexual disorder* of the *paraphilia* class involving erotic attraction to an inanimate object or specific body part, especially clothing, shoes, and hair. See also *erotic orientation*.

fetology   The science and medical specialty that deals with the study, care, and treatment of the *fetus* during prenatal development.

fetus   An unborn infant; usually the term is applied to developing human organisms from the third month after conception until birth. Development from the ninth week consists primarily of the refinements of existing organ systems and an increase in size.

fetus personhood debate   The controversial issue about the rights of the unborn; one side holds that human life and full personhood begins at *conception*, and the other side holds that, although human life in all forms is important, the fetus is not yet a person with full rights that might subordinate the rights of the mother. See also *abortion, prochoice movement,* and *right-to-life movement*.

feudalism   The socioeconomic and political system in medieval Europe in which people of high social rank were given land grants (fiefs) by people of even higher rank in exchange for tax payments and the military services of those who managed and worked the land.

fibromyalgia   A *chronic pain* condition with symptoms such as muscle aches and tender points on examination, sleep disturbance and fatigue, headaches, vascular reactivity, and urinary and bowel irritability. Many sufferers also experience *depression* and decreased social functioning.

fidgetiness   Restless movements and increased motor activity, often seen in people experiencing anxiety, hyperactivity, anger, or impatience. It also occurs in *tics* and gross motor disturbances.

fiduciary   A trustee who is entrusted with the rights and powers of another person and who is responsible for exercising those rights and powers on behalf of the beneficiary. The fiduciary relationship exists between trustee and beneficiary; in certain circumstances it also exists between lawyers and their clients, clergy and their parishioners, and social workers and their clients.

field instruction   In *social work education,* an integral part of the *BSW* and *MSW* educational curricula—providing students with supervised opportunities to engage in direct social work practice with individuals, families, groups, communities, and organizations. Students are helped to refine professional skills, acquire and solidify social work values, and integrate the knowledge acquired in the academic setting with that obtained in the field.

field placement   A part of the social work student's formal educational requirement, consisting of ongoing work in a community social agency. The *MSW* student typically is given a work assignment (of 16 to 20 hours weekly) in one agency during the first training year and assigned to another agency with about the same time requirements during the second year. The student receives close supervision by agency personnel and has the opportunity to integrate, use, and apply classroom content to practical experiences. Field placements also exist in undergraduate (baccalaureate social work) programs and in some doctoral programs. See also *concurrent placement* and *block placement.*

field study   A social research method of investigating subjects in their natural environments instead of in a laboratory or clinician's office. For example, a social worker doing research in a ghetto would stay in that neighborhood to make systematic observations for an extended period.

fields of practice   The social work term pertaining to the profession's various practice settings and the special competence needed to work in those settings. Fields of practice were established by the 1920s when it became apparent that social work practice itself was so far-reaching that it was becoming difficult for individuals to encompass. The first fields of practice included *family welfare, child welfare, psychiatric social work, medical social work,* and *school social work.* These fields have, to some extent, changed their names and their focus (for example, from *psychiatric social work* to "social work in mental health" and from *medical social work* to "social work in health care"), and new ones have emerged. They now also include *occupational social work, gerontological social work, rural social work, police social work,* and *forensic social work.*

Fifth Amendment rights   Protections under the Fifth Amendment of the U.S. Constitution guaranteeing that no citizen may be compelled to give self-incriminating testimony for a court or congressional committee. This amendment also protects the individual from being tried a second time for the same crime *(double jeopardy)* or being deprived of life, liberty, or property without *due process of law.* See also *self-incrimination.*

filial responsibility   See *relatives' responsibility.*

filial therapy   The use of parents in a structured intervention for children with mental, social, or behavioral disorders. The therapist meets with small groups (six to eight parents) in didactic and information-gathering sessions. The parents then rehearse treatment techniques in the group before using them at home with their children. They discuss the ongoing results with the group.

fine motor skills   The ability of muscles to make small movements, increments, and adjustments to achieve delicate manipulations such as threading a needle or tying a shoelace. See also *gross motor skills.*

fines   Payment of money as a punishment for wrongdoing. In the corrections field, fines are the most common penalty imposed on lawbreakers. See also *community-based corrections.*

First Amendment rights   Protections under the First Amendment of the U.S. Constitution guaranteeing that government will not abridge the rights of free speech and press, worship, peaceable assembly, or petitioning the government for redress of grievances.

First Nations Peoples   The descendants of the original inhabitants of what is now referred to as Canada and the United States. See also *Native Americans.*

FirstGov   The U.S. federal government Internet homepage (http://www.firstgov.gov) that provides links to all federal government agencies, programs, laws, benefits, and services of the U.S. government.

first-order change   In *systems theories,* a temporary or superficial change in a system and the way it functions. See also *second-order change.*

fiscal intermediaries   Organizations that provide third-party and fourth-party financial services between recipients and providers of a benefit. For example, whereas a government organization *(third party)* provides funds for Medicaid health care providers, a private insurance company such as Blue Cross–Blue Shield *(fourth party)* may provide the related administrative support.

fiscal policy   A nation's economic goals and the manipulation of its finances to reach those goals, usually through the raising or lowering of taxes, spending levels, and interest rates.

fiscal welfare   A system of redistributing income through tax exclusions, exemptions, deductions, and credits. In the United States, fiscal welfare is administered primarily through the *Internal Revenue Service,* and the tax expenditures it controls are revenue losses to the public in favor of those who meet the criteria for special exclusion from taxation. Among these exclusions are tax deductions for dependents and older people, medical expenses that exceed 7.5 percent of adjusted gross income, mortgage interest, local property taxes, and many other exemptions. See also *corporate welfare* and *occupational welfare.*

fiscal year   A 12-month accounting period used by governments, business organizations, and social agencies that often does not coincide with the calendar year. The fiscal year of the U.S. government begins October 1st and ends September 30th.

501(c) organizations   A type of nonprofit public interest or public service organization, such as a lobbying group, social welfare group, or charitable foundation, identified by the U.S. Internal Revenue Service to indicate its tax status. Lobbying organizations are 501(c)(4) groups and not exempt from paying taxes. Contributors to *political action committees (PACs),* which are 501(c)(5) groups, cannot deduct their contributions from their taxes. Charitable foundations are 501(c)(3) groups and are tax exempt. To take advantage of tax laws, many 501(c) organizations form foundations outside of their functions. For example, the Sierra Club comprises several organizations, including a PAC that is a 501(c)(5) organization and a foundation that is a 501(c)(3) organization.

Five Promises Movement   A national effort to mobilize Americans to fulfill five major obligations to its young people. The promises are to provide them with (1) ongoing relationships with caring adults, (2) safe places after school, (3) opportunities for good health, (4) marketable skills through effective education, and (5) opportunities to give back through community service. The movement was founded in 1997 by Colin Powell, the living former presidents, and many others. The movement is facilitated by an alliance of thousands of public and private service organizations and by the America's Promise Alliance for Youth and the *AmeriCorps Promise Fellows.*

"504 student"   A term applied to some public school students who meet criteria established in the *Rehabilitation Act of 1973* (P.L. 93-112), in which Section 504 prohibits discrimination against any person with physical or mental impairment that substantially limits one or more of such person's "major life activities," including education. The term came into use by professionals after schools were pressured to provide accommodations and services for students with impairments such as *attention-deficit hyperactivity disorder (ADHD)* who did not qualify for special education services.

fixation   1. A continuing mode of behavior, persistent thought, or enduring emotional attachment that has become inappropriate for one's present circumstances or age. 2. In psychodynamic theory, the partial or complete arrest of personality development at one of the psychosexual stages.

fixed assets   An organization's or social agency's financial holdings, such as land, buildings, and properties, that are not readily negotiable. Fixed assets exclude valuable things such as accessible cash, expertise of personnel, and the agency's reputation or goodwill factors.

fixed-interval schedule A procedure used in *behavior modification* in which a *reinforcement* is delivered when a specified period has elapsed after a response has occurred. For example, a child may be given a reward 10 minutes after completing a homework assignment.

Fizdale, Ruth (1908–1994) A social work practitioner, administrator, and scholar who encouraged efforts to extend social work services to nonpoor clients and led the profession's movement toward more accountability, licensing, peer review, and competence certification.

flashback A mental sensation of a sudden recurrence of a previous experience or perception. See also *hallucinogen persisting-perception disorder.*

"flasher" Slang for a certain type of exhibitionist who suddenly opens and closes articles of clothing, such as an overcoat, to reveal flashing glimpses of genitals. See also *exhibitionism* and *indecent exposure.*

flat affect The appearance of *apathy* in *mood*. For example, an individual may show no emotion when told of bad news or take good news with indifference. It is sometimes a symptom of *schizophrenia* or *depression.*

flat tax rate A tax system in which everybody pays the same percentage of taxes on their income. Although this would simplify calculating how much one owes, it is a regressive tax and would be a disadvantage to less affluent people.

flat-rate fee A predetermined amount of money charged by a professional for providing a particular service. The amount assessed is related to the service itself rather than to the client's unique economic circumstances. See also *sliding fee scale.*

Flexner Report An influential paper delivered to social workers in 1915 by Abraham Flexner (1866–1959) that declared that social work was not yet a *profession* because it lacked a unique technology, specific educational programs, a professional literature, and practice skills. Although it was controversial, the report stimulated social work to make the changes that eventually resulted in the fulfillment of Flexner's criteria of *professionalism.*

flextime A work schedule in which employees can use their own discretion as to the time on the job as long as they complete the specified number of hours within a work period (that is, one month, one week, or one day). In such circumstances, the workers usually must begin and end work within a prescribed band of time.

flight into health A phenomenon in which the client's symptoms or problems suddenly seem to cease without intervention. At that point, the client wants to terminate treatment or change the focus of attention in the treatment. This seems to occur primarily because the client fears some material or emotions that the therapy is uncovering and hopes to avoid the revelation by ending the work. Other causes are that the client is being pressured by financial or family constraints to end treatment.

flight into illness A phenomenon in which the client whose therapy is coming to an end suddenly exhibits new symptoms. It is considered a manifestation of overdependency, a *transference* experience, or fear of *abandonment.*

flight of ideas Rapid skipping from one thought or mental association to another without much basis for connection. It is sometimes a symptom of *hyperkinesis, bipolar disorder* (manic type), and drug-induced *euphoria.*

float The period between when a check is written and when the bank funds are collected; sometimes individuals write checks when there are insufficient funds to cover them, hoping to make deposits in time to cover the amount.

flooding A procedure used in *behavior therapy* in which stimuli that elicit anxiety are presented, either in reality or imagery, with such regularity or intensity that the subject eventually stops responding with anxiety. See also *implosive therapy.*

"flophouse" A derisive term sometimes applied to cheap transient hotels, mission homes, and shelters for homeless people.

Florence Crittenden Association A social services and residential treatment program to care for unwed mothers and to facilitate *adoption* of children.

In 1976 it merged into the *Child Welfare League of America (CWLA)*. See also *maternity homes*.

fluid intelligence The mental skills and abilities that pertain to problem solving, adaptability, and integration of ideas. Unlike *crystallized intelligence*, which continues to develop throughout life, fluid intelligence tends to decline in later adulthood. See also *multiple intelligences*.

focus group A group convened to discuss a specific issue or single topic, often with the aid of questionnaires and a moderator who actively keeps the conversation oriented to that topic. Such groups are often established to acquire information and generate ideas that would not be as accessible through individual interviews. Focus groups are frequently used in *social group work* and *community organization* and may include the *nominal group technique*, the *Delphi method*, and *brainstorming*.

folie à deux The sharing of delusions by two people. For example, a husband and wife may come to believe and help reinforce one another's conviction that they are being ridiculed secretly by their neighbors. This phenomenon is also known as *shared psychotic disorder*. See also *codependency* and *conjugal paranoia*.

folk medicine Alternative health care procedures and ideas, commonly using "natural" remedies, healing rituals that sometimes may entail supernatural elements, and extracts from plants to alleviate specific symptoms. This is also known as ethnomedicine.

folklore The traditions, legends, beliefs, and sayings of a group of people (such as an ethnic group, a tribe, a nation, a regional group, or an extended family).

Folks, Homer (1867–1963) A child welfare reformer who worked at the *Children's Aid Society* in New York but disagreed with their methods. He became an advocate of home placement of orphans and juvenile delinquents and urged an end to child dumping in *orphanages* and *almshouses* and unsupervised placing-out programs. In 1904 he wrote the influential text *Care of Destitute, Neglected, and Delinquent Children*.

folkways Informal, traditional, and not strongly enforced patterns of behavior and standards of conduct in a *culture*.

Follett, Mary Parker (1868–1933) A social activist in the *vocational guidance* movement, she also developed many of the principles used in *administration in social work* and wrote the posthumously published text *Dynamic Administration* (1941).

following responses In the social work *interview*, the process of giving clients immediate *feedback* that their messages have been heard and understood. The social worker does this not by asking questions or directing discussion but by *paraphrasing* the client's words, conveying *empathy*, and showing attentiveness through verbalizations such as "I see," "I understand," or "You did?"

Food and Agriculture Organization (FAO) An agency of the United Nations established in 1945 to improve the world's agricultural production and distribution and to enhance the nutritional level of all peoples. It devises plans for improving yields in agriculture, oceans, and forests and also supervises research to improve seeds and hybrid crops and to develop fertilizers and pesticides. Their Web site address is http://www.fao.org

Food and Drug Administration (FDA) A federal program, established in 1931 and now part of the *U.S. Department of Health and Human Services (HHS)*, that maintains standards and conducts research on the safety, reliability, and value of food and drug products available for human consumption. Their Web site address is http://www.fda.gov

Food and Nutrition Service The U.S. Department of Agriculture organization that administers the nation's nutrition assistance programs. Its programs include the *Food Stamp program*, the *WIC program*, the *Child Nutrition Programs* (including the *School Lunch Program*, the *School Breakfast Program*, the *Special Milk Program*, and the *Summer Food Service Program*), the *Child and Adult Care Food Program*, and *Team Nutrition*. Their Web site address is http://www.fns.usda.gov/fns/

food assistance programs Benefits for eligible people to ensure that their nutritional requirements are met. The major food assistance programs in the United States are managed by the *Food and Nutrition Service* of the USDA. USDA also arranges the donation of surplus agricultural products to some charitable institutions and nonprofit summer camps.

food bank A facility and program in which excess food from the donations of restaurants, grocery stores, private individuals, farmers, gardeners, and governments is collected and dispersed to needy individuals, soup kitchens, shelters, and organizations that help distribute food.

Food for Peace Act   The 1966 U.S. federal legislation (P.L. 89-808) to liquidate surplus food by donating it to poor nations. The program allows the government to give the food outright, or at significant discount, or it may provide loans or grants to nations so they may purchase the food from American farmers or agribusinesses. In its first 10 years the programs distributed about 27 percent of the total value of all U.S. farm exports. The current version of the program allocates foreign aid funds to combat hunger rather than provides surplus food.

food poisoning   Sickness from food-borne bacteria, yeasts, molds or viruses, and unsanitary food handling. The consequences range from short-term headache and stomachache, nausea, and diarrhea to long-term abdominal pain and sometimes death. The most common of these poisonings includes salmonella, staphylococcus, *cholera,* infectious hepatitis, and *botulism.*

Food Safety and Inspection Service (FSIS)   The USDA organization that ensures that commercial food is safe, wholesome, and correctly labeled and packaged. FSIS supervises inspection and grading of meat and poultry and food imports.

food security   The ability of an individual, family, community, or nation to obtain, consistently, enough food to maintain for all its people a level of nutrition needed for good health and productive lives.

Food Stamp program   The primary *food assistance program* of the United States that ensures that all people, regardless of need, will have adequate nutrition. Food programs originated in 1939 with actual distribution of surplus food products to eligible needy families. Food stamps began with 1964 legislation (P.L. 88-525). The stamp booklets were distributed to needy eligible individuals and families to be used like cash in participating stores to purchase most foods, plants, seeds, and sometimes *meals-on-wheels,* but not alcohol or tobacco products. The objective was to improve the diets of low-income households by supplementing their food-purchasing ability. The welfare reform legislation,

Personal Responsibility and Work Opportunity Reconciliation Act of 1996, placed significant restrictions on the program. Since then the states have more control in determining eligibility and amount of benefits and may deny benefits to those who, during the preceding 31 months, have received them and have not worked or participated in a work-training program. Most participants pay a deductible for the allotments. Coupons or debit cards (electronic benefit transfers) are used in transactions.

force field analysis (FFA)   A problem-solving tool often used in social welfare planning, administration, and *community organization* for assessing the degree of resistance or receptivity to a proposed change. FFA includes listing the social forces that push for change (such as high costs of the existing program or ineffectiveness in reaching stated goals) and then listing those forces expected to obstruct change (such as the existing personnel's fear of losing job security or authority). FFA then delineates actions that can be taken to increase or decrease certain forces so as to facilitate movement toward the desired goal.

foreclosure   The legal termination of the right to a specified property, usually as a consequence of nonpayment of the obligation.

Foreign Equivalency Determination Service   A program of the *Council on Social Work Education (CSWE)* that evaluates the academic credentials of people educated in nations other than the United States to determine their equivalency to CSWE-accredited education programs. These evaluations are used to establish qualifications for *certification, licensing, employment,* graduate school admission, and membership in social work–related *professional associations.*

forensic social work   The practice specialty in social work that focuses on the law, legal issues, and litigation, both criminal and civil, including issues in *child welfare, custody of children, divorce, juvenile delinquency, nonsupport, relatives' responsibility, welfare rights,* mandated treatment, and legal competency. Forensic social work helps social workers in *expert witness* preparation. It also seeks to educate law professionals about social welfare issues and social workers about the law. Many social workers in this field belong to the *National Organization of Forensic Social Workers.* Its Web site address is http://www.nofsw.org

forgery Counterfeiting or fabricating an object of value, such as a signature, document, or work of art, with the intent to commit *fraud.*

formal operations stage In *Piagetian theory,* the developmental stage that occurs during *adolescence* and that is characterized by greater flexibility in thought, increasing ability to use logic and *deductive reasoning,* the ability to consider complex issues from several viewpoints, and a reduction of *egocentrism.*

former migratory child See *migratory child.*

fossil fuels Burnable products, including oil, natural gas, and coal, formed from ancient living organisms extracted from the earth.

foster care The provision of physical care and family environments for children who are unable to live with their natural parents or legal guardians. Foster care is typically administered by county social services departments. Their social workers evaluate children and their families to help legal authorities determine the need for placement, evaluate potential foster homes as to their appropriateness for placing the particular child, monitor the foster home during the placement, and help the legal authorities and family members determine when it is appropriate to return the child to the natural family. The precedent for foster care in the United States originated largely with *apprenticing* and *indenture,* procedures in which homeless youths were placed in the care of a merchant or craftsperson for instruction and lodging in exchange for work. The term "foster care" also applies to full-time residential care for adults who are older, have developmental disabilities, or have a mental illness. See also *adult foster care* and *Title IV Foster Care.*

Foster Care Independence Act The 1999 federal law (P.L. 106-169) that assists children who age out of foster care programs to make the transition to independent adult living. Money is provided to eligible 18- to 21-year-olds who leave foster care for education, vocational training, training in daily-living skills, substance abuse prevention, pregnancy prevention, preventive health activities, and connections to dedicated adults. Funding for each individual comes from the federal government (80 percent) and the state in which the individual has been in the foster care system.

Foster Grandparents A U.S. *Senior Corps* volunteer program administered by the *Corporation for National Service* to employ low-income citizens over age 60 to provide care and emotional support for children with special needs. See also *intergenerational care center.*

Foundation Center An independent organization established in 1956 to collect and communicate information on U.S. philanthropy. The center lists foundation grant possibilities and information on how to obtain them. Information about its services, including its major publication, *The Foundation Directory,* can be obtained at the center's Web site, http://www.fdncenter.org

foundations Institutions through which private funds are distributed for public purposes such as education, international relations, health, welfare, research, the humanities, and religion. Several types include independent foundations (family and private foundations with fewer areas of focus), community foundations (organizations for administering separate charitable funds in one geographic region), company foundations (set up by, but legally independent of, business organizations), and operating foundations (to directly conduct research and provide services).

foundling hospitals Institutions that care for abandoned children. The first foundling hospital was established in Milan, Italy, in 787. *Thomas Coram* established the first one in England in 1739. St. Vincent's Infant Asylum was established in 1856 as the first such facility in the United States. For the most part, these hospitals have been replaced by *foster care* programs.

four-fifths rule The U.S. *Equal Employment Opportunity Commission (EEOC)* formula to determine whether an employer's hiring practices have a *disparate impact* on protected groups; if deemed unfair it is an *adverse impact.* For example, if African Americans are hired at a rate of less than four-fifths (80 percent) of white people, the practice is illegal.

four freedoms President Franklin D. Roosevelt's 1941 proposed goals for all the peoples of the world and the major objectives for the forthcoming United Nations: freedom of speech, freedom of religion, freedom from want, and freedom from fear.

4-H Club An international organization for young people interested or involved in agriculture or homemaking through the development of one's head, heart, hands, and health. Their Web site address is http://www.4-H.org

fourth party A fiscal intermediary between the provider of a health care or social service, the consumer of that service, and the organization that pays for the service. The fourth party does not provide the cash to cover the charges but provides administrative services for the cash provider *(third party)*.

Fourth World The underdeveloped nations, colonies, and protectorates that have extremely low per capita incomes and rates of literacy, few natural resources, and low financial reserves. Countries including Afghanistan, Bangladesh, Sudan, and Chad are called "Fourth World" to distinguish them from nonaligned *(Third World)* countries, which have resources and are working toward more economic sufficiency.

Fragile X Syndrome A genetic disorder in which an arm of the X chromosome is constricted or damaged, often resulting in mental retardation, developmental disabilities, or other handicaps.

frail elderly Older men and women who suffer from or are vulnerable to physical or emotional impairments and require some care because they have limited ability or opportunity to provide entirely for their own needs. See also *elderly* and *oldest old.*

franchising The process by which one organization grants another organization, group, or individual the right and obligation to fulfill one of its customary functions. For example, a state government contracts with a private company to provide penal facilities to some of its convict criminal population, or a county government engages a group of private social work practitioners to conduct the investigations for *foster care* placements.

Francis of Assisi (1181–1226) Founder of the Franciscan Order, in which members lived in poverty while serving people who were poor or ill.

Frankel, Lee (1867–1931) An early social work educator and developer of family casework theo-

ries and practice, he was a national leader in many health and welfare organizations, including New York's Training School for Jewish Social Work.

fraud Intentionally deceiving someone who thereby is injured.

fraudulent contract 1. An explicit or implied agreement between two closely related people that is repeatedly violated by one person, forcing the other to adopt new behaviors to accommodate. 2. In law, the term refers to a written document, to which both parties agree, that contains deceptive statements or information.

Frazier, Edward F. (1894–1962) Director of the social work program at Howard University who was a nationally known advocate for racial justice and author of numerous books about multiculturalism and the black family as well as the popular 1955 book *Black Bourgeoisie.*

free appropriate public education (FAPE) Public school education for children with disabilities at no cost to their parents that allows students to progress to their potentials. This is a requirement of the *Individuals with Disabilities Education Act (IDEA).* See also *individualized education plan, inclusion,* and *mainstreaming.*

free association A therapeutic procedure, most commonly used in *psychoanalysis* and other *insight therapies,* in which the professional encourages the client to express whatever thoughts or emotions come to mind. The client verbalizes at length, and the therapist gives no distracting external cues that could influence the material being presented. See also *catharsis* and *Freudian theory.*

free-enterprise system An economic orientation of a nation or community that permits open competition for customers with minimal government regulation or involvement in the economy. This is a relative concept, because any social system except anarchy must have some public regulation or controls.

free-floating anxiety Pervasive tension not attached to specific threats, situations, or ideas.

free-trade systems Markets between nations without tariffs, import quotas, or other restrictions. This usually results in greater economic integration between the trading partners. Some argue that the practice costs jobs in the higher-wage nation and cultural imperialism in the other.

free-trade zones   Also called "enterprise zones," an area within a nation that is exempted from certain taxes and other regulations to encourage the development of businesses therein. Usually these zones are established in cities and parts of cities that are especially economically depressed or in areas on national borders.

Freedmen's Bureau   Originally known as the Bureau of Refugees, Freedmen, and Abandoned Lands, this U.S. War Department organization was established in 1865 to assist former slaves in the transition to freedom by providing food rations and social services to those in need, finding employment opportunities, developing educational and medical institutions, and providing legal assistance. The bureau was the nation's first federal welfare agency but was eliminated in 1872.

Freedom Corps   A U.S. Executive Department initiative to enlist Americans for public service through full- or part-time volunteer programs. USA Freedom Corps encourages all Americans to serve their country for two years or 4,000 hours during their lifetimes, through local community volunteer programs or in national organizations such as the *Citizen Corps, AmeriCorps, Senior Corps,* and the *Peace Corps.* Volunteers may maintain an online *Record of Service* to spell out one's volunteer time and experiences. Their Web site address is http://www.usafreedomcorps.gov

freedom fighter   One who engages in political or military tactics designed to overthrow or change what is perceived to be an oppressive government or social system; to their opponents they are called "insurgents," "rebels," or "terrorists."

Freedom of Information Act   U.S. federal legislation, enacted in 1966 (P.L. 89-487), that permits citizens some rights to access nonclassified government documents and records. This can include case records of social work clients who were treated in federally funded settings, thus severely curtailing some forms of worker–client *confidentiality.* The law was revised as the Privacy Act of 1974 (P.L. 93-579), which further refined the requirements (that is, that disclosure can occur only with that individual's written consent).

freedom riders   *Civil rights* activists who rode buses into the American South in the 1960s to challenge racial *segregation* laws and practices. See also *Michael G. Schwerner.*

freestanding social services   Agencies and programs that operate independently of other social services providers and usually offer a wide range of *personal social services.* Examples include *child welfare* and *family services organizations.* Freestanding social services are contrasted with those provided within "host" organizations, such as the social services departments of hospitals and schools.

frequency distribution   In social research, the depiction of tabulated scores or other data showing the number of subjects who achieved each score.

frequency table   In social research reporting, a one-way table to analyze categories of data. For example, if a social agency surveyed its clientele according to age categories, the tables would depict in a simple way the age distribution.

Freudian slip   See *parapraxis.*

Freudian theory   An integrated set of principles about human behavior and the treatment of *personality disorders* based on the ideas of Viennese neurologist Sigmund Freud (1856–1939) and his followers. Central concepts about personality development include the growing organization of drives *(instincts, libido, pleasure principle,* and *reality principle),* personality structure *(unconscious, preconscious,* and *conscious),* personality dynamics *(id, ego,* and *superego),* and the stages of psychosexual development (the *oral phase,* the *anal phase,* and the *phallic phase).* Treatment concepts include *free association, catharsis, transference,* and *countertransference.* See also *psychoanalytic theory* and *psychosexual development theory.*

frictional unemployment   One of the four kinds of unemployment (the others being *seasonal unemployment, cyclical unemployment,* and *structural unemployment*) that occurs when people are moving geographically or occupationally from one job to another with only slight intervals of time with no work.

friendly societies   Volunteer organizations and self-help groups that formed in England in the early 1800s to help their members during times of sickness and death.

friendly visitors Volunteers and, later, paid employees of the *charity organization societies (COSs)* who eventually became known as social workers. Their primary job was to investigate the homes of needy people, determine the causes of problems, provide guidance for solving problems, and—as a last resort—provide material assistance to those clients deemed "worthy." Friendly visiting was supplanted by *casework* as the "visitors" developed greater *professionalism,* more thorough training, and better understanding of the causes of problems.

"frigidity" An obsolete term used to describe sexual disorders of women who do not experience sexual arousal or orgasms. Whereas the terms now used to describe these problems include *sexual aversion disorder, dyspareunia,* and *vaginismus,* the preferred term is *female sexual arousal disorder.*

frisk The action of a police officer to pat down a criminal suspect to determine if there is a concealed weapon. This action is usually considered legal without a search warrant.

frotteurism A *sexual disorder* characterized by strong and recurring sexual urges and erotic fantasies involving touching and rubbing against a nonconsenting person. The individual usually acts on these urges (commits frottage) in crowds where the behavior is less noticeable—except to the victim.

frustration A state of tension that occurs as a result of some goal-directed behavior being thwarted or postponed.

frustration tolerance The capacity to endure having a goal thwarted or postponed.

Fry, Norah (1871–1960) An advocate in England for people with developmental disabilities, learning disorders, and mental dysfunctions, she led the effort for legislation for those who were mentally disabled and later founded the University of Bristol Department of Mental Health.

FTE Full-time equivalent, determined by the number of hours that staff work measured against the hours in a workweek. For example, if an agency's workweek is 40 hours and a program employs one staff person 40 hours a week and another 20 hours a week, the program employs 1.5 FTEs.

fugue Amnesic flight; a *psychogenic* condition in which individuals, usually after experiencing intolerable internal or external stress, develop amnesia and abandon their homes, jobs, or familiar environments. The more appropriate term is *psychogenic fugue.*

Fulbright fellowships U.S. government grants to teachers, researchers, and students participating in educational programs abroad. Named for Senator William Fulbright (1905–1995), the program also helps teachers and students from other nations study in the United States.

full disclosure A requirement in business transactions, such as real estate sales, to tell the prospective buyer the entire truth so that a decision to buy can be made without being deceived.

full family sanctions A requirement in some state public welfare programs to reduce or terminate benefits to all members of a family when one of its members fails to adhere to all the program's requirements.

full-time employee One who works for the same employer at least 35 hours per week.

functional assessment Systematic procedures and criteria used by social workers and other professionals, especially in health care and institutional settings, to determine the capacity of clients to provide for their own care and well-being. The client is evaluated as to his or her ability to carry out needed *activities of daily living (ADLs)* and possession of the tools needed to fulfill those activities.

functional autonomy The tendency of organization rules, group mores, and individual behavior patterns to eventually become independent of the reasons that led to their original creation.

functional community A class of people or organizations that has common purposes, goals, or orientations toward their achievement. Examples are the education, military, business, religious, or medical communities. Social workers and others belong to the welfare or human services functional community.

functional dyspareunia   Painful sexual inter-course resulting from *psychogenic* rather than *organic* factors.

functional encopresis   Uncontrolled bowel movements resulting from *psychogenic* rather than *organic* factors.

functional enuresis   Involuntary urination result-ing from *psychogenic* rather than *organic* factors.

functional illiteracy   See *illiteracy, functional.*

functional impairment   The inability of an indi-vidual to meet certain expectations or responsibilities because of temporary or permanent physical or mental incapacitation. The term also refers to one who is only partially disabled and can effectively carry out most, but not all, normal functions.

"functional mental illness"   A term that pertains to psychological disorders for which there is no ap-parent physical or *organic* basis. With increased rec-ognition of the importance of physiological factors in mental processes, this term is becoming obsolete.

functional requisites   In *social policy* develop-ment, the process of identifying anticipated pro-gram activities and services, service targets, and types of intervention to be used.

functional school in social work   A theoretical and practice orientation in social work based partly on the "will" concept of Otto Rank and the ideas of *Virginia Robinson* (1883–1977), *Jessie Taft* (1882–1960), and *Ruth Smalley* (1903-1979). It is also known as the *Rankian School* and the *Pennsylva-nia School* to distinguish it from the *diagnostic school in social work.* Most influential from 1930 to 1950, the approach de-emphasized diagnostic in-quiry, history taking, and *Freudian theory;* instead, it stressed a strategy that was time limited and fo-cused on those issues that came from within the function of the agency.

functional vaginismus   A sexual pain in women in which continuing involuntary spasms of the musculature of the outer third of the vagina inter-fere with coitus. This term is now replaced by the term *vaginismus.*

functionally disabled   A person with a physical or mental impairment that limits the individual's capacity for independent living.

function-versus-cause issue   See *cause-versus-function issue.*

fundamentalist movements   The religious-based political and social cause activities of people with strong religious convictions who espouse their faiths to be the basic and only truthful tenets and who work toward convincing others likewise. These movements tend to be politically conserva-tive and often are led by charismatic clergy who cite the holy writings of their faiths to justify and advocate for social change.

funding   Allocation of a specific amount of money to be used in carrying out an organization's program for a certain amount of time.

fundraising   The process of soliciting and acquir-ing income through *philanthropy* and other pri-vate donations, grants, fees for services, invest-ments, and other means.

fundraising firm   A private company that per-forms fundraising services for nonprofit organi-zations, including planning campaigns, writing and distributing promotional literature, training vol-unteers, and soliciting contributions. Such firms are often compensated with a percentage of the funds raised.

fungibility   The degree of flexibility or restric-tiveness inherent in the funding of a program. When a program has low fungibility, for example, it is not authorized to deviate much from the ex-act requirements specified by the administrator of the allocation.

Fürsorge   The principle, in Germany, that it is the responsibility of a collective society to meet the basic minimal needs of its members, regard-less of any financial or other contributions the individuals may make. This principle is the foun-dation for the German welfare state, in which payments for disability or impoverishment are not tied to insurance contributions (as in the United States) but come from the nation's treasury.

furthering responses   The interview strategy of encouraging clients to communicate with more clarity, depth, and focus and to enhance the work-ing relationship. These activities are based on at-tentive listening and stimulating the client's ver-balization. Furthering responses include minimal prompts ("I see" and "And then . . .?") and accent responses (repeating a word or phrase from the client's verbalization to encourage further elaboration). See also *following responses.*

fusion In *family systems theory,* the obscuring of separate identities among family members. See also *differentiation.*

futurist One who specializes in predicting what the environmental and social conditions of the next decades will be based on past and current trends.

fuzzy logic The process by which a person comes to understand some phenomenon using incomplete facts, uncertain information, inference, preconceptions, and intuition.

gag order Instructions from some authority to refrain from disclosing, discussing, or advocating specified information. The order is sometimes issued by judges to witnesses or jurors during a trial, by military officers to their troops, and by social agency administrators to their staffs during budget hearings with legislators.

Gaia The earth and its ecosystem seen as a single, living creative system (named after the Greek goddess of the earth).

Galarza, Ernesto (1905–1984) An advocate for the social justice of farm workers and social policies that enhance the well-being of migrant workers and working poor people.

gallstones A common disease in which pebble-sized stones form in the gallbladder (the organ that stores bile secreted by the liver) or in ducts leading to the small intestine. Gallstones may cause intense abdominal pain and inflammation and infection of the pancreas and gallbladder. Surgical removal of the stones is often required.

"GALS" The informal name used in some juvenile court systems for lawyers and other people who are appointed *guardians ad litem*.

Gamblers Anonymous A *self-help organization* for people who experience problems as a result of gambling. Patterned after the *Alcoholics Anonymous (AA)* program, the organization was founded in 1957 and has chapters in many nations. See also *12-step programs*. Their Web site address is http://www.gamblersanonymous.org

gambling, compulsive A behavior disorder in which the individual becomes preoccupied with wagers and develops a progressively worsening urge to bet money. The urge often becomes uncontrollable and occurs even when funds for making bets are unavailable.

gamines Homeless children in Latin American countries who usually live together in groups in urban areas and survive through begging, stealing, and working at menial jobs.

gaming A process in which participants are *role playing* potential or actual life simulations in which problems must be resolved. The term "simulation" refers to an analogy to some process in the real world, however it is perceived. Unlike other role-playing situations, gaming has specified rules that are used to govern actions.

gang A group that originally forms spontaneously and whose members maintain a relationship because they share certain attributes. These attributes usually include age, ethnicity, residence in a neighborhood, or common values that lead to mutual bonding.

gang crime Unlawful activity by groups whose mutual encouragement leads to behavior that is unlikely to occur individually. Law authorities describe "gang-related" crimes as those in which a gang member is the offender or victim and "gang-motivated" crimes as those that serve the interests of the gang collectively. See also "*wilding.*"

Ganser syndrome Client behavior involving conscious or unconscious attempts to give wrong answers to the professional; often such behavior is for the purpose of denying responsibility for wrongdoing or to establish an insanity defense to avoid legal punishment.

GANTT chart A scheduling technique commonly used in social work and social planning to show graphically each of the activities of an organization and the time taken to complete each of them. For each activity, there is a horizontal line drawn under calendar dates, and a horizontal bar is drawn to show the duration of time spent on the task. Because the GANTT chart does not show interconnections between activities, the *Program Evaluation and Review Technique (PERT)* chart tends to be used for more complex planning.

garnishment A legal process by which a creditor may have a judgment against a debtor's money or other property (such as wages, salary, or savings) in the possession or control of a third party. Under state law, the court may order the employer, banker, or other holder of the property to remit such funds to an agent of the court or to the creditor until the obligation has been fulfilled.

Garrett, Annette Marie (1898–1957)   A systematizer of the concepts of social casework practice and a developer of field work as an educational experience and *industrial social work* concepts. She authored the influential 1942 book *Interviewing: Its Principles and Method.*

gastroenterology   The medical specialty that focuses on diseases of the digestive system, stomach, and intestines.

gatekeeper   One who facilitates or obstructs movement from one status to another or communication between one group and another. In *community organization,* the term refers to an indigenous member of a community who permits or precludes real access by the organizers to those in the target population. In this sense, gatekeepers are typically the natural leaders of a community, or they work in key positions that permit them to know what and who is influential. They may be playground workers, traffic patrol people, gang leaders, bartenders, or neighborhood "busybodies."

gateway drugs   Easily accessible drugs that are legal (such as nicotine, caffeine, and alcohol) or illegal drugs for which use is not well enforced by law officers (such as marijuana, glue inhalants, and mushrooms), so called because they are said to open the way to other drugs.

***Gault* decision**   The 1967 judgment rendered by the U.S. Supreme Court *(In re Gault)* that affirmed the right of juveniles to the same legal protections as adults in criminal court proceedings. This decision gave juveniles the right to proper advance notification of the charges, the right to counsel, freedom from *self-incrimination,* and the opportunity to have their counsel confront witnesses. Before the *Gault* decision, juvenile proceedings were regarded as civil, not criminal.

"gay"   The term preferred by many people with a homosexual orientation, primarily males, in describing themselves and their sexual orientation. Females with a homosexual orientation usually prefer the term *"lesbian."* See also *homosexuality* and *GLBT community.*

GBMI offender   One who has been found guilty of a crime but is mentally ill. The person is placed in a mental hospital for necessary treatment of the mental disorder, but once the condition is successfully treated, the offender either goes to prison or can be transferred to a correctional facility to serve out the sentence.

GED certificate   General equivalency diploma, a program by which people who did not obtain high school degrees can demonstrate to prospective employers, college admissions boards, and others that they have achieved an equivalent level of education. In some educational institutions, "GED" refers to graduate equivalency diploma.

gemeinschaft   The concept of an idealized community in which the members share strong values and beliefs and maintain personal and direct social bonds as well as a tradition of small-scale and local ties. The concept (from the German term for "community") was developed by sociologist Ferdinand Tonnies (1855–1936) to contrast with *gesellschaft,* a complex, impersonal type of society.

gender bias   Favoring one sex over the other, most frequently males over females. Gender bias may be manifested in granting more privileges and rights to boys than girls in a family, facilitating more educational and occupational opportunities, overt sex discrimination, or, in some countries, maintaining laws that explicitly forbid women from exercising the rights that are granted to men. See also *gender discrimination* and *gender role stereotyping.*

gender dysphoria   An aversion to the physical or social characteristics associated with one's own sex.

gender equity   A fair and appropriately balanced distribution of resources and responsibilities between the sexes. In many nations and cultures, gender equity is unrealized in that vocational and educational opportunities are heavily weighted in favor of males. Gender inequities may be explicit, as a part of national policy, or implicit, as in the existence of the *"glass ceiling."* See also *Title IX.*

gender gap   A nonspecific term referring to disparities between men and women in employment and promotion opportunities, pay, and gender-based discrimination.

gender identity   The relative degree to which an individual patterns himself or herself after members of the same sex. See *sexual identity* and *sex roles.*

gender identity disorder A strong and persistent self-identification with members of the opposite sex and feelings of discomfort and denial about one's ascribed *sex role*. In gender identity disorders of childhood, children often "cross-dress" and may become convinced they will grow up to be members of the opposite sex. They tend to maintain their preoccupations with the stereotypical activities of the opposite sex despite pressure against this behavior from parents, peers, teachers, and professionals. In adults, *transsexualism* is the most common of these disorders. Many individuals and organizations dispute the existence of such a disorder. See also *reparative therapy*.

gender roles The behaviors and personality characteristics that are attached, often inaccurately, to people because of their sex. For example, men often are expected to be more competitive and aggressive, and women often are expected to be more emotional and nurturing. These gender role distinctions are criticized by feminists and others, but many in society use them to define what is considered "socially appropriate" male and female behavior. Gender role is used, for example, in identifying *gender identity disorder*.

gender violence Causing harm to women through physical cruelty, sexual assault, abuse, humiliation, and practices such as selective abortion of female children, female *infanticide*, and *female genital mutilation*.

gene pool The totality of genetic information within any species, people, or other biological group.

General Accounting Office (GAO), U.S. The independent federal agency within the legislative branch of government that assists the Congress in determining whether public funds are efficiently and economically administered and spent and in evaluating the results of existing government programs and activities. As such, GAO has general rights of access to and examination of any records of the federal departments and agencies for which Congress has allocated funds. Their Web site address is http://www.gao.gov

General Allotment Act The legislation enacted in 1887 (Indian General Allotment Act, Ch. 19, 24 Stat. 388) that gave the U.S. federal government unilateral power to revise treaties with Native American tribes and nations and take away their lands.

general assistance (GA) A residual or emergency welfare program operated under state and local auspices to provide means-tested financial and other aid to individuals who are ineligible for any *categorical program*, such as *social security; Old Age, Survivors, Disability, and Health Insurance (OASDHI); Temporary Assistance to Needy Families (TANF);* or *Supplemental Security Income (SSI).* Local departments of *public welfare* (also called departments of *human services* or *social services* in some counties) determine *eligibility* and help coordinate the distribution of these funds. See also *emergency basic-needs services.*

general equivalency diploma See *GED certificate.*

general medical condition The relative health and presence of one or more diseases in a client. The term is used by psychiatrists and other physicians in diagnosing mental disorders that are the direct result of specific organic and physiological disorders, for example, "dementia, due to (the general medical condition of) Parkinson's disease."

general practitioners Nonspecialist licensed *physicians* whose practices usually involve initial contact (primary) medical care. In the United States, nearly all new physicians qualify in one of the 23 medical specialties. Primary medical care is provided by doctors who specialize in internal medicine or family practice. Other aspects of the general practitioner's role have been taken over by *registered nurses (RNs), physician's assistants (PAs), paramedics,* and other *allied health professionals.*

General Services Administration (GSA) The U.S federal agency responsible for procuring the goods and services needed and ordered by other government agencies. Their Web site address is http://www.gsa.gov

General Social Care Council (GSCC) In England the organization that regulates the social care workforce. Established in 2001 through a consolidation of other organizations, GSCC establishes and monitors codes of conduct and practice for social care workers and their employers, registers and certifies workers, and regulates social work education and training. The equivalent bodies elsewhere in the United Kingdom are the Scottish Social Services Council, the Northern Ireland Care Council, and the Care Council for Wales. Their Web site address is http://www.doh.gov.uk/gcc. See also *DipSW.*

general systems theory   A conceptual orientation that attempts to explain holistically the behavior of people and societies by identifying the interacting components of the system and the controls that keep these components *(subsystems)* stable and in a state of *equilibrium.* It is concerned with the *boundaries, roles, relationships,* and flow of information between people. General systems theory is a subset of *systems theories* that focuses on living entities, from microorganisms to societies. See also *ecological perspective* and *life model.*

general welfare clause   Part of the U.S. Constitution, in Article I, Section 8, that authorizes Congress and the government to "provide for the common defense and general welfare of the United States." Social workers traditionally have cited this clause to justify improvements in the nation's welfare programs.

generalist   In social work, a practitioner whose knowledge and skills encompass a broad spectrum and who assesses problems and their solutions comprehensively. The generalist often coordinates the efforts of specialists by facilitating communication between them, thereby fostering *continuity of care.* See also *generic social work.*

generalization   1. The process of forming an idea, judgment, or abstraction about a class of people, things, or events based on limited or particular experiences. 2. In *psychotherapy,* an act or pattern of behavior in which an individual avoids discussing personal problems by characterizing them as being universal. For example, a client may say "Every couple fights" to conceal current marital conflicts. 3. Generalizations are also used in social work practice to connect or clarify a client's experiences with others. For example, the social worker might say "Everyone feels depressed at times."

generalization, behavioral   In *behaviorism* or *social learning theory,* the tendency of a *response* to occur in the presence of a *stimulus* that is similar to one that was present when the response was learned.

generalized anxiety disorder   A type of *anxiety neurosis* (or anxiety state) characterized by symptoms such as *motor tension,* apprehension (fear and worry), autonomic hyperactivity (sweating, clammy hands, dizziness, light-headedness, upset stomach, flushing, and increased pulse and respiration rate), inability to concentrate, insomnia, irritability, and general impatience.

generation gap   The differences in values, lifestyles, and economic opportunities that exist between people of different age cohorts living in the same society.

Generation X   People born in the years 1962 to 1978, identified as unique because of the claim that although they are less well-prepared educationally to cope with future realities, they are expected to assume a disproportionate burden of repaying the national debt, to pay the social security entitlements for prior generations, and to deal with decaying infrastructure and international competition. The members of this generation are the children of the *baby boom generation.*

generational equity   A fair and appropriately balanced distribution of resources and responsibilities between age groups. Where such equity does not exist, for example, younger people might be unfairly burdened with high taxes and future national indebtedness to provide a standard of living for older people that is higher than what they can expect when they become old. Conversely, in a "pay-as-you-go" economy, older people could be required to pay high taxes for the education and infrastructure used by young people without commensurate assurance that their own economic needs will be met in their older years.

generativity   An orientation and activity involving some contribution to the quality of life for future generations. According to *Eriksonian theory,* this orientation develops as a normal stage of life in healthy people and most commonly occurs toward the end of middle *adulthood.*

generativity versus stagnation   According to the *psychosocial development theory* of Erik Erikson (1902–1994), the longest stage of a person's psychosocial development, occurring roughly from ages 24 to 54. In it, the individual tries to reconcile conflicts between egocentric desires and the need to contribute to the well-being of future generations. See also *Eriksonian theory.*

generic drug   A medical compound that possesses no proprietary or brand name. The active ingredients of the drug are chemically identical to the brand name medicine but are less expensive because the consumer does not pay for advertising or promotion.

generic social work   The social work orientation that emphasizes a common core of knowledge and skills associated with social services delivery. A generic social worker possesses basic knowledge that may span several *methods in social work.* Such a social worker would not necessarily be a specialist in a single *field of practice* or professional technique but would be capable of providing and managing a wider range of needed client services and intervening in a greater variety of systems.

generic–specific controversy A debate among social workers since at least the 1920s. One faction sees the profession as comprising a group of different *specialists,* each with a unique body of knowledge and highly refined professional skills that require considerable training and practice to master and that are applied to a specific and defined area of social welfare needs. The other faction sees professional social work as being made up of *generalists* who have a *macro orientation* and who develop and integrate services. The generalist faction also believes that social work skills are sufficiently similar from one specialty to another so that a social worker can be effective in a variety of settings. The 1929 *Milford Conference* attempted to resolve the controversy, saying most social workers fall somewhere between these extremes. See also *content-and-process issue.*

genetic conditions Diseases or dysfunctions that have resulted from defective genes, genomes (constellations of genes), or chromosomes. There are four categories of genetic conditions. First are the single-gene disorders, in which a defective gene results in diseases such as *cystic fibrosis, sickle-cell anemia, Tay–Sachs disease, Huntington's disease, Marfan's syndrome, hemophilia,* neurofibromatosis, and Duchenne's *muscular dystrophy.* Second are the multifactorial inheritance disorders, in which several genes and environmental factors interact to sometimes result in disorders such as *cleft palate, spina bifida,* congenital heart disease, and some cases of *mental retardation.* Third are the *chromosomal disorders,* resulting from the faulty structures or incorrect numbers of chromosomes, which can cause miscarriage, stillbirths, neonatal death, *congenital abnormalities,* and *Down syndrome.* Fourth are environmentally induced genetic disorders, in which factors potentially damaging to an embryo or fetus, such as alcohol, infections, drugs, tobacco, and some prescription medicines, harm fetal development.

genetic counseling The specialty in medicine and related fields that helps people who have or risk having physical problems as a result of inherited defects. Such problems include *Down syndrome, cystic fibrosis, diabetes, sickle-cell anemia, hemophilia,* and *Huntington's disease.* Counseling includes prevention of new problems by advising individuals about their reproductive risks and alternatives. See also *carrier screening.*

genetic engineering The planned modification of genes or genetic material in living organisms to produce desirable traits and eliminate undesirable ones.

Geneva Convention A periodically updated humanitarian agreement by nearly all nations on Earth regulating the treatment of people in wartime, including prisoners, those who are wounded, and civilians. The first Convention was signed in 1864 with subsequent revisions. The 1977 revision covers victims of civil conflicts and "undeclared wars."

genital personality In *psychoanalytic theory,* one who is excessively preoccupied and concerned about *sexuality;* the term is also known as the *oedipal personality* or genital character. The individual is seen as having personality problems involving self-image, *sexual identity, sexual orientation,* and sometimes a *paraphilia.* See also *anal personality* and *oral personality.*

genital stage In *psychodynamic* theory, the last significant phase of psychosexual development that begins with *puberty* and continues for several years thereafter. Sigmund Freud (1856–1939) postulated that, with the onset of adultlike sexual feelings, the individual has an opportunity to resolve the *Oedipus complex,* sever erotic attachments to parents of the opposite sex, and transfer sexual drives to peers of the opposite sex.

genitalia The internal and external male or female reproductive organs.

genitourinary disorders The dysfunctions or anomalies of the urinary or genital anatomy. These include disorders of the bladder, kidney, and prostate gland; anorchidism (lack of testes); circumcision problems; and urostomy (diversion of the urinary tract) and other ostomy procedures.

"genius" A nonspecific lay term that refers to a person of one or more extremely superior traits, especially intellectual and creative.

genocide The systematic elimination of racial, religious, ethnic, or cultural groups, usually through mass extermination by the government of the nation in which they reside. See also *Holocaust* and *"ethnic cleansing."*

Genocide Treaty The Convention on the Prevention and Punishment of the Crime of Genocide agreement enacted in the United Nations in 1951 calling for an end to any intentional destruction of a national, ethnic, racial, or religious group.

genogram A diagram used in *family therapy* to depict family relationships extended over at least three generations. The diagram uses circles to represent females and squares for males, with horizontal lines indicating marriages. Vertical lines are drawn from the marriage lines to other circles and squares to depict the children. The diagram may contain other symbols or written explanations to indicate critical events, such as death, divorce, and remarriage, and to reveal recurrent patterns of behavior.

genophobia The fear of sexual intercourse. The term preferred by professionals is *sexual aversion disorder.*

genotype The inherited traits common to a biological group.

gentrification The social phenomenon in which homes in formerly poor, overcrowded ghettos are purchased and privately rehabilitated by more affluent families for their personal dwellings or for investment. This has the effect of raising the property values, rents, and property tax rates of all the homes in the neighborhood, forcing the removal of the remaining less-affluent people and their replacement by those who can afford to live there. See also *urban homesteading* and *redlining.*

genuineness Sincerity and honesty; one of the important qualities in developing an effective therapeutic relationship. Genuineness includes being unpretentious with clients, speaking honestly rather than only for effect, acknowledging one's limitations, and providing only sincere reassurances.

geriatric mental status interview A systematic procedure for assessing the possibility and type of mental deterioration in an older person. The procedure is nearly the same as in any other *mental status exam,* except that the interviewer tends to use shorter, more frequent sessions, a more formal

and gentle manner, and is careful to assure the older person about why such questions are being asked.

geriatricians Board-certified physicians who specialize in treating older people, especially *frail elderly* people with complex, age-related medical problems.

geriatrics A branch of the medical profession that specializes in the prevention and treatment of diseases of old age. Physicians practicing geriatrics are known as *geriatricians.*

geriopharmacotherapy The prescription and administration of medications to prolong the physical and emotional health of older people. This process includes monitoring, counseling, and educating the older person about health factors and the use of the medicine.

Germain, Carel Bailey (1916–1995) A social work theorist, she developed the *life model* of social work practice. This orientation uses a systems approach and the ecological perspective to guide group and individual practice interventions.

gerontocracy Authority or rule of a culture or group by older people.

gerontological social work An orientation and specialization in social work concerned with the psychosocial treatment of older people—the development and management of needed social services and programs for older individuals. See also *Association for Gerontological Education in Social Work (AGE-SW).*

gerontology The multidisciplinary study of the biological, psychological, and social aspects of aging.

gerontophobia Fear or loathing of older people.

Gerry, Elbridge Thomas (1837–1927) Founder of the *Societies for the Prevention of Cruelty to Children (SPCC)* in 1885. As a lawyer, he worked in cases of *child abuse* and discovered the only relevant laws and programs were those protecting animals. He modeled the society, also called "Gerry Societies," after the Society for the Prevention of Cruelty to Animals.

gerrymandering The creation of political boundaries of unusual or unnatural shape so that some groups are politically under- or overrepresented. For example, a city might divide its legislative districts so that residents of an inner-city *ghetto* are divided among five other districts, making them minorities in each new district.

gesellschaft The concept of a model society in which members possess few shared values and have social bonds that are impersonal, narrow, and strictly functional. These societies are large scale and complex and have strict divisions between the individuals' private and public lives. The concept (from the German term for "society") was developed by sociologist Ferdinand Tonnies (1855–1936) to contrast with *gemeinschaft*, a local, closely integrated community.

gestalt psychology A group of theories that emphasizes the whole of an organism or environment rather than its parts and focuses on the interrelationships in mental perceptions. It is a school of psychology influenced by Kurt Lewin and Wolfgang Kohler in the 1920s and 1930s. Gestalt psychology has influenced, but is not synonymous with, *gestalt therapy.*

gestalt therapy A form of psychotherapeutic intervention developed and popularized by Frederick S. Perls and others in the 1960s. The approach seeks to help individuals integrate their thoughts, emotions, and behaviors and orient themselves more realistically toward their current perceptions and experiences. Emphasis is placed on becoming aware of and taking responsibility for one's own actions, on spontaneously expressing emotions and perception, and on recognizing the existence of gaps and distortions in one's own thinking.

gestation The period from *conception* to birth. For humans, the healthy gestation period is between 266 and 294 days, with 280 the average.

ghetto A geographic and usually poor section of a city, inhabited predominantly by ethnic groups or people of color. Ghettos originated in Spain in the late 14th century to segregate Jewish people, often behind guarded walls, to minimize their influence on Christian people. Ghettos for Jewish people continued to exist in various European cities until after World War II.

ghost sickness A *culture-bound syndrome* sometimes related to witchcraft, found most commonly among some Native American tribes whose individuals experience anxiety, hallucinations, loss of consciousness, feelings of futility, fainting, and sleep problems.

GI In medicine the common designation for gastrointestinal (the stomach and intestines). In popular usage, GI also may refer to armed forces personnel (from "government issue").

GI Bill The common name for the Serviceman's Readjustment Act (Ch. 268, 58 Stat. 284), the laws and programs begun in 1944 to provide educational, housing, insurance, medical, and vocational training opportunities for U.S. military veterans.

Gideon v. Wainwright The 1963 U.S. Supreme Court ruling that all indigent defendants in criminal cases have the right to free legal counsel.

gifted child A child who possesses one or more talents, exceptional skills, or high *intelligence.* This designation has come to be preferred by parents of such children over the former designation, *exceptional children,* which also included children with disabilities or below-normal intellectual functioning.

Gilbert Act The 1782 English welfare reform laws that classified needy people into groups including the elderly, infirm, children, and the "idle." The legislation repealed the right of *overseers of the poor* to contract them out to private caretakers. Overseers were to find jobs for employable people or maintain them in the community rather than the *workhouse.*

gingivitis A disease of the gums that may lead to inflammation, bleeding, and tooth loss.

Ginnie Mae The informal name for the *Government National Mortgage Association (GNMA).*

Ginsberg, Mitchell (1915–1996) An educator and welfare administrator. As New York's Social Service Commissioner in the 1960s, Ginsberg reformed policies, improved administrative procedures, and advocated a federal takeover of the nation's welfare system.

Girl Scouts/Girl Guides The national and international organization to help girls become healthy, productive citizens and develop high ethical standards, leadership abilities, skills, and effectiveness in community service. Girl Guides began in

England in 1909 and spread to other nations thereafter. Juliette Gordon Low established the Girl Guides in the United States in 1912 and soon changed its name to Girl Scouts. The four levels of Girl Scouts are Brownies (ages six to eight), Junior Girl Scouts (ages nine to 11), Cadette Girl Scouts (ages 12 to 14), and Senior Girl Scouts (ages 14 to 17). Girl Guides in some nations, such as Canada and Great Britain, have six levels: Brownies (ages six to nine), Guides (ages nine to 12), Pathfinders (ages 12 to 15), Rangers (ages 15 to 17), Junior Leaders (all ages, but mostly ages 14 to 18), and Cadets (ages 15 to 18). Their Web site address is http://www.girlscouts.org

Girls Clubs of America   See *Boys and Girls Clubs of America.*

glasnost   The Russian term, roughly implying "openness" and "public relations." Government officials and social agency administrators in many nations increasingly use the term to describe their own organization's intent to be more candid and forthright about policies and activities.

"glass ceiling"   A popular term referring to barriers to advancement in industry and government leadership positions that tend to restrict women and people of certain racial and ethnic groups. The term implies that the barrier cannot actually be seen and is not part of the organization's official policy but is manifested in failure to promote women and people of color who have equal or greater competence. See also *gender equity.*

glaucoma   An eye disease in which fluid builds up between the cornea and the iris, and the resulting pressure on the eyeball injures certain nerve cells. It is the leading cause of blindness in older persons.

gleaning   The recovery of usable food from excess harvests, storage facilities, and food handling organizations such as food processing companies and restaurants. Recovery includes handling the food more efficiently and sanitarily, separating out waste, transporting the food, and keeping it wholesome until use.

GLBTQ community   Those who self-identify as gay, lesbian, bisexual, or transgendered. Many members of this community also prefer the designation GLBTQ. The final letter refers to "queer," and the community is reclaiming that formerly derogatory term to encompass others who may feel they are not covered in the GLBT designation.

Global Assessment of Functioning (GAF) Scale   A tool used by mental health professionals to rate the relative degree to which a client is able to function psychologically, socially, and occupationally, not due to physical or environmental limitations. The practitioner rates the client's functioning on a rating scale with a continuum from 100 (superior functioning in a wide range of activities and no symptoms) to 0 (persistent danger of severely hurting self or others or persistent inability to maintain minimal personal hygiene, or serious suicidal act with clear expectation of death). The GAF Scale is used in the Axis V part of the *DSM* in completing a clinical *assessment.* See also *Global Assessment of Relational Functioning (GARF) Scale* and the *Defensive Functioning Scale.*

Global Assessment of Relational Functioning (GARF) Scale   A 100-point scale developed by the American Psychiatric Association to judge the functioning of a family or other relationship group on a hypothetical continuum ranging from competent, optimal relationship functioning to a disrupted, dysfunctional relationship. Those relational units that function most satisfactorily (from self-reports and perspectives of observers) score highest (81–100), whereas those that become too dysfunctional to maintain attachment and contact score lowest (1–20).

Global Burden of Disease   A World Health Organization report comparing the severity of different diseases by ascertaining their extent in each population group, the proportion of the population group in the total population, and the number of years of productive life that the population group has lost to the disease.

global village   The interconnectedness of all the world's people because of technological advances in communication, travel, cultural exchanges, and economic integration.

global warming   The gradual increase in the earth's temperature, said to be a result of burning fossil fuels, releasing excessive carbon dioxide, chlorofluorocarbons and nitrous oxide into the air, and leading to the *greenhouse effect.* See also *ecological overstress.*

globalization   The movement to make economic and cultural activity worldwide in scope and application. Proponents argue that this fosters economic development for all through enhanced trade, lower costs, efficiencies, and competitiveness.

Critics argue that the internationalization of corporations may enable them to circumvent a nation's worker protection and environmental laws and that it lowers wages and working conditions by the threat of moving employment opportunities to other countries.

glucose tolerance test A common examination of the blood to help determine the existence of conditions such as diabetes mellitus, hypoglycemia, or other conditions. The patient fasts overnight, then swallows glucose, and the blood is monitored for three hours or more to see how long it takes before the glucose level returns to the pretest level.

go-between role The process of *mediation* that occurs when a social worker or other professional intervenes between conflicting parties (such as husband and wife, parent and child, buyer and seller, landlord and tenant, or two members of a therapy group) and seeks to enhance mutual understanding and reduce tensions.

go-round The procedure used in some social work groups in which each member is specifically asked, in turn, to discuss a particular topic or respond to a specific stimulus. Often the go-round is a structured exercise or technique aimed at helping members get acquainted and keep oriented to one another. It is also used to get a group started or to establish the topics for the session's agenda. See also *check-in.*

goal-directed behavior Any activity that is directed toward conscious or explicitly defined objectives.

goal-setting A strategy used by social workers and other professionals to help clients clarify and define the objectives they hope to achieve in the helping relationship and then to establish the steps that must be taken and the time needed to reach those objectives. The community organizer–social worker uses goal-setting by helping key members of the target population or client community define their objectives and spell out the goals they want their people to achieve.

gold coast An affluent neighborhood, often where a city's most influential families live.

gold-collar workers Professionals who are in such high demand they are awarded bonuses, higher pay, and greater benefits as inducements for employment.

"goldbricking" A pejorative term indicating that an individual is only appearing to be working on a job but is actually loafing.

Golden Rule A guiding principle of human behavior that is considered a foundation for many religions, philosophical systems, and the practice of social work. The rule, as expressed by Jesus, states "Do unto others as you would have them do unto you." In Islam it is expressed as "Whatever is hurtful to you, do not do to any other person."

Goldstein, Howard (1922–2000) A social work educator, researcher, and scholar, he was influential both in the profession's movement toward integrating theory and practice and experiential learning and in promoting the value of the arts and humanities for social work practice. He was editor-in-chief of the journal *Families in Society* and numerous books and articles on social work education and practice.

gonorrhea A *sexually transmitted disease (STD)* that causes inflammation of the genitals and may eventually lead to sterility. The gonococcus organisms are highly vulnerable to most antibiotics. The disease was once a major cause of blindness among newborn children whose mothers were infected, but the routine use of silver nitrate solution in babies' eyes at birth has largely overcome the problem. See also *chlamydia.*

good-faith bargaining The requirement that both parties in a dispute, such as a couple or members of a family or community, discuss issues with open minds and make the possibility of discussion equal for all participants.

Good Samaritan laws Legislation enacted in many states and jurisdictions to provide immunity to individuals or groups from lawsuits if they provide emergency assistance to people who have been injured.

good works A term formerly used to describe activities to help disadvantaged people through *philanthropy, charity, volunteerism,* and personal examples of moral behavior. These activities were viewed by religious and political leaders and social philosophers as moral obligations to God and society, a view that motivated many of the social welfare activities that preceded government-funded welfare programs.

goodness of fit The degree of congruence between people's needs, capacities, and goals and the properties of their social and physical environments. See also *adaptation, ecological perspective,* and *life model.*

Goodwill Industries The organization, founded in 1902, with branches throughout the United States and other nations, that trains people with disabilities in job skills by employing them to collect, recycle, repair, and sell usable household goods. Their Web site address is http://www.goodwill.org

governance group A type of group, often found in residential settings (psychiatric hospitals, correctional facilities, and boarding schools) to involve residents in the daily running of the organization. The regular meetings not only help facilitate a more smooth operation, but also help members learn and practice social skills, mediation, conflict resolution, and communication.

government The established institutions and formal processes by which a society or organized group determines, implements, administers, and evaluates its decisions.

Government National Mortgage Association (GNMA) A U.S. *HUD* agency that finances or ensures financing for the purchase of low-cost housing or homes in areas where conventional loans are difficult to obtain. Mortgages issued by the association are informally known as "Ginnie Maes."

Government Performance and Results Act (GPRA) of 1993 The federal legislation (P.L. 103-62) that mandates all agencies of the federal government develop systematic measures of performance, including measures for outcome, and relate these results to actual and anticipated expenditures.

grace period A time after a decision or agreement is reached and before its terms must be implemented.

graduate equivalency diploma See *GED certificate.*

Graduate Record Examination (GRE) Standardized tests administered by the Educational Testing Service and used as part of the admissions process of many graduate schools, including MSW programs. The general test, which measures verbal, quantitative, and analytical abilities, may be taken in paper-based or computer-based format.

graduated tax See *progressive tax.*

graft Misappropriation of public money by one or more public officials.

grand jury A group of citizens selected by the justice system of a jurisdiction to decide together whether there is enough evidence to justify accusing a person of a crime (which would result in a trial before a *petit jury*). Most grand juries have 23 members.

grand larceny *Larceny* that involves property valued in excess of a certain amount. Each jurisdiction legislates the cutoff amount at which a larceny becomes grand larceny (in most U.S. states it is between $50 and $500).

grandiose-type delusional disorder A subtype of *delusional disorder* characterized by nonbizarre delusions, particularly an exaggerated sense of self-importance and the conviction of having some great mission, talent, insight, or potential.

grandiosity An exaggerated sense of self-importance; in its more extreme forms, it is equivalent to *delusions of grandeur.*

grandparenting clause Also known as a "grandfather clause," an exemption to a new agreement, rule, or requirement so that those who were already engaged in the relevant activity before a certain time need not fulfill the new requirements. For example, some states that passed laws to license social workers excluded certain older social workers from having to pass the exams required to qualify for the license.

Granger, Lester (1896–1976) A social and *civil rights* activist and proponent of equal opportunity for *African Americans.* Granger was a longtime leader of the *National Urban League;* he also helped the U.S. Armed Forces become racially integrated and served as president of several national and international social work organizations.

"granny flats" The informal name for *ECHO housing,* they are temporary, mobile-home–style living units for one or two people usually installed on the grounds of their offspring and connected to the utilities of the main house. These facilities are designed to give older people privacy and security while enabling them to be close to their children or others who care about them.

grant A transfer of funds or assets from one government, organization, or individual to another for fulfilling some broadly specified function or purpose (usually to enhance knowledge or otherwise provide for the well-being of people and their cultural institutions). See also *block grant* and *categorical grant.*

grants-in-aid Payments made by one organization, such as a government agency, to another to achieve a specified purpose. For example, the federal government might grant payments to states or states might make such payments to cities to help fund and ensure the existence of the local organization's *public assistance* programs. See also *block grant.*

grantsmanship In social administration, the ability to develop proposals for special project funding. The ability includes skills in research design, verbal communication, sales, writing, needs assessment, innovation of new techniques for problem solving, coordination of plans, and political and administrative activity, as well as knowledge about the appropriate sources of project funds.

graphology Analysis of handwriting to identify the writer or to determine aspects of the writer's personality. Many professionals are skeptical that such interpretations can be very accurate in assessing personality characteristics. It has more acceptance in criminal detection to determine whether a given person was actually the writer of a particular document.

GRAS "Generally recognized as safe," the U.S. *Food and Drug Administration (FDA)* acronym referring to their list of food additives in long-term use that seem to have few or no risk factors.

grass roots The public, especially the voters, and those who provide the basic support for a political movement or social cause. See also *political activism.*

Grass Roots Organization for Welfare Leadership (GROWL) The national movement and advocacy group made up of social welfare professionals, welfare recipients, and welfare rights organizations dedicated to furthering economic justice. GROWL sponsors research, monitors legislation affecting poor people, tracks the effects of welfare legislation, and provides training and consultation to those working for welfare justice. Their Web site address is http://www.ctwo.org/growl/index.html

grassroots organizing The *community organization* strategy of helping at the local level the members of a neighborhood or geographic region develop stronger relationships, common goals, and an organization that will help them achieve those goals. The focus is on organizing the people who will be affected by change, rather than on organizing only the community leaders. This involves educating and mobilizing people for action toward agreed-on goals. See also *political activism.*

gray ghettos 1. Neighborhoods or housing projects, often in older, decaying areas of inner cities, whose residents are primarily poor and elderly. 2. Private retirement villages and communities zoned for the exclusive use of people older than a certain age.

gray-market adoption The *adoption* of dependent children outside the legitimate social agencies and legal institutions. Such adoptions are often arranged by physicians, lawyers, or other professionals who personally know the couples who seek to adopt and the birth mothers who choose to give up their children for adoption. See also *private adoption.*

Gray Panthers An intergenerational advocacy group founded by Maggie Kuhn (1905–1995) in 1970 to work on behalf of the social and economic needs of older people. The group's major focus is on state and national legislation affecting older people and on issues affecting all ages. It also acts as watchdog in implementing legislation. Their Web site address is http://www.graypanthers.org

Great Depression The severe and extended economic crisis that occurred in the United States and many other nations during the 1930s, ending with reindustrialization in preparation for World War II. In 1933, 16 million people were unemployed (nearly one-third of the U.S. workforce). Largely in response to the resulting hardship, President Franklin D. Roosevelt established the *New Deal* programs, which redefined the role of the federal government in helping individuals and ensuring the general welfare.

Great Society The name given by President Lyndon B. Johnson to *social welfare* goals and programs established as a *War on Poverty* during his administration. Some of these efforts included the *Model Cities program, Head Start,* the *Office of Economic Opportunity (OEO), Medicaid,* and *Medicare.*

green card   The name commonly used for the registration card issued by the U.S. government that identifies the holder as a permanent U.S. resident who is a citizen of another nation. The card (no longer green), which is issued by the *Bureau of Citizenship and Immigration Services,* is officially U.S. Government Form I-551, "*Alien Registration Recipient.*"

green papers   Documents intended to stimulate debate and launch a process of consultation on a particular topic, such as social policy. These consultations may then lead to the publication of *white papers,* which translate the conclusions of the debate into practical proposals for community action.

green politics   A *social movement* initially concerned with pursuing environmental goals through political action. Its major goal is protecting the environment and enhancing endangered systems, as well as fighting organizations whose actions and products are considered harmful to the environment. This ideology has led to formation of several political parties, especially in Germany, Italy, France, the United Kingdom, Belgium, and New Zealand.

green revolution   The movement throughout the world to increase food production, especially in *developing countries,* by using high-yield hybrid seeds, plants that are resistant to destruction, crop rotations, fertilizers, and biotechnology.

greenhouse effect   *Global warming,* or the heating of the environment as a result of the burning of fossil fuels (such as coal and oil). Burning these fuels results in an atmospheric gain in carbon dioxide molecules. The excess carbon dioxide in the atmosphere does not prevent the sun's rays from reaching the earth's surface but prevents the escape of heat radiating from the ground. Some scientists believe that, unless there is a drastic reduction in the use of fossil fuels, the earth's weather and heat level are likely to increase by five degrees in the next 30 to 100 years, an increase that could significantly change climatic patterns.

greenlining   A tactic used by community organizers in which residents of a neighborhood are mobilized to withdraw their funds from banks that are not equal opportunity lenders or that practice *redlining.* See also *Equal Credit Opportunity Act (ECOA).*

Greenpeace   An international social activist organization devoted to preserving the environment and wildlife habitats through education, lobbying, political campaigning, and overt obstruction of those activities that it considers environmentally destructive.

gregariousness   A preference for living in groups and being in frequent contact with others; friendly, approachable, sociable.

"greystocking"   A term applied, somewhat derisively, to social workers and other helping professionals and volunteers in Great Britain and some other English-speaking nations. The term was originally applied to welfare investigators who supposedly made unexpected visits to the homes of welfare recipients but were usually identified by their neighbors in advance because of their predictable attire. The most similar term in the United States has been "*lady bountiful.*"

grief   Intense and acute sorrow resulting from *loss.* It has many of the same symptoms as physical or mental illness, although it tends to diminish with time. However, like all illnesses, grief can end in complete or partial recovery.

grief reaction   Experiencing deep sadness as the result of an important *loss.* This emotional response is normal and in healthy people will gradually subside in a limited time.

grief work   A series of emotional stages or phases following an important *loss* that gradually permit adjustment and recovery. The individual typically reminisces, expresses emotions, accepts, adjusts to the new situation, and forms new relationships.

grievance   A perceived injustice or wrong that results in a formal complaint.

grievance committee   A formal group established to evaluate whether an organization's policies and activities have resulted in harm to a complainant, to recommend changes in the policy or activity that has been deemed harmful, and to recommend ways to make amends for those harmed. Grievance committees usually comprise members of the organization.

grippe   Influenza, or sometimes colds. The term is used by older people and people from nations in the former British commonwealth.

Griscom, John (1774–1852) The founder in 1817 and longtime leader of the Society for the Prevention of Pauperism, the most influential of the early efforts to understand, resolve, and prevent problems of poverty.

gross motor skills The ability to cause effective movement of the body's large muscle groups. See also *fine motor skills.*

gross national product (GNP) The total value of a nation's annual output of services and goods.

groundswell A sudden rise in popular support for some cause, candidate, or policy.

group A collection of people, brought together by mutual interests, who are capable of consistent and uniform action. Major types of groups include the *primary group* and the *secondary group.*

"group balance" A term used in *social group work* or by group therapists for achieving the optimal mix of group members to achieve the group's goals. For example, if the group consists of so many socially withdrawn people that its norm is silence, more outgoing members are added to give it better balance.

group climate The social–emotional atmosphere of a group, also called the "group mood." Group leaders often describe the group in terms of its climate: angry, depressed, celebrative, serious, flighty, suspicious, caring, and so forth. Leaders often try to influence climate or use it to influence individual members in desirable ways. The group achieves its climate when the attitudes, ideas, and feelings of one or more members of the group become those of the other members by association. See also *reciprocal interactions.*

group cohesiveness The degree of mutual attraction or reciprocal benefit experienced or anticipated by individuals in relation to a social collective with which they identify. See also *reciprocal interactions.*

group contagion The process of association and interconnectedness among members of a group that leads to the *group climate* or group mood. See also *reciprocal interactions.*

group development Changes through time in a group's internal structures, norms, processes, and culture.

group development phases In *social group work,* the stages through which the group grows in its normal life cycle. Various group work theorists have identified five phases: (1) the *preaffiliation phase,* (2) the *power-and-control phase,* (3) the *intimacy phase,* (4) the *differentiation phase,* and (5) the *separation phase.*

group dynamics The flow of information and shifts of power influence among members of a social collective. These exchanges can be modified by group leaders or helping professionals and used to achieve certain predetermined objectives that may benefit the members.

group eligibility Being qualified for benefits or obligations as the result of membership in some association or occupation of a defined social *status.* For example, everyone who reaches a certain age may become qualified for specified social insurance benefits.

Group for the Advancement of Doctoral Education in Social Work (GADE) The association of social work educators in the nation's *doctoral programs.* These educators began meeting in 1974 to synchronize their efforts to coordinate and standardize doctoral requirements. The organization became official in 1977, and its members now have annual meetings, conduct workshops, and prepare materials to assist doctoral programs in schools of social work. Their Web site address is http://www.cosw.sc.edu/gade

group goals model A concept about different types of group work and therapy groups based on the overall objectives of the group. The delineation was originated by Catherine Papell and Beulah Rothman and emphasized three major types: *social goals model, remedial goals model,* and *reciprocal goals model.*

group health insurance A plan for insuring against the cost of illness all members and dependents of an established group who want to enroll (for example, all employees of a company, all government workers, or all members of an organization).

group identity The degree to which an individual affiliates with, feels part of, and emulates the characteristics of a social collective.

group leader An individual who facilitates group processes. The leader can be an indigenous member (for example, one of the students in a class) who, through charisma, skill, or other attributes, influences the others. The leader also can be external (for example, a group therapist) whose position or expertise usually results in some influence over the group. Each group has a leader (whether or not the group recognizes it as such), but the leader may change from one meeting to the next or even from one minute to the next.

group leadership roles   Activities that an indigenous or professional *group leader* uses to accomplish the group's goals include giving and seeking information and opinions, proposing tasks and goals, summarizing, coordinating, diagnosing, energizing, testing reality, and evaluating whether goals have been accomplished. Activities that leaders use to maintain the group's social and emotional bonds include encouraging participation, compromising, relieving tension, helping members communicate, setting standards, listening actively, and building a climate of trust for others to emulate.

group practice   A consortium of professionals who provide their services as a single entity. Those who use the services of the group pay the practice as a whole, and the professional's income derives from the group rather than the individual client. This is contrasted with solo or independent practice.

group psychotherapy   A form of *psychotherapy* that treats individuals simultaneously for emotional and behavioral disorders by emphasizing interactions and mutuality. Most professionals consider the term to be synonymous with *group therapy*. Some writers, however, make a distinction among *group psychotherapy, group therapy,* and *social group work;* they consider group psychotherapy to be only one type of group therapy. Whereas group psychotherapy uses group treatment techniques to help individuals resolve emotional problems, group therapy uses a wider range of intervention strategies to help individuals deal with both social maladjustment and emotional disorders. Social group work, although sharing some of these objectives and techniques, is not limited to treating disorders and problems but includes education support groups and positive group experiences that help healthy individuals achieve greater personal fulfillment and change conditions in the environment and society.

group, structured   A purposeful bringing together of clients, who meet some predetermined criteria, for *social group work* or *group therapy* membership. Because effectiveness is achieved largely by the characteristics each member brings to the group, the social worker or therapist may seek the right balance or structure. For example, the structured group might include at least one outgoing and talkative person, one who is quiet, one who is tense, and one who is relaxed. The opposite of a structured group is not an *open group* but a *blanket group.*

group support systems   Computer-based technologies designed to assist groups that are convened to accomplish specific tasks. For example, the group support system known as "electronic brainstorming" asks the group participants to interact in idea formation and development using integrated computers and programs that often hasten the process and give equal credence to those who may be reluctant to discuss ideas or suggestions in face-to-face encounters.

group therapy   An intervention strategy for helping individuals who have emotional disorders or social maladjustment problems by bringing together two or more individuals under the direction of a social worker or other professional therapist. The individuals are asked to share their problems with other members of the group, discuss ways to resolve their problems, exchange information and views about resources and techniques for solving the problem, and share emotional experiences in a controlled (by the professional) setting that enables the members to work through their difficulties. A typical format in group therapy is to have six to eight members meet with a professional therapist in a facility provided by the therapist for 90 minutes once each week. Among the many variations of group therapy are *closed group* and *open group.* Group therapy is a format used by practitioners of many orientations, including *behaviorism, transactional analysis (TA), family therapy, gestalt therapy,* and *psychoanalysis.* See also *sensitivity group* and *marathon group.*

group, transitional   See *transitional group.*

group-type conduct disorder   One of the three types of *conduct disorder,* in which the maladaptive behavior occurs as part of a gang or group of peers. The other types are *solitary aggressive–conduct disorder* and "undifferentiated type."

group work   See *social group work.*

GROW mutual help group   A *mutual help* organization founded in Australia in 1957, now with thousands of groups throughout the world, to provide reciprocal support for people who have shared the experience of emotional or *mental disorder*. In communities where it exists, it is a vital part of the mental health care system and usually maintains 24-hour support, long-term availability, regular group meetings, and social activities. See also *support system*.

growth group   A group whose primary goal is to help members develop their strengths and learn more effective patterns of thinking and behaving. The focus of the growth group is on enhancing and promoting existing strengths rather than treating illnesses or overcoming problems. Types of growth groups include *encounter group, values clarification* groups, and *consciousness-raising* groups.

GSAs   Gay–straight alliances; formal and informal organizations of persons interested in fostering greater understanding of and tolerance for people of diverse sexual orientations. GSAs have been established notably in high schools and colleges as extracurricular clubs to receive school sponsorship.

guaranteed annual income   A proposal made by some social policy experts to eliminate the *means test*. Rather than evaluate each person's resources and needs as the basis for assistance, every individual or family would receive a specified amount of money or service each year from the relevant government agency, regardless of need. See also *negative income tax* and *Family Assistance Plan (FAP)*.

guardian   A person who has temporary or ongoing legal responsibility to care for another person or to manage that person's property and affairs, in whole or in part. Courts appoint guardians to protect the interests of minors or legally incompetent adults.

guardian ad litem   An individual appointed by a judge to protect a party to litigation who is assumed to be unable to protect his or her own interests, such as a child in a custody dispute or an adult who is alleged to be incompetent. The responsibilities of the guardian ad litem are temporary and limited to the course of the litigation. See also *"GALS."*

guerrilla warfare   Military operations within an area controlled by the opposition, often in the form of surprise raids and harassment of the people and facilities protected by the controlling force. The strategy is to patiently wear down the ruling force and replace it after it has lost its power to rule. "Guerrilla" is a Spanish term for "small war."

"guest worker"   The term used especially in continental European nations for foreign workers who enter and work in a country for a specified time.

guidance counselor   A professional who is knowledgeable and skilled in delineating alternatives, articulating goals, providing information and advice, and facilitating client self-awareness. Guidance counselors are frequently employed in educational institutions and personnel offices of business organizations to provide guidance in vocation opportunities, work and study habits, and problem resolution.

guilt   An emotional reaction to the perception of having done something wrong, having failed to do something, or violating important social norms. The reaction is often a loss of *self-esteem* and a desire to make *restitution*. In *psychodynamic* theory, this reaction can be *unconscious* and can be based not on any actual wrongdoing but on concealed drives and motives that are contrary to the prohibitions established by the *superego*.

Gulf War syndrome   A series of symptoms, including vision loss, headaches, skin rashes, and joint pain, found in a significant number of soldiers who served in the Kuwait–Iraq military action in 1990–1991.

gun control   Laws and other efforts by governments and citizens to regulate the acquisition and use of firearms. Most nations have stringent gun controls that make it difficult to possess firearms; firearm use for those who get permission is strictly monitored. The United States is an exception. The Second Amendment of the U.S. Constitution states, "A well-regulated Militia, being necessary to the security of a free State, the right of the people to keep and bear Arms, shall not be infringed." Although gun control advocates interpret this amendment to refer to the military, opponents say the amendment gives citizens the right to possess and carry guns with only limited, if any, controls. See also *Brady Bill* and *CAP laws*.

"gun lobby"   The term applied to organized activists, especially members of the National Rifle

Association, who try to influence legislators to repeal gun control laws or try to convince them not to pass laws restricting access to guns. The gun lobby cites the Second Amendment of the U.S. Constitution, which states, "A well-regulated Militia, being necessary to the security of a free State, the right of the people to keep and bear Arms, shall not be infringed."

Gurin, Arnold (1917–1991)   An advocate and conceptualizer for *community organization* in schools of social work. Gurin served as dean and organizer for several graduate schools of social work and helped develop social work education in Israel.

Gurteen, Steven Humphreys (1836–1898)   A founder of the first of the *Charity Organization Societies (COSs)* in the United States in Buffalo in 1877. Gurteen later helped several other COS programs in various cities and in 1882 wrote *A Hand-book of Charity Organization,* which some have called the first social work textbook.

gustatory hallucination   An imagined perception of taste; tasting something that does not exist outside subjective experience.

gynecology   The branch of medicine specializing in female reproductive health.

Gypsies   An ethnic group of people thought to have originated in the subcontinent of India and who now live in most nations of the world, while retaining their unique culture rather than adopting that of their host nations. Primarily because of their nomadic traditions and cultural isolation, they have remained outsiders in most of these nations and have suffered discrimination, expulsion, and genocide. Many still speak the native language, called Romany, and many Rom people live in groups of related families, or bands.

H

habeas corpus A court requirement that the custodian of a prisoner (or otherwise institutionalized individual) bring the person before the judge. The court may then determine whether the party is being held in violation of his or her constitutional rights to *due process of law*. See also *Fifth Amendment rights*.

habilitation A practice orientation of the social worker that views the client as a competent and coequal problem solver who is empowered through education, newly developed coping skills, and resources. This view is in contrast to the *rehabilitation* orientation, in which the social worker sees clients as dysfunctional or dependent recipients of treatment.

Habitat for Humanity The volunteer organization, established in 1981, to build homes for needy, eligible people. Sponsors pay for materials, land, and fees; supply most of the labor; and charge the residents small monthly payments, much of which goes into a revolving fund to finance other projects. Former President Jimmy Carter is one of the group's predominant participants. Their Web site address is http://www.habitat.org

habituation 1. A type of *adaptation* in which an individual has learned to eliminate responses to repeated and distracting stimuli. For example, an abused child might appear to become indifferent to continued physical punishment. 2. Some social workers and other professionals also use the term to refer to a form of *drug dependence* in which the individual has more of a psychological craving than a physical addiction (manifested by *withdrawal symptoms*).

hacker One who uses computers and Internet systems to explore and exploit the information of others.

Hague Convention on Child Abduction An agreement among signatory nations to honor and enforce the legal decisions made in local jurisdictions about child custody. The Convention was established primarily to prevent a noncustodial parent from moving to another country with the child to circumvent the rights of the custodial parent. In 1988 the United States became the 44th signatory.

halfway houses Transitional residences for individuals who require some professional supervision, support, or protection but not full-time institutionalization. Such facilities are used primarily by formerly hospitalized mental patients and those under parole or who have problems with alcohol dependence and drug dependence. Other transitional residences are *quarterway houses* and three-quarterway houses, which offer more or fewer services, according to need.

Hallowitz, Emmanuel (1920–2000) A social work expert in the theory and practice of group psychotherapy and training for group workers, he was president of the *American Group Psychotherapy Association* for many years.

hallucination An imagined perception of some object or phenomenon that is not really present. Often a symptom of a *psychosis*, it may involve hearing nonexistent voices *(auditory hallucination)*, seeing objects that are not there *(visual hallucination)*, smelling *(olfactory hallucination)*, tasting *(gustatory hallucination)*, and touching *(haptic hallucination)*.

hallucinogen A drug or chemical that, when ingested, results in *hallucination*. Examples are *LSD*, *mescaline*, psilocybin (from some types of mushroom), and peyote (from some types of cactus plant).

hallucinogen abuse Ingestion, usually orally, of an *illicit drug* that is known to result in *hallucination*. Such drugs include *LSD* (lysergic acid diethylamine), dimethyl-tryptamine (DMT), and *mescaline*. The resulting *hallucinosis* is accompanied by other symptoms such as intensification of perceptions; depersonalization; and sometimes tremor, tachycardia, sweating, blurred vision, and poor coordination.

hallucinogen affective disorder A depressive or manic mood disturbance and accompanying recurrent hallucinations, all occurring as a result of *hallucinogen abuse* but lasting longer than the period of direct effect.

hallucinogen persisting-perception disorder A substance-related disorder characterized by a *flash-back* reminiscent of the experiences (hallucinations) during earlier intoxication by a *hallucinogen*.

hallucinosis Disorders characterized by *hallucination* resulting from a substance abuse, psychotic disorder, or general medical condition.

halo effect The tendency to evaluate individuals either too favorably or too negatively on the basis of one or a few notable traits. See also *devaluation* and *idealization*.

Hamilton, Gordon (1892–1967) A social work educator and writer who advanced *social casework* in the profession. As an educator, she helped develop doctoral training in social work, and as a writer, she produced the classic text *Theory and Practice of Social Casework* (1940, revised in 1951).

handicap A physical or mental disadvantage that prevents or limits an individual's ability to function as others do. A handicap refers to the disadvantage or restriction that results from a disability.

handicapism Prejudicial behavior that promotes unequal or unjust treatment of people because of apparent or assumed physical or mental disability; a synonym for *able-ism*. The behavior most commonly occurs in speech ("He's a moron . . . a spastic"), behavior (avoiding contact with a person with a disability), and policies (unequal access to facilities).

Handicapped Children Act of 1975 See *Education for All Handicapped Children Act.*

"handout" Disparaging term for welfare payment.

"hang-up" A popular term referring to any psychological disturbance, especially one that inhibits a positive behavior.

hangover Physical aftereffects of consuming alcohol or other drugs, which often lead to temporary symptoms such as nausea, tremor, headache, dry mouth, anxiety, and depression.

haptic hallucination An imagined perception of touching something or being touched by something that does not exist outside of subjective experience.

harassment The act of tormenting, intimidating, threatening, or badgering an individual using physical, mental, emotional, or economic coercion or influence. See also *sexual harassment.*

harboring a fugitive The illegal practice of concealing someone wanted by law enforcement authorities or providing a refuge or shelter for one who should be in police custody.

"hard sciences" The name sometimes attached to empirically based bodies of knowledge, including natural sciences such as biology, chemistry, and physics. This is contrasted to what are called the *"soft sciences,"* including social sciences such as economics, psychology, and sociology.

hard-core unemployment The lack of job availability, even when ample employment opportunities exist, for those people who lack appropriate education or social skills or who have a physical or mental disorder.

hardship allowance Funds or goods paid to an employee whose job is located in an area of high cost or difficult living conditions or with a lack of amenities.

hard-to-reach clients Individuals, families, and communities who need and are eligible for professional assistance and social work intervention but who are unaware of, unmotivated for, or fearful of the service offered.

hardware In computer technology, the physical machinery—including the computer, keyboard, monitor, modem, and other equipment.

***Harlow v. Fitzgerald* decision** The 1982 U.S. Supreme Court decision (457 U.S. 800) granting to public employees immunity from civil suits for damages. The Court held that public servants performing discretionary functions are generally shielded from liability if their conduct does not violate existing laws or constitutional rights.

harm reduction strategy A pragmatic, public health approach to reducing the negative consequences of some harmful behaviors rather than eliminating or curing the problem. For example, in alcohol or substance abuse problems, the strategy is less concerned with achieving total abstinence and more concerned with helping clients take whatever steps they are willing to take to reduce their risks (for example, substituting methadone for heroin, beer for vodka, and nicotine gum for cigarettes, or using clean needles rather than those that others have previously used).

Hart, Hastings Hornell (1851–1932)   A prison reformer and leader of the child-saving movement. Hart helped develop the *juvenile court* system, championed defendant's rights, and established the federal parole system.

Hartley, Robert M. (1796–1881)   Founder of the Association for Improving the Condition of the Poor in 1843 and its longtime leader. Hartley believed the major causes of poverty were intemperance, improvidence, and extravagance and worked to correct these characteristics in individuals. His advocacy resulted in laws requiring school attendance and parental responsibility.

hashish   A resin produced in the tops of *marijuana* plants, which contains the most powerful concentration of tetrahydrocannabinol *(THC)*, the active ingredient in *marijuana*.

Hatch Act   U.S. federal statutes established in 1939 and updated periodically restricting the political activities of most federal employees and state employees whose organizations receive federal funding.

hate crime   The illegal act motivated by the wish to harm groups or individuals whose affiliations, values, or actions are intolerable to the perpetrator. Such crimes include vandalizing synagogues or black churches, killing physicians who perform abortions, and terrorizing or intimidating people who speak out on a certain political issue. Three types of hate crime are thrill, defensive, and mission. Thrill hate crimes are perpetrated for pleasure against any member of an identifiable group who is at the moment vulnerable; defensive hate crimes seek to discourage the intrusion of members of a group (such as a black family moving into a formerly all-white neighborhood); and in mission hate crimes, the perpetrator specifically targets an individual or member of a group. See also *ethnoviolence.*

Hawthorne effect   The phenomenon that often occurs in *social research* in which subjects behave differently from their norm because of their awareness of being observed. For example, a social worker who observes the interactions of the members of a psychiatric ward may not be seeing the same behaviors that occur when the ward is not being observed.

Haynes, Elizabeth Ross (1883–1953)   A pioneer social worker, politician, and community activist for the rights of women and people of color. She began her career in leadership positions with the *Young Women's Christian Association (YWCA),* the *U.S. Women's Bureau,* and the U.S. Employment Service, where her special concern was for African American domestic workers.

Haynes, George E. (1880–1960)   Cofounder, with Ruth Standish Baldwin, of the *National Urban League* and an authority on the effects of migration on black people.

hazardous substances   Manufactured materials or their residue (or some products of nature) that can lead an exposed person to immediate or gradual illness or death.

head injury   A *trauma* that temporarily or permanently damages tissue in or near the cranium, possibly resulting in brain or nerve damage. Internal head injury may affect some cognitive or motor functions or result in some functional impairment, even though there may be no overt symptom of damage.

head lice   Skin parasites found in the scalp hair, especially among school-age children, and spread by direct contact and sharing combs, hats, pillows, and so forth. The tiny lice and lice eggs may be seen attached to hairs, and the major symptom is severe itching. Although the condition is mostly associated with children from poor and unhygienic environments, it is also seen in children from affluent families. Lice infestations are called "pediculosis." The disease *typhus* is transmitted by lice to humans.

head of household   A family member or other resident of a dwelling unit who is regarded by the other residents and relevant outsiders as the arbiter and ultimate decision maker for those belonging to the group. Usually, but not always, this person is the household's primary income producer or money manager.

Head Start   The U.S. program to provide preschool children of disadvantaged families with compensatory education to offset some of the effects of their social deprivation, including medical, dental, mental health, nutrition, and parental involvement assistance. Established in 1965 as a *Great Society* program, Head Start is administered by HHS's *Administration on Children, Youth, and Families (ACYF)*. The program has been expanded to include *Early Head Start* and Head Start-IHS (for Native American preschoolers). Their Web site address is http://www.acf.dhhs.gov/programs/hsb. See also *Upstream Head Start program, Migrant Head Start program,* and *Project Follow Through*.

head tax   See *poll tax*.

"headshrinker"   A slang expression applied to *psychiatrists, psychologists,* and clinical *social workers* who seek to develop insight and to bring about behavioral changes in their clients.

health   The state of complete physical, mental, and social well-being and, according to the *World Health Organization (WHO)*, not merely the absence of disease or infirmity.

Health and Human Services, U.S. Department of (HHS)   The cabinet-level federal department formed in 1979 when the U.S. Department of Health, Education and Welfare divided. The department coordinates the U.S. government's effort to ensure the health and welfare of the populace. The major components of HHS include the *Administration for Children and Families (ACF), Administration on Aging (AoA), Centers for Medicare and Medicaid Services (CMS), Agency for Healthcare Research and Quality (AHRQ), Centers for Disease Control and Prevention (CDC), Agency for Toxic Substances and Disease Registry (ATSDR), Food and Drug Administration (FDA), Health Resources and Services Administration (HRSA), Indian Health Service (IHS), National Institutes of Health (NIH),* and the *Substance Abuse and Mental Health Services Administration (SAMHSA)*. Their Web site address is http://www.os.dhhs.gov

health care   Activities designed to treat, prevent, and detect physical and mental disorders and to enhance people's physical and psychosocial well-being. The health care system includes personnel who provide the needed services (physicians, nurses, hospital attendants, medical social workers, and so on); facilities where such services are rendered (hospitals, medical centers, nursing homes, hospices, and outpatient clinics); laboratories and institutions for detection, research, and

planning; and educational and environmental facilities that help people prevent disease.

health care facility   Organizations and structures in which the detection and treatment of physical and mental disorders take place, including hospitals, medical centers, nursing homes, outpatient clinics, and hospice centers.

Health Care Financing Administration (HCFA)
See *Centers for Medicare and Medicaid Services*.

health care proxy   A form of advance directive in which individuals name others to make all their health care decisions in situations in which they cannot make their own wishes known. The proxy thus has the same rights as the patient would have to request or refuse treatment. See also *living will*.

health care workers   The generic name for all the professional, paraprofessional, technical, and general employees of a system or facility that provides for the diagnosis, treatment, and overall well-being of patients. Informally, this designation is more commonly used when referring to nonprofessional hospital staff. When referring to professionals other than physicians and nurses in such settings, the term most commonly used is *allied health professionals* or allied health workers. Those included in this designation are home health aides, medical records personnel, nurses aides, orderlies, and attendants.

Health, Education and Welfare, U.S. Department of (HEW)   The former federal agency formed in 1953, replacing the Federal Security Agency, to administer, develop, and improve the national programs for social welfare, health, and education. When the autonomous *U.S. Department of Education* was created in 1979, the remaining components of the agency became known as the *U.S. Department of Health and Human Services (HHS)*.

Health Insurance Portability and Accountability Act (HIPAA)   The U.S. law (P.L. 104-91) that enables people to obtain or retain health insurance coverage despite moving from one job to another or having preexisting medical conditions. A major concern for social workers and other professionals who serve clients is the protection and confidentiality of electronically stored and transmitted information and records.

health maintenance organization (HMO)   A comprehensive health care program and medical group that offers services for a fixed annual fee. In this alternative to the fee-for-service model, enrollees voluntarily prepay for medical and health care, including treatment and prevention of physical and mental illness. HMOs usually have their own medical care facilities, staffed by physicians of all specialties, as well as social workers and other health care providers. See also *managed health care program* and *independent practice associations (IPAs)*.

health planning   Rational efforts to ensure that people's physical care and mental health care needs are being met and that available health care resources are used as effectively as possible . Health planning is conducted in government organizations, private medical and research organizations, and educational institutions. It includes prevention and early-detection activities as well as treatment and follow-up care. Health planning also involves deciding how many health care personnel will be needed in the future, how to finance and control health care costs, where to locate medical facilities, and what methods are most effective and cost-effective. It also considers proper sewage treatment, air quality, and the provision of nutritious food.

Health Professions Educational Assistance Act of 1976   The U.S. federal legislation (P.L. 94-484) that provides financial help to students in health care–related professional schools, including social work.

Health Resources and Services Administration (HRSA)   The organization within the *U.S. Department of Health and Human Services (HHS)* to maintain and improve the utilization, quality, and cost-effectiveness of the nation's health care system. HRSA helps fund the training of health care personnel and facilitates the equitable distribution of these personnel throughout the nation. The component organizations within HRSA include the *Bureau of Primary Health Care (BPHC)*, the *Bureau of the Health Professions (BHP)*, and the *Maternal and Child Health Bureau*.

Healthfare   A welfare proposal in which benefits would be withheld from those who fail to comply with specified medical and health care requirements, such as obtaining immunizations for family members. See also *Workfare* and *Learnfare*.

Healthy Homes and Lead Hazard Control Office   An office within the U.S. Department of Housing and Urban Development, created in 1991, to protect children's health and safety in low-income dwelling units against risks such as lead-based paint hazards, toxic molds, allergens, carbon monoxide, and other hazardous agents. Their Web site address is http://www.hud.gov/offices/lead

Hearn, Gordon (1914–1979)   A social work educator and theoretician, Hearn developed theories about *social group work* and *general systems theory* into social work thought. He wrote *Theory Building in Social Work* in 1958.

hearsay evidence   Statements made by witnesses in courts of law based not on their direct observation but on what they have heard others say. When social workers or other professionals testify as expert witnesses, they are sometimes challenged about the conclusions they have reached on the basis that it is hearsay.

heart attack   Partial failure of the pumping action of the heart. Generally, an event in which the blood vessels that feed the heart become blocked and the heart muscle does not receive enough blood. Symptoms usually include severe chest pains, sweating, hot flashes, and nausea. See also *myocardial infarction*.

heart disease   Disorders affecting the heart muscle, adjacent tissue, and the circulatory system. Heart disease is the leading cause of death among men older than age 40. Those with increased risk include smokers, people with diabetes, people with high blood pressure, and individuals with high serum cholesterol.

Heavily Indebted Poor Countries (HIPCs)   A designation of the World Bank and creditor nations applied to those nations that owe more money than their economies can reasonably pay. The World Bank's HIPC initiative has been seeking arrangements to relieve debt obligations so that repayment can occur without eliminating needed educational and social programs. Others advocate complete debt forgiveness and making future financial transfers in the form of grants rather than loans.

hebephrenic schizophrenia   A type of *psychosis* characterized by wild excitement, giggling, silly behavior, and rapid mood shifts. This disorder is known as "schizophrenia, disorganized type" in current diagnoses. See also *disorganized schizophrenia*.

Hebrew Immigrant Aid Society (HIAS)   The international refugee organization to help Jewish and other peoples whose lives and freedom are endangered, assisting in rescue, relocation, family reunification, and resettlement. Their Web site address is http://www.hias.org

hedonistic behavior   Pleasure-seeking activity without much concern about the accompanying responsibilities or consequences.

hegemony   The political, cultural, and economic influence or domination of one nation, society, or group by another.

HELP Committee   The U.S. Senate's standing Health, Education, Labor and Pension Committee, which processes legislation most relevant to social work.

help line   A telephone-based social service to provide contact between people in need of assistance and professionals or volunteers who provide encouragement and access to necessary services. Trained listeners are available for callers, especially those at risk of suicide and family violence, runaways, and those seeking information about how to get needed services. The term is often used interchangeably with *hot line*, although the latter may also emphasize communications such as *whistle blowing*. See also *Nineline*.

helping network   A *linkage* comprising various combinations of individuals, groups, families, organizations, government offices, social agencies, and so forth, all of which work together or autonomously to provide a person with the supports, resources, information, and access required for problem solving or meeting a need. Helping networks differ from *social networks* in that they are linked only with respect to the help they seek to provide, whereas social networks have far more bases for their existence. See also *natural helping network* and *collaboration*.

helplessness, learned   See *learned helplessness*.

help-rejecting complaining   Appeals for help followed by explanations about why the assistance was deficient. One who engages in this behavior is often dealing with emotional conflicts and seeks help to disguise unconscious feelings of hostility and self-pity. The pattern is often seen in *hypochondriasis* and *narcissistic personality disorder*.

hematology   The scientific study of blood and blood disorders. A hematologist is a physician who diagnoses and treats disorders of the blood and organs that form blood constituents as well as the microorganisms that infect blood.

hematophobia   The pathological *fear* of blood.

Hemlock Society   The organization, founded in 1980, concerned with right-to-die issues and advocating consensual *euthanasia* for terminally ill or suffering individuals. See also *Society for the Right to Die*. Their Web site address is http://www.hemlock.org

hemodialysis   The medical process of purifying the blood of patients who have had kidney failure. This process involves a machine through which the body's blood circulates past a semipermeable membrane. Waste products in the blood are absorbed through the membrane and discarded.

hemophilia   A *genetic disease* in which the blood has insufficient capacity for rapid clotting, often resulting in excessive bleeding when injuries occur.

hemorrhage   Bleeding. The term is often used to indicate an unusual flow of blood. In an internal hemorrhage the bleeding occurs within the patient's body and is invisible to observers. Cuts on the skin are external hemorrhages.

hemorrhoid   An enlarged vein around the anus or rectum that may lead to fissures and intense pain, usually the result of untreated constipation or chronic diarrhea. This condition was once commonly known as "piles."

Henrician Poor Law   English legislation, enacted in 1536 during the reign of King Henry VIII, the primary purpose of which was to organize the ways the nation would deal with its "able-bodied" poor population. Officially named "The Act for the Punishment of Sturdy Vagabonds and Beggars," it placed responsibility for the care of poor people with local officials who could collect taxes for the purpose. The officials furnished work for unemployed people and restricted begging to people with disabilities. Penalties for begging by able-bodied individuals included branding; enslavement; removal of their children; and, for repeated offenses, execution. Many provisions of these laws remained until they were modified in the 1782 *Gilbert Act.*

hepatitis   A viral disease resulting in swelling and inflammation of the liver. Symptoms include nausea, fever, weakness, loss of appetite, and often jaundice. Treatment involves extensive bed rest and controlled diet. The virus is spread by contact with contaminated food or water (infectious hepatitis), injections of contaminated blood, or the use of contaminated needles (serum hepatitis). It also sometimes occurs as a complication of other diseases, such as *cirrhosis* of the liver, *mononucleosis,* and *dysentery.*

heredity   1. The transmission of characteristics from parents to offspring through chromosomes that bear their genes. 2. The tendency of an individual to manifest the traits of his or her progenitors. See also *chromosomal disorders* and *genetic disorder.*

heroin   A potent narcotic synthesized from *morphine.* It can be snorted or injected under the skin or into a vein *("mainlining").* Its effect on the user is euphoria or apathy, and for some a "rush"—a sensation described as similar to an orgasm throughout the entire body. Once addicted, the user seeks further doses to avoid the intensely discomforting experience of *withdrawal symptoms.* Heroin is highly addictive and, partly because of its high cost and nonexistent quality control, contributes to an increased death rate and to higher incidence of organized and street crime. Heroin use is illegal in most nations. See also *opioid abuse* and *methadone treatment.*

herpes   A viral infection resulting in blisterlike eruptions. Herpes simplex takes the form of recurring blisters filled with clear fluid, known as cold sores when they appear around the lips and as canker sores when in the mouth. Herpes genitalis is a viral infection in the genital area. Herpes zoster, also called "shingles," is a painful viral infection of the nerves, most commonly appearing on the chest–abdomen area and sometimes following other nerve pathways.

heterogeneous   Possessing dissimilar traits.

heterogeneous groups   Groups whose memberships comprise people with different traits, such as a wide age range, different ethnic backgrounds, and divergent political orientations. Some group leaders who hold the *dissonance theory of groups* seek to have a disparate membership as a catalyst for more dynamic interactions. See also *homogeneous groups.*

heteronomy   The opposite of autonomy. Those who are heteronomous are completely influenced by forces outside their control, such as compelling mental or emotional urges, or totally under the influence of a charismatic leader.

heterosexism   The belief that gay men and lesbians are deviant, abnormal, or inferior to heterosexual people, usually manifested as bias against gay men and lesbians. The term *homophobia* is similar but implies a stronger feeling involving feelings of fear, anger, or disgust.

heterosexuality   Association with and orientation toward sexual activity with members of the opposite sex.

heterostasis   The tendency of a system or organism to become unstable.

heuristics   A hypothesized mental or cognitive strategy for storing and accessing information by reducing more complex concepts to simpler ones.

HHS   The familiar name for the *U.S. Department of Health and Human Services.*

hidden agenda   The underlying goals, expectations, and strategies of members within a group, as opposed to the overt purposes of the meeting.

hidden inflation   An economic situation in which costs for products or services apparently remain constant while the quality or quantity declines. For example, the price for a box of cereal stays the same, but the manufacturer puts less in each box.

hierarchy of needs   The view developed in 1954 by Abraham Maslow and other professionals with a *humanistic orientation* that people's needs occur in ascending order. One fulfills physiological needs first, followed by needs for safety, belonging, self-respect and self-worth, and finally *self-actualization* or achieving one's full potential. See also *motivation.*

high blood pressure   See *hypertension.*

higher law An allusion to some moral or spiritual guideline that is supposedly superior to laws created by legislative bodies; also referred to as "natural law" or "natural justice." The allusion is sometimes used by social activists and religious fundamentalists to justify disobeying laws (for example, pacifist tax protesters who withhold funds from governments that wage war on others).

high-rise slums Groups of multifloored apartment houses, usually surrounded by bare earth or asphalt, in disrepair and crime ridden, and most often part of *public housing* projects.

high-risk screening Outreach efforts by social workers and other professionals to identify, locate, and offer services to individuals who belong to groups that are vulnerable to illness and social problems.

high-tech home health care The use of specialized medical equipment, supplies, and professional knowledge in the patient's home for diagnosis, treatment, and rehabilitation.

hijos de crianza In Spanish-speaking cultures, "the children of upbringing," a term that refers to the traditional practice of everyone in a community assuming responsibility for helping raise a child as one's own without the necessity of blood or even friendship ties. See also *compadrazgo* and *padrinos*.

hilfsbedürftig In German, a term meaning "needy."

Hilfskassen German for "aid funds." In the mid–19th century, many German guilds and corporations informally collected voluntary funds to be used for needy people. As this became more centralized and formally organized, along with the *Krankenkassen* (sickness funds) organizations, they were incorporated into Germany's social insurance programs established in the 1880s.

Hill, Octavia (1838–1912) An advocate for better housing for poor people in England, Hill developed principles for more equitable landlord–tenant relationships. She founded the London Society for the Prevention of Pauperism, a forerunner of the first of the *Charity Organization Societies (COSs)*.

Hill–Burton hospitals Health care facilities built under the 1946 Hospital Survey and Construction Act and named for the legislation's sponsors. The act provided low-cost government-insured loans to build hospitals and encouraged states and localities to build new facilities in underserved areas.

"hillbilly" A disparaging term referring to an individual who comes from mountainous regions or other nonmetropolitan areas.

hippocampus A part of the brain believed responsible for storing or discarding memories and processing threatening or traumatic stimuli.

Hispanic Persons who identify themselves as coming from or being descended from people from Mexico, Puerto Rico, Cuba, Central America, or South America. Hispanic-origin persons may be of any race and in census statistics may be included in any one of these racial groups. The term refers to Spanish language users rather than any racial or ethnic identity.

histogram A bar graph depicting a *frequency distribution*.

histology The study of microscopically small structures of the body.

historical research The systematic collection and evaluation of data about past events. It follows the procedures of all research (defining the problem to be studied, posing hypotheses, collecting data in a systematic way, analyzing the information obtained, and interpreting it within the limits of generalizability). Because the data that survive are so limited and the studied phenomena are not replicable, the potential for *bias* is great.

histrionic personality disorder One of the 11 types of *personality disorders* with all or many of the following characteristics: overly dramatic behavior, overreaction to minor events, craving for attention and excitement, tantrums, appearance to others of shallowness and lack of genuineness, apparent helplessness and dependence, proneness to manipulative gestures, and threats of suicide. A person who has this disorder is commonly referred to as a "hysterical personality" or a "*hysteric*."

histrionics Manipulative behavior that is overly dramatic, demanding, volatile, self-indulgent, and attention seeking.

HIV/AIDS Bureau The bureau within the HHS Health Resources and Services Administration that provides funding for HIV/AIDS care for low-income individuals, education for caregivers and patients, access to treatments, development of AIDS policies, and administration for most of the *Ryan White CARE Act.*

"HIV cocktail" An evolving treatment regimen for people with HIV disease involving several assorted medications, all administered simultaneously, to attack the HIV virus in various ways. HIV cocktails have many benefits for significantly reducing the viral load, prolonging life, and reducing the risk of opportunistic infections. The cocktail is not available to all because it is expensive and occasionally presents adverse drug reactions and side effects.

HIV disease See *human immunodeficiency virus (HIV)* and *acquired immune deficiency syndrome (AIDS).*

HIV negative A result of a blood test to detect antibodies to the *human immunodeficiency virus (HIV)* when no antibodies are found. Care must be taken to gather an accurate history of risk practices or behaviors to ensure that the antibody test was not given during the *"window period."*

HIV positive A result of a blood test that has determined the existence of antibodies to the *human immunodeficiency virus (HIV).*

Ho, Man Keung (1940–1992) A social work author, educator, and expert on multiculturalism, the problems facing Asian Americans, and social work with nonwhite and non–middle-class clients.

hoarding Acquiring and holding goods, such as food, water, gold, and money. Disaster planners have to contend with a tendency of some people in impending crises to buy up all available supplies, leaving others without access to needed goods.

Hoey, Jane (1892–1968) A public welfare administrator and social researcher who influenced policy and legislation and led various social work organizations.

hold harmless agreement A signed legal document stating that the signer agrees to relieve another party of liability by assuming the liability. A hold harmless agreement is used as a defense in a lawsuit but usually will not prevent one from being filed. Many social workers use a form of this agreement in contracts with clients to ensure *informed consent.*

holding environment A metaphor for the helping relationship devised by psychoanalyst Donald Winnicott (1896–1971) and based on the world created by a mother for her newborn; she recognizes the infant's absolute dependence and meets her baby's physical and emotional needs on demand. In some situations, a therapist fulfills a similar role with clients.

holistic Oriented toward the understanding and treatment of the whole person or phenomenon. In this view, an individual is seen as being more than the sum of separate parts, and problems are seen in a broader context rather than as specific symptoms. One who maintains a holistic philosophy seeks to integrate all the social, cultural, psychological, and physical influences on an individual.

holistic medicine An approach to health care that stresses treatment of the whole person, with emphasis on the interconnections of the various physical systems, including the mind. It encourages the active involvement of the patient in the treatment process through diet, exercise, pleasurable activities, and positive attitude. See also *complementary and alternative medicine.*

Hollis, Florence (1907–1987) A social work educator and theoretician, she developed the typology of casework treatment and wrote *Women in Marital Conflict* and the classic text *Casework: A Psychosocial Therapy.*

Hollis–Taylor Report A 1951 study of *social work education* conducted by Ernest Hollis and Alice Taylor, demonstrating the profession's increasing specialization, fragmentation, and growing orientation toward the case-by-case treatment of problems. The report recommended social work education that emphasized a more generic orientation and a greater concern for social issues and social action. Many of the recommendations were accepted by the profession and became a foundation for the current objectives of social work education.

Holocaust Great destruction of the lives and property of a people. Today, the term is most often applied to the planned efforts of the Nazis during World War II to eliminate the Jewish population of Europe. See also *genocide, pogrom,* and *"ethnic cleansing."*

home-alone child A child whose parents or guardians leave him or her without needed care and supervision. See also *latchkey child.*

home-based instructional services Programs designed to provide education for children or adults who are unable to attend schools or other training facilities, usually as a result of illness or severe physical disability.

home care The provision of health care, homemaker, and social services to clients in their homes.

home care services Programs usually conducted by local and state departments of human services to assist people who have problems that preclude basic self-care needed to remain in their own homes. Such programs include *homemaker services, meals-on-wheels, chore service, home health services, respite care,* and *attendant care.* Some social workers also call this *domiciliary care services;* others use the term "home care services" as a synonym for "homemaker services" and "domiciliary care services" as a synonym for programs to help needy people with the physical repairs and maintenance of their homes.

home detention A *corrections* program in which as part of the sentence a convicted felon is confined to home or other restrictions outside of penal facilities. Many jurisdictions use electronic home-monitoring systems to ensure compliance. In these systems, convicts are fitted with small radio transmitters riveted on their ankles, which keep a central computer notified about the person's whereabouts.

home equity conversion plans Various methods for older homeowners to use some of the value of their homes for living expenses while continuing to live in them until death. Also known as HELP (home equity liquification plans), these plans include property tax postponement to be repaid upon death, *reverse annuity mortgages* (RAMs), and sale–leaseback arrangements in which investors buy the home for lump sum cash or monthly payments and allow the person tenancy for life.

home health aides Health care workers who provide personal care and homemaker services and some nursing to patients who are disabled or recovering on discharge from health care facilities.

Home Health Care Social Workers, The American Network of The independent professional association for social workers employed in home health care settings or interested in aspects relevant to it. The network sponsors workshops; an annual conference; and publications, including *Guidelines*

for Practitioners and Agencies. Their Web site address is http://www.homehealthsocialwork.org

home health services Programs that provide for medical, nursing, occupational therapy, physical therapy, speech therapy, and follow-up care of patients in their homes. Many of these services are provided in the private sector for a fee by health care personnel or by private nursing service care, financed in part by *third-party payment.* Public health care services in the patient's home are also available. This provides a system that often is more comfortable for the patient and more economical than hospitalization or *nursing home* care.

home purchase vouchers The HUD program, established in 2000, that enables persons who received *rental vouchers* to use this assistance toward buying new or existing houses or shares in housing cooperatives. If the homeowner sells or refinances during the first 10 years, a portion of the home's equity is returned to the local public housing authority. To qualify the applicant must have a minimal income, be a first-time home buyer, and attend free counseling sessions to learn about aspects of home ownership.

home relief A means-tested welfare program operated under state and local auspices to provide financial assistance to needy individuals and families who are not eligible for any other categorical program. The term is synonymous with *general assistance (GA).*

Home Responsibilities Protection (HRP) Program A benefit in the British social security system to protect the retirement pensions of people whose work income is low or who are out of the labor force to care for dependents.

home rule Governmental autonomy in the hands of the people who live in the region governed. The term is often used by residents of colonies or regions within a nation that seek control over their own governments.

home visits Going to clients' homes to provide social services, often because of clients' disabilities or because they are homebound or otherwise do not go to the social worker's office. Sometimes workers are required to make such visits unexpectedly to investigate the clients' normal living conditions (as in investigating concerns about child welfare, disability claims, or impoverishment). The procedure began in the pre–social work days of *friendly visitors.*

homebound   One who because of illness or disability must remain bedridden or within the confines of the home, institution, or immediate neighborhood. See also *location bound.*

homebound employment   Jobs that people who are *homebound* are paid to do in their homes. Typical jobs include babysitting and day care, telephone solicitation, direct mail marketing, secretarial work, and computer services.

homebound instruction   Individualized program for students whose permanent or temporary disability precludes their attendance in regular classrooms. The 1975 *Education for All Handicapped Children Act* requires that school-age children with such conditions be provided with such services by the appropriate educational authorities.

Homeland Security, U.S. Department of (DHS) The cabinet-level federal department created in 2002 (P.L. 107-296) primarily to prevent terrorist attacks within the United States, reduce vulnerability to terrorism, and minimize the damage from potential attacks and natural disasters. Most of the components of DHS had existed in other departments, often with different names and structures. Components include the U.S. Coast Guard, the Secret Service, the *Bureau of Immigration and Customs Enforcement,* the *Bureau of Customs and Border Protection,* the *Border and Transportation Security Directorate,* and the Emergency Preparedness and Response Directorate. Their Web site address is http://www.dhs.gov

Homeless Assistance Act of 1987   See *McKinney Act.*

homeless shelters   Private or publicly funded residential facilities for individuals and families who otherwise have no homes. The shelters typically offer beds, meals, and sometimes health and social services to as many needy people as possible, depending on available room, supplies, and demand. Some shelters have strict requirements about who is accepted, whereas others admit anyone on an as-available basis. Many shelters are highly dependent on private contributions of money, food, and volunteer workers.

homelessness   The condition of lacking a permanent residence and the means to obtain one. Generally, a homeless person is impoverished and transient and often lacks the social skills or emotional stability needed to improve the situation unless help is provided.

homemaker   A person whose primary role and activity is to maintain a comfortable and secure living environment for his or her family.

homemaker services   A health or social services program to help clients remain in their own homes. Usually, one or more helpers visit the clients' homes on predetermined schedules to prepare meals, do laundry, clean house, and provide transportation and some nursing care. These homemakers are usually public employees or volunteers, and their services often help keep clients out of more expensive hospitals or nursing homes. In many communities, the homemaker service program is oriented primarily to educating and training family members to do this work, and those in *chore service* do the work.

homeostasis   The tendency of a system or organism to maintain stability and, when disrupted, to adapt and strive to restore the stability previously achieved. See also *general systems theory.*

homeowner tax deferrals   State and local laws that allow property owners to postpone paying residential taxes until the homes are sold or the owners die. The program is designed to protect older people (whose property taxes have increased substantially because of the escalating value of their homes) from being forced because of taxation to vacate. See also *circuit-breaker tax relief.*

Homestead Act   The 1862 federal legislation designed to redistribute the population, provide opportunities, and settle the open lands in the West. The law authorized any U.S. citizen to receive 160 acres of unoccupied government land free of charge by agreeing to live on it for five years.

homestead exemptions   State and local laws that give property tax breaks to qualified homeowners to permit them to remain in their homes or encourage people to live in certain neighborhoods. The law subtracts some of the home's value from the property assessment to lower its taxes. The law is designed mostly to protect older people from being forced out of their increasingly valuable homes because of tax increases.

homicide   The killing of one human being by another.

homogeneous   Possessing the same or similar traits. See also *heterogeneous*.

homogeneous groups   Groups whose membership comprises people of similar traits; for example, members who are of the same age or gender or who share the same problem. Some group leaders believe homogeneity permits the members to focus on their core problem areas without having to deal so much with distracting side issues. See also *single-focus group, heterogeneous groups,* and *dissonance theory of groups.*

homophobia   The irrational *fear* or hatred of people oriented toward *homosexuality*. The term is often applied to people who have strong negative feelings about gay men and lesbians and to people who support antihomosexual activities. Three types of homophobia have been identified. Institutional homophobia is the covert and overt prejudice found in economic, political, educational, religious, social welfare, and family structures. Individual homophobia occurs when people show open hostility and violence. Internalized homophobia is contempt for one's own actual or imagined homosexual orientation. See also *heterosexism.*

homophyly   The tendency of most people to like and be more comfortable with people who are like themselves.

homosexual panic   Severe distress related to an individual's fear or delusion of being thought to be homosexual by others or of being raped or seduced by someone of the same sex. It sometimes appears as an initial symptom of *schizophrenia* (especially paranoid type) or as a manifestation of latent homosexuality.

homosexuality   The sexual or *erotic orientation* by some men and women for members of their same sex. This orientation is not considered to be a mental disorder. The term is used for men and women. See also *gay* and *lesbian*.

homosexuality, latent   In psychodynamic theory, the presence of erotic impulses outside the individual's conscious awareness toward one or more members of the same sex. The individual might give behavioral clues about this orientation but does not engage in overt homosexual activity. Some theorists suggest that latent homosexuality, accompanied by efforts by the individual to conceal the orientation from oneself and others, can result in *homophobia*. See also *latent homosexual.*

honor system   A principle followed by members of some organizations or associations based on mutual trust and the understanding that all members will fulfill their responsibilities without being monitored or coerced. This system is implicit in the *adult learner model* in *social work education.*

ho'oponopono   An indigenous Hawaiian form of family or group therapy. A method by which Hawaiian extended families or groups work to solve problems and restore harmony; the participants state and discuss the problem, confess wrongdoing, pray together, and offer forgiveness and release. See also *'ohana.*

Hoodless, Adelaide Hunter (1857–1910)   A Canadian social reformer who led the movement for dairy pasteurization after her child died from tainted milk. She became an expert and advocate for the YWCA, domestic arts training for Canadian girls, child welfare programs, and world health and welfare. She founded the Women's Institutes, which have hundreds of chapters in Canada and former British Commonwealth nations.

"Hooverville"   A term of derision for the *shantytowns* and encampments of poor people that formed near some cities during the *Great Depression*. They were named for President Herbert Hoover, who was president when the depression began.

Hopkins, Harry (1890–1946)   An administrator of the *Federal Emergency Relief Administration (FERA)*, President Franklin D. Roosevelt's adviser on *New Deal* programs, and director of the *Works Progress Administration (WPA)*. After completing his social work training, he worked for the *Association for Improving the Condition of the Poor (AICP)* and as a relief worker. He also served as the U.S. Secretary of Commerce in 1938.

Horatio Alger story   An expression referring to an individual's transition from poverty to affluence supposedly because of hard work, thrift, and honest character; based on the 19th-century "rags-to-riches" novels of the Reverend Horatio Alger, Jr.

horizontal career move   Taking a new job that represents the same level of attainment as the old, such as similar pay and benefits, responsibilities, and prestige, usually to fulfill nonvocational objectives. See also *vertical career move.*

horizontal disclosure   In *social group work,* the revelation by a member of a therapy group of some distressing information and the group's analysis of that information as it affects the relationship between the revealer and the other group members. This is the opposite of *vertical disclosure.*

hormone replacement therapy (HRT)   A medical treatment to replace hormones such as estrogen and progestogen when the body no longer adequately supplies them. The treatment is particularly helpful in reducing symptoms sometimes found in menopause, such as hot flashes and sleep disturbance, and the risks of osteoporosis and heart disease.

hospice   A philosophy of caring and an array of programs, services, and settings for people with *terminal illness.* Hospice services are usually offered in nonhospital facilities with homelike atmospheres where families, friends, and the significant other can be with the dying person. Organizations that foster the development of the hospice movement include the American Hospice Foundation and Children's Hospice International.

hospice care   The provision of health care and homemaker and social services in nonhospital, homelike facilities for people with a *terminal illness.*

hospital social work   The provision of social services in hospitals and similar health care centers, most often within a facility's department of social services or social work. The services provided include prevention, rehabilitation, and follow-up activities, as well as discharge planning and information gathering and providing. Other services include assisting patients with the financial and social aspects of their care and counseling patients and their families. In England the hospital social worker is a specialist in a hospital setting to ensure that patients' social needs do not interfere with their physical care needs.

hospitalist   A physician who cares for patients during their hospitalizations. This doctor takes over for the patient's primary care physician during the

hospitalization, keeps the primary care physician informed, and returns the patient to the primary care physician upon completion of the hospital stay.

host setting   An organization within which another organization provides specialized services. For example, a host setting for a hospital social services department would be the hospital.

hot line   A communications system that provides for immediate and direct telephone contact between certain people in times of emergency. Many communities have established such systems so that trained listeners are on hand to receive calls from people who experience emotional or social problems. There are also special-purpose hot lines such as those for runaways, *whistle-blowing,* suicide prevention, family violence, and other problems.

hot-seat technique   In social work with groups and other *group therapy* approaches, a procedure in which the group leader and all members focus exclusively on one member for an extended period.

house arrest   A method of *community-based corrections* in which the convicted lawbreaker, as part of the penalty for the wrongdoing, is confined to one's home rather than a *house of corrections.* The type of house arrest can vary from no monitoring to the requirement of periodic call-ins, unexpected visits, and electronic surveillance. House arrest is an increasingly popular alternative to the far more expensive institutional *incarceration.*

house of corrections   A jail or prison. Usually the term is applied to minimum-security facilities for incarcerating those convicted of minor offenses who have good potential for rehabilitation.

household   The *U.S. Bureau of the Census* term referring to all people, whether related or not, who live in the same dwelling unit. This includes individuals (single-person households) as well as groups of people.

housing allowance   Funds allocated and earmarked for payment of rent or mortgage on one's home, usually provided by an employer or human services agency.

Housing and Urban Development, U.S. Department of (HUD)   The cabinet-level department formed in 1965 to administer, develop, and improve national *housing programs,* including *urban* *renewal* and *community development*. Major divisions include the *Office of Fair Housing and Equal Opportunity,* the *Office of Community Planning and Development,* and the *Government National Mortgage Association (GNMA).* Their Web site address is http://www.hud.gov

Housing Benefit in U.K.   The welfare provision in the United Kingdom for low-income families and individuals that provides financial assistance to cover rent payments and reduces property taxes on the residences of needy people.

housing expenditure   As used by the *U.S. Bureau of the Census* and HUD statisticians, the total amount a family pays to live in and maintain their home. If the family is renting, this includes the monthly rental charge, rent as pay (that is free or reduced rent in exchange for some services such as managing other dwelling units), maintenance, insurance, utilities, and other expenses for renters. If the family is purchasing their home, the housing expenditure includes payments for mortgage principal, interest, and other fees; property taxes; maintenance and repairs; insurance; and other expenses.

housing programs   Publicly funded and monitored programs designed to provide suitable homes, especially for those unable to find or pay for them themselves. In the United States, most of these programs are administered by the *U.S. Department of Housing and Urban Development (HUD).* These programs include low-rent public housing, rent subsidies, home ownership assistance for low-income families, home maintenance programs for low-income people, and other programs.

Howe, Samuel Gridley (1801–1876)   A social reformer and advocate for people with physical or mental disabilities, he founded the New England Asylum for the Blind (now the Perkins Institute) and led in the development of state bureaus for charities.

hózhó   The Navajo people's concept of ideal harmony with oneself, with others, with nature, and with spiritual forces.

H2A Program   A *U.S. Department of Labor* agricultural worker program that permits farmers to recruit and employ foreign workers when no American workers are available. An H2A Visa is issued to each foreign worker for the time he or she is employed.

Huantes, Margarita (1914–1994)   Social work educator who advocated against *illiteracy* and *functional illiteracy* and helped develop literacy training programs, especially in the Mexican American community.

HUD   The familiar name for the *U.S. Department of Housing and Urban Development.*

HUD McKinney Vento Grants   The U.S. federal homeless assistance program enacted in various revisions of the 1987 McKinney Homeless Act (P.L. 100-77). The program funds grants for building or renovating emergency shelter facilities and maintaining and staffing them. It also funds Section 8 rehabilitation of single-room occupancy dwellings for homeless persons. The program gives states wide discretion in how they use the funds and encourages local programs to compete with one another in providing *continuum of care* procedures for homeless persons. See also the *Education for Homeless Children and Youth Act (EHCY).*

huddle groups   See *buzz grouping.*

Hudson, Walter W. (1934–1999)   Social work researcher who advocated that social workers use more empirically based measures in assessment, treatment, and social interventions. He wrote influential textbooks about research methodology and statistical analysis and developed measurement scales to more objectively assess interpersonal and social problems and social work interventions.

Hull-House   The most famous of the *settlement houses,* founded in Chicago in 1889 by *Jane Addams* and *Ellen Gates Starr.* Among the first of its kind, it was a community center for poor and disadvantaged people of the area and was the setting for initiating various social reform activities.

human capital   The cumulative knowledge, skills, values, resourcefulness, and personal connections that are available in a society. Also, expenditures to enhance the quality of a people, which increase their productivity. Human capital is developed by investment in the citizens of a nation through public education, health and security programs, and job training, all of which ultimately contribute to a more economically healthy society. See also *investment-versus-consumption concept.*

human development   The physical, mental, social, and experiential changes that occur over a person's *life cycle.* These changes are continuous, occur in fairly consistent sequences, and are cumulative with other changes. Human development occurs in a predictable manner, but the rate of change is unique to each individual.

human development index (HDI) A composite index that measures a nation's progress in three factors—longevity, level of education, and standard of living—as indicated by the nation's life expectancy rate, average amount of education, and real gross domestic product per capita.

human diversity The range of differences among people in terms of race, ethnicity, age, geography, religion, values, culture, orientations, physical and mental health, and many other distinguishing characteristics.

Human Genome Organization (HUGO) The international consortium of scientists, government research organizations, and universities involved in the *Human Genome Project,* established in 1989. HUGO coordinates activity; collects and disseminates information; and addresses related issues about ethics, legal and social problems, and intellectual property rights.

Human Genome Project The scientific project begun in 1986 by the DoE to develop new procedures and tools for detecting and analyzing DNA. By 2001 the project, which was also carried out by the NIH, established an ordered set of DNA segments from known chromosomal locations and developed computer technology for analyzing genetic map and DNA sequence data.

human immunodeficiency virus (HIV) The *acquired immune deficiency syndrome (AIDS)* virus, which attacks the body's immune system and thereby leaves the HIV-infected person eventually vulnerable to a debilitating or fatal *opportunistic infection, cancer,* or neurological condition. Two types of HIV have been identified: HIV-1 is found worldwide and HIV-2 appears mainly in central Africa. The progression of infection is similar. Blood, semen, vaginal secretions, and breast milk have been implicated in transmission. HIV is transmitted by unprotected penetrative sexual intercourse with an infected person, by infected hypodermic needles, by medical transfusion of untreated blood, and from infected mother to child (in utero, during birth, or shortly after birth). HIV cannot be transmitted casually (for example, touching an infected person or sharing a drinking glass). HIV infection and infectiousness are presumed to be lifelong.

human papillomavirus (HPV) One of the *sexually transmitted diseases (STDs)* that causes genital warts, HPV is also known as "venereal warts." HPV affects up to 40 million people in the United States.

human resources The knowledge and skill that some people can and do make available to others for the improvement and enrichment of their lives. See also *natural resources.*

Human Resources Administration (HRA) The title used in many state and municipal governments, such as New York City, for their departments of *social services, public welfare, social welfare,* or *human services.*

human resources management In organizations, the activity concerned with "personnel management" (employee recruitment, training, assigning, compensating, promoting, retiring, or discharging) as well as with finding ways to achieve maximum utilization of the organization's *human resources.*

human resources planning The systematic process of defining the problems and personnel needs of an organization, establishing objectives relevant to those problems and needs, determining activities required to meet objectives, identifying and analyzing tasks, creating jobs and career ladders, and designing *in-service training.* The activity was once referred to as "manpower planning."

human rights The opportunity to be accorded the same prerogatives and obligations in social fulfillment as are accorded to all others without distinction as to race, gender, language, or religion. In 1948, the U.N. Commission on Human Rights spelled out these opportunities. They include the basic *civil rights* recognized in democratic constitutions such as life, liberty, and personal security; freedom from arbitrary arrest, detention, or exile; the right to fair and public hearings by impartial tribunals; freedom of thought, conscience, and religion; and freedom of peaceful association. They also include economic, social, and cultural rights such as the right to work, education, and social security; to participate in the cultural life of the community; and to share in the benefits of scientific advancement and the arts.

human rights organizations Formal associations of individuals, professional associations, unions, and other nongovernment groups that work toward the establishment and improvement of *human rights*. They work toward their goals by monitoring political and social institutions, lobbying governments, and publicizing human rights problems. Many organizations try to influence nations to ratify and comply with the major international human rights declarations, such as the rights of the child; the elimination of discrimination; women's rights; and economic, cultural, and social rights. Among the major human rights organizations are *Amnesty International*, Human Rights Watch, and the Simon Wiesenthal Center.

Human SERVE Human Service Employees Registration and Voter Education Fund, an organization founded in 1983 to encourage people to vote and to make the voting process more accessible. The organization educates people about how to register; brings registration facilities to potential voters; and places legal or political pressures on boards of elections that make it difficult for some groups, especially racial and ethnic groups, to register. See also *voter registration drives, National Voter Registration Act of 1993,* and *Richard Cloward.*

human services Programs and activities designed to enhance people's development and well-being, including providing economic and social assistance for those unable to provide for their own needs. Some social scientists identify the six basic human services as (1) personal social services, (2) health, (3) education, (4) housing, (5) income, and (6) justice and public safety. The term "human services" is roughly synonymous with the terms "social services" or "welfare services" and includes planning, organizing, developing, and administering programs for and providing direct social services to people. The "human services" term came into wider use in 1979 when the *U.S. Department of Health and Human Services (HHS)* was established to replace the *U.S. Department of Health, Education and Welfare (HEW).* It was thought that the term "welfare" had a negative connotation and that the organization would have more influence with the new name. Also, in 1991 the American Public Welfare Association changed its name to the *American Public Human Services Association.* Use of the term "human services" (and "human resources") instead of "social welfare services" is also part of the trend toward employing other professionals in addition to social workers in the services arena.

humanics Organized activities and employment that provide social and human services for both young and old people, people with disabilities, people in need, and all others. Humanics special-

ists work for people primarily in nonprofit organizations. Colleges and universities throughout the nation have established certificate programs to prepare entry-level professionals for careers in youth programs, human services agencies, social agencies, and nonprofit community development programs. The programs include extensive coursework, majoring in humanics, along with internships and leadership opportunities in volunteerism.

humanism A philosophical orientation that holds that morality and ethical judgments should be based not on divine spirits or supernatural forces but on human experience and reason.

humanistic orientation Concepts, values, and techniques that emphasize people's potential rather than their dysfunctions. Professionals with this orientation tend to help clients achieve their positive goals by developing the therapeutic relationship and by concentrating on the "here and now." See also *self-actualization.*

hunger The psychophysiological discomfort reaction to the lack of needed nourishment. Recurrent or prolonged hunger leads to the diseases of malnutrition, susceptibility to other diseases, and death. Organizations to provide food for those in need include Food for the Hungry, Interfaith Hunger Appeal, Second Harvest, LIFE (Love Is Feeding Everyone), Freedom from Hunger, *OXFAM*, Feed the Children, and *CARE.* See also *soup kitchen* and *food assistance programs.*

hunger strike Refusal to eat, as a protest against perceived injustices or unacceptable conditions.

Hunter, Robert W. (1874–1942) Social worker, Hull-House resident, and influential writer of the classic book *Poverty* (1904), the first statistical survey of America's poor. He later became disillusioned with his socialistic philosophy and became an advocate for right-wing politics and author of the book *Revolution* (1940), which denounced socialist and Marxist ideology.

Huntington's disease A *genetic disorder,* also known as Huntington's chorea, that is transmitted by a dominant gene and affects half the offspring of those who carry the genes. The symptoms, which include hallucination, profound mood swings, dementia, and *choreiform movements,* do not appear until about age 30. *Genetic counseling* is important for those who have the disease and for their offspring.

"hustling"   The term used by *"street people"* to describe any activities designed to extract money from those they encounter. Hustling may occur through prostitution, swindling, *panhandling,* "borrowing," gambling, stealing, and *extortion.*

hwa-byung   A *culture-bound syndrome* most commonly found among Korean people in which the individual experiences insomnia, fatigue, panic, fear, and various somatic complaints said to be the result of suppressing anger.

hygiene   Activities to preserve and maintain health and prevent disease. The term derives from the Greek "hygieia," meaning health, and the Greek goddess Hygeia, who provided clean and healthy environments.

hyperactive child syndrome   A term formerly used for *attention-deficit hyperactivity disorder (ADHD).*

hyperactivity   Excessive muscular activity, usually with rapid movements, restlessness, and almost constant motion, that may be a symptom of anxiety, neurosis, organic mental disorders, or physiological or neurological disorders.

hyperacusis   Extreme and sometimes painful sensitivity to sounds.

hyperhidrosis   Profuse and excessive sweating. This may be normal for an individual or symptomatic of a variety of physical or mental conditions.

hyperkinesis   A childhood disorder characterized by excessive motor activity, reduced attention span, and accompanying difficulties in learning and perceiving accurately. Roughly synonymous with *hyperactivity,* the syndrome has also been known as "hyperactive child syndrome," "hyperkinetic reaction of childhood," "minimal brain damage," "minimal brain dysfunction," and "minimal cerebral dysfunction."

hyperkinetic disorder   A synonym for *attention-deficit hyperactivity disorder (ADHD).*

hypersomnia   One of the *sleep disorders* that involves excessive sleepiness and sleep attacks during all daytime and nighttime hours; the condition is the opposite of *insomnia.*

hypertension   High pressure of blood pulsing against the walls of the blood vessels. This chronic disorder of the cardiovascular system is a predominant risk factor in *stroke, heart attack, renal disease,* and eye diseases. A person with high blood pressure generally cannot feel any symptoms, so it can be detected reliably only by using a blood pressure cuff (sphygmomanometer). Physicians are especially concerned when the systolic pressure (caused when the heart contracts) exceeds 140 or the diastolic pressure (caused when the heart relaxes) exceeds 90.

hyperthymia   Intensified emotional responses and activity and affect that are heightened beyond the norm but beneath the level of *mania* or *manic–depressive illness.*

hypertonia   Extreme muscle tension.

hyperventilation   Taking in more air than can be processed by the body, which results in lowered levels of carbon dioxide in the blood stream. Usually the behavior is the result of anxiety and often causes the individual to feel dizzy, light-headed, and faint.

hyphenated American   The designation of a U.S. citizen by racial or ethnic background, as in African-American, Asian-American, Native-American, or Polish-American. Once applied derisively to new immigrants, the term is now generally used proudly in self-description.

hypnosis   The phenomenon of being in a mental state of aroused concentration so intense that everything else in the subject's consciousness is ignored. All hypnosis is *self-hypnosis,* and the role of the hypnotist is to offer suggestions for deepening the level of concentration. Generally, hypnotized subjects will not do anything contrary to their moral or ethical codes and can come out of trances at will. Forms of hypnosis are used successfully in therapeutic interventions, such as *hypnotherapy.*

hypnotherapy   The use of *hypnosis* and *self-hypnosis* is an adjunct or central tool in the psychotherapy process. Hypnotherapy has been used in psychotherapy since Sigmund Freud's earliest analytic cases and is now used especially in the treatments of phobia, pain relief, weight loss, cessation of smoking, and anxiety.

hypoactive   Less active than what is considered normal.

hypoactive sexual desire disorder   A *sexual disorder* in which the individual has little or no urge

205

for sexual activity. In making this diagnosis, sex therapists and other clinicians specify whether the condition is lifelong or acquired, generalized or situational, and caused by psychological or combined psychological–physiological problems. See also *sexual arousal disorders.*

hypochondriasis Preoccupation with the details of one's bodily functions and excessive concern about the possibility of having a disease. It is generally believed to be caused by neurotic anxiety. Individuals with hypochondriasis typically present symptoms but no actual disturbance in bodily function. Symptoms such as dizziness, sweating, and rapid pulse arising from health concerns are common.

hypoglycemia Low level of sugar in the blood. Left untreated, it may cause the appearance of psychogenic symptoms that can lead to inappropriate treatment for emotional disorders. Because of the possibility of hypoglycemia, prudent social workers advise clients about to enter psychotherapy to get a physical exam first.

hypokinetic Fewer movements than what is considered normal.

hypomania Behavior that is similar to but less severe than that observed in individuals with *bipolar disorder,* manic type. The individual in this state seems euphoric, energetic, and creative but may also be impatient and grandiose and use poor judgment.

hypomanic episode A symptom found in some of the *mood disorders,* especially *bipolar disorder,* consisting of an abnormally and persistently elevated, expansive, or irritable mood lasting at least four days. This may include feelings of inflated self-esteem, grandiosity, pressured speech, flight of ideas, distractibility, and psychomotor agitation, all a clear departure from the individual's usual mood and functioning. The symptoms are identical to those in a *manic episode* except they are not as severe and do not include delusions or other psychotic features.

hypothalamus The part of the brain that controls the *autonomic nervous system (ANS)* and many of the body's regulating systems such as hunger, thirst, and temperature. It is also thought to play a major role in *emotion* and *motivation.*

hypothermia Unusually low body temperature of 96°F (35.5°C) instead of the normal 98°F (37°C). A serious and sometimes life-threatening condition that requires immediate medical care, hypothermia is more likely to affect older persons, poor people who have inadequate heating systems in colder climates, and people who take antidepressant or antianxiety medications.

hypothesis A tentative proposition that describes a possible relationship among facts that can be observed and measured. In research the proposition is often stated in negative fashion as a *null hypothesis* (for example, "There is no difference between the work of MSWs and BSWs as measured by . . ."). Social workers and other professionals also use the term informally to indicate a theory believed to account for what is not entirely understood.

hypotonia Minimal muscle tension; flaccidity.

hypoxia Less oxygen than is needed to maintain health. See also *anoxia.*

hysterectomy Surgical removal of the uterus.

hysteria A term originally used by Sigmund Freud (1856–1939) to describe patients with symptoms he believed to be the result of suppressed sexual and oedipal conflicts. Laypeople tend to use this term for any intensely felt and dramatically expressed range of emotions. See also *conversion disorder* and *anxiety hysteria.*

"hysteric" A historical term still used informally and inappropriately to describe a person with some or all of the following characteristics: overly dramatic behavior, overreaction to minor events, craving for attention and excitement, tantrums, appearance to others of shallowness and lack of genuineness, apparent helplessness and dependency, proneness to manipulative gestures, and suicide threats. In treatment, a person with these characteristics would likely be diagnosed as having a *histrionic personality disorder.*

hysterical neurosis, conversion type A *somatoform disorder* caused by anxiety and resulting in the appearance of some physical dysfunction that has no apparent physical cause. The individual is said to use the symptoms unconsciously to avoid some undesired activities or to get some support from others that might not otherwise be available. This term is no longer used in official diagnoses; the preferred term is *conversion disorder.*

iatrogenic A physical or mental disorder originating in the treatment or intervention process. Technically, the term refers to the action of a physician or to medication that results in the patient developing a new disease. However, the term now includes the disorders that individuals or groups develop as a result of intervention by helping professionals, including social workers.

ICD-10 The *International Classification of Diseases (ICD), Tenth Edition.*

"ice" A highly addictive methamphetamine that is smoked to produce a period of euphoria that is more intense and much longer lasting than with *cocaine* or its derivative *"crack."* Far less expensive than other drugs of abuse, ice often produces symptoms of acute depression and psychosis after the euphoria ends. When this substance is injected, it is known as *"crank."*

ice breaking In *social group work,* the activities originated by group leaders in the *preaffiliation phase* of *group development* to create a comforting and productive atmosphere and become usefully acquainted with one another. Structured exercises help achieve this. For example, the leader might ask the new members to describe their goals for the group or indicate what they would most like to know about or reveal to the others. Another exercise is for the leader to ask each member to describe to the group everything imaginable about another member of the group, without the subject indicating whether the speculation is accurate or simply a *projection* or *prejudice.*

id In *psychoanalytic theory,* the part of the mind or *psyche* that harbors the individual's instinctive or biological drive, libido, or psychic energy. The id is completely *unconscious,* but id wishes are always being discharged. Its demands are centered on the body, and it is governed solely by the *pleasure principle.* It attempts to force the *ego,* which is generally governed by the *reality principle,* to meet its demands without regard to the long-term consequences.

idealization The overestimation of another person or of that person's specific attributes. See also *devaluation* and *halo effect.*

ideas of reference Inaccurate beliefs that the behaviors of others or environmental phenomena occur to have some effect on the individual. For example, a man encounters two strangers who are conversing and assumes they are talking about him. This is a form of *delusion* and sometimes appears as a symptom in *delusional disorder, schizophrenia,* and *histrionic personality disorder* and in people who have profound *inadequacy feelings.*

ideation The process of developing a belief. For example, a person with *suicidal ideation* is one who starts thinking about death, about wanting to die, and about specific actions that will help to reach that goal.

identification A mental process in which a person forms a mental image of another person who is important and then thinks, acts, and feels in a way that resembles the other person's *behavior.* Identification often promotes *ego integration* and personal growth.

identification with the aggressor The phenomenon that sometimes occurs when the victims of rape, kidnapping, hostage-taking, and assault come to develop sympathy or approval for the perpetrators and their aggression. For example, the victim may take on attributes of the aggressor.

identified patient (or client) The member of a family or social group for whom therapy, help, or social services are ostensibly sought. This person has typically been viewed by relevant others as "sick" or "crazy," even though he or she may have just as many or more problems and may implicitly need and receive just as much help from the perceptive therapist or social worker.

identity An individual's sense of *self* and of uniqueness, as well as the basic integration and continuity of values, behavior, and thoughts that are maintained in varied circumstances.

identity crisis Confusion about one's role in life. The individual enters a period of doubt about being willing or capable of living up to the expectations of others and is uncertain about what kind of person to be if those expectations are not met.

identity disorder   A *mental disorder* usually first observed in children and adolescents characterized by persistent and long-standing self-doubts. The individual experiences uncertainty about goals, moral values, sexual orientation, family, and friends. Symptoms of identity disorder are similar to the conflicts seen in *identity crisis,* except they have lasted longer and persist even when in supportive environments.

identity problem   An individual's personal confusion and conflict about goals, career choices, ethnic and group loyalties, moral values, sexual orientation, or spirituality. This term is used by counselors, therapists, educators, and social workers but is not a formal diagnosis.

identity theft   The crime of using another person's personal information to obtain access to that person's property, reputation, credentials, accrued benefits, or money. The Federal Trade Commission maintains a hot line to provide information about what victims of identity theft should do if such a theft occurs with their credit cards, social security records, and other data. The number is 1-877-IDTHEFT (1-877-438-4338). Information about identity theft is available at the Web site address http://www.consumer.gov/idtheft

identity versus role confusion   According to the *psychosocial development theory* of Erik Erikson (1902–1994), this fifth stage of human development occurs at about ages 12 to 18. The conflict facing adolescents is to establish clear ideas about their values, vocational objectives, and role in life, or there may be a lack of clarity about how to fit into the social environment. This is the period in which there is the greatest likelihood of an *identity crisis.*

ideologue   An individual who is preoccupied with one or more ideas and tends to see much of the world in terms of those ideas. Many effective social reformers have been called ideologues.

ideology   A system of ideas that is the product of one's values, experiences, political persuasion, level of moral development, and aspirations for humanity. For example, the ideology of a social worker is likely to include a concern for equal rights for all people and an interest in providing greater opportunities for less-privileged people.

idiopathic   Diseases or disorders with no known cause.

idiosyncratic   A term applied to a trait or characteristic that is unique to the subject or phenomenon being observed and unrepresentative of others of the same class.

idiosyncratic intoxication   A significant change of behavior in an individual who recently has consumed alcohol or other drugs. Typically, the substance ingested is too little to account for the degree of change.

idiosyncratic life-cycle transitions   Nonnormative changes in an individual's phases of life. These transitions are considered unusual; thus, they are not marked by celebrations or rituals, and the person generally has even more difficulty coping with the new circumstance than the normal transitions. Examples include unexpected death, birth of a child with disabilities, imprisonment, homosexual marriage, and migration.

"idiot"   An obsolete term once used to refer to a person with *mental retardation* having an *intelligence quotient (IQ)* score of 25 or less. People with very low intelligence who possess some special talents, once called "idiot savants," are properly referred to as persons with *"savant syndrome."*

idiot savant   An obsolete term once applied to individuals with *mental retardation* or a *mental disorder* who otherwise possess some highly specialized talent, such as playing a musical instrument or calculating mathematical equations. The preferred term is *"savant syndrome."*

IEP team   The professional staff in schools and other educational facilities who assess and facilitate the implementation of the *individualized education plan (IEP)* for students who have disabilities. The team is required by provisions of U.S. federal law in the *Individuals with Disabilities Education Act (IDEA)* (P.L.101-474) to evaluate each child with disabilities and create a unique plan before placement in any educational program. The team members usually include school social workers, school counselors, nurses, psychologists, speech and hearing therapists, special education teachers, regular teachers, parents, and school administrators.

illegal   A specific act that is contrary to the law and that can result in punishment imposed by the *justice system.*

illegal alien   A citizen of one nation who has unlawfully taken up permanent residence in another nation. This term is being replaced by "undocumented alien."

illegitimate 1. An activity that is against the law, norms, or values of a society. 2. An obsolete term once commonly applied to people born to parents who are not legally married to each other; the currently preferred term is *nonmarital birth.*

illicit drugs Chemical substances that are unlawful to use. In the United States, these include *cocaine, marijuana, opiates,* and *psychedelics.*

illiteracy Not knowing how to read or write.

illiteracy, functional Possessing some reading and writing skills but not of sufficient quality to permit their use in normal socioeconomic relationships. This term usually refers to those whose literacy deficits are the result of cultural factors rather than *mental retardation* or developmental expressive writing disorder.

image 1. A consciously experienced mental picture arising from one's memory. 2. The overall judgmental reaction of relevant others to an individual, institution, organization, or nation.

imagery relaxation technique A self-help and therapeutic procedure to reduce anxiety, in which the subject concentrates on being in an environment that is his or her ideal place for relaxation. Thinking about the place and recreating its sounds, colors, smells, and pleasures for about five to 10 minutes helps the person become more relaxed.

imago See *archetype.*

"imbecile" An obsolete term once used to refer to a person with *mental retardation* having an *intelligence quotient (IQ)* score between 25 and 50.

immigrant One who has moved to and intends to reside permanently in another country. See also *green card.*

immigrant visa An authorization granted by the U.S. Department of State or the *Bureau of Citizenship and Immigration Services (CIS)* to applicants to reside in the United States. A person with an immigrant visa may be given a *permanent resident card,* also known as a *green card.* Detailed and updated information about immigration eligibility, categories, and application procedures are available through the Web at http://www.immigration.gov

immigration Moving to a new country or region, usually for the purpose of permanent settlement.

Immigration and Customs Enforcement, Bureau of (ICE) An organization within the *U.S. Department of Homeland Security,* formed in 2003 to take over enforcement and investigative functions formerly conducted by the *Immigration and Naturalization Service* and other organizations. ICE works closely with the other law enforcement agencies to investigate potential immigration and customs violations and protect specified federal infrastructure. ICE is a component of the *Border and Transportation Security Directorate,* along with the *Bureau of Customs and Border Protection (BCBP).*

Immigration and Naturalization Service (INS), U.S. The former government organization, the functions of which were taken over primarily by the *U.S. Department of Homeland Security* and other federal offices in 2003. Most INS service programs were merged into the *Bureau of Citizenship and Immigration Services (CIS).* Most INS enforcement programs were merged into the *Border and Transportation Security Directorate (BTS).*

Immigration Appeals Board A quasi-judicial tribunal to hear appeals about judgments made in lower-court deportation cases or involving legal denials of visa petitions. The U.S. Attorney General appoints and empowers the board.

immigration quotas U.S. federal laws that determined the proportion of people from each country who were allowed to become residents, thus making it easier for Europeans to immigrate than for people of Asia, Latin America, or Africa. Quotas were eliminated in 1965 in an attempt to give people from every nation an equal chance of admission. Currently there are numerical limits for some types of visas. See also *Diversity Immigrant Visa Program.*

immunity Exemption from a responsibility or from legal prosecution, usually granted because of some service. For example, some people charged with crimes are granted immunity because they agree to testify against other people.

immunization Preventive medical procedures that reduce susceptibility to certain diseases. Immunization occurs most frequently through *inoculation* or a vaccine—that is, injecting into the body certain viruses or bacteria to cause a mild and controllable form of the disease so that the body develops *resistance* to the more serious forms.

impact analysis   The assessment used by social policymakers in determining the effect of a new law or policy on the relevant community.

impaired professional   An individual who is unable to fully carry out his or her professional responsibilities because of some physical or psychosocial disorder. The impairments may include *substance abuse, alcoholism, depression,* or *sexual disorder.*

impaired social functioning   The inability or diminished ability to fulfill one's social roles or responsibilities as a result of disease, mental disorder, stress, or preoccupation with personal concerns.

impaired social worker   One who is unable to function adequately as a professional social worker and provide competent care to clients as a result of a physical or mental disorder or personal problems, or the inability or desire to adhere to the *code of ethics* of the profession. These problems most commonly include alcoholism, substance abuse, mental illness, burnout, stress, or relationship problems.

impairment   A loss or abnormality in psychological, physiological, or anatomical structure or function, including blindness, loss of sight in one eye, deafness, paralysis of a limb, or mental retardation. See also *disability, handicap,* and *International Classification of Functioning and Disability.*

impeach   To accuse a public official of unlawful conduct before a legally constituted tribunal, such as a court of law or legislature.

imperialism   The political and economic domination by one country over another. It occurs when a ruling empire has colonized territories, through military force or economic power, or when a nation controls another nation's international trade and economic development. See also *colonialism* and *cultural imperialism.*

implanted memory   The unethical practice of influencing a client to "remember" events in the past that did not actually happen and to convince the client that the memory represents actual experience. This practice is sometimes associated with clients who eventually claim to have *recovered memory* of traumatic events such as incest, rape, and child abuse.

implied consent   An agreement to participate expressed by gestures, signs, actions, or statements that are interpreted as agreement, or by nonresistant silence or inaction. This is often used as a defense in rape trials in which the defendant claims to have acted in the belief that the victim consented to the defendant's advances. See also *informed consent.*

implosive therapy   In *behavior therapy,* the technique in which the client is presented with images of anxiety-producing stimuli and is encouraged to experience as much anxiety as possible. Because the anxiety-producing images do not result in any harm, the anxiety responses are not reinforced, and the symptoms are more likely to be extinguished.

impotence   A male *sexual disorder,* also known as *erectile dysfunction,* characterized by an inability to achieve or maintain an erection. See also *sexual aversion disorder* and *inhibited sexual excitement.*

impound   To seize funds, records, or property by an officer of the law or court, usually until some matter that involves those items can be legally determined and adjudicated.

impulse control disorder   A diagnostic group of *mental disorders* characterized by the repeated inability to resist some temptation that is harmful to oneself or others. In most cases, the individual becomes increasingly tense before succumbing to the temptation, feels pleasure and emotional release on completing the act, and then experiences regret after the act is over. Types of impulse control disorders are *pathological gambling, kleptomania, pyromania, trichotillomania,* and *explosive disorder.*

impulsiveness   The inclination to act suddenly, in response to inner urges, without thought and with little regard to the consequences of the action.

IMRAD   An acronym used by editors and referees of social work and other scholarly journals to remind them of the order and formats that some journals require for research articles. IMRAD stands for "Introduction" (What is the article about?), "Method" (How was the problem studied?), "Results" (What were the findings?), and "Discussion" (What do the findings mean?).

"in forma pauperis" A legal term in which a person is granted permission to sue without payment of court fees because of poverty. The term literally means "in the manner of a pauper."

"in loco parentis" The legal expression referring to the circumstances in which an organization assumes the obligations of parenting a child or other person without a formal adoption. Most commonly, such relationships exist when a child is in a residential institution such as a *reformatory* or boarding school.

in utero The being that lives in the uterus after conception and before birth.

in vitro fertilization Human *conception* by removing the woman's ovum surgically, placing it in a medium that preserves and nourishes it, introducing live sperm cells, maintaining the live cells until some growth and divisions occur, and then inserting the embryo in a woman's uterus.

in vivo assessment Evaluating client progress by directly observing the client in actual life situations. It is conducted either overtly or unobtrusively with the client's awareness and permission. For example, in overt in vivo assessment, a social worker may accompany a claustrophobic client into a crowded elevator. In unobtrusive in vivo assessment, the worker may enlist an associate to observe a passive client use newly learned assertiveness techniques in the marketplace. These assessments are used when situational assessments are difficult to create and *client self-monitoring* is unlikely to demonstrate client behavior accurately.

in vivo desensitization A *behavior therapy* procedure in which the subject gradually approaches a feared *stimulus* while in a relaxed state. The subject and worker make a list of situations that elicit fear and rank these items from least to most anxiety producing. The subject then enters a state of relaxation through *meditation,* deep-breathing relaxation, *imagery relaxation technique, muscle relaxation technique,* and so on. In this state, the subject is gradually desensitized to the feared stimuli.

inadequacy feelings An individual's *perception* of being inferior or of being incapable of fulfilling certain social expectations.

inadequate personality Obsolete term referring to one who has little ability to adapt to new or different social situations, few interests, and little physical or emotional stamina.

inalienable rights Rights that cannot be taken away or given away except by the person possessing them. Societies have varying concepts of these rights. In the United States, inalienable rights include the rights of life, liberty, the pursuit of happiness, the freedom of speech and worship, and *due process of law.* See also *First Amendment rights* and *Fifth Amendment rights.*

inappropriate affect A lack of consistency between one's words or ideas and the mood or feeling that accompanies it. This is often symptomatic of serious mental disorders such as *schizophrenia* or *bipolar disorder.*

incapacitation Lack of ability to provide sufficient care for oneself or to demonstrate adequate judgment as a result of diminished physical or mental functioning.

incarceration Confinement in an institution, such as a prison or mental hospital. Usually this occurs for the purpose of punishment or protection of society from the individual or to impose treatment or protective custody on the individual. See also *detention.*

incarceration alternatives Nonprison sanctions for convicted lawbreakers, including a *suspended sentence, probation, house arrest, restitution, community service work,* required participation in treatment programs, and similar alternatives.

incentive A reward or object of value that produces in an individual the motivation to act in a way that will lead to its acquisition.

incentive contracting A systematic method often used by public organizations to improve the delivery and quality of goods or services. The provider (contractor) is guaranteed more compensation if the goods or services meet predetermined time and quality standards.

incest Sexual intercourse or *sexual abuse* between close relatives—that is, people who are too closely related to be permitted by law to marry.

incestuous desire An individual's urge, whether conscious or not, to engage in erotic activity with a close relative.

incidence rate In population and demographic reports, the number of new cases of a physical or mental disorder, crime, or social problem that develops in an identified population group within a specific time frame. See also *prevalence rate* and *epidemiology.*

incivility The disregard for or ignorance of the norms and rules of conduct that are normally used to achieve effective interpersonal relationships; the opposite of *civility.*

inclusion An education policy that allows students with disabilities to be integral members of age-appropriate classrooms in neighborhood schools. In keeping with U.S. federal legislation, which requires schools to educate students with disabilities in the "least-restrictive environment" possible, needed special services and supports are brought to the student in the regular classroom.

inclusionary cultural model A technique to help those who work with ethnic groups understand their own biases. In classes or training groups of 18 to 45 members, participants identify ethnic stereotypes and then role-play themselves as being part of that ethnic group and subject to those stereotypes.

incoherence Disconnected thoughts, often a symptom of psychosis, bipolar disorder in the manic phase, and severe anxiety. Incoherent behavior includes talking about many subjects almost simultaneously, *loose association,* and nonlogical reasoning.

income distribution The division of moneys and other resources among individuals or family units in an economy. Economists also apply this term to the division of income among functions in the economy, such as labor, capital, and real estate. Income distribution is a primary indicator of the economic well-being of various demographic groups in society (such as women, older people, black people, people who live in the South, and divorced people).

income maintenance Social welfare programs designed to provide individuals with enough money or goods and services to maintain a predetermined *standard of living.*

income strategy A social welfare policy of providing direct monetary aid, based on predetermined objective criteria, to those in need. This is distinguished from a *service strategy* policy, in which social workers evaluate each person's situation and provide *counseling* and *in-kind benefits.* For example, an income strategy would be to pay each needy family a certain amount for housing so that the family can make their own choices. In this example, the service strategy would be to provide public housing or advice about living more frugally.

income test A financial test of *eligibility* for welfare benefits that considers only income (usually that reported for income tax purposes), in contrast to the *means test,* which considers income, assets, and other resources.

income transfer payments See *transfer payments.*

incompatibility A situation in which two persons in a relationship feel they should no longer be together, usually because of differences in goals, values, personality characteristics, desires, and lifestyle.

incompetent 1. Without the ability to fulfill obligations. 2. A legal term that has several connotations, depending on the circumstances. These include inability to consent legally to make or execute a contract, insufficiency in knowledge needed to carry out some legal obligation, inability to stand trial because the person is unable to assist rationally in his or her own defense, or inability to understand the nature of the charge or the consequences of conviction.

incontinence 1. Lack of *self-control.* 2. The inability to control elimination of body waste.

incorporation In psychosocial theory, a primitive *defense mechanism* in which the individual imagines he or she is ingesting or absorbing another person, part of a person, or an object to whom or for which there is great attachment. In the first months of life, this may be a literal goal, but later it is an unconscious fantasy.

incorrigible Not amenable to correction. This term once was applied to habitual criminals, juvenile delinquents, and unmanageable youths but is now rarely used by professionals.

incremental social change Gradual adaptation and adjustment made by social institutions to reflect changes in the values, needs, and priorities of people. Institutions retain their existence and basic character but modify their goals and means to accommodate to the demands of those served. This is the opposite of *structural social change.*

incrementalism   Gradual change in policies, attitudes, and behaviors. Social welfare planners tend to use incrementalism because of public resistance to adopting comprehensive programs all at once.

incubation   In the progression of a disease, the time between the onset of infection until the first symptoms appear. See also *"window period."*

indecent exposure   The crime of displaying one's genitals in a public place, usually to achieve some sexual gratification or to shock. See also *"flasher."*

indemnification   Protection or immunity from lawsuits or the penalties or liabilities stemming from an action, as in a *hold harmless agreement, malpractice insurance,* or payment for some damages to avoid incurring greater losses later.

indenture   An obligation in which one person is required to serve or work for another for a specified length of time. In colonial America, indentured servitude was a common practice by which immigrants would receive transportation to their new homes in exchange for working for several years. Later, the practice was frequently applied to parentless children who became indentured to a custodian. From this practice and that of *apprenticing* originated many of the principles of *foster care.* Indenture is still practiced, illegally or covertly, by some people who exploit the circumstances of an *immigrant* or *undocumented alien.*

independent adoption   The process of *adoption* outside of established social agencies. There are many variations in this process. In family adoptions, the *birth parents* place the child with a relative. In stepparent adoptions, the most common type of independent adoption, a stepparent adopts a spouse's child. In nonprofit intermediate arrangements, an individual or organization acts as a go-between for birth parents and adoptive parents who do not know each other. In *intercountry adoption,* a child from one nation is adopted by parents in another, with arrangements monitored with varying degrees of formality by authorities and individuals in the child's original country. A final category, that of for-profit intermediate arrange-

ments, is controversial. For-profit arrangement has been called *black-market adoption.* However, because the process is not "adoption" unless it is legal, it is a contradiction of terms. Thus, some child welfare specialists have used the term *gray-market adoption.*

independent living   The capability of an individual to be self-governing and not dependent on others for care, well-being, or livelihood. To be capable of independent living is seen as being able to manage one's own finances and to perform the necessary *activities of daily living (ADL)* without the necessity of continued reliance on others. Programs to help people achieve independent living provide for social and medical services and also for the modification of homes that permit people access to all rooms and facilities.

independent living centers   Facilities and programs to provide social and health care services for people with disabilities, as well as peer support and information for families. The centers are staffed largely by people who themselves have disabilities and offer services such as counseling for vocational, legal, financial, or mental health issues; transportation; wheelchair repair; and referrals.

independent practice associations (IPAs)   A consortium of individual health care providers, mostly in *private practice,* that represents all specialties and that provides for the health care needs of groups of people who contract for the service in advance. IPAs in some regions are also known as "individual practice associations." IPAs developed mostly as a competitive response to the proliferation of the *health maintenance organization (HMO).* See also *preferred provider organizations (PPOs)* and *managed health care program.*

independent social work   The practice of social work outside the auspices of traditional social agencies or government organizations. In addition to private practitioners, those engaged in such social work include self-employed proprietary social workers who have autonomous consulting firms or who organize and manage private, for-profit institutional facilities or educational institutions. See also *private practice* and *proprietary practice.*

independent variable   In systematic research, the factors that are thought to influence or cause a certain behavior, phenomenon, or reaction. The factor that is being influenced is the *dependent variable.*

indeterminant sentence   In the *criminal justice system,* the *incarceration* of an individual for an unspecified amount of time. Thus, the decision to release is based on the prisoner's demonstrated ability and willingness to satisfy certain standards.

indexing   The automatic adjustments of salaries, welfare payments, *social security,* and other benefits based on *inflation* rates and the changing *cost of living.*

India Integrated Child Services Development Scheme (ICDS)   The *social welfare* program established in 1975 to provide leadership and coordination of efforts in the provision of nutritional, health care, educational, and social services to needy children in India. Social workers administer these programs at the community level using volunteers, with added support from health care professionals.

Indian Child Welfare Act (ICWA)   Federal legislation enacted in 1978 (P.L. 95-608) to promote the best interests of Native American children and the stability and security of Native American tribes and families. Key provisions include the right of the child's parents or the tribe to be notified of and to intervene in child custody proceedings, higher standards of proof in termination of parental rights proceedings, and certain preferences when a Native American child is placed in foster care.

Indian Health Service (IHS)   An agency within HHS that provides federal health services to Indigenous Peoples in the United States. The program includes a network of hospitals and health care facilities, clinics, and personnel to provide direct care. The provision of health services grew out of the special relationships between the federal government and governments of federally recognized tribes. The Web site address is http://www.ihs.gov

Indian Self-Determination and Education Assistance Act   The 1975 federal legislation (P.L. 93-638) that removed most of the direct social services and educational functions from the *Bureau of Indian Affairs (BIA)* and permitted certain Native American organizations, commonly known as 638s, to provide such services or contract for them. This legislation was extended and amended slightly in 1988 (P.L. 100-472).

indictable offenses   Those felony crimes that are the most serious, carry substantial penalties, and are tried usually before juries.

indictment   A sworn written accusation submitted by a grand jury to a court charging an individual with a *crime.*

Indigenous Peoples   Descendants of earlier or original inhabitants of a nation or region, for example, *Native Americans* in the United States, *First Nations Peoples* in Canada, Aboriginal Peoples in Australia, Sami (Lapps) in Scandinavia, and Rom *(Gypsies)* in Eurasia. The term is mostly used by the currently dominant people or governments of the nation or region in referring to those who were there first or to peoples forced into migration or isolation from the original homeland.

indigenous worker   A member of a community who becomes active in helping professionals achieve some service goals for that community. Indigenous workers may be paid employees or volunteers, and their roles often include identifying sources of problems, educating residents as to the services being offered, linking clients with professional service providers, and counseling.

indigent   Poor and in need.

indigent care   Health, legal, or social services provided to poor people or those unable to pay. In health care, because many indigent patients are not eligible for federal or state programs, the costs that are covered by Medicaid are generally recorded separately from indigent care costs.

indigent criminal defense   Publicly financed legal services for poor people charged with felonies. The U.S. Constitution's Sixth Amendment establishes everyone's right to counsel in federal criminal prosecution. U.S. Supreme Court decisions, such as *Gideon v. Wainwright,* extend that right to all federal or state criminal prosecutions that carry a sentence of imprisonment. States and localities meet this requirement through *public defender* and assigned counsel programs.

indirect contact abuse   A form of childhood *sexual abuse* in which the perpetrator derives erotic pleasure by involving a child in some sexualized activity other than touching. Examples include covertly or overtly watching the naked child or displaying one's genitals, sometimes while masturbating. Such behavior is abusive, because studies show that children are harmed as a result.

indirect cost   Consequences, outcomes, or expenditures that are not immediately anticipated, apparent, or paid for by those who initiate an action. For example, although most of the *direct cost* of the U.S. drug problem is the funding that goes for law enforcement and treatment, an indirect cost is the lack of productivity on the part of the addicts.

indirect practice   Those professional social work activities, such as administration, research, policy development, and education, that do not involve immediate or personal contact with the clients being served. Indirect practice makes *direct practice* possible and more efficient; as such, it is considered essential and of equal importance to the mission of the profession.

indirect treatment   Work in the environment on behalf of the client, including *mediation,* education, *advocacy,* and the location of resources. These activities are said to require virtually the same skills and techniques as those needed in *direct treatment.*

individual development account (IDA)   A policy to provide incentives for the working poor population to save money for specified purposes such as retirement or home ownership. In the plan, the state or federal government would help the client set up the account in a financial institution and then match the amount the client puts into the account. IDAs are modeled somewhat after the individual retirement account system that tends to benefit more affluent citizens. See also *stakeholding.*

"individual initiative"   A term used especially by conservative politicians to suggest that people, through their own merits, can rise above social problems. The implication is that those who have not overcome such problems lack certain personal qualities and that, therefore, their problems are their own fault. See also *social Darwinism.*

individual practice associations (IPAs)   See *independent practice associations (IPAs).*

individual psychology theory   A school of thought about the development of personality and *psychopathology,* originated by psychiatrist Alfred Adler (1870–1937), that emphasizes a person's lifestyle and the individual's striving to overcome *inadequacy feelings.* This is also known as *Adlerian theory.*

individual racism   The negative attitudes one person has about all members of a racial or ethnic group, often resulting in overt acts such as name-calling, social exclusion, or violence. See also *institutional racism* and *institutional discrimination.*

individualism   The sociopolitical and philosophical concept that emphasizes the pursuit of people's own interests rather than the common or collective good. See also *rugged individualism.*

individualization   The ethical value in social work and other helping professions for understanding the client as a unique person or group rather than as one whose characteristics are simply typical of a class. In social work practice the term emphasizes the needs and welfare of each and every person as identifiable and unique and focuses on that which sets the person apart from all others. For example, a social worker adhering to this principle would treat a young unwed mother as though her background, needs, and values were hers alone and not necessarily the same as those of others in similar circumstances.

individualized education plan (IEP)   A legal requirement, based on provisions in the *Individuals with Disabilities Education Act (IDEA)* (P.L.101-474), that each identified child with disabilities must be evaluated and that a plan to meet his or her unique needs must be developed before placement in any educational program. See also *IEP team.*

Individuals with Disabilities Education Act (IDEA)   Federal legislation (P.L. 101-476) enacted in 1990 and expanded in 1997 to ensure appropriate services and a public education to children with disabilities from age three to 21. Special education services are to be provided for all children considered to have disabilities based on a school assessment procedure. If this assessment is deemed inadequate or inappropriate, parents may request that an independent evaluation be conducted at the school's expense. The child's apparent strengths and limitations are evaluated by school professionals known as the *IEP team,* including classroom teachers, special education teachers, psychologists and social workers, and school administrators, along with parents, to design an *individualized education plan.* IDEA also established an *ombudsperson* program to help resolve problems that create barriers for students. IDEA replaced the *Education for All Handicapped Children Act of 1975.*

individuation   The process by which individuals come to understand themselves as differentiated from others and the whole social system of which they are a part. The term is frequently used to describe the process by which toddlers and young children grow progressively independent from their mothers or other caregivers. See also *separation–individuation.*

indoor relief A historically important social welfare benefit that required recipients to reside in institutions to maintain their eligibility. The *almshouse* and *poorhouse* were the most common types of indoor relief. See also *relief* and *outdoor relief.*

induced psychotic disorder A delusional mental system that is brought about as part of a close relationship with one other person or many people. The term is roughly synonymous with *shared psychotic disorder* but is used by diagnosticians to imply some conscious intent by the other person to exacerbate the condition. See also *folie à deux* and *codependency.*

inductive reasoning The process by which theories and generalizations are evolved from a set of particular observations. Specific observations may be chosen to create explanations about a larger set of phenomena. See also *deductive reasoning.*

industrial policy A nation's plan and regulation of its entire means of production, marketing, and distribution of goods through laws, subsidies, tax incentives, *disincentives,* and access to privileges.

industrial social work Professional social work practice, usually conducted under the auspices of employers or *labor unions,* or both, for the purpose of enhancing the employees' overall quality of life within and beyond the work setting. The term is synonymous with *occupational social work.* See also *employee assistance programs (EAPs).*

industry versus inferiority According to the *psychosocial development theory* of Erik Erikson (1902–1994), the fourth stage of development occurring at about ages six to 12. The child may seek to acquire the basic social skills and competencies required for effective survival in the adult world or may come to feel unworthy and less able than peers to accomplish these tasks.

inequality Social disparity in power, opportunity, privilege, and justice. The term often implies the actual disparity of possessions, education, and health care.

inequity A disparity of power or opportunity to receive just treatment or equal rights. Social workers often apply this term to social conditions in which people face *institutional discrimination* or social barriers that impede their efforts to achieve the same goals available to others. The term usually differs from *inequality* in that inequity implies lack of opportunity for justice or privilege (such as fair court trials or opportunities to elect representative officials). See also *glass ceiling* and *generational equity.*

infant mental health A multidisciplinary specialty to understand and improve the factors that influence the psychological well-being of infants. Social work is joined by pediatrics, nursing, special education, psychiatry, and developmental psychology to develop methods of preventing future mental illness and to assess and treat those psychological problems that are found in infants. The focus is usually on at-risk infants, especially those who are potentially at risk of neglect, abuse, or deprivation, or whose parents have substance abuse or physical or mental illness.

infant mortality rate The demographic measure of the number of neonatal deaths that occur in proportion to the population as a whole or to the population of potential mothers (*fecundity* rate). The infant mortality rate is often used as a key factor in assessing the health and health care programs of a nation or community.

infanticide The killing of a baby. If the baby is less than 24 hours old, the term also used is *neonaticide.*

infantile autism See *autistic disorder.*

infantilization Overtly or covertly encouraging a person to behave in a manner more appropriate to an infant or small child. This pattern is often seen in parents or spouses who are overprotective. Examples are speaking to the person in baby talk or not requiring the person to behave with appropriate maturity. The term is also used to indicate behavioral regression or to indicate that a person's behavior is appropriate for a much younger person.

infectious disease A disease caused by the entrance of pathogenic microorganisms (bacteria or viruses). The disease may be contagious and enters the body through air, water, food, clothing, and insects. See also *opportunistic infection.*

inference Forming a conclusion based not on direct observation but on reasoning from something known. For example, a clinical social worker notes that a young child returns from a visit with a noncustodial parent covered with bruises and scars and laden with anxiety and fear. The social worker infers but has not seen child abuse.

inferiority complex An individual's persistent and extensive *inadequacy feelings* and a self-concept of being of a lower order than is expected.

infertility The inability to conceive despite at least one year of unprotected sexual intercourse. Infertility sometimes may result from a lack of sexual intercourse, the use of certain techniques in intercourse, effects of *contraception*, health factors, alcohol and drugs, radiation, and toxic substances. Infertility in men is attributed to problems related to testicular temperature, blockage of ducts, retrograde ejaculation, immunological problems, and *sexual disorders* such as *erectile dysfunction* or *premature ejaculation*. Infertility in women is attributed to problems such as blocked fallopian tubes, endometriosis, cervical conditions, hormonal problems, infectious disease, and sexual disorders including *vaginismus* and *inhibited sexual desire*.

inflation Increases in the *cost of living* in an economy and the resulting decrease in purchasing power.

influence peddling Facilitating access to policymakers for money or bribing public officials on behalf of third parties.

influence tactics See *tactics of influence*.

informal sanction The social pressure a family, group, or organization's members impose on its individuals to enforce rules of conduct, norms of behavior, and work performance. These *sanctions* take the form of disapproving looks, exclusion from social activities, isolation, and the disregarding of one's ideas. Informal sanctions also apply to groups and communities, especially to identifiable racial and ethnic groups.

informal sector 1. Economic activity that is outside the official financial system of a nation or community, that is, the underground economy. The informal sector is composed mainly of self-employed small entrepreneurs who buy, sell, and barter services and goods that may or may not be legal. Usually taxes are not paid, except as bribes, and government protections are not rendered. Many nations, especially the less developed ones, consider the informal sector a necessity for taking care of the poor people in the population. 2. A synonym for informal care—that which is provided by family or friends as opposed to established caregiving institutions. 3. A synonym for independent sector—welfare activities provided by charitable agencies or by private profit-seeking businesses.

information and referral (I&R) service A social agency or an office established within an agency that informs people about existing benefits and programs and the procedures for obtaining or using them and that helps people find other appropriate resources and sources of help. See also *access provision, citizen's advice bureaus (CABs)*, and *Alliance of Information and Referral Systems*.

information theory See *communication theory*.

informational therapy Counseling and psychotherapy oriented to and emphasizing growth through the acquisition of conscious knowledge. This orientation is contrasted with *insight therapies*.

informed consent The granting of permission by the client to the social worker and agency or other professional person to use specific intervention, including diagnosis, treatment, follow-up, and research. This permission must be based on full disclosure of the facts needed to make the decision intelligently. Informed consent must be based on knowledge of the risks and alternatives. One of the greatest risks in professional *malpractice* suits is failure to achieve informed consent. See also *implied consent*.

infrastructure The facilities, buildings, and systems that make up the foundation of a society, such as its highways, parks, public spaces, railroads, bridges, telephone lines, power plants, and water and sewage lines.

inhalant use disorder Abuse or dependence on the reaction resulting from inhaling vaporous substances such as gasoline, glue, paint thinners, spray paints, cleaners, spray-can propellants, or their combinations. Symptoms of intoxication include tremor; dizziness; psychomotor retardation; stupor or coma; sleep disturbances; nausea; irritability; fleeting illusions; and family, school, or vocational problems.

inhibited orgasm A *sexual disorder* in which the individual is unable to achieve satisfactory orgasm following a period of sexual excitement. In women, orgasm is delayed or absent even though the sexual activity is considered adequate in focus, intensity, and duration. In men, ejaculation is delayed or absent even though there may be an erection and adequate sexual arousal. This disorder is not caused by organic disorders. Sex therapists and other clinicians have replaced this term in diagnosis with the terms *male orgasmic disorder* or *female orgasmic disorder.*

inhibited sexual desire A *sexual disorder* involving the persistent lack of interest in or abhorrence for participation in *coitus* or *sexual foreplay.*

inhibited sexual excitement A *sexual disorder* in which the partner in *coitus* or *sexual foreplay* is unable to maintain the physical characteristics of arousal. Once labeled as *impotence* in men, there is failure to achieve or maintain an erection through to completion of coitus. Once described as *frigidity* in women, there is failure to achieve or maintain the lubrication–swelling response through to completion of the sexual act.

inhibition 1. Hesitancy or restraint in action or behavior. 2. In *psychoanalytic theory,* the term refers to the restraining of some instinctual impulse by the *superego.* 3. In behavioral terms, it is any process in which a response is restrained.

initiative versus guilt According to the *psychosocial development theory* of Erik Erikson (1902–1994), the third of the eight stages occurring at about ages three to six. The child may be encouraged for actively seeking to learn, discover, and experiment. On the other hand, the child may develop a pattern of passivity because rejection, punishment, and restrictiveness lead to a sense of wrongdoing or "badness."

injunction A court process and legal order by which a party is forbidden to take or is made to refrain from taking a particular action (for example, selling a contested property or visiting an unwilling former spouse). The order may be of temporary, permanent, or indefinite duration.

injustice Violation of the rights of an individual or collective; that is, unfair, discriminatory treatment, often by a government or its representatives or by social systems.

inkblot test See *Rorschach test.*

in-kind benefits See *benefits.*

inmate One who is confined in a prison, hospital, or other institution; a prisoner or patient.

innate Traits, abilities, or characteristics that are present at birth.

inner city An area within a city that is usually characterized by high population density, racial *ghettos,* and a decaying *infrastructure.*

innumeracy Inability to answer simple arithmetic problems or understand the meanings of numbers, that is, mathematical illiteracy.

inoculation The process of introducing, usually through injection or ingestion, a serum or *vaccine* into a living organism to create some *immunity* to disease. The process works by stimulating the organism's production of disease-resistant antibodies.

inpatient One who is receiving services while residing in a hospital or other care facility. See also *outpatient.*

input–output analysis A tool used by economists and planners to chart the *linkages* between organizations. In social welfare, the chart is constructed by listing all the social agencies in a column and then listing them in the same order in a row across the top. Numbers are written in the resulting columns to indicate the frequency with which any two agencies are linked according to some criteria. This method graphically reveals which organizations are isolated, which are sharing responsibilities and resources, and so on.

inracial adoption *Adoption* of a child of one race by adoptive parents of that same race (for example, an African American child being adopted by an African American couple). See also *transracial adoption.*

insanity A legal and lay term used to indicate the presence of a severe *mental disorder* in an individual. Used as a legal term, the mental disorder is considered to be so serious as to negate the individual's responsibility for certain acts such as criminal conduct. The person declared "legally insane" is thought to lack substantial capacity either to appreciate the wrongfulness of a crime or to act in conformity with the requirements of the law. Used as a lay term, insanity is roughly synonymous with "crazy" or "psychotic." The term is not used by mental health professionals in their diagnostic nomenclature. See also *McNaughten rule* and *Durham rule.*

insecure attachment In *attachment theory,* a pattern of attachment in which children are unable to comfortably explore their environments and interact with strangers even in the presence of their primary caregivers. Two forms of insecure attachment are *avoidant attachment* and *resistant attachment.*

insecurity A feeling of being unprotected or helpless as a result of economic or social realities, emotional conflicts, or other problems.

in-service training An educational program provided by an employer and usually carried out by a supervisor or specialist to help an employee become more productive and effective in accomplishing a specific task or meeting the overall objectives of the organization. Usually, but not always, such training occurs on the job and for short periods. See also *staff development.*

insight 1. Self-understanding and awareness of one's feelings, motivations, and problems. 2. In several forms of *psychotherapy* and *clinical social work,* raising awareness of or illuminating the client's inner conflicts and their origins, areas that previously had not been well understood.

insight therapies Treatment approaches oriented to helping individuals achieve greater self-awareness and understanding of their own *conscious* and *unconscious* motivations, emotions, thought processes, and underlying reasons for their behaviors. These forms of therapy tend to be more long term, broader, and more general in goals and focused on one's historical psychosocial development. They are contrasted with *cognitive therapy, behavior therapy, problem-solving casework,* and *task-centered treatment.* Some types of insight therapies include *psychoanalysis, existential social work,* and *client-centered therapy.*

insolvency An individual's or business's inability to pay debts when they come due, even if the party has assets that are sufficient but inaccessible.

insomnia Inability to sleep. The term is most commonly applied to chronic and persistent sleep-lessness that interferes with social functioning and is a symptom of anxiety, depression, pain, or organic disorders. See also *hypersomnia.*

instincts Patterns of behavior that are characteristic of a given species and seem to derive from inherited rather than learned processes.

Institute for the Advancement of Political Social Work Practice (IAPSWP) The organization founded in 1995 by Nancy A. Humphreys to encourage more social workers to seek elective office, to further develop political social work as a professional specialization, and to facilitate the efforts of social workers to become more politically influential. The institute produces a newsletter and other publications, maintains an internship program for prospective political social work specialists, and provides educational resources. A primary goal is to help social workers learn more about empowering their clients through voter registration, mobilization, and education. Their Web site address is http://www.uconn.edu/iapsw.htm

Institute for the Advancement of Social Work Research (IASWR) An independent social work organization to promote the profession's research capacity and provide technical assistance to social work researchers, provide research training, establish linking and networking opportunities for researchers, and develop a researcher database. IASWR was organized in 1993 by the major social work organizations. Their Web site address is http://www.cosw.sc.edu/iasw

institution 1. A fundamental custom or behavior pattern of a culture, such as marriage, justice, welfare, and religion. 2. An organization established for some public purpose and the physical facility in which its work occurs, such as a prison. See also *social institution.*

institutional discrimination Prejudicial treatment in organizations based on official policies, overt behaviors, or behaviors that may be covert but approved by those with power.

institutional ethics committees (IECs) See *ethics committees.*

institutional network The aggregate of human services agencies that make up the service system in a community.

institutional population The U.S. Census Bureau label for all persons in the United States who reside for long periods in carceral institutions such as prisons, jails, and juvenile delinquency detention facilities; chronic disease hospitals, homes, and schools for people with mental and physical disabilities; nursing and convalescent homes; group homes for neglected, abused, or abandoned children; group homes for unwed mothers and dependent older persons; and residential treatment centers.

institutional racism Those policies, practices, or procedures embedded in bureaucratic structures that systematically lead to unequal outcomes for people of color. See also *individual racism.*

institutional review boards (IRBs) See *ethics committees.*

institutional-versus-residual model See *residual-versus-institutional model.*

institutional welfare provision The conception of *social welfare* as a "mainline" function of society (equal to other *social institutions,* such as family, religion, economics, and politics) in which programs are permanent and provide for the overall security and emotional support of people.

instrumental activities of daily living (IADL) The performance of more complex self-care activities than those in *activities of daily living,* such as using transportation, cooking, cleaning, managing money, and making repairs.

instrumental conditioning See *operant conditioning.*

instrumental means The tools and facilities necessary to complete a task or fulfill a *role* successfully.

insurance code gaming The fraudulent practice used by some physicians and health care providers to manipulate the insurance company diagnosis codes to receive more reimbursement than the care actually warrants. Common forms of code gaming include "upcoding" (exaggerating the extent of a disorder so that reimbursement is for a more expensive procedure), "exploding" (performing a series of tests on a single sample of tissue and submitting separate claims for each test), and "unbundling" (submitting to the insurer for several separate treatment procedures when they were

actually performed simultaneously and are considered a single procedure). See also *common procedural terminology (CPT).*

Insurance Trust, NASW The principal provider of malpractice and professional liability insurance for social workers. The program is sponsored by the *National Association of Social Workers (NASW)* and managed by a private insurance company. All licensed, qualified social workers may be enrolled for a moderate annual fee. The trust also offers group life and other insurance coverage to eligible members.

insurgency A nonbelligerent *social action* that attempts to depose and replace an existing government. The insurgents use political tactics, including *propaganda, demonstration,* strike, and *sabotage,* to seek legitimacy for some aspect of the political system that the ruling authority considers illegitimate.

insurrection An organized uprising against the established government or other authority.

intact reality testing The ability of an individual who is experiencing hallucinations to understand that they do not represent external reality. For example, this may occur with some people who are substance abusers or experiencing recurrent nightmares.

intake Procedures used by social agencies to make the initial contacts with the client productive and helpful. Generally, these procedures include informing the client about the services the agency offers; providing information about the conditions of service, such as fees and appointment times; obtaining pertinent data about the client; interviewing to get a preliminary impression of the nature of the problem; arriving at an agreement with the client about willingness to be served by the agency; and assigning the client to the social worker or social workers who are best suited to provide the needed services.

integrated method Social work practice that brings together the concepts and techniques used in serving individuals, families, groups, and communities.

integrated welfare state A national system in which public assistance expenditures are indexed to the spending capacity of the state and the purchasing capacity of the currency. See also *postfisc welfare state.*

integration   1. The process of bringing together components into a unified whole. 2. Psychologically, an individual's internal connection of values, ideas, ideals, knowledge, motor responses, and relevant social norms. 3. Sociologically, the process of bringing together diverse social or ethnic groups and achieving harmonious relations.

integrity versus despair   The last of the eight stages in human psychosocial development, according to the *psychosocial development theory* of Erik Erikson (1902–1994), occurring from about age 54 to death. The individual may develop a sense of integration with humanity and of the unique meaning of his or her own life, or there may be a sense of regret about how that life has been lived and a fear of death.

intellectualization   A *defense mechanism* and personality tendency in which the individual ignores feelings and emotions and analyzes problems or conflicts as objectively as possible but usually in a stylized or overly rational manner.

intelligence   The ability to learn from experience and respond effectively to new situations, mentally store and retrieve information, solve problems, successfully manipulate the environment, and find ways of producing desired results. See also *multiple intelligences, fluid intelligence, constructive intelligence,* and *crystallized intelligence.*

intelligence quotient (IQ)   An index of a person's relative level of *intelligence,* as determined by performance on a specialized test. The tests are designed to determine a person's abilities to use abstract concepts effectively, to grasp relationships, to acquire information about the relevant environment, and to meet and adapt to novel situations. The resulting IQ scores are said to indicate the individual's mental potential, and test subscores are sometimes used in psychiatric assessments. The mean IQ score is 100, and those with scores between 90 and 110 are considered "average." Those whose scores are below 70 are often considered to need special education. Major intelligence tests include the WAIS (Wechsler Adult Intelligence Scale) and the WISC (Wechsler Intelligence Scale for Children).

intensive family preservation services (IFPS)   A program using a *multisystems orientation* to provide a holistic range of social services to families in crisis, usually through the involvement of *social work teams* and social agencies involved in *interorganizational collaboration.* Several agencies are organized to collaborate when a family enters any one of their systems and meets the appropriate criteria. The family is assigned to a social work team of workers from each agency.

interactional model   A *holistic* orientation to social group work and other forms of social work practice developed by William Schwartz and Lawrence Shulman *(Social Work, 38,* pp. 91–97) that emphasizes the reciprocal influences of each person and system involved in the helping process, including the worker, the client, the worker's supervisor and agency, the client's family, and relevant others as they are all engaged or acknowledged as participants in the service provided. The skill of the worker leads to the client's perception of the worker as a caring professional, which positively affects the relationship and the outcome of practice.

interactional problems   A term used by social workers as a category for the difficulties clients are having in their relationships with others as a consequence of some acts of commission or omission. In the *Person-in-Environment (PIE) System,* nine types of interactional difficulties are indicated: power type, ambivalence type, responsibility type, dependency type, loss type, isolation type, victimization type, mixed, and other.

interactive group therapy   A form of *group psychotherapy* that is usually long term and focused on developing insight and uncovering emotionally laden material buried in the psyche. The relatively unstructured therapeutic group culture facilitates member interactions that encourage catharsis, the exploration and comparison of earlier psychic trauma, and exploration of one's core values and ways of understanding the world.

Inter-American Children's Institute   An office within the *Organization of American States (OAS)* devoted to the social development and welfare of North and South American children, adolescents, and families. With headquarters in Montevideo, Uruguay, the organization sponsors the Pan American Child Conference every four years and helps coordinate the child welfare policies and activities of OAS member nations.

Inter-American Commission on Women   An office within the *Organization of American States*

(OAS) that works toward educational and vocational opportunities for women, consciousness-raising about the problems of women, and the development of *Women's Bureaus* in member nations.

Inter-American Human Rights Commission The agency within the *Organization of American States (OAS)* that seeks to ensure that the rights of the peoples of all its member nations are not abused.

Inter-American Indian Institute An office within the *Organization of American States (OAS)* that coordinates the policies and activities of Western Hemisphere nations pertaining to their Indian populations. The institute emphasizes education and consciousness-raising about the problems of Indians and helps Indian groups provide for their economic, health care, and social services needs.

Inter-American Social Development Center (CIDES) The principal educational and research facility of the *Organization of American States (OAS)*, with headquarters in Buenos Aires, Argentina. CIDES sponsors national and regional instruction for social planners on effective social development activities and program evaluation.

intercountry adoption *Adoption* in which a child from one nation is placed with couples in another country. Subject to the laws of the country of the child's birth, arrangements are monitored with varying degrees of strictness by authorities and individuals in the child's original country. Most nations have signed the 1993 Hague Convention on Protection of Children in Intercountry Adoption, which spells out acceptable intercountry adoptions procedures.

intercultural training The educational process of informing people about those of different nations, ethnic groups, or racial groups. Such training, often conducted by social workers, occurs particularly in organizations whose members are assigned to work among people of different nations or cultural backgrounds.

interdenominational agency A social services agency funded and administered by a coalition of religious groups in a community. The boards of these agencies are usually composed of representatives of the participating faiths and churches. See also *church social work*.

interdependence The sharing of responsibilities and benefits that are required for survival or well-being.

interdisciplinary teaming Team intervention or collaboration on behalf of a specific client or client system that involves members of different professions or disciplines. For example, a social agency might call on a social worker, psychologist, clergy member, nurse, and physician to coordinate their respective specialties to help a multiproblem family. See also *social work team* and *interprofessional team*.

interest group A segment of the population or members of a formal or informal association who have common interests, goals, concerns, or desires that often lead to purposeful and united action; also known as a *special-interest group*. See also *constituencies*.

interest inventory A form of questionnaire designed to measure the degree to which one is motivated for a particular activity. Such tests are widely used in *vocational guidance*.

interface The point of contact or communication between different systems or organizations.

interferon Chemical substances produced naturally in the white blood cells that prevent the spread of viral infections. Interferon now is produced in laboratory cultures and has proved useful in the treatment of some cancers, *leukemia*, and *HIV disease*.

intergenerational care center An agency or facility that provides care for infants and children and for senior citizens in the same building, often together (such as a section of a nursing home). See also *Foster Grandparents*.

intergenerational relations The degree to which members of different age groups engage with one another. See also *age segregation, gray ghettos, gerontophobia,* and *generational equity*.

intergroup relations Programs and groups to improve mutual respect between various sectors in the population, especially ethnic, racial, religious, geographic, socioeconomic, and other kinds of groups. These activities are also known as "race relations," "interreligious relations," and "intercultural education." Intergroup relations groups include the National Conference of Christians and

Jews, American Friends Service Committee, and the *Southern Christian Leadership Conference (SCLC)*.

Interior, U.S. Department of the   The cabinet-level federal department established in 1849 to conserve and develop the nation's natural resources, including its fish and wildlife, minerals and land management, national parks, government and public buildings, and many other programs. Components include the *Bureau of Indian Affairs (BIA)*, the National Park Service, the Geological Survey, the Fish and Wildlife Service, and the Bureau of Land Management. At various times in its history, this department was also in charge of the nation's educational system, hospitals, and interstate commerce as well as the *U.S. Bureau of the Census*, which is currently under the *U.S. Department of Commerce*. Their Web site address is http://www.doi.gov

interlocutory decree   In law courts, an interim decision that does not determine the final outcome of the case.

intermarriage   Legal wedlock between couples of different races, ethnic groups, religions, or social classes.

intermediate-care facilities (ICFs)   Nursing residences for older people who are not fully capable of living alone but do not require full-time nursing home care. ICFs usually have medical and nursing care conveniently available and provide social programs and room and board, but the residents can usually handle *activities of daily living (ADL)*. See also *skilled-nursing facility* and *continuing-care retirement communities (CCRCs)*.

intermittent explosive disorder   Numerous repeated episodes of a loss of control of aggressive impulses and fits of rage out of proportion to any stressor. See also *explosive disorder.*

intermittent reinforcement   In *behavior modification*, a schedule of *reinforcement* in which one type of *response* is reinforced at some times but not at others.

internalization   1. The process of incorporating the norms of one's culture; taking in and accepting as one's own the values, attitudes, style, and social responses of one's primary group or other reference groups. 2. In *psychoanalytic theory*, this term refers to the taking in of attitudes, feelings, and traits of significant others and making them one's own.

internally displaced persons (IDPs)   People who leave their homes under threat of war, terrorism, famine, or other disaster and who wander or resettle in their own countries (as contrasted with *refugees*, who leave their homes for other countries). In some ways many IDPs endure even greater hardships because they tend to be too poor to leave their own country, which may have few resources or inclinations to help them. Whereas international organizations including the United Nations may help refugees, IDPs usually receive little or no international assistance as they are the responsibility of their own countries.

International Association of Schools of Social Work (IASSW)   An organization of social work schools and educators founded in 1928 to improve training and ensure consistent standards for the higher levels of social work education. IASSW holds a biennial world conference, encourages research and dissemination of knowledge, and helps in the development of new schools in underserved nations. It produces, periodically, the *World Guide to Social Work Education* and, with the *International Federation of Social Workers (IFSW)* and the *International Council on Social Welfare (ICSW)*, the journal *International Social Work*. Their Web site address is http://www.iassw.soton.ac.uk

International Bank for Reconstruction and Development   See *World Bank.*

International Classification of Diseases (ICD)   A statistical classification of all human diseases, including *mental disorders*, that is compiled by the *World Health Organization (WHO)*. The publication, generally referred to as the ICD and followed by an edition number, is issued about every 10 years. The first edition, called the *International List of Causes of Death*, was completed in 1900. The most recent edition, *The International Classification of Diseases and Related Health Problems, Tenth Revision* (ICD-10), was published in 1992.

International Classification of Functioning and Disability (ICIDH-2)   A codification by the *World Health Organization (WHO)* that identifies and describes everything that the human body can do and any disturbances of those functions. The codification, completed in 1992, replaces the

WHO's International Classification of Impairment, Disability and Handicap (ICIDH-1).

International Conference for the Advancement of Private Practice in Social Work (I–CAPP) A professional social work organization the goals of which include promoting *private practice,* maintaining and improving standards for its members, providing members with learning and communication opportunities, developing the knowledge and skills of private practitioners, enhancing licensing and certification, and advocating for greater client access to private practice and social workers.

International Council on Social Welfare (ICSW) An interdisciplinary organization of community organizations, professionals, and volunteers interested in social welfare and social development. ICSW, founded in 1928 as the International Council of Social Work, hosts biennial meetings and frequent regional seminars. It is affiliated with the *International Association of Schools of Social Work (IASSW)* and the *International Federation of Social Workers (IFSW),* which together sponsor the journal *International Social Work.* Their Web site address is http://www.icsw.org

International Federation of Social Workers (IFSW) The association of social workers (who belong through their respective national social work organizations) established to promote the social work profession, establish standards, provide a forum for exchanging ideas among social workers around the world, and present social workers' views to governments and *nongovernment organizations (NGOs).* IFSW developed the *International Ethical Standards for Social Workers* and cosponsors, with the *International Council on Social Welfare (ICSW)* and the *International Association of Schools of Social Work (IASSW),* the journal *International Social Work.* IFSW provides consultation to the United Nations on issues of human development and human rights and also pairs social work organizations in economically developed and developing nations for an exchange of social work practice experience. IFSW originated in Paris in 1928 as the International Permanent Secretariat of Social Workers; the present organization was formed in 1956 and includes professionals from social work associations in over 80 nations. IFSW is also known by its French title Internationale des Travailleurs Sociaux, and by its Spanish name, Federacion Internacional de Trabajadores Sociales. Their Web site address is http://www.ifsw.org

International Federation on Aging (IFA) The nongovernmental international organization comprising national associations of and for older people that provides advocacy and education and promotes social and economic well-being for the world's older populations. IFA works closely with other organizations, especially the *World Health Organization (WHO),* the *International Labour Organization (ILO),* and other U.N. organizations. Their Web site address is http://www.ifa-fiv.org

International Labour Organization (ILO) A specialized agency within the United Nations concerned about employment, economic security, and social services among people in the world's nations. ILO helps nations develop programs for economic development and social security, especially in old-age insurance, workers' compensation, and unemployment programs, as well as health care and education benefits. Their Web site address is http://www.ilo.org

International League for Peace and Freedom The organization established in 1915 as the Women's International Peace Congress under the leadership of *Jane Addams* and *Emily Greene Balch* to protest the entry of nations into World War I. The group currently focuses on problems such as refugees, human rights violations, genocide, and antiwar activities. Their Web site address is http://www.wilpf.int.ch

International Network for School Social Work The independent professional association of social workers in nations around the world, established in 1990 to promote the field; facilitate communication; sponsor research and conferences; and inform parents, school administrators, taxpayers, and professionals about aspects of serving students with problems that affect their opportunity to learn in school. Their Web site address is http://www.internationalnetwork-schoolsocialwork.htmlplanet.com

International Rescue Committee An NGO established in 1933 by Albert Einstein and others to assist refugee victims of war, famine, and persecution. It is supported by private philanthropies, foundations, organizations, and individuals. Their Web site address is http://www.theirc.org

International Social Security Association (ISSA) A forum founded in 1927 for institutions responsible for the administration and development of *social security* programs. ISSA disseminates information about social security among nations and promotes, protects, and helps develop social programs in all nations. ISSA publishes the *International Social Security Review.* Their Web site address is http://www.issa.int

International Social Service (ISS)   The international NGO based in Geneva with branches in 100 nations that provides cross-national casework services. ISS helps with individual and family problems that require coordinated efforts among countries, especially adoptions, domestic child welfare issues, family reunification, refugee situations, and migration problems. ISS was founded in 1924 as the International Migration Service and took its present name in 1946. Their Web site address is http://www.iss-ssi.org

international social work   A term loosely applied to (1) international organizations using social work methods or personnel, (2) social work cooperation among countries, and (3) transfer among countries of methods or knowledge about social work. Virtually every country has a national department responsible for some phase of social services and personnel to carry out the functions of those departments. Organizations that have been active in international social work include the *United Nations Children's Fund (UNICEF)*, the *Organization of American States (OAS)*, the *International Labour Organization (ILO)*, the *International Social Security Association (ISSA)*, and the *United Nations Educational, Scientific, and Cultural Organization (UNESCO)*. Many *nongovernment organizations (NGOs)* also have international social work aspects, including the *Red Cross* and *Red Crescent*. A major forum for international social work is the *International Federation of Social Workers (IFSW)*. See also *comparative social welfare*.

International Society for Rehabilitation of the Disabled   A federation of voluntary organizations in more than 80 nations to improve *rehabilitation* services and provide education and knowledge about people with disabilities and their care and rehabilitation.

International Trade Administration   The U.S. Department of Commerce organization that furthers the growth of U.S. exports, monitors imports, develops fair-trade practices between nations, and collects and disseminates economic data. Their Web site address is http://www.ita.doc.gov

International Union for Child Welfare (IUCW)   An organization, with headquarters in Geneva, comprising government, public, and private organizations of many nations that are concerned about *child welfare*. The union facilitates research, provides training, and disseminates information that can benefit children.

Internet addiction   Compulsive misuse of the computer and Internet, characterized by at least five of the following symptoms: fairly continuous preoccupation with computers, dysphoria (anxiety, depression, restlessness, irritability, and so forth) when not engaged in computer activities, the need to spend increasing time on computers to change moods, being neglectful of obligations, having to lie to others about the amount of time spent on computer activities, lost relationships and opportunities because of computer activity, failure at repeated efforts to control computer activities, decline in physical well-being, and continued use of the computer despite experiencing personal problems because of its use.

Internet therapy   The procedure of using computer communications technology for interactions between a helping professional and a client. The typical procedure is for the therapist and client to exchange questions, thoughts, information, and insights through e-mails or similar interactions. The procedure has the advantages of convenience, lower cost, anonymity, and more immediate access. The disadvantages include nonpersonal interaction, less opportunity to assess or diagnose serious crises or illnesses, confidentiality problems, and the risk to clients of unscrupulous or untrained service providers. Also known as online therapy and *cybercounseling*.

internment   Confinement to *relocation camps*, prisons, or other designated places during wartime of a group of people thought to be dangerous or potentially sympathetic to the enemy. Often such actions are based on mass hysteria or racism rather than evidence.

interorganizational collaboration   A system whereby social workers and other professionals from different agencies work together to make decisions about and provide a more extensive range of services for the same client than would be possible or efficient when one agency or one worker alone engages the client. They also work together to develop new programs and services of mutual interest.

interpersonal skills   See *social skills.*

interpersonal theory   Concepts developed by American psychiatrist Harry Stack Sullivan (1892–1949) that emphasized conflicts between people as a primary factor in the development of psychopathology. Systematic interventions by professionals symbolically reverse the development of the pathogenic conflicts.

interpretation   Explanations offered to the client by a social worker or psychotherapist to enhance understanding, make connections, and facilitate the development of *insight.*

interprofessional team   A small, organized group of people, each trained in different professional disciplines, working together to resolve a common problem or achieve common goals. The interprofessional team may include but is not limited to the members of a *mental health team* (such as psychiatrists, psychologists, social workers, and psychiatric nurses). For example, a team formed to provide disaster relief could consist of social workers of various specializations as well as physicians, nurses, engineers, sanitation specialists, and political scientists. See also *social work team, interdisciplinary teaming,* and *collaboration.*

interrater reliability   In systematic research, the degree to which different people give similar scores for the same observation. For example, a researcher might give all the social workers in an agency identical lists of a client's problems and then ask them to rank those problems according to which must be dealt with first. If the social workers identify the same problems for immediate attention, this would be described as "high interrater reliability."

intersectoral planning   The coordination and integration of the efforts of single-issue organizations, which focus their efforts on one problem *(sectoral planning).* See also *social planning.*

interstate compact   An agreement between states to pass legislation on specific areas of the law concerning all the states involved. The law is drafted with input from all the participating states and then voluntarily enacted into state law intact or with slight modifications. When these laws are enacted they help to standardize state laws across the nation on covered topics. Some of the major compacts that have been established cover parental abandonment and custody, child support, adoption and medical assistance, and child placement.

Interstate Compact on the Placement of Children (ICPC)   An *interstate compact,* or agreement between jurisdictions, to ensure uniform protections and procedures for children who are lawfully moved from one state to another for the purposes of adoption or foster care placement. Both the originating state (where the child is born or resides) and the receiving state (where the adoptive or foster parents live) must approve the child's movement in writing. The compact has been enacted into law by all 50 states in the United States and the District of Colombia. The Association of Administrators of the Interstate Compact on the Placement of Children was established in 1974 to help carry out these laws.

Inter-State Parole and Probation Compact   An association of the *parole* and *probation* offices of all 50 states established in 1934. The organization makes it possible for parolees and probationers to return to their home states and remain under supervision by local authorities.

Inter-University Consortium for International Social Development (IUCISD)   An international association of scholars, practitioners, and students in human services and institutions of higher learning and allied organizations committed to advancing *social development.* Their Web site address is http://www.sc.edu/swan/iucisd

Inter-University European Institute on Social Welfare   A research and educational organization oriented to acquiring, developing, and disseminating information about European social welfare. The multidisciplinary organization, founded in 1970 and headquartered in Marcinelle, Belgium, comprises members from universities in most European nations and seeks a uniform European social welfare policy.

interval measurement   In research, a level of measurement that includes the properties of *nominal measurement* and *ordinal measurement* but also requires that there are equal intervals between the units of measurement. Most of the well-standardized psychological tests use interval measurement.

intervention   1. Interceding in or coming between groups of people, events, planning activities, or an individual's internal conflicts. 2. In social work, the term is analogous to the physician's term "treatment." Many social workers prefer using "intervention" because it includes "treatment" and other activities to solve or prevent problems or achieve goals. Thus, it refers to *psychotherapy, advocacy, mediation, social planning, community organization,* finding and developing resources, and many other activities.

interview　A meeting between people in which communication occurs for a specific and usually predetermined purpose. When the interview is between a social worker and client, the most typical purpose is some form of problem solving. To achieve that purpose, there are many types of social work interviews, including *directive therapy, nondirective therapy, fact-gathering interview,* and *intake.* Interviews may be of individuals, groups, families, and communities. Most interviews often combine different types in the same sequence of contacts.

interview schedule　A tool used especially in fact-gathering conferences or surveys to guide the interviewer toward the information that is sought. For example, schedules may consist of specific yes–no or *closed-ended questions* that are to be read to the respondent, or they may consist of *open-ended questions* that stimulate the respondents to answer in their own words.

intestate death　To die without a valid will. This means the state has control over the distribution of a person's assets according to its own rules, and court-appointed administrators settle the deceased person's estate.

intimacy　A strong sense of physical and emotional closeness, empathy, and attachment that permits mutual caring and communication about the most personal feelings and needs.

intimacy phase　In group work and group therapy the third of five *group development phases* in which group members tend to lose their mutual guardedness and struggle to establish their roles and power within the group and become genuinely concerned about the well-being of the other members. In most groups this is the longest phase and the time when most of the individual and group goals are reached.

intimacy versus isolation　According to the *psychosocial development theory* of Erik Erikson (1902–1994), the sixth of eight stages that occurs at about ages 18 to 24. The individual faces the challenge of developing one or more close and warm relationships or facing life alone.

intoxication　The state of being inebriated as a result of ingesting *exogenous* substances. These substances include alcohol and drugs, and the resulting behavior ranges from temporary euphoria, slurred speech, and impaired motor functioning to maladaptive behaviors such as ineffective job performance, impaired judgment, and deteriorating social functioning. See also *substance intoxication.*

intrapsychic　Occurring within one's personality or *psyche.*

intrinsic anxiety　The *anxiety* of the client that derives from the necessary focus on unpleasant material that is uncovered, analyzed, and processed. This is contrasted with *extrinsic anxiety.*

introjection　In *psychoanalytic theory,* a mental mechanism in which the individual derives feelings from another person or object and directs them internally to an imagined form of the person or object. For example, an individual may introject parental criticism, turning it into some type of self-criticism.

introspection　Self-examination of thoughts, values, and feelings.

introvert　One whose psychic energy, interests, thoughts, and feelings tend to be directed inward rather than toward the social and physical environment; the opposite of an *extrovert.*

intuition　An informal, lay term referring to an individual's perceptiveness, awareness of characteristics and feelings within another person, and accurate sense of what is going to happen.

Invalid Care Allowance　A British Social Security program for people under 65 years old who earn less than £50 per week while caring for a severely disabled person for more than 35 hours a week.

inventory　In social research, a type of *interview schedule* used to guide the researcher in assessing the presence or absence of specific phenomena, behaviors, or attitudes.

inverse relationship　1. An association between two phenomena in which a higher frequency in one variable accompanies a lower frequency in another. 2. In social research, it is sometimes called negative correlation.

investment-versus-consumption concept　A controversy about the ultimate objectives of social services, often faced in *social planning*. The one view (investment) holds that social programs should exist as an economic and social investment by enabling recipients to become more economically productive and that social services programs that serve this purpose should have priority. The other view (consumption) holds that social programs should provide goods and services to disadvantaged people to improve their standard of living and that this is a worthwhile goal in itself. See also *human capital*.

invisible government   Individuals and organizations with extensive, covert influence over legislative, executive, or judicial branches of government and other policymaking or policy-influencing entities. Such groups are not elected by the public and are usually not recognized to have such power.

invisible hand   The premise of some economic theorists, beginning with Adam Smith in the 18th century, that unrestricted trade and the free economic market, in which people can pursue their self-interests, will ultimately (invisibly) lead to the general welfare.

invisible loyalties   Alliances between family members that occur outside the *conscious* awareness of any of them. Most commonly this *family therapy* term refers to *unconscious* commitments that children acquire to support one or both parents or other family members.

involuntary client   One who is compelled to partake of the services of a social worker or other professional. For example, an individual may be required to seek a social worker's services by a court decision, by the fact of *incarceration*, or by family or employer pressure. See also *mandated client*.

irreconcilable differences   Disputes between parties that make it impossible for them to maintain their relationship. The term often applies to conflicts or problems between divorcing couples that cannot be resolved.

irresistible impulse test   A legal question used in insanity defense cases. A defendant who knew that an act was wrong may still be acquitted under this test if, because of some mental disorder, the person was unable to control behavior. See also *McNaughten rule*.

irritable bowel syndrome   A health condition with symptoms such as constipation, diarrhea, abdominal pains, and other digestive disorders that occurs when the contractions that push waste through the intestines become irregular.

irritation response theory   The view, held by some economists and social planners, that people will strive harder to improve their circumstances if social welfare is punitive and minimal.

"isms"   As used in social work, this suffix has become a term in itself and refers to the group of ideologies and prejudgments that most affect social work clients. Some social workers think of the "isms" only as negative belief systems and resulting behaviors (such as *racism, ageism, fascism,* or *speciesism*). However, there are many other "isms" that many people do not consider negative (such as heroism and *altruism*).

isolated explosive disorder   See *explosive disorder*.

isolation   1. The condition of being separated and kept apart from others. 2. Psychologically, it is aversion to or fear of contact with others. 3. In psychodynamic theory, it is a *defense mechanism* in which memories are separated from the emotions that once accompanied them. For example, a client may have been terrified when subjected to child abuse, but when relating the incident to the social worker 20 years later, the client seems to feel indifferent to it.

isolationism   The political view advocating the avoidance of relationships with foreign nations, especially military alliances and economic treaties.

IST defendants   In legal terminology, those people alleged to have committed crimes who are considered "incompetent to stand trial." Such people may be held pending completion of the IST evaluation within 90 days or treated as an outpatient until their competency status is resolved. See also *NGRI patients*.

"It takes a village"   An African expression popularized by First Lady Hillary Rodham Clinton referring to the optimal way to raise children involving not just the parents, but also relatives, neighbors, and everyone in the community acting together to provide nurturance, guidance, and positive role models.

IV drug user   An individual who takes *controlled substances* or sometimes legal drugs in an inappropriate way, through intravenous (IV) injections, usually self-administered. See also *needle exchange program.*

IVD program   Interactive video program; a CD-ROM computer-assisted instruction program *(CAI program)* used by social workers and other professionals, especially in medicine, engineering, and the physical sciences. This program is used to simulate real situations and develop practice experiences under laboratory conditions. For example, social work students can try different interview techniques with simulated clients shown on a monitor and immediately see the results.

IWW   The Industrial Workers of the World. See *"Wobblies."*

Jacobs, Frances Wisebart (1843–1892) A charity organizer and welfare worker, she developed and led Denver's movement to consolidate its charitable organizations. She formed the Denver Federation of Social Agencies, which became the model for the national *Community Chest* and *United Way* organizations.

Jaffee v. Redmond decision The 1996 U.S. Supreme Court decision that federal courts must recognize the absoluteness of social workers' right to *privileged communication;* social workers could no longer be compelled to disclose confidential information in civil lawsuits filed in federal court. This ruling may not extend to certain actions in state courts (many of which do not provide absolute confidentiality for social workers or other mental health professionals). See also *Tarasoff* and *confidentiality.*

Japanese Association of Social Workers (JASW) The professional association of social workers in Japan, established in 1960 and headquartered in Tokyo. Its purpose is to improve social workers' professional skills and standards and promote and develop the profession throughout the nation. Members must have completed a four-year professional education program in an accredited college and one year of supervised social work experience.

jargon The special language that is used by various professional groups as a shorthand method of communicating complicated concepts, which usually seem obscure and confusing to those outside the group. Social work jargon includes many of the terms found in this dictionary. See also *"psychobabble."*

Jarrett, Mary Cromwell (1876–1961) Developer of *psychiatric social work.* On the basis of her own work in mental hospitals, she developed a training course for social workers who worked in these facilities, which became part of the curriculum at the Smith College School for Social Work. In 1923, she founded the organization that became the *American Association of Psychiatric Social Workers (AAPSW).*

jaundice A symptom of diseases, such as liver disorder, in which the skin and whites of the eyes are yellow, caused by an excess of the pigment bilirubin in the bloodstream.

Javits Gifted and Talented Students Education Act The 1994 U.S. legislation (P.L. 103-382) to provide grants for programs and research for intellectually gifted and specially talented students. The program was named for U.S. Senator Jacob K. Javits and is administered by the U.S. Department of Education.

jealous-type delusional disorder A subtype of *delusional disorder* characterized by nonbizarre delusions, particularly an intense belief that one's spouse or significant other is being secretly unfaithful. The delusion often leads one to exhibiting hypervigilant behavior, seeking evidence, and threatening attacks.

jealousy A combination of uncomfortable emotions and reactions to the perceived threat of losing someone or something to a perceived rival.

Jewish communal agencies Social services agencies that serve indigent members of the Jewish community and others; resettle immigrants and help them become more acculturated to local customs; respond to international crises; fight anti-Semitism; and help Jewish people and other members of the community with social, health, and psychological problems. These agencies include Jewish Community Centers, *Young Men's and Women's Hebrew Associations,* the *Hebrew Immigrant Aid Society (HIAS),* Jewish Family Service, Jewish-affiliated hospitals, and many other organizations. Most of these agencies are united within the *Jewish Communal Service Association (JCSA).*

Jewish Communal Service Association (JCSA) The primary professional association for social workers and other professionals employed by *Jewish communal agencies.* Founded in 1899 as the National Conference of Jewish Communal Service, the JCSA provides a forum for issues of interest to the affiliated agencies, sponsors conferences and publications, and publishes a quarterly scholarly journal *(Journal of Jewish Communal Service).* Their Web site address is http://www.jcpa.org. See also *Council of Jewish Federations (CJF)* and the *United Jewish Appeal (UJA).*

Jewish federations See *Council of Jewish Federations (CJF)*.

Jewish social agencies Private organizations originally established in larger cities to serve the unique social welfare needs of Jewish families as well as people of all faiths and ethnicities. The organizations included Jewish Family Service Agencies, Hebrew Benevolent Associations, and Jewish Welfare Societies.

"jihad" An Arabic term for striving or overcoming adversity. The word is also interpreted as "holy war," a term that some terrorist groups use to justify violence against their enemies. Many Islamic scholars claim this is an illegitimate or distorted version of Islamic values.

"Jim Crow" laws Statutes requiring or condoning racial *segregation* in the United States. Such laws have been ruled unconstitutional.

jinglao lou Chinese term for a home respectful to elderly people. Such facilities are established in many local communities in China, generally to care for older people who have no families, income, or work skills (called *"San Wu"*).

Jinnah, Fatima (1893–1967) A Pakistani social reformer, she worked for the social emancipation and welfare of women, opposing the conservative orthodox attitudes toward women in her country. She helped establish industrial schools, social agencies, collectives, and the Women's Medical College in Lahore, where social workers were trained. She was the sister of Ali Jinnah, Pakistan's first leader.

JINS Juveniles in need of supervision. See *persons in need of supervision (PINS)*.

Job Corps The federal program, established as part of the *Economic Opportunity Act of 1964*, designed to provide residential training, employment, and work skills to disadvantaged young people. Jobless youths between ages 16 and 24 work and study at training centers or in conservation camps. The Job Corps is managed by the U.S. Department of Labor's *Employment and Training Administration (ETA)*, which contracts with local public and private agencies to establish the training centers. The program was partially modeled after the *Civilian Conservation Corps (CCC)* and similar *New Deal* programs. Their Web site address is http://www.jobcorps.org

Job Creation and Worker Assistance Act of 2002 The legislation (P.L. 107-147) popularly known as the Bush administration's "economic stimulus package." The law provides for money to states to help improve employment services to workers and employers, to help them reduce payroll taxes, and to fund and expand unemployment insurance eligibility and benefits. Critics claim that most of the money is in the form of tax breaks to money-losing corporations.

job description Explicit obligations and specific tasks required of an employee as conditions of employment. Some job descriptions also state certain educational, experiential, and skill requirements expected of the incumbent.

JOBLINK A nationwide clearinghouse for social workers seeking employment and employers recruiting social workers. Sponsored by NASW, applicants may use the telephone (888-261-2265) or the Internet (http://www.socialworkers.org), 24 hours a day, to locate social work jobs listed by location and specialty; they also may record mini-résumés, including their names and addresses and brief summaries of their experience, education, and credentials. Prospective employers pay a small fee for their listings and candidate information.

Jobseeker's Allowance A British social security benefit for needy unemployed people older than 18. In 1996 the program replaced the contributory Unemployment Benefit.

Job Training Partnership Act (JTPA) The 1982 federal laws (P.L. 97-300 and P.L. 97-404) to encourage more private and local employment-training efforts. JTPA replaced the *CETA* programs and in 1998 was superseded by the *Workforce Investment Act*.

Johari window A strategy in counseling and psychotherapy using a model for understanding aspects of the client's behavior. The window consists of four quadrants, that is, the public self (known to self and others), the blind self (known to others but not to oneself), the private self (known to oneself but not to others), and the unknown self (unknown to self or others). The name comes from the first names of its creators, Joseph Luft and Harry Ingham.

joining The *family therapy* process, described in 1974 by Salvador Minuchin and others, in which the therapist becomes a part of the family's interactional system to help change the dysfunctional parts of the system.

joint budgeting   A form of interagency linkage in which two or more service providers share decisions about the financing of existing or new social services. For example, two organizations could decide to reduce their respective expenses by eliminating some of their duplicated services. See also *joint funding*.

Joint Commission on Accreditation of Healthcare Organizations (JCAHO)   Since 1951, the major accrediting organization for more than 18,000 health care organizations in the United States. JCAHO develops and continually refines its standards for accreditation, surveys facilities and programs to measure and encourage compliance with the standards, and accredits organizations that meet the standards.

Joint Commission on Interprofessional Affairs (JCIA)   An informal organization composed of members of the American Nurses Association, the American Psychiatric Association, the American Psychological Association, and the *National Association of Social Workers (NASW)*. JCIA shares information on and plans joint strategies to deal with mental health issues.

Joint Commission on Mental Illness and Health   The organization of health care and welfare agencies that in 1961 completed a five-year study of the nation's need for mental health services. The findings led to federal funding for community mental health centers and improvements in state mental hospital programs.

joint custody   A legal decision involving a divorcing husband and wife and the respective responsibilities each of them will have for the care of their children. Typically, both parents maintain permanent homes for the children, and the children live with each for relatively equal amounts of time. Joint custody can also refer to an arrangement whereby the child lives with one parent most of the time, although the other parent has an equal say in important decisions regarding upbringing.

Joint Economic Committee   A combined committee of the U.S. Senate and House of Representatives established in 1946 to obtain information and make recommendations to Congress on pos-

sible legislative action pertaining to the U.S. economy and the economic welfare of its citizens.

joint funding   A form of interagency linkage in which two or more service providers or two or more funding services help finance a project or ongoing service collaboratively. For example, agencies or foundations that might be unable to afford to establish their own outreach programs could establish one together. See also *joint budgeting*.

joint interview   Variations of the interview format in which more than a single interviewer and interviewee meet. In one form, the social worker or other professional meets with the client and his or her *relevant other* (for example, teachers, guidance counselors, and classmates). In another form, the social worker meets simultaneously with several clients who may have no relationship with one another. In a third form, the client meets with two or more workers simultaneously.

"jointly and severally"   A stipulation in legal agreements under which each of the signers becomes individually liable for payment of the remaining debt.

joint processing   A procedure in which welfare clients apply for more than one program at a time, thus reducing the waste of resources, number of interviews, and paperwork. The procedure works best in *categorically needy* programs in which the eligibility criteria are the same.

joint tenancy   Legal co-ownership of a property. At the death of one co-owner the survivor becomes the sole owner of that property.

Jones, Mary Harris (1830–1930)   A community organizer, agitator, and labor union advocate, better known as Mother Jones, she led many strikes against inhumane and dangerous working conditions in the mining and steel industries and advocated for child labor laws. Her *bucket-and-broom brigade* organized the wives of workers to help in the strike actions.

"jump bail"   A slang term referring to the actions of some defendants in failing to appear for their criminal trials after depositing significant funds with the court to ensure that they will appear for their trials or will remain in the jurisdiction. If they fail to appear or leave the jurisdiction, they forfeit the deposit.

Jump Program The Juvenile Mentoring Program, administered by the U.S. *Office of Juvenile Justice and Delinquency Prevention (OJJDP)*, established by law (P.L. 35-415) in 1992 to support local programs that offer one-to-one volunteer adult mentoring for at-risk youths. The program funds local educational agencies and nonprofit organizations.

Juneteenth A celebration held on June 19th, especially in many African American homes, to commemorate when the last slaves were freed in America. Many slaveholders and southern states had ignored President Lincoln's Emancipation Proclamation, made on September 22, 1862. However, after the Civil War ended, federal troops entered Galveston, Texas, and issued a general order enforcing emancipation on June 19, 1865. The date is recognized officially in Texas as the actual end of slavery. A movement exists to make it a national holiday.

Jungian theory Concepts about the development of human personality and *psychopathology* formulated by Swiss psychiatrist Carl Gustav Jung (1875–1961). These concepts emphasize the *conscious* and *unconscious* influences on behavior. Important concepts include the *collective unconscious* (collection of human thoughts and experiences that have developed through many generations, called an *archetype*), *dream analysis*, introversion and extroversion, and *anima* and *animus*. See also *introvert* and *extrovert*.

junket Travel by government officials (especially legislators) at taxpayer expense, supposedly to conduct official investigations.

"junk jobs" A term of derision applied to employment positions in which pay and benefits are insufficient to maintain an individual or family above the poverty level. A similar term is "McJob."

Junior League A nonprofit volunteer women's organization with chapters in hundreds of communities and several nations. Established in 1901 by Mary Harriman, a young college student, she enlisted many of her socially prominent friends to participate in the settlement house movement. Its original name was the Junior League for the Promotion of Social Settlements. The group expanded rapidly and now its thousands of members organize volunteer efforts to improve social conditions in communities. Areas of major focus have included help with victims of domestic violence and

school readiness. The Web site address of the international organization, the Association of Junior Leagues International, is http://www.ajli.org

junior life skills The ability to carry out the *activities of daily living (ADL)* that are expected of young people before emancipation in preparation for independent living. These include tangible *life skills* such as housekeeping, financial management, hygiene, personal appearance, and the ability to access public transportation. Intangible junior life skills include knowing how to greet people, form and maintain friendships, and behave compatibly according to parental and educator expectations.

jurisprudence The philosophy and science of law in terms of its origins, nature, and structure.

jurymandering The act of selecting and appointing people to serve on juries based not on their ability to be objective but on their likelihood of reaching a verdict favorable to one side or the other.

just cause Legal grounds, or other justification, for taking an action, especially one that results in hardship to an individual or organization. For example, when an employer wants to fire a worker and avoid the risk of litigation, the action must be taken within legally prescribed rules, applied fairly and consistently, and carried out only for deviating from explicit norms of conduct.

justice The principle of fairness and equity, especially in accordance with moral and ethical rightness, social standards, and law. See also *social justice* and *economic justice*.

justice of the peace A local magistrate or court official with the authority to try minor cases, administer oaths, and perform civil marriages.

justice system The social institutions, facilities, and people—including police, the prison and parole systems, the legal profession, the judiciary, and investigative organizations—that provide the means for enforcing and interpreting the laws of the land. In the United States, this system is coordinated and influenced, to a major extent, by the *U.S. Department of Justice*. The system also includes the judicial and court system, from the Supreme Court to the local *justice of the peace*. See also *criminal justice system* and *juvenile justice system*.

Justice, U.S. Department of The cabinet-level department, established in 1870 and headed by the

Attorney General, in which the primary mission is to enforce all federal laws, administer the nation's law enforcement and investigation system, advise the president in legal matters, argue suits involving the U.S. government in the Supreme Court, and supervise federal penal institutions. This department includes the *Drug Enforcement Administration (DEA)*, the *Federal Bureau of Investigation (FBI)*, and the *U.S. Parole Commission*. Their Web site address is http://www.usdoj.gov

justifiable homicide   Taking the life of another human under circumstances that usually do not make it a crime. Examples include killing in self-defense or in military combat and executing an individual convicted of a capital offense.

"Just Say No" campaign   An antidrug approach, initiated during the Reagan administration, that stressed exhortations to young people to reject the use of drugs when approached by dealers. The campaign was reviled by opponents as an attempt to avoid spending money to address a serious problem.

juvenile   For purposes of criminal law, a young person who has not yet attained the age at which he or she would be treated as an adult. The term is distinguished from *minor*, which is used to refer to legal capacity. The age differs from state to state, although the Juvenile Justice and Delinquency Prevention Act of 1974 defines a "juvenile" as one who has not yet reached age 18.

juvenile court   A court of law that has jurisdiction over abused, delinquent, dependent, or neglected children and their parents or guardians. Generally, the court is also responsible for determining whether the alleged offense was committed by the accused juvenile and for overseeing the resulting rehabilitation or penalty process. See also *Gault decision.*

juvenile delinquency   A pattern of *antisocial behavior* by people younger than age 18 (or 21 in some jurisdictions) that would be regarded as criminal in nature if committed by adults.

juvenile justice euphemisms   Language used in the juvenile justice system to soften or disguise the actual nature of dealing with young offenders. For example, juveniles are not arrested but "taken into custody." They have "adjudicatory hearings" rather than trials. They are "detained" rather than jailed and placed in "youth services centers" or "reform schools" rather than prisons. When released it is usually to "aftercare" rather than parole. Some social workers defend such terminology by saying it is less stigmatizing, while others say it is deceptive.

juvenile justice policy   A component of *criminal justice policy* involving guidelines and established procedures to be considered when deciding how to cope with the illegal conduct of minors. Elements of current U.S. juvenile justice policy include the same legal rights to trial and counsel granted to adults, incarceration in facilities that are segregated from adult institutions, shorter sentences, clearance of the juvenile's record after a specified period of good behavior, and an orientation that tries to be more therapeutic than punitive. See also *Gault decision.*

juvenile justice system   That part of the *criminal justice system* that is oriented toward the control and prevention of illegal behavior by young people (those younger than age 22 in some jurisdictions and younger than age 16 or 18 in others) and toward the treatment of a *minor* engaged in such behavior. See also *Borstal system, juvenile court,* and *family court.*

juvenile offenders   Young people, usually under the age of legal responsibility (age 18 in most states), who have been convicted of legal violations, including *felony, misdemeanor,* and any other form of *delinquency.*

juvenile parole   In the judicial terminology, the status of a juvenile who has been conditionally released from incarceration as a result of delinquency and placed in a supervised treatment or rehabilitation program while living at home, in foster care, or in a transitional living facility. The system is also known as *aftercare.*

Kai-Hoken The Japanese national health insurance coverage system established in 1961, which uses both a voluntary (employees and employers contribute to a national health insurance plan) and a compulsory (community-based insurance) program.

Kai-Nenkin In Japan, the national old age pension system. Established in 1959, the program is a contributory pension insurance system, paying a flat-rate benefit to retired people not covered by their employers. Eligibility is based on flat-rate contributions by citizens between ages 20 and 60.

kaizen The Japanese concept of improvement, betterment, reform, self-motivation, and personal growth. It refers not only to improvement of social conditions but also to self-improvement, especially in the workplace and in school.

Kaposi's sarcoma (KS) A form of *cancer* in which tumors grow in the blood vessel walls. Symptoms include purple or brown lumpy spots appearing on the skin and mucous membranes of the mouth. The condition was once seen primarily in older men of Jewish or Mediterranean ancestry but now occurs as a major symptom of *human immunodeficiency virus (HIV)* infection or *acquired immune deficiency syndrome (AIDS)* in people of all ages and ancestry.

kapuna Native Hawaiian female elders, considered in the traditional Hawaiian culture to be the custodians of family history, the primary sources of wisdom, and the arbitrators of family disputes.

karma The belief, originating in Eastern philosophies and religions, that one exists within a context of destiny and that one's life is understood as ultimately beyond the individual's control and determined by a series of trials throughout life. Thoughts and acts determine one's fate in the next life as these thoughts and acts were determined by experiences in previous lives. In this way, objects, situations, or people can emit good or bad feelings or "vibrations."

Kelley, Florence (1859–1932) A crusader for *child labor* laws and protections for workers, Kelley helped organize the *National Consumers League*

(NCL) and, with *Lillian Wald,* founded the *Children's Bureau.*

Kellogg, Paul Underwood (1879–1958) Founder and editor from 1909 to 1952 of *The Survey,* social work's unofficial and vastly influential journal. *The Survey* was one of the few national publications to give in-depth analyses of social problems and their solutions. Kellogg was also an active leader in the development of various social work organizations.

Kenworthy, Marion E. (1891–1980) A social work educator, physician, and psychoanalyst. She developed conceptual frameworks that integrated psychoanalytic theory with social work knowledge.

Keogh Plan A retirement pension system for self-employed people, including social workers in private practice, in which they set aside a specified portion of their net earnings each year. No income taxes on these funds must be paid until retirement. Payouts begin between ages 59 1/2 and 70, at which time taxes on the income and interest are paid. The plan holder must keep the funds in a qualified financial institution (such as a bank, insurance company, or securities firm) set up for this purpose and permit all full-time employees to participate in the retirement plan. The plan holder must report Keogh activity to the Internal Revenue Service annually and cannot withdraw the funds until retirement without a financial penalty.

Kerner Commission The National Advisory Commission on Civil Disorders, a fact-finding group appointed by President Lyndon B. Johnson in 1967 and headed by Governor Otto Kerner of Illinois to determine the causes of and make recommendations on solutions to the *civil rights* protests and riots of that period. The commission's report, issued in 1968, blamed white *racism* and the limited opportunities available to the African Americans who lived in ghettos. Few of its proposals were implemented.

Keynesian economics The theories of British economist John Maynard Keynes (1883–1946), including the recommendation that, during economic slumps, government should increase public spending to stimulate commerce and create employment.

237

keyworker In Great Britain a social care worker who is assigned the job of coordinating the activities of all those involved in the care of one person, including the provision of counseling, therapy, and sometimes an emotional relationship.

kibbutz A collective residential *community* in Israel. Residents own almost no personal property and work for the community not for a salary but for goods and services from other members. The needs of the residents, including food, housing, education, child care, and health care, are provided for by the combined resources of the community.

Kibei Japanese Americans who are born in the United States but travel to Japan for education or temporary or permanent residence. See also *Sansei generation.*

kidnapping The *crime* of taking persons by force or manipulation and holding them against their wishes or the wishes of their legal guardians.

kidney dialysis See *hemodialysis.*

kinesalgia Vivid pain that is experienced only with movement.

kinesics *Nonverbal communication* through body motions. See also *communication theory.*

kinesitherapy See *movement therapy.*

Kinsey Report The research of Alfred C. Kinsey (1894–1956) and others about human sexual activity that delineated many sexual patterns and practices. The two books, *Sexual Behavior in the Human Male* (1948) and *Sexual Behavior in the Human Female* (1953) disclosed information about homosexuality, masturbation, coital frequency, infidelity, promiscuity, and prostitution that had not been openly discussed before.

kinship A group of people bound by the same bloodline (genetic inheritance). Use of the term usually implies other characteristics shared by the family, such as similar behaviors, values, and talents.

kinship adoption Legal adoption in which the adoptive parents are biologically related to the child. Most commonly these are grandparents, aunts and uncles, or older siblings.

kinship care The full-time nurturing and protection of children or other dependent people by their relatives other than parents. These relatives may have family ties or other important bonds, such as being members of their tribes or clans, godparents, or stepparents. When a child must be separated from parents, kinship care may be provided informally—that is, without state involvement—by kinship caregivers or kinship foster parents under formal arrangement with the public child welfare system. See also *foster care.*

kleptomania 1. Compulsive stealing. 2. An *impulse control disorder* in which the person unlawfully takes property belonging to another. The theft act is motivated by emotional release, excitement, or gratification and not by need for the object or its material value. Explanations for this phenomenon vary, but most jurisdictions do not accept it by itself as justification or as a defense against punishment or other legal action.

Klinefelter's syndrome See *XXY males.*

"knee-jerk liberal" A disparaging term applied (mostly by conservatives) to people who, supposedly without thought, elect to raise taxes and mobilize resources to solve social problems. The term is similar to *"bleeding heart."*

knowledge base In social work, the aggregate of accumulated information, scientific findings, values, and skills and the methodology for acquiring, using, and evaluating what is known. The knowledge base is derived from the social worker's own research, theory building, and systematic study of relevant phenomena and from the direct and reported experiences of others.

Kohlberg moral development theory Concepts proposed by Lawrence Kohlberg in the early 1970s to explain the way an individual's ethics and ideas about "right and wrong" change with age. Six stages or levels of development are delineated: The rules are obeyed (1) to avoid punishment, (2) to obtain rewards, and (3) to avoid being disliked and to be seen as being "good." The individual comes to (4) appreciate society's need for rules and develops a conscience or sense of guilt at wrongdoing, (5) understand that there are competing and contradictory values and that some impartial judgments are necessary, and (6) appreciate the validity of universal moral principles and develops a commitment to them. Most individuals are believed to have completed the first two stages (preconventional level of moral development) by age nine. The next two stages (conventional level) are usually completed during early adolescence. Most people do not reach the last two (postconventional level) until after age 20, and many people never reach this level at all, according to Kohlberg.

Kohutian theory   See *self-psychology.*

K-1 Fiancée Visa   A document issued by the *Bureau of Citizenship and Immigration Services (CIS)* that allows someone to enter the United States for the purpose of marrying a U.S. citizen within 90 days. The applicants must document that they have met within the previous two years, and after the marriage they must apply for permanent residency. CIS also issues a K-2 Visa for the minor children of the person from the foreign nation who enters under the K-1 Visa.

koro   A *culture-bound syndrome,* found especially among people of Chinese and East Asian ancestry, in which a man experiences intense anxiety that his penis will recede into his body or in which a woman fears her vulva and nipples will recede into her body.

Korsikoff's disease   *Amnesia* related to the prolonged, heavy use of alcohol.

Krankenkassen   In Germany, the "sick fund." This program, originating informally in German localities in the 1850s, was based on money collected from voluntary public contributions, churches, employers, and employees to be set aside for those unable to work because of illness. The organization of this program was later modified and incorporated into Germany's national health care program, established in 1883. See also *Hilfskassen.*

Kübler-Ross death stages   The psychological reactions to impending *death* described by Elisabeth Kübler-Ross in 1969, based on her interviews with terminally ill patients. The five stages identified are (1) *denial* and *isolation,* (2) *anger,* (3) *bargaining,* (4) *depression,* and (5) *acceptance.* Some patients go through these stages in a different order, some go back and forth between some or all of the stages, and still others never go through any of them.

Ku Klux Klan (KKK)   A loose confederation of *white supremacist groups* and *secret societies* who oppose the advancement of African American and other racial and ethnic groups. This opposition is expressed through attempted intimidation and terrorism. The KKK formed after the Civil War to keep African Americans from exercising their newly won rights. Through burning crosses, wearing hoods and robes, and committing murder and assaults, the KKK accomplished some of their goals, but it has been in general decline since then.

kupah   In Jewish tradition, a community fund; members of a local Jewish community contributed to this fund as a form of *tzedakah* (social justice obligation) to be dispersed to those in need. See also *tamhuy* (community kitchen).

kurtosis   In statistics, the degree of flatness or pointedness around the mode of a frequency curve. For example, a social agency plots on a graph the times during a one-year period that new clients are accepted and finds that most come during the summer. A frequency distribution would show a peak during that period.

Kwanzaa   An annual seven-day celebration in many African American homes held from December 26 to January 1. Originated by African American Maulana Karenga in 1965, the holiday is based on an amalgam of several African harvest festivals. Participating families light candles each day to remember seven basic principles: unity, self-determination, collective work and responsibility, purpose, cooperative economies, creativity, and faith.

kwashiorkor   A disease of *malnutrition* caused by protein deficiency. It is found most commonly in *Third World* and *Fourth World* countries or in impoverished areas where children receive too little milk or other protein-rich foods. Growth retardation, anemia, abnormal distension of the abdomen, weakness, and apathy are major symptoms.

kyphosis   Progressive rounding of the upper back, seen more commonly among older people. See also *lordosis* and *scoliosis.*

la belle indifference An apparent form of *apathy* or lack of concern for existing or potential problems, noted as a symptom in people with certain mental disorders, including *schizophrenia.*

La Leche League An international advocacy and educational organization that encourages natural infant feeding and discourages widespread use of commercial baby formula. Their Web site address is http://www.lalecheleague.org

La Raza Unida The political movement and party, comprising mostly Mexican American people and others of Spanish-speaking heritage, that advocates for policies and candidates favorable to the needs of *Hispanic* people. Their Web site address is http://www.larazaunida.tripod.com

labeling The application of a name to a person or a person's problem based on observed traits or patterns of behavior. Some social workers view labels (for example, psychiatric diagnostic terms such as *passive–aggressive*) as a form of name-calling or generalization about people that leads toward stereotyping and away from individualization. Other social workers consider it a necessity to facilitate research and communication about a person's problem without having to include prolonged detailed descriptions. See also *psychiatric labels.*

labeling theory The hypothesis that when people are assigned a label, such as "paranoid schizophrenia," to indicate some kind of disorder or deviance, others tend to react to the subjects as though they were deviant. Also, the subjects may begin to act in a way that meets the others' expectations. This may be a type of *self-fulfilling prophecy* and an example of the *Hawthorne effect.*

labile Having the tendency toward emotional flexibility, freedom of movement, and abrupt changes in mood or affect. See also *emotional lability.*

labile affect Abrupt shifts and excessive variation in an individual's expression of *affect.*

labor force The segments of a society that can or do produce all its marketable goods and services. The *U.S. Bureau of the Census* includes in this definition employed and unemployed people. Those not in the labor force include some people who are retired, in school, raising families, disabled, "voluntarily idle," and others.

labor-force participation rate (LFPR) The *U.S. Bureau of the Census* designation for the number of people who produce marketable goods and services divided by the number of people eligible for *employment.*

labor intensive 1. Pertaining to those organizations in which the greatest outlay is for personnel. 2. Pertaining to corporations and agencies that require many workers to provide a service or manufacture a product and that do not or cannot replace personnel through automation. Social agencies and most other service providers tend to be labor intensive. See also *capital intensive.*

labor mobility The degree to which a society permits or encourages its workers to move from one job to another within the same employment organization, between organizations, and from one location to another. Economists generally believe that those societies with a relatively high level of labor mobility are likely to become more economically productive than those that are less flexible.

labor theory of value The concept suggested by Adam Smith, David Ricardo, Karl Marx, and others stating that the value of each product or service should be determined by the amount of labor required to produce it.

labor union An association, primarily of wage or salary earners and employees in a particular industry (such as government employees or automobile workers) or craft (plumbers or teachers), whose purpose is to advance the economic interests and working conditions of its members. Many social workers belong to labor unions such as the *American Federation of State, County, and Municipal Employees (AFSCME);* the *American Federation of Government Employees (AFGE);* and the *Communications Workers of America (CWA).*

Labor, U.S. Department of The cabinet-level federal department created in 1913 to improve working conditions and worker safety and welfare, to secure employee benefits, to enhance employment opportunities, and to acquire and disseminate information about social conditions affecting employment. Its major offices and organizations include the *Occupational Safety and Health Administration (OSHA)*, the *Employment and Training Administration*, the *Job Corps*, and the *Bureau of Labor Statistics (BLS)*. Their Web site address is http://www.dol.gov

labor welfare Programs in industrial organizations to provide personnel- and employment-related social services. This is a term used in some *Third World* nations where social welfare services for the general public are limited, thus compelling some industries to provide such services for their employees.

lactose intolerance Deficiencies in the ability to digest lactose, a sugar found in milk and other dairy products. This may result in symptoms such as diarrhea, bloating, and gas. It occurs when the body does not produce enough lactase, an enzyme in the small intestine that is necessary to digest lactose. Some ethnic groups have significantly higher rates of lactose intolerance than others, and the rate tends to increase among all people as they grow older.

Ladies Physiological Society A 19th-century volunteer organization that focused on women's health interests, pregnancy, childbirth, natural childbirth, child rearing, nutrition, and health care reform. The organization started in Boston in 1840 and was based on the model of England's *friendly societies*. Eventually the societies were merged into other organizations, especially the more comprehensive *Charity Organization Societies (COSs)*.

"lady bountiful" A term once applied, somewhat derisively, to social workers and volunteer workers who provided goods and services to those in need. The term originated during the U.S. Civil War, when upper-class women donated and personally delivered food, clothing, and advice to those in need. Many of these women subsequently began working as *friendly visitors*, the precursors to professional *social workers*. See also *"greystocking."*

laissez-faire 1. In *social policy*, the idea that government should not interfere with the economy and that individuals will provide all services and fulfill all needs by means of financial incentives. 2. In social administration, the management practice of minimal involvement. A laissez-faire leader lets staff make their own decisions (compared to an autocratic leader, who makes the organization's decisions).

Lamaze method Natural childbirth without the use of anesthetics or other medication but with the use of exercise, systematic breathing, and relaxation procedures.

lame duck An office holder or manager whose time of departure has been specified and announced. This announcement sometimes weakens the power of the incumbent among those who know they soon will be dealing with a different leader.

LAMM A chemical compound (L-alpha-acetylmethadol) used in the *maintenance therapy* of people addicted to an opiate drug. LAMM treatment is an alternative to *methadone treatment*. Because it is slower acting but longer lasting, the addicted person need not stay at or make daily trips to the methadone maintenance clinic.

LAN Local area network; a connection of mainframe and personal computers within the same building or general area. See also *WAN*.

land despoilment The destruction of environment through activities such as *deforestation*, strip-mining, highway construction and urbanization, garbage dumping, topsoil erosion, oil drilling and spills, overgrazing by farm animals, and *slash-and-burn farming*.

Landmine Ban Treaty The international treaty, also known as the Ottawa Convention, developed in 1997 and signed by most nations (not including the United States and most Middle East countries), to comprehensively ban all antipersonnel bombs, mines, and related devices; destroy stockpiled mines; remove those in the ground within a decade; and help people who have been injured by them.

Lane Report The study, conducted in 1939 by Robert P. Lane, analyzing the field of *community organization* and describing it as a professional entity. The report influenced the social work profession to incorporate *community organization* as one of its three major practice methods, along with *social group work* and *social casework*. The report drew on earlier conceptualizations, especially those of *Eduard C. Lindeman* and Jesse F. Steiner.

language disorder An inability to use language to communicate satisfactorily, caused by developmental, cognitive, or physical impairment. The term does not apply to people who have communication problems in areas where the languages are not in their native tongue. Language disorders include never having acquired any language (usually the result of *mental retardation*) and acquired disorders resulting from physical problems such as trauma, hearing disabilities, stroke, neurological disorder, and developmental language disorder. Developmental language disorders are of the expressive or receptive types and, more frequently, combinations of both. See *expressive language disorder* and *mixed receptive–expressive language disorders.*

Lanham Act The first U.S. federal program (the Lanham Public War Housing Act, Ch. 260, 55 Stat. 361) to help provide day care for working mothers, enacted in 1942 primarily to enable mothers to join the workforce and help in the war effort. The program provided 50 percent matching grants to local communities to establish and operate day care centers.

laparoscopy A surgical procedure that uses a laparoscope (a fiberoptic instrument) inserted in small incisions into the peritoneal cavity. The procedure, sometimes colloquially termed "Band-aid" surgery, obviates the need for large abdominal incisions; it has been used for *in vitro fertilization,* female *sterilization,* and removal of gallbladders.

larceny Stealing or theft; the unlawful taking of property that belongs to another person. See also *grand larceny* and *petit larceny.*

Lassa fever A highly contagious, acute, and potentially fatal febrile viral infection found especially in tropical Africa. The first symptoms appear one to three weeks after contact with the virus (from rat droppings, contaminated food, contact with infected persons, or virus particles in the air). Symptoms include high fever, sore throat, pain, diarrhea, vomiting, hearing loss, tremors, and encephalitis. Patients need to be quarantined for long periods, but usually they live in areas where such isolation is virtually impossible to achieve.

Lassalle, Beatriz (1882–1965) A social activist for *suffrage* and other rights for Puerto Ricans, she headed the Puerto Rico Emergency Reconstruction Administration during the *Great Depression* and led the successful campaign for Puerto Rico to be the first state or territory to have social work licensing.

l'assistenza sociale Social worker in Italy.

last-hired/first-fired principle *Seniority* as the criterion in employment retention. This principle has been criticized, especially by women and people of color, as being discriminatory because it works against those who have more recently entered the *labor force.*

latah A *culture-bound syndrome,* noted especially in Indonesia, Malaysia, Thailand, Japan, and the Philippines, in which the individual enters a trance-like state, imitates the speech and manner of others, and seems highly sensitive to fright.

latchkey child A youngster who comes home from school to spend part of the day unsupervised because the parents are still at work. See also *home-alone children.*

latency-age child A child who has passed about age six but has not yet reached puberty. Common in social work usage, the term refers to the *latency stage* in the *Freudian theory* of psychosexual development. The term was used originally to suggest that the individual's sexuality is latent or dormant, although this premise is now questioned.

latency stage In the *Freudian theory* of psychosexual development, the stage of personality development in the child that follows the *phallic* (oedipal) *phase* and precedes the *genital stage (adolescence).* Sigmund Freud (1856–1939) viewed this as a time in which no new conflicts are introduced, but the child consolidates previous progress. Other analytic theorists, such as Harry Stack Sullivan (1892–1949) and Erik Erikson (1902–1994), saw this stage as important for the child's developing *social skills* and *sexual identity.* See also *psychosexual development theory.*

latent homosexual A term sometimes applied to an individual who believes himself or herself to have a heterosexual orientation but who has *unconscious* desires for erotic gratification with members of the same sex. Latent homosexuals may be in deep conflict about their *sexual orientation* and expend great psychic energy in denying to themselves and others that such conflicts exist. Such denial might take the form of overt hostility toward people who are gay or lesbian, avoidance of them, or avoidance of any behaviors that seem more appropriate for members of the opposite sex. See also *homosexuality, latent* and also *homosexuality* and *homophobia.*

latent schizophrenia An imprecise and obsolete term, rather than a diagnostic entity, referring to early or mild signs of *schizophrenia* (sometimes *flat affect,* some *paranoid ideation,* and *thought disorders*) but no clear-cut psychotic episodes or gross breaking with reality. Other obsolete terms also in common use by professionals to describe this condition have been "borderline schizophrenia," "prepsychotic," or "incipient psychosis."

Lathrop, Julia C. (1858–1932) An advocate for *child welfare* and a leader in establishing the U.S. *juvenile court* system, Lathrop was the first director of the *Children's Bureau* and later became active in the *women's suffrage movement.*

Latino One who identifies or is identified with the languages and certain cultural characteristics of the people of South America, Central America, and the Caribbean. There is considerable diversity among the groups who fit under the Latino rubric.

Latino Social Work Educators, Association of (ALSWE) The autonomous association of faculty members at graduate and undergraduate schools of social work in the United States and Puerto Rico who have Spanish-speaking backgrounds. The goal of ALSWE is to develop education for and represent the concerns and interests of Latino clients and to provide information about them to social work professional organizations, educational institutions, students, and professionals.

Latino Social Workers Organization (LSWO) An independent U.S. national association of social workers, primarily of Spanish-speaking backgrounds, established in 1992 to provide greater opportunities for Latino professionals to share information and work toward common goals, particularly on behalf of Latino clients. Their Web site address is http://www.lswo.org

***Lau v. Nichols* decision** The 1974 unanimous U.S. Supreme Court ruling that public schools must provide programs for students who speak little or no English. See also *Bilingual Education Act.*

law A system of rules and legislative pronouncements established and recognized by a state, nation, tribe, society, or community as binding to its members.

Law Enforcement Assistance Administration (LEAA) The former program created in 1968 (P.L. 90-351) to fund the efforts of states and localities to upgrade correctional facilities and personnel. LEAA was discontinued in 1982 as its functions gradually merged into other government organizations.

Law of Settlement and Removal The historically significant English statute, enacted in 1662, that led to the widespread use of *residency laws* in determining eligibility for *public assistance.*

lay analysis *Psychoanalysis* as practiced by one who does not have a medical degree but who has acquired special training in its theory and technique. Social workers and others with this training and experience may be considered lay analysts.

layoff A temporary but indefinite separation from employment, not associated with job performance but with the employer's economic situation, supply shortages, or market declines.

LBW baby See *low-birthweight (LBW) baby.*

LCA level In Britain the concept of "low cost, but acceptable" standard of living. This level refers to the minimum amount an impoverished individual or family needs to meet basic British standards of living. Social security benefits seek to ensure that everyone's income reaches the LCA level; income below that level (that is, nonacceptable) theoretically may be supplemented through payments, tax credits, commodities, and other programs.

LDS Social Services The organization of social agencies affiliated with the Church of Jesus Christ of Latter-Day Saints, with branches in major communities throughout the United States, that provides family, child welfare, and gerontological services as well as other social services for all individuals in need. See also *sectarian services.*

lead poisoning The absorption of quantities of lead, sometimes resulting in brain damage, respiratory illness, other health problems, or death in the affected individual. The lead may come from sources such as lead-based paint or the exhaust of automobiles that burn leaded gas. The population at greatest risk for lead poisoning is young children who live in older buildings in which lead-based paints were used.

League of Red Cross Societies   An organization founded in 1919 comprising 60 national *Red Cross* and *Red Crescent* societies to coordinate *disaster relief* activities by member societies, including raising funds, procuring emergency provisions, distributing resources to populations experiencing natural or human-made disasters, and training relief workers. Their Web site address is http://www.lrcrc.org

League of Women Voters   A voluntary organization established in 1920 to educate citizens about the political process and to scrutinize and conduct research on the electoral process and government structure at the national, state, and local levels. An outgrowth of the Woman's Suffrage Association, the league originally sought to educate women in the rational use of their newly acquired right to vote. The league, which opened its membership to men in 1974, has chapters in most cities in the United States. See also *suffrage* and *women's suffrage movement*. Their Web site address is http://www.lwv.org

leak   Anonymous intentional transferring of information to the media, usually by an insider, to achieve some public relations purpose. It is done anonymously to weaken the position of an opponent; to avoid sanctions or disapproval by the holder of the information, who may have power over the leaker; or to assess the impact of the information before it is officially disclosed.

Learn and Serve America   A program of the *Corporation for National and Community Service* to facilitate *service learning* by America's students in schools and colleges. Local school administrations, in cooperation with private community service organizations, enable students to participate in specified projects for school credit. Their Web site address is http://www.learnandserve.org

learned helplessness   A pattern of behavior, frequently seen in victims of *spouse abuse* and *child abuse*, in which the individual responds passively to risks of harm. The person may behave without obvious symptoms in every other way but has come to believe there is nothing that can be done and that no effective help is available. See also *self-defeating personality disorder*.

learner   One who purposefully or unintentionally acquires knowledge, skills, values, and concepts.

Learnfare   A plan and program in various public assistance systems that ties the client's benefits to participation in specified educational programs. The idea is to encourage recipients to acquire additional education to enable them to achieve greater economic independence. The program is sometimes part of *Workfare* welfare benefits. See also *Healthfare*.

learning curve   A graphic representation of the amount and frequency with which skill or information is acquired; usually the horizontal axis indicates time and the vertical axis indicates the activity learned, the skill demonstrated, or the errors involved.

learning disability   A descriptive term for children of normal or above-average *intelligence* who experience a specific difficulty in school, such as *dyslexia* (reading difficulty), *dysgraphia* (writing difficulty), or *dyscalculia* (math or calculation difficulty).

learning disorder   A level of achievement in reading, writing, and mathematics that is substantially below that expected for age, education, and intelligence. The condition may be related to low self-esteem, discouragement, cultural factors, or other diagnosable mental disorders, especially *conduct disorder, oppositional defiant disorder, attention-deficit hyperactivity disorder (ADHD)*, major depressive disorder, or *dysthymic disorder*. Learning disorders were formerly called "academic skills disorder."

learning style   The predominant way one acquires knowledge and processes information. Each person is said to have a unique learning style. Some learn best through reading, whereas others do better when information is transmitted orally. Some learners do better through the use of pictorials and video, whereas others prefer language, discussion, and personal interaction.

learning theory   Concepts that underlie *behaviorism, behavioral therapy,* and *behavioral modification,* based on the premise that human behaviors result from finding success or failure with certain responses to various environmental stimuli.

least-developing countries   A designation by the United Nations for countries with low economic growth, literacy rates, and per capita incomes and few natural or human resources with which to progress. See also *Fourth World.*

"least-restrictive environment" (LRE)   The term educators use for the legal requirement to place children with disabilities in learning situations that meet their special needs while most closely approximating that of the child without disabilities. Many educators think LRE is a synonym for *mainstreaming.* However, even though most children with disabilities under this provision are placed in normal classrooms, in some circumstances some restrictions may be necessary. See also *inclusion.*

Leboyer method   A system designed to minimize the infant's birth trauma by maintaining a quiet postdelivery environment in a dimly lit room and by placing the newborn on the mother's abdomen with the umbilical cord intact. Physicians do not spank or hold the infant upside down.

Lee, Porter (1879–1939)   A social work educator and leader in curriculum development for schools of social work. Lee helped organize the *American Association of Schools of Social Work (AASSW)* in 1919 and advocated the integration of multidisciplinary knowledge into social work. He wrote many early social work texts, including *Mental Hygiene and Social Work* and *Social Work: Cause and Function.*

"left-brain thinker"   A term applied to people who are supposed to rely more on the left hemisphere of their brains—the apparent origin of linear thoughts and adherence to formal rules of logic—scientifically and systematically, as opposed to the *"right-brain thinker,"* who is supposedly more creative, artistic, intuitive, and emotive.

leftist   An individual whose sociopolitical orientation is more liberal than those in the mainstream. The label also has been applied to anyone considered sympathetic to *Marxism.* See also *liberalism.*

legal adoption   The legal process by which a parent–child relationship is created between people genetically unrelated. Those who are legally adopted become heir to all the privileges with the parents that natural children would have. Technically, because *adoption* is a legal process, the term should be redundant. However, it often is used by social workers, necessitated by the practice of *black-market adoption.*

legal aid   The provision of free or reduced-fee legal counsel to a *litigant* who cannot afford a private attorney. Legal aid offices exist throughout the United States and many other nations and are sponsored by local bar associations, law schools, and government organizations. See also *Legal Services Corporation.*

legal defense fund   Monies collected and held to pay the expenses of individuals or groups who are or who may become involved in *litigation.* Those for whom such funds are established are usually unable to meet these expenses themselves.

Legal Defense Fund (LDF) of NASW   The program established by the National Association of Social Workers in 1972 to provide financial and legal assistance and services for those involved in cases of concern and interest to the social work profession. The member-funded program also supports educational projects to improve the legal status and knowledge of the profession. To be eligible for LDF assistance, the applicant must be an NASW member and the case must have some legal difficulties relevant to NASW's standards, goals, and mission, and legal precedents might be established with the outcome of the case.

legal regulation   The control of certain activities, such as professional conduct, by government rule and enforcement. In social work, legal regulation occurs through *licensing, certification,* or *registration of social workers.* In each of these activities, the public is assured by the relevant legal jurisdiction that the social worker possesses the knowledge or qualifications required by law to receive that designation.

legal risk adoptions   A program available in some states that allows prospective adoptive parents to become foster parents to children who are not legally free for adoption. Adoption can take place only if the rights of the biological parents become terminated. The foster parents understand in advance that they may never be able to adopt but are willing to assume the risk.

legal separation   An agreement between a husband and wife, enforced by law, that permits them to live apart without being divorced.

Legal Services Corporation   The federal agency, established in 1974, that provides funding for local programs that furnish legal services to eligible clients, especially poor people. Their Web site address is http://www.lsc.gov

"legally blind" A nonmedical expression referring to various deficiencies in vision and used primarily to define eligibility for certain benefits or concessions. What constitutes legal blindness varies depending on the country, condition, or benefit. In the United States a visual acuity test result of over 20/200, or a field restriction within 20 degrees diameter (tunnel vision), may be considered blindness for legal purposes.

Legionnaire's disease A pneumonialike disease of the respiratory system that tends to attack groups of people in closed spaces, caused by the bacteria *Legionella pneumophila,* which thrives in the mist sprayed from air conditioners and humidifiers and infests airplanes, well-insulated buildings, and self-contained rooms. The name originated in 1976 when an outbreak attacked many people who attended an American Legion convention in Philadelphia.

legislative advocacy The process of influencing the course or content of a bill or other legislative measure. This may be facilitated by individuals, agencies, organizations, or coalitions to protect or establish the rights and entitlements of their clients. Legislative advocacy may occur directly by using specific *legislative advocacy tactics* or indirectly by mobilizing community groups.

legislative advocacy tactics Procedures used to influence lawmakers and the legislative process and to modify, pass, or defeat legislation. Seven specific procedures have been delineated by Ronald B. Dear and Rino J. Patti ("Legislative Advocacy: Seven Effective Tactics," *Social Work, 26,* pp. 289–296) to be used by advocates, staff, agencies, community groups, and lobbyists to influence state legislators: (1) introduce a bill as early as possible, preferably before the legislative session; (2) obtain multiple sponsorships and avoid solo sponsorship; (3) obtain bipartisan sponsorship with the prime sponsor in the majority party; (4) seek an influential prime sponsor, such as a committee chair, but only if that person will use available power to promote the bill; (5) obtain the support or neutralize the opposition of relevant state agencies and the governor; (6) press for open hearings and organize effective testimony; and (7) be ready to compromise and support the amendatory process to obtain a favorable outcome. Other activities to enhance the chances of a bill's passage are to clearly define the problem that the bill addresses; fully assess the fiscal impact of the bill's passage; provide clear, concise, and relevant information to committee members and staff; support the sponsors to help move the bill through the legislative process; mobilize constituencies; and use the media to publicize the problem and the legislative remedy.

legislative casework Intermediary interventions performed by members of Congress or other legislators, or their aides, on behalf of constituents who seek assistance with their disputes with the government; also known as constituency services.

legitimation The acquisition of rights or authority to fulfill specified functions or pursue specified goals.

leishmaniasis A skin disease that leaves large, open sores. Transmitted by infected sand flies that live especially in dry desert areas, refugee camps, or bombed-out buildings in war-torn arid areas, the disease is not life threatening but often reaches epidemic levels. Victims are frequently stigmatized for life and ostracized by their peers.

leisure class The socioeconomic group that has sufficient resources to enable the group to devote most of its time to recreational or hedonistic pursuits.

lending out a license The practice in which a licensed professional employs an assistant to perform functions that would lead a reasonable-thinking client to consider the assistant a licensed professional. Social workers sometimes practice dubious ethics by hiring unlicensed assistants to see some of their clients. It is more commonly done by psychiatrists who hire social workers to do psychotherapy with their clients while charging the client the higher physician's rate. In such cases, the supervisor or employer may be liable for any damages even if that person has never seen the injured client.

Lenroot, Katharine F. (1891–1982) A longtime leader of the U.S. *Children's Bureau,* she was an advocate especially in resolving problems of juvenile delinquency, child labor laws, child welfare, and school health services. She succeeded *Grace Abbott* as director of the bureau but saw its various programs and initiatives be eliminated, dismantled, or placed within other government departments.

LePlay, Pierre Guilluame Frederic (1806–1882) A French political economist who may have been the first to address the problems of *poverty* using the scientific method of inquiry; in the 1850s and 1860s, he collected and analyzed the budgets of hundreds of French workers and wrote about how some of them became impoverished.

leptokurtic In the graphical depiction of data, a frequency distribution that is more peaked or pointed, as opposed to a normal "bell-shaped curve" or one that is *platykurtic* (flattened).

lesbian A woman whose sexual or *erotic orientation* is for other women. See also "*gay*" and *homosexuality.*

less-developed countries (LDCs) The poorest nations on Earth, including those with the fewest natural resources and the lowest level of education among the population. The United Nations term for such nations is *least-developing countries.* See also *Fourth World.*

less-eligibility principle The premise that poor people should not be given financial assistance that raises them to a level exceeding that of the lowest-paid employed person in the community.

lethality The degree to which someone or something is capable of causing *death.* Social workers primarily apply the term to clients who are *homicide* or *suicide* risks. For example, a client might be said to have a high degree of suicidal lethality if symptoms include feelings of depression and hopelessness, the recent loss of loved ones, development of a suicide plan, failing health, and deprivation of a supportive family or friends.

lethologica Recurring inability to remember a person's name; a temporary inability to recall proper names.

leukemia *Cancer* of the blood-producing tissues—including bone marrow, lymphatics, liver, and spleen—resulting in increased production of white cells and a commensurate reduction of red cells and other blood elements. The onset of leukemia can occur at any age.

level of care (LOC) The degree of assistance needed by clients that may determine their eligibility for programs and services. For example, clients may require protective, intermediate, or skilled levels of care.

level of measurement In research, the range and degree of complexity with which data collected about a phenomenon are observed, processed, classified, and systematically evaluated. Levels of measurement include *nominal measurement, ordinal measurement,* and *interval measurement.*

levels of significance See *significance level.*

lewd and lascivious A description used by law authorities for conduct considered immoral, including *indecent exposure,* solicitation for prostitution, the sale of pornography, and men and women living together without being married.

LGBT persons The community of people who are lesbian, gay, bisexual, or transgender.

liability A legal obligation to perform some duty, pay for some action, or refrain from doing something. Professional liability can take the form of paying clients who have been harmed by the intervention, and the liability can extend beyond the direct practitioner to that person's supervisor, as in *vicarious liability.* See also "*respondeat superior*" *doctrine.*

liability insurance A plan to protect one from the financial risks of a lawsuit. For professionals it is an important protection against claims of violations of *professional conduct.* Other important liability insurance plans include premises liability (covering accidents at sites where the service is performed), agency liability (covering all agency personnel, consultants, and volunteers), errors and omissions protection (shielding board members and executives), and fidelity bonding (covering those with financial authority).

libel Writing and publishing a statement that is untrue, misleading, malicious, and damaging to the person being written about. To win a lawsuit against a libel charge, an individual must prove that the statements were either true or nonmalicious and undamaging. See also *slander.*

liberal arts education Undergraduate education designed to give students a foundation of knowledge that equips them to make free, informed choices about themselves and the world in which they live. Liberal arts education is distinguished from vocational training or professional or technical education. Originally, the liberal arts consisted of language, logic, rhetoric, arithmetic, geometry, astronomy, and harmony but now are studies of the natural sciences, social sciences, and humanities. One requirement for admission to accredited graduate schools in social work in the United States is a degree signifying liberal arts education.

liberalism The sociopolitical orientation that currently emphasizes the development of opportunities for all people—especially those who are disadvantaged, poor, elderly, children, and racial or ethnic minorities—through economic, educational, and social programs that are principally financed, regulated, and administered by the government. Use of this term, as well as that of *conservatism,* has accurate meaning only in the context and time frame in which it is used. This is because the orientation and goals of liberalism have changed through the centuries (see *classical liberalism*), have been associated with many political movements along the way (see *leftist*), and may be about to change once again (see *neoliberalism*).

libertarian A political movement and party that advocates minimal government outside of police and military forces, the cessation of all welfare programs, greater privatization of education and health care, and an unregulated economy. The movement is centered in the Libertarian Party, founded in 1971, whose candidates for most public offices advocate the gradual elimination of all taxes, an end to government regulation of all personal matters, and quarantines for patients with HIV disease.

liberty A people's freedom from arbitrary controls, slavery, ignorance, or government interference with private actions.

libido In *psychoanalytic theory,* sexual instinct (energy toward expression of pleasure and the seeking of a love object as well as erotic gratification); a basic psychic energy.

licenciado The credential or license to practice professional social work awarded in many South American nations to those who have completed required university social work training. The term also applies to the credentials for other professions.

licensed clinical social worker (LCSW) A professional social worker who has been legally accredited by a state government to engage in *clinical social work* in that state. The acronym LCSW after a professional's name indicates possession of the license and the relevant qualifications. Qualifications for the license vary from state to state. Many states require an *MSW* degree from an accredited graduate school, several years of supervised professional experience, and successful completion of the state's social work licensing exam. Information about these requirements can be obtained from the relevant state's board of professional licensing or from the *Association of Social Work Boards'* Web site at http://www.aswb.org

licensed independent clinical social worker (LICSW) A designation used by some state professional licensing bodies and some third-party financing institutions to indicate that the practitioner is qualified for independent practice. The designation is sometimes used for social workers who have been granted the status of an independent vendor, requiring neither referral nor supervision as a condition of *third-party payment.* See also *independent social work.*

licensing Granting a formal government authorization to do something that cannot be done legally without that authorization. Before one can legally engage in the practice of clinical social work in any jurisdiction in the United States, one must obtain a license in that jurisdiction.

licensing board An official organization that regulates a professional or technical practice in a specific jurisdiction. State licensing boards are usually composed of a combination of professional and public members appointed by the governor. Social work licensing boards usually regulate social work practice through providing formal *licensing examinations,* issuing licenses to practice, overseeing license renewals, and disciplining social workers who have violated the law or its rules and regulations.

licensing examination The formal test a profession's licensing board requires for a professional to become licensed in that state. Most states license social workers at multiple levels according to education and professional experience earned and use different examinations for each level. The licensing examinations used by states are objective tests developed by the *Association of Social Work Boards (ASWB)* and are designed to measure minimal competence.

lie detector A machine used in police investigations designed to record physiological rates of change in pulse, blood pressure, skin moisture, and respiration. The subject answers questions, and the physiological rates of changes are recorded for expert analysis. Answering a question falsely is said to be emotionally charged for most people and stimulates the *autonomic nervous system (ANS)*, over which one has no control. Because accuracy is possible in about 75 percent of those tested, the machine is used more to help in the investigation process than as evidence in courts of law.

Liederman, David (1936–2001) An advocate for neglected, abused, and at-risk children, he was longtime head of the *Child Welfare League of America* and later led the Accreditation Board for Child Service Agencies. He was also a leader of the movement for intergenerational equity and a member of the review board for this dictionary.

lien A claim on some property placed there to secure payment of a debt. Until the lien is cleared, the property holder risks having the property sold to pay the debt if payment terms are not followed.

life adjustment groups Educationally oriented groups for people or their families who face some chronic condition (that is, irreversible medical or developmental disability). Similar to a *family life education program (FLE)* with a professional leader and six to 12 members for time-limited sessions, these groups provide information about the condition, advice for dealing with its consequences, and mutual support. Those using such groups have included families of people with head injuries, people with multiple sclerosis, parents of children with specific disabilities, and families of Alzheimer's patients.

life cycle The age-related sequence of changes and systematic development undergone by an individual from birth to death. Although most people are said to go through similar changes in a fairly predictable order, the life cycle concept also includes individual and cultural differences.

life expectancy The average length of time before death of people belonging to specified statuses, such as age group, occupation, gender, race, mental state, and health factors.

life model The social work practice approach that uses the *ecological perspective* as a metaphor for focusing on the interface between the client and the environment. The social worker who uses this approach views stressful problems in living (life transitions, interpersonal processes, and environmental obstacles) as consequences of person–environment transactions. According to *Carel B. Germain* and Alex Gitterman (*The Life Model of Social Work Practice,* New York: Columbia University Press, 1980, p. 5), the approach uses an integrated method of practice with individuals and groups to release potential capacities, reduce environmental stressors, and restore growth-promoting transactions.

life review The process of looking back over one's own life, analyzing it, uncovering the hidden themes, and understanding the meaning of the life. This occurs naturally among most older people, especially those approaching death. Conflicts that were unresolved during earlier years are addressed and dealt with. Reintegration occurs as conflicts are resolved. For some people, the life review process is effective and helpful when a therapist facilitates it through a systematic questioning and listening process. This type of life review therapy has been an important part of *existential social work.*

life script A concept originated by psychiatrist Eric Berne in the 1970s to describe a person's lifelong pattern of behavior, predominant roles, orientation regarding choices, and manner of interacting (transacting) with others. Life scripts have themes (such as martyr, victim, lover, failure, or nurturer), which the person tends to act out regularly. Four general life scripts that Berne-popularizer Thomas Harris identified as guides to transactions are as follows: (1) I'm OK—You're OK, (2) I'm OK—You're not OK, (3) I'm not OK—You're OK, and (4) I'm not OK—You're not OK.

life skills The relative abilities to carry out *activities of daily living (ADL)*, such as home management, budgeting, meal planning and preparation, home maintenance, personal hygiene, the finding and maintenance of appropriate educational and vocational opportunities, the use of the social system to obtain needed assistance, and the maintenance of positive social interactions. See also *junior life skills.*

life skills education Individualized and classroom instruction, practical training, and guidance to help people correct deficits in their *life skills.* Such education often is provided under the auspices of local departments of social or human services.

life–space interview The interview procedure designed to take place around the time and place of important symbolic events in the interviewee's life. The premise is that the effect of the meeting at such times and places is so powerful that it more than makes up for the time taken by the interviewer to be available at such times.

life–space social work Professional social work intervention based on the concepts of the *life–space interview* that takes place outside the walls of the agency and in the environment of the client at times that are important to the client.

lifestyle One's manner of living, as influenced by learning and culture; age and physical abilities; socioeconomic status; ethnic, religious, and sexual orientation; personality characteristics; and geographic and environmental opportunities. The term was coined in 1929 by Austrian psychoanalyst Alfred Adler (1870–1937). See also *quality of life* and *standard of living*.

lifestyle-associated disorder A health problem brought about by an individual's manner of living rather than a specific disease. Examples of such disorders may include *obesity* and physical weakness as a result of a lack of exercise.

light therapy The use of artificial bright light for the treatment of winter *depression* and *seasonal affective disorder (SAD)*.

limbic system That part of the brain beneath the cortex that helps regulate long-term memory functions and emotions, especially rage, fear, and sexual arousal. The limbic system also is involved in the transmission of information between the brain and the body's peripheral sensory and motor systems.

limited beneficence In social work practice, actions to enhance the well-being of others that are carefully circumscribed to protect clients from harm without interfering with their basic liberties (for example, important medical or financial decisions). See also *beneficence* and *selective beneficence*.

"limousine liberal" A term of disparagement applied to affluent citizens who advocate programs for poor and disadvantaged people but who do not tend to personally work or associate with them. It is similar to the term *checkbook activism*.

Lindeman, Eduard C. (1885–1953) A social work theorist and educator at the New York School of Social Work from 1924 to 1950. Lindeman developed many of the conceptual foundations of *com-munity organization* and *social group work*. He fought to keep the social context within social work during its movement toward intrapsychic concerns and sought to develop the integrated, holistic view of social work. He was also called the "father of adult education" in the United States. See also *Lane Report*.

line-item budget A financial statement listing each of the objects of expected expenditures for the forthcoming year, often presented by comparing the expenditures for each item with those of the previous year.

line-item veto The action of a nation's chief executive to exclude a portion of a spending bill that the legislative bodies have passed. The executive rules out that portion of the total bill (by crossing a line through the rejected budget item and initialing the line). This action would presumably enable the overall budget to be implemented without having to include all the minor attachments that individual legislators have added to the budget proposal.

line of business A *health maintenance organization (HMO)*, *preferred provider organization (PPO)*, or other health plan set up within a company, often an insurance company. A line of business is differentiated from a subsidiary or separate company.

linear causality The idea that one event is the cause and another is the result or response. This notion has been questioned by many family systems theorists who suggest that it is too simplistic, at least where families are concerned. They say *circular causality* is a more accurate depiction of the way people, especially families, influence one another—that is, not in a cause–effect relationship but through a series of repeating cycles and interacting loops.

linear perspective The term used by family therapists with a *systems theories* perspective to describe people who think in cause–effect terms. To have a linear perspective is to view behavior and events as resulting directly from specific causes rather than as being part of an endless cycle in a system. The linear perspective is said to be narrow and rigid because it does not consider the myriad influences and circularity of patterns that exist in social and environmental systems.

linkage In social work, the function of bringing together the resources of different agencies, personnel, voluntary groups, and relevant individuals and brokering or coordinating their efforts on behalf of a client or social objective. See also *collaboration*.

linking The procedure used in group therapy and social work with groups to encourage clients to relate more closely with others in the group by pointing out how one client's experience seems similar to that of another group member's.

liquidation Dismantling of an organization or estate by settling all its obligations and debts and distributing its remaining assets.

listening skills The ability to acquire and process the verbal and other cues of another and generally comprehend the meaning of the communication. When such skills are effective they include looking at and acknowledging the communicator; hearing and noting the other's words and accompanying gestures; and providing feedback, questions, and expressions of understanding when appropriate.

listening training Formal or informal educational activities to help individuals enhance their listening and attending skills. This training usually includes assessing the individual's current attending or hearing habits, demonstrating more effective habits, and providing practice opportunities and exercises.

listeriosis An illness caused by the listeria bacteria, usually due to consuming improperly handled contaminated food. The resulting flulike symptoms are especially dangerous to pregnant mothers, unborn babies, and people with weakened immune systems.

literacy The ability to read and write.

literacy test Examination of an individual's capacity for reading and writing. Often such exams have been used to keep some people of color, ethnic groups, and disadvantaged people from access to voting, jobs, education, or other opportunities.

literacy volunteer programs National organizations of trained volunteers who provide, at no cost, individualized and peer-group tutorial services to people who need help with reading and writing skills and, in cases of limited English proficiency, help in the English language. The largest of these

are Literacy Volunteers of America and the Literacy Program of Laubach.

lithium carbonate The chemical compound that in carbonated form is used in the treatment of bipolar disorder. It is generally taken more than once a day and must be monitored closely by trained medical professionals. There is a narrow range of effective dosage above which toxicity occurs and below which it is ineffective. Common trade names are Eskalith and Lithane.

litigant An individual or organization actively involved in a lawsuit either as a plaintiff or defendant.

litigation 1. Civil and other disputes contested in courts of law. 2. The process of being involved in legal action.

litigious client A recipient of professional services who indicates a predisposition to initiate a lawsuit. See also *malpractice*.

litigophobia The excessive *fear* of being sued or otherwise involved in legal actions.

little people The minority group comprising people who, as adults, are no taller than 4 feet 11 inches or who have disproportionately shorter limbs. The Little People of America (LPA) provides information to average-size parents of these children; raises funds for medical research; sponsors recreational activities; and advocates for equal opportunities for little people in jobs, housing, and civil rights. The LPA wants the public to call its members "little people," not "dwarfs" or "midgets."

live supervision A technique for enhancing clinical skills whereby the supervisor sits in on sessions or observes them in progress through one-way mirrors or closed-circuit television monitors and periodically points out various client dynamics and suggests different approaches or techniques.

living wage Income received by a worker that is enough to cover the costs of housing, food, health care, and other social and physical needs. What is generally considered a living wage tends to be much higher than a federally sanctioned *minimum wage*.

living will A formal statement made while the person is mentally competent that specifies an individual's wishes about the management of his or her own death. The statement is made particularly about the possibility of maintaining life, when viability and cognitive functions are impaired, by means of life support systems. State-specific documents are available from *Partnership for Caring.* See also *Patient Self-Determination Act* and *death with dignity.*

loan shark A moneylender who charges excessive interest for instant cash and sometimes recovers the money by taking the client's property or through threats or actual violence. See also *fence, usury,* and *predatory lending.*

lobbyist One who seeks direct access to lawmakers to influence legislation and public policy. The term derived from their use of legislative house lobbies where they sought out lawmakers. See also *legislative advocacy.*

Local Indian Child Welfare Committee (LICWAC) A legally mandated group (by federal and tribal laws) made up of American Indians from the relevant geographic region and tribe who provide input in cases involving the possible removal of Indian children from their families. LICWACs are established to help enforce the *Indian Child Welfare Act of 1978* (P.L. 95-561), and their recommendations (to keep the family intact if possible or otherwise to place the child with another Indian of the same tribe) are almost always followed.

localized amnesia See *psychogenic amnesia.*

location bound An individual who is constricted to living in a region or area because of social or health factors. Some reasons include a spouse's employment or preferences; the need to care for aging parents; the need for children to be near special-education facilities; and breathing disorders requiring residence in a clean, dry climate. See also *homebound.*

lockjaw See *tetanus.*

locura A term used by Spanish-speaking people to describe individuals who experience severe psychotic symptoms, including hallucinations, incoherence, unpredictability, and sometimes violent behavior.

"log rolling" Legislators helping one another to get bills passed. For example, Senator A votes for Senator B's bill not because of the virtues of the bill but because Senator B has agreed to support Senator A's bill in turn.

logical positivism The orientation that accepts as meaningful only that which can be verified by empirical procedures or logic.

logorrhea Excessive and frequently incoherent verbalization, sometimes a symptom of *anxiety, paranoia,* and *schizophrenia.*

logotherapy The meaning-oriented philosophy and treatment method developed in 1967 by Victor Frankl and others and used by members of many disciplines to help people search for the humanistic and spiritual significance of their lives.

loneliness A feeling of discomfort, longing, depression, or anxiety that people sometimes experience when they are, or believe they are, lacking the company of others. The term is not synonymous with aloneness or isolation because people sometimes seek to be alone and feel good when they achieve it.

long-range planning Efforts to assess objectives and examine proposed programs, services, and resources to establish priorities for an extended period in the future. The long-range planner supplements the normal year-by-year decision-making process with a comprehensive overview of goals and the means needed to achieve them over periods often exceeding five or 10 years.

long-term care (LTC) A system of providing social, personal, and health care services over a sustained period to people who in some way suffer from *functional impairment,* including a limited ability to perform *activities of daily living (ADL).* LTC services are required mostly by older people, adults with developmental disabilities, people with mental illness, and people with *HIV disease.* It is provided by professionals, family members, and volunteers under public or private auspices in nursing homes, boarding houses, assisted-living centers, day care centers, and community-based facilities. In addition to health care and case management services, LTC services include transportation, escort, *homemaker services,* night sitting, recreation, *home health services,* home meals, and *ombudsperson* services. See also *long-term long-term care (LTLTC).*

long-term long-term care (LTLTC) A designation applied by health care providers to indicate *long-term care (LTC)* that lasts 90 days or more and to distinguish it from *short-term long-term care (STLTC)*, which is fewer than 90 days.

long-term therapy   *Psychotherapy* or other forms of intervention in which the professional and the client expect to meet regularly for longer than three months, often years. In this form of therapy, the goals are extensive and usually not specified or even precisely known in advance, and the issues dealt with in the sessions are not restricted. See also *short-term therapy*.

longevity   The length or duration of life.

longitudinal study   Repeated testing of the same phenomenon or group of subjects over an extended period.

Lookout Book   The computer list compiled by the *Bureau of Immigration and Customs Enforcement (ICE)* that identifies specific people who are barred from entering the United States. The official name is National Immigration Lookout System (NAILS).

loose association   The tendency to shift abruptly from one thought to another with little, if any, apparent direct connection between the thoughts. Loose association is sometimes a symptom of severe anxiety or depression and in its more severe forms can be a symptom of psychotic processes or *primary process thinking*.

loose coupling   A concept administrators use to understand the nature of social welfare organizations and their environments. Although the organization is necessarily interdependent with the environment (coupled), its response can be flexible. Its self-modifications need not be immediate or extensive because environmental effects are usually unclear and incremental. See also *ambiguous mandate*.

Lord Shaftesbury   See *Shaftesbury, Lord*.

lordosis   Excessive curvature in the lower back. See also *scoliosis* and *kyphosis*.

Lorenz curve   A graphic representation, developed by economist M. O. Lorenz, of a nation's existing degree of income inequality. The vertical axis of the graph represents the percentage of the nation's total family income. The horizontal axis indicates the percentage of families that receive a specified level of income. Thus, a nation with perfect income equality would be represented by a 45-degree line, because 10 percent of the nation's families receive 10 percent of total income, and so on. The amount of deviation from that line indicates the degree of inequality.

loss   The state of being deprived of something that was once possessed, as a result of death, divorce, disaster, or crime. Social workers and other professionals consider loss to be the crucial element in crisis and a major precipitator of many forms of depression.

loss of consortium   The inability of one's spouse to have sexual intercourse as before, due to some accident, negligence, or mistreatment.

lottery visa   See *Diversity Immigrant Visa Program*.

love   A combination of biologically based, culturally modified perceptions, feelings, and actions signifying strong affection and attachment. Every person's experience of love and ways of expressing it are unique. There is considerable variability among people and even within the same person from one time to the next. This is because each person's genetic makeup, physiology, stage of development, cultural background, and immediate stimuli, all of which contribute to the way love is experienced, vary. Thus, it is probable that when any two people profess love, they are not communicating about exactly the same thing; also, what one person means when professing love one minute is probably not what that person means when using the term later.

Love, Maria Maltby (1840–1931)   An early developer of the *Charity Organization Societies (COSs)*, she advocated for reform in housing conditions for poor people and outreach programs for impoverished families. In 1881 she developed the Fitch Crèch, the first day care nursery for the children of working women.

low-birthweight (LBW) baby   A neonate condition in which the infant weighs less than 2,500 g regardless of gestational age. The *National Institutes of Health* identifies an LBW baby as one who weighs less than 5.5 pounds at birth and a very low birthweight baby as weighing less than three pounds, five ounces at birth. The condition may be related to nutritional deficiencies, neglect, disease, genetic factors, drug addiction, or other problems. LBW babies are at risk of premature death; central to their survival is control of fluid balances and modern neonatal hardware, including radiant warmers, phototherapy, ventilators, arterial catheters, and cardiorespiratory monitors. Some professionals also consider LBW babies to be any nonprematurely born infants who weigh significantly less than established norms.

Low-Income Home Energy Assistance Program The federal program of the *U.S. Department of Health and Human Services (HHS)* that helps poor families pay their heating bills.

Lowell, Josephine Shaw (1843–1905) A leader in the *scientific philanthropy* movement, a forerunner of professional social work. Lowell was a founder of the *Charity Organization Societies (COSs)* and a founder and first president of the *National Consumers League (NCL).*

lower class According to sociologists, the *socioeconomic class* in which people tend to have the least amount of income and financial security, the poorest job prospects, minimal educational attainments, and orientations that often include apathy and hopelessness.

LSD Lysergic acid diethylamide, also known simply as "acid," a synthetic *hallucinogen* that produces changes in sensation and perception, sometimes resulting in *hallucination,* changes in the thought process, flashbacks, and depression.

lucidity The degree to which a person seems to experience clear perceptions and the ability to communicate about the experience.

luddite One who avoids or does not understand technological advances and prefers the use of more familiar tools and traditional ways of doing things. The name comes from Ned Ludd, a mythical figure who was said to have led groups to destroy machinery.

"lumbago" A term, used mostly by older people, for lower back pain.

lunacy An obsolete term of ridicule, once used as a synonym for *psychosis* or *insanity.* The basis for words such as "lunatic," "loony," and "looney tune," it derives from "lunar" because of the erroneous belief by some people that the full moon frequently brought out psychoses in people.

"lunatic fringe" A term of disparagement applied to people and groups who are extremely devoted to their political or social causes. To those less zealous about the issue, these people seem likely to commit unreasonable or illegal actions in support of their views.

lupus A chronic disease in which the antibodies in the person's immune system attack the body's own substances. It can attack only the skin or any other organ. Symptoms include a butterfly-shaped rash on the face and tissue inflammation. Heart, joint, kidney, skin, and connective tissue disorders are also common. The disease is often misdiagnosed or not taken seriously.

Lutheran Social Services The organization of social agencies affiliated with the Lutheran Church, with branches in major communities throughout the United States, that provides family services, child welfare services, services for older people, and other social services for all families and individuals in need. See also *sectarian services* and *faith-based social services.* Their Web site address is http://www.lssnca.org

Lutheran World Federation (LWF) The international Lutheran Church–based organization that raises funds and provisions and distributes needed resources to those populations victimized by poverty and disasters. Their Web site address is http://www.lutheranworld.org

lygophobia Excessive and intense fear of the dark.

Lyme disease Disorder transmitted by infected ticks. Symptoms, which appear within seven to 10 days after the tick bite, may include an expanding skin rash, numbness, pain, fever, stiffness, headache, and, possibly much later, arthritis and heart problems. Prompt treatment with antibiotics is usually effective.

lymph nodes Pea-sized organs distributed throughout the body to facilitate the immune system; when antigens enter the body and enter the lymph fluid they are filtered out by the lymph nodes for attack by the immune system.

lymphoma One of the four major types of *cancer* (including *carcinoma, sarcoma,* and *leukemia*), which involves the lymphatic system.

Machiavellian A style of political leadership characterized by ruthless pragmatism and manipulation of the populace through propaganda, coercion, bribes, and appeal to religious and moral codes. These ideas originated in the work of Florentine political theorist Niccolo Machiavelli (1469–1526), especially in his 1513 book *The Prince.*

macho Public display, often exaggerated, of behavior and appearance considered masculine.

macro orientation In social work, an emphasis on the sociopolitical, historical, economic, and environmental forces that influence the overall human condition, cause problems for individuals, or provide opportunities for their fulfillment and equality. This perspective is contrasted with social work's *micro orientation.*

macro practice *Social work practice* aimed at bringing about improvements and changes in the general society. Such activities include some types of political action, community organization, public education campaigning, and the administration of broad-based social services agencies or public welfare departments.

macroeconomics The study of production, distribution, and consumption of a nation, society, or the world, as influenced by long-term trends, ecological changes, international relations, and large-scale technological advances. See also *microeconomics.*

macular degeneration An eye disease that primarily affects people older than 60, caused by breakdown of the light-sensitive thin tissue at the back of the eye, known as the macula. With this deterioration vision is impaired in the center of the retina, usually making it difficult for the person to read, drive, or perform tasks that require looking straight ahead. Those most at risk are older persons, women, smokers, people with high cholesterol, and people with family histories of macular degeneration.

MAGI Modified adjusted gross income; the annual amount of earned income less deductions one

reports to the *Internal Revenue Service (IRS),* plus any tax-free interest income received during that year. The resulting MAGI figure is used by the *Social Security Administration (SSA)* in calculating the retirement benefit one may receive.

magical thinking The pattern of reasoning and mental imaging in which an individual attributes experiences and perceptions to unnatural phenomena. For example, a client might attribute winning a lottery bet to wearing a lucky hat. Magical thinking is often seen in young children and in those with *schizophrenia.* It is the idea that one's thoughts or desires influence the environment or cause events to occur. It is normal in children younger than age five and is also commonly seen among some uneducated people and in certain relatively isolated societies. Among mature people in modern society, it may be a symptom of certain mental disturbances such as *paranoia.* See also *ideas of reference.*

magistrates court Local and lower courts, often officiated by justices of the peace or magistrates, to adjudicate minor crimes such as speeding, parking violations, and loitering and to perform civil marriages.

magnet school assistance program Federal grants and expertise to qualified local school districts to help them reduce minority group isolation. Schools encourage students from different socioeconomic, ethnic, and racial backgrounds to enroll by offering unique and special educational programs.

magnet schools Public schools established within public school districts to allow students to voluntarily participate in unique curricula and methods of instruction. Most magnet schools have well-defined educational goals and provide further education in special areas of interest such as science, the arts, business and technology, and vocational arts.

magnetic resonance imaging (MRI) A computer-based diagnostic tool physicians use to envision neurological activity and other physiological processes. MRI is replacing computerized axial tomography *(CAT scan)* because it provides cross-sectional, two-dimensional images of higher resolution without exposing the patient to radiation.

maim   Inflicting bodily injury or mutilation.

mainframe   A large-capacity, high-speed computer system, as opposed to "personal computers" or microprocessors.

"mainlining"   A slang expression to describe the injection of a narcotic drug, usually *heroin,* directly into the bloodstream through a vein.

mainstreaming   Bringing people who have some exceptional characteristics into the living, working, or educational environments to which all others have access. In education, for example, a child with certain learning or physical disabilities is permitted to attend classes and activities available to all the other children. Mainstreaming permits individuals to have greater opportunity for *socialization* and *integration.* However, it also subjects them to greater risks of social rejection and reduction of special care. See also *"least-restrictive environment" (LRE), inclusion, free appropriate public education,* and *Individuals with Disabilities Education Act (IDEA).*

maintenance   Money paid to a former spouse by the other in accordance with legal requirements to provide for independent living arrangements. Maintenance is the current term for *alimony* and is distinct from the obligation of child support payments.

maintenance therapy   In the treatment of persons with drug addictions, the use of substitute drugs, usually those that are less harmful and not illicit, to help wean the client from the original substance. Maintenance therapies ideally use the substitute drug along with professional intervention, peer support, and counseling. *Methadone treatment* for heroin users is the most well known of these therapies. *LAMM* and *naltrexone treatment* are similar programs.

major affective disorder   See *mood disorders.*

major depression   One of the *mood disorders* characterized by symptoms such as loss of interest in one's usual activities, irritability, poor appetite, sleeplessness or excessive sleeping, decreased sexual drive, fatigue, psychomotor agitation, feelings of

hopelessness, inability to concentrate, and *suicidal ideation.* Major depression can be subdivided into two groups: the "single episode" (at least four symptoms present almost daily for more than two weeks) and the "recurrent episode" (the episodes come and go for intervals of at least two consecutive months). Someone with major depression may be distinguished from someone with a *bipolar disorder* by the fact that he or she has not had a *manic episode.* Major depression may be distinguished from *dysthymic disorder* in that its symptoms are more severe but occur in discrete episodes that can be distinguished from the person's usual functioning; in dysthymic disorders, the symptoms are almost continuous.

major disaster   A natural or human-made catastrophe of such magnitude that damage, hardship, and suffering are widespread. When the U.S. president declares a major disaster, the area may be entitled to extensive government funding and assistance, including crisis counseling, according to the Stafford Disaster Relief and Emergency Assistance Act (P.L. 100-707). Such disasters, by definition, include hurricanes, tornadoes, storms, high water, wind-driven water, tidal waves, tsunamis, earthquakes, volcanic eruptions, landslides, mudslides, snowstorms, droughts, fires, floods, or explosions, in the United States, that cause damage so severe as to warrant federal disaster assistance to supplement the efforts and available resources of local governments and disaster relief organizations in alleviating the resulting damages and hardships.

major tranquilizer   An *antipsychotic medication* prescribed by physicians to reduce, in people with schizophrenia or other psychoses, symptoms of severe anxiety and hallucination. In the mid-1950s, these drugs were found to be successful in reducing psychotic symptoms but not in curing the psychosis itself. Side effects include dry mouth, drugged feeling, respiratory problems, weight gain, and *tardive dyskinesia (TD).* Trade names for some major tranquilizers include Thorazine, Mellaril, Compazine, Stelazine, Trilafon, Prolixin, Vesprin, Sparine, and Largactil. Other major tranquilizers with slightly different chemical compositions include Haldol, Serpasil, Moderil, Harmonyl, Navane, Taractan, Raudixin, Moban, and Loxitane.

make-work   Nonessential employment provided not to produce something but to give a needy person some activity that results in payment or benefit. Many government programs have been labeled (often inaccurately) as "made-work" or make-work programs, including the *Civilian Conservation Corps (CCC)*, the *Works Progress Administration (WPA)*, the *Job Corps*, and various *workfare* plans.

mal de ojo Spanish for "evil eye," a *culture-bound syndrome* in which the individual, most often a child, experiences fitful sleep, diarrhea, vomiting, fever, and crying without apparent cause.

maladaptive Pertaining to behaviors or characteristics that prevent people from meeting the demands of the environment or achieving personal goals.

maladjustment The inability to develop or maintain the values, thoughts, and behaviors needed to succeed in the environment.

malaise A vague sense of uneasiness, discomfort, or minor depression.

malaria An infectious disease found mostly in tropical areas where *Anopheles* mosquitoes live. These mosquitoes may carry and spread a protozoan parasite that causes the disease. Symptoms include cycles of fever, chills, sweating, aches, vomiting, diarrhea, and jaundice. Left untreated the disease can lead to kidney and liver failure, disorders of the nervous system, coma, and death. Oral or intravenous medications can be effective in preventing or treating the disease.

male climacteric syndrome Often called the "male menopause," a time of adjustment for many men in their sixties and seventies when they are faced with declining physical energy and some diminution of sexual potency. The syndrome does not result from hormonal changes, as in female *menopause.*

male erectile disorder A *sexual disorder* in which a man experiences a persistent or recurrent inability to achieve or maintain penis rigidity (tumescence) sufficient for completion of sexual intercourse, causing marked distress or interpersonal difficulty. By definition this disorder is not the result of a general medical condition or substance abuse. When using this term as a diagnosis, sexual therapists and other clinicians specify whether the condition is lifelong or acquired, generalized or situational, and due to psychological or combined factors. See also *female sexual arousal disorder.*

male orgasmic disorder A *sexual disorder* in which a man experiences persistent or recurrent delay or absence of orgasm following a normal sexual excitement phase. See also *female orgasmic disorder.*

malfeasance Wrongful or unlawful conduct committed intentionally, usually by someone holding a public office. See also *misfeasance* and *nonfeasance.*

malingering The act of feigning disability or illness, usually to avoid some undesired obligations or to achieve some real or imagined personal benefit *(secondary gain)*. See also *factitious disorder.*

malnutrition A physical condition, usually but not necessarily evidenced by *emaciation,* due to an insufficiency of needed food elements. Primary malnutrition is caused by a deficiency in the quantity or quality of foods containing essentials such as protein, vitamins, and minerals. This may result from an overall scarcity of food, from the individual's economic inability to purchase food, or from poor eating habits. Secondary malnutrition is caused by the body's inability to use or absorb certain nutrients, as sometimes happens in diseases of the pancreas, liver, thyroid, kidneys, and gastrointestinal system. Some of the diseases of malnutrition are *rickets, scurvy, beriberi, pellagra, kwashiorkor,* and some forms of *anemia.*

malpractice Willful or negligent behavior by a professional person that violates the relevant *code of ethics* and professional standards of care and that proves harmful to the client. Among a social worker's actions most likely to result in malpractice are inappropriate divulging of confidential information, unnecessarily prolonged services, improper termination of needed services, misrepresentation of one's knowledge or skills, the provision of social work treatment as a replacement for needed medical treatment, the provision of information to others that is libelous or that results in improper incarceration, financial exploitation of the client, sexual activity with a client, and physical injury to the client that may occur in the course of certain treatments (such as group encounters).

malpractice insurance An *indemnification* agreement in which a financial organization protects a professional from specified economic losses due to *malpractice* or accusations of malpractice. Usually the insurer agrees to reimburse the practitioner, who is legally compelled to pay for harm done to the client up to a predetermined amount. In most coverages the insurer also helps cover the costs of a legal defense. See also *Insurance Trust, NASW.*

Malthusian theory Ideas proposed by English economist Thomas R. Malthus (1766–1834) stating that populations will increase in geometric ratio (2–4–8–16–32, and so on), whereas food supplies and other necessities can only increase in arithmetic ratios (2–3–4–5, and so on). According to the theory, this leads to overpopulation problems unless controlled by war, natural disasters, or sexual restraint. This theory was used, in part, to justify the sufferings of poor people, especially at the beginning of the Industrial Revolution.

mammography X-ray screening to detect breast cancer.

"man in the house" rule A provision, once common in many welfare programs, to curtail assistance if a man, whether related to the family or not, lived with them. Most states ended the practice in the 1960s through legislation and court rulings.

managed care Participation of third parties (beyond physician and patient) in the delivery of health care services and procedures for monitoring the delivery of health care and health care benefit plans. The goal is to control overuse of services and overcharging by professionals and to ensure that proposed health care is consistent with accepted standards. Monitoring is primarily done through peer review and utilization review, although for social workers the monitoring is sometimes conducted by physicians.

managed care organizations (MCOs) Regulated groups of health care professionals, administrators, and ancillary staff who provide for employers a full range of health care services for their employees. The MCO offers the services to the employer at negotiated rates directly or by subcontracting with networks of institutional and individual providers. Thus, employers avoid the costs and inconveniences of providing health care insurance for employees.

managed competition A system in which vendors are free to develop the most desirable services or products at the best possible price to attract consumers, but within the rules and constraints established in advance by the competing organizations or overseers, such as a government body. This term is not synonymous with *managed health care program.*

managed health care program 1. Health care delivery systems within the context of fiscal responsibility. 2. A formal network of health care personnel, third-party funding organizations, and other fiscal intermediaries that provide for health care costs in exchange for regular premium payments. Cost containment, effective marketing, and provider oversight are emphasized in many of these programs. See also *preferred provider organizations (PPOs)* and *health maintenance organization (HMO).*

management See *administration in social work.*

management by objectives (MBO) The administrative procedure in which an organization's members reach *consensus* about group results to be achieved, the resources to be devoted to each result, and the deadline for reaching objectives. Inherent in this managerial approach is a clear and accessible budget, specified performance criteria, managers to assess the criteria, and procedural monitoring that encourages individual group members to assess progress.

management information systems (MISs) An administrative method often used in social agencies to acquire, process, analyze, and disseminate data that are useful for carrying out the goals of the organization efficiently. MISs may be used to track staff activity and the services that are provided to clients.

management tasks The principal activities of a social welfare administrator or manager. The six basic management tasks are (1) planning and developing the program, (2) acquiring financial resources and support, (3) designing organizational structures and processes, (4) developing and maintaining staff capability, (5) assessing agency programs, and (6) changing agency programs.

mandamus A court order that requires the performance of an act.

mandate The authority, expectations, and requirements to carry out some order or desire expressed by those to whom the administrator is responsible, such as the voters, the customers, or the government entity that pays the agency for the services to be rendered. See also *ambiguous mandate, competing mandate,* and *conflicting mandate.*

mandated benefits   Health care benefits that the law requires health care plans to provide. Mandated benefits vary widely from state to state.

mandated client   One who uses the services of a social worker or other professional involuntarily, usually as a requirement imposed by some other authority. For example, a judge mandates a convicted felon to see a social worker as a condition of probation or a suspended sentence.

mandatory community service   Also known as "compulsory volunteering," the requirement to perform some specified task or activity for the good of the public that is imposed on an individual through the pressure of legal authority or social acceptance.

mandatory retirement   The requirement that employees who have reached a previously specified age relinquish their jobs. With passage of the *Age Discrimination in Employment Act (ADEA) of 1967* and enforcement by the *Equal Employment Opportunity Commission (EEOC),* mandatory retirement is generally prohibited. However, ADEA has some exceptions: Company executives older than 65, tenured university professors older than 70, and law enforcement officials older than the state age of retirement may be asked to retire under certain circumstances.

mandatory sentencing   Laws and policies imposed on judges and juries specifying the minimum amount of time in incarceration one must serve for each category of crime. Sentencing guidelines have been established to achieve greater consistency and fairness in sentencing offenders and to reduce unwarranted variability. Critics argue that these laws are necessary to constrain judges who are "soft on crime." See also *three strikes laws.*

mania   1. An intense preoccupation with some kind of idea or activity, as in *kleptomania, nymphomania,* and *pyromania.* Some other specific types of mania include ablutomania (washing hands), erotomania (sexual gratification), graphomania (writing), kleptomania (stealing), megalomania (being important), and pyromania (setting or watching fires). 2. A state of agitation,

accelerated thinking, hyperactivity, and excessive elation seen in some major affective disorders (such as the *manic episode* in *manic–depressive illness*) and certain *organic mental disorders.* 3. A lay term used in describing *insanity* or "mental breakdowns" in which the individual seems violent or highly agitated.

manic–depressive illness   A disorder characterized by profound *mood swings* ranging from deep, prolonged *depression* to excited, euphoric, agitated behavior. Genetic and chemical studies are beginning to suggest an organic basis for this illness. The term has been replaced in the diagnostic nomenclature of mental health professionals by the label *bipolar disorder.*

manic episode   A symptom found in some of the *mood disorders,* especially *bipolar disorder,* consisting of an abnormally and persistently elevated, expansive, or irritable mood lasting at least four days. This may include feelings of inflated self-esteem, *grandiosity,* pressured speech, *flight of ideas,* distractibility, and *psychomotor* agitation, all of which are a clear departure from the individual's usual mood and functioning. See also *hypomanic episode.*

manipulative behavior   Actions intended to control and often exploit the thoughts, feelings, or responses of others. The behavior may be intentional or unconscious, and it may be motivated by efforts either to help or to harmfully take advantage of the other person.

Mann Act   The federal laws ("White-Slave" Laws: 36 Stat. 263 and 36 Stat. 825) passed in 1910 that prohibit taking a person, usually a woman, across state lines for "immoral purposes," such as *prostitution.*

Manning, Leah Hicks (1917–1979)   After receiving her social work degrees, she helped establish Inter-Tribal Councils for Native American groups and, in her position with the *Bureau of Indian Affairs (BIA),* she helped establish the *Indian Child Welfare Act (ICWA)* of 1978 to keep Indian children on reservations with their families.

Manpower Development and Training Act of 1962   The federal legislation (P.L. 87-415) that funded state employment agencies and private enterprise for on-the-job training to help workers acquire needed employment skills. In 1973, these programs were incorporated into *CETA.* See also *Economic Opportunity Act of 1964* and *Job Corps.*

"manpower planning" An obsolete term for defining the problems and personnel needs of an organization. The preferred term is "human resources planning."

manslaughter The unlawful, but unpremeditated, killing of another person. Laws in most jurisdictions distinguish between voluntary and involuntary manslaughter. The involuntary type refers to causing death through criminally negligent acts such as reckless driving. The voluntary type is an intentional *homicide* under mitigating but not justifiable circumstances, such as killing someone who has provoked uncontrollable rage or terror.

mantengo Colloquial term used especially by people of Puerto Rican heritage for public assistance, welfare programs, and other forms of government aid.

MAO inhibitors *Psychotropic drugs* prescribed by physicians primarily to relieve the symptoms of *depression* in certain patients. These drugs reduce the metabolism of monoamine oxidase (MAO) after it has been released into the synaptic space, which ultimately eases neural transmission. The process takes up to three weeks before depressive symptoms can be relieved. Some side effects include dry mouth, fatigue, and impotence in men. MAO inhibitors are one of the two important types of *antidepressant medication,* the other being the tricyclics (for example, Elavil, Tofranil, Vivactyl, or Sinequan). Trade names of MAO inhibitors include Marplan, Parnate, and Nardil.

maquiladoras People who work in manufacturing and assembly factories owned by U.S. corporations and located in Mexican border towns. Many of these plants have exploited workers, paying them low wages with few benefits.

marasmus A gradual deterioration and *emaciation* found in some infants and young children, particularly those who are cared for in institutional settings. Often, the child appears to have the symptoms of *malnutrition.* Many investigators believe marasmus is sometimes caused by a child's not being touched, held, fondled, and parented.

marathon group A form of *group psychotherapy* or *sensitivity group* in which participants remain together for extended periods, often 18 to 24 hours or more.

March of Dimes The fundraising organization established in 1938 by President Franklin D. Roosevelt as the National Foundation for Infantile Paralysis. The early appeal was to children and their families by having them contribute 10 cents or more toward the eradication of polio. After development of the Salk and Sabin vaccines, the organization focused on the prevention of birth defects, maternity problems, and neonatal care. The organization is now known as the "March of Dimes Mother's March." Their Web site address is http://www.modimes.org/mothersmarch

Marfan's syndrome A hereditary congenital disorder of connective tissue characterized by abnormally long and slender limbs.

marginalized groups Relatively powerless people who, because they belong to a certain socioeconomic class, age cohort, labor organization, political affiliation, gender, racial or ethnic group, or religious group, are seen as being of little importance by the dominant cultural group.

marginally attached workers People who have been seeking jobs within the past 12 months but not for the past four weeks. They are no longer counted as unemployed by the U.S. Department of Labor because they have not been actively seeking jobs recently. (Marginally attached workers who are identified as not seeking employment recently because they believe no jobs are available for which they qualify are known as *discouraged workers.*)

Mariel boatlift The rapid influx of Cuban refugees into the United States during a six-month period ending in September 1980. Over 130,000 Cubans, mostly anti-Castro relatives of Cuban Americans, debarked from the Cuban port at Mariel Bay. Cuban leader Fidel Castro also placed 20,000 people convicted of crimes and patients of mental institutions on the boatlift, which placed a burden on U.S. health, justice, and social services organizations. Immigrants to the United States from this group are known as "Marielistas."

marijuana *Cannabis,* a plant in which the active ingredient, tetrahydrocannabinol *(THC),* induces mild *euphoria,* certain intensified sensory impressions, and drowsiness when taken into the system either by smoking or ingestion. Some research indicates that its harmful effects include increased risk of heart and lung diseases, increased likelihood of accidents, loss of motivation, and possibly a greater risk of genetic problems for succeeding generations.

marital contracts The expectations and motives that each partner brings to the marriage. These expectations and motives may be *conscious* or *unconscious* in the person who holds them and may or may not be known to the partner. In healthy marriages, each person's contracts become known to both, and agreements are reached so that the husband's and wife's individual contracts become jointly shared. In those marriages in which the contracts remain concealed and separate, the couple is prone to confusion, suspicion, and disappointment with one another. The term also indicates formal, written, and legally enforced agreements made between marrying couples, usually to specify the financial terms and obligations each partner is to assume. See also *prenuptial agreement* and *postnuptial agreement.*

marital property Assets acquired by a couple during the course of their marriage, but not including any property owned before that marriage.

marital skew A *family therapy* term indicating that a husband or wife dominates the other and controls the relationship or takes the lead in maintaining its healthy or unhealthy aspects.

marital therapy Intervention procedures used by social workers, family therapists, and other professionals to help couples resolve their relationship, communications, sexual, economic, and other family problems. There are many theoretical orientations, treatment models, and therapy techniques. The major theoretical approaches currently used by social workers include the psychosocial, behavioral, and systems orientations. Treatment models include *conjoint therapy, concurrent therapy, collaborative therapy,* and *couples group therapy.*

market basket A concept used in the *Consumer Price Index* to model the relative costs of living. The market basket is made up of goods and services that typical consumers must purchase to maintain their daily lives at their current standard of living. It is calculated based on reports about the amount spent on each item in the basket from a representative sample of households.

market strategy In social welfare policy development, the premise that the nation's free economic institutions can provide needed social ser-

vices without distracting from the work ethic, without the need for extensive public service delivery systems, and without centralized planning. Critics of this strategy contend that this method of delivery of benefits will favor those with the most resources and deprive those who have the greatest disadvantages. See also *social marketing.*

marriage A legally and socially sanctioned union between two people resulting in mutual obligations and rights. Traditionally this union has been between one woman and one man. However, some societies, subcultural groups, religious organizations, and legal jurisdictions have sanctioned unions between members of the same sex, between several people, or between one person and a spiritual entity.

marriage counseling A form of *marital therapy.* Many professionals consider the term "marriage counseling" to be synonymous with "marital therapy." Others believe that "counseling" is less intense and more directive and deals with couples who may be less troubled. Research has not demonstrated significant differences between the two. Nevertheless, many professionals who treat couples prefer the term "marital therapy" because they believe it conveys a more technical and sophisticated repertoire of techniques and has a more theoretical and professional orientation.

marriage encounter An *encounter group* comprising several married couples who explore feelings, mutual understandings, and *conflict resolution* to improve their relationships.

marriage enrichment Programs, which grew out of the human potential movement in the 1960s, to help couples achieve more satisfying and meaningful relationships with one another. A wide variety of formats, procedures, and techniques have emerged. Generally, the programs are group encounters that use techniques to improve communication and understanding for couples whose relationships are not especially dysfunctional. A variation of marriage enrichment is *relationship enrichment,* which uses the same procedures but applies them to domestic partners, dating couples, and other family dyads. The Association for Couples in Marriage Enrichment (ACME) sponsors training programs, conferences, publications, and couples workshops.

marriage penalty Financial disadvantages to married couples that exist in current U.S. tax laws and entitlement programs, including federal income taxes, social security, welfare eligibility, and the Earned Income Tax Credit (EITC) program. Many people choose not to marry, but otherwise live as though they are, to circumvent these financial disincentives.

Marsh Report   The 1943 recommendations by Canadian social workers and others that were a major factor in the development of Canada's present social welfare system. See also *Beveridge Report.*

Marxism   The sociopolitical ideology, based on the work of Karl Marx (1818–1883) and Frederick Engels (1820–1895), that advocates a classless society so that the efforts of workers (proletariat) are no longer exploited by those who control the means of production (bourgeoisie). In the Marxist scenario, a class struggle and revolution lead to the overthrow of *capitalism,* which is temporarily replaced by a socialistic system of dictatorship of the workers and finally by the classless society known as *communism.* The scenario has been influential in the political and economic systems of many nations but has never been fully realized, usually stopping at the dictatorship of the proletariat stage.

masochism   1. The *conscious* or *unconscious* tendency to seek opportunities to be physically or emotionally hurt. 2. A *sexual disorder* of the *paraphilia* class in which the individual becomes sexually excited through being harmed, threatened, or humiliated. See also *sadomasochism* and *self-defeating personality disorder.*

masochistic personality disorder   See *self-defeating personality disorder.*

mass destruction   The sudden killing of large numbers of people and severe damage to infrastructure through tactics such as detonating nuclear devices; releasing toxic chemicals into the environment; and planting bombs in dams, buildings, stadiums, and other places where people have congregated. Weapons of mass destruction include nuclear bombs, missiles, biological or chemical devices, and "conventional" weapons used in civilian spaces.

matching grants   A procedure for raising funds and motivating organizations to allocate funds for certain programs. To raise funds, a contributor promises to give the organization an amount of money that is equal to or a percentage of the amount received from other sources during a specified period. Federal and state governments also use the procedure to motivate localities to develop certain programs by promising to give a specified amount of money for every dollar the locality contributes.

Maternal and Child Health Bureau (MCHB)   The bureau within the U.S. Health Resources and Services Administration of HHS that promotes the health of U.S. mothers and children. Tracing its origins to the *Children's Bureau,* established in 1912, and the Social Security system, established in 1935, the MCHB provides block grant funding and facilitates emergency medical services for children, as well as reduces infant mortality though the Healthy Start Initiative. Their Web site address is http://www.mchb.hrsa.gov

maternity benefits   The provision of cash and social and health services to new mothers. Many nations, not including the United States, provide such benefits to all new mothers regardless of their economic status. See also *demogrant* and *family allowance.*

maternity homes   Temporary residential facilities for unwed mothers that often provide counseling, social services, health care, and education as well as shelter away from the expectant mother's usual environment during the pregnancy. Some maternity home personnel help facilitate *adoption, abortion,* reintegration into the community, and financial assistance.

maternity leave   Time off from employment during *pregnancy* and the *neonatal* period. Maternity leave policies vary widely. Some employers grant several months off before and after the birth with full pay and restoration of the job on return. Others permit virtually no paid time off or grant only a few days of "sick leave." Most social workers have long argued for more generous maternity leave policies, saying that their absence discriminates against women or does not recognize that the nation's future well-being depends on encouraging healthy reproduction. See also *parental leave* and *Family and Medical Leave Act (FMLA).*

mathematics disorder   A type of *learning disorder* in which a student is testably below the average in mathematical skills and in understanding numbers concepts that are expected of others of similar ages, intellectual levels, and educational levels and without physical or neurological problems.

For the condition to be diagnosable, it must significantly interfere with the student's academic achievement or activities that require math or calculations skills. Many educators call this disorder *dyscalculia.* The other major types of learning disorders are *reading disorder* and *disorder of written expression.*

matriarchy A social pattern in which mothers or other women are the leaders of the family or group.

matrifocal family A kinship group centered around the mother without a male regularly assuming a husband or father role. A group centered around a father is a *patrifocal family.*

matrilineal society A cultural group in which descent is traced through the mother.

maximum family benefit (MFB) The *Social Security Administration (SSA)* limit on the amount of benefit it will pay to a retired or disabled worker and his or her dependents. If the total benefits due exceed the amount of the MFB, then the worker's benefits are paid in full, but a dependent's benefits are reduced proportionately. MFB amounts are usually equal to 150 percent to 180 percent of the worker's *primary insurance amount (PIA).*

Mayors' Conference The U.S. Conference of Mayors, an organization founded in 1933 of mayors and staffs of the nation's larger cities (over 30,000 population) for which the primary function is to provide a national forum for discussions about federal–city relationships and urban problems. Members meet regularly to coordinate plans and educate political officials about issues including homelessness, economic blight, racial segregation, employment opportunity, transportation, and sanitation.

McJob Minimum-wage employment requiring few skills, with little career potential.

McKinney Homeless Act The first comprehensive U.S. homeless assistance program based on legislation passed in 1987 (Stewart B. McKinney Homeless Assistance Act, P.L. 100-77) to provide access to social services, nutrition, housing services, and especially health care for homeless persons. The program has added several services in recent years, including education and health care for homeless children, but funding has not kept pace with demand. See also *Education for Homeless Children and Youth (EHCY) program.*

McNaughten rule A set of legal principles for the guidance of courts in helping to determine whether or not a defendant may be declared innocent by reason of *insanity.* Based on the 1843 British case of Daniel McNaughten, the accused is considered not responsible for the crime if "laboring under such a defect of reason from disease of the mind as not to know the nature or quality of the act; or, if he did know it, that he did not know that what he was doing was wrong." Some jurisdictions use different criteria for judgments in insanity pleas. For example, the American Law Institute's formulation states that "a person is not responsible for criminal conduct if at the time of such conduct as a result of mental disease or defect he lacks substantial capacity either to appreciate the wrongfulness of his conduct or to conform his conduct to the requirements of law." See also *Durham rule* and *irresistible impulse test.*

meals-on-wheels A home health service, sponsored primarily by local departments of human services, health care facilities, senior citizens centers, or private organizations, to bring prepared food to the homes of people in need.

mean A *measure of central tendency,* also known as the arithmetic average, found by adding scores and dividing this sum by the number of scores. For example, if an agency wanted to know the mean, or average, amount of time each client was seen during a week, it would add the total amount of minutes the agency social workers spent with clients that week and divide this sum by the number of clients seen.

means test Evaluating the client's financial resources and using the result as the criterion to determine *eligibility* to receive a benefit. The client applying for certain economic, social, or health services will be turned down if the investigator determines that the person has the "means" to pay for them. Programs and services that use the means test to determine client eligibility include *Medicaid, Temporary Assistance to Needy Families (TANF),* and the *Food Stamp program.* Means test evaluators usually consider the client's income, assets, debts and other obligations, number of dependents, and health factors. See also *income test.*

measure of central tendency A way of summarizing data about the central portion of frequency distributions in statistics and research. The three types are (1) the *mean,* (2) the *median,* and (3) the *mode.*

measure of dispersion   A statistical depiction of the extent to which individual test scores are spread out or concentrated from a *measure of central tendency*.

Medi-Credit   A proposed health care financing program in which the costs of premiums paid to private health insurance companies could be credited directly against personal income taxes.

media campaigning   A strategy to raise public awareness about a problem or goal and mobilize *social action* toward its elimination or achievement by getting the relevant newspapers and radio and television stations to run stories about it. This is done through activities such as issuing press releases, arranging "photo opportunities" and interviews with reporters, writing letters to the editor, paying for advertising, and preparing free public service messages.

media event   Activity designed to gain publicity; an event that would not happen if reporters or cameras were not present. Social activists and politicians often stage such events to show graphically the extent of a problem or demonstrate their concern about it.

median   A *measure of central tendency,* the point in a distribution that has the same number of scores above and below it. Its advantage over the *mean* in reporting statistical data is that it is unaffected by a few extreme scores.

mediation   Intervention in disputes between parties to help them reconcile differences, find compromises, or reach mutually satisfactory agreements. Social workers have used their unique skills and value orientations in many forms of mediation between opposing groups (for example, landlord–tenant organizations, neighborhood residents–halfway house personnel, labor–management representatives, or divorcing spouses). See also *conciliation; mediation, divorce;* and *adversarial process*.

mediation, divorce   A procedure used by social workers, lawyers, and other professionals to help settle disputes between divorcing couples outside the courtroom adversarial process. In some states mediation occurs under the auspices of the courts, but in other localities it is done as a private service. The goals include helping the couple make mutually acceptable compromises, understand the nature of their marital difficulties, agree on equitable distribution of possessions, make custody arrangements for the children, and disengage emotionally from the unhealthy parts of the relationship.

mediator role   An activity of the social worker or family therapist who sometimes acts as a go-between in getting various members of the family to communicate more clearly and fairly with one another. This role is not the same as in *divorce mediation*. See also *conciliation*.

Medicaid   The health care program established in 1965 to pay for hospital and medical services to people who cannot afford them. Eligibility is based on demonstrating that one's income and resources are insufficient to pay for health care insurance. Funding comes from federal and state governments under the auspices of the HHS *Centers for Medicare and Medicaid Services*. In most areas, the program is administered through local public assistance offices. *Supplemental Security Income (SSI)* recipients may also be helped with Medicaid applications in their local social security offices. Current federal government information about Medicaid is available at http://www.cms.hhs.gov/medicaid

medical day care   A community health care service and facility to provide nursing and other health services to chronically ill or disabled people who do not require intense or frequent attention. The facilities are often located in long-term-care institutions such as state or county hospitals.

medical model   An approach to helping people that is patterned after the orientation used by many physicians. This includes looking at the client as an individual with an illness to be treated, giving relatively less attention to factors in the client's environment, diagnosing the condition with fairly specific labels, and treating the problem through regular clinical appointments.

medical necessity   Services or supplies that are appropriate and consistent with the diagnosis in accord with accepted standards of community practice and are not considered experimental. They also cannot be omitted without adversely affecting the individual's condition or the quality of medical care.

medical social work   The social work practice that occurs in hospitals and other health care settings to facilitate good health, prevent illness, and aid physically ill patients and their families to resolve the social and psychological problems related to the illness. Medical social work also sensitizes other health care providers about the social–psychological aspects of illness.

medical social workers Professional social workers employed in health care settings, primarily to provide for the psychosocial needs of patients and alert other health care providers to the social needs of the patients. For example, in a hospital setting the medical social worker might facilitate the doctor's plan for early discharge of the patient by implementing a program of family and volunteer home care.

medically assisted suicide The intentional act by a medical professional of providing someone with the means and information needed to commit *suicide*. See also *passive euthanasia*.

medically necessary A designation by health insurance and provider organizations to indicate that some treatment procedure is reimbursable. For a condition to receive this designation it must meet the following criteria: The treatment must be offered by a physician or other approved health care provider, it must be effective in treating the condition for which it is prescribed, it is generally accepted as a method of treatment by the professional community, it does not duplicate other services, it is not experimental, and it has the purpose of restoring health and extending life.

medically underserved area (MUA) Local communities, rural areas, reservations, and remote sites that the U.S. government designates as lacking in physician and other health services. The designation is based on factors such as infant mortality rates, mortality rates, percent of older persons in the population, and environmental risk factors of living in that location. With an MUA designation, incentives and special programs may be instituted until the problem is mitigated.

Medicare The U.S. national social insurance health care program for all people older than age 65, plus some other defined populations, administered within the HHS by the *Centers for Medicare and Medicaid Services*. Medicare benefits are in two parts: (1) hospital insurance, including extended care, home health service, and hospice care, and (2) voluntary medical insurance, covering physicians' fees, outpatient services, and other medical

services. Costs are met by social security contributions, monthly premiums from participants, and general federal revenues. Eligibility is not based on need, but on reaching age 65. Current information about Medicare is available online at http://www. cms.hhs.gov/medicare

Medicare/Medicaid Assistance Program (M/MAP) A volunteer program to help people complete their *Medicare* or *Medicaid* forms, sponsored in most states by the *American Association of Retired Persons (AARP)*.

Medicare SELECT A form of *Medigap* (insurance that pays the difference between Medicare benefits and actual costs) that limits benefits to selected health care professionals and is thus less expensive than other Medigap policies.

medication-induced movement disorder Movements, gestures, postures, or muscle rigidity related to the use of medications, usually those prescribed to help the individual with a mental disorder or general medical condition. Some of these disorders most frequently encountered by staffs in mental hospitals and health care facilities include "neuroleptic-induced Parkinsonism" (medications with dopamine-antagonist properties inducing *Parkinson's disease* tremors), malignant syndrome (severe muscle rigidity), acute *dystonia*, acute *akathisia, tardive dyskinesia (TD),* and *postural tremor.*

medications The term used in health care facilities for the medicine prescribed for each patient.

Medicins Sans Frontières See *Doctors Without Borders.*

Medigap Insurance coverage against health care costs that are not reimbursable by *Medicare*. See also *Medicare SELECT.*

medipards Physicians and other health care providers who accept assignment of *Medicare* payments. Many health care providers consider Medicare payments to be less than their services are worth, and the required paperwork to get reimbursed is so great that they decline to accept assignment to serve Medicare-eligible patients. Medicare thus provides a medipard directory listing those providers who will accept assignment; it is available at district social security offices or senior citizens centers.

meditation   A state of concentrated relaxation, the systematic practice of which reportedly leads to feelings of heightened well-being and reduced anxiety. Meditators typically concentrate on and repeat a word, phrase, or sound (for example, a mantra) for about 20 minutes while remaining in a passive attitude, in one comfortable position, and in an environment free of distractions.

MEDLARS   The Medical Analysis and Retrieval System, a program of the National Library of Medicine, *National Institutes of Health (NIH)*. MEDLARS has the ability to interface with the computers of most medical and university libraries so that qualified professionals can have access to the relevant literature and a specific database. Such databases include MEDLINE (biomedical journal articles), MEDLINE PLUS (links to consumer health documents), TOXLINE (information about toxicity, environmental pollution, and adverse drug reactions), and CANCERLIT (the current literature about *cancer* studies). Their Web site address is http://www.nlm.nih.gov/medlars

megalomania   A personality trait characterized by excessive *egocentrism,* grandiose plans for personal influence over many others, and an exaggerated view of self-importance.

Megan's Law   Federal, state, or local legislation requiring law enforcement authorities to notify residents when a convicted sexual offender moves into their community. These statutes are named after a young girl who was sexually assaulted and killed by a convicted sexual offender; the law enforcement authorities knew of his presence in the community but had not informed the residents. See also *sex offender registry.*

melancholic features   Loss of interest or pleasure in all or most activities, or a lack of reaction to usually pleasurable stimuli; *anhedonia.* Clinicians specify melancholic features when they exist in people with major depressive disorders or depressive episodes in bipolar disorders.

melanoma   Tumor composed of cells containing dark pigment. Melanomas are mostly benign, but malignant melanoma is a serious form of skin *cancer.*

meliorism   The belief or ethical doctrine that social conditions are gradually improving or can be made to improve.

melting pot theory   The idea that immigrants to a new nation become socialized and take on the values, norms, and personality characteristics of the majority culture while losing some of their unique cultural traits.

member assistance programs (MAPs)   Labor union–sponsored services for workers using the *employee assistance programs (EAPs)* model. MAPs were originally developed by unions whose members worked for companies without EAPs to provide them with needed social services and also to develop more membership loyalty by providing this benefit. As with EAPs, MAPs often include social services such as *counseling* for *alcohol dependence* and *drug dependence, marital therapy,* and *career counseling.*

membership theory   A formal theory of social work that synthesizes physiological functioning, social interaction, *object relations theory,* and symbolization and that views the professional role as rendering aid in the management of human membership. Humanness, according to this theory, does not rest on individualism but instead is possible only through membership in the community and social structures that are derived from it. The orientation, which was first delineated by Hans S. Falck (*Social Work: The Membership Perspective,* New York: Springer, 1988), emphasizes the common membership of clients and social workers; the mutuality of giving and receiving; the social (rather than individualistic) nature of *self-determination;* and reciprocity among members, institutions, community, and society.

memory   The mental function of recalling or reproducing what has been experienced or learned.

memory recovery therapy   A form of *psychotherapy* oriented to retrieving parts of a client's forgotten past experiences that had been concealed from consciousness by *suppression* or *repression.* This type of intervention has become controversial because, as a result of it, many clients have accused parents or others of *child molestation* or *sexual abuse.* The person thus accused has often blamed and sued the therapist for inserting false memories into the client. See also *false-memory syndrome.*

Ménière's disease   A disease of the inner ear semicircular canals (endolymphatic sac) resulting in symptoms such as dizziness, nausea, vertigo, vomiting, ringing in the ears (tinnitus), and deafness.

menarche The biological process that occurs in young women as menstruation begins.

mendicancy The act of begging. A "mendicant" is one who begs for money or goods.

mendigo In Spanish-speaking countries, one who begs. A female who begs is a mendiga.

meningitis Bacterially or virally caused inflammation of the membranes that surround the brain or spinal cord or both. Antibiotic drugs have greatly reduced mortality and the effects of the disease, such as paralysis, arthritis, deafness, and blindness. Symptoms of meningitis may include fever, headache, vomiting, delirium, severe rigidity in the neck and back, and convulsions.

menopause The biological process that occurs in middle-age women as menstruation ceases. In some women, the hormonal changes result temporarily in certain accompanying physiological and psychological symptoms.

men's liberation movement The organized efforts of disparate people and groups to eliminate *sex role stereotyping* and *gender bias* against men and to widen the range of acceptable behaviors identified with masculinity and male roles. See also *women's liberation movement.*

"mens rea" A legal term (literally "criminal mind") pertaining to the guilty intent to commit a *crime.*

"Mensch" 1. A Jewish expression for a person of integrity and character. 2. A Jewish person who has retained the Jewish identity.

mental abuse In cases of child or spousal abuse, the persistent belittling, ridiculing, blaming, or rejecting of another person; blatantly favoring other members of the family; and showing little regard for the abused individual's emotional well-being. This term is synonymous with *emotional abuse.*

mental cruelty A legal ground for *divorce* in many jurisdictions, in which the behavior of one spouse imperils the mental health of the other to the extent that continuing the relationship is considered unbearable.

mental disorder Impaired psychosocial or cognitive functioning due to disturbances in any one or more of the following processes: biological, chemical, physiological, genetic, psychological, or social. Mental disorders are extremely variable in duration, severity, and prognosis, depending on the type of affliction. The major forms of mental disorder include *mood disorders, psychosis, personality disorders, organic mental disorders,* and *anxiety disorder.*

mental health The relative state of emotional well-being, freedom from incapacitating conflicts, and the consistent ability to make and carry out rational decisions and cope with environmental stresses and internal pressures.

Mental Health Association (MHA) The voluntary citizen's organization, founded in 1909 by *Clifford W. Beers* (1876–1943) and others, the purpose of which is to promote social conditions that enhance the potential for good mental health and to improve the methods and facilities for treating mental illness.

mental health day care A health care service and facility that provides mental health services and a supervised daily environment to adults with mental illness. Patients typically go to the facility for medications; some counseling; and sometimes group therapy, recreation and socialization, and educational programs for assistance with coping skills.

Mental Health Parity Act The U.S. legislation (P.L. 104-274) enacted in 1996 that requires health insurance companies to reimburse for mental health care as they would for physical health care. The actual legislation does not mandate complete equality and is readily circumvented. It does not cover substance abuse and excludes companies with fewer than 50 employees.

mental health professional One who has specialized training and skills in the nature and treatment of mental illness and uses them to provide clinical, preventive, and social services for people who have, or may be vulnerable to, a *mental disorder.* Mental health professionals include *psychiatrists, psychologists,* psychiatric *registered nurses, social workers,* and members of some other disciplines that provide special expertise and help for emotionally disturbed people.

mental health self-help groups Formal voluntary organizations of people who have experienced

269

mental illness and, through mutual aid, provide education and support to their peers. Among the major groups are Recovery, Neurotics Anonymous, Sidran Foundation (for trauma victims), Obsessive–Compulsives Anonymous, Depressives Anonymous–Recovery from Depression, and Schizophrenics Anonymous. An organization that helps such groups develop is the Philadelphia-based National Mental Health Consumer Self-Help Clearinghouse (NMHCSHC).

mental health team   Professionals and ancillary personnel from several disciplines who work together to provide a wide range of services for clients (and the families of clients) who are affected by a *mental disorder*. Members of such teams include *psychiatrists* (who usually head them), *social workers, psychologists,* and *registered nurses.* In some psychiatric facilities the team members may also include physical and occupational therapists, recreation specialists, educators, personnel and guidance counselors, psychiatric aides, *volunteers,* and *indigenous workers.* See also *interdisciplinary teaming.*

mental health workers   Mental health professionals, paraprofessionals, volunteers, and aides who work in facilities or organizations concerned with meeting the needs of those who are mentally ill or those vulnerable to *mental disorder.* Mental health workers are distinguished from *mental health team* members only in that their efforts are not necessarily coordinated with those of other workers to achieve specified, focused goals.

mental hospitals   Institutions that specialize in the care and treatment of people suffering from a *mental disorder.* These institutions may be publicly or privately financed and may provide a full range of health care services or be limited in the type of care provided. Many of the existing public mental hospitals in the United States were established as a result of the influence of social reformer *Dorothea Dix* (1802–1887).

mental hygiene   A synonym for *mental health.* The term often implies efforts to develop facilities and procedures for the treatment of people with mental illness and to educate people to live in ways that foster emotional stability and psychological well-being. See also *Clifford W. Beers.*

mental illness   A synonym for *mental disorder.*

mental retardation   Significantly below-average intellectual functioning and potential, with onset before age 18, resulting in limitations in communication, self-care and self-direction, home living, social and interpersonal skills, use of community resources, academic skills, work, leisure, health, and safety. It may be the result of genetic factors, embryonic development, pregnancy or perinatal problems, trauma, organ damage, or environmental influences such as social deprivation. One diagnosed with this condition has an *intelligence quotient (IQ)* lower than 70. Degrees of mental retardation are delineated as follows: mild retardation (IQ range of 50–70), moderate (35–49), severe (20–34), and profound (below 20). The IQ scores have a plus or minus 5 points to account for potential measurement error.

mental status exam   A systematic evaluation of a patient's level of psychosocial, intellectual, and emotional functioning. The examiner, who is usually a psychiatrist or physician but may be a social worker, observes the patient's *affect,* thought content, perceptive and cognitive functions, and need and motivation for treatment. This may be done, in part, by asking questions of the patient such as "What day is today?" and "Where are you now?" The patient may also be asked to repeat a series of numbers forward and backward and to interpret several aphorisms, such as "People who live in glass houses shouldn't throw stones."

mercenary   An individual who performs services, which often are distasteful or dangerous, for money. The term is most commonly applied to soldiers employed by countries other than their own.

"mercy diagnosis"   The ethically suspect practice by some social workers and other professionals of deliberately misdiagnosing a client on the supposed grounds that the appropriate label will lead to serious difficulties for the client or that the new, more gentle diagnosis will avoid those difficulties. For example, a diagnosis of *bipolar disorder* is replaced by one of *seasonal affective disorder (SAD).*

mercy killing   See *euthanasia.*

Merici, Angela (1474–1540)   Also known as St. Angela, a Catholic religious worker who advocated for poor and sick people, organized programs for their care, and provided educational programs for young girls. She founded the

Ursuline Order, whose primary mission was to serve ill and destitute people.

merit system An organization's set of rules, regulations, and policies used in personnel management to assure employees that their opportunities for promotion and retention on the job will be based fairly on performance. Federal government workers are protected in this system by the *Merit Systems Protection Board.* See also *spoils system.*

Merit Systems Protection Board An independent organization in the U.S. government designed to protect the integrity of the federal *merit system.* Appeals by federal workers who charge unfair treatment and other violations of federal regulations are evaluated by the board, and violators may be prosecuted. Their Web site address is http://www.mspb.gov

meritocracy Leadership theoretically based on achievements, talent, skill, intelligence, and other relevant virtues rather than on inheritance (aristocracy), wealth (*plutocracy*), or the will of the majority (democracy). What is sometimes called "meritocracy" is merely judging candidates for leadership roles based on their performance on some test scores or paper qualifications.

mescaline A psychedelic drug that produces *hallucination,* perceptual distortions, and thinking disorders. Although mescaline is considered one of the *drugs of abuse* in some societies, in others it is used in religious ceremonies. See also *psychedelics.*

mestizo People from Latin American cultures whose ancestry is mixed native and European.

meta-analysis The assessment of the outcome of a study by systematically reviewing the findings across similar studies.

metamemory The mental mechanisms that regulate and process the way actual memory content is stored, organized, and retrieved.

metamessage Communications between people that extend beyond the explicit verbalizations and information that is being transmitted. For example, a client might say "I'm not angry!" (primary statement) while banging a fist (metamessage). The metamessage may be verbal or nonverbal, *conscious* or *unconscious,* and consistent with or contradic-

tory to the primary statement. See also *paralinguistics* and *communication theory.*

metaphor A type of analogy or figure of speech used to describe something to which it is not literally applicable. Metaphors are used by social workers and their clients to connote feeling and imagination as well as objective reality. For example, a social worker could describe a client as a "hurricane" to convey a variety of behavioral and personality characteristics. See also *dichos.*

metastasis The spreading of a disease, such as *cancer,* from one part of the body to others.

meth labs Facilities used for the illegal production of *methamphetamines.* Usually such places are set up in apartments, motel rooms, garages, and abandoned houses, often in urban, suburban, and rural neighborhoods. When the producers are apprehended or leave, the facility they leave is usually contaminated with dangerous toxins until an extensive and expensive cleanup occurs. The labs are often identified when their contents include large quantities of over-the-counter cold and asthma medications containing ephedrine or pseudoephedrine, drain cleaner, lye, battery acid, antifreeze, camp stove fuel, and hydrochloric acid.

methadone A synthetic pain-relieving drug used primarily in the treatment of *heroin* addiction.

methadone treatment The use of the synthetic narcotic *methadone* to help wean addicts from *heroin.* However, methadone itself is addictive, even though it has less severe *withdrawal symptoms.* Methadone clinics give methadone to patients and supervise their use of it. For such treatment to be truly effective, it must be accompanied by *psychosocial therapy.* See also *LAMM* and *naltrexone treatment.*

methamphetamine A highly addictive synthetic drug of abuse that has stimulant properties similar to adrenaline. Withdrawal is more intense and longer lasting than cocaine or other drugs and sometimes produces acute depression, psychotic episodes, and brain damage. It is sold in the form of pills, capsules, powder, and chunks and may be smoked (see "*ice*"), injected (see "*crank*"), or swallowed. It is less expensive than most other drugs and is often made in *meth labs* using easily obtained chemicals.

methodology The systematic and specified procedures by which a social worker or other investigator develops hypotheses, gathers relevant data, analyzes data acquired, and communicates the conclusions.

methods in social work The specific types of interventions and other activities used by social workers in their professional practices. The term is used especially by social work educators. Social work activities that have been identified as methods include *social casework, social group work, community organization, administration in social work, research, policy, planning,* direct clinical practice, family and marital treatment, other *micro practice,* and what is called "generic social work practice, combined micro–macro."

Metropolitan Statistical Area (MSA) A designation by demographers and urbanologists indicating a large population nucleus surrounded by the nearby communities, all of which have a high degree of socioeconomic integration.

Mexican American A resident of the United States whose parents or ancestors are from Mexico. See also *Chicano.*

Meyer, Carol H. (1924–1996) Social work educator, theoretician, and writer who advanced concepts about social work practice from the *ecosystems perspective* and developed theories and educational programs for in-service training, assessment, feminist social work, and community organization. She was editor-in-chief of many social work journals, including *Social Work* and *Affilia,* and was the author of many professional articles and textbooks, including *Assessment in Social Work Practice, Clinical Social Work in an Eco-systems Perspective,* and *Social Work Practice.*

mezzo practice Social work practice primarily with families and small groups. Important activities at this level include facilitating *communication, mediation,* and *negotiation;* educating; and bringing people together. This is one of the three levels of social work practice, along with *macro practice* and *micro practice.* All social workers engage, to some extent, in all three, even though they may give major attention to only one or two of the levels.

"mica" Slang term used especially in Latin American communities for *green card* or *permanent resident card.*

micro orientation In social work, an emphasis on the individual client's psychosocial conflicts and on the enhancement of technical skills for use in efficient treatment of these problems. This perspective is contrasted with social work's *macro orientation.*

micro practice The term used by social workers to identify professional activities that are designed to help solve the problems faced primarily by individuals, families, and small groups. Usually micro practice focuses on direct intervention on a case-by-case basis or in a clinical setting. See also *macro practice* and *mezzo practice.*

microeconomics The study of the way individuals and groups produce, distribute, and consume goods, usually on a small scale with simple technology and locally available resources. See also *appropriate technology (AT)* and *macroeconomics.*

microenterprise A small business activity ranging in size from self-employment to six workers. Examples include unlicensed child care, street-corner car washing, lawn mowing, recycling goods, and manufacturing and selling small products. Often those involved in such activities belong to *marginalized groups* and find mainstream employment opportunities very limited. Governments and foundations sometimes seek to encourage microenterprise by providing low-interest lending pools, technical assistance, and networking opportunities. See also *self-employment development* and *Personal Responsibility and Work Opportunity Reconciliation Act* of 1996.

micromanagement Administration of an organization by close supervision of employees who are given little authority or decision-making powers. Social agency administrators sometimes complain that government bureaucrats and lawmakers micromanage by making rules so specific and detailed that there is no room for administrative discretion or innovation.

midlevel practitioners (MLPs) Health care practitioners who do not have medical degrees. These include the *nurse practitioner, midwife,* and *physician's assistant.* Midlevel practitioners provide medical services, generally under the supervision of a physician, at lower cost.

midlife crisis The inner conflict and, often, the changed behavior patterns that occur in some middle-age individuals who are reassessing the meaning and direction of life, questioning their future goals, examining their relative progress toward achieving their goals, and coping with social demands made on them.

midwife   A nonphysician who assists a mother through the process of childbirth.

Migrant and Seasonal Agricultural Worker Protection Act   U.S. federal legislation (P.L. 97-470) enacted in 1983 to protect migrant farm workers from unfair labor practices or working, living, or housing conditions that are unhealthy or unsafe. The law also requires employers to inform workers, in writing, of their rights, their wages and benefits, and the length and terms of their employment.

Migrant Education Program (MEP)   The U.S. DoE program to help children of migrant families achieve state student performance standards and overcome cultural and language barriers, health and social problems, and other problems that result from repeated moves. The MEP establishes criteria, provides information, and awards funding grants to local education agencies to achieve these goals. Their Web site address is http://www.ed.gov/offices/oese/mhs

Migrant Head Start program   A type of *Head Start* program that serves children whose parents are migrant farm workers. The program coordinates and monitors the educational progress of children who may go from one geographic region to another during the time of eligibility. Their Web site address is http://www.acf.dhhs.gov/programs/mhs

migrant laborer   A worker who travels from place to place to take short-term or seasonal jobs, such as those in agriculture and construction. Often such workers travel in groups, typically with their families, and are vulnerable to exploitation by employers. They and their children have limited or minimal opportunities to obtain education, social skills, and health care.

migratory child   A minor who has moved with a parent or guardian seeking seasonal employment in an agricultural activity. Children who are so designated are entitled by U.S. law to compensatory education programs. If the child has not moved within the past five years and currently resides in an area where migratory children are served, the child may be entitled to the same benefits as a "former migratory child."

mild cognitive impairment   Impaired cognitive functioning with minimal impact on everyday functioning, due to a *general medical condition*. This is also known as mild neurocognitive disorder.

Milford Conference   The early 20th century study group, composed of social workers, agency executives, and board members, set up to determine whether social work was a disparate group of specialties or a unified profession with integrated knowledge and skills. The group published its conclusions in the book *Social Case Work: Generic and Specific* (New York: American Association of Social Workers, 1929), which emphasized that *social casework* in all settings used basically the same skills and knowledge and is thus one profession. See also *generic–specific controversy.*

milieu therapy   A form of treatment for people who are institutionalized with social and mental disorders. Treatment is not restricted to individual hours with a professional therapist but also occurs in the total environment of this closed setting, which is also referred to as the "therapeutic community." Those being treated attend group sessions for everyone in the facility, elect their own leaders, and provide one another with social and emotional support throughout the day. The entire environment is considered vital to the treatment process.

militant   One who seeks *social change* but who is considered less likely to compromise and more inclined to be an *agitator* or *dissident.*

militarism   An orientation to maintaining strong armed forces and being prepared and motivated to use them before all other options are exhausted. See also *pacifism* and *warism.*

military social work   Professional social work intervention on behalf of active-duty military personnel and their families. This form of practice is accomplished by social work officers and civilians in all branches of the U.S. military. Military social workers evaluate and treat emotionally disturbed military personnel or members of their families, find and develop social resources, and facilitate communications between military personnel and their relatives who live in other locations. See also *Uniformed Services Social Workers (USSW).*

mimesis   Imitation of the behaviors of another person, often seen among family members who tend to assume the same verbal and physical gestures, expressions, or postures. Social workers and other therapists sometimes imitate the movements and posture of clients, especially when working with families or groups, to facilitate *joining* or alliance building.

mind   The part of a person in which intellectual functions occur, including cognitive processing, information accumulation, memories, unconscious material, reasoning, emotional reactions, sensory input, and the personality.

"mind games"   A slang expression usually referring to *manipulative behavior,* especially involving attempts to provoke feelings of guilt, anger, confusion, or affection.

mind reading   The alleged ability of a person to know the thoughts and feelings of another person without direct communication. This term is used by social workers as a figure of speech in *marital therapy* and *family therapy* to describe the tendency of one family member to interpret or describe to the social worker what he or she believes are the views or the feelings of another family member.

"minimal brain dysfunction"   An obsolete term for *attention-deficit hyperactivity disorder (ADHD).*

minimal supervision home   A residential facility for people with mental retardation who can live outside of institutions and apart from families but who benefit from scheduled in-home visits by social workers to help them plan their shopping, money management, recreation, health care, and educational activities. These facilities are overseen by state departments of human services and other agencies and are staffed by professionals, case aides, and volunteers.

minimum market basket   A concept used by economists and social welfare planners to indicate the least quantity of food required for survival; a form of *minimum-needs estimation.*

minimum-needs estimation   The delineation by social welfare planners of the least quantities of food, clothing, housing, and goods that an individual requires for survival. This concept is used as a basis in establishing an income *poverty line.*

minimum standard of living   The lowest amount of money and quality of essentials that an individual needs to maintain a lifestyle that is tolerable to the society.

minimum wage   A payment made to employees that, by law or contract, is the lowest amount the employer is permitted to pay for specified work. U.S. labor policy establishes that employers may not hire workers unless they guarantee to pay at least the amount established by government regulations.

ministroke   See *transient ischemic attack (TIA).*

minor   The legal designation for a child or adolescent, used to distinguish the different rights, protections, and privileges that exist for adults and for these youths. Each jurisdiction establishes the age at which one legally becomes an adult and specifies any rights available to minors, such as driving, buying property, drinking alcoholic beverages, and marrying.

minor tranquilizer   *Psychotropic drugs* prescribed by physicians to relieve the symptoms of mild tension, sleeplessness, irritability, and especially anxiety. They are usually taken orally as a tablet, capsule, or liquid and sometimes administered intravenously. Although these medications do not cure the underlying sources of the problems, they do give patients enough respite to work more effectively on those problem sources. Trade names include Valium, Librium, Tranxene, Ativan, Serax, Xanax, Klonopin, and Atarax.

minorities of color   One term for people who have *minority* status because their skin color differs from that of the community's predominant group. In the United States, the term usually refers to *African Americans, Asian Americans, American Indians,* and certain other groups.

minority   One term for a group, or a member of a group, of people of a distinct racial, religious, ethnic, or political identity that is smaller or less powerful than the community's controlling group.

Minority Business Development Agency (MBDA)   The organization within the U.S. Department of Commerce, established in 1969, to facilitate business opportunities for *minorities of color,* women, and Native Americans. The MBDA provides management and technical assistance and initiates public–private partnerships to increase access to capital for minority-owned businesses. The agency has also administered laws that require a percentage of monies spent on government projects be *set-asides*. Their Web site address is http://www.mbda.gov

minority report A presentation of dissenting conclusions reached by some members of a committee to give reasons why they did not concur with the majority.

minority set-asides See *set-asides*.

minsei i'in In Japan, the nationwide system of community volunteers, appointed by the Minister of Health and Welfare for three-year terms, to help in the administration of welfare problems, especially those concerning children and older people. These individuals try to learn about the community's welfare needs, give advice about personal problems, provide information about available resources, act as liaisons with welfare offices and other community resources, and endorse those believed to qualify for public assistance. The system is based on Germany's *Elberfeld system*.

MIPRAs Mentally ill persons in recovery from addictions, a diagnostic term used by social workers and others helping clients who have drug problems and *mental illness*. Many clients have both disorders together, and this designation reminds professionals that treating one disorder without treating the other will likely be ineffective.

Miranda The 1966 U.S. Supreme Court ruling in *Miranda v. Arizona* requiring police to inform suspects of their constitutional rights before questioning them. Suspects must be told that they have the right to remain silent, the right to have an attorney present when being questioned, the right to a court-appointed attorney if they cannot afford a private attorney, and that any statements they make can be used against them in court.

mirror technique In social group work and family group therapy, a therapeutic procedure in which one group member reenacts a behavior of the protagonist, mimicking gestures, expressions, and vocalizations, to emphasize aspects of the behavior for more objective scrutiny.

misanthropy Hatred or aversion to humanity. The prefix is from the Greek "misos" (to hate) and may be attached to any group to indicate an individual's feelings about it; for example, a misogynist hates women, a misogamist hates marriage, and a misopedic hates children.

misappropriation The illegal acquisition of someone's property or money for one's own use. The term usually applies to the act of a public official, executor of a will, or administrator of an estate.

miscegenation Marriage or sexual relations between a man and woman of different races in violation of a law. Laws forbidding such marriages were common in the United States but were generally abolished by legislation or court decrees in the 1960s and by the U.S. Supreme Court in 1967.

misconduct Willful actions or omissions by persons who are obliged to fulfill certain duties or tasks.

misdemeanor A minor criminal offense generally defined by state law in terms of possible jail sentences of less than six months. Such acts as breaking streetlights, defacing property, and littering are usually misdemeanors. See also *felony*.

misery index A nation's or society's combined rates of *unemployment* and *inflation*. See also *Index of Social Health*.

misfeasance Performing a proper act in a way that is harmful or injurious, especially by public officials. See also *malfeasance*.

missing person A designation by law enforcement authorities applied to one whose whereabouts remain unknown to his or her family, significant other, or colleagues. If the missing person is a minor, the appropriate term is usually *runaway*.

mission statement A brief description of an organization's overall goals, direction and purposes, reasons for existence, and operating values, often used to support program review efforts and to inform the public about the focus of the organization.

mistrial In a court of law, a trial that is ended and declared void before a verdict has been reached. This occurs most commonly because of deadlocked jury deliberations (when the jurors cannot achieve necessary consensus) and sometimes because of prejudicial misstatements made by attorneys or illnesses of key participants.

mixed anxiety–depressive disorder   Persistent or recurrent *mood* of *dysphoria* lasting one month or more; it is accompanied by worry, irritability, fatigue or low energy, sleep disturbance, and difficulty concentrating.

mixed economy   A society or environment in which services and transfers of funds occur through the participation of public, nonprofit, and proprietary organizations.

mixed receptive–expressive language disorder   A *communication disorder* characterized by the presence of *expressive language disorder* combined with impaired receptive language development (difficulty understanding words, sentences, or types of words). This disorder may be developmental or acquired (as a result of medical conditions such as head trauma). If mental retardation, motor or sensory deficits, or sociocultural deprivation is present, the language difficulties are greater than usually found in just those problems.

mnemonics   Learning and cognitive strategies to improve the acquisition, retention, and retrieval of memories.

mobility   The ability to move with relative ease or flexibility. See also *social mobility.*

Mobilization for Youth   A multifaceted social services *demonstration program,* established in New York City in the early 1960s, designed to test the theory that poor urban youths will enter mainstream society if social barriers to opportunities are removed.

mobilizer role   In social work, the responsibility to help people and organizations combine their resources to achieve goals of mutual importance. This is accomplished by bringing clients together, enhancing lines of communication, clarifying goals and steps to achieve them, and devising plans for gaining greater support. Other roles are the *facilitator role,* the *enabler role,* and the *educator role.*

mode   A *measure of central tendency* in statistics and research, it is the number that occurs most often in a given series. For example, an agency wants to know how many clients are seen by most of its workers in a given day. A few of the 20 agency workers typically see about 12 clients daily, and a few others see only about five. But most of the workers see eight clients per day, which is the modal number.

model   A representation of reality. For example, social workers use the *life model* to represent the interplay of forces found in the client's environment that influence and are influenced by the client.

Model Cities program   A U.S. federal program established in 1966 to coordinate and integrate various government efforts in housing, urban renewal, community development of facilities, transportation, education, and economic opportunities in participating cities. Federal officials coordinated government programs and resources with local efforts. In the 1980s, the program was largely supplanted by federal *block grants.*

Model Licensing Act   Legislative guidelines that recommended the conditions and qualifications for jurisdictions to use in licensing social work practice. The *National Association of Social Workers (NASW)* developed the model law before most states had fully developed licensing laws for social work practice. Social workers and lobbyists with various state legislatures offered the Model Licensing Act to assist legislators in writing their own laws pertaining to social work licenses. The act specified what social work practice is and is not, outlined the recommended qualifications for doing it, and indicated the procedures to be taken to enforce compliance.

modeling   In *behavior therapy* and *social learning theory,* a form of learning in which an individual acquires behaviors by imitating the actions of one or more other people.

MOE expenditures   State funding for welfare recipients to supplement the federal monies spent under the TANF program. For states to receive their full TANF block grant funding they must fulfill a "maintenance of effort" (MOE) requirement: They must spend at least 80 percent of their historic level of expenditures for needy eligible families, or 75 percent if the state meets federal TANF participation rate requirements.

molestation   The crime of sexual fondling or similar abuse of a child, including rape, indecent exposure, inducement of sexual acts, and the touching of genitals. Molestation also may apply to unwanted sexual acts with adults. See also *pedophilia.*

"mommy track"   A term referring to the career path of some women who are viewed as placing their obligations to their children over those of their jobs. Those who are presumed to be on this path are often overlooked for promotions and given fewer opportunities to contribute to their organizations. When men espouse these priorities, they are said to be on a "daddy track."

monetarism   The theory in economics that attributes fluctuations in inflation rates and unemployment to changes in the supply of money. Monetarists are said to believe that governments can regulate the economy by controlling the supply of money and interest rates, without the need of other legal or bureaucratic regulations or protections.

money income   The sum of gross pretaxed cash, including net income from employment and any other form of cash income (such as interest and dividends) and all cash transfer payments (such as pensions, social security, public assistance, and unemployment insurance benefits). It does not include the value of one's assets, capital gains, or noncash benefits.

money laundering   Converting illegally obtained cash or other assets to different forms to conceal its origin or true ownership. For example, money obtained through organized crime activity may be placed within the supposed income of a restaurant.

"mongolism"   An obsolete and inappropriate term for *Down syndrome*.

monogamy   The state of being married to one person.

monolithic code   A belief often held by members of a dominant culture that suggests only one acceptable pattern of behavior and considers any other behavior as deviant. For example, someone who adheres to this code may consider divorce, working wives, innovative hair and dress styles, and associations with members of different ethnic or racial groups as deviant.

mononucleosis   A viral infection that most commonly affects adolescents and young adults with symptoms such as sore throat, fever, and chills; feelings of weakness and tiredness; and enlarged lymph nodes.

monopolists   Clients in groups who seek to be the constant center of attention.

monopoly   The market condition in which one producer of goods or services exists solely or in such predominance as to be able to dictate prices and distribution patterns.

monopsony   The market condition in which there is only one buyer for the products or services that many have to sell.

mood   An emotional state that influences an individual's perceptions, cognitive functions, and actions. To be in a "bad mood" is to be irritable, depressed, anxious, or— especially—angry. To be in a "good mood" is to be elated, happy, or—especially—cheerful. Social workers and other professionals sometimes describe a client as being in a mood of *dysphoria* or *euphoria*.

mood-altering drugs   A synonym for *psychoactive drugs*.

mood disorder NOS   "Not otherwise specified," a residual diagnostic category for the classification of *mood disorders*. This diagnosis is given when the individual presents with enough symptoms to warrant a mood disorder diagnosis but not enough to indicate any one of the specific types.

mood disorders   A group of serious mental disorders involving affective lability (*depression* or persistently elevated moods). The diagnosable mood disorders include *major depressive disorder, dysthymic disorder, bipolar disorder, cyclothymic disorder, substance-induced mood disorder,* mood disorder due to general medical condition, and *mood disorder NOS*. In diagnosing this condition, the term "mood disorder" has replaced the formerly used label *affective disorder*.

mood swings   Going from one general *mood* to another within a fairly short time.

moral citizenship   The responsibility to determine standards of ethical behavior as one's right and obligation as a member of the community and society.

moral development   Acquiring the values, feelings, and thoughts that lead to behaviors that are consistent with standards of right or wrong. Many theorists have proposed models about how this is accomplished, including Gilligan, Kohlberg, Piaget, Mischel, and Erikson. See also *Kohlberg moral development theory* and *values clarification*.

moral judgment   A choice made about right or wrong behavior based on a rational assessment and evaluation of consequences to oneself, to others, and to society.

moral turpitude   A gross violation of the local standards of conduct.

moralizing   Communicating a message about how someone should behave or think, often accompanied by *manipulative behavior* designed to stimulate feelings of guilt or obligation. The moralizer implies that the other person has a duty to some vague higher authority, such as "the family honor." Social workers who sometimes moralize with their clients tend to cause resentment and diminished receptivity in them.

moratorium   A time in a negotiation process during which both sides agree or are compelled to refrain from the disputed actions so that a fair settlement can be reached.

morbid   Diseased or disordered.

morbidity rate   The proportion of people in a specific population who are known to have a specific disease or disorder during a certain period.

morbidity risk   An individual's lifetime chances of having a specific illness.

mores   Social customs that are accepted as traditional and enforced by others in the social group.

"moron"   An obsolete term, once used to refer to a person with mild mental retardation with an *intelligence quotient (IQ)* score below 70 and above 50.

morpheme   In *communication theory,* a basic unit of meaningful language. Morphemes include words, prefixes, and suffixes.

morphine   An *opiate,* used medically to induce sleep and relieve pain.

morphogenesis   The concept used in *systems theories* to depict the tendency of a living system to change its structure and to evolve into a system that has a different structure. The tendency of a system toward morphogenesis is balanced by the system's equally powerful tendency toward *morphostasis.*

morphological analysis   A problem-solving method used in many organizations in which all possible alternatives to reaching a solution are broadly outlined and then broken into their components for further study and evaluation. Each component is depicted on a grid or three-dimensional cube that has intersecting axes. The most promising alternatives are then evaluated, modified, and developed as solutions.

morphostasis   The concept used in *systems theories* to depict the tendency of a living system to retain its structure and to resist change. The tendency of a system toward morphostasis is balanced by the system's equally powerful tendency toward *morphogenesis.*

mortality rate   The number or proportion of deaths in a specified population during a certain period. The mortality rate is also known as the *death rate.*

Mother Teresa (1910–1997)   Founder and long-time leader of the Missionaries of Charity, an international social services organization based in Calcutta, India, to assist those who are poor and unwanted. Born in Albania as Gonxhe Agnes Bojaxhui, she went to India as a young woman to help impoverished people. She opened and operated homes for those who are dying and destitute, orphanages, and mobile health clinics. She was awarded the Nobel Peace Prize in 1979.

Mothers Against Drunk Driving (MADD)   A national organization established in 1980 to influence legislation, police activity, judicial decisions, punishment, prevention, and education pertaining to the operation of motor vehicles while under the influence of alcohol or drugs. Their Web site address is http://www.madd.org

Mother's March   See *March of Dimes.*

motivation   A set of physical drives, desires, attitudes, and values that arouse and direct behavior toward the achievement of some goal.

motivation–capacity–opportunity theory   The assessment model used by social workers to predict the likelihood that a client will make effective use of the help offered. *Charlotte Towle* (1896–1966) first formulated the triad, and social work researchers *Lillian Ripple* (1911–1993), Ernestina Alexander, and Bernice W. Polemis studied its relevance. Their findings concluded that when clients have adequate motivation and the capacity to partake of services provided in an appropriate manner, they will make use of the services, unless there are restrictive or unmodifiable forces outside the agency or influences on the client.

motor skills disorder   Marked impairment in the development of motor coordination that significantly interferes with academics and daily activities. This disorder is not due to medical conditions such as *cerebral palsy* or *muscular dystrophy.*

motor tension   A symptom of anxiety that results in muscular contractions, stiffness, or uncontrollable movements such as shakiness and trembling.

motor tic disorder   See *tic disorder.*

motor voter law   Popular name for *National Voter Registration Act (NVRA).*

Mouravieff-Apostol, Andrew (1913–2001)   The Secretary General of the *International Federation of Social Workers (IFSW)* from 1975 to 1992 and lifelong honorary president, he developed programs to improve international cooperation and coordination between social workers and their goals, especially social justice, human rights, and social development. Prior to his IFSW work, Mouravieff-Apostle developed resettlement programs for refugees in many nations.

mourning   The psychological and cultural process of expressing sorrow about the loss of a loved one; breaking the emotional tie with that loved one; and gradually reinvesting the emotional energy in other people, activities, or things. See also *bereavement* and *grief.*

movement disorders   Unusual and persistent gestures, expressions, postures, and movements believed to be the result of medical conditions, effects of substances, or physiological or mental disorders. A professional can often begin to determine the type of problem by observing such movement patterns. Some of the more notable ones identified include *choreiform movements,* dystonic movements (slow twisting interspersed with prolonged muscle tension), athetoid movements (slow, irregular writhing, mostly in the fingers and toes), myoclonic movements (brief, shocklike muscle contractions), spasms (sterotypic, slower, and more prolonged movements involving muscle groups),

and synkinesis (involuntary movements accompanying voluntary ones). See also *medication-induced movement disorders* and *stereotypic movement disorder.*

movement therapy   A systematic procedure for helping patients with diminished strength, energy, and muscle disorders, as well as lethargy, depression, and sometimes arthritic conditions, through physical activity. Usually in groups, the patients perform dances and other movements designed for their needs. This is also known as kinesitherapy.

MSW   The master of social work degree awarded to students who have completed the requirements of accredited schools of social work. Requirements for the MSW typically include successful completion of 60 academic hours, including about 24 hours of field placement, taken over the equivalent of two full-time years. The student is often required to complete a thesis or research project. In some schools, the degree is known as the MSSW (master of science in social work or master of social service work), MSSA (master of social service administration), or MA in social work. All are essentially the same in educational requirements and standards.

muckrakers   The name first used by President Theodore Roosevelt to describe a group of journalists, speakers, agitators, and social activists who sought to make the public aware of abuses, unethical practices, and corrupt business and political activities that exploited and endangered people. The muckraking movement was especially prominent in the United States from 1900 to 1915 and resulted in many of the social reforms of the *Progressive Era.* The term is still used and often applied to social workers, writers, investigative reporters, and other reform-minded people who call attention to current examples of abuse and corruption.

mudslinging   An aspect of *negative campaigning* in which an opponent or opponent's supporters make unflattering public disclosures about a candidate that may be true, partly true, or entirely false.

"mug shot"   Front and side photographs of an individual's face taken upon being booked for an alleged criminal act. These photographs are usually kept on file by the local police authorities and often by the *Federal Bureau of Investigation (FBI)* and later may be shown to witnesses and victims to help them make identifications of criminals.

muina A *culture-bound syndrome,* found especially among Latino people, in which the individual experiences nervous tension, trembling, screaming, and various somatic complaints said to be the result of feeling intense anger or rage. This syndrome is also known as *bilis.*

mulatto One who is the offspring of a black parent and a white parent.

multi-infarct dementia *Dementia* resulting from *cardiovascular disease.* The dementia is caused by a series of strokes, causing a step-by-step deterioration of different mental functions, depending on which part of the brain is destroyed. The preferred term for this is *vascular dementia.*

multiaxial assessment system The system used in the *DSM* for assessing types of *mental disorder* on five axes, each of which refers to a different domain of information about the client: (1) Axis I, clinical disorders and other conditions that may be a focus of clinical attention; (2) Axis II, personality disorders and mental retardation; (3) Axis III, general medical conditions; (4) Axis IV, psychosocial and environmental problems; and (5) Axis V, global assessment of functioning.

multiculturalism An orientation that recognizes, supports, and accommodates a variety of sociocultural practices and traditions; also a socio-intellectual movement that promotes the value of diversity as a core principle and insists that all cultural groups be treated as equal.

multiethnic placement *Adoption* or *foster care* involving children of one ethnic origin and adoptive or foster parents of another ethnic origin.

Multiethnic Placement Act (MEPA) The 1994 federal legislation (P.L. 103-382) that prohibits using race to deny or delay adoptive or foster care placements. Race may be among the factors considered when placing a particular child, but multiethnic placement cannot be ruled out. The law also requires more diligent recruitment of potential foster and adoptive homes that reflect racial and ethnic diversity. The law was implemented partly in response to the thousands of children, especially children of color, waiting for years in foster care for adoptive homes because of race-matching policies. MEPA was revised slightly in a 1996 law (P.L. 104-188).

multifactorial inheritance See *genetic disorder.*

multifamily therapy A *family therapy* approach in which several families meet regularly in a *group psychotherapy* format, guided by one or more professional leaders or facilitators, to provide mutual understanding, exchange ideas, make recommendations, role-play, and perform psychodramas.

multifinality The systems theory concept in which subsystems have identical beginnings or origins but achieve different outcomes. This term is synonymous with *equipotentiality* and the opposite of *equifinality.*

multineeds clients People who seek the social worker's services because of the simultaneous existence of problems. Usually the different problems require the skills and resources of more than one worker or agency. Because multineeds clients constitute a high percentage of the social work clientele, the need for coordination of services and agencies is increasing.

multiple-causation theory The view that a given disorder or social phenomenon is the result of many factors operating simultaneously and in many cases somewhat independently of one another. This is a *holistic* view that is particularly emphasized by those who use *systems theories* as their orientation and by those who question the concept of *linear causality.*

multiple-drug use The simultaneous abuse of two or more drugs, often resulting in a mix of symptoms and contradictory progression in the treatment process.

multiple etiologies A condition that originated from the combination of several, not necessarily related, factors. For example, a diagnosis due to multiple etiologies could be the result of *head trauma* and *Alzheimer's disease.*

multiple-impact therapy A team form of treatment used by professionals, especially with the *multiproblem family.* It is typically intensive and relatively short term. Members of the professional team meet with various subgroups or individuals from the client system. Then different subgroups meet with the professionals, and so on, in a variety of combinations.

multiple intelligences   A conception about the different types of *intelligence* made by cognitive researcher Howard Gardner. There are seven distinct types of intelligence: (1) verbal/linguistic, (2) logical/mathematical, (3) visual/spatial, (4) body/kinesthetic, (5) musical/rhythmical, (6) interpersonal, and (7) intrapersonal. In this conception, all people have all these intelligences, but not all of them are developed equally; one or more of these intelligences are more fully developed than the others. Any of them may be developed or diminished through various circumstances and life stages. See also *fluid intelligence, crystallized intelligence,* and *constructive intelligence.*

multiple-personality disorder   A form of *dissociative disorder* in which an individual has two or more distinct personalities. The term preferred by professionals is *dissociative identity disorder.* The individual may not be aware of the existence of these other personalities. Nonprofessionals often inappropriately confuse *schizophrenia* for this disorder.

multiple-program participation   The involvement by clients in two or more social welfare services simultaneously. For example, in the United States most of those who receive *Temporary Assistance to Needy Families (TANF)* might also be eligible for *Medicaid* and food stamps; some TANF recipients might also qualify for housing assistance.

multiple sclerosis   A slowly progressive disease of the *central nervous system (CNS)* that usually begins to affect its victims during their twenties. The symptoms may include some of the following: paralysis or numbness of various parts of the body, convulsions, visual and speech disorders, emotional problems, bladder control disturbances, and muscular weakness. The symptoms have a tendency to increase and decrease in severity at varying intervals.

multiple-stressor debriefing (MSD)   A form of debriefing in which participants in crisis situations meet with interviewers individually or in groups soon after the stressful event to discuss their involvement as well as their effective and ineffective coping strategies and common reactions. Originated for disaster relief operations personnel, the purpose is to better prepare for future crisis situations and to help the participants overcome reactions to experiencing many stresses within a short period. MSD is similar to *critical incident stress debriefing (CISD),* except that the latter occurs usually in a one-session intervention in a group format only. It is also similar to *traumatic event debriefing (TED),* except that the latter focuses on only one stressor event.

multiple tic disorder   See *Tourette's disorder.* See also *tic disorder.*

multiproblem family   A kinship group whose members are seen by the social worker and treated for a variety of different social, economic, and personality difficulties at the same time. Viewing some family clients as "multiproblem" enables the social worker to use many intervention techniques to address more than one problem at a time. See also *multiple-impact therapy.*

multistage cluster sampling   A form of probability sampling in which the researcher identifies classes or groups of population members, selects some of the clusters at random, and then selects randomly from each of the chosen clusters. For example, in studying social work students, the researcher lists all the schools of social work, chooses some randomly, and then chooses some students randomly from each selected school.

multisystemic therapy (MST)   A treatment model, especially for serious offending delinquents, in which the social worker or other therapist works with the youth and family, often in their homes, and focuses on separating the youth from problem peers. MST therapists work at many system levels identifying family strengths; developing natural support systems; and addressing the needs of the youth, family, peers, and community.

multisystems orientation   In social work interventions, the approach that gives special recognition to the client as part of an interrelated–related series of systems, each of which influences and is influenced by other systems and the client. The intervention occurs at more than one of these systems and often requires a team of workers and a collaboration of agencies to provide the services needed for effectiveness in this orientation. For example, when the client is a family whose father has been arrested for child molestation, the intervention strategy might include economic and emotional support services for the children and mother, legal and mental health services for the father, and group work with the extended family. An example of the multisystems orientation is the *intensive family preservation services (IFPS)* program.

multivariate analysis In research, a group of statistical techniques, including analysis of covariance and factor analysis, that tests the results of two or more variables acting simultaneously.

mumps A contagious viral disease that results in painful swelling of the salivary glands, especially under the jawbone.

Munchausen syndrome An outdated term for *factitious disorder.*

municipal court A local court with jurisdiction over minor offenses (such as traffic violations, curfew violations, and loitering) and over civil disputes (such as landlord–tenant grievances and unpaid debts) in which damages claimed are small.

muscle relaxation technique A therapeutic and self-help approach to reducing *stress* and *anxiety;* it is accomplished when the subject first tightens and then relaxes a set of muscles while concentrating on those muscles. The procedure has many variations but basically consists of sitting in a quiet, private place and then flexing, holding for a few seconds, and relaxing different muscle groups in a predetermined sequence (such as right hand, right forearm, right shoulder, and so on) until all the muscle groups have been relaxed. The technique is also used in conjunction with other therapy approaches, such as *systematic desensitization.*

muscular dystrophy A progressive disease of the skeletal muscles that usually begins in early childhood. In some forms, patients are confined to wheelchairs by the time they reach adolescence. Early manifestations of the disease include progressive muscular weakness, waddling gait, coordination problems, and sometimes *learning disorder* and *mental retardation.* Causes are not well established for all types, but in many male victims it is an inherited disease, passed on through the mother.

music therapy Psychosocial intervention that emphasizes the use of music as a means of communicating with clients or helping them express themselves, reduce tension, validate feelings, and promote behavioral change. Often used as an adjunct to other forms of therapy, music therapy sometimes gets clients to discuss music and lyrics, play instruments, and write songs. Music therapists come from many professions, including social work. The professional association is the American Music Therapy Association (AMTA), which promotes the field; facilitates information-building, training, and dissemination of information; and certifies qualified music therapists. Their Web site address is http://www.amta.org. See also *dance therapy.*

mutism A refusal or inability to speak.

mutual-aid groups Formal or informal associations of people who share certain problems and may meet regularly in small groups to provide one another with advice, emotional support, information, and other help. Mutual-aid groups are similar to *self-help groups,* except they may have professional leaders. See *support system.*

mutual help The efforts of people who face similar problems to provide assistance for one another. Social workers often encourage and facilitate such efforts among client groups. For example, senior citizens in a *network* may provide mutual help by calling one another periodically throughout the day for reassurance. See also *mutual-aid groups* and *support system.*

mutual obligation Reciprocity between those who are helped and those who help. In social welfare concepts it is the obligation of both the recipient of benefits and the government. The government provides funds, social services, education, and other benefits, and the recipients are obliged to fulfill some social good. These obligations include regularly searching for employment; providing suitable homes and education for their children; and, if required, performing community service tasks.

mutual withdrawal The condition of indifference, boredom, noncommunication, and nonmotivation to resolve problems that sometimes occurs among troubled couples and family members.

mutualistas Formally and informally organized *mutual-aid groups* found primarily in Mexican American communities and other Hispanic neighborhoods. Members of these organizations pool resources to help families pay for funeral expenses, health care, and small business opportunities while also offering social activities.

mutuality The efforts of two or more people to act together in ultimate harmony to achieve benefits for each. In *systems theories* it is the concept of interdependence between various subsystems, such as social worker and client, landlord and tenant, or parents and children. See also *pseudomutuality.*

myasthenia gravis A chronic neuromuscular disease causing muscle weakness during periods of activity and improvement after rest. The symptoms are caused by a dysfunction in the transmission of nerve impulses to the muscles. It is not contagious or inherited directly.

myocardial infarction A circulatory system disease in which a blood vessel that carries blood to the heart muscles (for example, a coronary artery) becomes blocked as the result of a blood clot or hemorrhage. Often this occurs because the artery wall has become hardened or narrowed by *arteriosclerosis.* See also *heart attack.*

myoclonus Involuntary twitching of muscles.

myopathy Any disease of the muscles.

Myrdal, Alva Reimer (1902–1986) A Swedish social scientist and activist, and wife of Nobel laureate Gunnar Myrdal. She was a leader in the international peace movement and headed the United Nations Department of Social Welfare and UNESCO's Department of Social Sciences. She received the Nobel Peace Prize in 1980.

myth A traditional narrative in story form that helps explain characteristics of one's culture or history.

najda   Arabic for assistance in time of need.

naltrexone   A drug used in the treatment of people addicted to opium-based substances and those with alcohol dependence, in combination with supportive psychotherapy.

NAMI   The organization established in 1979 (as the National Alliance for the Mentally Ill) to advocate for more comprehensive mental health research and health insurance parity in coverage for physical disorders and to coordinate the activities of many foundations involved in mental health research. Most of NAMI's 200,000 members are relatives of persons with mental illness. Their Web site address is http://www.nami.org

narcissism   Excessive self-preoccupation and self-love; an extreme form of *egocentrism.*

narcissistic personality disorder   One of the *personality disorders,* characterized by excessive egocentrism, grandiosity, self-centeredness, preoccupation with feelings of envy, fragile self-esteem, and behavior that is often seeking approval or admiration. The person usually has little empathy, volatile interpersonal relationships, and periodic depression.

narcolepsy   One of the *sleep disorders* in which the individual is subject to brief attacks of sleepiness resulting in deep sleep, often at inopportune times.

narcosis   Drug-induced stupor.

narcotic antagonists   Drugs used in the treatment of opiate (morphine or heroin) addiction that prevent users from feeling euphoria and thus help motivated addicts to become deconditioned. The most widely used narcotic antagonists are naloxone and cyclazocine.

narcotics   Natural or synthetic drugs that have a depressant effect on the *central nervous system (CNS),* relieve pain and anxiety, and alter mood. The major narcotic is *opium* (and its constituents *codeine* and *morphine*), from which *heroin* is derived. Narcotics tend to result in *addiction,* and their side effects can often endanger the life of the user.

narrative family therapy   A therapeutic approach used with families and individuals that holds that people's views of themselves, which are developed in interaction with others and society, may be narrow and restrictive, which can lead to certain problems dominating their lives. According to Michael White, the Australian social worker who developed it, and American social worker Patricia Kelley, who further refined and applied its concepts, the major goal of narrative family therapy is for the clients to broaden their views of self and family, see more alternatives, and challenge the dominance of the problem over their lives by taking control of it.

narrative summary   A system of social case *recording* in which the social worker describes and consolidates all the relevant information obtained about the client system: the progression of the intervention, including procedures used and outcomes, and the interim and concluding *prognosis* and recommendations. The information is written as succinctly as possible and is based on the social worker's ongoing progress notes, findings before the intervention, and overall conclusion about the case. See also *process recording.*

narrative therapy   Psychotherapeutic intervention that emphasizes the use of client storytelling through writing assignments involving specific aspects of one's life, thought, or imagination and oral descriptions of various life experiences. See also *poetry therapy.*

NASW Board of Directors   The *National Association of Social Workers (NASW)* 23-member body elected by the membership for three-year terms. Its major functions are to determine ongoing policies and priorities, implement policies, allocate resources, establish national committees and task forces to carry out programs, determine membership policies and practices, set personnel policies and practices, and evaluate the executive director. The board is chaired by the president, who is elected for a three-year term following a year as president-elect.

NASW Code of Ethics   The explication of the values, rules, and principles of ethical conduct that apply to all social workers who are members of the *National Association of Social Workers (NASW)*. The original *code of ethics* for social workers was implicit in the 1951 Standards for Professional Practice of the *American Association of Social Workers (AASW)*. NASW developed a formal code in 1960 and has since made subsequent revisions, the latest in 2002.

natality Birthrate; the ratio of births to total population within a specified time period.

Nation of Islam The Muslim organization founded in 1930 to emphasize self-help among African Americans. Once referred to as the *Black Muslims*, the Nation of Islam sponsors many activities and programs to provide social services to the community and advocate for social change. Their Web site address is http://www.noi.org

National Abortion and Reproductive Rights Action League (NARAL) The organization founded in 1969 to protect and maintain the right to legal *abortion*. The organization was formed as the National Association for Repeal of Abortion Laws and took its present name after the 1973 Supreme Court decision to permit legal abortions. See also *Roe v. Wade* and the *National Right-to-Life Committee (NRLC)*. Their Web site address is http://www.naral.org

National Academy of Practice (NAP) A professional, scientific, and educational organization, established in 1981 and modeled in part on the National Academy of Sciences, that comprises distinguished practitioners from each of the major health professions, including social work. NAP's goals are to promote excellence in professional practice for the benefit of all people and to provide a forum to which government and society can direct public policy concerns in health care. One of the constituent organizations in NAP is the National Academy of Practice in Social Work.

National Aging Information Center (NAIC) A service of the U.S. *Administration on Aging (AoA)* to disseminate information about older Americans, aging policy, current approaches to professional practice with older people, statistical data, and other issues of interest and concern to the aging community. The program was established in 1995 under the *Older Americans Act*. Their Web site address is http://www.aoa.dhhs.gov/naic

National Alliance for the Mentally Ill See *NAMI*.

National Assembly of Health and Human Services Organizations (NAHHSO) An association of national nonprofit health and human services organizations that facilitates the exchange of information and plans for mutual goals, membership development, and advocacy. Their Web site address is http://www.nassembly.org

National Assessment of Educational Progress (NAEP) The program of the *U.S. Department of Education*, established in 1969, to test the progress of students across the nation in reading, math, science, writing, history, and geography. Called "the nation's report card," NAEP looks at 9-, 13-, and 17-year-olds over time and allows for state-by-state and regional comparisons of the 4th, 8th, and 12th grades.

National Association for the Advancement of Colored People (NAACP) The largest and oldest of the U.S. *civil rights* organizations. It was established in 1909 when social worker *Mary White Ovington* (1865–1951) and others helped organize African American and white people who were outraged about a series of lynchings. NAACP now has more than 1,500 local chapters throughout all 50 states and works to achieve its goals primarily through legal actions to protect the rights of black citizens, nonpartisan political action to enact civil rights laws, and education and public information. Their Web site address is http://www.naacp.org

National Association of Black Social Workers (NABSW) The organization of people interested in the goals of African Americans, particularly those employed in human services jobs. Membership is not limited to social workers. Established in 1968, NABSW has chapters throughout the nation and sponsors conventions, publications, and research. Their Web site address is http://www.nabsw.org

National Association of Deans and Directors of Schools of Social Work (NADD) The organization of social work educators who head schools of social work in the United States. NADD started in the 1970s as an informal annual meeting of deans and directors during conferences sponsored by the *Council on Social Work Education (CSWE)*. Its members meet at least twice yearly to confer about the problems and plans pertaining to social work education. Their Web site address is http://www.cosw.sc.edu/nadd

National Association of Oncology Social Workers   See *Association of Oncology Social Workers (AOSW)*.

National Association of Public Child Welfare Administrators (NAPCWA)   The organization for administrative leaders of state and local public child welfare agencies, founded in 1983. NAPCWA provides opportunities for administrators across the nation to communicate about their common concerns and to inform political leaders, clients, and the public about the needs of children and the policies affecting their well-being.

National Association of Puerto Rican/Hispanic Social Workers   The *professional association* of social workers of *Hispanic* heritages whose members work primarily toward the improvement of social conditions for Hispanics and for the professional goals of Spanish-speaking social workers. The group was formed in 1971 as the National Association of Puerto Rican Social Service Workers. Their Web site address is http://www.naprhsw.org

National Association of School Social Workers (NASSW)   The organization of social workers in elementary, middle, and high schools, established in 1919 as the National Association of Visiting Teachers. In 1955 NASSW merged into the *National Association of Social Workers (NASW)*.

National Association of Schools of Social Administration (NASSA)   The social work education organization founded in 1942 to establish standards and accreditation for colleges offering baccalaureate degrees in social work. NASSA grew out of dissatisfaction with the requirement that only schools offering two-year master's degrees in social work could be accredited by the *American Association of Schools of Social Work (AASSW)*. The two organizations, NASSA and AASSW, merged in 1952 to form the *Council on Social Work Education (CSWE)*.

National Association of Social Workers (NASW)   The organization of social workers established in 1955 through the consolidation of the *American Association of Social Workers (AASW)*, the *American Association of Psychiatric Social Workers (AAPSW)*, the *American Association of Group Workers (AAGW)*, the *Association for the Study of Community Organization (ASCO)*, the *American Association of Medical Social Workers (AAMSW)*, the

National Association of School Social Workers (NASSW), and the *Social Work Research Group (SWRG)*. NASW's primary functions include promoting the professional development of its members, establishing and maintaining professional standards of practice, advancing sound social policies for the betterment of the nation, and providing other services that protect its members and enhance their professional status. The organization has developed and adopted the *NASW Code of Ethics* and other generic and specialized practice standards. *Certification* and *quality assurance* are promoted through several credentials, including the *Academy of Certified Social Workers (ACSW)*, the *Qualified Clinical Social Worker (QCSW)*, the *Diplomate in Clinical Social Work (DCSW)*, and other specialty certification programs. NASW maintains a lobbying group to influence national policy and its *Political Action for Candidate Election (PACE)* organization. NASW also sponsors professional conferences and *continuing education* programs and produces journals, books, and major reference works such as *Encyclopedia of Social Work* and this dictionary. Their Web site address is http://www.naswdc.org

National Center for Missing and Exploited Children (NCMEC)   A national clearinghouse and resource center to provide assistance in cases of child abduction, parental kidnapping, *child snatching*, lost children, and victims of *child abuse*. Funding comes primarily from the Office of Juvenile Justice and Delinquency Prevention of the *U.S. Department of Justice*. The center may be reached by calling 1-800-THE LOST or 1-800-843-5678 or by going online at http://www.missingkids.org. See also *child find organizations* and *Amber Alert*.

National Civilian Community Corps (NCCC)   Also known as AmeriCorps*NCSSS, a voluntary program for men and women between ages 18 and 24 who serve 10 months while living in one of five regional campuses in the nation (primarily on deactivated military bases). Their primary work is on environmental projects, public safety, disaster relief, and other community needs. Volunteers learn valuable skills, give back to the community, and receive education grants to help finance college or pay back student loans. AmeriCorps*NCSSS, along with *AmeriCorps*VISTA*, are components of the *Corporation for National and Community Service*. Their Web site address is http://www.americorps.org/nccc

National Committees of NASW　A component in the governance of the *National Association of Social Workers (NASW),* this group of standing committees, mandated by the elected leadership and various ad hoc committees and task forces, serves at the will of the *NASW Board of Directors.* The mandated standing national committees are the Executive Committee, the *Committee on Inquiry,* the Committee on Nominations and Leadership Identification, the National Program Committee, the National Finance Committee, the National Committee on Racial and Ethnic Diversity, the National Committee on Women's Issues, and the National Committee on Lesbian, Gay, and Bisexual Issues.

National Conference of Charities and Corrections　A former name for the organization that came to be known as the *National Conference on Social Welfare (NCSW).*

National Conference on Catholic Charities　The former name for *Catholic Charities USA.*

National Conference on Social Welfare (NCSW)　A federation of social welfare agencies in the public and private sectors, including secular and religious agencies as well as individuals concerned about the social welfare of Americans. Established in 1879 as the Conference of Charities, it changed its name to the National Conference of Charities and Corrections in 1884, to the National Conference of Social Work in 1917, and to its last name in 1957. NCSW suspended operations gradually throughout the 1980s.

National Congress of American Indians (NCAI)　The *civil rights* and lobbying organization established in 1944 by leaders of the nation's largest tribes. With headquarters in Washington, DC, the congress evaluates government policies pertaining to American Indians and promotes programs to enhance economic, educational, and legal rights for its constituents. Their Web site address is http://www.ncai.org

National Consumers League (NCL)　The advocacy and educational organization founded in 1899 to protect those who make, sell, purchase, or use products or provide and use services. In its early years, it was led by social worker–lawyer *Florence Kelley* (1859–1932) and philanthropist *Josephine Shaw Lowell* (1843–1904) and successfully fought for improved working conditions, child labor laws,

a minimum wage, shorter working hours, and safe and effective consumer products. Their Web site address is http://www.natlconsumersleague.org

National Council of Senior Citizens (NCSC)　A federation of more than 4,000 senior citizens' clubs in the United States, founded in 1961 to coordinate the activities of older people in educating the public, lobbying, and developing services and programs. Their Web site address is http://www. ncscinc.org

National Council on Aging (NCOA)　An organization of individuals and agencies to serve older people. The council coordinates conferences and procedures for exchanging information between organizations and helps disseminate information to researchers, academicians, health care providers, family members of older people, and others interested in services to older people. Through its *National Institute on Aging, Work, and Retirement (NIAWR),* it strives to promote opportunities for middle-age or older people to obtain employment or prepare for *retirement.* Their Web site address is http://www.ncoa.org

National Disaster Medical System (NDMS)　Volunteer professionals in medicine, nursing, social work, veterinary science, mortuary service, and other fields who can be brought together quickly in cases of large-scale disasters. NDMS consists of volunteer response teams in all parts of the nation. Their Web site address is http://www.ndms.dhhs.gov/ndms

National Education Association (NEA)　A professional membership association of teachers, school administrators, and related personnel. Founded in 1857, its major objectives are improved educational practices, facilities, standards, and conditions for teachers and students. Their Web site address is http://www.nea.org

National Federation of Settlements　See *United Neighborhood Centers of America.*

National Federation of Societies for Clinical Social Work (NFSCSW)　The former name for the *Clinical Social Work Federation (CSWF).*

national health insurance　Programs to help the citizens of a country pay their health care costs in the existing medical marketplace. These programs vary in different nations but basically use taxes, payroll deductions, and contributions to pay an organization that reimburses for needed health care. Usually beneficiaries pay a portion of the health care provider's bill. A national health insurance program exists in many nations, but not in the United States. Other nations use a *national health service*.

national health service   Direct government provision of medical personnel and facilities for citizens to receive health care. This system is common in many countries, although not in the United States. However, a form of national health service is provided to certain groups in the United States, including needy veterans, members of the armed forces and their families, tuberculosis patients, and American Indians. Opponents of the service call it *"socialized medicine."* This system is not to be confused with *national health insurance*.

National Immigration Lookout System (NAILS) See *Lookout Book*.

National Incidence-Based Reporting System (NIBRS)   A data-gathering and reporting procedure developed in 1986 by the *Federal Bureau of Investigation (FBI)* to revise and modernize its *Uniform Crime Reports (UCR)*. NIBRS has added 21 crime categories to the eight in the UCR, including drug violations, weapons offenses, counterfeiting, hate crimes, juvenile kidnapping, and other less serious crimes. NIBRS also includes information about the victims, the amount and type of property lost, recovery, and multiple crimes within an incident. As it is in the UCR, information is obtained from local law enforcement agencies. See also *National Crime Victimization Survey (NCVS)*.

National Indian Child Welfare Association (NICWA)   The national organization, founded in 1983, to facilitate the proper implementation of the *Indian Child Welfare Act* and to promote healthy and culturally strong environments for American Indian children. The Portland, Oregon–based organization works primarily on behalf of tribal governments and urban Indian social services programs to help train professionals and others in providing services for American Indian children and families. Their Web site address is http://www.nicwa.org

National Institute of Child Health and Human Development (NICHD)   See *Child Health and Human Development, National Institute of (NICHD)*.

National Institute of Mental Health (NIMH)   A federal organization within the *National Institutes of Health (NIH)* to support research and training, oversee plans for the care and treatment of people with mental illness, and facilitate programs to enhance the nation's *mental health*. Their Web site address is http://www.nimh.nih.gov

National Institute on Drug Abuse (NIDA)   The *HHS* organization that funds and coordinates studies pertaining to the manufacture, transportation, distribution, use, and consequences of illicit drugs in the United States.

National Institutes of Health (NIH)   The organization within the *U.S. Department of Health and Human Services (HHS)* that supports, coordinates, and conducts research into the causes, prevention, treatment, and cure of diseases. NIH has many component institutes, each specializing in a particular disease or health concern. Major components include the National Cancer Institute; the National Institute of Child Health and Human Development; the *National Institute of Mental Health (NIMH)*; the National Institute of Allergy and Infectious Diseases; the National Heart, Lung, and Blood Institute; the National Institute of Arthritis and Musculoskeletal and Skin Diseases; the National Institute of Diabetes and Digestive and Kidney Diseases; the National Institute of Environmental Health Sciences; the National Institute of Alcohol Abuse and Alcoholism; the *National Institute on Drug Abuse (NIDA)*; the National Eye Institute; the National Institute on Aging; the National Institute of Neurological Disorders and Stroke; the National Institute on Deafness and Other Communications Disorders; the National Institute of General Medical Sciences; the National Institute for Nursing Research; the National Institute for Human Genome Research; the National Institute of Dental Research; and the National Library of Medicine. Their Web site address is http://www.nih.org

National League of Cities (NLC)   The public interest organization, founded in 1924 as the American Municipal Association, in which membership consists of nearly all the towns and cities in the United States and for which the goal is to advocate municipal interests before Congress and other government agencies.

National Network for Social Work Managers (NNSWM) An independent *professional association* of social work managers, administrators, educators, and others, founded in 1985, to provide a forum for common concerns, facilitate research, and disseminate knowledge about social work management. The network produces the quarterly journal *Administration in Social Work* and the quarterly newsletter *Social Work Executive*. At its annual conference, it presents its Lifetime Achievement Award and the Exemplar Award to recognize excellence in social work management. Their Web site address is http://www.socialworkmanagers.org

National Organization for Human Service Education (NOHSE) An association of human service professionals, particularly educators and students, that facilitates the preparation of human service workers. NOHSE was established in 1975 to provide resources for educators and clients. It has an annual conference and sponsors a newsletter and the journal *Human Service Education*. Their Web site address is http://www.nohse.com

National Organization for Women (NOW) A volunteer organization, with local chapters throughout the United States, established in 1966 to enhance the economic and social opportunities for women through educating the public, lobbying, taking legal action against discriminatory procedures, and helping elect candidates sympathetic to NOW's goals. Their Web site address is http://www.now.org

National Organization of Forensic Social Work (NOFSW) The professional association, established in 1982, to represent social work specialists in the law and legal aspects of social services. Their activities include evaluations of criminal defendants, expert witness testimony, civil litigation cases, child custody determinations, and consultation and training for other law authorities. Their Web site address is http://www.nofsw.org

National Recovery Administration (NRA) The federal organization established in 1933, early in President Franklin D. Roosevelt's first term, to take immediate action to solve problems arising from the economic crisis. Mostly involved with establishing new codes regulating businesses and labor, NRA was absorbed into other agencies by 1936.

National Right-to-Life Committee (NRLC) The organization founded in 1973 to oppose *abortion*, *infanticide*, and *euthanasia* and to provide education, counseling, and alternatives such as *adoption*. The committee seeks a constitutional amendment to make abortion illegal. Their Web site address is http://www.nrlc.org. See also *Roe v. Wade* and the *National Abortion and Reproductive Rights Action League (NARAL)*.

National Social Workers Exchange An early social work organization that began informally in various cities in the 1910–1920 decade to provide central gathering points for the exchange of ideas, job information, and social cause actions. The exchange grew more formal and in 1921 was organized as the *American Association of Social Workers (AASW)*, which merged into the *National Association of Social Workers (NASW)* in 1955.

National Urban League See *Urban League, National.*

National Voter Registration Act (NVRA) Popularly known as the "motor voter law," the 1993 act (P.L. 103-31) gives U.S. citizens the opportunity to register to vote when applying for driver's licenses, welfare assistance, and government services. The legislation was initiated by *HumanSERVE* and social worker *Richard Cloward*.

National Welfare Rights Organization (NWRO) An organization of public relief clients to improve welfare legislation and programs and combat bureaucratic policies. NWRO was established in 1966 and suspended operations in 1975.

National Youth Administration (NYA) The *New Deal* federal program of the 1930s to provide part-time jobs for high school and college students so they could complete their educations.

nationalism A value orientation and worldview that one's country and its perceived interests are the most important consideration and that the citizens of that country are obliged to do anything required for the sake of the country. Proponents of this orientation cite its patriotism, devotion, pride in one's own people and land, and willingness to make personal sacrifices for the betterment of all. Opponents indicate how this orientation makes it difficult to find compromises and a means of cooperation with other nations.

nationalization A government's assuming ownership, management, or both of one or more of a nation's industries. Industries most commonly nationalized include utilities, telephone and postal companies, and natural resource production industries formerly under foreign ownership.

"Native Americans" The name applied by some to the ethnic–racial–cultural groups of American citizens whose ancestors lived in the Western Hemisphere before its exploration and settlement by Europeans. The designation has been applied to 350 to 400 (some say up to 600) distinct ethnic groups that use more than 250 languages. Those opposed to the use of the term say it is a "politically imposed false racial label applied to indigenous peoples in the United States by American colonizers" and that "First Nations Peoples" or "Indigenous Peoples" should be used (Michael Yellow Bird, personal communication, June 4, 2002). A 1995 survey by the Bureau of Labor Statistics showed that these people prefer "American Indian" over "Native American."

nativism The idea that certain personality factors are not learned but are genetically transmitted or present at birth. See also *archetype*.

natural family planning Engaging in sexual intercourse, or abstaining from it, during the fertility cycle to achieve pregnancy goals.

natural helping network Informal linkages and relationships between people who voluntarily provide important services and supports to people in need and those to whom they provide the services. Most natural helping networks develop among members of the needy person's family or neighbors, fellow employees, members of the person's church, members of associations or social classes to which the person belongs, or altruistic people in the community.

natural law The idea that there are unchangeable truths that govern all human relationships and behavior and that they would exist even if there were no legal authority to enforce them. Natural law includes natural rights, which all people have regardless of their governments.

natural resources The products and features of the Earth that permit it to support life and meet human needs, including land, air, water, climate, minerals, and biological resources such as trees, wildlife, and vegetation. See also *human resources*.

naturalization The legal process of becoming a citizen or national of a country. See also *immigration* and *repatriation*.

"near-poor" population People who are employed but earn only slightly more than is received by those who benefit from *public assistance* or *social security*.

necrosis Death of bone or tissue.

needle exchange program A program to provide new hypodermic syringes to those considered most likely to reuse already infected needles. Its primary purpose is to protect *IV drug users* from diseases such as *HIV*.

needs The physical, psychological, economic, cultural, and social requirements for survival, well-being, and fulfillment. Types of needs include *normative needs, perceived needs, expressed needs*, and *relative needs*.

needs assessments (NA) Systematic appraisals made by professionals in evaluating their clients for problems, existing resources, potential solutions, and obstacles to problem solving. In social agencies, needs assessments are made on behalf of the clients who receive clinical services and in communities to document needs and establish priorities for service.

needs group Representative victims of a problem who are included in planning committees to discuss and decide how to assist others who have the problem.

needs hierarchy Abraham Maslow's concept of human *motivation*. He asserted in 1943 that people have five sets of goals or basic needs, each building upon others: physiological needs, safety needs, affiliation needs, ego needs, and *self-actualization*.

negative campaigning Conducting a political or social-change *campaign* by emphasizing the actual or claimed liabilities of the opposition. See also *mudslinging*.

negative feedback Critical, derogatory responses to one's efforts or communications. In *systems theories* and *communication theory*, a signal or message that maintains the system's characteristic or organized state.

negative income tax A program designed to standardize procedures for assisting poor families while eliminating a *means test* through use of the federal income tax system. Taxpayers whose incomes fall below a specified minimum are reimbursed up to that amount from the federal treasury. A version of this plan exists in the *Earned Income Tax Credit* program. See also *guaranteed annual income.*

negative reinforcement In *behavior modification,* the strengthening of a *response* through escape or avoidance conditioning.

negative transference *Transference* that results in expressions of hostility or distrust or feelings of ill will that a client may have for a psychotherapist or other person. In *psychoanalytic theory,* it is believed to always exist, whether it is latent or overt.

negativistic personality disorder A pervasive pattern of negativistic attitudes and passive resistance; the individual habitually resents, opposes, and covertly obstructs demands to fulfill obligations and appropriate expectations. This condition is also known as *passive–aggressive personality disorder.*

neglect Failure to meet one's legal and moral obligations or duties, especially to dependent family members. When such conduct results in potential harm to others, legal proceedings may be taken to compel the person to meet the relevant obligations or face punishment.

negligence Failure to exercise reasonable care or caution, resulting in others being subjected to harm or unwarranted risk of harm; also, failure to fulfill responsibility that is necessary to protect or help another. Contributory negligence may occur when a person's failure to exercise prudent caution, combined with the negligence of another, results in harm to a third individual. For example, if a social worker does not report knowledge about a person's neglect of a child who has been harmed, the social worker could be charged with contributory negligence. Criminal (or culpable) negligence may occur when one is so reckless, careless, or indifferent to others' safety that injury or death results.

negotiation The process of bringing together those who are opposed on some issues and arranging for them to communicate clearly and fairly, to bargain and compromise, and to arrive at mutually acceptable agreements. See also *arbitration, mediation,* and *alternative dispute resolution (ADR).*

neighborhood A region or locality in which inhabitants share certain characteristics, values, mutual interests, or styles of living.

neighborhood centers See *settlement house.*

Neighborhood Guild Another name for *settlement house.* Stanton Coit, who started the settlement house movement in the United States, used this name for his original facility and referred to all settlements by this name. Most settlement houses are now called neighborhood centers. See also *United Neighborhood Centers of America (UNCA).*

neighborhood information center A social program, similar to the British Citizen's Advice Bureaus (CABs), in which highly accessible and geographically convenient organizations are used as entry points to the total *social services* system. They provide information, advice, and referrals but do not replace the intake evaluation function of social agencies. The centers can be freestanding or located in post offices, libraries, municipal buildings, and shopping centers.

Neighborhood Networks A community-based program of the United States established in 1995 to develop and maintain local centers to help people locate opportunities for jobs, housing, social services, education, and small businesses. The centers use computers, Internet, classrooms, and volunteer mentors and are funded through federal and philanthropic grants.

Neighborhood Watch Program The local crime prevention program in which volunteer residents of a neighborhood provide "extra eyes and ears" to law enforcement officials. The national program was created in 1972 to promote the establishment of such groups in all residential areas, especially high-crime areas.

neo-Freudian A theoretical orientation that basically follows *Freudian theory* but puts greater emphasis on sociocultural factors, interpersonal relationships, and psychosocial development into and through *adulthood.* There is no single neo-Freudian school, because those who have been given this designation also diverge from one another. However, leading neo-Freudians include

Harry Stack Sullivan, Karen Horney, Alfred Adler, and Erich Fromm.

neo-Nazism   A political ideology and movement in which the philosophy of the National Socialist Party of the German Third Reich and its leader, Adolf Hitler, is promoted. Much of the ideology centers around racism and the view that only some Aryan peoples should rule and that many other peoples, such as Jews, Gypsies, people of color, gay men and lesbians, and people with genetic or health problems, should be exterminated. Because the ideology is so disfavored by most people, at least in public, much of its activity is accomplished through *secret societies.*

neoconservatism   A revision of certain aspects of traditional conservative philosophies and views that retains most other aspects of these views. Thus, there are many neoconservative philosophies rather than a single one. The term is often applied to an attitude that favors more controls on morality and financial incentives and subsidies to businesses to encourage their growth, rejecting the traditional conservative view that government should be unobtrusive and minimal. See also *conservatism.*

neoliberalism   A revision of certain aspects of traditional liberal philosophies and views while retaining most other aspects of these views. Thus, there are many neoliberal philosophies rather than a single one. The term is most commonly applied to those who change their traditional liberal views and espouse fewer direct welfare benefits and similar programs.

neonatal   Pertaining to newborn infants.

neonatal withdrawal syndrome   Symptoms revealed by newborns indicating drug addiction that began in utero. The symptoms include spontaneous body tremors, *arrhythmia,* insomnia, and abnormal breathing patterns.

neonaticide   The deliberate killing of an infant within 24 hours of its birth. Such acts are most commonly committed by young, unwed parents who are in extreme denial about the existence of the child and overwhelmed by the responsibilities of raising it. See also *infanticide.*

nepotism   Favoritism shown to an individual's relatives, especially in appointing them to desirable jobs.

nervios   A *culture-bound syndrome* among Spanish-speaking peoples referring to general "nervousness" and a wide range of emotional distresses, including anxiety, somatic complaints, headaches, tearfulness, sleep problems, and an inability to concentrate.

"nervous breakdown"   An imprecise lay term that carries many meanings, usually having to do with any emotional condition that has resulted in hospitalization or severe emotional disability interfering with normal functioning. Social workers or other professionals do not use this term in professional communications.

NES immigrants   People from non–English-speaking nations. This designation is used in some English-speaking nations, especially Australia and New Zealand, to refer to applicants for immigration who come from Asian and African nations.

net present value (NPV) analysis   A method used in program planning and budgeting to help determine what *benefits* are available in relation to costs when measured over time. NPV rates programs according to the difference between the present value of the benefits and the costs required to achieve those benefits. It is an alternative to *cost–benefit analysis.*

net worth   The value of an individual's or corporation's total possessions, including savings, real estate, stocks, bonds, and other monetary assets, minus all unpaid obligations, including capital gains taxes owed when assets are sold.

network   A formal or informal linkage of people or organizations that may share resources, skills, contacts, and knowledge with one another. Networks may be positive or negative in their effects on individuals and families.

network therapy   The family treatment procedure in which a large number of people who are important to an individual or to a nuclear family are brought together with that family to discuss how everyone can help resolve existing problems. Included in such meetings can be members of the *extended family,* neighbors, classmates, fellow employees, other professionals, and clergy members.

networking   Efforts to enhance and develop the social linkages that might exist between people. These efforts include strengthening the supportive quality of existing networks, establishing new ones, creating linkages among the various networks to promote more competent support, and mobilizing these networks.

neurobiological disorders (NBD) The category of mental disorders that are now considered to be based, partly or entirely, on physiological dysfunctions of the chemical, neurological, or biological makeup of the individual. These disorders include schizophrenia, bipolar disorder, and major depression. Many scientists and mental health advocates suggest that the term "neurobiological disorder" should replace "mental disorder" at least for these conditions.

neurogenesis The formation of new neurons or nerve cells. NIMH studies report that the brain can add nerve cells during adult life. It was formerly believed that nerve cells were always created prenatally.

neurolinguistic programming (NLP) A communications model of human behavior developed by Richard Bandler, John Grinder, and others and used by social workers and other psychosocial therapists, educators, and business personnel to assess, build rapport with, and help clients. Major components of the model are "neuro" (the processing of information perceived through the five senses by the nervous system), "linguistic" (the systems of verbal and nonverbal communication that organize the neural representations into meaningful data), and "programming" (the ability to organize the neurolinguistic systems to achieve specific outcomes). To assess someone's behavior, the NLP counselor must identify the way the client understands information. The International Association of Neurolinguistic Programming (IANLP) was formed in 1983.

neurological disorder Dysfunction of the *central nervous system (CNS)* caused by injury, disease, or drugs and resulting in some forms of *organic mental disorders* and diseases of the CNS such as *cerebral palsy, Parkinson's disease,* and *seizure disorders.* The term should not be confused with similar sounding terms such as "neurasthenia," "nervousness," *neurosis,* or "neurotic," which are more closely related to *anxiety disorder.*

neurologist A physician who specializes in the diagnosis, treatment, and health of the individual's nervous system. The *American Board of Psychiatry*

and Neurology (ABPN) is the major credentialing authority for qualified specialists in this field.

neuromuscular disorders A group of neurological diseases that result in progressive weakness or uncontrollability of the muscles and *atrophy.* Major diseases of this type include *muscular dystrophy, Huntington's disease, Tourette's disorder,* and *Parkinson's disease.*

neuron The nerve cell, the basic building block of the *central nervous system (CNS)* on which electrochemical impulses are sent and received. See also *synapse.*

neurosis A mental disorder characterized by persistent and disturbing symptoms of *anxiety,* such as nervousness, irritability, and *somatic complaints.* The anxiety is said to be a maladaptive way of dealing with internal conflict. The symptoms can range from mild to severe but are relatively amenable to *psychotherapy.*

neurotransmitters See *catecholamines.*

New Deal President Franklin D. Roosevelt's name for the plans, programs, and legislation enacted during his first administration in response to the *Great Depression.* New Deal programs included the *Social Security Act; Federal Emergency Relief Administration (FERA); Civilian Conservation Corps (CCC); Works Progress Administration (WPA);* rural electrification; and legislation that regulated banking and securities practices, farm management, and unemployment exchanges.

new federalism An ideology that advocates reducing national spending and taxation, deregulating national controls on businesses and institutions, and ceding more responsibilities to state governments. The term was used by the Reagan administration to describe some of its policies.

new poor People who have recently become impoverished or have had significant reductions in their living standards as a result of job loss or other economic problems. Some sociologists and economists consider these people different from other poor people in that they tend to share the values and backgrounds of middle-class people.

new property The guaranteed assets, services, and resources that are available to a resident of a jurisdiction or member of a specified group. Also known as the "social wage," the "new income," and *entitlement programs,* these assets are seen by social planners and economists as being as important in considering an individual's *standard of living* as income from work or assets from unearned income.

new religious movements (NRMs) Groups and philosophies that have emerged, especially since the 1960s, that may include some of the ideologies and formats of traditional Western and Eastern religions and elements of modern secular culture. Some organizations referred to as NRMs include the Unification Church, Divine Light Mission, Rajneesh Foundation, Krishna Consciousness, Synanon, and Scientology. Some prefer the term NRM to *"cult"* because of that term's negative connotations.

Newborns' Act The 1996 U.S. federal legislation, formally called the Newborns' and Mothers' Health Protection Act of 1996 (P.L. 104-204), that requires insurance coverage for hospital stays at least 48 hours after vaginal birth and 96 hours after cesarean birth.

Newburgh welfare plan The controversial system of providing *public assistance* services in Newburgh, New York, beginning in 1960. Designed primarily to reduce *welfare* costs, the system gave applicants minimal help, often with payments in kind rather than in cash, and subjected them to stringent residency requirements. After several years, the program was terminated. Many of its provisions and ideologies were incorporated into the *Personal Responsibility and Work Opportunity Reconciliation Act* of 1996.

Newstart Allowance (NSA) An Australian social insurance program that provides income and other services for unemployed Australians who seek jobs.

Newstetter, Wilber I. (1896–1972) Social work educator who helped develop many concepts in social group work and social work with youths. He was also founder and first dean of the School of Social Work at the University of Pittsburgh.

NGRI patients The legal term for people tried but found "not guilty by reason of insanity." Such people may be committed for indefinite periods to mental hospitals.

niche 1. In the *ecological perspective,* the position a species occupies in the biotic community. 2. In humans, the social position or status occupied in the existing social structure and in those social structures of a community by participating groups, relative to power and oppression.

nicotine dependence A *psychoactive substance abuse disorder,* the effect of which occurs primarily through inhaling the smoke of burning tobacco or ingesting chewed tobacco. The disorder is significantly related to physical diseases such as bronchitis, emphysema, coronary artery disease, peripheral vascular disease, and various forms of cancer.

nicotine-related disorders The resulting *substance dependence* and *withdrawal symptoms* that commonly occur through the use of nicotine, the psychoactive ingredient in tobacco. These disorders can develop with use of all forms of tobacco, including cigarettes, chewing tobacco, snuff, cigars, and pipes. Symptoms include depression, insomnia, irritability, anxiety, and difficulty concentrating.

nightmare disorder One of the *sleep disorders,* of the *parasomnia* type, characterized by frequent awakenings from sleep due to frightening dreams, resulting in ongoing distress, irritability, anxiety, or occupational and interpersonal problems. The individual usually becomes fully and rapidly awakened after the nightmare, which often involves an elaborate dream sequence of perceived danger. Nightmare disorder was formerly called *dream anxiety disorder;* it is not synonymous with *sleep terror disorder.*

nihilism A denial of the value of any and all social structures, governments and laws, norms and values, and moral principles. Such an orientation may lead one toward violence or terrorism against the established social system but more often results in passive resistance to everything with no alternatives in mind.

NIMBY "Not in my back yard!"—a slogan attributed to groups and individuals who oppose the location of an undesired facility (such as a halfway house, jail, garbage dump, or factory) in their neighborhoods.

Nineline A 24-hour-a-day free national hotline for troubled and *runaway* youths. The telephone number, 1-800-999-9999, is posted in areas where runaways tend to go. Volunteers from Covenant

House, the national social agency, and professionals provide support, guidance, information, and access to resources for all young people who call.

NIOSH   National Institute for Occupational Safety and Health, the *U.S. Department of Health and Human Services* organization within the *Centers for Disease Control and Prevention*, established in 1970, to conduct research and make recommendations for the prevention of work-related disease and injury. The findings and recommendations of NIOSH may be implemented and enforced by *OSHA*.

Nisei generation   Americans of Japanese ancestry, born mostly between 1910 and World War II, whose parents emigrated from Japan. Members of this generation were subject to problems of *acculturation* and *discrimination,* culminating in their being placed in *internment* camps during World War II. See also *Sansei generation.*

No Child Left Behind Act (NCLBA)   The education reform legislation (P.L. 107-110) signed into law in 2001 to help children and schools that are not meeting specified standards. The law requires annual state tests in reading and mathematics in grades three through eight, beginning in the 2004–2005 school year, and in science in 2005–2006. A school in which scores do not improve to the specified standard two years in a row could be restaffed, and low-income students in those schools could receive tutoring or transportation to other schools. Teachers must be qualified for their subject areas, and additional services for children with English as a second language are provided.

no-fault divorce   Legal dissolution of a *marriage* that occurs without the necessity of declaring that one or the other spouse is guilty of marital misconduct. Before the enactment of no-fault *divorce* laws in several states, most marriages could be legally terminated only when one party proved that the other was guilty of behavior that was grounds for divorce. The most common basis for no-fault divorce is voluntary separation for a specified amount of time.

no-spouse rule   A policy by some employers preventing married couples from working together; many judicial decisions in the United States have attacked the legality of this policy.

"noblesse oblige"   Originally a French term pertaining to the obligation of the nobility to help the peasantry. Now it refers to the obligation of affluent people to help those less fortunate.

noise pollution   An excessive and persistent volume of noise in the environment that may lead to hearing disorders, neurological damage, stress, or the inability to rest.

"nom de guerre"   A pseudonym used by some leaders of revolutionary movements and by guerrilla or terrorist groups as much for symbolic purposes as for concealment.

nomadism   The regular shifting of habitation by an individual or group, usually in search of a more suitable environment or better economic opportunities.

nominal group   A group whose members work in the presence of one another without verbally interacting, usually to establish goals of common interest. For example, a classroom instructor might use this approach by asking students in a new class to write their goals for the class or their objections to the curriculum so far.

nominal group technique   A tool used by social planners in *organization development (OD)* to assess existing problems, needs, interests, or objectives. Participants in a meeting write these factors on small cards. The leader collects and categorizes the cards and posts them on a board for all to see. Then the group members consider each issue and decide how to proceed. Alternatives are considered as to cost, readiness, motivation, acceptability, and availability of other resources.

nominal measurement   The lowest *level of measurement* used by researchers, consisting simply of classifying observations into categories (for example, gender, race, and religion) that must be mutually exclusive and collectively exhaustive. Appropriate statistics for nominal-level variables include chi-square, phi, lambda, and contingency coefficients.

noncontributory benefits   Income transfer payments to people who belong to a certain social security benefit category in which they were not required to make ongoing contributions to become eligible. Money for these benefits comes primarily from the nation's general fund. See also *contributory benefits.*

nonimmigrant visa   An authorization permitting one to enter the United States for a specific purpose for a specified time. The *Bureau of Immigration and Customs Enforcement* and the *Bureau of Citizenship and Immigration Services* have 13 major categories of these visas, each with specific codes. Among the more common categories of visas are business (B-1) and tourism (B-2), academic student (F-1), family members of the academic student (F-2), vocational student (M-1), exchange visitor (J-1), and temporary worker (H-1).

noncategorical grants Disbursements of funds from one organization to another without any specified objective or requirement for spending. An example is the federal government's *revenue sharing* with state governments.

nondirective therapy An approach in counseling or therapy that emphasizes a warm, permissive, accepting atmosphere to encourage the client to discuss problems freely. Also called *client-centered therapy*, the therapist asks very few questions and offers few, if any, suggestions or advice. Rather, the therapist prompts and encourages the client to initiate exploration and follow ideas and feelings.

nonfeasance Serious failure to fulfill some responsibility or duty (for example, failure of a social worker to keep scheduled appointments with a client). See also *malfeasance* and *misfeasance*.

nongovernment organizations (NGOs) Nonprofit institutions or agencies that work to serve some public interests. Funded mostly by private contributions, foundations, and grants from various nations, NGOs often seek to improve social problems that exist internationally; enhance the rights, knowledge, and economic opportunities of all people; and help nations and cultures in development efforts. They do so by educating the public about social problems, investigating conditions that may lead to social and environmental problems, mobilizing people to help resolve crises, and independently monitoring the actions various governments impose on their own people. Many NGOs serve as consultants to national governments on specific issues and to the United Nations and its specialized bodies. NGOs are also called private voluntary organizations (PVOs).

nonjudgmental A fundamental element in the social worker–client relationship in which the social worker demonstrates an attitude of tolerance and an unwillingness to censor the client for any actions. The social worker does not suspend judgment but conveys to the client that the working relationship takes precedence over any possible feelings of disapproval. Although affirming the

worth of the client, the social worker does not condone criminal or dangerous behavior and, under certain circumstances, may need to take preventive action. See also *acceptance* and *unconditional positive regard*.

nonmarital birth Having a baby outside of marriage, the term preferred over *"illegitimate."*

nonprofessional One who is not a *professional*. Generally, the term is applied to a *paraprofessional*, support staff, ancillary personnel, and *volunteers* who work with professionals in service organizations, such as social agencies and hospitals, and assist the professionals in accomplishing less technical tasks. Nonprofessionals usually have specific training or experience in the jobs they carry out. The term should not be confused with *unprofessional*.

nonprofit agencies Organizations established to fulfill some social purpose other than monetary reward to financial backers. Technically the term includes government or tax-supported agencies, but it is usually reserved for private, voluntary social agencies and excludes for-profit *proprietary social agencies*. Nonprofit agencies have explicit policies and established boards of directors. They are funded by a variety of sources, including revenue coming directly from clients, third parties, public contributions, philanthropic contributions, and government *grants-in-aid;* they are usually tax exempt. Most of the traditional social agencies, professional associations, and social change organizations are nonprofit.

nonstandard American English Variations in the way the English language is spoken in the United States by members of distinct sociocultural groups, including some African Americans, Hispanics, Cajuns, and Appalachian mountain people. Nonstandard American English differs from standard English in conventions of grammar, idioms, and pronunciation. See also *Ebonics*.

nonsupport 1. In legal terms, the intentional failure to provide food, shelter, and maintenance when legally obliged to do so. 2. Informally, the lack of providing needed emotional encouragement and educational guidance between people in close relationships.

"nontraditional family" A term, sometimes used pejoratively, to indicate families that fall outside some predetermined norm (one such norm would be two parents with the father in charge and no more than several children). So-called nontraditional families may be composed of myriad relationship patterns, including blended families, interracial groups, gay and lesbian families, matriarchal families, and communal groups.

nonverbal communication   Exchanges of information between people through gestures, facial expressions, posture, tone of voice, and vocal sounds other than words. See also *communication theory, kinesics, paralinguistics,* and *proxemics.*

nonviolence   An approach in campaigning for social change that stresses peaceful demonstrations, especially through *passive resistance.*

nonwhite   The *U.S. Bureau of the Census* term for population groups that are not Caucasian, including *African Americans, American Indians, Asian Americans, mestizos,* and other people of color.

NORD   The National Organization for Rare Disorders. See *rare disorders.*

Nordic Council   An international organization of Scandinavian nations, including Norway, Sweden, Denmark, Finland, and Iceland, established by treaty in 1962 to facilitate social, economic, and cultural cooperation. The council has facilitated many laws, including granting reciprocal social security benefits and a common labor market.

norepinephrine   A biochemical of the *central nervous system (CNS)* that in normal amounts facilitates neurotransmission but in abnormal amounts is related to some forms of *psychosis* and other *mental disorders.*

norm   In social research, a standard, criterion, or baseline by which to compare a subject's performance test score or production rate. See also *norms.*

norm-referenced   A score on an aptitude, achievement, or other test that is compared to an average or percentile rank, derived from a larger population of interest.

norm-referenced test   A data-gathering instrument that describes a subject's performance in relation to the performance of all others who have taken the test.

normal   A term denoting a culturally defined concept of behaviors or phenomena that are not markedly different from the average, usual, or expected.

normal distribution   An expected frequency distribution of cases or scores that when plotted on a graph is symmetrical and bell shaped. Most scores fall near the *mean,* forming the highest point of the bell, and fewer cases are located on either side of the slope as distance from the mean increases.

normal retirement age (NRA)   A *Social Security Administration (SSA)* term for the time when people can begin collecting their full *social security* benefits. The SSA planned that beginning in 2000 the NRA will rise gradually over 22 years so that by 2022 it will be age 67.

normative   Pertaining to the average or expected *behavior* patterns of a group or community.

normative needs   The requirements for a level of well-being that is comparable to the standards established in the community or culture to which one belongs. Usually, experts or outsiders decide what the standard is. See also *perceived needs, expressed needs,* and *relative needs.*

norms   The rules of *behavior,* both formal and informal, and expectations held collectively by a culture, group, organization, or society.

North American Association of Christians in Social Work (NACSW)   An interdenominational and international organization of professional social workers who profess belief in Christian thought and values. NACSW began in 1950 as the Evangelical Social Work Conference, became the National Association of Christians in Social Work in 1953, and adopted its present name in 1984. It sponsors the journal *Social Work and Christianity* and the newsletter *Catalyst.* Their Web site address is http://www.nacsw.org

NOS   "Not otherwise specified." The NOS abbreviation may appear after use of a general diagnostic label to indicate that the presenting symptoms or available information do not permit further delineation about the disorder. For example, a *mood disorder NOS* diagnosis would suggest affective lability but not indicate whether depression or bipolar episodes predominate.

nosology   The science of classification, particularly of diseases and disorders.

nostalgia   Longing to return to an earlier time or place. Social workers often see this as a symptom in people who are aged, in crisis or pain, or immigrants from other nations.

notch babies   Social security insurance recipients who could receive more benefits, because of their birth dates, than other recipients who have made equal contributions. The *Social Security Administration (SSA)* has periodically changed the formula for calculating benefits from work histories, which has resulted in some inequalities. The SSA claims that people born from 1912 to 1916 received benefits that were greater than intended.

nuclear complex   Freud's original name for the *Oedipus complex.*

nuclear family   The kinship group consisting of a father, a mother, and their children.

nuclear-free zone   A nation or political region that has declared itself to be outside the world's involvement with nuclear weapons. Such zones permit no activities that advance the science of nuclear weaponry, nor do they allow the building, storing, or launching of such weapons.

null hypothesis   A negative statement about proposed relationships in research data. A typical *hypothesis* stated in null fashion would be "There is no difference between the results of A and B." The null hypothesis permits statistical tests of significance and demands more rigorous testing procedures than needed to prove an affirmative statement.

nuncupative will   An oral or spoken will. Many states do not recognize the validity of these wills, and others do only when specific other conditions are met, such as reputable noninterested witnesses.

nurse practitioner   A professional nurse who completes additional training, such as a master's degree or certificate program, and acquires skills and performs tasks that were traditionally performed only by physicians, including doing routine physical examinations, taking complete medical histories, providing independent psychotherapy, and coordinating health and social services resources.

nursing home   A residential facility that provides extended health care, skilled-nursing care, and inter-mediate care for people who are ill or unable to take care of themselves. See also *skilled-nursing facility.*

nurturance   Behaviors and activities that further the growth and development of another person, family, group, or community.

nutrition   The process by which living organisms assimilate materials that are necessary for sustenance, energy, and growth. Human nutrition involves the use of food substances (nutrients) that include the proper balance of proteins, carbohydrates, and fats, as well as vitamins, minerals, and water. Good human nutrition requires a well-balanced diet containing an adequate but not excessive amount of food and calories. Failure to achieve this balance can result in various diseases, dysfunctions, deficiencies, or death. See also *malnutrition.*

Nutrition Services Incentive Program (NSIP)   The program of the *U.S. Department of Agriculture* Food and Nutrition Service to help provide for the nutritional requirements of older Americans and others in need. NSIP reorganized the administration and distribution procedures of the *Elderly Nutrition Program* when the *Older Americans Act* was amended in 2000 (P.L. 106-501). NSIP emphasizes involvement by states, tribes, and welfare organizations by reimbursing cash and providing commodities for meals served to those in need. Their Web site address is http://www.fns.usda.gov/fdd/programs/nsip

nutritional assessment   An evaluation conducted by a dietitian or other professional of the food needed by a client to achieve certain health goals and of the food actually prepared and consumed. The assessment usually includes recommendations about what foods to eat and avoid and how they should be prepared.

nyctalopia   The inability to see well in dim light or at night. In some people this is caused by a deficiency in vitamin A.

nyctaphobia   A pathological *fear* of darkness.

"nymphomania"   An obsolete term referring to an insatiable and uncontrollable desire for sexual intercourse. Usually, the term was applied to women, with "Don Juanism" the equivalent term for men. The term *sex addiction* is more appropriate.

obdachloser In Germany, a homeless person (literally, a person without a shelter).

obesity An excessive accumulation of fat in the body, caused by the consumption of too much food, too little exercise, or glandular disorders. Obesity is determined not by a person's height–weight ratio or subjective appearance but by the percentage of fat in body tissue. Obesity increases the risk of diseases such as adult-onset diabetes, hypertension, stroke, heart attack, heart failure, cancer of the colon or rectum, gallstones, gout, osteoarthritis, sleep apnea, and many other conditions.

object permanence The understanding that something exists independently of the observer and continues to exist even when it can no longer be seen or otherwise perceived.

object relations theory A psychoanalytic concept about an individual's relationship with others based on early parent–child interactions and internalized self-images that are focused on these interactions. The *neo-Freudian* view is that *libido* and aggressive drives toward self-pleasure are no more important than are the child's object-seeking drives.

objective test A data-gathering instrument or examining device in which scores do not depend on the examiner's judgment (for example, a multiple-choice exam rather than an essay exam).

objective tree A technique in *social policy* analysis for graphically delineating the various goals of an organization and priorities to be used in their fulfillment. The administrator creates a box at the top of a page with the primary objective of the organization and below that lists in descending order the lesser objectives. The resulting diagram shows an inverted treelike figure that outlines serially the goals and their relative importance, permitting the administrator to establish the dates by which each objective is to be reached.

objectivity The ability to evaluate a situation, social phenomenon, or person without *prejudice* or subjective distortion. Often what is considered to be objective is only *bias* that is widely accepted.

obscenity The production, distribution, or use of materials that are designed to stimulate *prurient interest;* that lack serious artistic, literary, political, or scientific value; and that deviate from the standards of acceptance by the average person in the relevant community. See also *pornography.*

obsession A repetitive and persistent thought, action, or ritual that is believed to occur as a mechanism for controlling or relieving anxiety.

obsessive–compulsive disorder A type of *anxiety disorder* in which the individual experiences unwanted, recurrent, and persistent ideas, impulses, or images (an *obsession*) or engages in seemingly intentional behaviors that are performed ritualistically (a *compulsion*) as a reaction to conflict or other sources of anxiety. Obsessive–compulsive disorder is to be distinguished from *obsessive–compulsive personality disorder.*

obsessive–compulsive personality disorder One of the *personality disorders* that is characterized by perfectionistic behavior, insistence on having others submit to a certain way of doing things, limited ability to express warm feelings or tenderness, preoccupation with trivial details and rules, stinginess, stiff formality in relationships, and poor ability to prioritize and make decisions. This disorder is also known as *compulsive personality disorder.* It is to be distinguished from the *anxiety disorder* known as *obsessive–compulsive disorder* in that the perfectionistic behaviors are not responses to or attempts to overcome anxiety.

obstruction of justice The *crime* of preventing or attempting to prevent officers of the law and court from accomplishing their duties. Specific activities include attempting to bribe or intimidate jurors, witnesses, or officers of the court; interfering with police when they are in pursuit of a criminal suspect; and concealing or destroying evidence.

occupancy rate The number of persons per room, per dwelling, or per household; a figure for determining actual housing density and housing needs.

occupational hazard A danger directly associated with one's job. For example, an occupational hazard for some social workers is the risk of violent attack by disturbed clients or by interested third parties, such as the client's spouse.

occupational health The preservation of physical and mental well-being in the *workplace* through the maintenance of sanitary and safe facilities and conditions.

occupational illness Acute or chronic sickness or disease caused by exposure to factors in the work environment, such as those caused by inhalation, ingestion, absorption, or contact. When the worker sustains a job-related cut, fracture, sprain, or other injury, it is an occupational injury.

occupational provident funds In some English industries in the period 1830–1870, a system of compulsory savings withheld from employee wages, managed by employers, and used for workers who became aged or infirm.

Occupational Safety and Health Administration (OSHA) The *U.S. Department of Labor* organization, established in 1970, to ensure safe conditions in the workplace. OSHA administers training programs on occupational safety and health standards, conducts inspections, and issues citations to noncomplying employers. Their Web site address is http://www.osha.gov. See also *NIOSH*.

occupational social work A specialty within social work to provide professional services to employees and their families. The service may include clinical activities (such as family therapy, psychotherapy, educational counseling, and treatment for drug addiction) or macro practice (such as interventions on behalf of employee groups). These programs are usually employer funded, as in *employee assistance programs (EAPs)*, or labor-union funded, as in *member-assisted programs (MAPs)*. The term is sometimes used synonymously with *industrial social work.*

occupational therapy A profession for helping people with physical disabilities use their bodies more effectively and people with mental impairment overcome emotional problems through specially designed work activities. For example, a recently blinded person may be taught to perform household activities through guided practice in a model kitchen. Most occupational therapists work in hospitals, nursing homes, schools, and rehabilitation centers.

occupational welfare Subsidies from the public, usually in the form of special treatments under income tax laws, to employees as a benefit of their jobs. Examples include delayed taxes on private pensions and tax deductibility of costs for meals while away on business.

ocholophobia Pathological *fear* of crowds or crowded places.

oedipal personality A descriptive term from *psychoanalytic theory* referring to an individual who seems conflicted about sexuality and sexual identity; guilty about erotic impulses; and, as an adult, often regressive into unresolved issues of the *Oedipus complex.*

Oedipus complex In the *Freudian theory* of psychosexual development, the erotic interest and attachment developed by a young child (usually between ages three and seven) for the parent of the opposite sex and the concomitant feelings of rivalry with and envy of the parent of the same sex. The child's feelings are repressed and *unconscious* but are often manifested in flirtatious behavior toward one parent and hostile behavior toward the other. See also *Electra complex* and *phallic phase.*

Oettinger, Katherine (1903–1997) Longtime chief of the U.S. *Children's Bureau,* followed by service as deputy secretary of the *U.S. Department of Health, Education and Welfare (HEW)* for family planning and population. She was also a founder of the *National Association of Social Workers (NASW)* and dean of the Boston University School of Social Work, as well as a prolific author of family policy texts.

offender registration A legal requirement in many jurisdictions in the United States that requires people convicted of crimes, most often *child molestation* and *rape,* to notify the local law enforcement authorities of their plan to live in the community. Residents of some of these communities are notified so they may take precautions.

offentlig forsorg The Danish Law on Public Welfare, the 1933 legislation in Denmark to provide for general financial assistance of Danish people in need. Payments were based not on the recipients' insurance contributions but on their previous standards of living.

Office of Consumer Affairs The U.S. agency that informs the public and government officials about the needs and problems of consumers. The office does not directly test products or enforce food and drug laws but serves as an advocate–ombudsperson–mediator among consumers, manufacturers, and public officials. The office is administratively within the *U.S. Department of Health and Human Services (HHS)* but reports directly to the president.

Office of Domestic Preparedness (ODP) A U.S. federal organization, enacted in 1998 (P.L. 105-119) under the *U.S. Department of Justice* to help states and localities prevent and respond to terrorist acts involving weapons of mass destruction and *bioterrorism*. ODP became part of the *U.S. Department of Homeland Security* in 2002.

Office of Economic Development (OED) The federal organization, within the *U.S. Department of Health and Human Services*, established in 1969 to stimulate the growth of private profit-making businesses in neighborhoods of high unemployment. OED financed the establishment of urban and rural community development corporations. The office has been absorbed into other government agencies, and many of its functions were eliminated in the 1980s.

Office of Economic Opportunity (OEO) The organization created by the *Economic Opportunity Act of 1964* to implement President Lyndon B. Johnson's *War on Poverty*. Various programs originally within the organization included *Head Start, Volunteers in Service to America (VISTA)*, and the *Job Corps*. By 1969 much of OEO had been dismantled, and many of its programs were transferred to other federal departments. The remaining part of the office became the *Community Services Block Grant Program*, which itself was drastically curtailed with the *Personal Responsibility and Work Opportunity Reconciliation Act* of 1996.

Office of Family Assistance (OFA) See *Family Assistance, Office of*.

Office of Human Development Service (OHDS) The former organization within the *U.S. Department of Health and Human Services* to oversee federally sponsored programs for delivering personal social services. The office was eliminated in 1991, and most of its functions were taken over by the *Administration for Children and Families (ACF)*.

Office of Juvenile Justice and Delinquency Prevention (OJJDP) The organization, within the *U.S. Department of Justice*, established by law (P.L. 93-415) in 1974 to coordinate local efforts to prevent juvenile delinquency. The office sponsors research, disseminates information, assists in training, facilitates collaboration between local programs, and funds local programs for at-risk youths. Their Web site address is http://www.ncjrs.org/JuvenileJustice/

Office of Management and Budget (OMB) The organization to assist the U.S. president prepare the federal *budget* and formulate the nation's fiscal program. OMB also helps the president administer the budget and determine if allocated funds are sufficient for achieving their goals. OMB keeps the president informed about how various government agencies' funds are being spent and helps in proposing legislation for congressional action. Their Web site address is http://www.whitehouse.gov/omb

Office of Personnel Management (OPM) The federal organization that administers most of the federal employment system. Its functions include recruiting, training, testing, promoting, firing, and laying off federal workers, as well as maintaining criteria for employment, pay grades, and benefits. OPM was established by the Civil Service Reform Act of 1978 (P.L. 95-454). Their Web site address is http://www.opm.gov

Office of Refugee Resettlement (ORR) The *U.S. Department of Health and Human Services* program that assists refugees to live and become self-sufficient in the United States. To be eligible for ORR services, the person must experience well-founded fear of persecution in his or her native country due to race, religion, nationality, membership in a particular social group, or political opinion. The office sets standards and awards grants to state and voluntary agencies that help the refugees with employment programs, cash assistance, food stamps, and other benefits. Their Web site address is http://www.acf.dhhs.gov/programs/orr

Office of Special Education and Rehabilitation Services *U.S. Department of Education* organization to implement federal legislation pertaining to school-related rehabilitation programs such as *IDEA*. Their Web site address is http://www.ed.gov/offices/OSERS

Office of Technology Assessment (OTA) A former federal organization to inform the U.S.

Congress about the beneficial and adverse effects of technological change and help Congress anticipate and plan for the uses of technology and policy alternatives. OTA was established in 1972 and disbanded in 1995.

'ohana The family system among native Hawaiians. 'Ohana is a multigenerational kinship value orientation that extends over time and defines age-appropriate roles, pays homage to ancestors, strives for family sustainability, and emphasizes the wisdom of elders and the welfare of children. Although the name may be different, this system also exists among most Polynesian cultures throughout the Pacific region. See also *ho'oponopono*.

Old Age and Survivors Insurance (OASI) A central part of the *Social Security Act* of 1935 under which certain people older than age 65 or their surviving dependents were covered by the federal insurance program. With subsequent revisions in the Social Security Act, the insurance coverage was expanded to include workers who become disabled and ill *(Old Age, Survivors, Disability, and Health Insurance [OASDHI])*.

Old Age Assistance (OAA) A public assistance program for needy older people. Once the major form of *outdoor relief* in the United States, OAA was administered and financed by the states, leading to a wide variation both in benefits and in stringent residency and *relatives' responsibility* requirements. The *Social Security Act* of 1935 and its compulsory insurance program to protect retired workers reduced but did not eliminate the need for OAA. In 1972, the state OAA programs were consolidated, along with the *Aid to the Blind (AB)* and the *Aid to the Permanently and Totally Disabled (APTD)* programs, into the federal *Supplemental Security Income (SSI)* program for needy older, blind, and disabled people. Many SSI provisions for older people were curtailed with passage of the *Personal Responsibility and Work Opportunity Reconciliation Act* of 1996.

Old Age, Survivors, Disability, and Health Insurance (OASDHI) The federal government's *social insurance* program under the *Social Security Act* of 1935. Under the provisions of the *Federal Insurance Contributions Act (FICA)*, the government collects payroll and employer taxes from most adult Americans and uses the funds to partially finance the payments made to retired, surviving, and disabled beneficiaries and *Medicare* recipients.

"old-boy network" A term of disparagement referring to the way groups of men who belong to the same clubs, alumni associations, interest groups, or families help one another to advance in jobs or other opportunities.

Older Americans Act of 1965 The federal legislation (P.L. 89-73), with several subsequent amendments, that defined U.S. policy toward older people and created the *Administration on Aging (AoA)* to carry it out. The administration oversees state and city agencies that contract with private providers such as *Area Agencies on Aging (AAA)*, as well as directly offers *homemaker services*, transportation, socialization programs in senior citizens' centers, and *legal aid* services for older people.

Older Women's League (OWL) A national organization, founded in 1980, that provides a united voice on behalf of middle-age and older women. Of particular concern are issues such as pension equity, social security provisions, and health care for women. Their Web site address is http://www.owl-national.org

oldest old The *cohort* of people older than age 85. Previously, this group was described as "the *frail elderly*."

olfaction impairment Inability or limited ability to perceive smells; sometimes related to schizophrenia.

olfactory hallucination An imagined perception of smell; smelling something that does not exist outside of subjective experience.

oligarchy A system of government or organization in which an elite group (such as a wealthy family, a military group, or a religious order) holds the power and rules dictatorially. In an oligopoly, a group of large companies dominates an economy.

ombudsperson An advocate or spokesperson for the people who are served by an organization to ensure that the organization's obligations, ethical duties, and rules are being followed. Also, an individual employed by a government or other organization to investigate possible illegal, unethical activities or harmful unforeseen consequences of that organization's actions and to facilitate negotiations or actions toward satisfactory solutions. The term is gender-neutral for "ombudsman."

omen formation   Belief in one's ability to accurately predict future events.

omerta   The unwritten code within organized crime families that requires silence, loyalty, and the following of orders without question.

omnibus bill   Legislation that includes several, often unrelated, measures.

oncology   The medical specialty that studies and treats *cancer* and tumors.

O*NET   The *U.S. Department of Labor* online database that is the nation's primary resource of occupational information. O*NET replaced the *Dictionary of Occupational Titles,* which had described thousands of jobs and their qualifications, and added up-to-date interactive resources about job descriptions and availability, qualifications, and training opportunities. O*NET is widely used by job seekers, students, career counselors, and social workers. The O*NET Web site address is http://www.onetcenter.org

one-worldism   The view that the Earth is a single unit and that only through international cooperation rather than nationalistic rivalries can it achieve optimal well-being for all.

online support group   Computer- and Internet-facilitated interaction that enables participants to share information, advice, resources, and encouragement. Using e-mail, chat rooms, and listservs, the participants can communicate anonymously on specific issues of mutual concern or general topics of common interest.

ontology   The study of the ultimate nature of existence or reality.

open adoption   The legal and social services process of *adoption* in which adoptive parents and the birth mother or birth parents become known to each other and, in many instances, continue some contact throughout the child's development. See also *closed adoption* and *cooperative adoption.*

open-door policy   In international relations, minimal or no restrictions on *immigration.* In *social administration,* free access to supervisors and board members, not necessarily on immediate demand but at times that are regular and convenient. In institutional settings, the permission extended to residents that they are free to leave the facility whenever they desire.

open-ended questions   In systematic opinion research and clinical interviews, a form of questioning that permits respondents to give extensive answers. This is in contrast to *closed-ended questions* (such as yes–no or multiple choice). For example, the social worker asks "Why do you think it is difficult to get a job?" instead of "Is it difficult for you to get a job?" Both types of question are useful in the social work interview, depending on the goals of the working relationship. See also *questioning.*

open-ended service   A pattern in social work intervention procedures in which the social worker and client maintain the working relationship indefinitely. See also *time-limited service.*

open-ended service versus time-limited service   The debate about whether clients are better served with or without time limits on the intervention. Arguments for the open model include the following: It is possible to address "deeper" issues; an individual cannot know in advance what will be uncovered in the intervention; clients' problems cannot be compartmentalized, as is required in the closed model; and social workers and clients are more familiar and comfortable with the more traditional open model. Arguments for the time-limited model include the following: Effectiveness studies show time-limited work is at least as effective and much less costly, thus more clients can be served; clients intensify their efforts under time constraints (even in long-term treatment most of the gains are accomplished within the first six sessions); and most clients drop out of treatment after a few sessions anyway. It is possible that some clients and some social workers do better in one model while others do better in the other.

open enrollment   A period of time during which individuals or families may sign up for health care insurance in group plans.

open group   In *social group work* and *group psychotherapy,* the type of group that permits the inclusion of new members to replace those who have left the group. Some social workers also use this term for group meetings that have no predetermined ending time. See also *closed group.*

open system   In *systems theories,* a system that accepts input from outside and is amenable to change based on conditions in the environment. For example, an open family system is structured so that its members can become involved with outsiders, bringing them and their ideas into the family unit to effect some changes in the way the family interrelates. The open system concept is generally applied to living systems rather than nonliving or mechanical ones. See also *closed system*.

operant conditioning A type of learning defined by B. F. Skinner (1904–1990) in which behaviors are strengthened or weakened by altering the consequences that follow them. Operant conditioning differs from *respondent conditioning*, which has the effect of controlling antecedent rather than consequent conditions. See also *Skinnerian theory*.

operant therapy The use of *operant conditioning* as a form of treatment.

operational definition In research, the explanation of the phenomenon to be studied in terms of how it will be measured, that is, if it is specific enough to allow a researcher to measure it.

operational tasks In *task-centered treatment*, one of two types of tasks (the other being general tasks) that calls for the client to undertake a specific action that is spelled out and understood before it is accomplished. For example, the task-oriented social worker asks the client to request a raise from his or her supervisor.

opiates Drugs containing *opium*.

opinion survey A systematic data-gathering technique used to determine what people at a given time in a given area think about a certain subject. A representative *sample* of the *population* being investigated is interviewed verbally or by means of a structured and sometimes self-administered *questionnaire*. Opinion surveys of certain communities are often made by social activists, planners, and community organizers to understand and later influence the concerns, problems, and goals of the people.

opioid abuse The use of opium-based drugs, such as *heroin* and *morphine*, taken intravenously, orally, by sniffing, or through *"skin popping."*

opioid dependence Addiction to one of the *opiates* as manifested by *opioid abuse, tolerance*, and *withdrawal symptoms*.

opioid intoxication The mental and physical symptoms resulting from recent opioid depression or *opioid abuse*. The symptoms include *euphoria* or depression, sluggishness, apathy, dilation or constriction of the pupils, drowsiness, impaired memory or attentiveness, slurred speech, poor judgment, and impaired social functioning.

opium A *narcotic* drug extracted from the juice of the opium poppy. It has been used for centuries as an effective painkiller; however, because of its habit-forming properties, the drug is restricted in most nations. Opium is processed to produce *morphine, codeine, heroin,* and laudanum.

opportunistic infection An attack by microorganisms (that could not normally bring about disease) after the body's immune system has been weakened. The immune system is most commonly weakened by malnutrition, organic dysfunction, or other disorders.

opportunity costs A *social planning* concept in which the value of the resources that must be expended to achieve a certain objective is weighed against the cost of alternatives that would have to be forgone to achieve that objective.

opportunity programs *Social welfare* programs and organizations with an orientation toward preparing client groups for greater access to the opportunities that exist for others. The goal of such programs is not necessarily to help clients "adjust" or gain insight but to acquire skills and resources.

opportunity theory The hypothesis that deviant behavior is more likely to occur among specific groups (for example, youths who are at risk for juvenile delinquency) when the opportunities to achieve socially acceptable goals are restricted and opportunities to behave in socially unacceptable ways are more available.

oppositional defiant disorder Persistently negative and disobedient behavior usually including provocative hostility to authority and resistance to rules. Oppositional defiant disorder is similar to *conduct disorder* (a pattern of truancy, theft, physical *aggression*, vandalism, and so forth), except it is not as severe and more typically involves refusal to cooperate rather than destructiveness of others.

oppression The social act of placing severe restrictions on an individual, group, or institution.

Typically, a government or political organization in power places restrictions formally or covertly on oppressed groups so they may be exploited and less able to compete with other social groups. The oppressed individual or group is devalued, exploited, and deprived of privileges by the individual or group who has more power.

oral personality   Also known as "oral character," a descriptive term from *psychoanalytic theory* referring to an individual who tends to be overly dependent or greedy and demands to be "filled up." This individual's satisfactions come largely through activities such as eating, smoking, drinking, and talking. These personality characteristics are thought to become fixed during the individual's first two years of life.

oral phase   The first stage in the psychosexual development of the personality, which occurs at ages up to two years. During this phase, the infant seeks pleasure by stimulating the mouth and oral cavity and experiences the world through literal or psychic incorporation. According to *Freudian theory,* during this age the zone of sexual pleasure is the oral cavity, which explains the intense satisfaction the infant derives from nursing. Self-concept and feelings of personal worth are usually said to develop during this stage.

ordinal measurement   In research, a level of measurement that entails classifying observations into mutually exclusive categories.

ordinal position   See *birth-order theories.*

ordinance   A local law that applies and is enforced only within the municipality where it was made. Local ordinances usually cover laws such as driving speeds, refuse disposal, loitering, and disturbing the peace.

organ donation   The act of bequeathing a vital body part for transplantation into another human being. Typically, the organ is surgically removed from someone who has agreed to donate it so that it can help preserve the life or health of another person. Organizations such as The Living Bank International promote organ and tissue donation and maintain an international database at no cost. See also *United Network for Organ Sharing (UNOS).*

organic   Pertaining to the biological aspects of an individual. The term is used most commonly by professionals to distinguish between physiological disorders and psychosocial problems. See also *functional mental illness.*

organic mental disorders   Mental disturbances thought to be caused by permanent or temporary damage to the brain. The disorders may be related to the aging process, to the ingestion of toxic substances such as alcohol and other drugs, or to certain physiological dysfunctions.

Organisation Mondial de la Santé   The French name for the *World Health Organization.*

organization   In social work and *community development (CD),* the process of helping individuals and groups arrange their activities, communication, and structure so that they can work together in a coordinated whole to achieve mutually beneficial goals.

organization development (OD)   The administrative technique that draws on *systems theories* and human relations orientations to enhance the group members' ability to solve problems together, communicate more effectively, and achieve greater efficiencies in production by encouraging innovation and coordination. OD is both a long-term process and a management style. It uses a variety of techniques, including the *sensitivity group, T-group, feedback* systems, process consultation, and team building.

Organization of American States (OAS)   The political association of most nations in the Western Hemisphere, founded as the International Conference of American States in 1989 and later called the Pan American Union. In addition to its role in mutual self-defense and economic cooperation, OAS is actively engaged in social welfare, human rights, and social justice. Some of its specialized social welfare agencies include the *Inter-American Human Rights Commission, Inter-American Children's Institute, Inter-American Commission on Women, Inter-American Indigenous Institute,* and the *Inter-American Social Development Unit (CIDES).*

organizational theory   Conceptual frameworks about the ways an *organization* fulfills its functions, which several theories or schools have tried to explain. The classical school emphasizes bureaucratic structure, defined lines of *authority,* specialized functions by employees, and criteria for performance evaluations. The scientific management school emphasizes the use of measurements of human activity and uses time and motion studies and "efficiency experts." The human relations school emphasizes the interrelationship of the work-group members, the informal *network* of workers, and the relationship between the organization's goals and the workers' social needs. The structuralist or systems orientation sees the organization as an adaptive whole within a changing environment. *Human services* organizations differ from others in that their "raw material" and product are the people being served.

organizations Formally structured arrangements of people, tools, and resources brought together to achieve predetermined objectives through institutionalized strategies.

orgasmic disorders The *sexual disorders* characterized by persistent or recurrent delay or absence of orgasm following a normal excitement phase, or *premature ejaculation,* causing marked distress or interpersonal difficulty. These disorders occur in both men and women. Diagnosticians indicate whether the condition is lifelong or acquired, generalized or situational, and due to psychological or combined factors. In diagnosis the term replaced *inhibited orgasm.*

orgasmic impairment See *female orgasmic impairment.*

orphan A dependent child with no parent or caretaker. This term is outdated in the United States except in one context. The *Bureau of Citizenship and Immigration Services (CIS)* defines an orphan as a child in a foreign country who has no living parent or guardian or whose parents have disappeared or abandoned the child or cannot care for the child. Adoptive parents who are U.S. citizens may seek to adopt these orphan children if they meet the CIS Bureau criteria.

orphan trains Railroad facilities and other modes of transportation used by some child welfare agencies (before 1915) in the eastern United States for *placing out* homeless and family-less children with families in the western United States.

orphanage A residential institution for parentless or poor children. In the United States, most such facilities have been dismantled in favor of various foster care programs, although they are still common in many other nations.

orthopedic impairment The permanent or extended loss or dysfunction of bones through conditions such as amputation, bone tuberculosis, cerebral palsy, poliomyelitis, or limb destruction.

orthopedics The branch of medicine dealing with injuries and diseases of the bones. The alternative spelling, which is preferred in most English-speaking nations other than the United States, is "orthopaedics."

orthopsychiatry An interdisciplinary field that emphasizes the development of mental health from early childhood on, prevention of mental illness, and the early (childhood) treatment of those who have a *mental disorder.* The American Association of Orthopsychiatry, which was founded in 1924 and is based in New York, publishes the quarterly journal *Orthopsychiatry.*

osteoarthritis A degenerative joint disease characterized primarily by inflammation and wear and tear of the joints. This is the most common form of arthritis, and it usually affects the hands, feet, spine, hips, and knees. See also *rheumatoid arthritis.*

osteogenesis imperfecta A rare genetic disorder characterized by fragile bones, often resulting in fractures in infants and very young children. When this disorder remains undetected, parents are sometimes wrongfully accused of child abuse. The disorder is more commonly known as "brittle bone disease."

osteomyelitis An infection of the bone marrow.

osteopath A doctor of osteopathy (DO), a physician who is equivalent to an MD in training, licensure, and health care responsibilities but is more oriented to the body's natural ability to defend itself against diseases.

osteoporosis A disorder of the bones associated with calcium deficiency and characterized by increasing porosity and brittleness and decreased density in the bone matter. The major at-risk populations are middle-age and older women. See also *osteogenesis imperfecta.*

OTC drugs Nonprescription medications purchased "over the counter," including aspirin, mild sedatives, nasal decongestants, and vitamin supplements.

otologist   A physician who specializes in the ear.

otorhinolaryngologist   A physician who specializes in ear, nose, and throat disorders.

outcome-based education   Educational or training programs in which success is determined not by the number of hours or classes taken, but by the students' demonstration of having reached specified learning goals.

outcome evaluation   A process aimed at determining if a program is achieving its objectives and whether the results are due to the interventions provided. Outcome evaluations range from subjective judgments made by clients and staff to rigorous experimental investigations.

outcome variables   In research, phenomena that are seen as the consequences of experimental manipulations or interventions.

outdoor relief   A historical term referring to a form of welfare assistance that occurs outside an *almshouse, orphanage,* and other residential facilities. Most forms of *public assistance* are of this type. See also *indoor relief.*

outing   Publicly disclosing a person's *homosexuality* to achieve some political or social objective. The term often refers to the practice by members of the gay community of revealing the homosexual orientation of an influential opponent of their goals. See also *"passing," "coming out,"* and *"Don't ask, don't tell policy."*

outpatient   One who receives professional services without residing in the care facility. See also *inpatient.*

outreach   The activities of social workers, especially in neighborhood-based agencies, to bring services and information about the availability of services to people in their homes or usual environments. See also *case finding.*

outsourcing   Employing individuals from outside the organization's permanent workforce to accomplish specific tasks for a set fee. In contrast to permanent employees, these temporary employees usually do not receive benefits. Outsourcing is also known as *contracting out.*

over-the-counter (OTC) drug   A medicine that may be purchased without a doctor's prescription.

overanxious disorder of childhood   A disorder of childhood or adolescence characterized by persistent anxiety, including worry about the future, overconcern about appropriateness of past behavior, extreme self-consciousness, inability to relax, and the excessive need for reassurance.

overbedding   The practice of building more hospital facilities than are needed in a given community. This contributes to increased charges for inpatient care costs, because the full beds have to carry the costs of the empty ones.

overcompensation   A *defense mechanism* characterized by an individual's extreme efforts to counterbalance a real or imagined deficiency.

overdetermination   The concept used by psychoanalysts to explain a phenomenon, such as dreams or neurotic symptoms, as being caused by combinations of factors.

overdose   The taking in of too much medication or drugs, usually resulting in serious side effects such as unconsciousness, extreme pain, anxiety, confusion, heart or respiratory failure, or even death.

overgeneralization   The thought or act of forming broad principles from small or limited details. For example, a client says, "My son stayed out late last night. I know he's always going to do that from now on." When an overgeneralization is an *unconscious* attempt to avoid facing some painful truths, it is considered to be a *defense mechanism.*

overloving   Intense emotional investment in another person, including the wish to control that person "for his or her own good." The term was coined by Sophie Freud, who pointed out that it is a feeling or state experienced as love but is also narcissistically motivated.

overprotectiveness   The tendency of some parents or parent surrogates to shelter their children excessively through avoidance of situations they believe have the potential for psychological or physical harm. The result is that these children often do not learn to become sufficiently independent. Overprotection may also occur between marital partners or other family members.

overrepresentation   Inclusion of a disproportionate number of observations in a sample relative to a population. For example, if 80 percent of social workers in a population were female, yet a research study used a sample in which only 50 percent were female, then males would be over-represented.

overseers of the poor   People who in 16th- and 17th-century England and Colonial America were appointed as public officials to help collect local taxes and use these funds to provide *relief* for those who were destitute and, primarily, jobs for people who were unemployed and not disabled. Over-seers of the poor were established in the *Henrician Poor Law* of 1536 and served as local officials for the government and for churches. The *Gilbert Act* of 1782 modified their role, requiring them, whenever possible, to find jobs and housing for the poor population in the community rather than placement in workhouses or almshouses. Some social welfare historians trace the evolution of the modern social work profession to the over-seers of the poor.

oversensitivity   A response pattern of behavior and often a symptom of *depression, paranoia, anorexia nervosa, obsessive–compulsive disorder,* and many other *mental disorders,* characterized by heightened awareness of reactions by others, social fragility, embarrassment, and anxiety about perceived disapproval by others and defensive verbalizations or withdrawal in anticipation of rejection by others.

overt behaviors   An individual's actions that are observable to others. Such actions are now described by behaviorists as "overt" to distinguish them from behaviors that are not observable but that can be recorded or registered by various instruments (such as electroencephalographs, blood pressure gauges, *lie detectors,* and so forth).

overutilization   See *utilization review.*

Ovington, Mary White (1865–1951)   A principal founder and longtime leader of the *National Association for the Advancement of Colored People*

(NAACP). She began as a settlement house worker, where she was exposed to the problems facing black people and became active in anti-lynching campaigns. She was the NAACP board chair for 10 years.

ovulation   Release of a female reproductive cell, that is, the ovum or egg, into one of the two fallopian tubes. This takes place in women about 14 days, on the average, after the onset of menstruation.

Owen, Robert (1771–1851)   Welsh philanthropist and social advocate who worked toward elimination of exploitative working conditions for paupers and apprentices, improved *child labor* conditions, and aided in the establishment of national old-age and sickness insurance programs.

own recognizance   Releasing from *incarceration* someone accused of a crime without requiring *bail.*

Oxford Committee for Famine Relief (OXFAM)   An international voluntary *nongovernment organization (NGO)* based in London that raises and distributes funds and emergency supplies to those nations and peoples who lack sufficient food or nutrition to maintain quality of life. Their Web site address is http://www.oxfam.org.uk

Ozanum, Antoine Frederic (1813–1853)   A social reformer and founder of the *St. Vincent de Paul Society.* He sought to develop a rational program for helping poor people in France. He established the nonsectarian Conference of Charity, later renamed the St. Vincent de Paul Society (after the 16th-century reformer who helped the poor population and freed slaves and helped them establish new lives).

ozone layer   A layer of ozone gas in the atmosphere between 10 and 30 miles above Earth that absorbs many of the solar ultraviolet rays that would otherwise harm life on the planet. Some scientists believe various manufactured chemicals are depleting this layer.

"p-funk" Street jargon for a synthetic form of *heroin*.

pacemaker An electronic device surgically implanted to regulate a patient's irregular contractions of the heart *(arrhythmia)*. Most often, they are used to increase the rate of heartbeats when the heart is below 60 beats per minute *(bradycardia)* and sometimes to slow heartbeats that are too rapid *(tachycardia)*. The device is battery powered (and requires replacement every 7 to 15 years in a routine outpatient procedure). See also *defibrillator*.

Pacific Islanders Indigenous residents of and immigrants from the islands and islets in the Pacific Ocean, including those in the areas known as Polynesia, Melanesia, and Micronesia. In the United States, the term is most often applied to people native to Hawaii and to people from the U.S. Trust Territory of the Pacific Islands, including the Marshall and Marianas Islands, and from Guam and American Samoa.

pacifism The *value orientation* or policy of universal peace and the resolution of all differences between nations by peaceful means. The term is sometimes confused with passivism (the passive unwillingness to negotiate differences; appeasement), but "pacifism" implies a much more active effort to find solutions that are alternatives to war. See also *militarism* and *warism*.

padrinos In Spanish-speaking cultures, a child's godparents. Usually, they are kin or adult friends of the family bonded by a long tradition of friendship *(compadrazgo)* and have an important role in the care and upbringing of the children. See also *hijos de crianza*.

padrone An overseer of farm workers or unskilled laborers. The term originally applied to employment agents for unskilled Italian immigrants.

pain disorder A medical and psychological condition in which the predominant symptom is continuous, recurrent, or intermittent sensations of pain, either localized in specific parts of the body or body systems or generalized throughout. Because pain is usually symptomatic of a medical condition or mental disorder, the relevant diagnosis is of that disorder. Otherwise, the formal diagnosis would be "pain disorder associated with psychological factors" or "pain disorder associated with both psychological factors and a general medical condition." The former term was *psychogenic pain disorder*.

palimony An award, granted in a court of law, that is similar to *alimony*. Palimony requires support payments to one partner in a couple that formerly lived together in a nonmarital relationship or otherwise maintained an intimate relationship. See also *cohabitation*.

palliative care Providing for the common physical and emotional needs and comfort of a patient with a terminal illness after efforts to cure are no longer successful. See also *hospice*.

palsy A form of paralysis or diminished ability to move or control motion, often accompanied by *tremor*.

pan-ethnic Pertaining to the identification with more than one ethnic group or with a collective of national origin groups, that is, European, Hispanic, Latino, Mediterranean, or East Asian.

Pan-Indian Characteristic of multitribe groups and individuals; an individual whose ancestry belongs to two or more tribes and who seeks identity as an Indian rather than as a member of one tribe. Such people seek to maintain the traditions of all the tribes of their heritage or residential area. Although many Pan-Indians are more accepting of a variety of different tribal traditions, they are less inclined to adopt or accept Anglo-American ways.

panacea A cure-all; a plan that would solve all problems. Often, opponents of a social reform movement deride the plan as "no panacea" because it hopes to solve only part of a problem.

PANDAS A form of obsessive–compulsive or tic disorder that begins in childhood (three years to puberty), with the patient exhibiting neurological abnormalities such as motor hyperactivity, and is associated with strep infection or scarlet fever. PANDAS is an acronym for pediatric autoimmune neuropsychiatric disorder associated with streptococcus.

pandemic A term applied to *social problems, disease,* or *mental disorder* that appears on a broad scale throughout a specific large area (such as a city, a nation, a continent, or the entire world).

pandering The *crime* of inducing a person to become a prostitute or procuring customers for a prostitute. An individual who does this is usually called a "pimp."

panhandling Begging for money or food, usually in face-to-face encounters on streets, usually to sustain the personal needs of the one who is soliciting.

panic attack The sudden onset of intense fear and anxiety, usually accompanied by symptoms such as sweating; palpitations; tremor; nausea; chills; dizziness; *derealization;* and fears or feelings of losing control, going crazy, and dying. The attack occurs suddenly and builds to a peak within a few minutes. It occurs in several types of *anxiety disorders,* including *panic disorder, social phobia, specific phobia, posttraumatic stress disorder (PTSD),* and *acute stress disorder.* Onset of the attack may be unexpected with no particular stressor (uncued), or it may occur almost always when confronted by or in anticipation of a stressor (cued). Panic attacks may also be situationally predisposed, in which the attack is more likely but not invariably going to happen when confronted by or in anticipation of a stressor.

panic disorder An *anxiety disorder* characterized by recurrent *panic attack* or fear of having further panic attacks for more than one month over an extended period in situations in which there is no life-threatening stressor. Symptoms include choking and breathing difficulties, palpitations and chest pains, sweating, trembling, dizziness, and faintness. Often, the individual anticipates the onset of such attacks and becomes fearful of places or situations in which such attacks previously occurred. Abnormal avoidance of these places may be diagnosed as "panic disorder with *agoraphobia*."

Pap test The microscopic examination of cells collected from a woman's cervix to detect early stages of cancer. Finding premalignant or malignant cells makes early treatment possible. The test is routinely administered to women during physical examinations and has saved countless lives. The name refers to the originator of the test, Dr. George Papanicolaou.

paradigm A model or pattern containing a set of legitimate assumptions and a design for collecting and interpreting data. For example, the psychosocial paradigm begins with an assumption that behavior is determined largely through learning the experiences of interpersonal relationships.

paradigm shift A process of reconceptualizing about some model, pattern, or perception, leading to significant changes, or "reinventions." For example, the 1996 welfare reform laws are said to represent a paradigm shift from traditional *AFDC* payments to time-limited work preparation programs.

paradoxical directive In certain types of *family therapy,* an approach in which the social worker or other therapist tells the family members to continue their symptomatic behavior and sometimes to "improve on it." This makes them more aware of the existence of the behavior and the gains they derive from it and finally gives them more control over it.

paralegal An individual who performs routine legal tasks under the supervision of an attorney. Paralegals usually have some legal training but not a law school degree or bar exam certification.

paralinguistics Nonverbal vocalizations accompanying speech that give additional meaning to communications and convey the speakers' emotions and cultural stances. Paralinguistics include tone of voice, tempo, pauses, loudness, sighs, laughs, clearing the throat, and so on. See also *communication theory* and *metamessage.*

paramedics Health care professionals who provide assistance in emergency situations, more highly trained than *emergency medical technicians (EMTs)* but with less training than emergency room physicians.

paranoia A symptom of *mental disorder* in which the most prominent characteristics are permanent and unshakable suspiciousness and persecutory *delusion* but in which the individual is otherwise clear thinking. Paranoia is a prominent feature of *persecutory-type delusional disorder, paranoid schizophrenia,* and *paranoid personality disorder.*

paranoid disorders   A general class of *mental disorder* characterized by inappropriate suspiciousness. Diagnosticians tend to use more specific terms to describe patients with *paranoid ideation,* such as *paranoid personality disorder, paranoid schizophrenia,* and *paranoia.*

paranoid ideation   An unfounded suspicion that one is under surveillance or is being followed, talked about, or persecuted. This behavior may be but is not necessarily symptomatic of several mental disorders.

paranoid personality disorder   One of the 11 types of *personality disorders,* characterized by pervasive distrust and suspiciousness of others. These people rarely become close to others or confide in them, often refuse to disclose personal information to anyone, bear grudges, and retain hostile feelings over imagined insults and slights. They devote time to gathering evidence of the malevolence of others and often question the loyalty, fidelity, or intentions of spouses, family members, or others. The condition differs from *paranoid schizophrenia* or *delusional disorder* of the persecutory type in that they include psychotic symptoms such as *delusion* and *hallucination.*

paranoid schizophrenia   Technically known as "schizophrenia, paranoid type," one of the five major subtypes (also including *disorganized, catatonic, undifferentiated,* and *residual*) of *schizophrenia,* characterized by prominent *delusions of persecution* or *delusions of grandeur* and *auditory hallucination.*

paraphilia   A *sexual disorder* in which unusual fantasies, bizarre acts, or the use of nonhuman objects are necessary for sexual arousal. The acts or fantasies may include repeated or fantasized sexual activity involving suffering, humiliation, and nonconsenting partners. Also referred to as "sexual deviations" and "perversions," paraphilias include *fetishism, transvestism, pedophilia, exhibitionism, voyeurism, sexual masochism, frotteurism,* and *sexual sadism.*

paraphilic coercive disorder   A *paraphilia* in which an individual derives erotic gratification primarily from imposing brute force or threats of violence on another or from watching them im-posed. When the victim is compelled to participate in sexual activity, the term used is *paraphilic rapism.*

paraphilic rapism   A *mental disorder* in men who are aroused only when forcing sexual activity on others. The resulting behavior is *rape.*

paraphrasing   A technique used in a helping interview in which the interviewer expresses the idea of what the client has just said so that the relevant points are pulled together and emphasized. This helps clients clarify their own thoughts and assures them that the interviewer understood the message.

paraphrenia   Late-onset *psychosis,* a disorder in which symptoms begin in older people and resemble those of *paranoid schizophrenia,* except there is a minimum of debilitating *hallucination* and personality disorganization.

paraplegia   Motor or sensory paralysis of half the body, usually the lower half of the body, usually due to disease or injury to the spinal cord.

parapraxis   An error in verbalization that is thought to reveal what is in the subject's unconscious. It is informally known as a Freudian slip. For example, a client who fears that a social work investigator is going to reduce some welfare benefit refers to him or her as the "social worrier."

paraprofessional   One who has specialized knowledge and technical training who works closely with and is supervised by a *professional* and who performs many tasks formerly carried out by the professional. Such people include paralegals, *physician's assistants (PAs),* and *social work associates.*

parapsychology   The study of paranormal behavior and psychic events that are not explained through the *scientific method.* This includes mental telepathy, extrasensory perception (ESP), *intuition,* precognition, clairvoyance, and memory experiences of being in other worlds or generations.

paraquat   A herbicide often used to kill illicit crops by spreading it from airplanes. People in the surrounding region may experience lung damage when inhaling this product or smoke from the burning residue.

parasomnia   A *sleep disorder* in which psychological or physiological events occur during sleep or during transitions from sleeping and awakening. Cognitive, motor, and *autonomic nervous system (ANS)* processes are activated during sleep stages in these disorders, resulting in specific types of parasomnia, including *nightmare disorder, sleep terror disorder,* and *sleepwalking disorder.*

parasuicide   Unsuccessful attempts at ending one's own life.

parataxic distortion   Inaccurate perceptions about the behaviors, attitudes, thoughts, and goals of those with whom emotional relationships exist. The concept was developed by Harry Stack Sullivan (1892–1949).

pardon   A decree to specific people that frees them from being tried or punished for criminal offenses, granted by a state's chief executive. See also *amnesty* and *clemency.*

parens patriae   A legal doctrine that refers to the role of the state as guardian of people who are unable to care for themselves. The concept is used legally in deciding to intervene in family matters, such as *custody of children, divorce* disputes, and removal of children to *foster care.* Under this authority, the child is not the absolute property of a parent but a trust granted to a parent by the state.

parent abuse   Infliction of physical or psychic injury on a parent or guardian, through beating, sexual abuse, degradation, or exploitation. Usually, such acts are committed by teenage or adult offspring against older and *frail elderly* parents. See also *elder abuse.*

Parent Effectiveness Training (PET)   An educational program designed by Thomas Gordon to help parents learn to interact with their children more effectively.

parent self-help associations   Private voluntary organizations made up of parents who provide mutual support in dealing with their children's problems. Some organizations of this type help parents deal with the death of their children, including The Compassionate Friends, Parents of Murdered Children, HOPING (Helping Other Parents in Normal Grieving), and SHARE (for pregnancy and infant loss support). Other groups focus on problems of child rearing, such as National Parents Association, Parents Helping Parents, *Parents Without Partners (PWP),* Tough Love International, Unwed Parents Anonymous, and *Mothers Without Custody.*

parent training   Didactic and experiential educational programs to teach parents how to be effective in child rearing and socialization, parent–child communication, and problem solving. The best known of these programs include PET (*Parent Effectiveness Training*), STEP (Systematic Training for Effective Parenting, developed by D. Dinkmeyer and G. McKay on the basis of the recommendations of Rudolph Dreikurs), PIP (Parent Involvement Program, developed by William Glasser on the basis of his *reality therapy* concepts), and *behavior modification* approaches (developed from *social learning theory*).

parental child   See *parentified child.*

parental consent laws   Legislation limiting the rights of minor children to actions explicitly and knowingly permitted by parents, legal guardians, or legal caregivers.

parental leave   An employment policy of granting a mother or father time off before, during, or after a child's birth or adoption. This leave may be granted to one or both natural or adoptive parents (partly to facilitate the neonatal bonding process). Parental leave policies were established after there was some acceptance of *maternity leave,* when it was recognized that fathers and adoptive parents and their children have essentially the same rights and needs as do new birth mothers and their infants.

parental liability   The amount of financial restitution parents may be compelled to make to compensate for any damages caused by their minor or dependent children. Each jurisdiction specifies the amount of *liability,* if any, that a parent can be compelled to pay. See also *relatives' responsibility.*

parental responsibility   A moral, ethical, and often legal obligation of parents (and others who have assumed parental roles) regarding the care and development of their children. These responsibilities include the provision of adequate nutrition, shelter, safety, and protection from physical and emotional harm; exercise; opportunities for education and social development; experience in problem solving; development of social skills; moral and spiritual guidance; and role models for effective social functioning.

parentified child   A child who is placed in the role of an adult to fulfill responsibilities that are normally the obligation of the mother, father, or other adult caregiver. These duties typically include caring for younger siblings, preparing food and cleaning up, and meeting the emotional needs of immature parents. Some social workers refer to such persons as a "parental child."

parenting capacity assessment   The systematic evaluation of the extent to which parents are capable of meeting the developmental needs of their children, including physical and emotional care, safety, warmth, stimulation, guidance, boundaries, and stability.

parenting skills   Behaviors by mothers and fathers or parent figures who provide adequately for the physical, educational, moral, and emotional needs of their children. In addition to meeting basic physical and emotional needs, good parenting includes quality time with children, enjoyable mutual activities, family fun, problem solving and conflict resolution with the child, communication, reduced family stress, planning together, effective discipline, verbal and tangible rewards, clear and consistent directions, positive role modeling, avoidance of physical punishment, positive attention and praise, scheduled regular play time with children, empathy, stability, and consistency.

parenting style   The predominant characteristic manner by which parents or parent surrogates provide the opportunities for their children's psychological and social development. Various family therapists, writers, and commentators have given myriad names for these styles. Some of the better known are laissez-faire, indulgent, strict, domineering, inconsistent, abusive, overprotective, or detached parenting styles.

Parents Anonymous (PA)   A national self-help organization whose members help one another restrain themselves from abusing their children. PA maintains a *hot line* and "buddy systems" and holds regular meetings, patterned partly on the *Alcoholics Anonymous (AA)* program. Their Web site address is http://www.parentsanonymous.org

Parents Without Partners (PWP)   A national self-help organization, with chapters in most U.S. communities, most of whose members are divorced or widowed people raising children. PWP members share mutual concerns about child rearing and maintaining healthy social relationships. Their Web site address is http://www.parentswithoutpartners.org

paresis   Partial or complete paralysis.

paresthesia   An abnormal burning or tingling sensation that occurs when inadvertent pressure is placed on a nerve.

Parish Poor Rate   An early system of national taxation to help pay for the needs of eligible poor people, which started in England in 1572. The system included a register of persons needing assistance and made efforts to create jobs and change social conditions to help reduce the incidence of *poverty*. See also *poor law*.

parity   Equivalence or equality. In wage parity, a city might be required to pay its firefighters on the same scale as police officers. In international relations, a nation wants military parity with its major rivals. Farmers seek a parity price support from the government so that their spendable income is proportionate to the incomes of previous generations of farmers. In employment parity, an organization's workers at every level are from each racial–ethnic group in the same proportion as that group's percentage of the population.

parity in mental health care   *Third-party* coverage to pay for mental health care services equivalent to the payment for physical health care services. To social workers, the term also suggests reimbursement for social work services as well as for psychological and psychiatric services. See also *Mental Health Parity Act*.

Parkinson's disease   A disease characterized by progressive motor disability and manifested by *tremor* or shaking, muscle stiffness, poor coordination, and sometimes *dementia*. The initial onset occurs most frequently among people between ages 50 and 65. Some patients become severely incapacitated but live long lives, and others may die within a few years as a result of complications.

parochialism   1. Narrowness of interests, opinions, or knowledge. 2. The policy of delegating social plans and government policies to local interests rather than centralized or national ones.

parole   The release of a prisoner before completion of full sentence because of good conduct in prison, promised good conduct, and continued supervision by an officer of the legal system (often a social worker) once out of prison. See *probation, incarceration,* and *community-based corrections.*

Parole Commission, U.S. The independent agency within the *U.S. Department of Justice,* established in 1930, to oversee the parole process of federal and District of Columbia prisoners. The Parole Commission also oversees the victim and witness protection programs to ensure their confidentiality, safety, and right to be informed. Their Web site address is http://www.usdoj.gov/uspc

partial hospitalization Health care within an inpatient medical setting for a specified period (usually from three to six hours) each day. Such programs give patients needed medical, psychological, or psychosocial treatment in a supervised setting but advance a transition from institutional to community living by encouraging the patient's developing independence and *coping skills.*

partial reinforcement In *social learning theory,* the pattern of providing a reward, not every time a desired response is emitted, but with sufficient frequency to encourage the behavior. This increases the likelihood of such behaviors continuing without *extinction,* even when no immediate rewards are forthcoming.

partialization The social work process of temporarily considering a client's interconnected problems as separate entities so that work toward their solution can be more manageable. The process includes developing priorities or distinguishing those problems or needs that demand immediate attention from those whose resolution can be postponed for a time.

participant modeling A technique used in *behavior therapy* and *behavior modification* in which the client directly observes the social worker or some other person interacting with a feared *stimulus* without being harmed. The client is then gradually encouraged to interact with the same stimulus without fear of harm.

participant observation A technique in social science research in which the investigator systematically becomes as much as possible a member of the group being studied.

participative management A decision-making strategy used by some social agency administrators to involve all those who are likely to be affected by desired organizational change. This strategy includes building voluntary *consensus* and commitment among the organization's personnel, clientele, sponsors, and other interested groups to achieve organizational goals.

Partnership for Caring (PFC) The end-of-life advocacy organization for the dying and for improved ways of caring for the dying. PFC originated as the Choice in Dying organization and took its present name in 2000. It originated and distributes the *living will* and lobbies and campaigns for legalization of *physician-assisted suicide* and other reforms. Their Web site address is http://www.partnershipforcaring.org

"passing" The process in which gay men and lesbians present themselves to others as being heterosexual. The practice is common among the gay and lesbian population to avoid stigma, hostility, and discrimination. See also *"coming out."*

passive–aggressive The behavior of an individual who uses covert actions to fight another person or organization. The individual may feel angry but powerless in direct confrontations and so becomes obstructionistic, obstinate, and inefficient and tends to pout and procrastinate. Because the anger is often unconscious, the reaction is also usually unconscious. When this behavior is deeply ingrained and persists through many situations and life phases, it may indicate the presence of a *personality disorder.*

passive–aggressive personality disorder Also called *negativistic personality disorder,* a pervasive pattern of negative attitudes and passive resistance. The individual habitually resents, opposes, and covertly obstructs demands to fulfill obligations and appropriate expectations.

passive congenial relationship A pattern in some marriages and domestic partnerships in which both partners have little overt conflict but also little affection or interest. Inertia, plus their personalities or general level of contentment, precludes any attempts to end or change the relationship.

passive–dependent The behavior of an individual who tries to get others or one other person to assume all the relevant responsibilities in the individual's life. When deeply ingrained and persistent in many situations, the behavior may indicate the presence of *dependent personality disorder.*

passive euthanasia The withdrawal of life supports to a patient with terminal illness, usually following the use of the patient's prestated wishes, as in a *living will* or *advance directive.* This process is not considered synonymous with *physician-assisted suicide.* In passive euthanasia, the withdrawal of supports does not cause the death but allows the natural process of dying.

passive resistance A nonviolent form of social activism in which individuals or groups stop using or cooperating with the institutions to which they object. For example, in the late 1950s, when African American people in the South objected to the rule requiring them to sit in the back of buses, they banded together to *boycott* the buses.

passive smoking Involuntary inhalation of the residue of burned materials, most commonly occurring when one is confined in an enclosed space where tobacco products are being smoked. Several disorders, especially respiratory diseases such as lung cancer and *emphysema,* have been correlated with sustained passive smoking. See also *smoke-free society.*

passivity A behavior pattern in which the individual seldom initiates action but submissively responds to forces in the environment.

pastoral counselor Clergy or former clergy who provide *counseling* and *psychotherapy* to clients, either within the auspices of their churches or in autonomous practices. Many of these professionals obtain their training as counselors within theological schools, whereas others obtain additional education in schools of social work and other fields. They tend to specialize in *marital therapy,* premarital guidance, and *spiritual counseling.* The nonsectarian American Association of Pastoral Counselors (AAPC) was founded in 1963 to certify pastoral counselors and accredit pastoral counseling centers.

paternalism Making decisions for others without their consent, usually with good intentions.

paternity establishment The legal procedure to determine if a man, outside of marriage, is the father of a particular child and to establish his rights and responsibilities in regard to that child. The pro-

cedure is relatively easy and accurate through genetic testing and is an important activity in the U.S. *Office of Child Support Enforcement.*

paternity suit A legal proceeding to determine whether a man is the father of a certain child.

path analysis In *social research,* a statistical technique for analyzing the direct and indirect relationships between variables and representing them in a diagram.

pathogenicity In public health, the proportion of persons who become infected after being exposed to a disease-carrying agent.

pathological gambling An *impulse control disorder* in which the individual continues to make wagers on games of chance despite continuous disruption in life responsibilities, such as financial problems, disrupted family relationships, and nonviolent criminal behavior, to pay for debts. Typically, these individuals believe that money can cause and solve their problems and continue gambling, often secretively, to recoup their losses. See also *Gamblers Anonymous.*

pathology The study of the nature of physical or mental diseases, including causes, symptoms, effects on the subject, and the circumstances in which the disease occurs. The term is also used more broadly in referring to physical or behavioral deviations from the norm that can or do result in *disease* or *dysfunction.* See also *psychopathology.*

patient government Participation in the management of a hospital ward by those being treated therein. This system is prevalent in mental hospitals and other residential health care centers and is integral to the therapeutic community or *milieu therapy.*

Patient Self-Determination Act The 1990 U.S. federal legislation (P.L. 101-508) that requires health care providers receiving federal funds to inform patients of their rights to advance directives and to indicate in the patients' charts that such a directive has been established. See also *living will.*

patients Those who are receiving care and treatment from physicians and health care personnel. Social workers generally use the term "client" when referring to the individuals they are serving. However, the term "patient" is more commonly used by social workers who are employed in health care settings (for example, hospital and *medical social workers*).

patients' rights The legal, moral, and ethical standards that protect patients from improper or unwarranted treatment and allow for participation in decisions affecting their care. The *American Civil Liberties Union (ACLU)* has delineated eight legal rights of patients: the right to (1) informed participation in all decisions involving one's health care; (2) privacy, respecting the source of payment for treatment and care; (3) prompt attention, especially in emergency situations; (4) clear, concise explanation of all proposed procedures in understandable terms, including the risk of death or serious side effects, and the right not to be subjected to any procedure without voluntary, competent, and understanding consent; (5) clear, complete, and accurate evaluation of one's condition and prognosis before being asked to agree to any test or procedure; (6) access to all information contained in one's medical record while in the health care facility and the ability to examine the record on request; (7) refuse any drug, test, procedure, or treatment; and (8) leave the health care facility at will regardless of physical condition or financial status, although the patient may be requested to sign a release stating that he or she is leaving against the medical judgment of the doctor.

patria potestas The tradition, especially strong in Latino cultures, in which the father has a high degree of authority over the other family members.

patrifocal family A kinship group centered around the father. See also *matrifocal family*.

patrilineal society A cultural group in which descent is traced through the father.

patron One who supports a charity, social cause, artistic endeavor, or other activity considered socially worthwhile.

patronage In political terms, the privileges a government official bestows on others, usually in exchange for their past or future support. Often, these privileges are government jobs, contracts, or access to lawmakers.

pauper A poor person. The term originated in Europe in the early Middle Ages from "pauperes," referring to dependence. Those called paupers were not necessarily in need but could be in their de-

pendent state voluntarily. The "pauperes Christi" spent their time praying near churches and depending on donations.

pauper schools Public schools established for the children of poor people. Currently, such schools are common in some nations; they were prevalent in the United States and Europe in the 19th century.

pavement people Those who live in primitive and makeshift shacks on sidewalks or streets, most often near urban areas of poor nations.

pavor nocturnus See *sleep terror disorder*.

pay equity The principle that people who do the same jobs should receive the same wages or salaries, regardless of gender, age, ethnic or racial backgrounds, or need. See also *comparable worth*.

payroll tax A tax levied on wages or salaries that is paid by employers and employees and usually designated for programs such as *unemployment compensation* and *Old Age, Survivors, Disability, and Health Insurance (OASDHI)*. Some economists also refer to this as an income tax. See also *earmarked taxes* and *Federal Insurance Contributions Act (FICA)*.

PC 1. See *political correctness (PC)*. 2. See *professional corporation (PC)*. 3. PC also commonly refers to a personal computer.

PCBs Environmentally hazardous chemicals (polychlorinated biphenyls) known to cause cancer in some animals and dangerous health effects in humans. PCBs are now banned in the United States but widely used elsewhere in the production of electrical and refrigeration equipment, fluorescent fixtures, and oils. PCBs enter the atmosphere during their production and shipment, through leaks and fires, and from toxic dumps. PCBs degrade extremely slowly and accumulate in microorganisms, which are taken up or consumed by fish and wildlife.

PCP Phencyclidine hydrochloride, an illegal drug (except as an animal tranquilizer) that in low doses produces *euphoria* and numbness but in higher doses may produce *delirium*, convulsions, violent behavior, and changes in the users' perceptions of their bodies. Also known as *"angel dust,"* "lovely," and "loveboat," the drug can have severe and permanent effects such as psychosis, coma, or heart failure.

PCP abuse   A *substance-use disorder* involving *PCP* (phencyclidine hydrochloride), or similarly acting arylcyclohexylamines, which leads to sensations of *grandiosity, emotional lability, euphoria,* psychomotor agitation, and diminished responsiveness to pain. When PCP is used repeatedly, by smoking, snorting, or swallowing, the individual may develop *impaired social functioning.*

peace   A state of tranquility in the social order and freedom from civil disturbance, violence, war, strife, social enmity, and mutual agreements between governments and peoples. Peace is usually achieved or maintained only when relative *social justice* exists or is perceived to exist for most of the people and nations with competing interests.

Peace Corps   The independent federal volunteer organization established by President John F. Kennedy in 1961 that sends American volunteers to *less-developed countries (LDCs)* for two years to provide training in more than 300 skills, particularly in agriculture, natural resource development, science, and public administration. Their Web site address is http://www.peacecorps.gov

peace dividend   Funds that are no longer needed to maintain the *Cold War* military budget that could be allocated for nondefense public purposes such as education, infrastructure, and social welfare. At the end of the Cold War in 1990, many political leaders and voters assumed that more of these funds would be available than has proved to be the case.

Peace Institute   The independent U.S. government organization founded in 1984 to help find ways to resolve international conflicts. The U.S Institute of Peace, as it is formally called, trains and prepares negotiators for mediation work, educates the public through changes in curricula, and organizes information to be used for these purposes. Their Web site address is http://www.usip.org

peace movement   The organized efforts of individuals, organizations, and governments to achieve conflict resolution without wars, terrorism, or social injustice. Social workers, including *Jane Addams* and *Jeannette Rankin,* have been at the forefront of such movements. Many organizations coordinate peace efforts, including the Jane Addams Peace Association, Women's International League for Peace and Freedom, and the National Peace Foundation. Religious groups include Clergy and Laity Concerned and the Interfaith Center to Reverse the Arms Race. Professional groups include Physicians for Social Responsibility, Psychologists for Social Responsibility, International Association of Educators for World Peace, and Lawyers Alliance for World Security.

Pearson's *r* correlation   Also known as the Pearson product–moment correlation coefficient, a statistical measure of the strength of relationships between two variables (such as weight and height) that are measured at intervals.

pederasty   Anal sexual contact with boys.

pediatric AIDS   *HIV disease* that infects fetuses and infants to preadolesecents. The federal Maternal and Child Health Services program, under the *U.S. Department of Health and Human Services (HHS)* and the *U.S. Public Health Service,* manages a major pediatric HIV/AIDS program to help with community-based care, education, and technical assistance.

pediatrics   The branch of medicine pertaining to the care and treatment of children. The physician who so practices is known as a "pediatrician." See also *physician.*

pediculosis   See *head lice.*

pedophilia   Erotic interest in children. When this attraction is restricted to inner fantasy, it is considered by clinicians to be a serious mental disorder known as *paraphilia.* When the attraction is acted upon, usually in the form of child sexual abuse, it is a crime. Some clinicians suggest that if the individual is attracted to adolescent boys or girls rather than prepubescent children, the condition should be referred to as *ephebophilia.* However, most professionals do not consider this a distinct disorder.

"Peeping Tom"   Vernacular for one who participates in *voyeurism.*

peer   An equal, as in age group, educational level, ethnic group, or other classes of people.

peer group   An association of people who have the same social status (for example, profession, occupation, age group, or gender).

peer pairing   A therapeutic technique used especially for socially isolated children and adults who might have difficulty relating to a social worker on a one-to-one basis or who cannot tolerate small groups. The therapist sees the client and another person who has similar characteristics (such as age, gender, or type of personality) together and treats both simultaneously. This model has been used most frequently in schools, residential facilities, hospitals, and clinics.

peer review A formal evaluation by a specific group of one's fellow professionals to determine general competence or specific actions. In social work and other professions, the term refers to a formal periodic process in which professional standards of intervention have been spelled out and practices are monitored by colleagues. For example, if a client or someone making a *third-party payment* (such as an insurance company) suspected some wrongdoing by a social worker and complained to the person's professional association or state licensing authority, a panel of fellow social workers could review the case to determine appropriate action. See also *professional review organizations (PROs)* and *accountability.*

peer review organization (PRO) A formal and sometimes legally mandated association of people who are members of one profession, brought together to evaluate the work of other members of that profession in accomplishing a specific set of tasks or objectives. The evaluation is commonly done by reviewing the professional's case records to determine if the type of treatment plan, methods, and outcome are commensurate with the organization's objectives and the client's needs. The U.S. government has required the establishment of PROs in hospitals and nursing homes that receive federal funds to oversee the administration of the *diagnosis-related groups (DRGs)* system.

Pell Grants A U.S. government financial aid program for qualified low- and middle-income students, primarily for those who have not yet received baccalaureate degrees. Administered by the U.S. Department of Education, Pell Grants are paid directly to the student's college and do not have to be repaid. Their Web site address is http://www.pellgrantsonline.ed.gov

pellagra A disease of *malnutrition* that results from a dietary deficiency of niacin. Its symptoms include inflammation of the skin and mucous membranes, gastrointestinal disturbances, and, often, cognitive disturbance.

pelvic inflammatory disease (PID) Infection of the female pelvic organs, commonly caused by *sexually transmitted diseases (STDs)* such as *gonorrhea* and *chlamydia.* PID often causes scarring of the fallopian tubes and *infertility* in 20 percent of the infected women.

penal institution Penitentiary; a facility for the *incarceration* of convicted criminals that sometimes provides them with education and other resources that might reduce the *recidivism rate.* See also *carceral organization.*

penetration rate The proportion of an organization's workforce who belong to a particular minority group. The *Equal Employment Opportunity Commission (EEOC)* reviews an organization's minority hiring practices by this rate.

penis envy theory In *psychoanalytic theory,* the idea that women and girls resent the males' possession of penises and sometimes feel inferior because they lack them. Modern psychoanalytic theorists emphasize the symbolic aspect of this resentment, indicating that women and girls are more envious of the opportunities available to males that frequently are lacking for females in most cultures. See also *castration theory.*

Pennsylvania School The theoretical and practice orientation in social work based on the ideas of University of Pennsylvania School of Social Work educators *Virginia Robinson, Jessie Taft, Ruth Smalley,* and their colleague, psychoanalyst Otto Rank. Also known as the *functional school in social work,* the approach de-emphasized *Freudian theory* and suggested a goal-oriented approach to problem solving.

penology The study of prison and reformatory management, crime prevention, and the *rehabilitation* of criminals and delinquents. See also *corrections.*

pension A payment made regularly to an individual because of *retirement,* age, loss, or incapacitating injury or to dependents in the event of the beneficiary's death. *Social security* benefits as well as retirement income provided by employers are generally considered to be forms of pensions.

penury *Destitution* or extreme *poverty.*

peonage Forced labor or involuntary servitude, frequently because of debt or legal obligation.

Although such practices are forbidden in the United States by the 13th Amendment of the Constitution, the practice is widespread in some societies, especially in some resource-poor countries, *Third World* and *Fourth World* developing nations, or some totalitarian dictatorships.

People for the Ethical Treatment of Animals (PETA) A national and international nongovernment organization working to protect animals from abuse, primarily through education and publicity. PETA also has engaged in militant actions directed at research labs that experiment with animals, furriers, meatpacking plants, and industries using animal products. Their Web site address is http://www.peta-online.org

People-to-People Committee for the Handicapped A voluntary organization that provides information to families of people with disabilities about available services and self-help activities. The committee publishes the *Directory of Organizations Interested in the Handicapped,* which contains an extensive listing of organizations that give information about treatments, training, equipment, and techniques used to help people with disabilities.

pepper spray The chemical oleoresin capsicum (OC) and an aerosol widely used in self-defense and by law enforcement authorities to subdue dangerous suspects by using relatively little force.

perceived needs The requirements that people believe they must have to achieve an acceptable level of well-being. See also *normative needs, expressed needs,* and *relative needs.*

percentile The score in a *frequency distribution* to indicate the percentage of cases that falls below that score. For example, the 33rd percentile indicates the point below which falls 33 percent of the scores.

perception The psychic impressions made by the five senses (sight, sound, smell, taste, and touch) and the way these impressions are interpreted cognitively and emotionally, based on one's life experiences.

perceptual distortion Incongruity between a physical reality and the way it is perceived, understood, or interpreted cognitively by the individual.

perestroika The Russian term, roughly meaning "restructuring." Social agency administrators

and other organization officials in many nations increasingly use the term to describe their own organization's intent to change policies and practices.

performance budgeting A plan used by administrators to allocate resources based on predicted or observed results rather than on costs of maintaining existing structures.

performance evaluation The systematic determination of the degree to which an employee or public servant achieves the goals specified in the employee's job description or performance objectives. This is done by a supervisor or administrator through peer interviews, rating scales, and performance tests.

perimenopause A transitional stage of life leading to menopause. Hormone production starts to fluctuate, menstruation and menstrual periods become less regular, and hot flashes and other symptoms begin.

perinatal Pertaining to the phase of life that encompasses the several months or so before and after birth.

perinatal social work A professional specialization within social work that focuses on the psychosocial treatment of the mother, fetus, and newborn. Perinatal social workers are employed primarily in hospital settings and maternity medical facilities, but many also serve in public health settings, AIDS clinics, ethics centers, and private practice. Many belong to the *National Association of Perinatal Social Workers (NAPSW).*

Perinatal Social Workers, National Association of (NAPSW) The professional association of social workers who help individuals, families, and communities deal with the problems that occur from pregnancy through an infant's first year of life. NAPSW was incorporated in 1980 to facilitate its members to work effectively with pregnancy and family counseling, high-risk pregnancies, premature and sick newborns, dysfunctioning parents, and related issues. NAPSW issues publications, sponsors research, and hosts an annual conference. Their Web site address is http://www.napsw.org

perinatologist A *physician* who specializes in the care and treatment of the mother and child several months before and after birth.

period prevalence   See *epidemiology.*

peripheral nervous system (PNS)   That part of the nervous system outside the *central nervous system (CNS)*, that is, the entire network of nerve fibers.

peritoneal dialysis   See *dialysis.*

perjury   The *crime* of making false statements while under legal oath to tell the truth.

Perkins, Frances (1882–1965)   The first woman to serve as a U.S. cabinet member, Perkins was President Franklin D. Roosevelt's Secretary of Labor during the *Great Depression* and World War II. Using her social work background, she promoted and helped develop the *social security* system, *child labor* legislation, and *unemployment compensation.*

"perks"   See *perquisites.*

permanency planning   In *child welfare* work, a systematic effort to provide long-term continuity in dependent children's care as an alternative to temporary foster placements. This might be done by facilitating *adoption,* by establishing clear guidelines for remaining in *foster care,* or by helping the children's natural families become capable of meeting the children's needs. Permanency planning goals include efforts to prevent out-of-home placements whenever possible; promote family restoration; and implement placement guidelines such as placement in the least restrictive (most familylike) setting available, in close proximity to the parents' homes, and consistent with the child's best interests and special needs.

permissiveness   A high degree of tolerance by those in control for the behavior of an individual or group.

permitted disparity   The U.S. federal pension and tax law provision that allows employers to include their employees' *social security* benefits when calculating total retirement benefits. This provision is also known as *social security integration.*

pernicious   The term health care workers use for life-threatening.

pernicious anemia   A serious form of *anemia* in which the red blood cells decrease as a result of the body's inability to use vitamin B_{12}. Early symptoms include paleness, fatigue, digestive problems, and anxiety.

perpetrator   Among law enforcement authorities, a person considered to have committed the crime being investigated.

perquisites   Special benefits given to one who holds a particular office, job, or status. Often, such "perks" are tax exempt and granted to top executives or other privileged employees. Examples include the use of company cars and set-aside parking places.

persecutory-type delusional disorder   One type of *delusional disorder* characterized by nonbizarre delusions, particularly an intense belief that one is being plotted against, harmed, spied on, followed, or obstructed. The person focuses on an imagined injustice and often seeks remedy through appeals to authorities, legal action, or threatening and violent behavior.

perseveration   Preoccupation and intense focus on one thought, word, or act.

person-in-environment perspective   Among social workers and other professionals, an orientation that views the client as part of an environmental system. This perspective encompasses the reciprocal relationships and other influences between an individual, the *relevant other* or others, and the physical and social environment.

Person-in-Environment (PIE) System   A tool social workers use to describe and classify problems of *social functioning.* The system is used for the systematic collection of relevant information that can produce a comprehensive assessment of the social-functioning problems adult clients bring to social workers (James Karls & Karin Wandrei, *Person-in-Environment System,* Washington, DC: NASW Press, 1994). The system also helps the worker draw conclusions about the interrelated factors contributing to the client's problem and select interventions that might relieve or solve problems. PIE calls for a description of the client based on four factors: Factor I—social-functioning problems (including four categories of social role problems: family, other interpersonal, occupational, and special life situation roles); Factor II—environmental problems (including economic–basic needs; educational, legal, health, safety, and social services;

voluntary association; and affectional support systems); Factor III—mental disorders; and Factor IV—physical health problems. The degree to which these problems require social work intervention is rated in a *severity index*. The length and recency of the client's problem is rated in the *duration index*. The *coping index* is a rating of the client's resources for dealing with the problem.

person-oriented record   A format used by some social workers and some social agencies to keep specific, accountable, and goal-directed records of the intervention process for each client. An adaptation of the physician's *problem-oriented record (POR)*, the person-oriented record contains an initial database, treatment plan assessment, progress notes, and the progress review (to evaluate a client's progress over a specified time, such as every 6 or 12 weeks).

person–situation configuration   The concept used in *social casework* pertaining to the threefold interrelationship consisting of the person with the problem, the situation in which the problem exists, and the interaction among them. The interaction is influenced by internal conflicts or reactions and environmental pressures.

personal advisor   In the British Social Security system, professionals who provide individual counseling and *ombudsperson* services, especially for those dependent on welfare benefits, to help them become active participants in society and, when possible, fully employed paid workers.

personal capability assessment   In the British Welfare Reform and Pensions Act of 1999, the test given to applicants for employment disability benefits to determine if they are eligible. Information about the person's work capabilities comes from the doctors and others who examine him or her and from the applicant in interviews with his or her *personal advisors*. They focus on the applicant's ability to perform a range of work-related activities such as walking, sitting, lifting, hearing, seeing, and concentrating. The findings are incorporated into a capability report and used in determining the extent of benefits. This was called the All Work Test before 1999.

personal care services   A program, usually under the auspices of local departments of welfare or human services, that provides basic nonmedical care, such as bathing, grooming, and assistance in dressing, to needy people in their homes.

Personal Earnings and Benefits Estimate Statement (PEBES)   A summary of the *Social Security Administration (SSA)* financial record of each beneficiary. SSA recommends that people periodically review their PEBES while still working to ensure that all information is properly recorded. SSA furnishes this statement free to anyone who calls 1-800-772-1213 or uses the Web address http://www.ssa.gov

personal response systems (PRS)   The use of communications devices, monitors, and on-call personnel to provide emergency assistance to persons who are alone but in need.

Personal Responsibility and Work Opportunity Reconciliation Act   The federal legislation enacted in 1996 (P.L. 104-193) to reform the U.S. welfare system. Programs such as *Aid to Families with Dependent Children (AFDC), Emergency Assistance*, and the *Job Opportunities and Basic Skills (JOBS)* training programs were repealed and other welfare programs were curtailed. The replacement *Temporary Assistance to Needy Families (TANF)* program placed restrictions on recipients. Parents were required to work after no more than two years of receiving cash assistance, with a lifetime limit of five years; unmarried parents younger than 18 were ineligible for assistance unless they lived in the homes of adult relatives; and states were allowed to deny cash payments to additional children born into families already receiving assistance (that is a *family cap*). Medicaid eligibility was no longer guaranteed, except at the state level. Legal immigrants were barred from receiving *Supplemental Security Income (SSI), Medicaid*, and *food stamp* benefits until they became U.S. citizens. Future immigrants were ineligible for means-tested benefits for five years. State controls over the food stamp program were increased. Eligibility criteria for SSI payments were more restrictive. Subsequent reauthorization of the act has increased the required hours of work from 30 to 40 hours per week and eliminated the distinction between two-parent and single-parent families. Some new funds were authorized to promote and experiment in innovative approaches to family formation and healthy marriage activities. The *Administration for Children and Families (ACF)* of the U.S. HHS provides detailed and updated information online. Their Web site address is http://www.acf.hhs.gov/news/welfare

personal social services *Social services* with a basic purpose to enhance the relationships between people and between people and their environments and to provide opportunities for social fulfillment. Personal social services are distinguished from institutional services (*income maintenance* programs, *health care*, education, employment, and housing) and include *counseling* and guidance, development of *mutual help* and *self-help groups*, *family planning*, and services for older people and for children.

personal unconscious In *Jungian theory*, one of two parts of the *unconscious* (the other part being the *collective unconscious*). The personal unconscious is the region of the mind that is not subject to the individual's immediate awareness but that is developed through the individual's unique experiences, drives, and circumstances.

personality An individual's entire intellectual and emotional structure, including abilities, attitudes, interests, and enduring patterns of understanding and relating to the environment.

personality change A significant deviation from one's previously characteristic pattern of behavior, thinking, and communicating, usually symptomatic of an underlying mental or physical problem. Among the more common changes are increased *emotional lability*, disinhibition, aggressive or apathetic behaviors, and paranoid behaviors. When using this term as a formal diagnosis, the clinician indicates the predominating behavioral change and the general medical condition thought to underlie the change.

personality disorders Patterns of relating to and understanding others that are so maladaptive, inflexible, and deeply ingrained that they produce significant social impairment. Personality disorders are usually recognizable in one's adolescence. There are 11 major types of personality disorder: (1) *paranoid personality disorder*, (2) *schizoid personality disorder*, (3) *schizotypal personality disorder*, (4) *histrionic personality disorder*, (5) *narcissistic personality disorder*, (6) *antisocial personality disorder*, (7) *borderline personality disorder*, (8) *avoidant personality disorder*, (9) *dependent personality disorder*, (10) *obsessive–compulsive personality disorder*, and (11) the atypical personality disorder.

personality inventory A psychological test, usually using a questionnaire, in which the subject answers personal questions to reveal characteristics and individual behaviors and sometimes to derive diagnoses. The individual's scores are often compared to norms based on the responses by many others who have taken the same tests. The most widely recognized of these tests is the Minnesota Multiphasic Personality Inventory (MMPI).

personnel standards A formal delineation of the rules, behaviors, qualifications, and manner of interrelationships that are expected of each employee as a condition of employment. Often, these standards are used to fire workers, hire applicants, and adjudicate grievances between employer and employee.

persons in need of supervision (PINS) A designation used by social workers for adults who require monitoring because they have certain physical or mental health care needs, diminished capacities, or legal status. See also *children in need of supervision (CHINS)*.

perturbation Agitation or distress; the degree to which a person is disturbed about some environmental or internal phenomenon.

pertussis A highly communicable *infectious disease*, popularly known as whooping cough, occurring predominantly in young children. The person develops respiratory difficulty and eventually begins coughing rapidly. This causes the individual to gasp for air, during which a high-pitched, whooping sound occurs. In most developed nations, pertussis has been controlled to a great extent by *immunization* during infancy.

pervasive developmental disorder A physical or mental dysfunction that appears before maturity and is characterized by severe and inclusive impairment in areas such as communication and social interaction skills or by the presence of stereotyped behavior, interest, and activities. Pervasive development disorders include *autistic disorder*, *Rett's disorder*, *childhood disintegrative disorder*, and *Asperger's disorder*.

perversion See *paraphilia*.

pestilence Any epidemic, highly contagious disease; a synonym for *plague*.

petit jury A group of 12 (sometimes 6) citizens selected by the justice system of a jurisdiction to hear evidence and, from that only, decide on the guilt or innocence of an accused person. See also *grand jury.*

petit larceny *Larceny* that involves goods of relatively small value. Each jurisdiction legislates the amount that determines whether a theft is petit (or petty) or *grand larceny.* In most states, that cutoff amount is usually between $50 and $500. The punishment for petit larceny tends to be much less than that for grand larceny.

petit mal seizures See *seizure disorders.*

phallic phase The third stage in *psychosexual development theory* that occurs approximately between ages three and six. During this phase, the child's zone of pleasure centers in the genitalia. The *Oedipus complex* is a culmination of this phase, during which the healthy child works through rivalry with the parent of the same sex so that a loving relationship can exist with both parents and *self-esteem* can develop in the child.

pharmacotherapy The administration of medications to help maximize the physical or mental health potential of a patient. This includes educating the patient about the need for the drug and its proper use, monitoring, and taking efforts to modify the prescription as needed. Counseling and support are also important.

phase-of-life problem A normative transition in the *life cycle* that requires the individual to use *coping skills* to adapt to unfamiliar but virtually inevitable circumstances. Examples include entering school, getting married, having a first child, and retiring. See *idiosyncratic life-cycle transitions.*

phatic communion The exchange of gestures and verbalizations, with strangers, about neutral subjects (for example, "It's a nice day, isn't it?"). Both participants do this, not to actually discuss the neutral topic, but to provide and receive information about the other's statuses and roles. A common synonym is "small talk," although the function of this communication is important in the structure of society.

phencyclidine-related disorders See *PCP abuse.*

phenylketonuria (PKU) A genetically transmitted metabolic disorder in which the victim's body fails to produce enzymes needed to break down certain natural amino acids. Skin disorders, neurological problems, and mental retardation are common results.

philandering Consorting with members of the opposite sex, usually in extramarital relationships.

philanthropy A term derived from the Greek, meaning "love of humanity," that has come to refer to practical efforts to promote the public welfare by donating funds or resources to worthy causes. Philanthropic activity, especially in the secular community, was rather spontaneous and haphazard until the late 19th century. The field of social work was born, in part, as an effort to make these activities more systematic and effective in their raising and distributing funds. Today, philanthropy constitutes a sophisticated and highly complex number of organizations and groups. See also *alms* and *charity.*

Philippine Department of Social Welfare and Development (DSWD) The Philippine government division (established in 1915 as the Philippine Public Welfare Board) that administers the nation's six human services programs, including (1) Assistance to Socially Disadvantaged Communities, (2) Women, (3) Children, (4) Families, (5) Relief and Rehabilitation of Victims of Natural Calamities and Social Disorganization, and (6) Disability Prevention and Care of Disabled Persons.

phlebitis Formation of clots within veins, usually caused by local injury, coagulation disorders, and, especially, inactivity.

phobia An intense and persistent fear of an object or situation. Psychosocial theorists think this is caused by displacement of a conflict onto an external object, where it will be presumably more tolerable and avoidable. Behavioral theorists think it is a consequence of a chain of associations of various negative stimuli. Phobias are the main symptom of a *phobic disorder.* There are an infinite number of identifiable phobias because every potential experience and *stimulus* could result in a fear. Some examples are *acrophobia, agoraphobia, claustrophobia, nyctaphobia, xenophobia,* and *zoophobia.* Other phobias include the following: achluphobia (irrational fear of the dark); acousticophobia (sounds); aerophobia (drafts of fresh air, airborne diseases, or flying in airplanes); agyiophobia (crossing streets); aichmophobia (pointed objects); ailurophobia (cats); algophobia (pain); amathophobia (dust); androphobia (men); anthophobia (flowers); apiphobia (bees or being stung); arachnophobia (spiders); astraphobia (lightning and thunderstorms); autophobia (being alone); bathophobia (deep water or other deep places); bibliophobia (books or places of study); coitophobia (sexual intercourse); coprophobia (feces); cynophobia (dogs or dog bites); demophobia (crowds); gamophobia (marriage); genophobia (sex); gynephobia (women); haptephobia (being touched); hemophobia or erythrophobia (blood); homophobia (homosexuals); hydrophobia (water); hypnophobia (sleep); kleptophobia (being robbed); necrophobia (dead bodies); neophobia (new situations, places, or unfamiliar things); nosophobia (disease); ochlophobia (crowds); ophidophobia (snakes); osmophobia (odors); panophobia (everything); pathophobia (disease); phengophobia (daylight); pyrophobia (fire); and thanatophobia (death).

phobic avoidance   A symptom of *phobic disorder* in which the individual attempts to stay away from the feared object or situation (*phobic stimulus*) or avoids even thinking about such things. This often results in such social and mental constriction that psychosocial functioning is impaired and *activities of daily living (ADL)* are not fulfilled.

phobic disorder   A condition in which the essential feature is a persistent and irrational *fear* of a specific object or situation, resulting in serious attempts to avoid it. The three types of phobic disorder are *agoraphobia, social phobia,* and *specific phobia*. Specific phobias were once called "simple phobias."

phobic stimulus   Clearly discernible, circumscribed objects or situations that produce an immediate *anxiety* response. The stimulus can be an actual object (for example, snakes, high places) or a situation (for example, giving a public speech), or it may be anticipation of an encounter with it. The level of anxiety or *fear* usually varies according to the proximity of the stimulus and the degree to which escape from it seems possible. Types of stimuli in *specific phobia* are animal type (generally with a childhood onset), natural environment type (storms, heights, water), blood-injection type (the sight of blood, needles, medical operations), situational types (entering elevators or tunnels, crossing bridges, flying), and other types (fear of contracting illness, loud noises, falling down). See also *agoraphobia* and *social phobia*.

phonological disorder   A *communication disorder* (formerly known as developmental *articulation disorder*) characterized by one's failure to use developmentally expected speech sounds that are age and dialect appropriate. The individual may have difficulty pronouncing certain sounds clearly or pronouncing sounds such as *r, sh, th, f, z, l,* or *ch,* often making substitutions for these sounds. See also *expressive language disorder, mixed receptive–expressive language disorder,* and *stuttering.*

phototherapy   The human services intervention that emphasizes the use of photographs, film, videotapes, and other graphic depictions to help clients achieve greater understanding about themselves and their world and to express themselves artistically. Phototherapy is often used in conjunction with other forms of psychotherapy to achieve these goals. The International Phototherapy Association (IPA), founded in 1981, promotes the use of this method, facilitates professional interactions, encourages training, and disseminates information. The term also refers to a specialized form of medical treatment in which controlled dosages of light are used, especially by dermatologists, in the treatment of diseases such as psoriasis and vitaligo.

physiatrist   A *physician* who specializes in rehabilitation medicine or physical medicine and works primarily with patients who have impairments and disabilities arising from musculoskeletal, neuromuscular, or vascular disorders.

physical therapy   The treatment of a disorder, injury, or disability by using mechanical or physical intervention, such as massage, controlled exercise, heat application, water, movement, and manipulation.

physician   A health care professional with an educational degree of doctor of medicine (MD) or doctor of osteopathy (DO) and the highest level of responsibility in patient care. Training to be a physician begins after receiving an undergraduate degree. Medical school typically consists of four years of academic and clinical training. This is followed by an in-hospital residency training period of three or more years, depending on the specialty. The first residence year (once known as the internship) is known as the PGY-1 (first postgraduate year). After successful completion of PGY-1, the student may take exams for medical licensure. In the United States, medical licensure is state regulated. The new physician then completes three to six years of in-hospital residency training in an area of specialization. In the United States, many physicians become board certified in one of 23 specialties: allergy and immunology, anesthesiology, colon and rectal surgery, dermatology, emergency medicine, family practice, internal medicine, neurological surgery, nuclear medicine, obstetrics and gynecology, ophthalmology, orthopedic surgery, otolaryngology, pathology, pediatrics, physical medicine and rehabilitation, plastic surgery, preventive medicine, psychiatry and neurology, radiology, surgery, thoracic surgery, and urology. Physicians known as *general practitioners* are now rare, and physicians who are family practitioners or internists usually perform primary care. See also *osteopath.*

physician-assisted suicide (PAS)   A patient's use of a medical doctor's willful knowledge, facilities, or lethal drug prescriptions to consciously and deliberately take his or her own life. The physician may write a prescription for a lethal dose, which the patient can use directly without further help, but the patient actually carries out the suicidal act. In many jurisdictions, this may legally implicate the physician as an accomplice to a crime. Oregon, where PAS has been legal since 1997, is the exception in the United States. Physician-assisted suicide is not the same as *passive euthanasia.*

physician's assistant (PA)   A licensed health care professional qualified to perform physical examinations, provide counseling, and prescribe certain medications under a physician's supervision.

physiotherapist   An alternative name for physical therapist.

Piagetian theory   A theory of *cognitive development* proposed by the Swiss psychologist Jean Piaget (1896–1980) to explain the processes by which humans come to perceive, organize knowledge, solve problems, and understand the world. According to this theory, human cognitive development is the product of a consistent, reliable pattern or plan of interaction with the environment, known as a *scheme.* Schemes are goal-oriented strategies that help the person achieve some intended result. These schemes are sensorimotor (occurring in infancy and early childhood, in which reflexes and motor responses are prevalent) and cognitive (based on experience and on mental images, reflecting the person's ability to develop the use of abstract reasoning and symbolism). Two

processes in cognitive development are *assimilation* and *accommodation.* Piaget delineated four stages of cognitive development: (1) *sensorimotor stage,* (2) *preoperational stage,* (3) *concrete operations stage,* and (4) *formal operations stage.*

pibloktoq   A *culture-bound syndrome* found most commonly among indigenous peoples of arctic and subarctic regions, in which the individual behaves irrationally and sometimes dangerously for up to 30 minutes, shouting obscenities, tearing off clothing, eating feces, or fleeing. The behavior often follows a period of withdrawal or irritability and frequently ends in convulsive seizures and coma for up to 12 hours. The individual usually remembers nothing about the event.

pica   An *eating disorder* involving the frequent consumption of inorganic or nonnutritive substances such as dirt or paper.

picketing   A demonstration by an individual or group wishing to call public attention to some social problem, political goal, grievance, or labor dispute. The demonstrators typically carry signs and march in front of some facility where the grievance occurs or where publicity is most likely.

Pickle Amendment   A provision in a 1977 U.S. law (P.L. 94-566) that allows certain clients who have lost their *SSI* eligibility to continue receiving *Medicaid* benefits. SSI eligibility is frequently used as a criterion to establish Medicaid eligibility, as long as the client does not exceed certain income thresholds. When SSI cost-of-living allowances or other income sources pushed these clients beyond this threshold, they were deemed ineligible for Medicaid, until the Pickle Amendment was passed.

Pick's disease   A degenerative brain disease particularly affecting the frontal and temporal lobes and resulting in symptoms such as *dementia,* deterioration of social skills, behavioral disinhibition, primitive reflexes, and extreme apathy or agitation.

piles   See *hemorrhoid.*

pilfering   Stealing small items, often from storerooms, luggage, hotel rooms, coin boxes, and similar places.

pilot study   In social research, a procedure for testing and validating a questionnaire or other instrument by administering it to a small group of respondents from the intended test population (who will then not be part of the sample). The procedure helps determine whether the test items possess the desired qualities of measurement and the ability to discriminate other problems before the instrument is put into widespread use. This is not the same as a *pretest.*

placater role   A recurrent pattern of *communication* one assumes in relating to others, characterized by talking in an ingratiating way, apologizing, avoiding disagreements, and attempting repeatedly to gain the approval of the *relevant other.* This role was delineated by *Virginia Satir* (1920–1987), who described this person as a "yes-man" who feels worthless without the approval of others (*Peoplemaking*, Palo Alto, CA: Science and Behavior Books, 1972, p. 63). Other roles are the *blamer role,* the *computer role,* and the *distracter role.*

placebo   An inert preparation that is made to appear identical to or presented to patients as an active drug. In research that is *double blind,* the investigator tests the effectiveness of a drug by giving it to half the subjects and the placebo to the others. Sometimes, placebos are also given to patients who apparently do not need an active drug but who seek the attention or *secondary gain* that comes from using one. A physical effect based on an individual's belief that the inactive substance is working is called a "placebo effect." The term used in most English-speaking nations outside the United States is "dummy."

placement   The assignment to or location of an individual in a setting that is suitable to achieve a specified purpose. Social workers use the term mostly to indicate the assignment of a child or dependent adult to a facility or person who can provide for that person's needs. The term also refers to the social work student's assignment to a *social agency* for practice in *field instruction.*

placing out   The practice of finding new homes and families in distant areas for institutionalized children or those who can no longer remain with their own families.

plagiarism   The act of appropriating the scientific or literary writings of another person and presenting it as one's own work. Plagiarism is a *crime* when such work has been copyrighted or when state laws specify conditions in which such acts are

unlawful (as in selling term papers). The act is considered unethical by social workers.

plague   A highly contagious, rapidly spreading, and virulent disease. The disease is caused by the bacteria *Yersinia pestis,* which was spread mostly by rats carrying fleas; when people become infected, their coughs and sneezes can also spread it. Once the most devastating killer of human life on Earth, preventive and treatment methods now keep it well under reasonable control.

planned parenthood   A *social movement* advocating population control and reproductive restraint. The term is also used as a synonym for *contraception* or *birth control.* See also *family planning.*

Planned Parenthood Federation   An international organization established by Margaret Sanger (1883–1966) in 1921 to promote planned *birth control* and *contraception.* The original name, until 1939, was the American Birth Control League. Their Web site address is http://www.ippf.org

planning   The process of specifying future objectives, evaluating the means for achieving them, and making deliberate choices about appropriate courses of action. This process of choice involves two aspects: (1) rational decision making, which seeks to examine all relevant alternatives and select from among them, and (2) incremental decision making, which encompasses a more limited range of alternatives and practical considerations. See also *social planning* and *social policy.*

platform   A formal public statement by a political party or social cause organization of its guiding principles and goals for the future.

platica   Spanish term for friendly conversation, the purpose of which in initial contacts is to build the relationship rather than exchange information. When conducting interviews with many Latino clients, social workers find that the platica process is essential in establishing the working relationship or *confianza.*

platykurtic   In graphically depicting data, a *frequency distribution* that is more flat topped than a normal bell-shaped curve or one that is *leptokurtic* (more peaked).

play therapy   A form of *psychotherapy* to facilitate communication with clients, usually children and some speech-reticent adults. The client uses toys to act out conflicts or to demonstrate situations that cannot be verbalized.

plea bargaining *Negotiation* between a prosecuting attorney and a person accused of a crime (and his or her defense counsel), resulting in a disposition of the case. Typically, the accused agrees to plead guilty to a lesser charge and forgoes a jury trial. The advantage to the accused person is that the case is resolved sooner and at less risk of serious penalty. The advantages to the public are that court dockets are less backlogged and cases can be resolved with less cost.

pleasure principle A principle in *Freudian theory* stating that the individual begins life seeking only gratification and pleasure and the avoidance of pain and discomfort. The developing child eventually learns that immediate gratification sometimes has to be subordinated, so the *reality principle* starts to emerge. Thereafter the person faces a lifelong conflict between both. The healthy *ego* tries to adhere to the reality principle while allowing some room for the pleasure principle.

plebiscite A vote by the entire electorate of a nation or other jurisdiction on an issue (rather than on a candidate).

plenary session A meeting for everyone who attends a conference. Most conference participants spend part of their time at smaller gatherings called workshops or sessions but occasionally meet in the plenary sessions with all the other participants, usually to hear some notable speaker or vote on issues pertaining to the whole group.

Plessy v. Ferguson The 1896 U.S. Supreme Court decision upholding a state law permitting *segregation* of the races in public transportation. The ruling, which was extended to other public places, held that segregation was permissible under the Constitution as long as "separate but equal" facilities existed. The ruling was not reversed until the 1954 Supreme Court decision in *Brown v. Board of Education.*

pleurisy A condition of the respiratory system involving swelling and irritation of the membrane that surrounds the lungs. Symptoms include severe chest pain, especially when taking deep breaths. Usually symptomatic of another disease, the causes of pleurisy include viral or bacterial infections, tu-

berculosis, chest injury or trauma, blood clots in the lungs, or cancer.

pluralism Cultural diversity in a society, organization, community, or group, along lines such as race, age, gender, ethnic background, educational level, language, or appearance. In an idealistically pluralistic society, each type of group has some power or influence. Those who oppose pluralism tend to advocate *assimilation.* See also *melting pot theory.*

pluralistic society A society that includes people of many racial, ethnic, religious, and cultural characteristics.

plutocracy Social or government control by those who are wealthy.

podiatrist Specialist in foot and feet-related problems. Podiatrists are not MDs but are licensed practitioners with extensive training.

poetry therapy The use of language arts, metaphor, narrative, and the reading of and listening to the reading of poetry in clinical treatment, either as an adjunct or a central part of the intervention process. The terms "poetry therapy" and *"bibliotherapy"* are often used synonymously. The National Association of Poetry Therapy was founded in 1969 and is headquartered in Port Washington, New York.

pogrom An organized attack on or massacre of a group, usually Jews, residing in a nation or *ghetto.*

point prevalence See *epidemiology.*

Points of Light Foundation An organization established by President George Bush in 1990 consisting of 500 volunteer centers across the United States that bring together people who can help with those who need help. Its goal is to combat people's disconnection from their communities and their sense of alienation and to facilitate their efforts to alleviate social problems. Their Web site address is http://www.pointsoflight.org

polarization A phenomenon in which two or more objects, individuals, or groups develop opposing or contrasting tendencies. In social activism and community organization, it may refer to the process in which an organization's members split into opposing camps over an issue or policy, leading to stalemate or to stronger coalitions.

police social work Professional social work practice within police precinct houses, courthouses, and jails to provide social services to victims of crimes, people accused of crimes, and their families. Some workers counsel police officers and members of their families under job-related stresses. They sometimes act as advocates and public relations specialists for police departments and help in *mediation* with various community groups. A major activity is helping resolve domestic troubles for which the police are called. Some police social workers are civilians, and others are police officers as well as professional social workers.

policy The explicit or implicit standing plan that an organization or government uses as a guide for action.

policy analysis Systematic evaluations of a *policy* and the process by which it was formulated. Those who conduct such analyses consider whether the process and result were rational, clear, explicit, equitable, legal, politically feasible, compatible with social values, cost-effective, and superior to all the alternatives in both the short and long term. Three approaches to policy analysis are (1) the study of process (sociopolitical variables in the dynamics of policy formulation), (2) the study of product (the values and assumptions that inform policy choices), and (3) the study of performance (cost–benefit outcomes of policy implementation).

policy decision-making theories Explanations for the sociopolitical influences and considerations that are translated into specific policies and laws. Five models are used to explain how policy decisions are made: (1) "traditional model" (public-spirited citizens form planning groups, hire a planner, make rational decisions, and propose fair plans); (2) "power pyramid model" (a few business leaders influence politicians and impose decisions on those lower in the social structure); (3) "Yale polyarchic power model" (different issues each have different leadership patterns); (4) "qualified diffused-influence model" (influence is spread among many interest groups that change in size and importance over time); and (5) "decision process model" (the systems approach that sees decision making as a flow in which final decisions are the result of a series of interactions among various systems that all have interest in the decision).

policy practice In social work, professional efforts to influence the development, enactment, implementation, modification, or assessment of social policies, primarily to ensure social justice and equal access to basic social goods.

policy statement A formal and accessible explication of the policies that guide an organization or any of its relevant aspects.

poliomyelitis A contagious viral disease that can cause nerve damage, resulting in permanent paralysis of affected muscles; formerly known as "infantile paralysis." Polio, as it is more commonly called, has been controlled in nations where preventive vaccines are administered to all young children.

political action Coordinated efforts to influence legislation, election of candidates, and social causes. Social workers engage in political action by running for elective office, organizing campaigns in support of other candidates or issues, fundraising, and mobilizing voters and public opinion. Political action also includes lobbying, testifying before legislative committees, and monitoring the work of officeholders and government workers.

political action committees (PACs) Finance groups organized to raise and disburse funds to political candidates.

Political Action for Candidate Election (PACE) The *political action committee* of the *National Association of Social Workers (NASW)*. The organization helps coordinate personnel and financial resources of interested members to elect political officials.

political activism Engaging in activities that influence the decisions and viewpoints of elected officials or their appointees, civil servants, and the electorate. Such activities include holding *voter registration drives,* performing social *consciousness-raising* activities, raising funds to help finance legislators' campaigns, lobbying, running for political office, engaging in *media campaigning,* and helping monitor elections to ensure their fairness.

political correctness (PC) Verbal or written statements to avoid offending any person from a racial, ethnic, religious, or cultural group; any person with a disability; any person with a disease; any person from a geographic region or other entity; and their supporters.

political prisoner An individual held in confinement by a state for views and actions that its leaders think will jeopardize the continued existence of that state.

polity The institutions and people who directly shape the way a society is governed, including political parties, interest groups, government, non-government organizations, and the media.

poll tax A tax of a fixed amount that each person in a jurisdiction is obliged to pay; also called a "head tax." It is regressive in that those with lower incomes pay a higher proportion of their income than do those who earn more.

polydipsia Excessive water drinking, a common symptom among psychotic populations.

polygamy Plural marriage; a social custom that permits having more than one wife or husband at the same time. If the marriage involves one man with more than one wife, it is also called "polygyny." If it involves one woman with more than one husband, the term is "polyandry." Polygamy is not synonymous with *bigamy*. Polygamy is legal in some societies. See also *monogamy*.

polypharmacy The use of two or more drugs in treating one illness.

polysubstance dependence A *substance-use disorder* in which at least three groups of substances other than caffeine and nicotine are used within the same 12-month period, with no single substance predominating.

Ponzi scheme An illegal investment practice in which the operator uses money collected from new participants to pay promised returns to earlier investors. The name comes from Charles Ponzi, who originated it in 1919.

poor law A generic term technically referring to any government statute pertaining to the economic and social care of and control of poor people or measures to reduce the extent of *poverty*. However, the term is primarily used to refer to a group of repressive statutes in Colonial America and in England before the 20th century. These laws established the *almshouse, indoor relief,* and concepts about the *"unworthy poor"* and were generally conceived to discourage people from seeking relief. See also *Elizabethan Poor Laws, Henrician Poor Law, Statute of Labourers, Gilbert Act,* and *Poor Law of 1834.*

Poor Law of 1834 The English legislation enacted to revise the *Elizabethan Poor Laws* of 1601. The new law was punitive and based on the premise that poor people lacked strong or moral character. The laws discontinued public assistance for all able-bodied citizens except those in public institutions and imposed the *less-eligibility principle* so that no beneficiary would receive as much as the lowest wage earner. The program was taken from local authorities and administered nationally. The principles of the Poor Law of 1834 had a significant influence on public welfare policy in the United States for more than a century. See also *Chartist Movement* and *Edwin Chadwick.*

poorhouse 1. A form of *indoor relief* funded by government organizations or by private charities in which needy people are provided with temporary or permanent residential care. 2. An *almshouse.*

"pop psychology" The oversimplified descriptions of the theories and empirical findings from the sciences of psychology, psychiatry, sociology, and related fields. "Pop psych" is often used as a modern technique of name-calling, by using diagnostic terminology to label a person's behavior. It is also used as a basis for self-help and inspirational guidance books.

"poppers" Slang in the drug subculture for nitrite inhalants, which produce in the abuser *euphoria,* relaxation, erotic feelings, and other symptoms, but which can lead to toxic reactions, irritation of the respiratory system, and impairment of the immune system.

population 1. The total number of people in a nation or other specified geographic region; also, the number of people of a specified class or group (such as women, Roman Catholics, African Americans, and people with disabilities) in a specified place or geographic region. 2. In *social research,* all people or cases that could theoretically be available for an investigation. It is from the population that a *sample* is taken for research. See also *universe.*

populism A political orientation in which the interests of wage earners, farmers, and less affluent families take precedence over those of business and professional groups.

"pork" Political jargon referring to government appropriations for a lawmaker's pet projects in exchange for past or future support of another lawmaker's pet projects. The appropriations are said to come from the "pork barrel" (the government's treasury or national debt).

pornography The depiction of erotic acts, sexual intercourse, sadistic or masochistic activities, and other presentations in writing and pictures designed especially to appeal to one's *prurient interest.*

Port Royal Experiment The 1862 U.S. Civil War program to aid slaves who had been abandoned on island plantations when Northern soldiers arrived. The program was federally authorized, but because it was voluntarily funded, it could not meet the needs of those affected. It was discontinued when the *Freedmen's Bureau* was established in 1865.

portability A feature of insurance programs and other benefit systems in which the contract remains in effect despite a change of residence, work or other status. See also *Health Insurance Portability and Accountability Act (HIPAA).*

position paper A written statement declaring one's views on a certain subject and the rationale and documentation for maintaining such views.

positive connotation The *family therapy* technique in which a therapist or family member ascribes virtue to some act that may or may not be beneficial to family functioning. This sometimes causes the person who performed the act to look at it more carefully, re-evaluate it from the new perspective, and gain control over when it is performed.

positive reinforcement Strengthening a desired *behavior* or *response* by presenting a reinforcing *stimulus* contingent on performance of the response. The reinforcer may be a desired object, a privilege, verbal approval, or any other stimulus that strengthens the response.

positive transference *Transference* that results in expressions of affection, love, erotic desire, or feelings of warmth and closeness that a client may have for a psychotherapist or other person.

positron emission tomography (PET) scan A computerized diagnostic device using radioactive isotopes that are injected intravenously to evaluate cerebral metabolism.

"POSSLQ" Partner of the opposite sex sharing living quarters, a term devised by the *U.S. Bureau of the Census* and first used in 1970.

postabortion syndrome (PAS) A woman's psychological reaction to having an abortion. Some researchers and many antiabortion advocates claim the reaction usually includes depression, anxiety, eating disorders, sexual dysfunction, feelings of guilt, substance abuse, and suicidal ideation. Other researchers and most abortion rights advocates claim that no such syndrome exists and that the idea of it is just another attempt at abolishing abortion rights. None of the major professional associations dealing with mental health issues has recognized PAS as a diagnosable disorder.

postconcussional disorder Impaired cognitive functioning and neurobehavioral symptoms as a result of a closed head injury.

postconventional morality In *Kohlberg moral development theory,* the last two of the six stages of development. In stage five, moral thought is based on understanding the validity of universal moral principles and the social context in which they must operate. In stage six, the individual understands and becomes committed to universal moral principles. These stages, if they occur at all, usually do not do so until the individual is older than age 20.

postfisc welfare state A national system of public assistance in which benefits to a given population are calculated only after the government's taxation capacity and budgetary provisions are determined. See also *integrated welfare state.*

postindustrial society A stage of economic development in which a nation or region becomes oriented to producing services rather than manufactured goods. In such societies, fewer blue-collar workers are employable, and economic advantages go to those with more education, investment capital, and technological knowledge.

postnuptial agreement A written notice by a husband and wife who disclose all their assets and state that, in the event of death or divorce, they will seek no more of the other's assets than the amount specified. Such agreements usually are validated only when both parties have retained separate legal counsel in the preparation of the agreement. See also *prenuptial agreement* and *separation agreement.*

postpartum depression Feelings of sadness experienced by some new mothers in the first few weeks or months after giving birth. The symptoms are thought to be related to hormonal changes and other physiological and psychological adjustments.

postplacement contact Follow-up activity by a social worker or social agency that has facilitated a new *placement* for a client to ensure that the needs of the placed individual and the new caregiver are being met. The activity normally includes telephoning or personally visiting the client and the caregiver in the new setting. Usually, such contacts are prearranged, but in certain circumstances they take place without prior notice. Postplacement contact is most often done in *foster care* for children; *nursing home* care for older people; and *halfway houses* for people who were incarcerated or institutionalized because of illness, disability, or criminal behavior.

postpsychotic depressive disorder of schizophrenia A major depressive episode occurring during the residual phase of *schizophrenia.*

posttest A questionnaire or other data-gathering instrument administered to a subject at the end of a specific period of inquiry (for example, after a training program, health regimen, or psychological treatment intervention). Usually, the subject has received a *pretest* at the beginning of the inquiry, and the pre- and posttest results are compared.

posttraumatic stress disorder (PTSD) A delayed psychological reaction to experiencing an event that is outside the range of usual human experience. Stressful events of this type include accidents, natural disasters, military combat, rape, and assault. Stresses that are not unusual to people, such as marital problems, *bereavement,* and illness, are often excluded from this class of disorders. Individuals may react to these events by having difficulty concentrating; feeling emotionally blunted or numb; being hyperalert and jumpy; and having painful memories, nightmares, and sleep disturbances.

postural tremor Rapid, regular, and rhythmic oscillation of the hands, fingers, mouth, and limbs that seem most apparent when the individual tries to hold a body part in a sustained posture. This is most commonly a *medication-induced movement disorder.*

potable water Drinking water that is clean and palatable enough for human consumption without dangerous amounts of pollutants, contaminants, or infective agents.

potlatch A cultural tradition rooted in Native cultures in which large groups of participants gather to celebrate community. Possessions and food are given away to promote community and increase one's prestige among peers.

poverty The state of being poor or deficient in money or means of subsistence. Various types include *absolute poverty* (below a *subsistence level* of income) and *relative poverty* (below the living standard of the person's mainstream community). People who are impoverished may be considered transitional poor (a brief, temporary poverty related to specific events in one's life or environment), marginal poor (moving in and out of poverty because of job insecurity, inadequate skills, or limited education), and residual poor (long-term and intergenerational poverty).

poverty cycle A pattern of living in which the children of poor families grow up to become poor and raise their own children to also become poor. An implicit and unproven premise, often used by critics of the U.S. welfare system, states that poverty occurs by choice and that some welfare programs foster *dependency* and teach children to live the way their parents live.

poverty line A measure of the amount of money a government or a society believes is necessary for a person to live at a minimum level of subsistence or *standard of living.* The original poverty line, issued in 1962, was determined by figuring three times the cost of a subsistence food budget. Since 1989 the poverty line, or threshold, has meant the previous year's poverty line adjusted for the change in the *Consumer Price Index (CPI).*

power The possession of resources that enables an individual to do something independently or to exercise influence and control over others.

power-and-control phase The second stage in *group development* in which group members tend to lose their guardedness and ambivalence and begin to establish their respective roles in the group, as leaders, followers, talkers, passive members, and so forth. In this conception about the various stages through which groups progress, this phase follows the *preaffiliation phase* and is followed by the *intimacy phase*, the *differentiation phase*, and the *separation phase*.

power group   Members of a community who, because of their social status and positions, influence the decisions made on behalf of the community and have the greatest access to resources. Power group members usually include political leaders, financial and industrial executives, members of the clergy, and local indigenous leaders.

power of attorney   A written and properly witnessed statement in which one person grants another person the authority to perform specified acts on behalf of the first. See also *durable power of attorney*.

PQSW credential   In the United Kingdom, the "post-qualifying award in social work" credential for professional social workers who have completed any or all of the following: accredited post-qualifying courses, work requirements, and work-based learning experiences. See also *DipSW*.

practical nurse (PN)   A *paraprofessional* specialist in the care of people who are ill and in the maintenance of health and well-being. PNs complete training programs that last one year or more, after which they carry out important but less technical nursing duties such as administering medication, monitoring tests, and feeding and cleaning patients. See *licensed practical nurse (LPN)* and *registered nurse (RN)*.

practice theory   Concepts that systematically pull together what is known about behavior and social systems and their interaction, the relevant values and goals to be achieved, and the specific techniques and skills available to permit purposeful action.

practice wisdom   The accumulation of information, assumptions, ideologies, and judgments that are practically useful in fulfilling the expectations of the job. Practice wisdom is often equated with "common sense" and may or may not be validated when subjected to empirical or systematic analysis and may or may not be consistent with prevailing theory.

practicum   Part of the professional education of students in which they apply the knowledge and skills acquired primarily through classroom assignments to direct practice with clients. In *social work education*, this occurs primarily in *field placement* assignments.

praxiology   The study of custom and practice in human relationships.

Pray, Kenneth (1882–1948)   Social work scholar who developed *community organization* as a social work method. Pray led the first comprehensive survey of social work education done by the *Council on Social Work Education (CSWE)*.

preaffiliation phase   The first stage in *group development* in which group members tend to be ambivalent about belonging, fearful, guarded, distant, and reluctant to engage in self-disclosure and risk taking. The subsequent stages have been described as the *power-and-control phase*, *intimacy phase*, *differentiation phase*, and *separation phase*.

preauthorization   A health care insurance requirement that links prior approval for prescribed services to reimbursement for those services. The process requires providers to evaluate the necessity of the medical procedure before it is performed.

precedent   A decision made by a government organization, agency, or court of law that has become the basis for subsequent policies, judgments, or arguments on behalf of some position.

precipitating cause   An event or change that seems to result in an individual's disorder or problem; the "last straw" that leads the person to seek the social worker's help.

precocity   Significantly earlier development of intelligence, skills, talents, or emotional maturation than the norm. A precocious child may continue to be advanced in the trait through adulthood or may plateau at a certain stage and eventually show only average abilities as in *asynchronous development*.

preconscious   Thoughts, images, and perceptions that are not in one's immediate awareness but that can be recalled with relative ease.

preconventional morality   In *Kohlberg moral development theory*, the first two of the six stages of development. In stage one, moral thought is based on fear of punishment; in stage two, it is based on the desire to obtain rewards. Preconventional morality development usually occurs before age nine.

predatory lending The practice of loaning money on terms that are disadvantageous to the borrower. These lenders use aggressive sales tactics with promises to improve credit ratings and lower monthly repayment obligations but often commit borrowers to excessive interest rates, unknown balloon payment requirements, prepayment penalties, and negative amortizations. Predatory lending often uses deceptive or obscure contracts and is concentrated in poor and minority neighborhoods where fair loan practices are less accessible. See also *loan shark* and *usury*.

predelinquency A pattern of behaviors and social circumstances that, when found in some youths, significantly increases their chances of *juvenile delinquency*. Such behaviors include attending school erratically, disrupting class, fighting, "borrowing" things from peers, associating with older delinquents, and being unmanageable by parents. Circumstances include living in a crime-plagued neighborhood, having little or no supervision or guidance, and having role models who glamorize antisocial behavior.

predictor variable In *social research,* a systematically measured performance, rating, or score that is used to estimate the likelihood that a subsequent objective is accomplished. For example, many schools of social work require student applicants to take academic aptitude tests. The resulting scores are predictor variables to indicate the likelihood of a student's success in the program.

predisposition A tendency to develop a trait or attribute under the right circumstances. For example, an obese child who has obese parents could have a predisposition toward adult obesity.

pre-elderly A diagnostic term applied to people who show some of the physical, mental, and behavioral characteristics of old age but whose chronological age is below that of the older person. The specific age depends on the function being evaluated.

pre-existing condition A disorder or incipient health condition that occurred before the patient signed on for coverage by an insurance company or third-party organization. Many insurance companies refuse to enroll people with pre-existing

conditions or to reimburse for any health problems related to that condition. The 1996 *Health Insurance Portability and Accountability Act* (P.L. 104-191) limits the degree to which health insurance companies are legally permitted to do this.

preferred provider organizations (PPOs) Affiliations of professionals, often in *private practice,* who fulfill contracts to receive *third-party payments*. PPO members agree to provide professional services to members of a designated group at a favorable fee-for-service rate, and the *third party* agrees to channel members of its group to the PPO. See also *independent practice associations (IPAs)* and *managed health care program*.

pregenital In *psychoanalytic theory,* the *oral phase* and *anal phase* of personality development and the manifestations of those stages that recur in later life.

pregnancy The reproductive state of carrying a *fetus* within the body; that is, the time between *conception* and birth. Human pregnancy normally lasts about 280 days, during which time rapid changes in the development of the fetus occur in the mother's uterus. Determining the existence of pregnancy may be based on observation of certain symptoms. Physicians use three categories of pregnancy criteria: (1) Presumptive symptoms include failure to experience the anticipated menstrual period, nausea or vomiting ("morning sickness"), fatigue and need for excessive sleep, frequent urination, alteration of skin pigmentation around the nipples, and softening of the cervix. (2) Probable symptoms include positive results of laboratory tests for pregnancy (urine sampling for the presence of a specific level of the hormone chorionic gonadotropin), abdominal enlargement, and uterine changes. (3) Positive signs include fetal heartbeat, fetal movements within the uterus, and the presence of a fetal skeleton as shown by ultrasound. It is important to determine the existence of pregnancy fairly soon after conception and to determine the relative health of the fetus. See also *amniocentesis* and *chorionic villus sampling (CVS)*.

pregnancy discrimination Singling out for harassment or unfair treatment—or denying equal opportunities in the workplace or in commercial, recreational, or educational facilities—to women who are, or who may become, pregnant. U.S. laws forbid this in most employment situations and require employers to treat pregnant employees (who, as a result of pregnancy, are unable to perform their job duties) as they would any other temporarily disabled employee.

prejudice An opinion about an individual, group, or phenomenon that is developed without proof or systematic evidence. This prejudgment may be favorable but is more often unfavorable and may become institutionalized in the form of a society's laws or customs. See also *bias, discrimination, separatism, individual racism,* and *institutional racism.*

preliminary examination An evaluation of an individual or situation made in advance of acquiring all the relevant information that eventually will become available. Such examinations are made to evaluate emergency medical situations, to begin some intervention processes, to determine if sufficient evidence exists to hold a person for trial, or to determine if an individual seems ready to proceed to the next stage of evaluation. The slang term for this is "prelim." Social workers make preliminary examinations primarily during *intake* and initial client contacts. The social worker always tries to determine at least four facts in the prelim: (1) Is the client suicidal? (2) Should the client also seek medical care? (3) Does the client constitute a danger to others? and (4) Does the client need any emergency social services to maintain health, safety, and security?

premature aging See *progeroid syndromes.*

premature birth The birth of a baby significantly before completion of the normal *gestation* period or of a baby with very low body weight (usually less than four pounds).

premature ejaculation A *sexual disorder* in which the man recurrently reaches orgasm before he wishes to, resulting in unsatisfactory *coitus.*

premature termination Discontinuing services to clients who are still in need. This is considered unethical, and many *malpractice* suits have been made over this action. See also *"client dumping."*

premenstrual dysphoric disorder (PMDD) A markedly depressed mood, anxiety, affective lability, and decreased interest in activities that regularly occur during the last week of the luteal phase of the menstrual cycle (the period between ovulation and the onset of menses), which significantly interferes with usual social activities and relationships. This disorder is considered far less common than *premenstrual syndrome (PMS)* but may be more discomforting or impairing.

premenstrual syndrome (PMS) Feelings of discomfort and related personality fluctuations that affect some women during the several days of their menstrual cycles immediately before menstruation. Some medical researchers indicate that hormone secretions peak during these days and hypothesize that this may influence the feelings and behaviors of some, but not all, women.

prenatal Before birth.

prenuptial agreement A contract entered into by two people who plan to marry, delineating ownership of property and rights and obligations of each. See also *postnuptial agreement* and *separation agreement.*

preoccupation Conscious and prolonged attention to a worrisome event or general mental self-absorption so that the individual's contact with current responsibilities or relationships is hindered. Preoccupation is often symptomatic of mental disorders, especially *depression, schizophrenia,* and *narcissism.* However, it is also common in healthy, but concerned or absent-minded, people.

preoperational stage The second stage of development described in *Piagetian theory,* lasting from about age two to seven. During this time, the child begins to use symbols and some reasoning ability but still cannot group objects and must deal with each item individually.

presbycusis Age-related degeneration of the inner ears resulting in some hearing loss, a condition that occurs in most people older than 40.

presbyopia Age-related condition of the eyes in which the lens becomes less able to focus on close objects. Presbyopia exists in varying degrees in nearly everyone older than 40.

prescribing the symptom A technique in *family therapy* in which the therapist directs one or more members of a family to continue their symptomatic behavior under specified circumstances. For example, the therapist might tell certain family members to pout every Tuesday. This helps them realize the existence of the symptom and that it is under their voluntary control.

prescription, medical   A physician's written order to a pharmacist or patient describing the type and amount of drug or other treatment to be used, the duration of use, and other special directions. Physicians often use some of the following abbreviations in writing prescriptions: ad lib. (as needed), a.c. (before meals), b.i.d. (twice a day), dieb. alt. (every other day), o.d. (every day), p.c. (after meals), q.h. (every hour), q.2h (every two hours), q.3h (every three hours), t.i.d. (three times a day), q.i.d. (four times a day), q.s. (as much as needed), stat. (immediately), and p.r.n. (when needed).

presenile   The mental and physical characteristics of a person immediately before old age. The term "presenile dementia" once was used to describe mental deterioration in people who had symptoms of *senility* but who were not of advanced years; however, this term now is rarely used because of its lack of precision.

presenium   Just before old age.

presenting problem   The perceived symptoms, overt issues, or difficulties the client believes to constitute the problem and for which help is sought. The one who presents the problem may be the person for whom help is sought, or others may recognize the need for helping that person. Because the social worker recognizes that the problem may be the result of underlying causes or that there can be inaccuracies in the way the problem is understood by the client, consideration of the presenting problem is only the beginning of the *assessment* phase.

pressure group   An organization or collective of like-minded individuals that seeks to influence the policies of governments, political candidates, agencies, or the general public. Such groups present their views through the use of a *media event, legislative advocacy tactics, lobbyists, political action committees (PACs), fundraising,* and voter campaigns. Two types of pressure groups are the *public-interest group* and the *special-interest group.* See also *interest group.*

pretermitted child   A legal concept referring to a child born after a deceased parent's will has been executed and who is not named in the will.

pretest   A questionnaire or other data-gathering instrument administered to a subject just before a specific period of inquiry, such as a training program, health regimen, or psychological treatment intervention. Usually, the pretest results provide a baseline level for comparison with the *posttest* results. A pretest is not the same as a *pilot study.*

pretrial detention   Confinement of a person who is accused of a *crime* before a conviction has been reached in a court of law. This happens when a defendant cannot raise the amount of *bail* or is held without bail.

pretrial services agencies   District court facilities generally designed to make prebail investigations for judicial officers and to supervise defendants who are released pending trial. In smaller jurisdictions, these agencies are part of the probation offices; in larger jurisdictions, they are independent.

prevailing charge   The customary fees physicians and other professionals in the area require for their services and the amount most insurance providers, including Medicare, will approve.

prevalence rate   A measure of the number of cases of some problem or disease that exists in a given *population* during a specified period. See also *incidence rate* and *epidemiology.*

preventative detention   A form of *pretrial detention* applied to a person who is considered likely to be found guilty at the trial and who poses an immediate threat to the public if released.

prevention   Actions taken to minimize and eliminate social, psychological, or other conditions known to cause or contribute to physical and emotional illness and sometimes socioeconomic problems. Prevention includes establishing those conditions in society that enhance the opportunities for individuals, families, and communities to achieve positive fulfillment. See also *primary prevention, secondary prevention,* and *tertiary prevention.*

preventive health programs   Activities in the public and private sectors to ensure that people remain in good health and are protected from disease. The *U.S. Public Health Service,* state and local health departments, private health and welfare organizations, and foundations are the primary coordinators of these programs in the United States. The activities include vaccinating against disease, providing instruction in hygiene, enforcing standards of sanitation, and researching the causes and cures of diseases.

preventive social work   Professional social work practiced to achieve the goal of enhancing human potential, maintaining and protecting the individual's psychosocial resources, and promoting competencies that enable people to avoid or overcome the predictable and unexpected problems of living. This approach emphasizes *habilitation* rather than *rehabilitation* and uses proactive rather than reactive measures in helping healthy clients remain that way.

price controls   Government regulations that limit the amount of increase or decrease in the prices consumers are charged for goods and services. The purpose is to control inflation and increase employment. This policy is often accompanied by *wage controls*.

price discrimination   Charging different people different prices for the same goods or services. See also *means test* and *sliding fee scale*.

price supports   Government regulations that specify the least amount that may be charged for a product or service regardless of the costs of production or the amount people would pay on the open market. Governments usually do this by giving direct financial assistance to producers of the goods or services or by purchasing them at a set price. See also *subsidy* and *Commodity Credit Corporation (CCC)*.

prima facie evidence   Information that can be used in a court of law that requires no further support to establish its credibility or validity.

primal therapy   A form of *psychotherapy* based on intense *catharsis*. The therapist may encourage *regression* in clients by focusing on early childhood experiences to the extent that the client expresses primitive (primal) emotions through dramatic means such as loud, prolonged screaming.

primary alcoholism   One of the three major types of *alcoholism* (the other two being *secondary alcoholism* and *reactive alcoholism*) in which the individual has high tolerance for alcohol, drinks in response to physiological withdrawal symptoms, and puts drinking ahead of all other activities. This appears to be a genetically influ-

enced disease and begins, in most people, between ages 25 and 35.

primary care   In the *health care* delivery system, the first contact type of intervention that occurs in hospital emergency rooms, outpatient clinics, and doctor's offices. Primary care usually includes monitoring symptoms, screening for diseases, treating minor injuries, and managing chronic diseases. See also *secondary care* and *tertiary care*.

primary degenerative dementia   A *mental disorder* in which *dementia* begins gradually with steady deterioration thereafter. Symptoms begin for most people in their mid-60s and are rare before age 50. *Alzheimer's disease* is the most common of the primary degenerative dementias.

primary gain   Direct relief from anxiety achieved by using a *defense mechanism*. See also *secondary gain*.

primary group   People who are in intimate and frequent face-to-face contact with one another, have norms in common, and share mutually enduring and extensive influences.

Primary Insurance Amount (PIA)   The term used by the *Social Security Administration (SSA)* for the full monthly amount of money one receives when beginning to collect social security benefits at age 65. If the beneficiary retires earlier than 65, the PIA is lower; if retirement is delayed past 65, the benefits are more than 100 percent of the PIA.

primary prevention   Actions taken to keep conditions known to result in *disease* or *social problems* from occurring. For example, a community's development of sanitation facilities, recreation centers, and parks helps prevent diseases and stress-related disorders. Social welfare efforts in primary prevention include the development of social insurance programs and settlement house activities that help socialize and educate people so they can avoid problems and enhance their opportunities. See also *prevention, secondary prevention*, and *tertiary prevention*.

primary process thinking   Disorganized and irrational thoughts expressed without reference to the individual's external world. Psychoanalytic theorists believe that such expressions represent thoughts from the deepest parts of the *psyche* and include *unconscious* thoughts that have not been screened or "processed" by the *ego*. Such expressions are sometimes seen in psychotic patients and in some people who speak while asleep.

prior restraint Preventing one from issuing a statement before it is made. Most nations permit prior restraint by court order if the statement is considered defamatory or dangerous. In the United States, free speech protections have precedence, with lawsuits for libel, slander, and criminal advocacy acting as the restraint.

private adoption *Adoption* that occurs outside of legally regulated agencies. Also known as *independent adoption,* the process is often facilitated by a physician, lawyer, or broker who, usually for a fee, places a child with the adoptive parents. See also *gray-market adoption.*

private case management The employment of autonomous organizations or professionals to help clients negotiate and use a wide range of needed health and social services. Private case managers may serve in nonprofit or for-profit organizations and work independently or for industrial organizations. Fees may be paid by the client, the employing company, or insurance companies.

private income maintenance Programs financed by employees, their employers, insurance, and savings to cover risks of retirement, illness, disability, and death. These include individual retirement plans (IRAs), 401(k) plans, and employee stock ownership plans.

private practice In social work, the provision of professional services by a licensed/qualified social worker who assumes responsibility for the nature and quality of the services provided to the client in exchange for direct payment or third-party reimbursement. Also, the process in which the values, knowledge, and skills of social work, acquired through sufficient education and experience, are used to deliver social services autonomously to clients in exchange for mutually agreed payment.

private social agencies Nonprofit agencies that provide social services, mostly to members of targeted groups (such as residents of a certain neighborhood or members of a certain religious affiliation, ethnic group, or age category). These agencies are funded by voluntary contributions and government grants. They are generally incorporated

and have elected board members to represent the community and establish policy.

private voluntary organizations (PVOs) See *nongovernment organizations (NGOs).*

privatization The transfer of economic resources from the public to the private sector to meet the social needs of people. In the United States, this tendency is seen in the reliance on private health, educational, and social institutions and entrepreneurs to provide services.

privatized prisons Nongovernment-controlled, for-profit, correctional institutions. They are used primarily to incarcerate lawbreakers less expensively than can be achieved in public prisons and to rapidly bring needed new facilities into use.

privileged communication The premise and understanding between a *professional* and *client* that the information revealed by the client will not be divulged to others without expressed permission. In fact, the laws and judicial interpretations in each state are not always consistent or clear about this premise. Courts in many states have honored privileged communication for social workers and other professional groups, except when there is a risk of public danger or a threat to the public good. See also *confidentiality, absolute confidentiality, relative confidentiality,* and *Jaffee v. Redmond* decision.

pro bono publico "For the good of the public," the Latin phrase used primarily by lawyers in reference to providing professional services at no charge to a needy recipient, especially one whose case has broader social implications.

pro se Legal term referring to people who represent their own cases without lawyers, that is, "on one's own behalf."

probability sampling In *social research,* the systematic selection of cases in a way that allows the researcher to calculate the likelihood, or level of probability, that any given case would be selected from the *population.* This makes it possible to estimate the degree to which the sample is likely to represent the population. See also *random sample.*

probation 1. A specified time during which an individual is to demonstrate possession of certain abilities or qualifications. 2. In the *corrections* field, probation is a status in which *incarceration* is suspended on the condition that the subject fulfills certain requirements. These requirements often include periodic visits to a court-designated probation officer, who may be a social worker. See also *community-based corrections.*

problem An unanswered question or unresolved circumstance involving deficiency from a norm or ideal. Social problems pertain to any deficiency from an ideal social structure or social institution. A client's presenting problem is a perceived deficit between the existing situation and the norm or ideal.

problem-oriented record (POR) A format used by physicians, social workers, nurses, and other professionals to develop and maintain efficient case records. The record contains four components: (1) the database (*face sheet* information; *presenting problem;* relevant demographic, cultural, and medical data; and relevant addresses); (2) the problem list (each problem is numbered so that when it is resolved it is convenient to identify and check off); (3) the plan (possible steps to take in resolving each numbered problem); and (4) the follow-up action (what has actually been done to implement the plan). POR is highly focused on specific problems and their progress and resolution and thus makes the professional more easily accountable than do less focused, chronological summaries. See also *process recording, SOAP charting method,* and *person-oriented record.*

problem-pregnancy counseling Therapeutic intervention with women who have psychosocial conflict about their pregnancies. The process is most often applied to young unmarried women and is oriented to educating them about available options. This occurs after determining, as early as possible, whether there actually is a pregnancy. If tests are positive, then the options discussed include *abortion, marriage, adoption,* and rearing the baby alone. The father and family members are included in these discussions whenever possible and helpful, but the pregnant woman makes the ultimate decision.

problem-solving casework A form of *social casework,* developed primarily by Helen Harris Perlman (*Casework: A Problem-Solving Process,* Chicago: University of Chicago Press, 1957). This model stresses clear delineations of the goals of the casework intervention, focused and time-limited intervention, and concern for the environmental

and social forces that influence and are influenced by the client.

Procedural Terminology for Psychiatrists (PTP) A systematic listing and coding of procedures and services performed by psychiatrists on behalf of their patients. PTP is a part of the physician's *Current Procedural Terminology (CPT).* Services of nonphysicians are not included in the *PTP* codes, and nonphysicians should not use them to report services.

process-and-content issue See *content-and-process issue.*

process recording A method of writing about the social worker–client interactions during the *intervention* process. The *case record* using this format begins with a *face sheet* of factual data about the client and relevant social, environmental, economic, and physical factors. Then it briefly describes the *presenting problem* and includes documenting data about the problem. The social worker then includes a statement of goals, obstacles to reaching the goals, means to reaching them, and—where applicable—a written contract signed by social worker and client. The record then contains entries for each contact the client makes with the social worker or agency, including telephone calls and messages from other family members. The entry is headed by the date and time of the visit or contact and a summary of the factual information obtained as well as any subjective impressions the social worker has developed. These entries are not as elaborate as those in *verbatim recording* but are more chronologically stated than in the *problem-oriented record (POR)* or *person-oriented record.* Because of recent legislation, court rulings, and ethical principles, social workers are often advised to prepare their records so they are accessible to other social workers, clients, peer reviewers, or providers of *third-party payments.* This is to protect the client's rights during emergencies, when the social worker is inaccessible, or in cases of *quality assurance* evaluations and *peer review.* See also *narrative summary.*

prochoice movement Organized efforts to influence public opinion, legislation, judicial interpretations, and legal enforcement and to gain financial support and medical access that are considered necessary for maximizing reproductive choices, especially keeping the option of *abortion* legal and accessible. The name of this movement came about primarily as a response to the name used by those who were fighting against abortion, known as the "prolife movement." The prochoice movement advocates education, *family planning,* and opportunities for pregnant women to choose abortion or *adoption* or to keep their babies. See *National Abortion and Reproductive Rights Action League (NARAL)* and *Planned Parenthood Federation.*

prodromal phase   The early stages of a *disease.* See also *schizophrenia.*

prodrome   In the diagnosis or assessment of a psychiatric or other medical condition, the period before the criteria of the disorder are fully met but during which some signs or symptoms of the disorder have begun to appear.

Producer Price Index (PPI)   A measure of the selling prices received by those who produce goods and services. The amount received by the producer is not synonymous with the amount consumers and other purchasers pay because of sales and excise taxes, distribution costs, government subsidies, and other intervening factors. See also *Consumer Price Index (CPI).*

productivity   In economic theory, the actual output per unit of input. For example, labor productivity is usually described as the amount of value that is achieved per hour of work. Capital productivity is the number of dollars obtained for the dollars invested. Total factor productivity is the average real output per unit of capital and labor.

profession   A group of people who use in common a system of *values,* skills, techniques, knowledge, and beliefs to meet a specific social need. The public comes to identify this group as being suited to fulfill the specific need and often gives it formal and legal recognition through *licensing* or other sanctions as the legitimate source for providing the relevant service. The group enhances its public credibility by expanding its body of knowledge, making the knowledge accessible to its members, refining its skills and values, ensuring that its members comply with its established standards, and making public the actions it takes to reach these goals.

professional   An individual who qualifies for membership in a specific *profession* and uses its practices, knowledge, and skills to provide services to client systems and, in so doing, always adheres to its *values* and *code of ethics.*

professional association   A membership organization of qualified individuals from the same profession that represents the profession throughout the nation, with national headquarters and local chapters, the purposes of which are to maintain ethical standards, to educate the members about advances in their fields, to educate the public and the membership about issues of concern to the profession, to advocate for better working conditions for members and for the well-being of their traditional clientele, and to help legal bodies establish and maintain laws regulating the profession's type of practice. Examples include the *American Medical Association (AMA),* the *American Bar Association (ABA),* and the *National Education Association (NEA).* Social work professional associations include the *National Association of Social Workers (NASW),* the *National Association of Black Social Workers (NABSW),* the *Clinical Social Work Federation (CSWF),* the *Canadian Social Workers Association (CSWA),* the *British Association of Social Workers (BASW),* and the *International Federation of Social Workers (IFSW).*

professional certification   The public assurance by a recognized professional association, consisting of a significant part of a profession's membership, that a member of that profession has attained a specified level of knowledge, experience, and skill. Professional certificates offered by NASW include the *Academy of Certified Baccalaureate Social Workers (ACBSW),* the *Academy of Certified Social Workers (ACSW),* the *School Social Work Specialist (SSWS)* credential, the *Qualified Clinical Social Worker (QCSW),* the *Diplomate in Clinical Social Work (DCSW),* and several specialty certificates.

professional conduct   Behavior in accordance with a profession's *code of ethics.* Most professions set forth explicit standards of professional conduct and provide processes for reporting, reviewing, and sanctioning violations. State social work licensing boards receive, investigate, and adjudicate complaints about a licensed social worker's professional conduct.

professional corporation (PC)   A corporation or legal association formed to practice a *profession.* The *professional* or professional group that is incorporated has the letters PC or PA after the names and degrees. Members of the corporation are shareholders, and all are members of the profession being practiced. Individuals as well as groups can incorporate. Professional corporations allow professionals certain tax advantages unavailable to individuals and permit professionals to join together without assuming personal liability for the practices of other members.

professional review organizations (PROs) A federally mandated system established under the Peer Review Improvement Act of 1982 (P.L. 97-248) to evaluate social and health care services provided by professionals in hospitals, nursing homes, and residential care facilities that receive third-party payments from federal funds. The reviewers periodically scrutinize case records, medical charts, and other documents and sometimes interview providers and local peer reviewers to help determine if procedures are necessary and implemented competently and cost-effectively.

professional sanctions Punishments levied against a *professional* for violation of that profession's *code of ethics.* The most common punishments levied against social workers belonging to NASW include the requirement of retraining and professional counseling for a specified length of time, public notification of the violation, probation of membership status, and expulsion from membership.

professionalism The degree to which an individual possesses and uses the knowledge, skills, and qualifications of a profession and adheres to its values and ethics when serving the client.

profiling A law authority's aggressive and intense scrutiny of a class of people in an attempt to apprehend a lawbreaker or potential lawbreaker. The procedure is justified (in the authority's view) by narrowing the search and focusing limited resources on those considered most likely to be persons of interest. See also *racial profiling.*

profoundly handicapped Individuals who have been diagnosed as severely mentally retarded, autistic, or mentally disturbed such that minimal *social functioning* is expected.

progeria Premature aging.

progeroid syndromes Disorders and conditions resulting in premature aging. Usually, these are genetic conditions and include some forms of *Down syndrome,* Werner syndrome, Cockayne syndrome, and progeria. Progeria patients usually appear normal at birth but with each passing year take on

characteristics of some very old people, such as baldness, age spots, wrinkles, and *atherosclerosis.* The average life span is 12 to 13 years, and most deaths are due to heart failure.

prognosis A professional's prediction of the likely course, direction, and outcome of the problem that is being addressed.

program 1. A plan and guideline about what is to be done. 2. A relatively permanent organization and procedure designed to meet ongoing client needs (as opposed to a "project," which is more flexible and short term in scope).

Program Evaluation and Review Technique (PERT) A procedure commonly used in organizational management to relate goals to means in a rational and systematic way. PERT looks at program objectives and indicates all the activities that need to be performed, the time required for each, the sequence in which they should take place, and the resources required. This may be charted and posted so that all personnel are informed.

Program Planning and Budgeting System (PPBS) An administrative procedure that specifies objectives and measures progress in achieved end products, including amounts and distributions. More commonly used in federal government agencies and departments as well as other large organizations, PPBS relates costs to outputs (goods, services, and other products) rather than to inputs (labor, capital, and interest on debt).

progression Movement or development, as in the client's changes in symptoms or results of the therapeutic intervention.

Progressive Era The name given by historians to the period (roughly 1890–1915) in the United States when social reformers and advocates for socioeconomic justice were effectively demanding changes. The reformers and *muckrakers* sought and achieved changes in corrupt political practices at the local and national levels; established *settlement houses* in many poor neighborhoods; enacted laws for occupational and consumer safety; and influenced enactment of *social welfare* laws and programs for children, women, and disadvantaged people.

progressive social work An orientation in social work that focuses on the injustices in institutions, culture, and social practices that cause further disadvantage to the poorest and most vulnerable groups. Progressive social workers, who sometimes call their effort *radical social work,* seek to change oppressive institutions and practices primarily through social and political activism and organizing communities rather than through case-by-case interventions. Progressive social workers, throughout the history of the profession, have been at the forefront of social change activities. Writings of progressive social workers have been found in the journals *Social Work Today* (1934–1942), *Catalyst: A Socialist Journal of the Social Services* (1978–1989), and currently the *Journal of Progressive Human Services.* See also *Social Welfare Action Alliance (SWAA),* formerly the Bertha Capen Reynolds Society.

progressive tax A government's revenue-collecting system in which those in a higher income bracket pay a higher percentage (as well as a higher amount of money) in taxes than do those in lower income brackets. For example, a person with a taxable income of $20,000 would pay 10 percent of that amount in taxes, and a person with a taxable income of $100,000 would pay 30 percent of that amount in taxes. See also *regressive tax.*

Project Follow Through A *Great Society* research–education program, from 1967 to 1995, to study and help children from low-income families receive additional compensatory education through the elementary years. The program was primarily for children in the *Head Start* program.

projection A *defense mechanism* in which unacceptable aspects of one's own personality are rejected or attributed to another person or entity, such as a parent, a colleague, or the government.

projective identification A process whereby an individual uses *projection* onto another member of his or her family, group, or organization and then induces that person or the others to behave in accordance with the projected attitudes. This process also may occur when the individual comes to perceive that others are behaving accordingly, whether or not they actually are doing so.

projective test A procedure that uses systematic but unstructured *stimulus* objects or situations designed to elicit the subject's way of perceiving and understanding the world. The premise is that the subject will project *unconscious* thoughts onto

the stimulus object and reveal possible *psychopathology.* Major projective tests are the *Rorschach test* and the Thematic Apperception Test (in which the subject is shown a series of vague pictures and tells a story for each). Certain forms of *play therapy* are also considered to be types of projective tests.

prolife movement See *right-to-life movement.*

promiscuity Casual, frequent, and indiscriminate sexual encounters.

Promise Fellows A volunteer program within *AmeriCorps,* whose members provide a year of service developing and expanding community programs for children and youths in exchange for a living allowance and other benefits, including money for education or to pay off student loans. Most Promise Fellows are recent college graduates or advanced-degree candidates; professionals looking for a new challenge; and alumni of other AmeriCorps programs, the *Peace Corps,* or the military. Promise Fellows also work with programs in the *Five Promises Movement.* Their Web site address is http://www.americorps.org/promisefellows

propaganda Planned efforts to convince segments of the public about certain opinions or beliefs. Usually, this is done with powerful slogans, testimonials, attractive images, and promises of better circumstances and the ending of problems. Propaganda is usually an important part of any political or social movement.

property-tax-relief programs State and local laws that reduce, defer, or cancel property taxes on the homes of needy older people. These programs are designed for people whose houses have escalated in value during their residency to the point that the taxes are more than they can afford. Three such programs are *circuit-breaker tax relief, homestead exemptions,* and *homeowner tax deferrals.*

proprietary practice In social work, the delivery of social services for profit, generally in nonclinical settings by self-employed professionals. The term "proprietary practice" is essentially synonymous with *private practice,* except that the latter usually refers to clinical practice. Proprietary social workers typically offer their own facilities and professional skills in capacities such as private consultants, organizers of special-interest groups, and caregivers for specific client groups. Some establish profit-making institutions for clients who require physical care, along with special social services (for example, a private facility for adolescent substance abusers).

proprietary social agencies Organizations or facilities that are usually owned or staffed by social workers and other professionals and that are intended to make a profit by providing a specified social service. These agencies provide essentially the same services as traditional nonprofit agencies, except that the charges to the recipient or recipient's agent may be higher. Examples of such organizations are private *halfway houses,* residential and educational facilities, camps, inpatient mental health facilities, training centers, research institutes, consultation services, *privatized prisons,* and *social action* and *community organization* programs.

proprietary social services The use of the knowledge, training, skills, values, ethics, and methods of professional social work to make a profit for providing *social services.* See also *privatization* and *private practice.*

prosocial behavior Actions an individual, organization, or society takes to benefit society without the anticipation of external reward. What is considered to be of social benefit is relative and based on one's cultural values.

prospective utilization reviews A procedure used by health care organizations, including *managed care organizations (MCOs),* to determine the medical necessity of treatment and its payment. This review occurs prior to medical intervention and often uses a second opinion. Prospective utilization reviews also assess and determine the efficacy of the actual services to be used. See also *concurrent utilization reviews* and *retrospective utilization reviews.*

prosthesis The replacement of a missing body part with an artificial one. The part, such as a leg, tooth, or hand, is a "prosthetic device," and the professional who administers such treatment is a "prosthetic surgeon" or "prosthodontist."

prostitution The illegal act of offering oneself for sexual contact with another in exchange for money or other benefits. See also *pandering.*

protected class Groups specifically identified for protection from discrimination in employment or provided with equal employment opportunities

under federal, state, or local laws. See also *affirmative action groups.*

protective custody The *placement* of an individual by legal authorities in a facility to keep him or her from the danger of harm by others or from self-inflicted injury.

protective services Interventions by social workers and other professionals on behalf of individuals—such as children, people with disabilities, older people, and people with mental retardation—who may be in danger of harm from others or who are unable to take care of their own physical needs. The social workers are usually employed by the local *Department of Social Services (DSS)* or a similar agency, or they may work with the courts or law enforcement agencies. The primary job is to investigate situations in which a person may be at risk (as in *child abuse* or neglect of a disabled person), to help ameliorate the situation, to minimize further risk, and to find and facilitate alternative placements and resources for the person at risk.

protest movement An organized effort by a part of the public to show dissatisfaction and possible noncompliance with a new law, policy, or situation. Those involved in the movement use a variety of tactics to inform their political leaders, policymakers, or people in positions of authority over them of their dissatisfaction. The tactics include strikes, *propaganda,* marches, and *political action.*

Protestant ethic A value and behavioral orientation that is generally associated with hard work, self-discipline, deferred gratification, and the belief that such efforts will result in rewards, possibly including more money, higher social status, greater freedom, and eventual entry into heaven. This orientation derives its name from the moral teachings of Protestant leaders such as John Calvin, Martin Luther, and Charles and John Wesley and has guided the conduct of many middle-class U.S. families since colonial times. See also *Puritanism.*

provider The term used by *third-party payment* organizations in referring to the professionals and institutions that have served the client and to which reimbursement is made. See also *vendor.*

provision systems The interacting social organizations that supply the products and services that people need, want, and demand; also, the *network* of social relationships that, together or individually, identify products and services needed and demanded, develop the necessary natural and social resources, distribute those resources, and evaluate the effects. In different societies, these systems may have a competitive, self-interested orientation or an egalitarian, cooperative orientation.

proxemics   Spatial behavior; the study of the way humans influence one another through the use of space. This includes factors such as the distance people need between one another for various types of *communication* and the arrangement of their furniture, homes, and streets to facilitate certain kinds of communications. See also *communication theory, sociofugal arrangements,* and *sociopetal arrangements.*

Prozac   A psychotropic drug widely used in the treatment of *depression.*

prurient interest   Attention devoted to erotic materials or situations that stimulate erotic interests. See also *pornography.*

pruritus   Itching.

PSA victims   Children harmed by pediatric *sexual abuse.*

pseudocyesis   False *pregnancy;* a woman's sensation of being pregnant or showing some of the symptoms of pregnancy when she is not. Symptoms might be due to psychogenic factors, physiological changes, or both.

pseudomutuality   A facade of harmony among members of a family, group, or organization when the members are actually antagonistic. According to the *family therapy* approach, pseudomutuality may result in serious internal conflict within individual members.

psyche   The mind and soul, including the totality of one's conscious and unconscious mental processes. See also *ego* and *spirituality.*

psychedelics   *Drugs of abuse* that produce intensified and distorted sights and sounds, *hallucination, delusion, euphoria,* and other symptoms. *LSD, mescaline,* psilocybin, and peyote are psychedelics.

psychiatric emergency   Sudden or unexpected behavior in a person that indicates symptoms of mental disorder requiring immediate action by a psychiatrist or members of a mental health team. The most common behaviors that result in psychiatric emergencies include *suicide* attempts or threats, active *hallucination* that seems threatening, *fugue* states, drug-induced harmful behavior, and precipitous deterioration of the mental faculties. Sometimes, this deterioration is related to the misuse or discontinuance of prescribed *psychotropic drugs.*

psychiatric labels   Descriptive or diagnostic terms applied to people by *psychiatrists, physicians,* or mental health professionals to characterize a person's psychiatric processes. They may be formal diagnostic terms (such as *bipolar disorder* or *borderline personality disorder*) or less formal characterizations (such as "phobic" or "drug addict"). Critics of psychiatric labels say their use is inaccurate and dehumanizes people, precludes the principle of *individualization,* oversimplifies problems, and minimizes the impact of the psychosocial and environmental systems in which they occur. Proponents of psychiatric labeling say it is necessary for efficient communication among helping professionals and important for the conduct of research. Formal diagnostic terms apply to illnesses and should not be used as descriptive nouns to characterize people (such as "a schizophrenic").

psychiatric social work   Social work in a mental health setting. The psychiatric social worker provides psychosocial therapy and other social services for those with mental disorders and, in collaboration with the psychiatrist and other members of the mental health team, works with the patient's family members. The worker usually has an *MSW* or higher degree and additional experience in working with psychiatric problems. The "psychiatric social work" designation has largely been replaced by the term *clinical social work.* See also *American Association of Psychiatric Social Workers (AAPSW).*

psychiatrist   A *physician* who specializes in the treatment of mental disorders. The psychiatrist makes specific diagnoses of the mental disorder and prescribes, supervises, or directly provides the necessary treatment, which may include *psychotherapy,* psychotropic drugs, and hospitalization with *milieu therapy.* Qualifications to be a psychiatrist include four years of medical school and four or more years of approved residency training, usually in mental hospitals or hospital psychiatric wards.

psychic energy An individual's mental and physical drives and forces that lead to the processes of the mind, including thinking; remembering, storing, and retrieving information; providing ego defense mechanisms; acting willfully with determination; and many other functions.

psychoactive drugs Drugs that induce changes in the user's *mood,* cognitive ability, or perceptions. They include both *psychotropic drugs* and many *illicit drugs* or *controlled substances.*

psychoactive substance abuse disorder Any one of a group of disorders involving a continuing pattern of maladaptive behavior resulting from the chronic ingestion of a *psychoactive substance.*

psychoactive substances Compounds or chemicals that produce an alteration of the mental or affective processes of the user. These chemicals may be illegal, as in *drugs of abuse,* or medically prescribed, as in *psychotropic drugs.*

psychoanalysis A method for diagnosing and treating mental illness and achieving better self-awareness using the principles of *psychoanalytic theory* originated by Austrian physician Sigmund Freud (1856–1939).

psychoanalyst A professional who uses the theories of *psychosexual development* and personality structure as well as the special *psychotherapy* techniques originated by Sigmund Freud (1856–1939) and his followers. Most psychoanalysts in the United States are psychiatrists, but the specialty also includes social workers and other mental health professionals who have qualified to practice through advanced psychoanalytic training and personal psychoanalysis. Typically, psychoanalysts see their patients for 45 or 50 minutes, four or five times weekly, for an indefinite period, sometimes lasting several years. The client often reclines on a couch and verbalizes through *free association.* The psychoanalyst interprets the patient's dreams and the expressions of emotions related to *drive,* unconscious motives, and unhealthy use of *defense mechanisms.*

psychoanalytic enactment Symbolic and reciprocal interactions between the client and the analyst that have *unconscious* meaning to both. Typically, the enactment occurs when the client's transference reactions provoke unconscious responses in the analyst, although theoretically the opposite interaction can also occur.

psychoanalytic theory The hypotheses and treatment applications about human personality and its development as proposed by Sigmund Freud (1856–1939), with later elaborations and modifications by many theorists and analysts such as Carl Jung (1875–1961), Alfred Adler (1870–1937), Otto Rank (1884–1937), Wilhelm Stekl, Melanie Klein, and Ernest Jones (1879–1958). Most of the concepts now recognized as psychoanalytic are from *Freudian theory* (that is, the *pleasure principle,* the *reality principle,* the *libido,* the *unconscious,* the *id,* the *ego,* the *superego,* and *psychosexual development theory*). Concepts that were emphasized by other analysts include *defense mechanisms* (Anna Freud, 1895–1982); *object relations theory* (H. V. Dicks); *inferiority complex* (Adler); *collective unconscious* and *archetypes* (Jung); *psychosocial development theory* (Erik Erikson, 1902–1994); *separation–individuation* (Margaret Mahler); and *parataxic distortion* (Harry Stack Sullivan, 1892–1949). Psychoanalytic theory and especially its progenies, *ego psychology* and *neo-Freudian* theory, have been influential in the theories of clinical social work practice and social casework, particularly in the *diagnostic school in social work* and especially between 1940 and 1965.

"psychobabble" A term of disparagement referring to the indiscriminate use or misuse of psychological words or concepts. Often, such language is used by pseudosophisticates who have incomplete understandings of the concepts or who use the terms as a form of name-calling.

psychobiology The science that studies the interrelationships between mental and biological functions, especially as they influence personality.

psychodrama A technique used primarily in certain forms of *group therapy* in which clients perform roles, often playing the parts of themselves in various socially stressful situations and sometimes playing the parts of their antagonists. This gives them the opportunity to act out their inner feelings to relieve anxiety, to practice handling situations better, and to experience the situation from another person's viewpoint. The other group members or psychodrama participants play roles, too, which gives everyone a chance to relate to one another from different perspectives.

psychodynamic Pertaining to the cognitive, emotional, and volitional mental processes that consciously and unconsciously motivate one's behavior. These processes are the product of the interplay among one's genetic and biological heritage, the sociocultural milieu, past and current realities, perceptual abilities and distortions, and one's unique experiences and memories.

psychoeducation The process of teaching clients with mental illness and their family members about the nature of the illness, including its etiology, progression, consequences, prognosis, treatment, and alternatives.

psychogenic A disorder or condition that originates in an individual's mind or psyche rather than in the body's physiological mechanisms. The term is generally used as the antonym for *organic*.

psychogenic amnesia An obsolete term for the sudden onset of *amnesia* that was thought not to be the result of organic disorders. The current diagnostic term is *dissociative amnesia.*

psychogenic fugue A *dissociative disorder* characterized by an individual's sudden travel away from familiar places or inability to recall past events and sometimes by the assumption of a new identity. The condition is not the result of organic mental disorders or malingering, although it is difficult for professionals to determine if the individual is feigning or actually unable to remember previous life experiences and the location of his or her home.

psychogenic pain disorder Recurrent symptoms of severe pain not resulting from physical disturbances. Often, the symptoms are associated with some environmental stressors or the wish to avoid some responsibility *(secondary gain)*; however, the individual is apparently not pretending to have pain symptoms, as in *malingering*. In current clinical use, the preferred terminology is "*pain disorder* associated with psychological factors."

psychogeriatric clients Older people who are cognitively impaired.

psychogeriatrics The branch of psychiatry that specializes in the mental disorders of older adults.

psychographics A depiction of the psychosocial characteristics of a given *population*, including things such as lifestyle, value orientations, and ideological commitments. In *social planning* and *social marketing*, psychographics often are as important as *demographics.*

psycholinguistics The study of language, *communication,* and metacommunication as they are affected by psychosocial factors. See also *communication theory.*

psychological morbidity A rarely used term for *mental illness* or *mental disorder.*

psychological profiling An effort to identify criminals by examining the behavioral clues provided in the commission of a crime. See also *profiling* and *racial profiling.*

psychologist A professional who studies behavior and mental processes and may apply that knowledge to the evaluation and treatment of a mental disorder. Psychologists have many specialties, including experimental, educational, counseling, industrial, and clinical orientations. Clinical psychologists are those who apply their knowledge about human behavior to the treatment of various psychosocial disorders, usually in offices, hospitals, or mental health settings. To become a clinical psychologist, a person must obtain an academic degree in psychology (either a master's degree or a PhD or PsyD degree from an accredited academic institution). This is usually followed by a requirement of two years of supervised work experience.

psychometrics The study of the scientific measurement of human behavior.

psychomotor Pertaining to muscular activity coming from or directly related to mental processes.

psychoneurosis A synonym now rarely used for *neurosis* or *anxiety disorder*. In the 19th century, Sigmund Freud (1856–1939) and other neurological researchers needed to distinguish between disorders that were apparently caused by physical problems and those that seemed to come from the *psyche*. The term "psychoneurosis" was coined to refer to nervous symptoms of a psychological origin, whereas "neurosis" was used for somatic neurological problems. See also *neurosis.*

"psychopath" An imprecise lay term for one who has a serious mental disorder. The word is derived from the word *psychopathology,* the study of psychological pathology or disease, and was once used by mental health professionals to refer to a person with a diagnosis of *antisocial personality disorder.*

psychopathic personality See *antisocial personality disorder.*

psychopathology The study of the nature of mental, cognitive, or behavioral disorders, including causes, symptoms, effects on the subject, and the psychosocial circumstances in which the *dysfunction* occurs. The term is also used in referring to personality or behavioral traits that may lead to problems or underachievement for the individual or for those in contact with the individual. Virtually every mental or behavioral disorder or any social relationship problem that prevents an individual from reaching his or her potential for well-being can be considered psychopathological.

psychopharmacological violence A type of crime identified by the *U.S. Department of Justice* that occurs when the perpetrator or victim ingests specific substances that lead to excitability or irrationality that results in the commission of a violent criminal act. This category of crime also includes people who ingest substances purposefully to reduce anxiety or boost courage and thus facilitate the previously planned crime.

psychopharmacology The study and use of drugs to bring about changes in behavior and personality. See also *psychotropic drugs.*

psychosexual development theory The concepts derived from *psychoanalytic theory,* which describe the process by which much of the individual's personality is formed. According to this theory, the individual is motivated by innate drives and instincts toward pleasure and immediate gratification. As the individual matures, there is a transformation through various stages of development. These stages are the *oral phase* (up to age two), *anal phase* (ages two to three), and the *phallic phase* or oedipal stage (ages three to seven). These are followed by a *latency stage* (from age seven to *puberty*) and the *genital stage (adolescence).* If the individual resolves the conflicts inherent in each of these stages, the mature *adult* is relatively free of psychic pathology. If not, then adult *intrapsychic* conflict, *fixation,* and potentially serious emotional problems may result.

psychosexual disorder Disturbances of human *sexuality* that are considered primarily *psychogenic.* The degree to which these disorders are psychogenic or *biogenic (organic)* is still being debated. For this reason the preferred term is *sexual disorder.*

psychosis A serious and frequently incapacitating mental disorder that may be of organic or psychological origin. These disorders are characterized by some or all of the following symptoms: impaired thinking and reasoning ability, perceptual distortions, inappropriate emotional responses, inappropriate *affect,* regressive behavior, reduced impulse control, impaired *reality testing, ideas of reference, hallucination,* and *delusion.* See also *schizophrenia* and *organic mental disorders.*

psychosocial assessment The social worker's summary judgment as to the problem to be solved; also referred to as the "psychosocial diagnosis." This description may include diagnostic labels, results derived from psychological tests and legal status, brief descriptive expressions of the problem configuration, a description of existing assets and resources, the prognosis or prediction of the outcome, and the plan designed to resolve the problem. Throughout the intervention process, the psychosocial assessment is a "work in progress" in that it is revised continually as new information is acquired, as circumstances and goals change, and as progress toward goals is made.

psychosocial crisis An important turning point or role change in one's life for which the individual has had little previous coping experience. The concept is that individuals go through predictable phases or stages of development mentally and socially throughout their lives and that each stage presents unique circumstances and challenges that the person must meet to make healthy developmental progress. The crisis occurs when the individual has not yet learned how to meet the demands of the new stage and may become conflicted and less effective until the necessary social and psychological adjustments are made.

psychosocial development theory The concepts delineated by Erik Erikson (1902–1994) and others to describe the various stages, life tasks, and challenges that every person experiences throughout the *life cycle.* The phases and life tasks are *trust versus mistrust, autonomy versus shame and doubt, initiative versus guilt, industry versus inferiority,*

*identity-versus-role confusion, intimacy versus iso-
lation, generativity versus stagnation,* and *integrity
versus despair.* Some other psychosocial theorists
describe different ages and life tasks.

psychosocial diagnosis   See *diagnosis* and *psychosocial assessment.*

psychosocial study   The process of acquiring the
relevant information needed to decide on and develop a rational plan for helping the client (an individual, family, group, or community). This information may include the client's description of the
problem, corroboration from other sources (such
as medical records, school and personnel files, letters, telephone communication, and direct meetings
with the client's family members and others who
know the client), psychosocial history taking, information about the client's cultural and subcultural
groups, information about the environment in
which the client lives, and information about resources that might be used to help the client. The
information obtained in the psychosocial study is
used in arriving at the *psychosocial assessment.*

psychosocial therapy   A relationship that occurs
between a professional and an individual, family,
group, or community for the purpose of helping
the client overcome specific emotional or social
problems and achieve specified goals for well-
being. Psychosocial therapy is a form of *psychotherapy* that emphasizes the *interface* between the
client and the client's environment. The psychosocial therapist tends to focus on interpersonal and
social *relationship* problems in addition to intrapsychic concerns. Psychosocial therapy also seeks
to mobilize available resources or create needed
ones and combine them with individual, group,
and familial relationships to help people modify
their behaviors, personalities, or situations. This is
done to help attain satisfying, fulfilling functioning within the framework of one's values and goals
and the available resources of society.

psychosomatic   The interrelationship of the
mind and body. Usually, the term refers to an
individual's symptoms that appear to be physical
but are partly or fully the result of psychological
factors.

psychotherapist   A mental health professional
who practices *psychotherapy.* The major disciplines
in which members practice psychotherapy include
social work, psychiatry, and clinical psychology.

Some members of other professions are also psychotherapists, including nurse practitioners, physicians, family therapy specialists, clergy, guidance
counselors, and educators. The legal qualifications
for use of this title vary in different jurisdictions.

psychotherapy   A specialized, formal interaction
between a social worker or other mental health
professional and a client (an individual, couple,
family, or group) in which a therapeutic relationship is established to help resolve symptoms of
mental disorder, psychosocial stress, relationship
problems, and difficulties in coping in the social
environment. Some specific types of psychotherapy
are *psychoanalysis, family therapy, group psychotherapy, supportive treatment, gestalt therapy, experiential therapy, primal therapy, transactional analysis (TA), psychosocial therapy, psychodrama,* and
cognitive therapy.

psychotic   Characteristic of a *psychosis.*

psychotropic drugs   Drugs used by psychiatrists
and other physicians to help their patients achieve
psychological or emotional changes. These drugs
include *antidepressant medications* (such as *Prozac,*
Elavil, Norpramin, Pertofrane, Sinequan, Aventl,
and Vivactil), *antianxiety drugs* (such as Valium,
Librium, Tranxene, Ativan, Serax, and various barbiturates), *antipsychotic medications* (such as
Thorazine, Haldol, Compazine, Selazine, Navane,
Mellaril, Serentil, Trilafon, and Prolixin), and
antimanic medications (lithium carbonate—that is,
Eskalith, Lithane, or Lithonate).

puberty   The period of biological development
in which the reproductive capacity of the male or
female is established.

puberty rites   Formal or informal socially institutionalized behaviors applied to or required
of youngsters to mark their newly established biological reproductive capability. In some cultures,
these behaviors are formal and ceremonial, such
as requiring the youngster to start wearing "adult"
clothing or to spend the night alone in the forest.
Many puberty rites exist in the United States today, but they are informal and vary greatly among
subcultural groups. Examples include beginning
to wear makeup, smoke, drink, drive, or have
sexual intercourse.

public assistance   Also known as *social assistance,*
a government's provision of minimum financial

aid to people who have no other means of supporting themselves. Funds come from the general revenues of the federal and state governments and not from any social insurance funds such as *Old Age, Survivors, Disability, and Health Insurance (OASDHI)*. Some public assistance programs are administered at the federal level, including *Supplemental Security Income (SSI)* payments, which cover the *Old Age Assistance (OAA)*, *Aid to the Blind (AB)*, and *Aid to the Permanently and Totally Disabled (APTD)* programs. Other public assistance programs are administered by states and localities, sometimes with the help of federal funding. These include *Temporary Assistance to Needy Families (TANF)* for those ineligible for any other *categorical assistance* programs.

public defender   An attorney for people who are accused of crimes or require legal services but are unable to pay for their own counsel. Public defender systems exist in most states largely as a result of the U.S. Supreme Court's ruling in *Gideon v. Wainwright* that indigent defendants must be furnished with legal representation.

public domain   Property of the society at large and, within specified limits, legally available to all. Uncopyrighted software, books with expired copyrights, and some national park lands are examples.

public health   A system of programs, policies, and health care personnel in which the goal is to prevent disease, prolong life, and promote better health. Efforts to achieve these goals are made through public health measures such as improving sanitation, controlling communicable diseases, educating people about personal hygiene, organizing medical and nursing services for early diagnosis and prevention of disease, and developing health care facilities and access to these facilities. Public health programs are administered by many federal, state, and local agencies.

Public Health Service, U.S.   The federal organization under the *U.S. Department of Health and Human Services (HHS)* that initiates and coordinates the nation's effort to maintain and improve the health and health care of its people. The service is involved in improving sanitation and health education, facilitating *primary prevention,* setting and enforcing standards for food and drug processing and handling, investigating imported organic products, controlling epidemics, and overseeing and conducting health research. Within the

U.S. Public Health Service are the *Centers for Disease Control and Prevention (CDC)*, the *Food and Drug Administration (FDA)*, the *Health Resources and Services Administration (HRSA)*, and the *National Institutes of Health (NIH)*. The Public Health Service originated in 1798 as a health service for merchant sailors, was formally established in 1870 as the Marine Hospital Service, and acquired its current name in 1912. Their Web site address is http://www.hhs.gov/phs

public housing   Residential facilities that are built, maintained, and administered by a local or federal government to provide low-rent or no-rent homes for needy people. In the United States, most of these programs are under the authority of the *U.S. Department of Housing and Urban Development (HUD)* and local housing agencies. "Public housing" is a term that could theoretically apply to many additional federally subsidized programs designed to help people obtain residences, such as the Rent Supplement Program, Lower Income Housing Assistance, Rural Housing Loans, Farm Labor Housing Loans and Grants, and the Indian Housing Improvement Program, as well as the *Federal Housing Administration (FHA)* homeowners' loans and the home loan programs of the *U.S. Department of Veterans Affairs.*

public-interest group   An organization or collective of like-minded individuals seeking to influence the policies of governments, political candidates, agencies, or the general public toward changes that are believed to benefit the whole society rather than one *special-interest group.* Such groups often employ *lobbyists* to present their views through the use of a *media event, legislative advocacy tactics,* lobbying, *political action committees (PACs), fundraising,* and voter campaigns. See also *pressure group* and *interest group.*

public-interest research group (PIRG)   Organizations funded by private and philanthropic contributions to identify the existence of particular *social problems,* determine their causes, evaluate proposed solutions, and present findings to the public and those institutions that can address the problems.

public law (P.L.)   An act created by a legislative body and signed by the chief executive (president) that applies to everyone in the relevant jurisdiction and is executed, administered, and paid for by and on behalf of the citizens. This is in contrast to a private law, which applies only to a specified person or entity. When a public law is enacted in the United States, it is known by its title and the designation P.L. or Pub. L. and a specific number. The first two numbers indicate the specific Congress in which it was passed, and the last numbers indicate the order in which the act became law. For example, the Social Security Act (P.L. 74-271) was the 271st law passed by the 74th Congress. The act that created Medicare, P.L. 89-97, was the 97th law passed by the 89th Congress. A new Congress is convened every two years.

public policy institutes   Independent and privately funded research and educational organizations established to obtain, interpret, and disseminate knowledge about economic, political, and social issues. Many of these organizations publish journals and books, maintain libraries and speakers' bureaus, and monitor the decision-making processes of governments and social institutions. Among the larger of these organizations are the Brookings Institution (founded in 1916), the Carnegie Endowment for International Peace (1910), the Hudson Institute (1961), the Cato Institute (1977), the *Urban Institute* (1968), the Center for Policy Alternatives (1975), the Institute for Policy Studies (1963), and the Center on Budget and Policy Priorities (1981).

public welfare   The relative well-being of a society and its people as manifested by a nation's policy of providing for the protection and fulfillment of its citizens. To most people this term is now also a synonym for *social welfare* and *public assistance.*

public works   The existing and ongoing construction, under government auspices, of that part of the infrastructure that is built for public use, such as highways, parks, irrigation projects, power plants, and canals.

Public Works Administration (PWA)   The *New Deal* program established in 1935 to stimulate depressed industries and cope with the unemployment of their former workers by contracting with private organizations to build public facilities such as parks, recreation centers, post offices, and government buildings.

pulmonary disorders   A group of diseases associated with decreased ability to inhale oxygen into the lungs and expel carbon dioxide. Such disorders include bronchial *asthma, emphysema,* pneu-

monia, chronic obstructive pulmonary disease, and acute respiratory distress syndrome. These conditions have varying causes, including smoking, injury to the respiratory system, and obstructions of the airways.

punishment   1. A penalty imposed for misbehavior (for example, a parent spanking, isolating, or withdrawing privileges from a child) or illegal acts (for example, *incarceration*). 2. In *behavior modification,* the presentation of an unpleasant or undesired event following a *behavior,* the consequence of which is that there is decreased probability that the behavior will be repeated.

punitive damages   A legal judgment requiring a person who has harmed another to compensate the other for the actual harm caused, plus an additional sum as a punishment for intentional and malicious misconduct that led to the harm.

pupil services team   The professional staff of public and sometimes private school programs to provide for the physical, emotional, and social needs of students so they can participate in the educational process. The members of this team include school social workers as well as school counselors, psychologists, nurses, speech therapists, special education teachers, and other specialists, as well as the pupils' regular education teachers. See also *IEP team.*

purchase-of-service (POS) agreements   Fiscal arrangements or contracts between two or more organizations; one organization agrees in advance to pay a specified amount to the other for providing a predetermined number of services within a specified period. Purchaser organizations are thus able to extend services to their clientele, and provider agencies can increase their budgets, extend their services, and in some cases increase their profits. Such agreements are often between government entities as the purchaser and social agencies as providers. This term is also known as purchase-of-service contracts (POSCs).

purdah   The system of gender segregation and sex-role differentiation widely practiced in some Islamic and other cultures. The many variations of purdah include divided physical spaces within one household between the sexes; restrictions on women from entering certain areas of a city, building, or social center; and the obligation of women to wear veils and other concealing clothes.

Puritanism   The system of *values* and beliefs that was prominent in the 17th century, characterized by severe penalties for nonconforming behavior, strict discipline, and controls on what was considered immoral. Much of the Puritan philosophy was implicit in the English *poor laws* and was imported into Colonial America. See also *Protestant ethic.*

purposeful expression of feelings   One of the fundamental elements of the social worker–client *relationship*, in which the social worker encourages the client to communicate certain emotions. The client is helped to express those emotions that may be debilitating when not communicated. The worker encourages purposeful expression of feelings by listening, asking relevant questions, listening intently to answers, and avoiding any behavior that seems intolerant or judgmental.

pushout youth   Adolescent and younger children who, through psychological or physical pressure, are compelled to permanently leave the homes of their custodial caregivers.

putative father   A man who has been named father of a child born out of wedlock even though paternity has not been legally established.

PWAs   People with *AIDS.*

pyramid schemes   The fraudulent practice of enticing people to join a hierarchy and make small payments to the originator with the expectation of receiving payments from a greater number of new participants. These arrangements frequently take the form of chain letters, "gifting clubs," and investment services. See also *Ponzi scheme.*

pyromania   An *impulse control disorder* in which the person frequently has compelling urges to start or watch fires.

q-sort technique   A tool used in *social research* in which subjects are given a series of statements—each written on a separate card—and asked to sort them into various piles to indicate the degree to which they apply to the subject.

QCs   Quarterly credits, the name used by the *Social Security Administration (SSA)* for the work credit units that a future beneficiary pays into the *Federal Insurance Contributions Act (FICA)* system for coverage eligibility. One QC is obtained by paying into the FICA system one quarter of a year. Workers born after 1929 must earn 40 QCs to be fully and permanently insured for retirement, survivors, and disability benefits. A worker born before 1929 needs slightly fewer QCs for full benefits.

qi-gong psychotic reaction   A *culture-bound syndrome,* found mostly in China, in which the individual experiences an acute psychotic episode or nonpsychotic dissociative or paranoid reaction, often after intensive involvement in the "exercise of vital energy" practice known as qi-gong.

"quack"   A term of disparagement applied to some medical professionals and to unqualified persons who fraudulently provide medical care.

quadriplegia   Paralysis of all four limbs or paralysis from the neck down. The correct terminology is "a person with quadriplegia" rather than "a quadriplegic."

Qualified Clinical Social Worker (QCSW)   The professional credential sponsored by NASW signifying advanced experience and education for clinical social work practice. Minimum requirements for admission are a master's degree from a CSWE-accredited school, two years of paid post-master's clinical social work experience in an agency or organized setting under the supervision of a social worker with two years of experience, and a current state license or membership in the *Academy of Certified Social Workers (ACSW).* The holder must document these requirements and sign an agreement to practice according to NASW's *Code of Ethics* and the *NASW Standards for Continuing Professional Education.*

qualified domestic relations order (QDRO)   A legal document or judicial decree that authorizes legal officers to enforce judgments pertaining to alimony, child support, or marital property rights of a spouse, in compliance with the jurisdiction's domestic relations laws.

qualified medical child support order (QMCSO)   In divorce cases, a ruling that requires the non-custodial parent to pay the health care costs or provide health insurance coverage for the dependent child.

qualified mental retardation professional (QMRP)   One who provides professional services for persons with developmental disabilities, including counseling, assessment, advocacy, benefits finding, and training. QMRPs are licensed in some states, are usually employed in nursing homes or special facilities, have bachelor's degrees or higher, and have specialized training in mental retardation and working with persons with developmental disabilities.

qualitative research   Systematic investigations that include inductive, in-depth, nonquantitative studies of individuals, groups, organizations, or communities. Examples include *field study, ethnography,* and *historiography.*

quality assurance   The processes and measures an organization takes to determine that its products or services measure up to the standards established for them. This may be accomplished when supervisors, peers, consumer advocates, or legally designated overseers inspect the work, review the description of the work, or evaluate the system for producing the work. Products or services that fail to meet standards may be rejected, procedures for their completion may be revised, and sanctions can be brought against the provider. Quality assurance measures used for social workers include the following: sufficient education from accredited schools of social work, entry-level work experience under qualified *supervision, licensing* and *certification,* competency examinations, and *continuing education* requirements. For the profession, measures include a professional *code of ethics* that is accessible to the public, *peer* *review, utilization review,* program evaluations, professional *sanctions,* civil *malpractice* suits, and criminal *negligence* charges. Quality assurance programs tend to be more concerned with compliance than with client outcome. This term is synonymous with quality control.

quality assurance programs in social work Those measures taken by the social work profession to determine and demonstrate that its practitioners meet the standards that have been made explicit. These programs contain one or more of the following components: a patient or client information system (which tends to record physical and social characteristics of the client, problems or goals, and services received and outcomes), a *peer review* system (which evaluates the social worker's initial contact, *assessment,* formulation of goals, actual *intervention,* and *termination* and outcomes), and various systems for ensuring that social work coverage is available. In the process, reviewers outline the standards of care, evaluate cases to determine if standards are being met, make recommendations for improvements, and have a follow-up review to see if improvements were achieved. See also *quality improvement teams (QITs).*

quality circles In organizational management, a procedure in which a small number of employee volunteers, usually 6 to 12 people from the same work area, meet regularly to discuss positive ways to solve problems. The organization usually provides advance training in decision making for these volunteers, but it has no direct decision-making power. Quality circles are considered effective alternatives to the anonymous "suggestion box" method of gaining new insights from the employees' perspective.

quality control See *quality assurance.*

quality improvement teams (QITs) In organizational management, a *total quality management (TQM)* procedure in which employees from different organizational levels, departments, and functions within the organization meet regularly to consider how to improve conditions and quality of output. QITs are similar to *quality circles* but usually draw different employees rather than those from within the same work groups.

quantitative research Systematic investigations that include descriptive or inferential statistical analysis. Examples are experiments, survey research, and investigations that make use of numerical comparisons.

quarantine Isolation of potential carriers of communicable infections, including people and animals. The term is also used by computer technicians to denote the isolation of computer viruses before deleting them so that they do not contaminate or otherwise harm existing programs or data.

quarterly credits See *QCs.*

quarterway houses Transitional residences for individuals who require more *supervision,* support, or protection than is available in *halfway houses* but less than full-time institutionalization.

quartile In *social research,* any one of three scores or points that divide a distribution into four equal parts, each constituting 25 percent of all the cases. See also *decile.*

quartile range In research reporting, a way to depict the middle 50 percent of the cases. The range of the variable is the value to the 25th percentile, subtracted from the 75th percentile.

quasi-experimental studies Systematic research inquiries made without complete controls, as is attempted in *experimental studies.*

"queer" A vernacular term for *homosexual.* Once a pejorative name used only by intolerant and homophobic individuals, "queer" is being reclaimed and used as a positive self-identifying term, especially by younger gay men and lesbians involved in civil rights activities (for example, the "Queer Nation").

questioning A primary tool in the social work *interview,* the procedure in which the worker systematically requests from the client information, *feedback,* and emotional expression. The social worker's questioning process gives focus and direction to the client and to the working relationship and is a medium through which the client develops self-understanding and learns new skills and insights. Questioning takes many forms, depending on the immediate and long-term goals of the interview.

questionnaire A set of written questions seeking specific facts or subjective opinions on a given subject, used by social work interviewers and researchers to guide and systematize the information being gathered. Questionnaires may be so highly structured that they can be self-administered by the client, who merely gives yes–no responses. Conversely, they can be relatively unstructured, consisting of a list of subjects that remind the investigator to ask relevant questions.

questions, closed-ended See *closed-ended questions*.

questions, direct *Questioning* that compels the client to address a certain topic, often one that the client may wish to avoid or minimize. Direct questions may be closed-ended ("Did you drink any liquor this week?") or open-ended ("How do you think you are affected by alcohol?").

questions, indirect *Questioning* that helps the client feel less pressured and bombarded and permits him or her not to respond if desired and to have more flexibility about how to respond. An example is when a social worker comments to a client "It must be difficult to have to work all day and then take care of the kids all night."

questions, open-ended See *open-ended questions*.

quetiapine An antipsychotic drug.

quick relaxation techniques Simple self-administered methods for achieving a state of greater calm and reduced stress. Four techniques are (1) the countdown (sitting quietly, eyes closed, counting numbers or imaginary objects); (2) imagery (imagining beautiful scenes or pleasurable remembrances); (3) the turtle (the yoga-inspired practice of sitting straight, letting the chin fall to the chest and exhaling, inhaling while moving the head back as though trying to touch the shoulders, then pulling the shoulders up as though trying to touch the ears); and (4) scanning (while sitting during normal daily activities, inhaling slowly while thinking about each muscle group in the body and purposefully relaxing all the muscles that are tense).

quorum The minimum number of members required to be at a meeting before the meeting can conduct its official business.

quota system An organizational plan, social policy, or legal doctrine that specifies how many or what proportion of people of an identified status will be included in an identified group. The system may be designed to exclude people (as in some past U.S. immigration laws that permitted a higher number of Europeans than Africans or Asians to enter the country) or include people (as in some *affirmative action* programs). For example, a city may decide that half its police officers should be African American to reflect the population and overcome past discriminatory policies, so it mandates that efforts will be made to reach the 50–50 quota.

race   The major subdivisions of the human species, whose distinguishing characteristics are genetically transmitted. Races are divided in myriad ways, including the three traditional groups (Negroid, Mongoloid, and Caucasian); the "geographical races" (African, American Indian, Asian, Australian Aborigine, European, Indian, Melanesian, Micronesian, and Polynesian); and the groupings of various national ancestries, tribes, and even families. Many characteristics by which people seek to distinguish racial groups are not genetically transmitted but culturally learned. The U.S. government, through various entities, has recognized specific groups of people as composing a racial group, at least for purposes of legal protection. For example, the U.S. Supreme Court has held that people of Arabian ancestry and Jewish ancestry are to be protected from racial discrimination. For reporting purposes, the *Equal Employment Opportunity Commission (EEOC)* delineates many race categories, including white, not of Hispanic origin; Hispanic (people of Latin and South American and Spanish culture origin, regardless of race); African; *American Indian* or *Alaska Native;* and Asian and *Pacific Islander.*

race relations   See *intergroup relations.*

racial preferences   Laws or institutional advantages for one race over others, as in "whites only" covenants in new neighborhoods. The term has been used as a synonym for *affirmative action,* especially by its opponents.

racial profiling   A law authority's focus on members of a specific racial or ethnic group for suspected criminal activities or to seek possible criminal offenders. The term also applies to the actions of laypersons, such as store owners and civil servants, who focus on members of specific minority groups. For example, a shop clerk might be told to closely watch all members of a designated racial or ethnic group to prevent shoplifting. See also *profiling* and *psychological profiling.*

racism   Stereotyping and generalizing about people, usually negatively, because of their *race;* commonly a basis of *discrimination* against members of racial groups. Racism is an ideology that a group's genetic (racial) physical characteristics are linked in a direct causal way to psychological, intellectual, or behavioral traits, and these distinguish superior and inferior groups. See also *institutional racism, individual racism,* and *able-ism.*

Racketeer Influences and Corrupt Organizations Act (RICO)   U.S. law (P.L. 91-452) designed to combat organized crime and illegal conspiracies. RICO gives law enforcement authorities greater leeway in investigating and prosecuting crimes by groups characterized by a hierarchical structure. The act permits more leniency in obtaining wiretaps, protecting witnesses, granting immunity, and *plea bargaining.*

racketeering   Organized *crime;* the process by which a group of people conspires to acquire the property of others unlawfully through various crimes, especially *extortion,* smuggling, and sales of illicit goods and services, often facilitated by *bribery,* murder, intimidation, and the influencing of corrupt officials.

radical environmentalism   Social activist movements advocating militant measures to protect the natural world. Activities include *demonstration, boycott,* obstruction of developments, and highly confrontational actions against those considered to be engaged in ecologically harmful activities. See also *Greenpeace* and *ecotage.*

radical social work   The ideology among some social workers that the most effective way to achieve goals of equality and solutions to social problems is to eliminate or make major changes in existing institutions. Radical social work, which is now mostly referred to as *progressive social work,* includes techniques for peaceably bringing about these changes, including *passive resistance, demonstration,* strikes, and political and social activism. The major social work organization to promote this ideology, the *Bertha Capen Reynolds Society (BCRS),* is now known as the *Social Welfare Action Alliance.*

Ragged School Movement   The educational and social development program started by *Lord Shaftesbury* in England in the 1850s to help educate poor children, who previously had little access to any schooling. The Ragged Schools provided schooling, social services, vocational development, and health care and were originally staffed by volunteers. Later, as education became more accessible to all British children, the role of these schools changed to focus on providing social services and assistance for children with disabilities and poor families. The Ragged School organization was renamed the Shaftesbury Society in 1944.

rainbow coalition A group of people from different racial backgrounds working together to achieve specific political or social goals.

Ramabai, Pandita (1858–1920) A pioneer for women's rights in India and the founder of Sharada Sadan, a residential school and vocational training program for widows.

Ramadan The ninth month in the Islam calendar during which Muslims fast during daylight and seek spiritual renewal.

***Ramona* decision** The 1994 judgment in a California court that psychotherapists may be held liable and sued by "indirect victims of the therapy." In the case, a father claimed his career and marriage were destroyed because his daughter's therapist convinced her that the father had sexually abused her. Some legal scholars believe such decisions make therapists liable for the negative effects of therapy on third parties (for example, a husband suing because his wife decides to divorce him as a result of therapy).

random sample A group of subjects or cases systematically taken from a *population* so that each one is as likely to have been selected as any other one. In this way, the resulting sample is likely to be a valid representation of the population from which the cases were selected. See also *stratified sample*.

randomization In *social research,* the assignment of subjects to experimental and control groups in such a way that each subject has an equally likely chance of being assigned to either of the groups.

rank and file The masses, or that group of people who are outside leadership roles.

Rank and File Movement A coalition of public welfare workers, social work unions, and welfare client groups active in the United States from 1925 to 1940. The movement began when welfare workers sought better working conditions, better pay, and more manageable caseloads, but it grew into an activist movement for massive social change.

Rankian School See *functional school in social work.*

Rankin, Jeannette (1880–1973) The first woman elected to the U.S. Congress (she served two terms in the House of Representatives: 1917–18 and 1941–42) and a leader against the U.S. participation in World Wars I and II. She was trained and employed as a social worker prior to her political career. She also led successful campaigns in the *women's suffrage movement* and protective legislation for children and in the 1930s campaigned for social security programs.

RAP model An orientation used especially in social group work in multiracial and multicultural settings. RAP is an acronym for recognize, anticipate, and problem solve, which are seen as the critical tasks effective group leaders and members perform.

Rapaport, Lydia (1923–1971) Social worker who helped integrate *psychodynamic* theory with social work theory. Later she developed theoretical underpinnings for *crisis intervention* and *short-term therapy.*

rape The *crime* of forcing a nonconsenting person to engage in some form of sexual contact, usually involving penetration. The force may take the form of violent assault or real or implied threat. The victim most frequently is a woman or girl but may be a man or boy, and the *perpetrator* is almost always a man. See also *acquaintance rape, statutory rape,* and *sexual assault.*

rape crisis centers Organizations and facilities to help victims of *sexual assault* and educate potential victims and the public about the problem and its prevention. Many centers are nonprofit and work with health care facilities, social agencies, and police departments. They are usually staffed by a core of professionals and trained volunteers. These programs also assist the victim's partners and families as well and usually provide emergency *hot line* services, preventive educational programs, and outreach services to the public.

rape trauma syndrome A specific type of *post-traumatic stress disorder (PTSD)* following *sexual* *assault* victimization. Many victims experience, at first, a sense of shock and numbness, followed by some superficial adjustment and, after several weeks, an increased sense of emotional distress, including terror, startle response, insomnia, fits of crying, and fear of others. Then, after a phase of anger at the assailant and society, the victim may adjust to the experience and become a survivor rather than a victim.

rapport   In the social work *interview,* the state of harmony, compatibility, and *empathy* that permits mutual understanding and a working *relationship* between the client and the social worker.

rapprochement   The fourth subphase in the *separation–individuation* process of human development proposed by Margaret Mahler, which lasts from about the age of one month to two years. If *fixation* or deviation occurs during this phase, according to Mahler, it is likely to lead to *borderline* or narcissistic disturbances in later life.

rare disorders   Diseases that are found in few people and thus receive little attention, research funding, or awareness of their existence. More than 5,000 of these diseases have been identified, and more than 20 million Americans are affected by them. Some may be fatal or severely disabling, incurable, or untreatable. Because they are rare, some health care providers, as well as the victims themselves, do not recognize them. The National Organization for Rare Disorders (NORD) coordinates efforts to deal with these diseases. NORD's Web site address is http://www.rarediseases.org

rate review   A procedure in which *third-party* funding organizations such as government or insurance companies attempt to contain the costs of health care and social services by periodically evaluating the charges and procedures made by providers. The third parties and providers agree in advance about how much to charge for each specified service, and this is reconsidered usually every year. See also *fourth party.*

ratification   The formal confirmation and approval of an agreement or treaty. Each participant in the ratification process carries out the confirmation in accordance with its own constitution and system.

rating errors   In *social research* using evaluators to rate responses to tests, the tendency to give

higher or lower ranks than is objectively deserved. Various types of rating error include "errors of central tendency" (when raters tend to assign average scores to most respondents), "errors of contrast" (when raters tend to compare subjects with each other in the test rather than to some predetermined standard), "*halo effect* errors" (when raters tend to generalize some positive or negative characteristic of the subject to other characteristics of the same person), "errors of inconsistency" (when raters do not use the same method or evaluation instructions), "errors of projection" (when raters allow their own values or orientations to influence their ratings), "errors of recency" (when raters give more importance to factors that occurred more recently, downplaying the overall performances), "stereotyping errors" (when raters classify subjects inappropriately because of their membership in a minority group), and "errors of subjectivity" (when raters give inappropriate evaluations because of improper training, bias, values, or thought processes).

ratio   A mathematical relationship of one number to another, found by dividing one of the numbers into the other. For example, if an agency has 10 social workers and 500 clients, there are 50 clients for every social worker, and the ratio is 50 to 1. In social agency management, ratios are frequently used for the ratio of assets to liabilities, of revenue to expenses, and of salaries to total budget. When the base number (for example, the total agency budget) is expressed as 100, the ratio is expressed as a percentage (for example, 80 percent of the total agency budget goes for salaries).

ratio scale   In research reporting, a scale that permits one not only to quantify and compare the sizes of differences between values but also to interpret both values in terms of absolute measures of quantity. For example, a social agency reports that the 1,000 hours its therapists worked the previous month was only half the 2,000 hours they worked the month before that.

rational casework   A type of clinical social work intervention, based on the concepts of *cognitive theory* and delineated especially by Harold D. Werner. This approach concentrates on the client's rational thinking processes.

rational–emotive therapy   A psychotherapeutic method based on the *cognitive theory* of psychologist Albert Ellis, in which the client is encouraged to make distinctions between what is objective fact in the environment and the inaccurate, negative, and self-limiting interpretations made of one's own behavior and life. The Institute for Rational–Emotive Therapy, founded in 1968, is headquartered in New York.

rationalization   1. Presenting in logical terms, or interpreting the reasons for, some action or event. 2. A *defense mechanism* in which a person explains or justifies an action or thought to make it acceptable when it is unacceptable at a deeper psychological level.

rationing   A process of allocating goods and services from limited available supplies. Rationing has been used when famine, war, disasters, or unexpected shortages of needed goods disrupt normal marketing price and distribution systems.

raw score   In research, the original and unprocessed quantitative result of a test. For example, a student's raw score on a test of 25 items would be the number of items answered correctly. See also *scaled score.*

RDA   Recommended dietary allowance or recommended daily allowance; the amount of nutrients needed every day to maintain optimal health, according to the *Food and Drug Administration (FDA).*

reaching out   Activities by the social worker to gain the trust or motivation of fearful, unmotivated, or *hard-to-reach clients.* Such activities might include tangible gifts (a cup of coffee or a piece of candy), *concrete services* (cutting through some *red tape* with another agency), or special favors (extending the length of a session, telephoning the client between meetings, and so on). Reaching out also includes making services known and more accessible to people in need.

reaction formation   A *defense mechanism* in which the person behaves or thinks in ways or assumes values that are the opposite of the original *unconscious* trait. Thus, a social worker who has an unconscious dislike for children might specialize in working with them.

"reactionary"   A term of derision applied to an *activist* or an *ideologue* who opposes all forms of *social change* except those that go back to some former, idealized system.

reactive alcoholism   One of the three major types of *alcoholism* (the other two being *primary alcoholism* and *secondary alcoholism*) characterized by heavy or excessive drinking that starts soon after experiencing a perceived crisis such as the death of a loved one, surviving an accident, or crime victimization. No prior indication of a drinking problem is noted, but after the traumatic event, the individual may or may not become and remain addicted to alcohol. See also *posttraumatic stress disorder (PTSD).*

reactive attachment disorder (RAD)   A condition in which the individual is unable to form normal and needed emotional bonds with caregivers and others, brought about by early childhood experiences such as trauma, abuse, neglect, inconsistent caregiving, or similar factors. The disorder is most commonly seen among children who have been sexually or physically abused or who have had multiple placements in foster homes. The resulting symptoms may take different forms. Some RAD children are clingy and show separation anxiety; others are very compliant and superficially bonded but lack emotional engagement; and others may be angry, oppositional, and defiant.

reading disorder   A type of *learning disorder* in which there is a deficiency in reading skills not resulting from limited education or cultural deprivation. The person may lack these skills because of visual or hearing impairment, cognitive or intellectual functions, or *organic mental disorders.* If the individual has been unable to develop reading skills, the condition is known as developmental reading disorder. See also *dyslexia.*

reality principle   An idea in *Freudian theory* stating that the young child soon learns that the satisfaction of immediate impulses must be reconciled with the often competing demands of the environment. Thus, the *ego* finds ways to compromise between the demands of the environment and the internal drives that are related to the *pleasure principle.*

reality testing   One's relative ability to judge and evaluate objectively the external world and to distinguish between it and the ideas and values that exist in one's mind.

reality therapy   Psychosocial and behavioral intervention, developed by William Glasser, that focuses on the client's behavior rather than feelings and on the present and future rather than the past. Therapists encourage working out alternative solutions to problems. They do not accept client excuses, rarely ask "why," and place little emphasis on taking case histories.

realpolitik   Practical *social planning* that is acceptable to enough voters that it has a chance of being legislated. The term derives from a German expression for "realistic politics," or the subordination of idealistic policies for practical sociopolitical achievements.

reapportionment   The political process of changing the boundaries of a legislative district or the number of representatives to which a district is entitled. See also *gerrymandering*.

reasonable accommodation   The U.S. federally mandated requirement of employers to help employees with disabilities to work unless the action would cause a hardship for the employer. For example, the employer arranges for adequate workspace for an employee in a wheelchair.

reassurance   In the social work *interview*, the expression by the social worker of positive belief in the client and in the client's activities and motivations to improve the situation.

recalls   The request issued to purchasers of some product to return it to the place of purchase for repair, replacement, or refund. The U.S. federal government, as well as various manufacturers, periodically issues recalls when a product has later been found to be hazardous, defective, or ineffective. Products most frequently recalled are automobiles, toys, food products, tools, electronic goods, and furniture.

recertification   The *quality assurance* measure in which experienced professionals are required to demonstrate that they have maintained their ability to provide competent services. This is often done by compelling professionals to pass examinations at designated times during their careers, to take a specified number of qualified training and retraining programs or units of continuing education, or to demonstrate continued practice competence to peers. See also *continuing education, CEUs,* and *grandparenting clause.*

recession   A socioeconomic condition characterized by lowered business activity, higher unemploy-

ment, and reduced purchasing power. Recession is considered a milder or shorter version of economic *depression.* See also *stagflation.*

recidivism rate   The number of people in a specified period who return to an institution relative to the population of that institution. For example, a mental hospital with a 50 percent annual recidivism rate would see half of its discharged patients return within a year.

recidivist   1. An individual who relapses or returns to a former condition or tendency. 2. One who returns to an institution because of a recurrence of the behavior or condition that led to the original *incarceration.*

reciprocal causality   A concept emphasized in the *ecological perspective* that views social interrelationships and transactions as occurring not in a simple, linear cause–effect outcome but with circular *feedback* so that cause becomes effect and effect becomes cause all around the circular loop. In this view, the individual's problems are the consequence of people–environment exchanges rather than the sole result of personality or environmental factors.

reciprocal goals model   In *group work* and therapy group conceptions, a model in which the group is seen as an integral element in the social system, and all its members and leaders influence and are influenced by the system, including one another. The leader's role is to mediate between the group and society. The group process is as important as any of its outcomes. See also *remedial goals model* and *social goals model.*

reciprocal inhibition   A technique used in *behavior modification* in which suppression of an undesired *response* or *behavior* is accomplished by associating it with a dominant antagonistic response. For example, in *systematic desensitization,* relaxation responses are paired with anxiety responses until the anxiety is inhibited. The technique was developed by Joseph Wolpe.

reciprocal interactions   Mutual responsiveness. For example, the *behavior* of one person toward another leads to a behavior by the other, leading to a behavior by the first, and so on.

reclassification   Formal and official changes made by an employer organization in the job descriptions, educational requirements, and personnel standards of its current and potential employees. Social workers in public agencies have been particularly affected by such actions, which have included reducing educational requirements for entry-level jobs, equating formal education with experience, and using non-BSWs and non-MSWs to perform tasks once reserved for them. See also *declassification.*

reconstituted family A family unit consisting of a husband and wife, one or both of whom have children from a previous marriage or relationship who live with them. See also *stepfamily* and *blended family.*

recording In social work, the process of putting in writing and keeping on file relevant information about the client; the problem; the *prognosis;* the *intervention* plan; the progress of treatment; the social, economic, and health factors that contribute to the situation; and the procedures for *termination* or *referral.* There are many types of recording, depending on the agency's requirements, the social worker's social style, and the type of intervention. These may include the *narrative summary,* the *psychosocial assessment,* the *behavioral assessment, verbatim recording,* the *problem-oriented record (POR),* and the *SOAP charting method.*

recovered memory Retrieved parts of a client's forgotten past experiences that had been concealed from consciousness due to *suppression* or *repression.* See also *memory recovery therapy, false-memory syndrome,* and *implanted memory.*

"recovering addict" The preferred term for one who has been addicted to alcohol or other substances but who has maintained longtime sobriety. Because of the chronic relapsing tendency in addictions, the person is never referred to as "recovered."

Recovery, Inc. The *self-help organization,* with chapters in most larger communities in the United States, Canada, Israel, and some European nations, in which members meet regularly to help one another recover from emotional problems or the effects of mental illness. The Chicago-based organization was founded by Dr. Abraham Low in 1937. Their Web site address is http://www.recovery-inc.com

recreation skill group In *social group work,* the type of group that exists to improve members' skills

in specific tasks while enjoying recreational activities, such as in crafts, arts, and sports activity groups.

recurrent expenditures The amount an organization must pay out on a regular basis, including salaries, costs of expendable supplies, interest on loans, and so on.

recycle Preparing disposable items for reuse.

Red Crescent *Disaster relief* and humanitarian organizations in Muslim nations, affiliated with the International *Red Cross.*

Red Cross The international organization and federation of more than 100 autonomous national societies concerned with the alleviation of human suffering and the promotion of public health and civil rights. The organization was founded in Switzerland in 1863 by Jean Henri Dunant, and its emblem is based on the Swiss flag. The International Red Cross often acts as a neutral intermediary between nations at war or in conflict and works to ensure humane treatment of prisoners of war. The American Red Cross, founded in 1881 by *Clara Barton* (1821–1912), emphasizes *disaster relief, social services* to military personnel and veterans, health and safety programs, and the coordination of blood and organ donations to hospitals. Their Web site address is http://www.redcross.org

red-light district In many cities, an area where there is a concentration of *prostitution,* sexually oriented shops and clubs, and drug-related *crime.*

Red Power The sociopolitical movement, prominent especially in the 1960s and early 1970s, to raise public consciousness and support for legislation to enhance the well-being of *Native Americans.*

red tape Bureaucratic procedures and rules.

redlining The practice by certain financial institutions of designating an area of a city as being too risky and unprofitable to lend money to those who want to rebuild or refurbish buildings there. The term came from the red line that various institutions drew on maps around *ghetto* areas to identify those locales that would not be funded. The practice was made illegal with passage of the *Community Reinvestment Act of 1977.* See also *greenlining.*

"redneck" A disparaging term applied to people who seem angry, racially prejudiced, and dogmatic.

reduction-in-force (RIF) Action by an organization to reduce the size of its workforce through firings, layoffs, employee reassignment, position downgrades, or the provision of incentives for voluntary terminations.

reductionism A method of explaining a theory, a methodology, or data by reducing the more complex aspects to less complex ones. Often, the effect of doing this is to oversimplify the phenomenon and give it an inaccurate interpretation.

referee A peer reviewer of some written material to help editors and publishers determine its suitability for publication. Publishers of serious scholarly journals, textbooks, and other professional documents usually ask several of the author's professional colleagues, usually those with some expertise in the topic discussed in the proposal or submitted manuscript, to evaluate the material. The publisher commonly uses the *double blind* process to help ensure that the decision to publish or not to publish is based only on the merits of the writing. Reputable social work journals and textbooks, as well as those of other professional groups, use referees to determine if the material should be published.

reference group A social status, culture, subculture, or association of any type in which behaviors, values, and lifestyles are emulated by an individual. The person may or may not be a member of the group with which he or she is identifying.

reference individual One whose appearance, values, lifestyle, or behavior is chosen as a model for imitation or emulation.

referendum A direct vote by the citizens on a proposed law, constitutional amendment, or funding measure.

referral The social work process of directing a client to an agency, resources, or a professional known to be able to provide a needed service. This process may include knowing what the available resources are, knowing what the client's needs are, facilitating the client's opportunity to partake of the service, and following up to be certain that the contact was met.

"referral fatigue therapy" A facetious term for the practice of sending clients to other helpers so often or with so many complications that the cli-

ent eventually becomes discouraged and discontinues the search for help or obtains it from other sources. This reduces the social worker's caseload and appears in records as a success in providing service.

reflection of feeling An *interview* technique in which the social worker clarifies and shows the client what his or her feelings are at the moment and encourages further expression and understanding of those feelings. Often, the social worker reflects the client's feelings by *paraphrasing*, pointing out revealing *parapraxis,* and displaying *paralinguistic* expressions of concealed feelings.

reflex An involuntary response to some *stimulus.*

reform movement A coordinated social or political activity to bring about changes in existing institutions or government structure. Usually, such movements are formed to eliminate *corruption* or unethical business practices.

reform school See *reformatory.*

reformatory A *carceral institution* in which young people convicted of delinquent or criminal activity are confined and given special training, therapy, and education to help them overcome *antisocial behavior* tendencies; also known as *reform school.*

reformer A *social activist* who seeks to bring about changes in institutional structures or human behavior.

refractory depression *Depression* that seems resistant to treatment.

reframing A technique used by family therapists to help families understand a symptom or pattern of behavior by seeing it in a different context. For example, a family might see a child diagnosed as depressed as being disrespectful and detached from them. Reframing changes the understanding of the problem from an individual's illness to a family problem.

refugee One who seeks safety or protection from previously experienced dangers, such as immigrants to the United States who have sought to escape religious, ethnic, or political persecution in their native lands. See also *United Nations High Commissioner for Refugees (UNHCR), immigrant,* and *asylee.*

refugee resettlement programs Organizations and agencies, both government and private, to assist refugees in making the transition to healthy, productive lives in the new country. Major U.S. programs are provided through the U.S. State Department and *U.S. Department of Health and Human Services' (HHS) Office of Refugee Resettlement (ORR)*. The State Department's Bureau of Refugee Programs provides for the movement, reception, assessment, and placement of refugees and, with the help of voluntary agencies, operates refugee camps. The ORR helps refugees achieve economic self-sufficiency through employment programs, cash assistance, food stamps, and other benefits.

refugees, economic or political An important distinction to those seeking to enter and stay in the United States. Political refugees (those who are in grave danger from their own governments because of political ideology or action) are granted entry fairly readily. Those identified by the *Bureau of Citizenship and Immigration Services* as economic refugees (those seeking entry because they want to end their impoverishment or to have access to financial opportunities) must go through a much longer and more rigorous process.

regional planning The process, usually sponsored by a group of local or adjacent state governments, by which goals for a geographic area are specified and the means and timetables for achieving them are delineated.

Register of Clinical Social Workers, NASW A publication and online database listing more than 7,000 professionals who are at the level of *Qualified Clinical Social Worker* or *Diplomate in Clinical Social Work*. The *Register* describes each worker's qualifications, specialties, preferred methods of treatment, geographic location of practice, address, telephone number, and other information to facilitate referrals and collaborations. To be listed, clinical social workers must be verified as meeting national standards for education and experience established by the NASW *Competence Certification Commission*. The *Register* may be purchased through NASW Press as a book or CD-ROM and is reissued about every three years.

registered nurse (RN) A *professional* who practices the science of providing continuous care for people who are ill and facilitates the health and well-being of individuals, groups, and communities. Many nurses become specialists, working with psychiatric patients, newborn infants, and maternity patients; specializing in emergency room care; or providing skilled assistance to surgeons. See also *practical nurse (PN)* and *nurse practitioner.*

registration of social workers An organization's or government's listing (or registry) of people who identify themselves or are identified as *social workers*. This is a form of *quality assurance* and, sometimes, public regulation that has a minimal degree of regulatory power (compared to *licensing* and *certification*). The organization usually specifies some qualification criteria to permit a worker to be included in the registration. For example, in the *NASW Register of Clinical Social Workers*, the applicant for registration must pay a fee, have a master's or doctoral degree from an accredited school of social work, have two years or 1,500 hours of post-master's professionally supervised *clinical social work* practice, and be a member of the *Academy of Certified Social Workers (ACSW)* or be licensed or certified in a state that requires an examination.

regression Behaviors and thought patterns that indicate a return to earlier or more primitive levels of development. This phenomenon is often seen in people who are exposed to severe stress, trauma, or conflicts that go unresolved.

regression analysis In *social research,* a statistical technique for assessing the contribution of one or more independent variables in predicting the outcome of a *dependent variable.* This is also referred to as multiple regression analysis. See also *independent variable.*

regressive social welfare National policies in which the benefits of public assistance are transferred from poor to more affluent people. For example, a policy might be to compel public assistance beneficiaries to work on farm harvests at low wages, thus subsidizing the consumer of the farm products by keeping these prices down.

regressive tax A government's revenue-collecting system in which less affluent people pay taxes on an equal or higher percentage of their taxable incomes than do more affluent people. For example, one whose taxable income is $20,000 might pay 20 percent of that amount for taxes, whereas one whose taxable income is $100,000 would pay only 15 percent. See also *progressive tax.*

regulatory agency   In the U.S. government, the groups charged with oversight of a specific industry or system (such as communications, trade, and civil rights). These agencies are independent of the president and Congress, theoretically bipartisan, and have quasi-judicial and quasi-legislative powers.

Rehabilitated Offender Program   The U.S. federal government program to promote fair opportunity for federal employment of qualified applicants convicted of crimes who have completed sentencing and been declared rehabilitated. The employer makes the final decision about hiring such an applicant.

rehabilitation   Restoring to a healthy condition or useful capacity to the extent possible. Social workers usually use this term in the context of helping people who have been impaired through injury, disease, or dysfunction. This process may include physical therapy, *psychotherapy,* exercise, training, and lifestyle changes. See also *habilitation.*

Rehabilitation Act of 1973   The federal legislation (P.L. 94-112) that defines handicaps and, under the U.S. Office of Civil Rights, enforces laws that prohibit unfair treatment of individuals with disabilities. See also *Section 504.*

reinforcement   In *behavior modification,* a procedure that strengthens the tendency of a *response* to recur. If a reinforcer is arranged to follow a *behavior,* there is increased probability that the behavior will be repeated. Similarly, if performance of a response removes an aversive event, there is increased probability that the behavior will be repeated.

rejection   Refusal to grant, acknowledge, or recognize something or someone. Individuals may experience rejection when their ideas, presence, or requests are not accepted by a *relevant other.* Social workers find that some of their clients with low *self-esteem* or poor self-confidence believe they are experiencing rejection when being ignored or not being given what they want.

relabeling   A technique used by family therapists to make a family problem more amenable to treatment by defining a symptom. By considering the problem from an alternative perspective, the family members may change the way they understand the symptom or behavior and begin to respond to it in a different, often healthier way.

relapse   The recurrence of symptoms.

relational aggression   Actions to assert power or authority over others in a social circle, such as a school or neighborhood, typically by spreading rumors and gossip, being manipulative, maintaining cliques, stigmatizing, and colluding to exclude others.

relationship   In social work, the mutual emotional exchange; dynamic interaction; and affective, cognitive, and behavioral connection that exist between the social worker and the client to create the working and helping atmosphere. It is created by adhering to certain ethical behaviors, including *acceptance, confidentiality, individualization,* and *nonjudgmental* view of the client, as well as through permitting the client ultimate *self-determination, purposeful expression of feelings,* and controlled emotional involvement. The term "relationship" was first described for social workers by *Virginia Robinson* (*A Changing Psychology in Social Casework,* Chapel Hill: University of North Carolina Press, 1930).

relative confidentiality   A position held by some social workers and other professionals that, under certain circumstances, they may ethically disclose information about a client. The circumstances include putting the information in records and computers for review, but only by colleagues who are involved in the case; audio- or videotaping of sessions, but letting the tapes be reviewed by others only with client consent; providing information to law enforcement and other legal officials in accordance with relevant regulations; or when *privileged communication* has been waived by the client. See also *absolute confidentiality* and *Tarasoff.*

relative needs   The requirements that people must have to achieve an acceptable level of well-being as compared to other people's requirements. This term is often used in reference to apparent gaps between needs and services or between equity of services available to different groups of people in need. See also *normative needs, expressed needs, perceived needs,* and *LCA level.*

relative poverty   Assets and income that are so little the person or group cannot maintain a *standard of living* in accordance with the standards of the mainstream community. For example, a family living in *public housing* on *Temporary Assistance to Needy Families (TANF)* may be considered poor in relation to other U.S. citizens but not so poor in comparison with malnourished, homeless people in a *Fourth World* nation. See also *absolute poverty.*

relatives' responsibility   Laws and moral codes that compel specified members of the family to care for or pay for the care of another family member who is in need. Also called "filial responsibility," the legal requirements in this area vary widely from state to state. All states have such laws pertaining to the care of minor children. Most states have eliminated or relaxed their laws requiring a person to care for parents, siblings, or more distant relatives, although a few have recently activated or enforced them. See also *parental liability.*

release agreement   Another term for *hold-harmless agreement.*

relevant other   In *role theory,* the individual who makes the expectation that defines the role. For example, the relevant other of a wife is the husband; of a mother, the child; of a client, the social worker. This term is often incorrectly confused with *significant other.* Although it can include others who are emotionally significant, it also includes others who are generally insignificant but important in a single context (such as a grocery store cashier when one is in a checkout line).

reliability   1. In *psychosocial assessment,* the individual's degree of dependability and consistency. 2. In *social research,* the dependability and consistency of scores on a test that is repeated over time with the same group. Researchers use three types of reliability: *test–retest reliability, split-half reliability,* and *interrater reliability.*

relief   A historical term referring to money, goods, or services provided to needy people by government or private philanthropic agencies.

relief organizations   Government and *nongovernment organizations (NGOs)* that provide emergency provisions and long-term developmental support for individuals and communities in need because of war, famine, natural and environmental disaster, civil crisis, and economic declines. International and national governments provide support through publicly supported aid programs. NGOs, funded by individuals, philanthropies, and fundraising drives, include the *Cooperative for American Relief Everywhere (CARE),* the International *Red Cross, OXFAM, Americares Foundation,*

and Humanity International. See also *sectarian relief organizations.*

religious right   The movement in many societies that combines conservative ideologies (small nonintrusive government, autonomy of the individual, and free-market economics) with the views of many fundamentalist religious organizations (antiabortion, traditional family hierarchies, intolerance of homosexuality, tougher responses to crime, permitting of organized prayer in schools and commencements, and opposition to separations between church and state).

relinquishment adoption   *Adoption* in which a parent's rights to the child are voluntarily or involuntarily severed. This process is also known as "agency adoption."

relocation camps   Temporary living facilities for groups of people who are compelled to or choose to move. Such camps usually are established by governments, with the assistance of private organizations and volunteers, to help people become re-established in a new area. These people often are displaced from their previous homes by war, famine, natural disaster, or political and economic conditions. Some are involuntarily held in such facilities because they are considered too dangerous to be assimilated into the new country. See also *internment* and *sociocultural dislocation.*

remarried family   See *reconstituted family.*

remedial goals model   In *social group work* the objective of bringing about change within individual members who experience problems. Also known as the "treatment goals model," the group goal in this case is to help each member achieve more effective social functioning and to help at-risk members prevent problems. See also *reciprocal goals model* and *social goals model.*

remediation   The elimination or reduction of an existing problem or its effects.

reminiscence therapy   A treatment procedure used primarily for older people, especially in *existential social work* and *logotherapy,* in which the client remembers and describes life events to the professional and sometimes to others in a group setting. Presenting this material enables the client to achieve greater insight and recognize the meaningfulness of life.

remission   Cessation or abatement of the symptoms of a physical or mental disease.

remote memory   Very long-term memory.

renal disease   Malfunction of the kidneys.

renewable resource   A natural resource that is constantly replenished so that its distribution, if administered properly, does not result ultimately in depletion. Forests, agricultural products, fisheries, and hydroelectricity are examples. See also *sustainable development.*

rent control   A government's regulation of the amount of money tenants are required to pay landlords and the conditions under which evictions may occur, and the general oversight of relationships between landlords and tenants.

rent strike   A strategy, often used in *community organization,* in which tenants withhold rent payments to pressure their landlords into improving the conditions of their housing.

rental vouchers   A housing subsidy program in which eligible poor families find their own dwelling units and pay the negotiated rent, some or all of which is covered by a monthly assistance grant. In the United States, the rental voucher program, administered by HUD, is an alternative to public housing and permits recipients more flexibility to pursue job and living opportunities without relinquishing places to live. See also *home purchase vouchers.*

Renticare   A proposal within President Lyndon B. Johnson's *Great Society* program to subsidize rent payments to poor people. The program was never funded but, later, elements of the program were incorporated into the *rental vouchers* part of the *Section 8 Housing* program.

renunciation   The legal or official act of giving up a right.

reparation   1. Compensation by a country or political entity defeated in war for the damages caused. 2. The legal procedure whereby money, property, or services are given by one person to another for damages in a crime or civil action (for example, *restitution*).

reparations movement   Organized legal and public relations efforts to compel governments and corporations to award monetary compensation and other benefits to those people, or their descendents, whose labors and assets had been exploited for the financial benefit of others. The slavery reparation movement, whose leaders seek actual and punitive damages from those governments that maintained legal slavery (in the United States for 244 years), would distribute the awards directly to individual descendents of slaves or to the community of slave descendents for general social, educational, and economic programs.

reparative therapy   A form of psychosocial intervention that attempts to change lesbians, gay men, or those with *gender identity disorder* into people of heterosexual orientations. Such interventions emphasize behavior modification, counseling, and education and espouse goals of celibacy or heterosexual marriage. Opponents of such interventions claim that the method is a "treatment in search of a disease," uses "brainwashing" and guilt-based coercion, and is ineffective and possibly harmful.

repatriation   The act of voluntarily returning or being sent back to one's country of birth or citizenship. This is the preferred outcome in many *refugee* situations because the person returns to a familiar *culture* and *social networks.*

Repatriation Program   A U.S. program to provide temporary assistance to U.S. citizens who need to return from a foreign country, because of illness, impoverishment, or threatening situations, but lack needed resources. The program is administered by the Department of Health and Human Services (HHS) in cooperation with the U.S. State Department.

repetitive checking behaviors   A pattern of self-reassurance activity in which one frequently returns to a former setting to be sure all is well. The behavior is considered a symptom of *anxiety* or *obsessive–compulsive disorder* when it is particularly time-consuming or interferes with *activities of daily living (ADL).*

repetitive motion disorder (RMD)   Bone and muscle conditions that result from making the same movements repeatedly, usually in the course of work, intense recreation, or other activities. Most often affected are the hands and arms, but it can occur all over the body. At-risk patients include those who work in factories, type, sew, or play musical instruments. The condition is also known as repetitive stress injury. See also *carpal tunnel syndrome, tendonitis, aburaitis,* and *ergonomics.*

replacement cost   The amount of money, work, or services that must be provided to maintain the status quo if and when some loss occurs. In management and budgeting, it is often less important to calculate the current value of something that has been lost than to calculate the amount needed to get back its equivalent.

replication   In *research,* the process of duplicating an experiment—in which the same *hypothesis,* variables, sampling procedure, testing instruments, and techniques for analysis are used—with a different *sample* of the same *population.*

Report on the World Social Situation   A *United Nations* publication, issued every four years since 1952, that documents the status of social welfare, health, and environmental programs in U.N. nations and progress toward solving specific social problems.

repossession   The legal process of seizing a debtor's property and holding it or selling it to recover the funds owed. To repossess, the creditor files a complaint with the legal authorities, and fair hearings and opportunities are given to the debtor to make *restitution* and recover the property. Otherwise, the creditor may proceed with a sale after informing the debtor and potential buyers about the sale.

representativeness   A concept in *social research* pertaining to the extent to which the information gathered is unbiased and typical of the entity from which the information was extracted.

repression   A *defense mechanism,* derived from *psychodynamic* theory, in which the individual unconsciously pushes out of the consciousness certain memories, ideas, or desires that are unacceptable or cause a high level of anxiety. Once these ideas or desires are contained in the *unconscious,* they cannot be recalled directly. However, they may emerge in one's behavior in disguised forms, and their effects are sometimes seen in slips of the tongue (*parapraxis*) or dreams. Because repression is, by definition, a mechanism of the unconscious, it should not be confused with the *conscious* act of *suppression.*

reproductive technology   Medically supervised systems of artificially facilitating a fetus's *conception* and development through to birth. These technologies include *artificial insemination, surrogacy, in vitro fertilization,* and embryo freezing.

request for proposal (RFP)   A statement issued by a federal, state, or local agency; private corporation; or philanthropic or other organization seeking detailed bids from consultants, educational centers, and vendors to meet some need or service. RFPs usually include a statement of the technical requirements and specifications of the service or product needed, time frames, cost estimates, and other criteria. After a specified time, the agency selects the most suitable proposal from all those submitted.

rescission   Cancellation of the funds and budget authorizations that had previously been allocated.

research   Systematic procedures used in seeking facts or principles.

resettlement   The act of moving and establishing a new, permanent residence in another area.

residency laws   Statutes that specify what qualifications must be fulfilled before an individual can be considered eligible for the privileges and obligations of that jurisdiction. For example, a person must live in a state for a specified time before becoming eligible to receive lower public college tuition rates or being able to obtain a divorce in that state.

residential care facilities   Structures that house people who are without homes or who, for a variety of reasons, cannot stay in their homes. These facilities include boarding schools, *shelters* for abused women, *orphanages,* homes for juvenile delinquents, and centers where *residential treatment* occurs.

residential treatment   Therapeutic intervention processes for people who cannot or do not function satisfactorily in their own homes. Such treatment typically occurs in certain environments such as private schools, medical centers, penal institutions, and *shelters.* It usually includes a variety of professionally led assistance, such as individual or group psychotherapy, formal schooling, social skills training, recreation, and fulfillment of the needs usually met in one's home.

residual phase The stage often found in the *progression* of various mental illnesses when the symptoms have ceased or diminished considerably.

residual schizophrenia One of the five subtypes of *schizophrenia* (also including *paranoid, disorganized, catatonic,* and *undifferentiated*), in which there has been at least one episode of schizophrenia but the current clinical picture is without prominent psychotic symptoms. There is an absence of prominent delusions, hallucinations, and disorganized or catatonic behaviors found in the other subtypes, but the other major symptoms of schizophrenia such as thought disorder and flat or inappropriate affect are present. If these symptoms have occurred for less than six months, the diagnosis would be *schizophreniform disorder.*

residual versus institutional model The dichotomy described by H. L. Wilensky and C. N. Lebeaux (*Industrial Society and Social Welfare,* New York: Free Press, 1958) involving two concepts of *social welfare.* The residual model views social welfare as being primarily a *safety net* function in which programs are temporary substitutes for the failures of individuals and institutions. The institutional model views social welfare as having a "mainline" function (equal to the other social institutions, such as family, religion, economics, and politics) in which programs are permanent and provide for the overall security and emotional support of humans.

residual welfare provision The idea that the public should provide *social services* and *public assistance* only to those people who, because of unusual circumstances, are unable to receive needed help through the family or the normal social structure and marketplace. See also *safety net.*

resiliency The human capacity (individual, group, and/or community) to deal with crises, stressors, and normal experiences in an emotionally and physically healthy way; an effective coping style. For example, a successfully resilient child might deal with parental neglect and a hostile environment by cultivating healthy relationships with other relatives or friends, whereas one who is not resilient might withdraw and become isolated and lonely. Resiliency is a factor that social workers consider in assessing their clients and in developing prognoses and treatment plans.

resistance 1. *Avoidance* behavior used by a client to defend against the influences of the social worker. 2. In *psychoanalytic theory,* the mental process of preventing one's *unconscious* thoughts from being brought into the consciousness. Resistance may be *conscious* or unconscious, and the client uses it for protection against self-realization. It is an inevitable facet of therapy.

resistant attachment A form of *insecure attachment* seen in children who seem angry at their *caregivers* after any separation but obstruct the caregivers' efforts to provide reassurance and comfort. See also *attachment, secure attachment,* and *avoidant attachment.*

resocialization Preparing someone to enter and live in a *culture* and environment that is or has become unfamiliar because of crises, trauma, or life-stage transition. For example, an immigrant becomes resocialized into a new culture partly by learning the new language, or a recently divorced woman re-enters the job market after familiarizing herself with the expectations of a potential employer.

resocialization group A type of *group therapy* or *self-help group* that helps people adapt to unfamiliar roles and statuses. Such groups exist for people like *displaced homemakers,* recently widowed or divorced people, people who become physically disabled, and adults who must care for their elderly parents.

resolution 1. A formal statement made by the members of an organization, usually after a vote, to express their sentiments, goals, or intentions to the public or to officeholders. 2. The outcome or conclusion of an event, as in the resolution of a client's problem.

resource allocation The distribution of goods and services based on systematic decision making and predetermined criteria.

resource-based relative value scales (RBRVS) U.S. national system of health care reimbursement based on the provider's time, skill, training, effort, and overhead in providing the service. Some medical insurance and health care financing organizations, including *Medicare,* changed their reimbursement structures in 1996 from the former "usual, customary, and reasonable" criteria to the

RBRVS system. The system gives comparatively higher values to time-consuming (but formerly less lucrative) services such as taking thorough medical histories and counseling patients. RBRVS are also known as "revenue-based relative value scales."

resource mobilization   In social agency administration, the process of bringing together and making available the organization's assets, including existing funds, funds to be raised from the constituency and other sources, information base, personnel and volunteers, and the knowledge and talents of board members and others who can be called on for assistance. This process depends on the organization's making clear its needs and mission, identifying the population to be served, and communicating this information to the public.

resource systems   The biopsychosocial and environmental sources of the material, emotional, and spiritual needs required for a person to survive, to realize aspirations, and to cope with life tasks. The three types of resource systems are (1) the informal type (family, friends, and neighbors), (2) the formal type (membership organizations), and (3) the societal type (social security programs and educational and health care systems). A basic purpose of social work practice is to enhance the functioning of these resource systems and their linkages with people. See also *networking*.

resources   Any existing services or commodities that can be called on to help take care of a need. A primary skill of social workers is their ability to know of and use the existing community resources that can help their clients. Resources used by social workers typically include other social agencies, government programs, other professional or volunteer personnel, self-help groups, natural helpers, and individuals in the community who possess the qualities and motivations that can help the client.

respiratory distress syndrome (RDS)   A common, sometimes fatal, disease mostly affecting newborns (especially premature infants). Treatment includes concentrations of oxygen; intravenous fluids; and, sometimes, mechanical breathing apparatus to keep the lungs from collapsing.

respite care   The temporary assumption of responsibilities of a person who provides for the *home care* of another. For example, the parents of an adult child with mental retardation are relieved every few weeks by someone who comes to their home to help, or the child goes to a facility for a few days. The goal is to give the caregiver a break from the responsibility so that tensions are minimized, the caregiver can have some other interests or take care of personal crises, and the client can stay out of institutional care.

respondeat superior doctrine   The legal *liability* of employers or supervisors for the job-related actions of the employees. The term is Latin for "let the superior answer" and has the effect of requiring supervisors to monitor their workers. Social work supervisors have been held liable, along with their supervisees, for practices found to be damaging to clients.

respondent behavior   *Behavior* that is elicited by specific stimuli and subject to the principles of *respondent conditioning*.

respondent conditioning   The procedure in *behavior modification* in which a *stimulus* (such as food) that automatically results in a *response* (such as salivation) is presented repeatedly along with a neutral stimulus (such as a ringing bell) to elicit essentially the same response from the previously neutral stimulus. This term is a synonym for *classical conditioning* (or Pavlovian conditioning).

response   A *behavior*. Usually, the term is used to indicate a discrete form of behavior such as a knee jerk, salivation, or the pressing of a key, but the term also applies to broadly defined behaviors such as bringing home flowers for one's spouse or expressing anger to the social worker after being turned down in a request for assistance.

response prevention   A procedure commonly used in *behavior therapy* to eliminate a *maladaptive* behavior by distraction, persuasion, or redirection of activity whenever the behavior is anticipated. Often, the procedure requires hospitalization or a controlled environment and participation by family members to be effective.

response repertoire   The accumulation of knowledge and skills that a person has learned and can perform effectively, comfortably, and without trial-and-error behavior.

restitution   The restoration of property or rights that had previously been taken away. People who have committed theft or property destruction are sometimes compelled to provide restitution to those they victimized. See also *victim compensation* and *community-based corrections.*

restitution center A small residential facility in which people convicted of a felony live while engaged in community service work or other employment. The residents' incomes are budgeted and allocated in such a way that living expenses are met and remaining funds are withheld to help compensate the victims.

restraining order A temporary decree, made by a judge or other legal authority without a prior hearing, prohibiting an individual or organization from performing some action pending the outcome of a trial or hearing. Law authorities refer to this as a "T.R.O." (temporary restraining order). See also *injunction.*

restricted affect Diminished variability and intensity with which emotions are expressed.

restricted funds Monetary or other gifts or grants and the income generated by them, which may be expended only for purposes specified by the donor or grantor.

retardation 1. The slowing of an individual's physical or mental development or social progress. 2. A significantly lower-than-average capacity for intellectual functioning (*mental retardation*) or a slowing of physical and emotional reactions (*psychomotor* retardation).

Retired and Senior Volunteer Program (RSVP) A *Senior Corps* program of the *Corporation for National and Community Service* that uses the talents and knowledge of older and retired people by placing volunteers in a variety of settings such as hospitals, schools, and senior citizens' centers, often on a short-term basis. Their Web site address is http://www.seniorcorps.gov/rsvp. See also *Senior Companion Program* and *Foster Grandparents.*

retrenchment Cutting back, as in reducing an agency's expenditures or services to a previous and reduced level. See also *cutback strategies.*

retribution The dispensing of *punishment* for wrongdoing. The term can also refer to future rewards for good works.

retroactive seniority A policy mandated in *Title VII* of the *Civil Rights Act of 1964* in which

employees who prove they have been discriminated against may be granted seniority from the date of the discrimination.

retrograde amnesia The inability to recall experiences that have occurred only before a certain time, usually before some physical injury or psychic stress. See also *amnesia.*

retrospective data Information collected through indirect means, such as rekindling subjects' memories, reviewing records, comparing the study findings from previous eras with contemporary results, and re-evaluating current information from different perspectives.

retrospective utilization reviews A *managed care* procedure to determine whether a completed medical treatment had been necessary and effective. Reimbursement for the service would be withheld if the review concluded that the treatment had not been necessary or effective. Usually, this was done by reviewing the professional's records and sometimes by interviewing the professional and the patient. Retrospective utilization reviews were considered unfair if performed solely after the treatment; thus, these reviews are now more commonly used in conjunction with *prospective utilization reviews* and *concurrent utilization reviews.*

Rett's disorder One of the *pervasive developmental disorders* in which, following a few months of normal development and functioning after birth, the child (usually female) declines. There is deceleration of head growth, loss of previously acquired motor skills, and severely impaired language development. The disorder begins before age four, and in most cases recovery is limited. See also *autistic disorder.*

reunification service Interventions in *foster care* to help children and their *birth parents* develop mutual relationships to facilitate being able to live together again. After the problems that led to the separations are resolved or improved, the social workers often act as go-betweens to restore lines of communication. Then they may act as facilitators of face-to-face communication and finally as monitors and consultants in follow-up after the reunion has taken place.

revenue sharing The government process of dividing a proportion of its income, which comes from taxes, and contributing those funds to another level or sector of government that provides needed services to people. The State and Local Fiscal Assistance Act of 1972 (P.L. 92-512) used revenue sharing to provide states and localities with specified portions of federal income tax collections for certain local health, education, welfare, and criminal justice programs. See also *apportioned tax.*

reverse annuity mortgages (RAMs) A procedure to allow older homeowners to increase their incomes while staying in their homes until death; they sell their homes and use the money to create a lifetime annuity payment. Upon death the investor takes possession of the home. See also *home equity conversion plans.*

reverse brainstorming A procedure used especially by *task groups* in which the negative consequences of proposed actions are quickly discussed. Members of the group are asked "what could go wrong" with the ideas presented in brainstorming sessions. These are listed and later considered, along with ideas for overcoming the obstacles.

"reverse discrimination" The term sometimes used to describe the preferential treatment of a previously victimized *minority* group or person to the disadvantage of the majority. Generally, the practice has been used to withhold opportunities from white people and men to give more opportunities to people of color and women. See also *affirmative action.*

reverse mortgage A financial arrangement that permits older homeowners to obtain money from their house's equity. It is essentially a loan against the value of the house that is not repayable until the homeowner moves or dies. The total loan must be paid back when the last surviving borrower dies, sells the home, or permanently moves away. Reverse mortgages are usually available from state or local governments or from the private sector (banks and mortgage companies) and may be made for purposes such as home repairs, payment of taxes, or needed income. They may be federally insured (home equity conversion mortgages) or, if in the private sector, insured through commercial arrangements.

revolution A sweeping change in the established order of things, usually after those who preferred the status quo are forced to relinquish their authority to those who sought change. Major types of revolution include political (in which a civil war

or protest movement results in a new government structure), industrial (in which new technologies and inventions change the way economic institutions are administered), and cultural (in which changes occur in *values, norms, mores,* and tastes).

revolving credit system A capital acquisition system funded through the savings of individuals and groups from the same ethnic or kinship group and dispersed to those in the group for use in starting businesses, getting an education, or overcoming emergencies. Once the borrower has started the business or used the funds in the way specified, the money is repaid to the system for use by another member of the group for a similar purpose. This system has been most effective in those close-knit groups in which failure to reimburse would be unthinkable.

Reynolds, Bertha Capen (1885–1978) A social work educator, author, and advocate for the rights of workers. She sought to establish labor unions for social workers and others. An avowed Marxist, she was fired from her position in social work education and eventually worked for labor unions. The *Bertha Capen Reynolds Society (BCRS),* for progressive social workers, was established in her name.

rheumatic fever An *infectious disease* in which symptoms often include inflammation of the joints, fever, nosebleeds, and skin rash. In its more serious forms, there is inflammation of the heart valves, which may become scarred and deformed (rheumatic heart disease).

rheumatoid arthritis A form of *arthritis* that affects the joints and sometimes the lungs, nervous system, and other parts of the body. This disorder can affect young as well as older people and is often extremely painful.

Ribicoff children People younger than 21 who meet the criteria of poverty but who are not considered dependent children. More commonly referred to as *"street kids,"* such children can be considered *categorically needy* and thus eligible for some *Medicaid, Supplemental Security Income (SSI), Temporary Assistance to Needy Families (TANF),* or other benefits. The name refers to Senator Abraham Ribicoff, who initiated legislation that made these young people eligible.

Richmond, Mary E. (1861–1928) Considered one of the principal founders of professional social work. Richmond led the *Charity Organization Societies (COSs)* movement to develop schools to train social caseworkers. She taught volunteers and paid employees in various settings and developed some of the first teaching programs for social work. Her books were among the first to be used in training for social work. They included *Friendly Visiting Among the Poor* (1899), *Social Diagnosis* (1917), and *What Is Social Case Work?* (1922).

rickets   A bone disease caused by vitamin D deficiency. In children, the disease's symptoms include softening of the bones, enlargement of the cartilage, bowleggedness, and deformities in the chest and pelvis. With the addition of vitamin D to milk and the use of vitamin supplements, prevention of rickets has been effective in the United States.

"right-brain thinker"   A term applied to people who supposedly rely more on the right hemisphere of their brains—the apparent origins of emotions, creativity, and imagination—as opposed to the *"left-brain thinker,"* who supposedly depends more on logic, mathematical rigor, and linear thinking.

right of self-determination   The ability to decide one's own actions, goals, lifestyles, and ideologies, as long as these decisions do not harm others. Invariably, in human society this is a limited right, mitigated by one's age, gender, culture, opportunities, and personality.

right to die   Opposition to artificial life support and extreme treatment measures to prolong the life of one who is incurably ill. See also *death with dignity.*

right-to-life movement   A loosely coordinated body of groups, institutions, and individuals working to change laws and norms that permit and facilitate *abortion.* The movement is also referred to as the *"prolife movement."* Supporters of this movement emphasize the rights of the unborn embryo/fetus and encourage *adoption* and other alternatives to abortion for unwanted pregnancies. Religious and philosophical beliefs about the point at which human life begins are important in this movement. The movement is opposed by the *prochoice movement.* See also *National Right-to-Life Committee (NRLC).*

right to refuse treatment   The legal principle, upheld in numerous court cases or contained in explicit statutes in several states, that an individual may not be compelled to undergo any form of *treatment,* including social work intervention, unless there is a life-threatening emergency or the person exhibits seriously destructive behavior. This principle has been applied to people who are involuntarily committed to mental hospitals, prisons, and other institutions. It has also influenced the way social work services are integrated with *income maintenance* programs in *public assistance* programs. Thus, a public assistance recipient is no longer compelled to receive counseling to obtain financial aid.

right to treatment   The legal principle, established in the *Wyatt v. Stickney* decision, that an individual who is confined in an institution has the right to receive the *treatment* necessary to offer a reasonable chance for improvement so that the person can function independently and be released from that institution. This right has led many facilities that lack the resources for individual treatment to discharge their clients. See also *deinstitutionalization.*

right-to-work laws   Statutes in various jurisdictions that make it illegal for membership in a *labor union* to be a condition of *employment.*

"right wing"   A slang expression for a conservative sociopolitical orientation.

rights   1. The obligations of society to each of its members. 2. That which is legally or morally due to an individual by just claim. These are more specifically identified as *civil rights, equal rights,* and *human rights.*

rigidity   Inflexibility of attitude, behavior, movement, and *adaptive capacity.* One manifestation of rigidity is to persist in a behavior or idea that was appropriate in one circumstance or time frame even when it is inappropriate in another.

Riis, Jacob (1848–1914)   A writer and social reformer whose descriptions of slum conditions awakened America to the need for economic reforms and better assistance for poor people. His most influential book, *How the Other Half Lives* (1890), led to widespread support for the *Charity Organization Societies (COSs)* movement, which in turn helped develop social work as a profession.

riot   A collective violent uprising in which property and sometimes people are the target of mob attack.

Ripple, Lillian (1911–1993) A pioneer in social work research and principal author of *Motivation, Capacity, and Opportunity,* one of the profession's first systematic attempts to determine how clients succeed. A longtime social work professor at the University of Chicago and a leader of the *Council on Social Work Education (CSWE),* she began her career as a volunteer at *Hull-House* and as a juvenile court caseworker.

risk pool All the individuals and families an insurance company is obligated to cover against the financial consequences of a specified problem. In the climate of competition among insurance companies, the tendency is to make these pools highly restrictive, limited only to the youngest, most healthy people. This eliminates coverage for those most likely in need and ultimately places the financial burden on the general taxpayer population. When risk pools are larger and more inclusive, the cost burden for those at greater risk is reduced, but it is usually increased for those less at risk.

rite of passage A formal or informal activity, ceremony, or behavior that a group uses to recognize the movement of one of its members into another *role* or set of expectations. Examples include graduation ceremonies, bar mitzvahs, retirement parties, and mothers helping their daughters apply makeup for the first time. See also *puberty rites.*

road rage Aggressive, hostile, and violent behavior sometimes displayed by automobile drivers, often during periods of heavy traffic congestion or right-of-way disputes.

robbery The *crime* of forcible stealing. Robbery differs from theft in that it occurs through direct *violence* or intimidation.

Robinson, Virginia (1883–1977) A social work theoretician and educator who wrote influential textbooks on casework, supervision, and training. With her longtime partner *Jessie Taft,* she developed the *functional school in social work.*

Robison, Sophie Moses (1888–1969) A social work researcher and activist whose studies in *juvenile delinquency* led to redefinitions about how the problems can be addressed. Her works became models for social work research.

Roe v. Wade The 1973 decision by the U.S. Supreme Court that state laws forbidding *abortion* were unconstitutional under specified circumstances. The Court held that, in the first *trimester,* abortion must be left to medical judgment. In the second trimester, the state may, if it chooses, regulate abortion to protect maternal health but may not prohibit abortion. In the third trimester, the state may regulate or prohibit abortion except when necessary to preserve the mother's life. The decision has been the source of considerable controversy, and there have been numerous challenges in the courts. *Political action* in support of the decision is led by the *prochoice movement,* and the opposition is led by the *right-to-life movement.*

role 1. A culturally determined pattern of *behavior* that is prescribed for an individual who occupies a specific *status.* 2. A social *norm* that is attached to a given social position that dictates reciprocal action. For example, a person who occupies the status of social worker is expected by others—that is, clients, supervisors, the profession, the general public, and so on—to behave in the manner generally prescribed for all social workers.

role ambiguity A situation in which the expectations of a *role* are unclear or diffuse either to the person enacting it or to the *relevant other.* For example, a new client goes to a social worker but is not sure what social workers do to help and thus does not know quite what to expect from the meeting.

role boundary The dividing line that distinguishes one's *role* from all other roles. For example, there are specific and normative expectations of one who occupies the status of social worker, and the worker who meets those expectations but does not go beyond them is behaving within the boundary. Workers who develop *dual relationships* with clients go beyond the professional boundary. Role boundaries are most commonly violated in situations of *role ambiguity,* often resulting in problems of *role conflict* or *role discomplementarity.* See also *enmeshed family.*

role complementarity See *complementarity.*

role conflict The experience of one who occupies two or more social positions that carry incompatible expectations. For example, a social worker may be expected by the client to be immediately available during times of crisis but is expected by the supervisor to see clients only according to a predetermined schedule.

role discomplementarity The condition that exists when an individual's various *roles* are inconsistent with one another or with the expectations held by a *relevant other*. For example, the client and the supervisor have certain expectations of the social worker but have not made clear what those expectations are, so they cannot be fulfilled. Social scientists identify five conditions in which role discomplementarity occurs: (1) cognitive discrepancy, which is based on a lack of knowledge of what the appropriate expectations are (for example, the social worker or client does not know what the other expects and thus cannot fulfill those expectations); (2) status discrepancy, in which one person expects another to fulfill expectations that are inappropriate to that person's social position (for example, the client expects the social worker to provide medical information); (3) allocative discrepancy, in which one person does not choose to accept responsibility for fulfilling the other's expectations even though he or she is capable of doing so (for example, the client wants the social worker to treat the whole family, and the worker wants to work only with the individual); (4) discrepancy of value orientations, in which those who have expectations of one another have incompatible values (for example, the client expects the social worker to help her end her marriage, and the worker expects to help save the marriage); and (5) absence of instrumental means, in which the reciprocal expectations are compatible but the people lack the tools necessary to carry them out (for example, the client and social worker both want the welfare department to increase the financial supports to the family, but there is not enough money to do this).

role model One whose conduct, accomplishments, personality, or social position serves as a standard for emulation by others. The standard may be socially beneficial (for example, a basketball star who shows young people how to avoid drugs) or not (for example, a wealthy and charismatic figure who is a crime boss).

role modeling Purposeful demonstration of behaviors that one wants others to emulate. This demonstration is often done in *social group work, group psychotherapy, counseling,* and various educational programs to assist a client in learning more effective ways to achieve desirable goals.

role overload A situation in which a person is expected to behave in many different, often conflicting, ways so that it is difficult to fulfill any of the expectations satisfactorily.

role playing 1. A rehearsal of behaviors that can be useful in a subsequent situation to fulfill some expectation or achieve some goal. 2. A re-experiencing of the past as one imagines being another person (a parent, a sibling, and so on); a technique to elicit self-awareness and understanding of others. Social workers often help their clients rehearse for real situations. For example, a social worker asks a client to pretend she is going to ask her boss for a raise to make it easier for the client to actually confront her boss. Role playing is a technique developed in the 1920s by J. L. Moreno in his *psychodrama* method of therapy and is now used in various *group work, social group work,* teaching, *group therapy* systems, game analysis, and leadership training programs to help individuals test certain behaviors and receive immediate feedback about approaches to the situation.

role re-equilibration The process that takes place between two or more people to end *role conflict* or *role discomplementarity*. Usually, this is achieved by clarifying mutual expectations.

role reversal A situation in which one person changes behaviors and begins to act in a way that is expected of another person. For example, a father might begin to act childishly around his son, who in turn acts with more maturity around his father.

role strain Any form of *role conflict, role discomplementarity,* or social relationship difficulty that prohibits or limits the enacting of a *role* in a stress-free manner. This can arise from *role ambiguity,* role conflict, role discomplementarity, or lack of access to information necessary for the role.

role theory A group of concepts, based on sociocultural and anthropological investigations, that pertain to the way people are influenced in their behaviors by the variety of social positions they hold and the expectations that accompany those positions. See also the related terms used in this dictionary, including all those beginning with *role,* as well as the terms *status, norms,* and *sanctions.*

role vigor The relative degree of deviation from a role's expectations permitted by the culture. For example, more role vigor is permitted for women in large, pluralistic urban areas than in small towns.

rootwork A *culture-bound syndrome* found most commonly among Caribbean societies and people of the southern United States of European and African ancestry in which the individual is believed to be placed under a spell or hex. This results in the individual experiencing anxiety, fears, dizziness, and various somatic complaints until the "root doctor" removes the hex or root.

Rorschach test A *projective test*, designed in 1921 by Swiss psychiatrist Hermann Rorschach (1884–1922), in which clients are given a series of 10 standardized inkblots and asked to report what they see. Responses can indicate personality traits, interests, thought processes, and so forth.

Rothman, Beulah (1924–1990) One of social work's major conceptualizers and systematizers of social work with groups, who was also a prominent educator and administrator. She helped found several group work organizations, including the *Association for the Advancement of Social Work with Groups (AASWG)*, and was a founding editor of the journals *Social Work with Groups* and the *Journal of Teaching in Social Work*.

rough sleeping The condition of *homelessness* in Britain. The term applies to people who sleep in building doorways, on park benches, and in other public spaces and unsheltered environments.

roundworm diseases Parasitic diseases in which a type of worm or its eggs are ingested or enter through the skin and eventually reside in the intestine, causing serious symptoms such as cramps, malnutrition, intestinal blockage, and diarrhea. The parasites include hookworms, pinworms, and other roundworms and often are contracted by walking barefoot in contaminated earth or eating unwashed contaminated vegetables.

RU 486 Mifepristone, a drug that induces *abortion* if taken within seven weeks of conception by impeding the progesterone hormone, which is necessary for the fetus to stay implanted in the uterus. It has been available since the 1980s and is widely used in Europe and Asia. Although approved by the U.S. *Food and Drug Administration (FDA)* in September 1996, the drug is not generally available in the United States owing to the reluctance of pharmaceutical companies to produce or distribute it. The drug has been the focus of attacks by antiabortion groups because it makes abortion more easily available, cheaper, safer, and more private than currently available surgical methods.

rubber-fence concept A *metaphor* used in *family therapy* to describe how some families maintain *boundaries* between themselves and others. A boundary may seem to stretch to incorporate what is seen as positive and to contract when apparently threatened. For example, if a social worker makes suggestions to such a family, the members might appear to expand in incorporating the new ideas into the family dynamics but would later contract to their original configuration.

rubella A short-term, mild form of measles, also called German measles or three-day measles. Although rarely fatal to children or adults, this disease is particularly dangerous to the fetus of an infected pregnant woman and can result in miscarriage, deafness, or other conditions.

Rubinow, Isaac Max (1875–1936) An economist and social work educator who helped draft legislation leading to the *Social Security Act* of 1935. He helped found the *Anti-Defamation League of B'nai B'rith* and was editor of the *Jewish Social Service Quarterly*.

rugged individualism The *ideology* espoused by certain economists, politicians, and others that people should be left to their own initiative in providing for their needs. According to this view, even though difficulties might be experienced, it strengthens a person's character and capacity to cope more effectively with any other problems that might be faced in the future.

rumination disorder One of the *eating disorders* in some infants and young children, characterized by repeated regurgitation, in which the infant loses weight or fails to gain weight and may develop nutritional deficiencies. The cause of this condition is not understood, but it is not the result of gastrointestinal illness or nausea.

runaway A minor who has departed the home of his or her parents or legal guardians contrary to their wishes and who intends to remain independent of their control. A major program to help these youngsters and possibly reunite them with their parents is the *National Center for Missing and Exploited Children (NCMEC)*, which maintains a free 24-hour daily hot line at 1-800-843-5678 (or 1-800-THE-LOST).

"running a group" A metaphor commonly applied to the activity of social workers who lead groups. Usually, it is an inappropriate expression because when the group process is effective the group is not controlled or run by the leader.

Rural Development The organization within the USDA to improve the quality of life for rural Americans by helping to finance and build water and sewer systems, housing, electricity service, health clinics, and other facilities, as well as to provide technical assistance for cooperative and community empowerment programs.

rural social movement Efforts and organizations that raise the consciousness of citizens and professionals about the problems of rural areas and advocate legislation to correct rural social problems. The movement grew in the 1970s and is now active in forging coalitions with the grassroots community. Some of the rural advocacy organizations include Rural America, the Rural Social Work Caucus, and the National Association for Rural Mental Health.

rural social work Social work practice oriented to helping people who have unique problems and needs arising out of living in agricultural, nonmetropolitan, or sparsely populated areas or small towns. These people face many of the same problems and needs as do urban clients; in addition, however, they often encounter difficulties because of limited services and *resource systems,* less acceptance of any variations from the social norms prevalent in the area, and fewer educational and economic opportunities.

rural social workers Professional social workers whose predominant clientele and practice activities are in sparsely populated regions. The most successful workers in these settings are well-trained, creative professionals who can work in relative isolation with limited additional resources. The major professional association for this group is the Rural Social Work Caucus. Their Web site address is http://www.uncp.edu/sw/rural

ruralite A person who resides in a nonmetropolitan area, often the client of *rural social work.*

Russell Sage Foundation A philanthropic organization, founded in 1907 by *Margaret Slocum Sage* (1816–1918), the widow of entrepreneur Russell Sage, for the improvement of social and living conditions in the United States. The foundation funded many programs and research projects that helped to make social work a profession.

Ryan White CARE Act The federal legislation (P.L. 101-381), named for a young boy who died of AIDS, that provides federal funds to cities and states for planning, implementing, and evaluating programs to prevent transmission of *human immunodeficiency virus (HIV)* and to improve the quality and availability of health care social services for people affected by HIV and *acquired immune deficiency syndrome (AIDS).* The formal title of the act is the Ryan White Comprehensive AIDS Resources Emergency (CARE) Act, and it is now administered by HHS's *Health Resources and Services Administration.*

S-Night A night designated by U.S. Census Bureau enumerators to count those people living on the streets; in homeless shelters, missions, and emergency housing facilities; and at predetermined street locations. The "S" refers to street/shelter.

sabbatical A period of paid leave, usually granted to some academics or other professionals, to achieve rejuvenation, conduct research, or experience new lifestyles. Qualified professors with *tenure* in many universities may be granted one year of leave after each seven years of service.

sabotage Purposefully causing damage to institutions, manufacturing facilities, or social procedures to achieve a sociopolitical objective. See also *insurgency* and *ecotage*.

sadistic Deriving pleasure from inflicting pain on or causing pain to others.

sadistic personality disorder A type of *personality disorder* in which a person frequently seeks opportunities to impose mental or physical cruelty on one or more other persons.

sadomasochism The presence, within an individual or between couples, of cruel, punishing behavior and behavior that is self-destructive. For example, in a sadomasochistic relationship, one person would persist in cruel behavior to the other, and the other would remain in the relationship and encourage more of the cruelty. See also *masochism, masochistic personality disorder,* and *folie à deux.*

Safe Haven A U.S. program that provides temporary refuge to people who have fled their home nations to escape persecution or other hardships until they can return safely or find permanent relief elsewhere.

"safe sex" Precautionary sexual practices that attempt to minimize the risk of sexually transmitted diseases or unwanted pregnancy. This usually means engaging in sex without penetration or using condoms and/or vaginal dams and avoiding any activity that may exchange bodily substances (blood, saliva, sperm, vaginal secretions,

and fecal matter). Because *sexually transmitted diseases,* such as *AIDS, syphilis, chlamydia,* and *gonorrhea,* are spread by such exchanges, sex that precludes or minimizes this is relatively safer though not guaranteed.

safety net The idea that if some social services programs are eliminated through economic cutbacks, then benefits and programs of last resort will remain for individuals or families who cannot find needed resources on their own. See also *residual welfare provision.*

Sage, Margaret Slocum (1816–1918) Philanthropist and creator of the *Russell Sage Foundation* to improve social and living conditions in the United States. As the widow of Russell Sage, she helped fund the early organizations, conferences, and publications that became the knowledge base of the new field of social work.

Salomon, Alice (1872–1948) One of the principal founders of professional social work in Germany and the creator of German social work education. As a young social reformer and feminist leader in 1893, she helped establish the Girls' and Women's Groups for Social Aid Work, and in 1899 she cofounded the first one-year course in vocational welfare training, which in 1908 became a two-year training program. She was a leader in the development of social work as a profession for women and for men before, during, and after World War I. She led in efforts to restore the nation after the war and fought the Nazi movement until being forced to emigrate in 1937. A leading German school of social work in Berlin bears her name.

Salvation Army An international religious service organization involved in philanthropic and evangelical work. Founded in England in 1878 by William Booth, it is patterned after military structures, including uniforms and military rank, because its goal is to wage war against evil and against human suffering. With programs in nearly 100 nations, it operates hospitals, community centers, social work agencies, alcohol and drug rehabilitation centers, emergency care facilities, disaster relief services, and the well-known *soup kitchen.* Their Web site address is http://www.salvationarmyusa.org

same-sex marriage *Marriage* between two men or two women. Advocates of same-sex marriage say it should be legally and publicly sanctioned and that all the benefits and obligations that occur in men–women marriages should exist for these marriages as well (such as widow's benefits, bereavement leave, and no-fault divorce and property settlements). See also *Defense of Marriage Act.*

sample In research, a part of a *universe* from which a representative selection is made. Researchers want to use the largest sample possible because the larger the sample, the smaller the likelihood of error or deviation from the universe or *population.* Larger samples give the principle of randomness a better chance to work. See also *random sample* and *stratified sample.*

sampling error Generalizing about the characteristics of a population from a *sample* that is not totally representative.

san wu A Chinese term (literally, three "no"s), usually referring to elderly people in China who have no family, no work ability, and no dependable sources of income. Those so designated are the primary recipients of public assistance and are often served in *linglao lou* houses.

sanction 1. Official permission to carry out a plan granted by the established authority. 2. A provision in law or organization bylaws to penalize an individual for noncompliance. For example, social workers who are found to have violated their professional *code of ethics* may be subject to sanctions in the form of suspension from the organization or of the license to practice. See also *informal sanction.*

sanctuary A place of refuge or protection.

Sanders, Daniel S. (1928–1989) Social work educator and dean at the University of Hawaii who advanced knowledge about international social work and helped organize and lead international organizations, including the *Inter-University Consortium for International Social Development.*

sandwich generation Men and especially women in their middle years who have the major caregiving responsibilities for their children and parents. This generation is growing dramatically because of the prolonged life spans of older people who tend to need increasing care and because of the trend among younger people to stay with their parents longer.

sangue dormido A *culture-bound syndrome* most commonly found in people of Portuguese ancestry in which the individual experiences pain, convulsions, *tremor, stroke,* blindness, heart attack, infection, and miscarriage. The term means "sleeping blood."

Sanitary Commission, U.S. The health and welfare agency set up during the Civil War to manage the welfare of Union soldiers and their families. Managed almost entirely by volunteer women, the agency established and maintained hospitals, supplied food, and raised money for destitute family members.

Sansei generation Third-generation Americans of Japanese ancestry, born primarily after World War II—the offspring of the *Nisei generation.* Members of the Sansei generation are integrated into American society and tend to adopt cultural values of mainstream America more than those of their Japanese ancestors. The children of the Sansei are known as the Yonsei generation.

Sarabhais, Anusyabehn (1885–1972) A social worker in India who helped Ghandi organize labor strikes and develop trade unions and social welfare advocacy. She helped establish schools of social work and the social work profession in India.

sarcoma One of the four major types of *cancer* (including *carcinoma, leukemia,* and *lymphoma*), characterized by spread of the disease into the bones, fat, or cartilage.

Satir, Virginia (1916–1988) A major theoretician and educator in *family therapy* who developed many of the innovative communications concepts of the field. She wrote the highly influential books *Conjoint Family Therapy* (Palo Alto, CA: Science and Behavior Books, 1964) and *Peoplemaking* (Palo Alto, CA: Science and Behavior Books, 1972) and led countless workshops to instruct social workers and others in the theory and practice of family therapy.

satisficing A decision-making process among disparate groups in which the option chosen is a "good enough" compromise rather than the best possible choice. The compromise is made to keep the group progressing and moving incrementally toward optimal goals.

"savage inequalities" The term education reformer Jonathan Kozol used to describe the disparity between opportunities available to students in affluent suburban schools and those in inner-city schools. He attributes this to the way American schools are funded mostly at the local level, resulting in more money for teachers, supplies, and infrastructure in affluent neighborhoods than in poor ones. The effect is that society places another obstacle before those who are already the most disadvantaged.

savant syndrome A condition in which an individual with mental retardation or mental disorders otherwise possesses some highly specialized talent, such as playing a musical instrument or calculating mathematical equations. The term has replaced the obsolete *"idiot savant."*

Save the Children Federation The organization founded in 1932 to provide social services, community development, and financial assistance to communities, families, and especially children who live in impoverished nations or areas that have suffered disasters or are undergoing economic problems. Their Web site address is http://www. savethechildren.org

scaled score A test score after it has been converted from a *raw score* to a number or position on a standard reference scale. For example, the raw score of a student taking a scholastic aptitude test is systematically converted to a score that indicates how the student compares with other students.

scam A fraudulent business scheme. Typically, the victim is enticed to purchase or contribute something, and the product or service is inferior to what was promised or nonexistent.

scapegoat A member of a family or group who has become the object of displaced conflict or unfair criticism.

"scared straight" programs An intervention for first-time juvenile offenders in which they are taken into adult prisons to hear those who are incarcerated describe their experiences. The premise that such exposure will deter the juveniles from further delinquency has not proved to be valid.

scarlet fever A contagious disease in which the symptoms include a red rash, sore throat, and high temperature.

scatter diagram In *social research,* the depiction of the relationship between two variables or events on an x and y graph. Each dot represents an individual, a test score, or an event for both variables. How the dots are clumped or dispersed illustrates the relationship between variables. This is also known as a scatter plot.

schedule of reinforcement In *behavior modification,* a plan determining when the subject will be reinforced. This may occur at regular intervals or according to the number and type of responses the subject makes. See also *reinforcement.*

scheme The mental structure, described in *Piagetian theory,* that allows information to be understood and processed if it fits the individual's cognitive processes.

schizoid Personality traits that include aloofness, social withdrawal, and indifference to others. If such traits seem deeply ingrained and relatively permanent, the individual might be diagnosed as having *schizoid personality disorder.* If a person with these traits is younger than 18, the diagnosis might be schizoid disorder of childhood or adolescence.

schizoid personality disorder One of the 11 types of *personality disorder,* characterized by an ingrained pattern of aloofness, social withdrawal, indifference to the feelings of others, and a restricted range of emotions. Often described as "loners," people with this disorder usually have no close friends and choose solitary interests and occupations.

schizophrenia A *psychosis,* not apparently the result of *organic mental disorder* or *mood disorder,* that has lasted more than six months and in which the active phase has begun before the subject is 45 years old. Typical features include thought disturbances (often including misinterpretation of reality, misperceptions, *loose association, delusion,* or *hallucination*); mood changes (*inappropriate affect,* blunted emotions, inability to empathize, and *ambivalence*); communication problems (incoherence or poverty of speech content); and behavior patterns that may be bizarre, regressive, or withdrawn. Many subtypes of schizophrenia have been identified, including *disorganized schizophrenia, catatonic schizophrenia, paranoid schizophrenia,* and *undifferentiated schizophrenia,* according to the symptoms. Complete recovery is extremely rare, although *psychotropic drugs, psychotherapy,* and help with *social functioning* enable most people to live fairly comfortable and somewhat independent lives. Many researchers believe schizophrenia is not a single disease but a group of disorders with similar overt features but differing etiologies. Laypeople often confuse schizophrenia with the rare and unrelated *dissociative disorder* known as *multiple-personality disorder.*

schizophreniform disorder   A disorder in which the symptoms are identical to those of *schizophrenia* except that its duration is more than two weeks but less than six months.

"schizophrenogenic parent"   An obsolete concept originated by psychoanalyst Frieda Fromm-Reichman to describe a mother who is domineering and inconsistent or a father who is submissive and inconsistent in such ways as to precipitate *schizophrenia* in their offspring. There is little, if any, scientific evidence verifying this theory, and most experts discount it.

schizotypal personality disorder   One of the *personality disorders* in which the client shows many of the symptoms of *schizophrenia,* including disturbances of thought, perception, and speech, but the symptoms are not as severe. Typical but not inevitable traits are *ideas of reference, paranoid ideation, magical thinking,* strange fantasies, eccentric or peculiar behavior, and social isolation.

Scholastic Assessment Test (SAT)   An examination required of students seeking admission to most colleges and universities in the United States to help facilitate admissions decisions. Administered by the Educational Testing Service, a private organization, it is used to predict how well a student will do in learning college-level academic subjects. The SATs, which were formerly called Scholastic Aptitude Tests, then Scholastic Achievement Tests, have been criticized as being culturally biased.

school-based health centers (SBHCs)   Facilities located within schools to provide students with confidential medical treatment services, health care and preventive health care information, mental health counseling, and social services. Funding comes from various sources, including Medicaid, Maternal and Child Health Block Grants, private foundations, and payments from the students.

School Breakfast Program   The U.S. federal program to provide low-cost or free meals before school to needy children. The program was estab-

lished in 1966 and is administered by the USDA's *Food and Nutrition Service.* Their Web site address is http://www.fns.usda.gov/cnd/breakfast

school leaver   An individual who discontinues formal education before high school graduation. This term is now preferred by many school social workers and educators over the pejorative "dropout."

School Lunch Program, National (NSLP)   A U.S. program to provide free or reduced-price lunches to needy children at participating schools and residential child care institutions. The program began in 1946 and is administered by the USDA's *Food and Nutrition Service* in collaboration with state and local governments, the U.S. Department of Education, and HHS. Federal funds, farm commodities, and donated food are supplied to public and nonprofit private schools and residential child care institutions. Other related initiatives are the *School Breakfast Program, Special Milk Program, Summer Food Service Program,* and the *Child and Adult Care Food Program.* Their Web site address is http://www.fns.usda.gov/cnd/nslp

school phobia   A young child's irrational *fear* of going to school, thought by some psychodynamically oriented therapists to be related to unresolved *dependency* needs or strong *separation anxiety.*

school social work   The specialty in social work oriented toward helping students make satisfactory school adjustments and coordinating and influencing the efforts of the school, the family, and the community to help achieve this goal. School social workers are often called on to help students, families, and teachers deal with problems such as *truancy;* social withdrawal; overaggressive behavior; rebelliousness; and the effects of special physical, emotional, or economic problems. They also interpret the methods and philosophy of the school to the parents and community. In many states, school social workers are certified or licensed, with the statutes often following the *NASW Standards for School Social Work Services.* School social workers were once known as "visiting teachers," and in 1919 the National Association of Visiting Teachers was formed. See also *visiting teacher service* and *Certified School Social Work Specialist (C-SSWS)* credential.

School Social Work Association of America (SSWAA)   The professional association of social workers employed in public and private schools in the United States. SSWAA offers its members opportunities for communication, professional development, and advancement of the goals of school social work. It sponsors annual conferences, publications, lobbying activities, and evaluation and research. Their Web site address is http://www.sswaa.org

School Social Work Specialist   See *Certified School Social Work Specialist (C-SSWS).*

school violence risk factors   Indicators that teachers and school staff look for in students that suggest they might be vulnerable to committing violent acts. When more than one of these indicators appear, school officials may initiate mechanisms for further evaluation or referral. The indicators are the following: history of violent or aggressive behaviors; frequent disciplinary infractions in school; bringing a weapon to school; a pattern of violent threats when angry; threats to hurt others or self; access to weapons or possession of weapons; history of abuse, neglect, or violence in family; social withdrawal, isolation, or poor peer relationships; history of depression or mental illness; academic failure or poor attachment to school; history of alcohol or substance abuse; history of cruelty to animals; and involvement in a street gang.

school vouchers   Redeemable notes paid by governments to parents who spend money on approved educational services. The controversial plan supposedly would enable parents who could not otherwise afford it to enroll their children in private schools. Opponents call this "welfare for the rich" and suggest that it might further damage public schools, especially those in underfunded inner cities. See also *"savage inequalities."*

Schottland, Charles Irwin (1906–1995)   A social welfare policy theorist and administrator who was the U.S. Social Security Commissioner and Director of the U.S. Children's Bureau and helped design social welfare education programs. He was dean of the School of Social Work at Brandeis University, NASW president, and the author of influential articles and textbooks on the social security system.

Schwartz, William (1916–1982)   Social work educator who developed many of the theories and principles of *social group work.* He wrote the influential textbook *The Practice of Social Group Work* (New York: Columbia University Press) in 1971.

Schwerner, Michael (1939–1964)   A civil rights martyr and *freedom rider.* He was a housing project social worker and social work graduate student when he became a summer volunteer in the South, where he helped organize blacks in Mississippi. Along with James Chaney and Andrew Goodman, he was assassinated by members of the *Ku Klux Klan.*

scientific method   A set of rigorous procedures used in social and physical *research* to obtain and interpret facts. The procedures include defining the problem, operationally stating in advance the method for measuring the problem, defining in advance the criteria to be used to reject hypotheses, using measuring instruments that have *validity* and *reliability,* observing and measuring all the cases or a representative *sample* of those cases, presenting for public scrutiny the findings and the methods used in accumulating them in such detail as to permit *replication,* and limiting any conclusions to those elements that are supported by the findings.

scientific philanthropy   A movement and social orientation that emerged in Europe and the United States between 1870 and 1900 to use systematic procedures for determining who was in need, raising private funds, coordinating the efforts of organizations and individuals who provide help, and providing the specific type of help that would be most effective and efficient. The movement eventually helped replace the haphazard method of raising and dispersing funds. When volunteers and *friendly visitors* began using these methods, their efforts led to the creation of a profession called "social work."

scoliosis   Sideways curvature in the back. See also *kyphosis* and *lordosis.*

screen memory   Thoughts and ideas that the client uses, consciously or unconsciously, to block more painful memories. Therapists often find that the screen memory is associated in some way with the more painful one.

screening interview   A preliminary interview to establish basic facts that will include or exclude some subjects or applicants from more in-depth interviews or further consideration.

scripts   Characteristic patterns of behavior that tend to accompany specific social situations or relationships and that are often followed despite the fact that they can lead to outcomes that are inconsistent with the individual's overt objectives. The term was popularized through *transactional analysis (TA)* theory, which is partly built around an examination and analysis of these patterns, the circumstances in which they occur, and their consequences.

sculpting   An experiential technique, used especially by group and family therapists, in which one member of a group or family is asked to depict his or her understanding of the relationship with others. This is done by moving the people into certain positions and asking them to hold certain gestures.

scurvy   A disease caused by vitamin C deficiency, resulting in symptoms such as *anemia,* weakness, bleeding in the mucous membranes, and spongy gums. See also *nutrition* and *malnutrition.*

SDAT   Senile dementia of the Alzheimer's type. See also *Alzheimer's disease.*

search warrant   An order by a judge authorizing specified law officers to examine a subject's premises or possessions and to bring any evidence found to the court. Search warrants can be issued only if there is probable cause to believe a *crime* has been committed and must explicitly describe the place to be searched and the items or persons to be seized.

seasonal affective disorder (SAD)   A *mood disorder,* characterized by many symptoms of *depression,* that affects some individuals during the colder, darker months of the year. Some researchers attribute SAD in some people to deficiencies in needed exposure to light for an extended period each day. Treatments include moving to sunnier climates or providing regular exposure to special light-emitting equipment.

seasonal pattern specifier   Onset and remission of major depressive episodes or bipolar I or II disorders at specific times of the year, with onset most commonly in the fall and winter and remission in the spring and summer.

seasonal unemployment   Unemployment related to regular changes in the weather or season. For example, farm workers, lifeguards, snow removal workers, and some construction workers cannot work at their jobs during certain predict-able times of the year in certain localities. This is one of the four types of *unemployment* (including *structural unemployment, cyclical unemployment,* and *frictional unemployment).*

seasonal worker   One who seeks or obtains employment for only specified periods of each year. Examples include a ski lodge employee, a fruit picker, or a department store Santa Claus.

Second Harvest   Voluntary hunger relief organization, based in Chicago, that obtains private donations of food and money to maintain more than 200 food banks nationwide. Their Web site address is http://www.secondharvest.org

second opinion   1. Consultation about a client by a professional with one or more colleagues and specialists to enhance the assessment and intervention process. 2. The process by which a client or patient seeks information from one or more other professionals. Clients and patients have the right to ask for second-opinion referrals. The American Medical Association says second opinions should be sought whenever surgery is proposed, the diagnosis is of a potentially fatal or disabling disease, symptoms persist unrelieved without explanation, risks and benefits of proposed procedures are not satisfactorily explained, diagnostic procedures seem unnecessarily complex or expensive, or the patient lacks confidence in the doctor. Clients of social workers could use similar criteria in deciding whether to seek second opinions about social work services.

second-order change   In *systems theories,* a fundamental and relatively permanent change in the structure of a system and the way it functions. See also *first-order change.*

secondary alcoholism   Alcoholism in which the individual has a major psychiatric disorder before the onset of drinking problems. The most common of the related mental illnesses are *affective disorder* and *antisocial personality disorder.* Secondary alcoholism is one of the three major types (including *primary alcoholism* and *reactive alcoholism).*

secondary care   In the system for delivery of health care, the type of intervention provided by specialists, usually in community hospitals, including obstetrics and gynecology, dermatology, and cardiology. See also *primary care* and *tertiary care.*

secondary gain The advantages or benefits one derives from a physical or mental illness, such as attention, freedom from responsibility, and disability benefits. See also *primary gain, tertiary gain, malingering,* and *factitious disorder.*

secondary prevention Efforts to limit the extent or severity of a problem through early identification of its existence, early case finding, isolation of the problem so that its effects on other people or situations are minimized, and early treatment. See also *primary prevention* and *tertiary prevention.*

secondary process thinking In *psychoanalytic theory,* the type of thinking that occurs in the *conscious* part of the *ego.* It is the refined, culturally influenced, environmentally responsive pattern of thought.

secondary trauma Also known as "vicarious trauma," the sense of trauma that comes often to those who are close to the victim of trauma, such as a family member, helping professional, or bystander near the trauma site. The person may feel guilt at having avoided the crisis event or overwhelmed with compassion.

secret societies Organizations in which the goals and procedures are kept from the general public. Some of these groups operate secretively as forms of elitism or social exclusivity. Others are secretive because they emphasize political ideologies or tactics deemed by the public to be threatening to society. Such groups include the Communist Party, the *Ku Klux Klan (KKK),* the American Nazi Party, the Posse Comitatus, and The Order.

sectarian relief organizations Church-based and interdenominational organizations to provide emergency and developmental assistance to individuals, communities, and groups who have become needy because of war, famine, environmental or natural disasters, economic problems, and religious and political persecution. Some of the largest of these organizations include Church World Service, Adventist Development and Relief Agency, Bishops' Fund for World Relief, Freedom Fellowship Foundation, and Friends Disaster Service.

sectarian services Social welfare programs that began their existence under the auspices of or with the financial support of religious organizations or that are oriented toward providing social services primarily to members of a specified religious group. Examples are *Catholic Charities USA, Jewish social agencies, LDS Social Services, Lutheran Social Services,* and the *Salvation Army.* See also *faith-based social services.*

Section 8 Housing A HUD program to help poor people live in homes in the private sector. The program comes from Section 8 of the Housing and Community Development Act of 1974 (P.L. 93-383). The program helps low-income renters by paying the difference between what they can afford and the fair-market rent for a living unit. Some Section 8 units are in new or rehabilitated housing, but most are in existing structures. Their Web site address is http://www.hud.gov/offices/pih/programs/hcv

Section 504 The common designation for the Rehabilitation Act of 1973, Section 504, which prohibits unfair treatment for individuals with disabilities in any U.S. programs or businesses that receive federal funds. The law defines the criteria for a "handicap" and encourages organizations that do business with the federal government to hire qualified workers who meet these criteria.

sectoral planning *Social planning* within a special problem area, usually involving the interests of a specified target population or geographic area (for example, older people, undernourished mothers, delinquent youths, unemployed Hispanics, inner-city residents, or all residents of Baltimore County, Maryland). See also *intersectoral planning.*

secular humanism An orientation and philosophy independent of religion that espouses morality, ethical conduct, and helping one's fellow humans and the environment.

secular society A people and its government and sociocultural institutions that are based on values and knowledge not necessarily derived from religious traditions or doctrine. There are degrees to which a society is secular, ranging from those that allow for the free expression of any and all religious beliefs and moral systems to those that forbid the recognition or practice of any religious belief system. See also *theocracy.*

secure accommodation A facility that involves physical confinement. These are usually used for at-risk children, some persons with disabilities, or some people with mental illnesses who might be vulnerable to danger from themselves or others if not confined.

secure attachment In *attachment theory,* one of the three general patterns of attachment (including *avoidant attachment* and *resistant attachment*) in which children are able to explore their environments and interact fairly comfortably with strangers while in the presence of their primary caregivers.

security deposit An advanced payment made to a landlord when a lease is signed to cover possible damages to the property or unpaid rent payments. The money repaid to the tenant is for the full deposit, less any repair expenses or unpaid rent. Depending on local market conditions, most landlords require a deposit proportional to the monthly rent, from one to three months.

security risk One whose beliefs, statements, associations, or actions are deemed to constitute a threat to a nation's government and constitutional authority. In most nations, even so-called democracies, an individual does not have to be convicted of subversive or criminal conduct to be given such a label; nevertheless, when individuals have been so identified, they have been fired from jobs, incarcerated, interred, and deported.

sedative use disorders A class of substance-related disorders involving the use of sleeping pills, tranquilizers, anti-anxiety drugs, barbiturates, and other brain depressants. Symptoms from *intoxication* by these chemicals may include *delirium, amnesia, psychosis, mood disorder, anxiety disorder, sexual dysfunction, sleep disorder,* and significantly reduced social effectiveness. *Withdrawal symptoms,* resulting from cessation or reduction of use, may include *hyperactivity, insomnia,* hand *tremor,* nausea, *hallucination, anxiety,* or seizures.

sedatives Drugs or procedures used to reduce *anxiety* or *psychomotor* activity. See also *tranquilizer.*

sedition The incitement of civil disorder and rebellion against the government.

Seebohm Report The 1968 study conducted for the British Home Office by Frederic Seebohm (leader of the British National Institute for Social Work Training). Officially titled *The Report of the Committee on Local Authority and Allied Personnel Social Services,* the document analyzed the struc-

tures of local social services departments and recommended ways to improve their efficiency. The report led to a unification of the social services in Great Britain.

segregation The separation or isolation of a group through social sanctions, laws, peer pressure, or personal preference. Voluntary segregation occurs when people choose to associate with others like them. Involuntary segregation occurs when legal, political, or normative requirements, usually established by a dominant group, are imposed on the members of a less powerful group. See also *Plessy v. Ferguson, apartheid, separatism,* and *discrimination.*

seigniorage In government financing, the "profits" from minting coins, that is, the difference between the cost of producing and circulating coins and their actual face value.

seizure disorders Disorders associated with abnormal electrical activity in the brain, often resulting in distressing *psychomotor* activity. The causes of these disorders, once commonly called *epilepsy,* are thought to include lesions in the brain, endocrine abnormalities, or neurological deficits. According to the manifestations that occur during attacks, the disorders may be classified into four major groups. Grand mal seizures usually begin with an "aura," which may include feelings of numbness and dizziness, then loss of consciousness and jerking movements of the limbs, followed by a period of deep sleep and, just after awakening, muscular stiffness, fatigue, and headache. The attacks may last from less than a minute to more than 30 minutes, and their frequency can vary from several per day to one in several years. Petit mal seizures are transient losses of contact with the environment. They may last only a second or up to two minutes, occurring infrequently or as often as 30 times per hour. Petit mal seizures usually occur in childhood and may disappear in adulthood. Psychomotor seizures, more commonly known as "partial seizures" or "temporal lobe seizures," are usually not characterized by loss of consciousness but by stereotyped movements and dramatic affective changes. Jacksonian seizures tend to begin with convulsive twitching in one part of the body that may spread to others. For most people with seizure disorders, medication can control or significantly reduce the symptoms.

selective amnesia See *psychogenic amnesia.*

selective attention   Concentrating on information, situations, or the like while ignoring other stimuli. Skilled social work interviewers use selective attention so they can attend to only the most significant information out of all the material that a client presents. See also *centration* and *decenter.*

selective beneficence   In social work practice, interventions designed to enhance the client's well-being only in specific areas. The premise is that unlimited beneficence might lead to *paternalism,* restricted client self-determination, or dependency, so the interventions are limited.

selective eligibility   A policy by which social services are provided only to those people who meet predetermined criteria, and the amount of benefit is related to the recipient's specific circumstances, economic status, or special needs, often determined by a *means test.* This policy may be contrasted with *universal eligibility* and *exceptional eligibility.*

selective mutism   A childhood disorder, formerly called *elective mutism,* characterized by the refusal to talk in social situations in which talking is expected for at least one month and to the extent that it interferes with educational or occupational achievement. An individual with selective mutism does not lack knowledge of the language or have another *communication disorder.*

selective programs   Social welfare programs based on individualized assessments to determine *eligibility.* This occurs in programs using the *means test,* including *Temporary Assistance to Needy Families (TANF), Medicaid,* and the *Food Stamp program.* Selective programs are so named to distinguish them from *universal programs.*

Selective Service System   The independent U.S. federal organization to ensure that the Armed Forces have adequate personnel to fulfill their missions. From 1940 until 1973, the Service could require (draft) eligible men (usually between ages 18 and 26) to enter the military or alternative service and serve for at least two years. Since 1973, the U.S. military has used only volunteers, and there is no draft system in effect. However, every male American citizen, and every alien who is a permanent resident of the United States, is required to register within 30 days of his 18th birthday. Registration forms are available at any post office or online. Their Web site address is http://www.sss.gov

self   An individual's unique identity; that part of the personality or character that distinguishes the person or entity from all others.

self-actualization   Achieving the full development of one's potential. According to Abraham Maslow, this is a basic human motivation toward which one strives, especially after fulfilling the *basic needs,* including physiological needs (food, air, water, and rest), safety needs (security, stability, and freedom from fear), needs of belonging (family, friends, affection, and intimacy), and esteem needs (self-respect and recognition of worth from others).

self-assertion   One's expression of thoughts and feelings that are direct rather than manipulative.

self-concept   The image or picture people have of themselves, including their own identity, body image, personality traits, and evaluation of self (that is, *self-esteem*).

self-control   An individual's relative ability to restrict impulses or behaviors to appropriate circumstances in the environment.

self-deception   Unawareness about some aspects of one's own personality characteristics, appearance, talents, capacities, or opportunities. The person may be in *denial* or in a condition of *dissociative disorder.*

self-defeating personality disorder   A pervasive pattern of behavior characterized by avoidance or subversion of pleasurable experiences and attraction to situations in which suffering is a likely result. The term is synonymous with *masochistic personality disorder.*

self-defense   Using reasonable force to protect oneself, one's family, or property from someone who poses an immediate physical danger.

self-determination   An ethical principle in social work that recognizes the rights and needs of clients to be free to make their own choices and decisions. Inherent in the principle is the requirement for the social worker to help the client know what the resources and choices are and what the consequences of selecting any one of them will be. Usually, self-determination also includes helping the client implement the decision made. Self-determination is one of the major factors in the helping relationship.

self-disclosure   In the social work interview, the social worker's revelation of personal information, values, and behaviors to the client. The profession does not declare that such revelation should or should not be made, and in certain limited circumstances it may be considered useful. However, there is some consensus that self-disclosure should not occur unless it serves a therapeutic purpose or is designed to help achieve the client's goal.

self-efficacy   A client's expectation and belief in his or her ability to accomplish specified tasks that are needed to reach therapeutic goals. The social worker seeks to enhance the client's belief by offering direct assistance, pointing out client strengths, breaking down the tasks into doable elements, and using all available resources.

Self-Employment Assistance Program, Philippines   A social welfare program in the Philippines that provides loans without collateral or interest to needy families to help them develop businesses or income-producing projects and thus enhance their self-sufficiency.

Self-Employment Contributions Act (SECA)   The federal program established in 1954 that allows a self-employed person to pay a portion of income taxes to the Internal Revenue Service for *social security* (*Old Age, Survivors, Disability, and Health Insurance [OASDHI]*). It is equivalent to a worker's *Federal Insurance Contributions Act (FICA)* payroll tax, except that with SECA the self-employed person pays the entire tax, whereas in FICA the employer pays part.

self-employment development   Planned, organized efforts to facilitate the movement of economically disadvantaged people into the workforce by empowering them to form small businesses. Governments in *Third World* nations, international economic organizations, and economically developed countries are establishing programs to facilitate *microenterprise*. This is done primarily through training, small loans, and the relaxing of ordinances against such activity. Obstacles to self-employment include lack of business skills and access to capital and also social welfare policy and psychosocial barriers.

Self-Employment Investment Demonstration (SEID) Program   A national project funded by federal and state grants to show whether public assistance recipients in several states can become economically independent by starting small businesses. SEID recruited people from *Aid to Families with Dependent Children (AFDC)* and *TANF* rolls and helped them obtain capital and business skills training and is evaluating the results in longitudinal studies.

self-esteem   An individual's sense of personal worth that is derived more from inner thoughts and values than from praise and recognition from others.

self-fulfilling prophecy   An expectation one has of another person, group, or social phenomenon that influences the way that person, group, or phenomenon is subsequently perceived. For example, a social worker may view all *Temporary Assistance to Needy Families (TANF)* recipients as too lazy to obtain jobs and thus may ignore a TANF client's request for advice about obtaining employment.

self-help groups   Voluntary associations of *nonprofessionals* who share common needs or problems and meet together for extended periods for the purpose of mutual support and exchange of information about activities and resources that have been found useful in problem solving. These groups usually meet without the direction of a professional.

self-help organizations   Formally structured organizations that provide mutual assistance for participants who share a common problem with which one or more of the participants has coped successfully. Some organizations of this type that have chapters throughout the United States and the world include *Alcoholics Anonymous (AA), Al-Anon, Batterers Anonymous,* Depressives Anonymous, *Gamblers Anonymous, Mothers Without Custody,* Narcotics Anonymous, Neurotics Anonymous, Overeaters Anonymous, Parents of Premature and High-Risk Infants, *Parents Without Partners (PWP), Recovery Inc.,* Stroke Club International, and *Women for Sobriety.*

self-hypnosis   The act of placing oneself in a mental state of aroused concentration such that everything else in one's consciousness is virtually ignored. Psychotherapy providers sometimes instruct their clients in ways to self-administer hypnotic suggestion for therapeutic purposes outside the formal sessions.

self-incrimination   Providing information directly to law authorities that can be used as evidence for one's own criminal conviction. The U.S. *Fifth Amendment rights* protect individuals from being compelled to provide such information. However, the individual may offer such information by voluntarily waiving these rights after being informed about them (see *Miranda*).

self-psychology A psychodynamically oriented theory and therapy based on the work of Heinz Kohut and others who delineated two forms of *narcissism,* one toward the self and the other toward the object. Self–objects are entities in the world that we experience as part of ourselves. Individual growth can occur when the client transforms positive healthy objects into an internalized self-structure, a process called "transmuting internalization." In therapy, through empathic attunement, the patient transforms the self–object functions of the therapist into an internalized self-structure.

self-report study In research, a method for gathering data in which representative samples of people respond to questions about their own behavior, attitudes, or perceptions. The resulting data may have limited validity due to subjectivity.

self-study An organization's evaluation of itself, especially to determine if its mission, governance, efficacy, finances, ethics, and other characteristics are in compliance with some predetermined standard. Often, that standard is imposed by outside organizations, such as accreditation bodies, financing institutions, and other organizations.

semantics The study and analysis of the meanings of words and the varying ideas conveyed by the words over time. The term is often used to suggest the twisting of words to confuse or mislead.

semicomatose Not fully conscious. An individual in this state usually drifts in and out of conscious awareness of the environment or has only partial awareness.

semiotics The study of signs and symbols in language and other ways of communicating. The focus is on signs and gestures used to clarify or obscure what is being communicated.

semiprofession An occupation that meets some but not all of the criteria the public and social scientists use to distinguish a *profession* from other entities. These criteria include the group's own theoretical *knowledge base,* autonomy from other

professions, unique skills, and a *code of ethics.* Some scholars once described social work, along with nursing, librarianship, engineering, occupational therapy, and various technical fields, as semiprofessions. Most now consider social work to be a profession.

Seneca Falls Convention The 1848 feminist meeting in Seneca Falls, New York, that outlined the right to *equality* for women. This "Declaration of Sentiments" spelled out feminist positions. The declaration helped lead to the passage of the 19th Amendment to the Constitution, which, in 1920, gave women the right to vote. See also *women's liberation movement* and *suffrage.*

senescence The normal biological process of human aging as evidenced by the decline in functioning of various organs and senses.

senile dementia A syndrome that occurs in some people in late life that is associated with deterioration of brain tissues, often leading to symptoms such as loss of memory, confusion, stubbornness, perceptual distortions, *personality disorders,* and *thought disorders.* It is a syndrome characterized by generalized irreversible disturbance of the higher cortical functions. Senile dementia is not a disease itself but a syndrome associated with several diseases. The most common types of senile dementia are *Alzheimer's disease* and *vascular dementia.* Senile dementia is also referred to as *senility,* "senile psychosis," "primary degenerative dementia, senile onset," and *organic mental disorder.*

senility The condition of old age. Although this term originally was simply a synonym for "old," it has become a pejorative and lay term implying deterioration of physical and mental faculties. Social workers, gerontologists, and other professionals prefer not to use this term. See also *age-related cognitive decline.*

senior boomers Members of the *baby boom generation* when they reach retirement age. Because American men and women who were born in the two decades after World War II constitute a population "bulge," planners, demographers, and especially those concerned about the social security system anticipate a challenge in meeting the increased financial and service needs of this cohort. On the other hand, these people are likely to be better educated, healthier, and more affluent than older people of previous generations.

senior centers Facilities and programs where older persons congregate to socialize with one another and participate in activities such as education, creative arts, recreation, health and nutrition awareness, and receipt of social services. The *Administration on Aging*'s National Institute of Senior Centers gives a national voice to and coordinates many of these programs.

Senior Community Service Employment Program (SCSEP) A program administered by the U.S. Department of Labor's *Employment and Training Administration* to facilitate part-time employment for people with low incomes older than age 55. Participants usually work in government agencies and programs for minimum wage and receive additional training. Their Web site address is http://www.wdsc.doleta.gov/seniors

Senior Companion Program (SCP) A *Senior Corps* program of the *Corporation for National and Community Service* in which people older than age 60 help other adults with special needs, particularly the *frail elderly*. Senior Companions provide support, assistance, and companionship to people in institutional and in-home settings, as well as *respite care* to caregivers. Their Web site address is http://www.seniorcorps.org/scp

Senior Corps The organization of the *Corporation for National and Community Service* that engages older people in serving those in need in their communities. There are three programs in the Senior Corps: the *Retired and Senior Volunteer Program (RSVP)*, the *Senior Companion Program (SCP)*, and the *Foster Grandparent Program*. Their Web site address is http://www.seniorcorps.org

seniority The achievement of a certain rank or status through length of time on the job.

senium The time of old age.

sensitivity group A training and *consciousness-raising* group rather than one that meets to resolve psychosocial or mental disorders. Such groups typically consist of 10 to 20 members and a leader, called a trainer or facilitator. The members participate in discussions and experiential activities to demonstrate how groups function, to show how each member tends to affect others, and to help them become more aware of their own and other people's feelings and behaviors.

sensorimotor stage The first phase of human development, according to *Piagetian theory*, which occurs from birth to about 18 months and is characterized by the formation of increasingly complex sensory refinements and motor skills that permit the child to understand and control his or her environment better.

sensorium The consciousness; that part of the *psyche* that organizes the input from the senses into a fairly coherent understanding of the immediate environment. When a psychiatric report describes a patient as having a "clear sensorium," it indicates that the individual is oriented accurately as to time, place, person, and memory.

sensuality Experiencing pleasure and gratification primarily through the senses.

sentient being An animal that has the sense of pain and other feelings.

sentiment group Individuals and groups that possess and express the predominant values, norms, and goals of the community. Sentiment groups often include fraternal and *civic associations*, *labor unions*, and ad hoc groups that have been brought together because of some problem or social cause.

separation The breaking off of a tie or relationship. Social workers use this term in several contexts, including marital separation (a husband and wife living in different residences), *legal separation*, *separation anxiety*, and *separation–individuation*.

separation agreement An informal understanding or, more commonly, a written and witnessed agreement between spouses who intend to live apart, specifying the future conditions of their relationship. Usually, the agreement describes how property is to be divided and covers *custody of children* and support payments. Formal agreements may be entered in official records and become legally enforceable and not subject to modification unless both parties want a change. The terms of a separation agreement are frequently incorporated into a *divorce* decree. See also *legal separation*.

separation anxiety The fear that a young child experiences when threatened by the loss of the primary caregiver. This fear decreases or ends as the child gets older but often returns during acute stress, crisis, or life-stage transitions. Older children and adults sometimes suffer separation anxiety.

separation anxiety disorder of childhood A childhood *mental disorder* characterized by excessive anxiety and fear when the major attachment figure goes away. The child becomes afraid that the caregiver will not return and will be harmed. The child also fears being lost, kidnapped, or victimized. Many children with this disorder develop somatic symptoms such as stomachache and nausea and are afraid of the dark and of sleep. These children will stay very close to the attachment figure and become tense when anticipating separation. The disturbance begins before age 18 and lasts more than four weeks.

separation–individuation According to Margaret Mahler, a psychosocial stage in human development in which the young child develops a sense of self-identity and a recognition that he or she is distinct from the mother. See also *individuation.*

separation phase The fifth and final stage in *group development* in which group members tend to regain their sense of individuality and autonomy from other members and become more oriented to life without the group. This phase occurs as preparation for termination and comes after the *preaffiliation phase,* the *power-and-control phase,* the *intimacy phase,* and the *differentiation phase.* Many other typologies also have been proposed to describe the phases in the typical life of group work or a therapy group.

separatism An ideology that espouses voluntary or compulsory *segregation* among people based on differences such as race, ethnic background, religion, age, or other statuses. See also *apartheid, ghetto,* and *gray ghettos.*

septicemia Blood poisoning (that is, the rapid release of toxins or germs into the bloodstream).

sequela The consequence or after-effect of a disease or condition.

Serious Crime Index Part of the *Uniform Crime Reports* issued by the Federal Bureau of Investigation (FBI) that lists eight crimes—four against persons (murder, forcible *rape, aggravated assault,* and robbery) and four against property (arson, motor vehicle theft, burglary, and *larceny* over $50). These crimes are more likely caused by people from the lower socioeconomic classes and do not reflect the types of crimes most commonly caused by more affluent people, such as fraud, embezzlement, false advertising, tax evasion, and environmental pollution.

serious emotional disturbance (SED) A label used by educators to identify students who persistently exhibit behaviors in the school setting that indicate emotional and/or behavioral disorders. One who is classified as an SED student may be eligible for special treatment, therapy, and special education alternatives under the *Individuals With Disabilities Education Act (IDEA).*

serotonin A naturally occurring molecule in the body, secreted by activated platelets and cells of the brain. Serotonin has been found to be related to mood, coronary artery disease, *myocardial infarction,* and *angina pectoris. Depression* occurs when the brain has too little serotonin; *manic episodes* can occur when serotonin levels are too high. Serotonin also acts as a potent vasoconstrictor and causes ischemia (localized tissue anemia) on normal human coronary arteries.

SERVEnet A Web site sponsored by Youth Service America (YSA) that enables users to enter their location, skills, interests, and availability and be matched with organizations needing volunteer help. The address is http://www.servenet.org

service club An organized group of volunteer members who meet regularly to socialize, network, and work on tasks that benefit the community. Many clubs are exclusively local, whereas others have national and international affiliations (for example, Rotary, Lions, Soroptimists, Kiwanis, Jaycees, and Junior League).

Service Corps of Retired Executives/Active Corps of Executives (SCORE/ACE) A volunteer program sponsored by the U.S. Small Business Administration. Its members use their skills and experience to help people start and develop their own businesses. Their Web site address is http://www.score.org

Service Employees International Union (SEIU) A labor organization, affiliated with the *American Federation of Labor–Congress of Industrial Organizations (AFL–CIO),* in which members generally are employed in public service agencies. Many social workers belong to SEIU, especially in California and the larger eastern states. Their Web site address is http://www.seiu.org

service integration (SI) The comprehensive process of coordinating the activities of social services organizations in communities to meet a range of needs by client groups so that duplication and service gaps are minimized. This process also includes establishing new organizations and service provider systems, identifying current and future unmet needs, and facilitating the efforts of various organizations to reach mutual predetermined goals. Communities include neighborhoods, geographic regions, ethnic groups, and other identified groups.

service learning An educational method in which students provide school-approved and school-monitored social services to their communities for school credits. Services such as preparing and serving food in homeless shelters, maintaining recycling programs, and preserving environments give students a greater sense of involvement in the community and its needs and enhance their academic instruction. The U.S. *Corporation for National Service* maintains the *Learn and Serve America* program, which helps fund and guide these programs for state and local educational agencies.

service strategy A social welfare policy designed to help clients obtain needed goods and services (such as food, housing, transportation, health care, or counseling) rather than direct monetary aid. For example, a service strategy would be to provide public housing for a needy client rather than provide the client with money for housing. This strategy is sometimes described as providing benefits in-kind rather than in cash. See also *income strategy*.

servidores In Latino communities, people who are formally or informally designated as neighborhood helpers who assist with a variety of local needs, including procurement of funds, food, and facilities and advocacy in negotiating the system.

set-asides The allocation of a certain percentage of business to companies owned by members of various racial and ethnic groups.

settlement houses Neighborhood-based facilities established in most urban centers to bring together people of different socioeconomic and cultural backgrounds to share knowledge, skills, and values for their mutual benefit. These centers are financed primarily through voluntary contributions and grants and are staffed primarily by people indigenous to the neighborhood, educators, recreation specialists, and social workers whose primary orientation is *social group work, community organization,* and *social planning.* The social settlement movement began in London in 1884 at *Toynbee Hall,* where university students lived and met with their neighbors to exchange ideas. Soon, hundreds of settlement houses were established in the United States with the same goals. Many have discontinued the residential aspect of the program, but some remain active in the establishment of neighborhood self-help programs and crime and delinquency abatement efforts and are involved in *political activism.*

706 agencies State or local government organizations designated by the *Equal Employment Opportunity Commission (EEOC)* to ensure fair employment practices. The term derives from Section 706(c) of Title VII of the *Civil Rights Act of 1964,* which requires employees who feel they have been discriminated against to petition the 706 agency before the case can be reviewed by the EEOC.

severance pay A payment received by employees who are laid off, discharged, or otherwise compelled to leave their places of employment.

severity index A rating system used to indicate the degree of seriousness of a client's problem. One of the several indexes of this type was developed for the *Person-in-Environment (PIE) System,* which delineates six levels on its severity index: catastrophic, very high severity, high severity, moderate severity, low severity, and no problem.

sex addiction A compulsive craving for sexual intercourse or stimulation, usually accompanied by extreme interpersonal dependence, preoccupation with romantic fantasies, inability to achieve or maintain true intimacy, and behavior that is ultimately demeaning and unacceptable. Self-help groups, 12-step programs, and professionals treat this compulsion as a form of *addiction.*

sex discrimination Treating people differently based on their gender. Usually, the term refers to favorable treatment of males and relegation of females to subordinate positions. Sex discrimination is manifested in activities such as promoting men over equally capable women or paying male employees more than female employees for the same or comparable work. See also *gender bias.*

sex education   Providing knowledge about the human reproductive system, often including information about the anatomy and physiology of the male and female reproductive organs, fertilization, fetal development, childbirth, *contraception, family planning, reproductive technology,* protection from *sexually transmitted diseases (STDs),* responsible sexual behavior, and concepts of eroticism and love.

sex offender registration (SOR)   An official list, compiled and maintained by federal and state law enforcement authorities, indicating information about people convicted of "sex crimes," such as *pedophilia,* child sexual abuse, *rape, voyeurism,* exposure, sex trafficking, and other offenses. The registry indicates the nature of the crime and the specific location of the offender. All jurisdictions in the United States have centralized sex offender registries, and the Department of Justice maintains a National Sex Offender Registry.

sex role stereotyping   Preconceived and relatively fixed ideas about all males or all females and the attribution of negative characteristics to people because of their gender. When these ideas are overtly acted on, the result is *sex discrimination.*

sex roles   Culturally defined expectations for "male behavior" and "female behavior."

sex therapy   Professional clinical treatment of the psychological and physiological dysfunctions of human sexuality. Such treatment is now typically provided to couples in *cotherapy* situations and provided by male–female teams of therapists. There are four levels of such therapy: (1) providing permission—conveying to the couple that their behaviors and desires are normal; (2) providing general information—helping the couple know how to get the most out of sexual relationships; (3) providing specific information—advising the couple about how to correct some sexual disorders or improve some unsatisfactory behaviors; and (4) providing intensive sex therapy. Intensive sex therapy begins with thorough physical examinations to rule out or correct physiological problems. This examination is followed by intensive psychosocial and sexual history taking. If the sex thera-

pists use *psychodynamic* perspectives, the treatment is likely to be more insight-oriented work toward resolving underlying conflicts that lead to the problem. If the sex therapists use behavioral perspectives, the treatment involves teaching the couple techniques for greater success and using *systematic desensitization* and other methods to achieve specified goals.

sexism   Individual attitudes and institutional arrangements that discriminate against people, usually women and girls, because of *sex role stereotyping* and generalizations.

sexist language   The use of written or spoken words that imply or convey the idea that one of the sexes is more important than the other. This use may occur intentionally or unintentionally and exists whether or not the producer of the words or the receiver of the words consciously recognizes that such an idea is being communicated. Sexist language is found most commonly in using males to represent humanity (for example, "Man is the most intelligent creature on Earth") or in applying generic masculine pronouns for both sexes (for example, "If a client is motivated, he will find a way to get help"). See also *unbiased writing.*

sexual abuse   The exploitation and mistreatment of children and adults in ways that provide erotic gratification for the abuser. Abusers tend to have serious psychological problems such as a *personality disorder, paraphilia* or another *sexual disorder,* or *psychosis.* Victims often cannot or are unwilling to understand or resist the advances of the abuser. Sexual abuse can include sexual intercourse without consent (or when the victim is younger than the age of consent), the fondling of genitalia, *frotteurism,* the taking or showing of pornographic pictures, and other forms of sexual *acting out.* Some social workers also include *rape,* seduction, *sexual harassment,* and sexual coercion as other forms of sexual abuse.

sexual arousal disorder   The *sexual disorders* characterized by the recurrent and persistent inability to complete satisfactorily all phases of the sexual response cycle, causing marked distress or interpersonal difficulty. See *female sexual arousal disorder* and *male erectile disorder.*

sexual assault   Nonconsensual, illegal sexual misconduct. Many writers use the term interchangeably with *rape;* others suggest that rape implies a more serious offense involving penile penetration, whereas sexual assault also includes attempted rape, sexual molestation, sexual coercion, criminal sexual exposure, *voyeurism,* and *frotteurism.* The legal definitions of rape and sexual assault vary by jurisdiction.

sexual assault survivor group (SASG)   A form of time-limited group therapy for women who have been victims of *sexual assault.* SASGs typically consist of six to eight women led by two female clinicians. The group meetings last 90 minutes per week for 12 weeks and focus on themes related specifically to sexual assault issues.

sexual aversion disorder   A *sexual disorder* characterized by active avoidance of and aversion to genital sexual contact with a sexual partner, causing marked distress or interpersonal difficulty. Individuals experience varying degrees of fear, disgust, or anxiety when in sexual situations, ranging from lack of pleasure to severe distress.

sexual desire disorders   Absence of fantasy or desire for sexual activity, leading to marked distress or interpersonal difficulty. The major types of sexual desire disorders include *hypoactive sexual desire disorder* and *sexual aversion disorder.* See also *sexual arousal disorder.*

sexual development   Anatomical, hormonal, physiological, cognitive, emotional, and social changes in an individual that are related to the reproductive function of life. Sexual development begins at *conception,* when the egg is fertilized by a sperm cell that carries either an XX (female) or an XY (male) sex chromosome. Sexual development continues through puberty and menopause and ends only at death. See also *psychosexual development theory.*

sexual deviation   See *paraphilia.*

sexual disorder   Disturbances of human sexuality, including the type of problem known as *paraphilia,* and *sexual dysfunction.* This type of disorder was once labeled a *psychosexual disorder;* however, because the degree to which it is *psychogenic* or *biogenic* (organic) has not yet been determined, sexual disorder is the preferred term.

sexual dysfunction   The inability of an individual or couple to experience sexual intercourse in a satisfactory way. The dysfunction refers both to objectively occurring deficits in an individual's sexual response cycle (in any part of the cycle, including excitement, plateau, orgasm, and resolution) and to an individual's subjective dissatisfaction with his or her sexual response, even if it falls within the normal range. The cause of the dysfunction may be psychosocial or physical (including effects of disease, injuries, or medications) or a combination of both. The most prevalent types include *orgasmic disorders, vaginismus, dyspareunia, erectile dysfunction, premature ejaculation, ejaculatory inhibition, sexual aversion disorder,* and *paraphilia.*

sexual equality   Opportunities, benefits, and rights that are uniformly available to people, regardless of gender.

sexual foreplay   Erotic or amorous stimulation before *coitus.*

sexual harassment   Abusive and unfavorable treatment or *sex discrimination* of a person because of his or her gender. Such treatment typically includes making lewd gestures and propositions, touching someone who does not want to be touched, or seeking to exchange sexual favors for employment opportunities. Sexual harassment is against the law in the United States and many other nations, and employers in those countries are required to provide workplaces that are free from it. See also *harassment.*

sexual identity   The degree to which an individual takes on the behaviors, personality patterns, and attitudes that are usually associated with male or female *sex roles.* This is a synonym for *gender identity.*

sexual masochism   The act of deriving erotic excitement or arousal by being subjected to pain, humiliation, or suffering. Excitement occurs by the actual, not fantasized, experience of being bound, tortured, or beaten.

sexual orientation   Inclination toward or preference for sexual activity with members of one's own sex (homosexual orientation), the opposite sex (heterosexual orientation), or both (bisexual orientation). Three components of sexual orientation are attraction, behavior, and identity. Attraction may be to partners of the same or opposite sex or, rarely, to partners of both sexes. Behavior refers to sexual activities with partners of the same or opposite sex. Identity refers to one's view of oneself as heterosexual (primarily attracted to opposite-sex partners), homosexual (primarily attracted to same-sex partners), or bisexual (equally attracted to partners of both sexes).

sexual pain disorder A *sexual disorder* in which the individual experiences unpleasantness or pain during some or all phases of the sexual response cycle. Also known as *dyspareunia,* the causes include infection, inflammation, after-effects of injury or surgery, and, in women, endometriosis. Psychological distress, including previous sexual trauma, also can lead to this disorder.

sexual predator A person who has committed or seeks to commit sexual assaults, usually on children or women. The legal designation of sexual predator is one who has been convicted of a sexual assault and, after release from incarceration, is still considered dangerous and likely to repeat the offense. Some communities and jurisdictions have brought about laws and judgments designating the person as a "sexual predator" as long as that individual remains in the neighborhood.

sexual sadism The act of deriving erotic excitement or arousal from inflicting pain on others. Excitement occurs by subjecting a consenting or nonconsenting partner to humiliation and simulated or actual injury and suffering.

sexual trauma A shocking experience involving sexuality that has a lasting effect on an individual's personality and mental health. The experience is usually *rape, incest, sexual abuse,* or exposure to a *psychosexual disorder* of others. The resulting symptoms of these experiences include inability to forget, *flashback, anxiety, shame, posttraumatic stress disorder (PTSD),* and difficulties in having intimate relationships.

sexuality Characteristics of an individual that essentially pertain to the reproductive function, including anatomy and physiology, primary and secondary sexual traits, sex role patterns, and behavioral characteristics.

sexually transmitted diseases (STDs) *Venereal diseases*—infectious illnesses passed from one person to another through *coitus* or other intimate contact. They occur by the exchange of bodily fluids and contact with mucous membranes such as those in the mouth, rectum, eyes, penis, and vagina. STDs include *gonorrhea, chlamydia,* genital *herpes, syphilis,* and *HIV disease.* See also *condom.*

shadow welfare state Taxpayer-supported social services and income maintenance programs that primarily benefit the middle classes, typically through tax policies (such as deductions for home loan interest, child care costs, and business expenses), federal subsidies for agriculture and businesses, and social security pensions.

Shaftesbury, Lord (Anthony Ashley Cooper, 1801–1885) Founder of the *Ragged School Movement* and England's foremost social reformer in the 19th century. Through his work as a member of Parliament, he guided legislation that improved conditions in housing, physical and mental illness care, slums, and education for poor children. He also helped found the Society for Improving the Conditions of the Laboring Classes and the *Young Men's Christian Association (YMCA).*

shaken baby syndrome A serious form of head injury that may occur when a baby is shaken forcibly enough to bruise or damage brain tissue within the skull.

shame A painful feeling of having disgraced or dishonored oneself or those one cares about because of an intentional act, involuntary behavior, or circumstance.

shame versus autonomy The basic conflict found in the second stage of human psychosocial development, occurring between ages two and four, according to the *psychosocial development theory* of Erik Erikson (1902–1994). During this time, the toddler experiences social controls and discipline and is helped by the *socialization* process to achieve recognition of his or her uniqueness.

shantytowns Densely populated settlements of impoverished people who have built homes of scrap materials on land they do not own. Because these people usually occupy the land illegally, they cannot demand public services and have little fire and police protection, water and sanitary facilities, or schools. Shantytowns are growing rapidly, especially in *Third World* nations, and are also found in more affluent nations that do not provide adequately for their poor populations. See also *slum, ghetto,* and *barriadas.*

shaping Procedures used in *behavior modification* in which new patterns of behavior are fashioned by reinforcing progressively closer approximations of the desired behaviors and not reinforcing other behaviors.

sharecropping Arrangements in rural areas in which landowners allow families to live on and work their land and both parties share in the harvest.

shared custody A court-ordered legal right of divorced parents to maintain approximately equal control of the children they had together. This usually means the child lives in the home of each parent for about the same amount of time, and both parents have equal authority in discipline, education, and all other decisions affecting the child's well-being. See also *visitation rights.*

shared psychotic disorder A psychotic disorder in which two or more people experience in common *delusions of persecution* or other delusions. The disorder is exacerbated because each participant fuels the delusions of the other. See also *codependency, folie à deux, conjugal paranoia, jealousy,* and *induced psychotic disorder.*

sheltered-care facility A program and agency that provides a protected and monitored environment for those unable to function independently. These facilities are similar to nursing homes, except their residents usually do not require such intensive health care services. Most are 24-hour residential centers, but others provide only *day care.* Many facility residents have mental illnesses or physical disabilities or are relatively healthy but vulnerable older people.

sheltered employment A program to provide a work environment for individuals who cannot otherwise obtain or keep jobs in the community. Clients work under close supervision and are usually paid at or below minimum wage or on a piecemeal basis (only for the amount produced).

sheltered workshop A program primarily for people with physical or mental disabilities to provide services such as vocational evaluation, *sheltered employment,* work adjustment training, counseling, and placement services.

shelters Facilities that provide and maintain temporary residences and protection for people or animals in need. Shelters exist in most communities for battered and abused women, homeless men and women, abandoned or abused children, victims of crimes and natural disasters, and people experiencing a variety of other circumstances.

shenjing shuairuo A *culture-bound syndrome* found most commonly in China in which the individual experiences anxiety and moodiness and various somatic complaints.

shenkui A *culture-bound syndrome* found most commonly among people of Chinese and Taiwanese ancestry in which the individual experiences *sexual disorders* such as *impotence* and *premature ejaculation,* dream disturbances and *insomnia,* and fatigue and weakness, said to be the result of excessive loss of semen through frequent intercourse, masturbation, and nocturnal emissions. See also *dhat.*

Sheppard–Towner Act The federal child welfare and maternity health legislation (Maternity Act, Ch. 135, 42 Stat. 224) enacted in 1921 and discontinued in 1929. Administered by the *Children's Bureau* under the leadership of social worker *Grace Abbott* (1878–1939), the act established almost 3,000 child and maternity health centers across the nation, mostly in rural areas. Despite great improvements in the nation's infant and maternal *mortality rates,* political pressure led to the act's abolition. See also *WIC program.*

Sherman Anti-Trust Act The federal law (Ch. 647, 26 Stat. 209) enacted in 1890 to eliminate business monopolies and conspiracies in the restraint of trade or commerce.

shin-byung A *culture-bound syndrome* found most commonly among Koreans in which the individual experiences *anxiety* and various somatic complaints, including dizziness, *insomnia,* and weakness, said to be the result of possession by ancestral spirits.

shingles A painful viral infection, formally called herpes zoster, resulting in blisters and inflammation along the path of a nerve. The virus can remain latent in the body for years before becoming active again.

shock Rapid loss of blood pressure, often due to traumatic injury and serious vessel damage. Symptoms may include weak pulse, chills, nausea, irregular breathing, faintness, and weakness. This term is also used to indicate sudden surprise, fright, and the feeling that one's bodily systems have temporarily come to a halt.

shock therapy See *electroshock therapy (EST).*

shoplifting   The *crime* of stealing goods from a store during its business hours.

short-term long-term care (STLTC)   Any health and social services program that provides *long-term care (LTC)* for fewer than 90 days.

short-term therapy   *Psychotherapy* or other forms of helping intervention that the professional and the client agree in advance to end within a set time, usually less than three months, and within 12 to 15 sessions. In this form of intervention, the goals and the issues addressed in the sessions tend to be more limited and focused. See also *long-term therapy.*

show cause order   A court order requiring one of the litigants in a civil case to explain why the court should not take a particular action in the case.

Shriners Hospitals   A network of hospitals established in 1922 and funded by the fraternal organization to provide orthopedic and burn care at no cost to children. Their Web site address is http://www.shriners.com

Shyne, Ann Wentworth (1914–1995)   A leader in the development of social work research. She directed research projects for various organizations and helped found the influential *Social Work Research Group.* She led the group's effort to promote research in social work practice and in the curricula of schools of social work. She also authored many articles and books on research, foster care, and the development of brief treatment models.

shyness   Reticence, timidity, and self-consciousness, especially in unfamiliar social situations. Although shyness is sometimes a symptom of more serious emotional disturbances, it is usually seen more as an indicator of insecurity, lack of self-confidence, or *anomie.*

sibling abuse   The physical, emotional, or sexual mistreatment of a child by a brother or sister. Usually, the abuser is older and stronger and has more influence with parents or other authorities. See also *child abuse.*

sibling rivalry   Competition between siblings, basically to gain parental favor or attention.

sibling therapy   The use of *family therapy* and other forms of helping interventions with a *multi-problem family,* working only with children. This model is sometimes used when parents are uncooperative, resistant, or so inconsistent that their presence is more disruptive than productive. The children are helped to develop and strengthen the bonds that exist between them so they can be more effective in providing one another with needed supports.

siblings   Brothers and sisters.

sickle-cell anemia   A genetically transmitted blood disorder in which a large proportion of red cells assume sicklelike shapes. The disorder affects primarily people of West African descent. In the United States, government grants have led to the establishment of free testing for the sickle-cell trait in health centers around the nation. See also *genetic counseling* and *genetic disorder.*

side effect   A drug's unintentional and nontherapeutic effect on the body. Almost every drug has some major or minor side effects.

side-taking   A technique used especially in family therapy in which the therapist actively and deliberately advocates for one family member over others to unbalance a dysfunctional system or break up a pattern in which both sides are stalemated.

sidetracking   In the helping interview, the client's or interviewer's intentional or unintentional shifts in focus of attention. Frequently getting away from the relevant subject impedes the helping process. The effective interviewer sometimes prevents this by intervening, reminding the client of the subject, and labeling the digression for what it is.

Sierra Club   The environmental and conservation organization founded in 1892 to work for protecting the wilderness, controlling pollution, reversing global warming, and protecting endangered species. Their Web site address is http://www.sierraclub.org

sigmoidoscopy   A medical procedure, using a sigmoidoscope, to inspect the rectum and sigmoid colon. This is the most common procedure to screen for colon cancer and other abnormalities (such as polyps) of the large intestine. The American Cancer Society, the National Cancer Institute, and the American College of Surgeons recommends that asymptomatic individuals have a sigmoidoscopic examination every three to five years in conjunction with an annual fecal occult blood test, beginning at age 50. The screening of individuals with a family history of colorectal cancer should begin at least by age 40 and should be repeated every five years.

sign in/sign out procedure   In *group psychotherapy* or social work with groups, the procedure of beginning or ending each session by having each member briefly offer a personal reflection that relates to the purpose of the group.

significance level   The degree to which a value that has been obtained through systematic data collection will not occur by chance. In research reporting, this level is expressed numerically to indicate the number of times out of a specified number of samplings that the result would probably occur by chance. In the social sciences, the significance levels are most often .01, .05, or .001, even though any other figure could be used as well. For example, if the .05 level is used, a specified outcome would occur by chance five times among 100 samplings.

significant other   A generic lay term referring to one who, because of affection, proximity, family relationship, or *codependency* need, is considered more important than others. See also *relevant other.*

silicosis   Respiratory disease and damaged lung tissue that result from extensive breathing of crystalline silica. Construction workers are the primary at-risk group for this condition through inhalation of the dust of crushed rock, cement, and abrasives.

simple deteriorative disorder   Also referred to as "simple schizophrenia," a progressive development within the past year of the following symptoms: marked decline in academic or occupational functioning, increasingly flattened affect, reduced quantity and quality of speech and activity, poor interpersonal rapport, and social withdrawal.

simple phobia   See *specific phobia.*

simple schizophrenia   See *schizotypal personality disorder.*

"sin tax"   An informal term referring to a tax to be paid on those particular goods and services that some citizens consider ignoble, such as cigarettes, alcoholic beverages, gambling winnings, and legal *prostitution* services.

single-focus group   An orientation in *social group work* or *group psychotherapy* in which all the group members share the same or closely related problems and, in single or ongoing sessions, work only on those problems. These groups, also called *homogeneous groups,* are becoming more common in mental health settings and predominate in *self-help groups.* See also *focus group.*

single-masked design   In research, a study plan in which the investigator or therapist, but not the participants, knows what is actually being investigated. Also called the "single-blind" design, this is contrasted with the double-masked or double-blind study, in which neither the investigator nor the participants know what is being investigated.

single-parent family   A family unit and household consisting of the children and the mother or father but not the other spouse. This family unit is not to be confused with the *reconstituted family,* in which the children and one parent are joined by a stepparent and perhaps that person's children.

single-payer health care plans   A health care financing program paid solely from one source, usually the government. This approach is used by many industrialized nations and typically has the following characteristics: Everyone in the nation is covered and has the same benefits; benefits are "portable" (that is, not linked to employment or residency requirements); coverage is comprehensive, including physical and mental health care and prevention; administration is nonprofit and nonduplicated and is based on negotiated fee scales; and patients are free to choose their providers. Some in the United States, which has a multitiered, privatized system with considerable administrative duplication, call this the "Canadian system."

single-room occupancy (SRO)   A one-room dwelling place, usually in an apartment, hotel, or house, occupied by a person not related to others in the same housing unit.

single-session group   A form of *group therapy* or *social group work* in which the members meet only once. Usually, such groups are highly structured and focused on one type of problem. Some groups of this type are scheduled to last only an hour or two, but others may be scheduled for many hours, as in a *marathon group.*

single-subject design   A *research* procedure often used in clinical situations to evaluate the effectiveness of an intervention. Behavior of a single subject, such as an individual client, is used as a comparison and a control. Typically, the results of progress or change are plotted graphically. Single-subject design is also known as $N = 1$ design or single-system design.

sit-ins   A method of *passive resistance* in which demonstrators occupy a public place and refuse to leave until action is taken to redress their grievances. Sit-ins were used extensively during the Civil Rights movement of the 1960s, especially in segregated restaurants, legislators' offices, and bus stations.

sit-down strike   Tactics used by labor unions and activists to interfere with the normal operation of some social organization by encouraging participants to occupy passively an important space to obstruct activities there. See also *passive resistance* and *work-in.*

situational ethnic identity   The process of changing one's self-identification as a member of a national-origin group one or many times to achieve advantages as circumstances arise. For example, a person of Puerto Rican origin might designate himself as such when with other Puerto Ricans and as Hispanic when with *"Anglos."*

situational tests   A procedure social workers in direct practice and research use to measure client behavior and behavioral changes in which they have the client perform some contrived tasks while under observation. The social worker describes a problem–situation and shows how a person might respond. Then, using tools such as videotape simulations, role plays, or written descriptions of problems, the client demonstrates probable responses when confronted with the actual situation.

"638s"   The commonly used term for American Indian social services and educational organizations that implement provisions of the *Indian Self-Determination and Education Assistance Act.* The term comes from the 1975 federal legislation (P.L. 93-638) that removed most of the direct social services and educational functions from the *Bureau*

of Indian Affairs (BIA) and permitted certain American Indian organizations to provide such services or to contract for them.

skew   A concept in *research* indicating that a distribution curve is not symmetrical.

"skid road"   A term once commonly used to describe areas, usually found in larger cities, frequented by homeless people and alcoholics and containing many tenement houses, cramped and deteriorating buildings, pawn shops, religious missions, and shelters. This term is also known as "skid row."

skill   Proficiency in the use of one's hands, knowledge, talents, personality, or resources. A social worker's skills include being proficient in communication, assessing problems and client workability, matching needs with resources, developing resources, and changing social structures. See also *social work skills, direct practice skills,* and *social skill.*

skilled-nursing facilities (SNFs)   Health care structures and programs for patients who need relatively intensive and often *long-term care (LTC),* staffed primarily by more highly trained and experienced professional nurses and nurse practitioners who may be specialists in certain types of health care. These facilities are sometimes described as hybrids between nursing homes and hospitals. The designation "skilled-nursing home" also has been used in federal legislation, especially in the *Medicaid* provisions of the *Social Security Act.* These provisions require Medicaid patients in need of nursing home care to be placed in skilled-nursing homes, which are defined as being headed by a nonwaivered practical nurse. Facilities that Medicaid calls "skilled-nursing homes" range from active treatment and rehabilitation programs to those that provide limited health care. See also *extended-care facilities (ECFs).*

skim   The illegal practice of concealing receipts or income from legitimate sources to avoid paying taxes or sharing the proceeds with others entitled to it.

"skin popping"   An activity of drug abusers who make small cuts in their flesh and place the substance under the skin.

skinheads   Members of *street gangs,* most of whom are white people with shaved heads, who tend to hate authority, immigrants, and members of nonwhite races. As they become older, many skinheads affiliate with *white supremacist groups.*

Skinnerian theory   The learning theories developed by American psychologist B. F. Skinner (1904–1990). His concepts, especially that of *operant conditioning,* have greatly influenced the development of modern *behaviorism* and its use in treatment.

slander   Spoken false statements that damage the reputation of another person. See also *libel.*

slash-and-burn farming   A method of gaining and fertilizing farmland by setting fire to vegetation that was cut out of forested areas. Harvests tend to be good soon after the burning, but in subsequent years the soil becomes eroded and nonproductive. See also *land despoilment.*

slave labor   Work an individual is compelled to do with no choice or no opportunity to select an alternative.

sleep disorders   Conditions involving chronic and persistent disturbances in sleep patterns, including abnormalities in the amount, quality, or timing of sleep; abnormal behavioral or physiological events in association with sleep; or sleep disturbance patterns resulting from a variety of specified conditions. Among these disorders are primary sleep disorders (including *dyssomnia* and *parasomnia*), sleep disorders resulting from other mental disorders (*insomnia* and *hypersomnia*), and sleep disorders related to another mental disorder or substance abuse.

sleep terror disorder   A *sleep disorder* characterized by repeated awakenings in a state of fright. The individual often cannot remember the source of the fear but awakens with a scream or with panicky escape movements. This condition, once known as "pavor nocturnus," differs from *nightmare disorder* in that the individual does not awaken as easily or remember the stimulus dream clearly.

sleep–wake schedule disorder   A *sleep disorder* in which the individual's opportunity for sleeping and ability to sleep at that time are mismatched. Clinicians use the term *circadian rhythm sleep disorder.*

sleepwalking disorder   A *sleep disorder, parasomnia* type, in which the individual arises from

bed during sleep and moves about. The individual has reduced alertness and responsiveness and limited recall of the episode, which usually lasts for several minutes to a half hour. The pattern is most common among children and ends in most people by age 15.

sliding-fee scale   The practice, found among many social agencies and workers, in which clients are charged fees for services based on their ability to pay rather than on a fixed rate established in advance for everyone who receives the same service. See also *flat-rate fee.*

"slow learner"   A descriptive term for students whose below-average academic achievements may not be attributable to mental illness, retardation, physical problems, or special needs. Most students who are so described have *intelligence quotient (IQ)* ranges of 75 to 90 (above those who are considered educable mentally retarded but below those who are considered average). However, many students begin to make progress after successful help with emotional or social relationship problems.

slum   A concentration of deteriorating buildings, many of which are inhabited by people who are economically and socially deprived.

slumlord   An owner of houses and buildings, usually in deteriorated or deteriorating neighborhoods, who realizes excessive profits by charging high rents and withholding repairs.

small claims court   A court of law that hears cases involving disputes over small amounts of money. The disputants typically represent themselves rather than hire lawyers.

small-group therapy   *Group therapy* with fewer than 10 members.

Smalley, Ruth (1903–1979)   A social work philosopher, practitioner, and educator who wrote extensively about social work methods. As dean of the Pennsylvania School of Social Work, she led that faculty's work in offering an alternative to Freudian theory–based casework theory with a more time-limited, task-centered, functional approach to problem solving.

"SMART"   Specific—Measurable—Achievable—Relevant—Time-limited; a mnemonic to help remember all the elements to be incorporated into the objectives part of a psychosocial record treatment plan.

Smith, Zilpha Drew (1852–1926)   An early developer of the *Charity Organization Societies (COSs)* and the friendly visitor approach to intervention. A strong advocate for training for *friendly visitors*, she helped *Mary E. Richmond* develop educational plans for them. She also developed programs for mothers' aid and wrote about problems of family breakdown.

smoke-free society   The absence of cigarette, cigar, and pipe-tobacco smoking in a community or nation through legislation, norms, or lack of access.

snorting   The ingestion of powdered forms of a drug of abuse, such as *cocaine,* by rapid inhalation into a nostril. Some users prefer this over other ways of ingesting the drug, such as smoking, chewing, swallowing, intravenous injecting, or *"skin popping,"* believing it produces more rapid or more intense effects.

SOAP charting method   A system used by professionals in health and mental health care settings to organize their patient charts or notes. Part of the *problem-oriented record (POR)* originated by Lawrence Weed in 1968, such charting involves classifying information according to the acronym SOAP, which arranges records in four elements: (1) subjective information (such as symptoms reported by the client or family members), (2) objective information (such as sociodemographic information or data obtained from medical tests), (3) assessments and conclusions that the professional draws from the data, and (4) the plan (what the professional or agency is doing to resolve the problem).

social accounting   Measuring the positive and negative influences a business has on society and reporting the findings in a "social impact statement." Factors taken into consideration include the company's environmental impact on the surrounding community, product safety, and personnel issues such as discrimination.

social action   A coordinated effort to achieve institutional change to meet a need, solve a social problem, correct an injustice, or enhance the qual-

ity of human life. This effort may occur at the initiative and direction of professionals in social welfare, economics, politics, religion, or the military, or it may occur through the efforts of the people who are directly affected by the problem or change.

social activist   A professional organizer or indigenous layperson skilled at raising the public consciousness about a social problem or injustice and mobilizing available resources to change the conditions leading to this problem.

social adult day care   Community programs and facilities for adults whose *social functioning* has become impaired and who can no longer function independently. Many such facilities provide transportation to and from the client's home, a midday meal, and a variety of recreational and social programs five days weekly while family members are at work. Most funding comes from federal or state allocations, Medicaid, or private insurance.

social agency   An organization or facility that delivers *social services* under the auspices of a board of directors and is usually staffed by human services personnel (including professional social workers, members of other professions, paraprofessionals, clerical personnel, and sometimes indigenous workers). The agency provides a specified range of social services for members of a population group that has or is vulnerable to a specific social problem. The agency may be funded by combinations of philanthropic contributions and privately solicited donations, by governments, by fees paid by those served, or by third-party payment. Social agencies are accountable to their boards through accessible financial records, statements of purpose, and representatives from the community who serve on the boards of directors. The board members set overall policy, and administrators coordinate activities to carry out those policies. The organization has explicit bylaws that determine which clients to serve, what problems to combat, and what methods to use in providing service. Public organizations, such as social security offices, hospitals, and community mental health offices, are considered social agencies, as are private organizations such as *Family Service International (FSI)* offices, *Lutheran Social Services,* and *Catholic Charities USA.*

Social and Occupational Functioning Assessment Scale (SOFAS) A 100-point scale in development by the American Psychiatric Association to assist in the clinician's evaluation of the degree to which an individual maintains job-related and social functions not directly related to existing psychological symptoms. Individuals who function most effectively score highest (81–100), whereas those unable to function independently and maintain minimal standards of personal hygiene score lowest (1–20). See also *severity index*.

social anxiety disorder See *social phobia.*

social assistance A synonym for *public assistance;* the provision of benefits financed from a nation's general revenues and usually subject to a test of the recipient's need and means. This is a *residual welfare provision* in most nations, such as the United States, because the funds do not come from *social insurance* programs. In countries that do not use the social insurance funding system, this is a primary welfare program.

social capital Economic value that is derived from the existence of relevant social networks that foster trust and promote cooperative exchange and collective action and the skills of the workforce within those networks. For example, an organization in which members have cooperative and trusting relations with people of power and influence has more value than one that has weak social networks. The collective value of all these networks and skills is the social capital. See also *human capital.*

social care The provision of concrete and especially relationship-based *social services* for those people with normal developmental needs as well as extraordinary dependency and deprivation problems. The social care concept emphasizes that all people, at least sometimes, have needs for some social services and that many of these services can be provided by a *volunteer, paraprofessional,* or *indigenous worker.* This system is more prominent in *international social work* than in the United States.

social care worker In the United Kingdom, a description of people, including social workers, who fulfill a wide range of social services, human services, and youth and recreation activities and who implement programs to care for human needs. Social care workers range from those who are highly educated in university settings to people without advanced formal education but who are qualified with training and experience in social care settings.

social casework The orientation, value system, and type of practice used by professional social workers in which psychosocial, behavioral, and systems concepts are translated into skills designed to help individuals and families solve intrapsychic, interpersonal, socioeconomic, and environmental problems through direct face-to-face relationships. Many social workers consider social casework to be synonymous with *clinical social work* practice.

social category A conceptual or statistical grouping of individuals who share a common trait, such as all the people in a specified society whose incomes are below the poverty line.

social causation theory The idea that insecure and stressful economic and social conditions strongly increase the probability that a given individual experiencing them will develop social problems or mental disorders. This theory is often advanced to explain why there is a higher *incidence rate* and *prevalence rate* of mental illnesses, *poverty, divorce, spouse abuse,* and so on among people of certain socioeconomic classes, ethnic and racial backgrounds, and geographic areas of residence.

social change Variations over time in a society's laws, norms, values, and institutional arrangements.

social class A category of people in a society, ranked according to criteria such as relative wealth, power, prestige, educational level, or family background.

social competence The acquired mastery of the social, emotional, and cognitive skills necessary to exist as a member of human society. This is a relative and constantly changing condition because the skills needed by a young child to be considered socially competent are different from the skills needed by an adult.

social consciousness Awareness of the needs and values of other people and of society in general, often accompanied by actions to meet those needs and enhance those values.

social control 1. The organized effort of a society or some of its members to maintain a stable social order and to manage the process of *social* *change.* 2. Efforts to constrain people, requiring them to adhere to established *norms* and laws.

social cost 1. The expenditures for certain programs or activities that are borne by society as a whole. For example, the rising unemployment rate among African American youths is considered a social cost of racial discrimination and social and educational inequalities. 2. Societal problems that do not easily lend themselves to financial calculations. An example is the social and emotional investment required for young couples to care for their disabled parents at home.

social Darwinism The philosophy first articulated by English sociologist Herbert Spencer (1820–1903), who coined the phrase "survival of the fittest" and applied Charles Darwin's theories of evolution to human economic conditions. The philosophy suggested that competition was normal and inevitable, that those who could not compete would be eliminated through natural selection, that only those who were inferior or inadequate to survive in society would be poor, and that the laissez-faire economic system was best because self-help was the only way out of poverty. This philosophy has had great influence in the development of social welfare policy in the United States.

social development Planned comprehensive social change designed to improve people's general welfare. The interrelatedness of major social problems requires the economic and cultural efforts of national and international government structures and society's institutions and all its citizens.

social distance The relative degrees of isolation, aloofness, intimacy, and *social mobility* among people that occur or are permitted within a society or part of that society (such as a family, a group of workers, or a socioeconomic class). For example, one culture might discourage and another might encourage physical embraces between men.

social ecology The study of the reciprocal and adaptive relationship between the natural environment and human society.

social engineering A term, often used disparagingly, for *social planning* and for efforts to change the law, norms, mores, and social institutions.

social exclusion Marginalization of people or areas and the imposition of barriers that restrict them from access to opportunities to fully integrate with the larger society. Those who are most vulnerable to social exclusion are people who are poor, inadequately educated or trained, physically handicapped, or ex-offenders and people of various racial and ethnic groups. Social workers, especially in Europe, attempt to address this combination of linked problems as a more rational strategy rather than deal with the various individual types of social exclusion (for example, unemployment, discrimination, family breakdown, and lack of access to opportunities that exist for others). The governments of many European nations have Social Exclusion Units to deal comprehensively with the problem. One Web site address in the United Kingdom is http://www.socialexclusionunit.gov.uk

social functioning Living up to the expectations that are made of an individual by that person's own self, by the immediate social environment, and by society at large. These expectations, or functions, include meeting one's own basic needs and the needs of one's dependents and making positive contributions to society. Human needs include physical aspects (food, shelter, safety, health care, and protection), personal fulfillment (education, recreation, values, aesthetics, religion, and accomplishment), emotional needs (a sense of belonging, mutual caring, and companionship), and an adequate self-concept (self-confidence, self-esteem, and identity). Social workers consider one of their major roles to be that of helping individuals, groups, or communities enhance or restore their capacity for social functioning.

social gerontology The scientific study of the societal and psychological aspects of aging.

social goals model In *social group work* and therapy group conceptions, the group objective of bringing about *social change* in those institutions, norms, and structures that affect the group's members. The goal in this case is to help each member become more effective in recognizing and bringing about desired social changes; this is seen as often being more effective than individual efforts alone. See also *reciprocal goals model* and *remedial goals model.*

Social Gospel The reform movement that occurred in the United States beginning in the 1870s under the sponsorship of Protestant leaders to advocate for improved conditions among workers, abolition of child labor, occupational protections for women, and the right to living wages. The movement declined when its goals were taken over by organized labor and by the federal programs established in the 1930s.

social group work An orientation and method of social work intervention in which small numbers of people who share similar interests or common problems convene regularly and engage in activities designed to achieve certain objectives. In contrast to *group psychotherapy,* the goals of group work are not necessarily the treatment of emotional problems. The objectives also include exchanging information, developing social and manual skills, changing value orientations, and diverting antisocial behaviors into productive channels. Intervention techniques include, but are not limited to, controlled therapeutic discussions. Some groups also include education and tutoring; sports; arts and crafts; recreational activities; and discussion about topics such as politics, religion, sexuality, values, and goals. Although social group work draws on the theoretical perspectives of existential theory, learning theory, psychoanalytic theory, and social exchange theory, its major theoretical perspective to describe group functioning is social systems theory. This orientation provides workers with a way to conceptualize the effect of group dynamics and interrelationships outside the group. Social group work theorists delineate three major conceptions of group work: (1) the *social goals model,* (2) the *reciprocal goals model,* and (3) the *remedial goals model.* See also *group development, phases of.*

Social Health Index See *Index of Social Health.*

social history An in-depth description and assessment of the current and past client situation, often included in the *case records* and medical records of clients. It is a document that describes the person's family and socioeconomic background and relevant developmental experiences. Typically, this document is prepared by social workers and social work assistants based on interviews with the client and members of the client's family, reviews of records and reports, consultation with other professionals and agencies, and direct observation of the client and the client's environment. The social history often precedes and forms the basis for social work assessment and service planning. It may also be used by other professionals, such as physicians, lawyers, and teachers, in their own decision making to serve the client. Many social histories are written in a narrative, chronological fashion.

Others are organized topically. They frequently include the information under specific headings similar to the following nine headings: (1) *presenting problem,* (2) symptoms of the problem, (3) history of the problem (including recurring situations or repetitious psychological events), (4) current situation (including family; job; economic status; and relevant environmental, social, and health factors), (5) family background (including parents, grandparents, and other close relatives and relevant health and psychological factors about them), (6) educational and vocational background, (7) client goals (including relevant goals of immediate members of the client's family), (8) social worker's assessment, and (9) social worker's recommendations (including social work treatment plans). The history also may include other information the social worker deems relevant to the presenting problem, goal, or agency function.

social indicators Quantitative measures about demographic, environmental, and societal conditions that are used in establishing comprehensive and balanced planning.

social inequality A condition in which some members of a society receive fewer opportunities or benefits than other members.

social institution A formal organization of relationships, the purpose of which is to serve a specific and unique sociocultural function. Examples of social institutions include religion, the family, military structures, government, and the social welfare system.

social insurance Government programs to protect citizens against statutorily stipulated risks, such as loss of income due to old age, disability, death of a breadwinner, unemployment, and work-related injury and sickness. Social insurance programs are characterized by compulsory contributions and participation, presumptive needs, clearly defined benefit formulas, and the absence of the *means test.* Unlike private insurance programs, benefits under social insurance programs are not necessarily proportional to contributions. Major social insurance programs in the United States are *Old Age, Survivors, Disability, and Health Insurance (OASDHI); Unemployment Insurance; workers' compensation;* and state temporary disability insurance.

social justice An ideal condition in which all members of a society have the same basic rights, protection, opportunities, obligations, and social benefits. Implicit in this concept is the notion that historical inequalities should be acknowledged and remedied through specific measures. A key social work value, social justice entails advocacy to confront discrimination, oppression, and institutional inequities.

social learning theory The conceptual orientation and treatment application that builds on and modifies principles of *behaviorism,* taking into account some internal cognitive processes. The major developer of this theory, which emphasizes reciprocal relationships and the ability to learn new responses through observing and imitating others, has been psychologist Albert Bandura.

social legislation Laws and resource allocations providing for human welfare needs, income security, educational and cultural progress, civil rights, consumer protection, and programs that address social problems.

social marketing Activities designed to generate interest and demand by consumers, resource suppliers, licensing and credentialing organizations, and the general public for the services of social agencies. The social marketer's role, unlike that of the traditional social planner, is to help the public find ways and resources to use those services as well as to facilitate their existence. See also *market strategy.*

social minded Having an active concern for the welfare of a society and its institutional services that enhance the well-being of people.

social ministry Activities and *sectarian services* carried out by clergy, religious workers, and volunteers to help poor and disadvantaged people and to combat social injustice. See also *faith-based social services.*

social mobility The degree to which a society permits, encourages, or forces people to change statuses, geographic residence, socioeconomic level, or cultural value orientations.

social movement An organized effort usually involving many people representing a wide spectrum of the population to change a law, public policy, or social norm. Examples of social movements include the *temperance movements,* the *Townsend Plan,* and various *equal rights* movements.

social networks Individuals or groups linked by some common bond, shared social status, similar or shared functions, or geographic or cultural connection. Social networks form and discontinue on an ad hoc basis, depending on specific need and interest. Included as some of the many types of social networks are the *support system,* the natural *helping network, self-help groups,* and groups of formal organizations that address a common problem.

social phobia An intense, continuous, and unreasonable *fear* of being observed or evaluated. Victims of this *anxiety disorder* are most commonly afraid of public speaking or performing before audiences, using public lavatories or bathing facilities, or eating in restaurants. Typically, they fear they will show *anxiety* and be humiliated, a condition that often leads to the outcome they fear (a *self-fulfilling prophecy*). See also *specific phobia.*

social planning Systematic procedures to achieve predetermined types of socioeconomic structures and to manage *social change* rationally. These procedures usually include designating some individual or organization to collect the facts, delineate alternative courses of action, and make recommendations to those empowered to implement them. Social planning is one of the methods of *social work practice.*

social policy The activities and principles of a society that guide the way it intervenes in and regulates relationships among individuals, groups, communities, and social institutions. These principles and activities are the result of the society's values and customs and largely determine the distribution of resources and level of well-being of its people. Thus, social policy includes plans and programs in education, health care, crime and corrections, economic security, and social welfare made by governments, voluntary organizations, and the people in general. It also includes social perspectives that result in society's rewards and constraints.

social problems Conditions among people leading to behaviors that violate some people's values and norms and cause emotional or economic suffering. Examples of social problems include *crime, social inequality, poverty, racism, drug abuse,* family problems, and maldistribution of limited resources.

social promotion An educational practice in some school districts of sending students to the next higher grade even though they have not mastered the needed skills or accomplished the prerequisites. The rationale is to protect the student from feelings of failure or low self-esteem or to portray the school as helping all students achieve educational goals whether they have or not.

social psychiatry   The orientation in the medical profession of psychiatry that emphasizes the family, economic, and environmental contributions to mental illness and a treatment approach that encompasses prevention and community treatment. This approach originated with Dr. Adolph Meyer in the early 1900s and involved social workers in patient aftercare.

social referencing   The process in which an individual observes and interprets the behaviors and emotional responses of others for subsequent emulation. Infants typically pick up from their parents cues about how to understand unfamiliar events, objects, or persons through this process.

social reform   Activity designed to rearrange *social institutions* or the way they are managed to achieve greater *social justice* or other desired change. The term is most often applied to efforts to eliminate corruption in government or structural inequities such as *institutional racism*.

social rehabilitation   Programs and activities that facilitate an individual's entry into a relatively unfamiliar society or cultural system. For example, former prison inmates are sometimes reacquainted with the norms and circumstances of society after long periods of *incarceration*. See also *deinstitutionalization*.

social research   A systematic investigation, using the principles of the *scientific method*, to test hypotheses, acquire information, and solve problems pertaining to human interrelationships.

social security   The provisions a society makes to provide income support for citizens whose incomes are lost because of encountering statutorily defined hazards, such as being old, sick, young, or unemployed. In the United States, the term "social security" refers to cash payments provided by *Old Age, Survivors, Disability, and Health Insurance (OASDHI)* and health benefits provided in the *Medicare* program. In other countries, it also includes health benefits for all residents regardless of need or circumstances and cash benefits to children regardless of their parents' income level.

Social Security Act   The federal legislation (Ch. 531, 49 Stat. 620) enacted in 1935, with several subsequent amendments, designed to meet many of the economic needs of older people, dependent survivors, people with disabilities, and needy families. In its original form, the act contained two major provisions—a compulsory insurance program for workers and a public assistance program financed jointly from the federal and state treasuries. The insurance program collected payroll taxes from certain groups of workers and matching contributions from their employers and, with those funds, established specific funds used to pay benefits to retired workers. Surviving dependents could also receive benefits. Benefits varied according to how much the worker had earned and contributed. Through grants to the states, the act also established an *Unemployment Insurance* program and awarded funds to states to develop uniform programs to care for poor children *(Aid to Dependent Children [ADC])*, needy older people *(Old Age Assistance [OAA])*, and blind people *(Aid to the Blind [AB])*. The Social Security Act has been used as the framework for much of the subsequent national legislation that provides for people's economic and social welfare needs. See also *Old Age, Survivors, Disability, and Health Insurance (OASDHI); Medicare; Social Security Administration (SSA); Federal Insurance Contributions Act (FICA);* and *Title XX*.

Social Security Administration (SSA)   The independent federal organization created to implement the provisions of the *Social Security Act.* It has more than 1,200 local service offices in nearly every county in the United States, and its central records are maintained in its Baltimore, Maryland, headquarters. The local offices are primarily oriented to helping people with its largest programs, *Old Age, Survivors, Disability, and Health Insurance (OASDHI)* and *Supplemental Security Income (SSI)*. The SSA was created in 1946, superseding the Social Security Board. The SSA maintains a Web site and a toll-free 24-hour telephone service to help clients recover lost social security cards, obtain information about social insurance and Medicare eligibility, and obtain an update about one's contributions and expected future benefits. The telephone number is 1-800-772-1213 and their Web site address is http://www.ssa.gov

social security integration   See *permitted disparity.*

social security number   The nine-digit number given to almost all people in the United States to identify them for future *social insurance* benefits. Because of its near-universality, the number is being used as an identifier for other official documents, including tax forms, licenses, passport applications, and other records. As of 1993, all children who are claimed as dependents on Internal Revenue Service (IRS) tax returns must have their own number. Certain working and nonworking aliens who need to report income to the IRS must also have these numbers.

social services   The activities of human services personnel in promoting the health and well-being of people and in helping people become more self-sufficient; preventing dependency; strengthening family relationships; and restoring individuals, families, groups, or communities to successful *social functioning*. Specific kinds of social services include helping people obtain adequate financial resources for their needs, evaluating the capabilities of people to care for children or other dependents, providing counseling and psychotherapy services, providing referrals and channeling, serving as a mediator, advocating for social causes, informing organizations of their obligations to individuals, facilitating health care provisions, and linking clients to resources.

social services employee unions   Labor organizations in which members are employed in public welfare offices and other public and private social agencies to maintain workers' rights and enhance working conditions as well as to advocate for clients. The largest two of these unions are *American Federation of State, County, and Municipal Employees (AFSCME)* and *Service Employees International Union (SEIU)*, both of which are affiliated with the *American Federation of Labor–Congress of Industrial Organizations (AFL–CIO)* and have many social workers among their memberships. Many independent social work unions also exist in larger cities, including New York's Social Services Employee Union and Chicago's Independent Union of Public Aid Employees.

social services technician   A preprofessional employee of a social agency who typically has a two-year degree in a human services field, a four-year degree in a non–social work program, or both.

social services vouchers   A system in which clients eligible for public *social services* are given authorizations for service providers to remit bills to the welfare or human services department for the care they provided to the client. Providers are reimbursed if they meet specified standards. The rates are negotiated in advance between the service providers and the department. This system is thought to give clients greater choice, cut costs, foster innovative service delivery procedures, and provide more efficient delivery of welfare services.

social skill   The ability to relate to and work with others in achieving specific social goals. Examples include speaking understandably, writing clearly, managing time and finances adequately, and empathizing with and influencing people.

social status   See *status.*

social stratification   The division of society into classes (for example, upper class, middle class, working class, lower class, and underclass) according to criteria such as economic level, educational level, or cultural value orientation.

social study   In earlier social work delineations, one of the three major working processes, including *diagnosis* and *treatment.* The study phase of the process consisted of the systematic collection and organization of information relevant to serving the client, which is then analyzed in the diagnostic phase.

social support   Formal and informal activities and relationships that provide for the needs of humans in their efforts to live in society. These needs include education; income security; health care; and especially a network of other individuals and groups who offer encouragement, access, empathy, role models, and social identity.

social therapy   A term often applied to the activities of social workers. In contrast to *psychotherapy,* it refers to providing concrete services, facilitating environmental supports for clients, and helping people deal with social problems and conflicts.

social utility   A way of looking at social services as part of the normal system of needs most people may use at some time in their lives. This construct sees social services as inherently the same as any other public utility and part of the infrastructure, including the transportation system, the educational system, the postal system, the water and sewer systems, libraries, and museums. People who use social utilities, and thus rely on others in society, are not considered deviant or helpless. In the social utility concept, the user of social services is seen as a citizen, not a patient or client.

social value The relative worth to society of a service or commodity. The term is used to differentiate between the cash or dollar value of some items that are measured objectively and the value of other items that enhance the social good but cannot be measured in dollars. For example, a library building and its contents may have the same dollar value as a liquor store and its contents, but their social values differ.

social wage See *new property.*

social welfare 1. A nation's system of programs, benefits, and services that help people meet those social, economic, educational, and health needs that are fundamental to the maintenance of society. 2. The state of collective well-being of a community or society.

Social Welfare Action Alliance (SWAA) The organization founded in 1985 as the *Bertha Capen Reynolds Society,* with chapters throughout the nation. Individual and organizational members of the SWAA, which include social welfare organizations, practitioners in professional social work, and welfare recipient groups, are committed to social, political, and economic justice; peace; and alliance building for fundamental change in existing class, racial, and gender hierarchies. Their Web site address is http://www.swaaction.org

Social Welfare History Archives Collections of records, notes, diaries, photographs, letters, and other material from individual social workers, social agencies, and social movements of the past 100 years or longer, archived and stored in retrievable form at the University of Minnesota since 1964. The Web site address is http://www.special. lib.umn.edu/swha/

social work 1. The applied science of helping people achieve an effective level of psychosocial functioning and effecting societal changes to enhance the well-being of all people. 2. According to the *National Association of Social Workers (NASW),* "Social work is the professional activity of helping individuals, groups, or communities enhance or restore their capacity for social functioning and creating societal conditions favorable to this goal. *Social work practice* consists of the professional application of social work values, principles, and techniques to one or more of the following ends: helping people obtain tangible services; providing counseling and psychotherapy with individuals, families, and groups; helping communities or groups provide or improve social and health services; and participating in relevant legislative processes. The practice of social work requires knowledge of human development and behavior; of social, economic, and cultural institutions; and of the interaction of all these factors" (*Standards for Social Service Manpower,* Washington, DC: National Association of Social Workers, 1973, pp. 4–5). 3. The International Federation of Social Workers adopted their official definition of the term at their General Meeting in Montreal, Canada, in July 2000: "The social work profession promotes social change, problem solving in human relationships, and the empowerment and liberation of people to enhance well-being. Utilizing theories of human behavior and social systems, social work intervenes at the points where people interact with their environments. Principles of human rights and social justice are fundamental to social work."

Social Work Abstracts A quarterly publication and database established in 1965 by the *National Association of Social Workers (NASW)* to provide summaries of recently published articles from social work and related journals. Between 1977 and 1993, it was part of the publication *Social Work Research & Abstracts.*

social work associates Members of the *social work team* who perform a specific task when so assigned by the professional social worker–team leader. Social work associates are similar to *case aides,* although the range of their activities can go beyond work on a specific case.

Social Work Curriculum Study The landmark report published in 1959 by the *Council on Social Work Education (CSWE),* under the direction of Werner Boehm, that delineated the components of graduate-level social work education. The 13-volume study was used as a guide by CSWE in establishing criteria for accrediting schools of social work and by the schools as a means of developing effective educational programs. See also *Hollis–Taylor Report.*

social work education The formal training and subsequent experience that prepare social workers for their professional roles. The formal training takes place primarily in accredited colleges and universities at the *baccalaureate social work* (bachelor's degree in social work) level and in accredited professional schools of social work in *MSW, DSW,* PhD, and other *doctoral programs.* Social work education includes extensive classroom activity as well as direct supervised work with clients *(field placement).* Social workers do not consider their education to be completed only because they have acquired their degrees. On graduation, most social workers provide services under the *supervision* of more experienced colleagues and then take additional formal courses *(continuing education).* See also *Council on Social Work Education (CSWE), curriculum policy statement, Group for the Advancement of Doctoral Education in Social Work (GADE), Hollis–Taylor Report,* and *Social Work Curriculum Study.*

social work fellow   A *National Association of Social Workers (NASW)* designation for a social worker who has achieved the highest professional level of advanced practice.

social work knowledge   According to the *Standards for the Classification of Social Work Practice* (Silver Spring, MD: National Association of Social Workers, 1982, p. 17), social work requires knowledge in some or all of the following areas: *social casework* and *group work* theory and techniques; community resources and services; federal and state *social services* programs and their purposes; *community organization* theory and the development of health and welfare services; basic socioeconomic and political theory; racial, ethnic, and other cultural groups in society—their values and lifestyles and the resultant issues in contemporary life; sources of professional and scientific *research* appropriate to practice; concepts and techniques of *social planning;* theories and concepts of *supervision* and the professional supervision of *social work practice;* theories and concepts of personnel management; common social, psychological, statistical, and other research methods and techniques; theories and concepts of *social welfare* administration; social and environmental factors affecting clients to be served; theories and methods of *psychosocial assessment* and *intervention* and of *differential diagnosis;* theory and behavior of organizational and social systems and of methods for encouraging change; community organization theory and techniques; *advocacy* theory and techniques; ethical standards and practices of professional social work; teaching and instructional theories and techniques; social welfare trends and

policies; and local, state, and federal laws and regulations affecting social and health services.

Social Work Month   A public information and media relations effort that occurs every March to educate the public about the social work profession, its mission, and social issues. In 1984, President Ronald Reagan officially designated March as National Professional Social Work Month. Each year since, the *National Association of Social Workers* sponsors the month-long campaign to increase public understanding of the profession while building pride among social workers. Over the years, the campaign has highlighted social work contributions in areas such as aging, child development, community building, international development, health care, and social justice.

social work practice   The use of *social work knowledge* and *social work skills* to implement society's mandate to provide *social services* in ways that are consistent with social work values. Practice includes *remediation,* restoration (rehabilitating those whose *social functioning* has been impaired), and *prevention.* Some of the most important social work practice roles are clinician, administrator, advocate, broker, caregiver, case manager, communicator, consultant, data manager, evaluator, mobilizer, outreacher, planner, protector, researcher, socializer, supervisor, teacher, and upholder of equitable social values. Social work practice may occur in *micro practice, mezzo practice,* or *macro practice.*

social work purpose   The *Working Statement on the Purpose of Social Work,* developed by the *National Association of Social Workers (NASW)* in 1981, which states that social work's purpose is to promote or restore a mutually beneficial interaction between individuals and society to improve the quality of life for everyone.

Social Work Research Group (SWRG)   The professional association founded in 1949 to facilitate the development of the research specialty in social work. In 1955, SWRG merged with six other associations to become the *National Association of Social Workers (NASW).*

social work skills   The *Standards for the Classification of Social Work Practice* (Silver Spring, MD: National Association of Social Workers, 1982, pp. 17–18) identifies 12 essential skills in social work. They are being able to (1) listen to others with understanding and purpose; (2) elicit information and assemble relevant facts to prepare a *social history, assessment,* and report; (3) create and maintain professional helping relationships; (4) observe and interpret verbal and nonverbal behavior and use knowledge of personality theory and diagnostic methods; (5) engage clients (including individuals, families, groups, and communities) in efforts to resolve their own problems and to gain trust; (6) discuss sensitive emotional subjects supportively and without being threatening; (7) create innovative solutions to clients' needs; (8) determine the need to terminate the therapeutic relationship; (9) conduct *research* or interpret the findings of research and professional literature; (10) mediate and negotiate between conflicting parties; (11) provide interorganizational liaison services; and (12) interpret and communicate social needs to funding sources, the public, or legislators. The same policy statement identified the abilities necessary for social work practice. Social workers should be able to speak and write clearly, teach others, respond supportively to emotion-laden or crisis situations, serve as role models in professional relationships, interpret complex psychosocial phenomena, organize a workload to meet designated responsibilities, identify and obtain resources needed to assist others, assess their own performances and feelings and use help or consultation, participate in and lead group activities, function under stress, deal with conflict situations or contentious personalities, relate social and psychological theory to practice situations, identify the information necessary to solve a problem, and conduct research studies of agency services or their own practices. See also *direct practice skills.*

social work team   A system for delivering social services in which several professional social workers, *social work associates, case aides, indigenous workers, volunteers,* and various ad hoc specialists work in an integrated and coordinated way to achieve a specified goal. The team members discuss in advance all the activities that can be accomplished to achieve the goal efficiently, and then various assignments toward that end are made by the social worker–team leader. Social workers also participate in interdisciplinary teams in fields such as mental health, health care, and developmental care.

Social Work Yearbook   The encyclopedic publication of social work knowledge published originally by the *Russell Sage Foundation* every two or three years beginning in 1929. Publication and distribution were taken over by the *American Asso-*

ciation of Social Workers (AASW) in 1951 with the 11th edition. In 1965, the 15th edition became the two-volume *Encyclopedia of Social Work,* published by the *National Association of Social Workers (NASW).*

social worker cooperatives   A form of *proprietary practice* in social work in which an organization is formed, staffed, and owned by a group of professionals and sometimes paraprofessionals who provide for-profit or nonprofit social services. The cooperatives' owner–workers participate equitably in decision making and direct practice. Income is often derived from grants or capitation fees from third parties or governments to provide specified social services.

social workers   Graduates of schools of social work (with either bachelor's, master's, or doctoral degrees) who use their knowledge and skills to provide social services for clients (who may be individuals, families, groups, communities, organizations, or society in general). Social workers help people increase their capacities for problem solving and coping, and they help people obtain needed resources, facilitate interactions between individuals and between people and their environments, make organizations responsible to people, and influence social policies.

Socialbidrag   The means-tested *income maintenance* program used in Sweden as a supplement to its *social security* program. It is administered and primarily funded at the local level; the rates and types of assistance are determined on a case-by-case basis. Usually, cash payments are made as part of a package of social and educational services.

socialism   A system of economic organization in which all or most of the planning is centralized, and most of the means of production are controlled by the government or a collective institution.

Socialist Workers Party   A national political organization founded in 1938 by a splinter group from other leftist organizations. It generally advocates abolition of capitalism and more rights for racial and ethnic groups, women, and workers. Because of the similarity of names, some people confuse the party with the social work profession. There is no connection between the two.

socialization   The process by which the roles, values, skills, knowledge, and norms of a culture are transmitted to individual members in the society.

socialization group   In *social group work*, one of the five major types of group (along with *support group, education group, growth group*, and *therapy group*). Socialization groups frequently use structured program activities such as games, outings, and recreation. A major purpose of such groups is to improve the interpersonal relationship skills of the members.

socialized conduct disorder   See *conduct disorder.*

socialized medicine   A *health care* system in which a national government directly employs health care providers, builds and maintains health care facilities, and pays for this care through public taxation and international trade revenues. This system is more commonly known as *national health service* and is used by many nations. It is not synonymous with *national health insurance* or the *single-payer health care plans*. The term "socialized medicine," rather than "national health service," is often used derisively by its opponents to convince the public that it is inefficient, lowers standards, increases government control and spending, and reduces accessibility.

Societies for the Prevention of Cruelty to Children (SPCCs)   Independent organizations in many larger communities that advocate for the rights and protection of children. The first SPCC was established in 1874 in New York after it was found that there were more legal protections against the abuse of animals than children. The well-established Societies for the Prevention of Cruelty to Animals began taking child abuse cases to court, holding that children were animals and deserved at least as much protection. Soon thereafter, SPCCs were developed in more than 250 communities. They were instrumental in early efforts to provide legal protections for children and in developing child welfare legislation.

Society for Social Work and Research (SSWR)   An independent professional association established in 1994 to facilitate, improve, and develop social work research. SSWR hosts an annual conference; issues awards for outstanding research contributions; maintains researcher databases; and sponsors publications, including a regular newsletter and the journal *Research on Social Work Practice*. Their Web site address is http://www.sswr.org

Society for Social Work Leadership in Health Care (SSWLHC)   A national professional organization for the development of social work values, practice, and leadership in health care organizations and for the promotion of standards and ethics for the field. The organization sponsors annual conferences, publications, and the newsletter *Social Work Leader*. Their Web site address is http://www.sswlhc.org

Society for Spirituality and Social Work   An independent, interdenominational organization of social workers and other helping professionals, established in 1990, to advocate for spiritually sensitive helping and to honor and encourage spiritual development and justice for all people of diverse religious and nonreligious paths. The society sponsors conferences and the quarterly journal *The Spirituality and Social Work Forum*. Their Web site address is http://sehd.binghamton.edu/affprograms/sssw/

sociobiology   The science of social behavior in humans and other animals and the genetic basis for that behavior.

sociocultural dislocation   The movement of an individual or group into a society that has unfamiliar or unacceptable norms. The move may be permanent and inclusive, as in migrating from a Third World nation to a wealthy one, or it may be temporary and partial, as experienced by some racial and ethnic groups whose members live in ghetto areas and have jobs in affluent offices dominated by Caucasian people. See also *relocation camps.*

socioeconomic class   Categorization of groups of people according to specified demographic variables, such as level of income or education, location of residence, and value orientation. Sociologists often categorize the classes as "upper," "middle," "lower," and *working class*. Other observers make further distinctions, such as "upper middle class" and *underclass.*

sociofugal arrangements   The physical design, setting, and decor of offices and facilities that tend to keep people apart and inhibit their interaction. For example, a social worker's sociofugal office and waiting room might contain stiff chairs lined straight against walls that are too far apart for easy communication. See also *sociopetal arrangements.*

sociogenic   Behavior that is motivated, influenced, or imposed by social conditions, values, and constraints.

sociogram A diagram or graphic presentation used by group workers and other professionals to display how members of the group feel about one another and how they tend to align themselves with some and against other members of the group or organization. See also *action sociogram.*

sociolinguistics The study of language in relation to the social context in which it is expressed. The social work interviewer can understand the context of the transaction much more fully through a microanalysis of sociolinguistic concerns such as repetitions, interruptions, silences, pause placements, word emphasis, and hesitations.

sociopath See *dyssocial.*

sociopetal arrangements The physical design, setting, and decor of offices and facilities that tend to draw people together and encourage interaction. For example, a social worker's sociopetal office might have comfortable chairs close to one another at attractive angles, have good lighting and music in the waiting area, and use file cabinets to form conversation nooks rather than barricades. See also *sociofugal arrangements.*

"soft sciences" The name sometimes attached to less empirically based bodies of knowledge, including social sciences such as economics, psychology, and sociology. This is contrasted to what are called the *"hard sciences,"* including natural sciences such as biology, chemistry, and physics. Social work is usually placed in the "soft science" category as an applied social science.

software In computers, the programs (or instructions) that make the physical equipment *(hardware)* execute the desired operations.

Solidarity Movement The labor movement that began in Gdansk, Poland, in the late 1970s to advocate for better working conditions and more efficient means of productivity. Many historians consider this movement to be the precipitator of the downfall of the Communist system of governing Eastern European (Iron Curtain–Warsaw Pact) nations and the end of the *Cold War.*

solipsism The view that one's knowledge must derive only from one's own personal experience and that everything outside one's experience is questionable.

solitary aggressive-conduct disorder That type of *conduct disorder* in which the person's pattern of *antisocial behavior* is harmful or threatening to others and does not take place within the context of a group or *gang.* This is considered usually more pathological than the *group-type conduct disorder.*

solution-focused social work An orientation in social work intervention that examines how progress is made rather than defines what problems exist. The focus is on the client's strengths, supports, and resources and considers how others with similar strengths have dealt with similar situations.

solvency The ability of an individual or organization to pay debts.

somatic complaints The description by a client or patient of physical symptoms or discomforts, such as headaches, dizzy spells, cramps, fatigue, or apparent injury or illness.

somatic-type delusional disorder A subtype of *delusional disorder* characterized by nonbizarre delusions, particularly an intense concern about bodily functions or sensations. The delusion takes different forms (for example, the conviction that one is emitting a foul odor, is infested with internal parasites or insects, possesses ugly or misshapen body parts, or is afflicted with an undiscovered disease). See also *taijin kyofusho.*

somatization disorder One of the *somatoform disorders,* characterized by a subject's long history of complaints about symptoms that are not caused by physical disease, injury, or drugs. Symptoms include being sickly for much of one's life, gastrointestinal symptoms (such as abdominal pain, nausea, vomiting, or diarrhea), and pseudoneurological symptoms (such as fainting, muscle weakness, blurred or double vision, or memory loss).

somatoform disorders Mental disorders that have the appearance of physical illness but, lacking any known organic basis, are generally thought to be *psychogenic.* The specific disorders in this category are *somatization disorder, body dysmorphic disorder, hypochondriasis, conversion disorder,* and *psychogenic pain disorder.* When the individual experiences only a few of these symptoms of a shorter duration, the diagnosis is "undifferentiated somatoform disorder."

somatoform pain disorder See *psychogenic pain disorder.*

somnambulism See *sleepwalking disorder.*

soporific A drug or procedure designed to induce sleep.

sosialrådgiver In Denmark, a professional social worker.

sosionomen In Sweden and Norway, the title for professionally educated social workers.

soup kitchen A facility, usually operated by a private charitable or religious organization, that prepares and serves food to poor people at little or no cost to the recipients. See also *bread line.*

Southern Christian Leadership Conference (SCLC) The *civil rights* organization, founded in 1956 by Martin Luther King, Jr., and others, in which the goal is the peaceful combat of racially motivated injustice. A Web site address is http://www.sclcmagazine.com

sozialarbeit Professional social work in Germany. A professional who is a male social worker is called a "sozialarbeiter" and a professional female social worker is a "socialarbeiterin."

Sozialhilfe The means-tested *income maintenance* program used in Germany as a supplement to its *social security* program. Sozialhilfe is funded primarily from local government taxes and is not related to the amount of contributions made by the recipient, as in the case of the German social security program. The amounts paid are consistent with the German policy of ensuring a "dignified existence."

span of control In administration, the number of people or activities under one person's supervision, including the amount of time the manager takes to supervise them effectively.

"Spanglish" A term describing the combination of the English and Spanish languages used by some Spanish-speaking immigrants to the United States and Canada.

spasticity A muscle disorder, usually caused by damage to the portion of the brain or spinal cord

that controls voluntary movement. Certain muscles are continuously contracted, often interfering with gait, speech, and movement. It is often associated with diseases such as spinal cord injury, multiple sclerosis, cerebral palsy, severe head injury, and some metabolic diseases.

Specht, Harry (1929–1995) Social work educator who was first exposed to social workers during his impoverished childhood, then entered the profession as a settlement house group worker and researcher. A longtime dean at the University of California–Berkeley, he coauthored influential books on social welfare policy, community organization, and the mission of the profession.

special education Any form of schooling, training, tutoring, or other educational formats to meet the needs of exceptional children and adults. The term has been most commonly applied to educational programs for people with visual impairments, hearing impairments, physical disabilities, cognitive disturbances, mental retardation, advanced talents, or intellectual giftedness.

special-interest group A formal or informal collective of like-minded individuals who seek to influence the policies of governments, political candidates, agencies, proposed laws, or the general public. The group has in common one issue that it seeks to promote through media events, legislative advocacy, lobbying, and political action committees (PACs).

Special Milk Program The *USDA* program in which half-pint containers of milk are supplied free or at cost to children who attend participating schools, especially those not in the *School Lunch Program* or *School Breakfast Program.*

special-needs adoption *Adoption* of children who have extenuating conditions or circumstances (such as older children; siblings; children of color; or children who have special physical, emotional, or developmental needs). Each state establishes its own definition of children with special needs. The *Adoption Assistance and Child Welfare Act of 1980* (P.L. 96-272) provides funding and services for eligible children with special needs if they cannot be placed with adoptive parents without such assistance.

special-needs clients People who, by reason of some mental or physical disability, require additional or different kinds of assistance to achieve their goals in seeking social services. For example, a couple seeks marital therapy and the wife has multiple sclerosis, or a child entering the adoption system has quadriplegia.

special populations   People and groups classified together because they share some distinguishing attributes, traits, talents, problems, disorders, obstacles, orientations, or other unique characteristics.

specialist   One whose orientation and knowledge are focused on a specific problem or goal or whose technical expertise and skill in specific activities are highly developed and refined. See also *generalist*.

specialization   A profession's focus of knowledge and skill on a specific type of problem, target population, or objective.

speciesism   The ideology that the human species is the only one with rights and that all other species and their habitats exist only to meet the needs and desires of humans.

specific development disorders   See *developmental disorder*.

specific phobia   An *anxiety disorder* characterized by marked and persistent *fear* of a clearly identifiable object or situation. Formerly called "simple phobia," this condition is one of three major types of phobias (including *social phobias* and *agoraphobia*). Some of the more common specific phobias are *acrophobia, algophobia, aquaphobia, claustrophobia, hematophobia, nyctaphobia, ocholophobia, thanatophobia*, and *zoophobia*. See also *phobia*.

"speed"   A slang term for *amphetamine*. When used illicitly, as in taking excessive dosages over extended periods or in intravenous injections, these drugs are dangerous and physiologically and psychologically addictive.

Speenhamland   An income subsidy system that originated in Speenhamland, England, in 1795 and was later widely imitated. Workers who earned less than a predetermined amount had the difference made up from public funds.

spell   A *culture-bound syndrome* found most commonly among European Americans and Afri-

can Americans in which the individual enters a trancelike state, often seeking to communicate with spirits or deceased significant others.

Spencer, Anna (1851–1931)   A feminist and social reformer who helped establish the American Purity Alliance and the New York School of Philanthropy, which became the nation's first school of social work. She also wrote influential texts, including *Woman's Share in Social Culture* (1912) and *The Family and Its Members* (1923).

spending down   Reducing one's total assets and income to become eligible for certain means-tested *social insurance* benefits. For example, people who have substantial savings would be ineligible for Medicaid, so they dispose of their funds to become eligible for Medicaid.

"SPICES"   Social—Physical—Intellectual—Cultural—Emotional—Spiritual; a mnemonic to help remember all the client's different needs when developing a case management plan.

spin control   A public relations effort to change the way the public understands some news event.

spina bifida   Failure of the spinal column to close properly during early fetal development. The disorder is frequently associated with other problems such as mental retardation and hydrocephalus and its complications.

Spinal Cord Injury Psychologists and Social Workers, American Association of   The professional association established in 1986 to promote the goals of those who provide for the psychosocial care of people with spinal cord injuries. The association facilitates information exchanges among professionals, advocates for the needs of patients, and sponsors publications and annual conferences. Their Web site address is http://www.aascipsw.org

spiritual counseling   Professional clinical intervention with an orientation to the client's moral, emotional, and religious perspective. See also *transpersonal social work*.

spirituality   Devotion to the immaterial part of humanity and nature rather than worldly things such as possessions; an orientation to people's religious, moral, or emotional nature.

splinter group   Those who dissent on one or more issues from a larger organization, break away, and form their own group.

split-half reliability   In research, the correlation between the scores achieved by a group of subjects in one part of a test (for example, the even-numbered items) and the group's scores on another similar part (for example, the odd-numbered items) of the same test.

splitting   In *psychoanalytic theory,* a primitive defensive process in which the individual is thought to repress, dissociate, or disconnect important feelings that have become dangerous to his or her psychic well-being. This may cause the person to get out of touch with his or her feelings and to develop a "fragmented self."

SPMI   Serious and persistent mental illness.

spoils system   A political and economic procedure in which those loyal to a winning candidate or organization leader receive more benefits than nonsupporters, regardless of merit. See also *merit system.*

spontaneous remission   The disappearance of symptoms of mental or physical disorders that is not attributable to outside help.

spousal impoverishment   Financial destitution of a married person whose spouse has been in nursing home care. Prior to 1988, older couples had to spend down their assets to zero to become eligible for *Medicaid* funding to help pay for nursing home care. In the 1988 legislation (P.L. 100-647), when a couple applies for Medicaid, an assessment is made of their combined resources, regardless of ownership, but it excludes their home, household goods, car, and burial funds. The rest is the couple's combined countable resources. A portion of that amount is the basis for determining if the nursing home patient is Medicaid eligible. Once resource eligibility is determined, any resources belonging to the community spouse are no longer considered available to the spouse in the medical facility.

spouse abuse   The infliction of physical or emotional harm on one's wife or, less frequently, on one's husband.

spurious correlation   A pattern of variation between two phenomena that seems to indicate causality or mutual reciprocity but results instead from other factors.

squatter   One who settles without title or right on rural or urban land belonging to another.

squatter's rights   The presumed entitlement of a person to own land or buildings merely by occupying them for a specified length of time. Such "rights" no longer have legal validation as they once did in some jurisdictions. See also *urban homesteading.*

St. Vincent de Paul Society   An international Catholic lay group established in France in 1833 by *Antoine Frederic Ozanum* to provide financial relief, counseling, and social services for needy people. The organization has local centers in most nations with significant Catholic populations, including the United States. Their Web site address is http://www.svdprvc.org

staff development   Activities and programs within an organization designed to enhance the abilities of personnel to fulfill the existing and changing requirements of their jobs. These activities often include short-term in-service training classes, distribution of relevant information, group conferences, use of outside consultants and speakers to meet with personnel, and funding of certain employees to participate in meetings or training programs outside the organization. Staff development, although usually related to the requirements of the employer, also helps personnel improve overall career objectives and opportunities. It also helps the organization attract and keep competent personnel and clarify and "humanize" the organization. See also *in-service training.*

staffing   In *social welfare* administration, an organization's activities designed to maintain and improve personnel effectiveness. These activities include recruiting and interviewing prospective employees and volunteers; assigning, promoting, transferring, and firing employees; and providing for *in-service training* and *staff development.*

stage theories   The concept that every period of life is characterized by some underlying challenges and orientations that modify one's behavior and priorities. Each stage has characteristics that make it unique, and each higher stage incorporates many of the gains made in earlier ones. The degree to which one reconciles the conflicts inherent in each stage largely determines the likelihood of coping successfully in subsequent life stages. Among the best known of these concepts are Erik Erikson's *psychosocial development theory;* Sigmund Freud's *psychosexual development theory; Kohlberg moral development theory;* and Piaget's theory of *cognitive development.*

stagflation A nation's economic condition in which there is *inflation* without accompanying economic growth. This is often an indicator of economic *recession* or *depression.*

stakeholding A social welfare policy in which poor people receive assets and incentives to accumulate assets instead of cash.

stalking Following, pursuing, and stealthily observing a person with persistence, often because of obsession or other mental disturbance.

stammering See *stuttering.*

standard deviation (SD) A statistical measure to indicate the degree of dispersion of a distribution. It is the average difference between individual scores and the mean score in a distribution, obtained by squaring the deviation scores, adding them together, dividing by one less than the number of scores, and taking the square root of the result. In a normal (symmetrical or bell-shaped) distribution, 6.2 percent of the cases will fall between +1 or –1 standard deviation from the *mean,* 95.4 percent will fall between +2 or –2 standard deviations, and 99.7 percent of the cases will fall between +3 or –3 standard deviations.

standard of living A concept comprising the necessities, luxuries, and comforts an individual, group, class, or society needs or uses to live in a particular circumstance. The concept is often confused with "standards of consumption." Consumption involves the availability of consumer goods to the individual or the society. "Standard of living" includes available consumer goods but adds choices and variety of these goods, normal working conditions, amount of leisure time, and opportunities for using that time. See also *lifestyle.*

standardized tests Measurement tools used by social researchers, educators, and clinicians. The tests have already been used on many subjects, permitting a high degree of confidence in their *validity* and *reliability.* Standardized tests provide in-structions, scoring procedures and standards, time limits, norms, and statistical data to make possible comparisons of the sample group with a much larger segment of society.

stare decisis doctrine The policy of courts of law to stand by precedence and not disturb settled points. Any decision made by the court is binding on that court and on other courts of equal or lower rank when the same or a similar issue arises in the future. Policies of courts do change, but only rarely and with good cause because of this doctrine.

Starr, Ellen Gates (1859–1940) A cofounder, with *Jane Addams,* of *Hull-House* in Chicago in 1889. Starr later worked as an advocate in the trade union movement and for improved conditions for workers. She also worked closely with *Florence Kelley* to improve *child labor* conditions.

State Children's Health Insurance Program (SCHIP) A program of the HHS, known as Title XXI, established as part of the Balanced Budget Act of 1997 to provide health insurance to children whose families earn too little to afford private health insurance but earn too much to qualify for *Medicaid.* The program is administered by the states and coordinated by the *Center for Medicare and Medicaid Services.* Their Web site address is http://www.cms.hhs.gov/schip

state terrorism A government's sanctioned use of violence to intimidate and weaken its opposition or those who espouse contradictory values. Tactics of state terrorism have included killing, torture, ethnic cleansing, kidnapping followed by "disappearances," and guerrilla warfare against other nations.

state's attorney A prosecutor in a court of law who represents the interests of the state and its people. The state's attorney may also be known as an attorney general or a district attorney or an assistant to one with that title.

statistical inference Systematically analyzing a *sample* and drawing conclusions about the *population* from which the sample was drawn.

statistical significance See *significance level.*

statistics 1. Data expressed in numerical form and the processes of analyzing these data and making inferences from the data. 2. In *research,* quantitative procedures (which may be descriptive or inferential) that are used to describe or assess *variables* or relationships between variables.

status   A social position that carries culturally defined expectations or *roles.* Statuses may be "achieved" (such as social worker, homeless person, or government bureaucrat) or "ascribed" (such as woman, Hispanic, or child). Laypeople use this term as a synonym for "prestige."

status offender   One whose actions would not be considered a violation of criminal law if they were committed by someone with a different *status.* For example, when children are truant from school, they are violating the law because of their status as children; if their status was "adult," their lack of school attendance would not be a violation.

Statute of Labourers   One of the world's earliest *public welfare* programs, initiated in England in 1349, it forbade giving charity to able-bodied people, compelled unemployed people to work for anyone who would hire them, forbade unemployed people to leave their hometowns or villages (or allowed them to go only to areas where there was work), and fixed the maximum wages that could be paid to workers.

statute of limitations   A law that specifies the amount of time within which a person must be charged with a *crime* or sued for damages. Courts do not hear cases involving acts that occurred beyond this time limit. The major exception is *homicide;* a person can be charged with this crime no matter how long after the event. Another exception is the doctrine of *contra non valentem,* which provides that the statute of limitations does not apply to one who is unable to bring an action.

statutory benefits   Entitlements (that is, cash and services) that federal and state laws mandate to qualified individuals. This includes benefits such as *social security, workers' compensation,* and *unemployment compensation* but not means-tested programs such as *Temporary Assistance to Needy Families (TANF)* or *Medicaid.*

statutory rape   A consenting sexual relationship with someone who is under the legal age of consent in a given jurisdiction.

Steering Committee for International Relief   An informal association of the five major private organizations for international relief—*Oxford Committee for Famine Relief (OXFAM), Catholic Relief Services (CRS),* the World Council of Churches, the *Lutheran World Federation (LWF),* and the *League of Red Cross Societies.* Headquartered in Geneva, the committee coordinates efforts of the private organizations with one another and with groups such as *United Nations Disaster Relief Organization (UNDRO)* and provides information and instruction to *disaster relief* workers.

stem cells   An unspecialized cell that can become a specialized cell when subjected to certain conditions.

stepfamily   A primary *kinship* group whose members are joined as a result of second or subsequent marriages. Such a family may include a stepfather (the husband of one's mother), a stepmother (the wife of one's father), a stepchild (the offspring of one's spouse by a previous marriage or relationship), and stepbrothers and stepsisters (the children of one's stepparent). As a result of increased divorce and remarriage rates, stepfamilies now constitute a major type of family constellation. See also *reconstituted family* and *blended family.*

stepparent adoption   *Adoption* of a child by the parent's spouse, the most common form of adoption and usually the least complicated legally and socially because the child is already in the family.

stepsibling   An individual whose family role is that of a brother or sister even though there is no biological connection. The stepsibling relationship occurs primarily when a mother of one child marries the father of another child. Stepsiblings may or may not live in the same home and may or may not be children.

stereotypes   Preconceived and relatively fixed ideas about an individual, group, or social status. These ideas are usually based on superficial characteristics or overgeneralizations of traits observed in some members of the group.

stereotypic movement disorder   A disorder of infancy, childhood, and adolescence characterized by intentional and repetitive gestures or activities that have no socially acceptable purpose. Some of these behaviors include teeth grinding, body rocking, head banging, hitting oneself, skin picking, or repetitive vocalizations, often performed in a rhythmic fashion. This condition was formerly known as "stereotypic habit disorder." See also *Tourette's syndrome* and *tic disorder*.

sterilization   1. A medical procedure that ends a person's ability to reproduce. This method of permanent *birth control* or *reproductive technology* usually involves *tubal ligation* or vasectomy (tying off a man's vas deferens). Attempts to reverse sterilizations have limited success rates. 2. The procedure of making something free of living germs or microorganisms.

steroids   Drugs based on natural hormones or synthetics intended for use in treating inflammation, arthritis, asthma, and other disorders. Steroids are rapidly becoming drugs of abuse, especially by athletes, bodybuilders, and others wanting to look more muscular but who risk serious long-term physical and social consequences of using them improperly. In prolonged misuse, the initial sense of enhanced well-being, strength, and energy is replaced by depression, irritability, low energy, and general medical conditions, especially liver disease.

stigma   The characteristic of an individual that is deemed by others as negative.

stillborn   A baby born dead after the 20th week of pregnancy.

stimulants   *Psychoactive substances* that produce in the user mild to intense feelings of *euphoria* and states of alertness, heightened awareness, and relief from feelings of sleepiness or tiredness. These substances tend to be habituating and addictive and often have serious side effects. Drug abusers know forms of substances such as *"uppers"* and *"speed."*

stimulus   Any event in the environment that is perceived by the individual. A stimulus may be discriminative, eliciting, reinforcing, punishing, or neutral. See also *response*.

stimulus discrimination   In *social learning theory*, the phenomenon in which the subject does not respond to a *stimulus* even though it is similar to one that had previously evoked a *response*.

stimulus generalization   The ability of a subject to respond to one *stimulus* in the same way he or she responded to another, similar stimulus; the opposite of *stimulus discrimination*.

sting operation   1. A method police officials use in apprehending felons by posing as businesspeople who buy stolen or illicit goods. 2. *Confidence crimes* in which victims pay for services to phony businesses.

Stockholm syndrome   The phenomenon in which the victim of a kidnapping or terrorist hostage situation becomes sympathetic with the perpetrators or their cause. The victim may later participate with the perpetrators in similar activities or try to defend or justify them. The response is thought to be based partly on relief and gratitude that the offenders did not kill or severely harm the victim. The term comes from a bank robbery incident in Stockholm in 1973. See also *survivor syndrome*.

stolen children   Youths who have been abducted from the legal custodial parent, usually by the other parent after a divorce and loss of custody. See also *child snatching*.

stonewall   To stubbornly refuse to give information or negotiate about debatable issues. An example is a client who remains noncommunicative or rigid about new ideas.

Stonewall   The incident that gay men and lesbians consider the beginning of the modern gay rights movement. The Stonewall Inn, a Greenwich Village, New York, bar, was frequented by gay men and lesbians. In 1969, after police arrested patrons for "indecency," gay men and lesbians worldwide showed support through demonstrations, passive resistance, and overt public relations campaigns.

stop-and-frisk laws   The limited legal right of a police officer to detain and search an individual who acts suspiciously or who may be carrying an unlicensed dangerous weapon. Any further search requires a warrant. In the United States, this right has been upheld in Supreme Court cases (such as *Terry v. Ohio*), but only when strictly related to the circumstances that justified the stop.

stranger anxiety   Fear or apprehension in the presence of unfamiliar people, most common among very young children. See also *separation anxiety*.

strategic family therapy   The orientation and procedure used by some family therapists to help families and their members discontinue reciprocal interactions in which recurring patterns of *symptomatic* behavior occur. The therapist designs an intervention to resolve specific problems, the resolution of which will require the family system to modify all other interactions.

strategic marketing   The development of a product or service that serves the interests of specific publics. Strategic marketing segments the public geographically, demographically, functionally, and psychologically to define an agency's or program's *niche* or market. It also involves pricing, placing, and promotions to regulate demand for a specific product or service.

strategic philanthropy   Contributions made by corporations to serve the interests of the company as well as the beneficiaries. For example, a software maker donates computer programs to schools so the students learn how to use that company's products.

strategic planning   The process of defining long-term goals and the alternative means toward their accomplishment. The goals are defined by specifying the target of intervention, auspices, value implications, feasibility, and interrelationships among various components of the social system. The goals thus established provide guidelines for looking at alternative means of achieving desired ends, which can often result in major modifications of existing programs and services.

strategies   Carefully designed and implemented procedures an individual or group uses to bring about long-term changes in another individual or group. Strategies refers to long-range approaches and ultimate goals, and *tactics* refers to short-term or day-to-day maneuvers.

stratified sample   In *research*, dividing a *population* into strata, randomly selecting from each of the strata, and pooling the result. This stratification ensures that a certain proportion of representation occurs from each component. For example, a stratified sample might consist of a random selection, except that an equal number of people were born in each decade.

streaming   Assignment of workers or students to distinctive paths of progression, supposedly based on their demonstrated abilities or aptitudes but often based more on characteristics such as race, gender, or social class. See also *mainstreaming*.

street children   Homeless or semihomeless children who are forced, or choose, to live away from their families. More common in urban centers of underdeveloped nations, but also found in cities of affluent nations, the children tend to congregate with each other in areas where they remain ignored by authorities and other adults. Many street children (including *runaways, thrownaway children,* and *pushout youths*) have menial jobs and are exploited for their labor. The *UN Convention on the Rights of the Child* requires signatory nations to ensure alternative care for them.

street gangs   Informal organizations composed mostly of younger people who tend to have common antisocial values, community residence, race, and symbols that distinguish themselves from other gangs and nongang members. Some predominantly African American gangs include *Crips and Bloods,* Vice Lord Nation, Disciples, Folk Nation, and People Nation. Some predominantly Hispanic gangs include 18th Street Gang, Latin Kings, and Maniac Latin Disciples. Southeast Asian and Caucasian groups, such as *skinheads,* also have significant gang memberships in some communities. Organizations established especially to deal with gangs and their victims include Mothers Against Gangs, Mothers Against Violence, the Gang Violence Reduction Project of the California Youth Authority, and the Gang Prevention Through Targeted Outreach program of the *Boys and Girls Clubs of America.*

"street kids"   Adolescents in the 16 to 21 age range who live on or near the streets of urban areas in relative independence from their parental homes. Whereas younger boys and girls are usually considered to be *runaways* or abandoned or lost children, these adolescents constitute a large subpopulation whose existence is generally unrecognized. For example, they are not counted among homeless people in the United States. (The *U.S. Bureau of the Census* counts only people older than 21 as homeless.) See also *Ribicoff children.*

"street people" A popular name for urban adults who congregate near centers of business activity and spend much of their time socializing, wandering about, seeking employment or assistance, or *"hustling."*

street-smart Possessing survival and coping skills, descriptive of some youths and adults who spend most of their time in public places. Their skills include being able to avoid exploitation by others, finding sources of money or goods whenever needed, avoiding unwanted contacts with authorities, and being able to live outside the established social system. This is a relative term, and everyone possesses or lacks some of these *social skills* or *coping skills* at times. The term is synonymous with "streetwise."

strengths perspective An orientation in social work and other professional practices that emphasizes the client's resources, capabilities, support systems, and motivations to meet challenges and overcome adversity. This approach does not ignore the existence of social problems, individual disease, or family dysfunction; it emphasizes the client's assets that are used to achieve and maintain individual and social well-being.

stress Any influence that interferes with the normal functioning of an organism and produces some internal strain or tension. "Human psychological stress" refers to environmental demands or internal conflicts that produce *anxiety.* People tend to seek an escape from the source of these influences—*stressors*—through means such as a *defense mechanism, avoidance* of certain situations, *phobia,* somatization, rituals, or constructive physical activity.

stress–diathesis theory The hypothesis that some mental disorders, including *schizophrenia,* are the result of genetic predisposition combined with some stressful situations in the environment.

stressful life events *Crisis* occurrences experienced by an individual that require coping responses but at a time when familiar sources of support or resources are no longer available. Major stressful life events include the death of a spouse or child, loss of a job, divorce, disease of a family member, and moving to a new neighborhood.

stressor A *stimulus* that leads to *anxiety* or other mental disorders unless the individual's *coping skills* are used effectively.

stroke A sudden interruption or blockage of the flow of blood to the brain, usually caused by the formation of a blood clot in the blood vessel. The resulting manifestations may include paralysis of

certain parts of the body, speech and language deficits, sensory loss, cognitive and communicative disturbances, convulsions, and coma. Stroke survivors vary in their recovery progress; approximately 50 percent retain some permanent disability, such as speech or motor coordination problems. Recurrence is frequent and often fatal. The term is also known as *cerebrovascular accident (CVA).*

structural approach A social work model developed by Gale G. Wood and Ruth R. Middleman (*The Structural Approach to Direct Practice in Social Work,* New York: Columbia University Press, 1989) in which the social environment is the primary target of change, and the intervention is to improve the quality of the relationship between people and their social environment by changing, creating, or using existing social structures.

structural family therapy An orientation and procedure in *family therapy* based on identifying and changing maladaptive arrangements, interactions, and the internal organization of subsystems and boundaries of a family. Structural family therapy was developed in the 1970s primarily by Salvador Minuchin. The therapy helps families understand the rules and roles they have developed for each member within the family unit and how those rules were developed; it also helps them understand how they have developed the rules and roles between themselves as a unit and the outside world.

structural social change Basic and relatively rapid changes in social institutions and social values, often brought about by revolution, great political upheaval, or natural disaster. This is the opposite of *incremental social change.*

structural social work A practice model that assumes that inadequate social arrangements are mainly responsible for many clients' problems. The model aims to help people modify the social situations that limit their functioning—for example, by connecting them with needed resources, negotiating difficult situations, and changing certain existing limiting social structures.

structural unemployment One of the four types of *unemployment* (including *cyclical unemployment, seasonal unemployment,* and *frictional unemployment*) caused by poor economic conditions in one industry or geographic area when employment elsewhere is good.

structured group   See *group, structured.*

structured observation   The practice of systematically witnessing those aspects of a social phenomenon that fit a predetermined plan. It may take place in a clinical setting, in a laboratory experiment, or in the field, and the observer usually has a checklist of categories to note. The categories were developed by the investigator on the basis of hypotheses or findings from previous research.

student aid programs   Financial assistance to people attending colleges or other educational institutions, mostly through grants or loans. Sources of funds are privately funded scholarships, foundation grants, and state and federal grant and loan programs. The major federal programs include *Pell Grants* (based on a formula of student need and expected family contribution); National Direct Student Loans (low-interest loans to needy students); Supplemental Educational Opportunity Grants (based on need); Guaranteed Student Loans (the government guarantees repayment to banks that lend money to students); and the College Work Study Program, which provides matching funds to colleges to hire students on campus.

stupor   A state of numbness and dazed confusion, often symptomatic of people with *organic mental disorders, schizophrenia,* and *intoxication.*

"sturdy beggar"   A designation used in *English Poor Law* for paupers who were considered to be able-bodied and therefore employable and ineligible for aid.

stuttering   One of the *communication disorders* characterized by disturbance of speech function, usually involving frequent repetitions of words or parts of words, disruptions in the flow of speech, and hesitation or prolongation of sounds. Stuttering, which also is known as "stammering," tends to be more intense when the individual is under scrutiny or feels under pressure to communicate. See also *cluttering* and *expressive language disorder.*

subemployment   The condition of having a job that pays below *subsistence level* or a job that does not use much of the worker's education or previous experience. Social workers describe many people who are *working poor* as being subemployed.

subject   An individual, group, organization, or entity that is being evaluated in the *research* design.

subjugated knowledge   The range of information and understanding that is acquired outside the established knowledge-building procedures (scientific method) and is possessed indigenously by people who are not considered "experts." Because this type of knowledge comes from and is maintained outside the academic or professional establishment, it is given little serious attention (that is, it is subjugated).

sublimation   In *psychodynamic* theory, a *defense mechanism* in which those desires and instinctive drives that are consciously intolerable and cannot be directly realized are diverted into creative activities that are acceptable to the individual and society.

subpoena   A legal document ordering an individual to appear in court at a certain time. Failure to comply may result in some penalty.

subpoena duces tecum   A type of *subpoena* requiring the witness who is called to bring to the court or deposition any relevant documents possessed. See also *case record* and *relative confidentiality.*

subsidized adoption   The provision of public financial assistance to families who adopt dependent children. Recent federal and state legislation has established criteria for subsidizing *adoption.* The two prominent criteria are that the child is unlikely to be returning to the birth parents or should not be returning to them and that adoptive placement without a subsidy has already been attempted for a specified amount of time by the proper authorities but has been unsuccessful because of the child's physical or emotional condition or racial or ethnic background.

subsidized employment   Work that is paid for partly by the employer and partly by another organization. For example, a government reduces its welfare expenditures and provides work and training opportunities by reimbursing an employer who has hired a recipient of *Temporary Assistance to Needy Families (TANF)* for part of that employee's wages.

subsidized guardianship   A program to provide financial assistance and social services for the *kinship care* of children who can no longer live with their parents. Even though kinship care has helped many needy, abused, or neglected children; kept them out of the overburdened foster care system; and saved large sums in public welfare budgets, kinship caregivers received little social or financial support. Subsidized guardianship provides money to kin who take permanent legal custody of a related child.

subsidy   Money or commodities granted by a government or other organization to another level of government, organization, industry, or individual. See also *grants-in-aid* and *block grant.*

subsistence economy   The economic system of a country or group that produces only the minimum amount of goods and services needed for survival, with few *resources* available for education, cultural advancement, or savings.

subsistence level   The lowest amount of money or *resources* one needs to survive.

substance abuse   A maladaptive pattern of using certain drugs, alcohol, medications, and toxins despite their adverse consequences. Substance abuse is considered less problematic than *substance dependence* in that *tolerance* and *withdrawal symptoms* have not yet occurred.

Substance Abuse and Mental Health Services Administration (SAMHSA)   The agency within the *U.S. Department of Health and Human Services (HHS)* that facilitates efforts and programs to assist people with substance abuse or mental illness problems. SAMHSA awards grants to local programs that serve the needs of these people and to research and demonstration programs. Their Web site address is http://www.samhsa.gov

substance dependence   Continued use; craving; and other cognitive, behavioral, and physiological symptoms that occur through the use of certain drugs, alcohol, medications, and toxins. Some of the symptoms include being preoccupied about the substance; taking greater amounts than intended; making persistent efforts to control its use; reducing occupational or social activities; and continually using the substance despite recognizing that it is causing recurrent physical, psychological, or social problems. If *tolerance* or *withdrawal symptoms* have not yet occurred, then the condition is known as *substance abuse.*

substance-induced anxiety disorder   Excessive apprehension, tension, fear, restlessness, sleep disturbance, difficulty concentrating, and other symptoms of *anxiety* that are judged to be due to the direct physiological effects of a drug of abuse, medication, or toxin.

substance intoxication   Specific behavioral patterns and symptoms (including cognitive impairment, *emotional lability,* belligerence, impaired judgment, and poor social or occupational functioning) owing to recent use of a drug, alcohol, medication, or toxin.

substance intoxication delirium   A *delirium* that occurs within minutes to hours after taking relatively high doses of medication or other substances. The delirium usually ends as the *intoxication* ends or within a few hours to days after the body has rid itself of the toxins. A formal diagnosis of this condition would specify the type of substance, as in "alcohol intoxication delirium." See also *substance-use disorders.*

substance-use disorders   A classification of disorders related to the taking in of a drug of abuse, alcohol, medication, or toxin resulting in undesirable symptoms and side effects. In the *DSM-IV* classification, the substances used or induced are alcohol, *amphetamine,* caffeine, *cannabis, cocaine, hallucinogen,* inhalant, nicotine, *opium,* phencyclidine, *sedatives,* polysubstances, and "other, unknown" substances. Disorders that result from this include substance-induced psychotic disorder, *mood disorders, anxiety disorder, sexual dysfunction,* and *sleep disorders.*

substance withdrawal   Significant patterns of physical discomfort and emotional distress, cognitive impairment, *emotional lability,* belligerence, impaired judgment, and poor social or occupational functioning because of reduced or discontinued use of a specific drug, alcohol, medication, or toxin.

substance withdrawal delirium   A *delirium* that occurs after termination or reduction of relatively high doses of certain medications or substances. Duration ranges from minutes after withdrawal begins to two to four weeks. When alcohol is the substance, the condition is also known as *delirium tremens (DTs).*

substandard housing   Dwelling places in which the physical or structural deficiencies preclude having a safe, secure, and reasonably comfortable home. According to the *U.S. Department of Housing and Urban Development (HUD),* a dwelling unit is severely substandard if it lacks electricity, hot or cold water, a flush toilet, a shower or bath, and effective heating equipment and possesses at least five basic maintenance problems such as holes in floors or walls, broken windows, water leaks, rodent or insect infestations, and so forth. A dwelling unit is moderately substandard if it does not have the aforementioned severe problems but does have maintenance problems such as frequently broken flush toilets; unvented gas or heating sources; and no sink, refrigerator, or stove.

substitution   In *psychodynamic* theory, the *defense mechanism* in which the individual replaces an unattainable or unacceptable goal with one that is attainable and acceptable.

subsystem   A part of a *system* that itself contains interacting and reciprocally influencing elements. For example, in the family system, such subsystems are the parents, the children, the females, the males, the *nuclear family* system, and the *extended family* system.

successive approximation   A technique commonly used in *behavior therapy* in which each small, incremental step toward the goal behavior is reinforced. See also *shaping*.

sudden infant death syndrome (SIDS)   The unexplained death of a young child, most frequently occurring between ages two and five months, sometimes referred to as "crib death." The cause is not yet well understood, but speculation centers on the possibility that some babies have not established adequate defense responses to respiratory problems. See also *apnea*.

sudden unexplained death syndrome (SUDS) Fatalities, not in infants, for which the causes cannot be determined.

suffrage   The legal right to vote. Many of the early social workers were women who advocated for this right and were called "suffragettes." See also *Seneca Falls Convention*.

suicidal ideation   Serious contemplation of *suicide*, or thought patterns that lead to killing oneself. Indicators of this include *depression*, especially when accompanied by a sense of hopelessness or unconnectedness with others in the present or past; major changes in sleep patterns; clear or implied statements indicating a wish to die or an intention

to commit suicide; substance abuse; a recent experience of irrevocable loss; absence of a support system; easy access to lethal means (weapons, drugs, and so on); previous suicide attempts; suicide or suicide attempts by role models; and strong feelings of failure and rejection.

suicide   The act of intentionally killing oneself.

suicidology   The scientific study of the act of taking one's own life—its motivations, progression, incidence, consequences, and prevention. Professionals who engage in such study and work with those affected by suicide or suicidal ideation are known as suicidologists. Most suicidologists are mental health professionals, including social workers. Many belong to the American Association of Suicidology, the Washington-based professional association founded in 1968.

Summer Food Service Program   A *USDA* child nutrition program started in 1968 to provide lunches during summer vacation months for needy children who are dependent on the *School Lunch Program*. Their Web site address is http://www.summerfood.usda.gov

sunk costs   In social agency administration and *social planning*, the investment of time and effort made by an organization's personnel to develop, maintain, and facilitate their relationship patterns, status and power arrangements, and traditional ways of doing things.

sunset laws   Statutes that require an organization to demonstrate periodically that it is achieving the goals it was established to achieve or be automatically discontinued.

sunshine laws   Legal requirements that government meetings and hearings are to be conducted in public. The law (P.L. 94-409) was enacted in 1976. This term now applies to the requirements that other organizations and levels of government also conduct their business open to the scrutiny of those affected.

superego   In *psychodynamic* theories, that part of the *psyche* or personality that regulates the individual's ethical standards, *conscience*, and sense of right and wrong. The superego is said to begin its development by identifying with the apparent *values* and rules established by parent figures. See also *ego* and *id*.

Superfund The Resource Conservation and Recovery Act of 1976 (P.L. 94-580), a federal program that allocates resources to be used in the cleanup of *toxic waste sites* and other environmentally hazardous conditions. The Comprehensive Environmental Response, Compensation, and Liability Act of 1980 (P.L. 96-510) assists individuals and communities affected by these sites.

superstition Beliefs and practices founded on nonrational expectations, *culture-bound syndromes,* folk tales, and fears of or answers for unexplained phenomena. Clinicians do not consider superstitious ideas or practices to be indicative of mental disorder unless they become so constricting or time-consuming that they interfere with *activities of daily living (ADLs).*

supervised community living The social structure of a group residential facility in which residents are monitored and assisted as needed to fulfill their *activities of daily living (ADLs).*

supervision An administrative and educational process used to help social workers further develop and refine their skills, enhance staff morale, and provide *quality assurance* for the clients. Supervisors often assign cases to the most appropriate social worker, discuss the assessment and intervention plan, and review the social worker's ongoing contact with the client. Educationally, supervision is geared toward helping the social worker better understand social work philosophy and agency policy, become more self-aware, know the agency's and community's resources, establish activity priorities, and refine knowledge and skills. Less experienced workers tend to be supervised according to a tutorial model, whereas more experienced workers use more case consultation, peer-group interactions, staff development, or *social work teams.* Educational supervision (oriented toward professional concerns and related to specific cases) is distinguished from administrative supervision (oriented toward agency policy and public *accountability*).

Supplemental Medical Insurance (SMI) A major component of *Medicare* to help pay the costs of physicians' fees, lab tests, ambulance services, prosthetic devices, and certain other medical services not entirely covered by Medicare. Those who elect to pay for additional coverage may be reimbursed for Medicare expenses not always covered, such as initial deductibles and coinsurance fees.

Supplemental Security Income (SSI) The federal *public assistance* program, established in 1972, that provides a minimum cash income for poor people who are elderly, have a disability, or are blind. Eligibility for SSI is determined by a *means test* and not related to one's previous work record. Funding comes from the federal treasury and is usually supplemented by state funds. It is administered primarily by the *Social Security Administration (SSA),* although its funds do not come from the money earmarked for financing *Old Age, Survivors, Disability, and Health Insurance (OASDHI).* The SSI program's benefits and eligibility were modified in the *Personal Responsibility and Work Opportunity Reconciliation Act* of 1996 (P.L. 104-193).

suppleness The degree to which the body's muscles and joints permit ease of movement.

supply-side economics The thesis in economic theory, popular during the Reagan administration, that lower taxes permit more money to flow into the economy and therefore result in more jobs and growth.

supply subsidy The concept of providing funds to organizations or allocating funds to establish new organizations so that they can provide services. This is in contrast to the *demand subsidy* concept, in which funds or vouchers are provided to individuals and families so that they can purchase goods and services in the existing service-providing market. Public housing is an example of the supply subsidy concept, and food stamps are an example of demand subsidy.

support group A structured ongoing series of meetings among people who share a common problem and who give advice, encouragement, information, and emotional sustenance. The group may be led by a professional social worker but more often comprises only the members themselves, and the degree of structure varies considerably.

support system An interrelated group of people, resources, and organizations that provides individuals with emotional, informational, material, and affectional sustenance. Members of a support system may include an individual's closest friends and family members, key members of the peer group, fellow employees, membership organizations, and institutions that can be called on for help in times of need.

supported employment An alternative vocational service for people with severe mental or physical challenges. Employees usually receive wages and benefits in the competitive marketplace; receive continuing on-the-job training, supervision, and transportation; and work in settings with nonchallenged employees.

supportive feedback In social work administration and *supervision*, the communication of approval when observing the fulfillment of desired behaviors. See also *corrective feedback*.

supportive treatment The helping interventions used by social workers and other professionals, designed primarily to help individuals maintain adaptive patterns. This is done in the interview through giving reassurance and advice, providing information, and pointing out client strengths and resources. Supportive treatment supposedly does not seek to reach unconscious material. However, the boundaries between supportive therapy and "deeper" *insight therapies* are unclear and overlapping.

suppression 1. In psychosocial theory, the conscious psychic mechanism of putting unpleasant thoughts out of one's mind. Suppression is similar to *repression*, except that the latter is a *defense mechanism* operating unconsciously to remove threatening ideas from one's awareness. 2. In social conflict theories, actions taken by one group or organization to prevent other groups or individuals from expressing their ideas, from assembling, or from developing political power.

Surgeon General The officer in charge of the public health of the American people. Administratively, the Surgeon General is the head of the *U.S. Public Health Service (PHS)* and its agencies, including the *Food and Drug Administration, National Institutes of Health,* and the *Centers for Disease Control and Prevention.* The Surgeon General reports to the *HHS* Assistant Secretary for Health and is the principal advisor to the President and spokesperson to the nation on matters concerning public health. Personnel in the Public Health Service are given military ranks and report to the Surgeon General, who is their commander. Their Web site address is http://www.osophs.dhhs.gov

surplus In government budgets, the amount of money left over after all the debts have been paid.

The term also applies to products that have been made and not sold and agricultural harvests that are greater than can be consumed.

surrogacy A form of *reproductive technology* in which a man donates his sperm or a woman donates her egg or use of her body so that a *fetus* can be conceived and developed through to birth. A male surrogate donates sperm to a "bank." The sperm, through *artificial insemination,* is used in conceiving a fetus in the biological mother. Male surrogacy generally is used when the man in a couple is sterile, so that the couple can have a baby that is 50 percent biologically related. A female surrogate donates an egg; the egg is artificially inseminated with the sperm in a Petri dish. The fertilized egg is then placed in the uterus. Female surrogacy generally is used when a woman's anatomy or physiology precludes development of a healthy fetus. Usually, the surrogate mother who carries the fetus to delivery is paid and is contracted to relinquish the baby soon after birth. Legal debates have challenged whether these contracts are irrevocable.

surrogate A person who has been granted the authority to act on behalf of, or substitute for, another.

surrogate parent 1. In the justice system, an individual who is not a child's biological parent but who voluntarily or through court appointment assumes the parent's rights and obligations. 2. A man who donates his sperm or a woman who donates an egg or temporary use of her uterus to a couple so that the couple can become parents.

survey A systematic fact-gathering procedure in which a specific series of questions is asked, through written or oral *questionnaires,* of a representative *sample* of the group being studied or of the entire *population.*

survival bonding Assigning shared responsibilities to two or more social workers in agencies with high rates of employee stress to provide them with the *mutual help* and collaborative opportunities needed to reduce the likelihood of *burnout.* Pairing gives both workers a degree of stress reduction through mutual ventilation, elimination of isolation, opportunities for the exchange of information, and mutual respect and dependence. This shared responsibility is particularly useful in working with nonmotivated multiproblem families and terminally ill clients.

survivor guilt A strong sense of *shame, depression,* and regret that often follows escape from some danger that harmed others. Survivors of war, earthquakes, group hostage taking, and similar experiences are particularly vulnerable. When this feeling persists and interferes with adequate social functioning, it is known as *survivor syndrome.*

survivor syndrome The behavior patterns, traits, and symptoms that tend to occur in people who have experienced dangerous, life-threatening events or *trauma.* Such people often have prolonged periodic anxiety, guilt feelings, anger, and fears, especially in situations that seem similar to the traumatic event. The syndrome has been experienced especially by *Vietnam veterans,* former prisoners of war, *Holocaust* survivors, sexual assault victims, crime victims, and people who have lived through serious natural disasters. See also *posttraumatic stress disorder (PTSD)* and *Stockholm syndrome.*

suspended sentence The deferral of a legally prescribed punishment, such as incarceration or payment of damages, until a probationary period is over. The sentence may be set aside if the conditions of the probation have been met.

suspicion The belief that someone has done or intends to do something wrong or harmful, often with little evidence. This is a major symptom of *paranoia* and the paranoid type of *schizophrenia.*

sustainable development (SD) The international goal of achieving more permanent economic well-being within the existing physical environment. An economy is sustainable only when it uses but does not deplete its resources or ruin its environment for immediate economic gain. See also *renewable resources.*

sustaining procedures Relationship-building activities used by the social worker to help the client feel more self-confident and confident of the worker's competence and good will, including listening with sincere interest and sympathy and conveying a sense of mutual respect rather than superiority over the client. *Acceptance, reassurance,* encouragement, and *reaching out* are other sustaining procedures.

susto A *culture-bound syndrome* most common to Latinos and Spanish-speaking people in which the individual experiences sickness and unhappiness, which is said to be caused by the soul leaving the body after a frightening event. Symptoms include *sleep disorders,* appetite disturbances, and various somatic ailments, sometimes days to years after the onset event. Ritual healings to call the soul back to the body sometimes reduce or eliminate the symptoms.

"sweatshop" A manufacturing facility in which employees work under inhumane conditions for low pay.

SWHSW Social Workers Helping Social Workers, a national mutual-aid group of social workers who have personal experiences with alcohol and chemical dependence. Established in 1980, SWHSW facilitates the efforts of affected social workers to help one another through mutual support, telephone contacts, workshops, meetings, conferences, and other contacts. Their Web site address is http://www.socialworkershelping.org

swindle The crime of acquiring someone's money or property by trickery, false statements, or other fraudulent methods.

Switzer, Mary E. (1900–1971) An administrator for various U.S. federal social welfare agencies who was chief of the Office of Vocational Rehabilitation and later the Social and Rehabilitation Service, in which she established the need for social work professionalism in such programs and effectively advocated legislation to serve people with disabilities.

symbiosis A relationship between two organisms in which there is mutual biological or psychological dependence. This may occur between different species (flowers depend on insects for cross-pollination and provide food necessary for the insects' survival) or within a species (termites help one another to survive). Symbiosis occurs between a parent and a child and to some extent between mature adults in certain mutually beneficial social relationships. The term also refers to a person's identification with others to such an extent that it blocks his or her differentiated identity. See also *codependency.*

sympathetic nervous system The part of the nervous system that controls the involuntary responses to perceived danger, such as the increase in the rate of heartbeat and dilation of the pupils.

symptom An indicator of the possible presence of an underlying psychological or physical disorder or of a psychosocial problem. For example, *flat affect* is *symptomatic* of *schizophrenia, ideas of reference* are symptomatic of *paranoia,* abnormally high fever is symptomatic of infection, repeated facial bruises are symptomatic of abuse, and *inflation* is symptomatic of a supply–demand imbalance.

symptomatic Indicators within an individual, family, group, society, or system of an underlying disorder, disease, or problem.

synapse The space between adjacent *neuron* fibers through which neurotransmitters travel.

syncope Fainting; a temporary loss of consciousness due to a sudden decrease of blood flow to the brain.

syndicalism The political ideology advocating better conditions and wages for workers and the elimination of state authority over economic organizations. It also advocated anarchy and revolution. The ideology developed in France in 1890 and spread throughout Europe and South America primarily in the trade union movement but lost influence at the beginning of World War I.

syndrome A cluster of behavior patterns, personality traits, or physical symptoms that occur together to form a specific disorder or condition.

synectics A creative problem-solving approach used in task groups. Members are asked to scrutinize the presenting problem outside the usual context. This is facilitated by including into the group's membership a variety of people with diverse interests and experiences. For example, a social agency board might invite former clients to attend a retreat to discuss more efficient outreach activities.

synergism 1. Cooperative effort by discrete organizations, social agencies, or subsystems that produces a more effective result than the sum of the output that could be achieved if the organizations acted independently. 2. The combined effect of two or more drugs that is greater than the total effect of each drug working alone. See also *systems theories.*

synergizing risk factors Multiplying the likelihood of contracting a disease by exposure to two or more factors that, by themselves, would not be as risky. For example, a person who smokes a pack of cigarettes a day and never drinks alcohol has a 52 percent higher risk of oral cancer than a person who does not smoke or drink, but if this person smoked one pack and had one drink per day, the risk would increase to 400 percent.

synoptic planning A model of *social planning* for economic, health, physical, and social needs that is comprehensive and rational. This is the planning "ideal," but many suggest that it can never be realized because of the limits of human rationality and the complexities of fully comprehensive planning.

syphilis A contagious *venereal disease* transmitted primarily by sexual contact and rarely by contact with an open wound or transmission of infected blood or plasma. Untreated, the disease causes lesions in subcutaneous tissue and internal organs and degeneration of the nerves, often causing blindness and psychosis. Treatment with penicillin has been effective in the early stages.

system A combination of elements with mutual reciprocity and identifiable *boundaries* that form a complex or unitary whole. Systems may be physical and mechanical, living and social, or combinations of these. Examples of social systems include individual families, groups, a specific social welfare agency, or a nation's entire organizational process of education.

systematic desensitization A *behavior modification* technique, designed by Joseph Wolpe in the 1950s, that gradually alleviates the fear and anxiety associated with an object or event. Using relaxation exercises and *imagery relaxation technique,* the client is exposed to stimuli from a gradation of anxiety-provoking situations. For example, if a client is afraid of heights of more than six feet, the social worker might encourage the client to stand on the lowest rung of a stepladder while thinking of some pleasant experiences long enough for anxiety to end at that level. This process would be repeated slowly until the client is comfortable at levels higher than six feet.

Systematic Multiple-Level Observation of Groups (SYMLOG) A method developed by social psychologist Robert F. Bales to assess client behavior graphically and to quantify systematically actions in the social worker–client system.

systemic requisites In *community organization* and social policy development, the identification of existing as well as potential *resources* and programs and the collaborative effort to link and coordinate these resources so that duplication and competition are avoided and the range and quality of service are expanded. See also *functional requisites*.

systems analysis The process of evaluating through the *scientific method* data about any set of dynamically interconnected elements and the environment in which the elements function.

systems theories Those concepts that emphasize reciprocal relationships between the elements that constitute a whole. These concepts also emphasize the relationships among individuals, groups, organizations, or communities and mutually influencing factors in the environment. Systems theories focus on the interrelationships of elements in nature, encompassing physics, chemistry, biology, and social relationships. See also *general systems theory, ecological perspective, life model,* and *ecosystems perspective*.

Szold, Henrietta (1860–1945) An American educator, writer, and social worker. She led the Youth Aliyah, a Zionist organization that rescued many thousands of Jewish teenagers from Nazi-dominated Europe in the 1930s and 1940s. She organized schools and facilities in America for Jewish immigrants who had escaped persecution in Russia. She helped found Hadassah, was a leader in the Zionist organization, and headed the department of social welfare for the Jews of Palestine.

T-group A training group, often made up of people who work together in one organization, that emphasizes communication, self-development, and cooperative problem solving. Some T-groups are structured, whereas others are unstructured to encourage the members to learn by experience how to be more effective in interpersonal relationships.

tabling A procedure in official meetings to dispose of a topic without decision or further debate, indefinitely or until a later specified time. To table a matter (to let a motion lay on the table) is a way to proceed with other business or to kill the proposal without discussion.

taboo A behavior or symbol prohibited by a cultural group. Every group teaches its members that certain actions, objects, persons, and words are not to be condoned. Although most societies have taboos against incest, cannibalism, and murder, each culture develops prohibitions against some behaviors that are acceptable in other cultures and subcultural groups. Some anthropologists use the alternative spelling "tabu."

tabula rasa The mind before it has any experience; a "clean slate." It is the absence of any preconceptions. The term is used by social workers to convey approaching something or someone without prejudice, that is, with a completely open mind; it also suggests that the way people think and behave is because of their various cultures rather than because of some inherent quality or instinct. This concept is the opposite of *nativism.*

tachycardia Excessively rapid heartbeat.

tactics Carefully designed and implemented procedures an individual or, more often, a group uses to bring about short-term changes in another group or individual. Tactics refers to short-term or day-to-day maneuvers, whereas *strategies* refers to the long-range approaches and ultimate goals. See also *legislative advocacy tactics.*

tactics of influence Activities of *community organizers, social activists,* and other social workers to encourage adoption of one policy over another. Some actions include holding case conferences with individuals and organizations to determine needs and needs provision, gathering facts, taking advocacy positions, convening and participating in committees, petitioning, *media campaigning,* providing expert testimony, working as *lobbyists, bargaining,* organizing a *demonstration,* initiating or coordinating a *class action suit,* and engaging in *disruptive tactics.* See also *tactics, strategies,* and *legislative advocacy tactics.*

Taft, Jessie (1882–1960) Social work educator and casework practitioner who developed the *functional school in social work* with her colleague, *Virginia Robinson,* and integrated the theories of psychoanalyst Otto Rank (1884–1937) into the social work curriculum. Her best known book is *A Functional Approach to Social Casework* (1944).

"tagger" A graffiti "artist" who uses spray-paint cans and other marking devices on large, highly visible surfaces, such as urban buildings, street signs, commuter trains, bridges, and water towers. Many "taggers" are members of *street gangs* and mark property to proclaim their gang's turf.

taijin kyofusho A *culture-bound syndrome* found most commonly in Japan in which an individual experiences intense fear of being offensive to others through physical appearance, body odors, or gestures. See also *somatic-type delusional disorder.*

take-turns format A procedure in which each member of a *social group work* or *group psychotherapy* session sequentially discusses an issue. This procedure is considered less effective because it discourages free interaction, forces premature self-disclosures, and produces undue anxiety in those waiting.

"taking the Fifth" Refusing to answer questions asked by law authorities by exercising the U.S. Constitution's *Fifth Amendment rights* against self-incrimination. See also *Miranda.*

tamhuy In Jewish tradition, a community kitchen in which those in need would never lack for food. Other needs were met in this tradition through the *kupah* (community fund). See also *tzedakah.*

TANF The popular designation, pronounced "tanif," for *Temporary Assistance to Needy Families.*

tantrum An episode of extreme anger, seen more commonly among young children and immature older people, manifested by screaming, violent body movements, ostentatious crying, and the throwing of objects.

***Tarasoff* decision** The 1976 ruling by the Supreme Court of California *(Tarasoff v. Regents of the University of California)* stating that, under certain circumstances, psychotherapists whose clients tell them that they intend to harm someone have a duty to warn the intended victim. Subsequently, this decision has been upheld in many other states. Some social workers have argued that the effect of the ruling is to make it more difficult for therapists to assure their clients of *confidentiality* and for clients to express certain hostile feelings to their therapists. Others argue that the effect of the ruling is to save the lives of innocent people. See also *relative confidentiality, code of ethics, Jaffee v. Redmond decision,* and *Ramona decision.*

tardive dyskinesia (TD) A *medication-induced movement disorder* that includes abnormal and uncontrollable physical movements, especially of the mouth, lips, and tongue, and sometimes repetitive movements of the head, hands, and feet. This neurological disorder is seen in many clients who have used antipsychotic drugs for extended periods.

target behavior In *behavior modification,* the behavior or behaviors selected for analysis or modification. Identifying the target behaviors is the first step in the therapist's *behavioral assessment.* This includes delineating the specific behaviors and the time and conditions in which they occur. For example, a social worker would list a target behavior for a youngster who frequently skips school as follows: "Student was absent from school an average of two times per week during the past two months." See also *unit of attention.*

target of intervention In social work practice, that which is to be changed so that the problems presented or recognized by the *client,* the *client system,* or the social worker can be solved or mitigated.

target segments of society In *social planning* and policy development, a category of people who are deemed most vulnerable to a given social problem or who are given special attention in efforts to find solutions or enhanced well-being. For example, a target segment might be all American mothers; everyone who is functionally illiterate; or all residents of Tacoma, Washington. See also *unit of attention.*

target system The individual, group, or community to be changed or influenced to achieve the social work goals. This is one of the four basic systems in social work practice (including the *change agent system,* the *client system,* and the *action system).* Target systems and client systems are sometimes but not always identical. They are different when the client is not to be changed. For example, a client may be a poor family that is being evicted, and the social worker's target system might be the landlord. Target systems and client systems may be the same when the client wants to achieve some self-change, such as relief from symptoms of emotional distress. See also *unit of attention.*

tariff A tax levied on imports to help protect a nation's or a community's business, labor, or agriculture from outside competition.

task-centered treatment A model of short-term social work intervention in which the social worker and client identify problems and the tasks needed to change them, develop a contract in which various activities are to occur at specified times, establish incentives and a rationale for their accomplishment, and analyze and resolve obstacles as they are identified. The client may also be helped to accomplish tasks by simulation and guided practice in the social worker's office before performing them independently during the week. The social worker also facilitates a contextual analysis by helping the client identify, locate, and use resources and modify distorted perceptions or unrealistic expectations.

task force A temporary group, usually within an organization, brought together to achieve some previously specified function or goal. An effective task force or task group knows why it is meeting, what jobs must be accomplished, who has responsibility for carrying out its decisions, and when the work is completed.

task groups In *social group work,* those groups in which the primary purpose is to accomplish some explicit goals that may or may not meet the individual emotional needs of members. The focus of group discussion is on the tasks at hand, with a formal agenda and rules for conducting the meeting.

task implementation sequence (TIS)   A systematic procedure for helping clients accomplish general tasks and *operational tasks* by enhancing the client's commitment to carrying out a specific task; planning the details for carrying it out; analyzing and resolving the anticipated obstacles; having clients rehearse the behaviors in carrying out the task; and summarizing the plan for task implementation, conveying encouragement and expectation that the client will carry out the task. TIS should be applied systematically but with flexibility to fit different client circumstances and models of intervention.

Tavistock group   A type of psychoanalytically oriented *group psychotherapy*, originated in 1944 by Wilfred Bion at the Tavistock Clinic in Great Britain, in which the group therapist assumes an apparently passive, almost bystander, role and makes interpretations only to the whole group. A major goal is for members to attain insight into the transference reactions that emerge.

tax   A mandatory charge, usually of money, imposed by a *government* to help pay for its operating costs. See also *regressive tax, progressive tax,* and *"sin tax."*

tax incentives   Government programs designed to encourage certain behaviors through policies of taxation. For example, a government may reduce or forgive taxes on a business that agrees to establish labor-intensive factories in its jurisdiction. A government may also attempt, through heavy taxation, to discourage actions such as smoking tobacco products or driving automobiles that consume great amounts of fuel, which is also known as a tax disincentive.

tax offset   A legal procedure to collect unpaid child support payments from noncustodial parents by intercepting their federal or state income tax refunds.

tax resistance movement   Organized and ad hoc responses to government taxation policies. The movement is worldwide and tends to mobilize in open societies in which tax increases occur or in which taxes are used for government actions that taxpayers dislike. The movement takes a variety of forms, from illegal tax avoidance and use of the underground economy to finding "loopholes" of dubious legality to supporting candidates who promise lower taxes and participating in antitax

lobbying groups. Among the largest of the U.S. groups are the National Taxpayers Union, founded in 1969; Americans for Tax Reform (1985); Citizens for an Alternative Tax System (1990); and the National Tax-Limitation Committee (1975). Many organizations advocate changes in or the elimination of the progressive income tax system, recommending a national sales tax system and the elimination of expensive government social services programs.

Tay–Sachs disease   A genetically transmitted metabolic disorder that results in fatal brain damage. It occurs mostly in infants of East European Jewish ancestry. See also *genetic disorder* and *genetic counseling.*

Taylor, Graham (1851–1938)   A *settlement house* founder and early developer of *social work education.* He developed the first training courses for volunteers and *friendly visitors* at the University of Chicago, which were incorporated into the first social work curriculum. He also founded and edited one of the first social work journals, *The Survey.*

Team Nutrition   The *USDA* initiative to help the nation's schools recognize and use more nutritious foods in their school food programs.

teams in social work   See *social work team.*

technique   The knowledge-based skills, methods, and procedures purposefully used to achieve explicit goals.

technocracy   A society led by scientists and *technocrats.*

technocrat   An official of a government or private organization whose decisions are based on scientific and technological findings rather than on sociopolitical ones. See also *apparatchik.*

technological disaster   A *disaster* caused by accidents within manufacturing plants or conveyances that causes mass destruction to people, property, or the environment in a widespread area. The designation is used by disaster experts to distinguish these kinds of problems from natural disasters, such as earthquakes, drought, famine, floods, and hurricanes, and from war or civil conflict. Technological disasters include events such as massive oil spills, nuclear power generator breakdown and contamination of an area, or dams bursting and flooding populated areas downriver.

teen court Justice system programs for juvenile offenders in which adolescents charged with crimes are prosecuted, defended, and sentenced by their peers in real courtrooms under the supervision of adult judges and court officials. These courts were conceived in Texas in the 1970s and are now found in nearly every U.S. state. Teenagers who serve as prosecutors, jurors, or spokespersons for defendants are volunteers or are often themselves serving teen court sentences.

teen living programs (TLPs) State-sponsored residential programs for adolescent parent welfare recipients who are unable to meet welfare eligibility living requirements of living in their family homes because of parental abuse, neglect, addiction, or other circumstances.

telehealth Professional consultation through telecommunication, provided by physicians, social workers, and other service providers. The program is used primarily by homebound clients who would face serious hardship if moved. Some third-party payers, including *Medicare,* reimburse social workers and others who provide this service (excluding telephone and facilities costs), and payments are shared between the referring and consulting health professional.

teleological 1. Purposeful; goal directed. 2. When used by clinical social workers and other psychotherapists, sometimes referring to the client's ultimate goal directedness and the worker's effort to help sort out goals and move purposefully. Workers influenced by Alfred Adler's (1870–1937) form of psychoanalysis emphasize the need to understand and modify goals.

telephone reassurance A program to provide daily contact for people who live alone and have concerns about their health and security. Local senior centers, social services departments, and city and state agencies on aging sponsor such programs, which are usually staffed by volunteers.

telephone scatologia A *sexual disorder (paraphilia)* involving the making of obscene telephone calls.

temperament The affective component of a person's personality.

temperance movements Organized efforts to influence people to abstain from or modify their consumption of alcohol. These movements were especially strong in the United States, Canada, and European nations in the years 1850 to 1930. The major groups in the United States were the Women's Christian Temperance Union, the Prohibition Party, and the Anti-Saloon League, which helped influence passage of many antiliquor laws, culminating in the 18th Amendment to the U.S. Constitution in 1919, or Prohibition. The influence of these groups declined when Prohibition was repealed by the 21st Amendment in 1933.

Temporary Assistance to Needy Families (TANF) The U.S. federally structured welfare program established in 1996 to consolidate the *Aid to Families with Dependent Children (AFDC)* program, the *Job Opportunities and Basic Skills Training (JOBS) program,* and Emergency Assistance. The program is part of the *Personal Responsibility and Work Opportunity Reconciliation Act* of 1996 (P.L. 104-193). TANF gives the states more authority to create and manage their own welfare programs. States are authorized to cut their welfare spending by up to 25 percent without losing the fixed federal block grants. Unlike the AFDC program, TANF cash assistance is not considered an entitlement. In its original law, lifetime eligibility of benefits was limited to a total of five years, and benefits to legal immigrants were restricted. One provision, which limited the amount a welfare recipient who moves into a state with higher benefits receives to the amount previously received in the lower-paying state, was invalidated in a 1997 Supreme Court decision. TANF was reauthorized in somewhat modified form in 2002 under the *Working Toward Independence* legislation. TANF is usually pronounced "tanif." Detailed information about TANF and its authorizing legislation are made available by the *Administration for Children and Families (ACF)* of the HHS. Their Web site address is http://www.acf.hhs.gov/news/welfare

temporary disability insurance State-run *social insurance* programs to protect workers from some of the financial consequences of being out of work because of injuries or disabilities that are not expected to last indefinitely. When the disability is expected to be permanent, federal disability insurance programs such as *Supplemental Security Insurance (SSI)* or *Disability Insurance (DI)* are used.

Temporary Inter-Association Council of Social Work Membership (TIAC)   The historical organization formed in 1950 to restructure the social work profession. Following its recommendations, various organizations merged by 1955 to form the *National Association of Social Workers (NASW)*.

tenant management   A program in *public housing* projects whereby residents participate in making and implementing decisions affecting their homes.

tenant organization   A formal or informal association of people, most of whom live in the same apartment building or housing complex and share an interest in maintaining or improving the conditions of their residence. Tenant organizations often present unity in confrontations with landlords or public housing authorities.

tendonitis   Inflammation of a tendon.

tenement house   A multifamily residential structure, usually old, run down, and rented to poor people.

tenure   A status achieved by some educators, government officers, and other employees ensuring continuing employment within the organization until retirement, subject to some qualifications. Also, in legal terms, the right to possess a property.

Terkel, Ida (1913–2000)   A social worker and activist who was a leader in various movements for civil rights, better housing, and social justice in Chicago. She also worked with her husband, writer Studs Terkel, in formulating, editing, and developing characters in his many influential columns and books.

terminal illness   A disease that is expected to result in a person's death.

termination   The conclusion of the social worker–client intervention process; a systematic procedure for disengaging the working relationship. It occurs when goals are reached, when the specified time for working has ended, or when the client is no longer interested in continuing. Termination often includes evaluating the progress toward goal achievement, *working through, resistance, denial,* and *flight into illness.* The termination phase also includes discussions about how to anticipate and resolve future problems and how to find additional *resources* to call on as future needs indicate. See also *premature termination* and "*client dumping.*"

terrorism   The systematic use of fear, intimidation, and disruption of social systems, usually by politically motivated or criminal groups, to gain publicity or concessions. See also *state terrorism.*

tertiary care   In the system for delivery of health care, the type of intervention provided by highly specialized professionals, usually taking place in large health care centers and university-based hospitals where sophisticated diagnostic and treatment equipment is found. Patients are referred to this level of care by primary- or secondary-level physicians. See also *primary care* and *secondary care.*

tertiary gain   The advantages and benefits a person with a physical or mental illness brings to others as a result of the illness. For example, a patient's sickness requires that the spouse remain home to provide care and avoid working at an unpleasant job.

tertiary prevention   Rehabilitative efforts by the social worker or other professional to assist a client who has already experienced a problem to recuperate from its effects and develop sufficient strengths to preclude its return. Most forms of clinical intervention can be considered forms of tertiary prevention. See also *primary prevention* and *secondary prevention.*

test bias   A tendency built into a test causing its results to be inaccurate. For example, some aptitude tests are said to be culturally biased against some racial and ethnic groups when those groups tend to score lower than do other test takers.

test case   A lawsuit to determine whether a law or legal practice is valid. Often, the case is brought intentionally by a cause-oriented group to test the validity of a newly passed law. For example, a state enacts a law stating that psychotherapy may be provided only by psychiatrists. A social work group might designate one of its members to provide psychotherapy and therefore be arrested. The resulting court case could test whether the law could be upheld.

test item distracter   One of the wrong answers to a multiple-choice test question.

test–retest reliability   In *research,* the degree to which a test or procedure achieves a similar outcome the second time it is administered to a group of subjects. For example, a group of social work students might be asked to take an aptitude test and, after a period of time, to retake it. *Reliability* is considered low if the second set of scores is very different from the first set.

tetanus   A disease characterized by violent *tremor,* spasms, muscle contraction and stiffness, and sometimes death, caused by certain bacilli entering the body through wounds. The disease is preventable by *inoculation.*

tetrogens   Factors that are potentially harmful to a developing fetus or embryo, sometimes resulting in miscarriage, neonatal death, congenital deformities, mental retardation, learning disabilities, and growth retardation. Tetrogens include drugs and chemicals (alcohol, cocaine, tobacco, and some antibiotics), infections (*rubella,* some *sexually transmitted diseases [STDs],* and *acquired immune deficiency syndrome [AIDS]*), and radiation. Tetrogenic effects vary with type of agent, duration and frequency of exposure, and stage of fetal development; some fetuses are more vulnerable than others to the same tetrogens. Fetal exposure to alcohol is a major cause of mental retardation.

thanatology   The systematic study of death.

thanatophobia   Pathological *fear* of death.

THC   Tetrahydrocannabinol, the active ingredient in *marijuana.*

theme group   A type of *group therapy* or *social group work* for which the range of discussion is highly focused around a single subject or theme that is of concern to all participants.

theocracy   A government or organization leadership system that is headed by religious clerics or by people who base their governing decisions on their assumption of Divine guidance. See also *secular society.*

theory   A group of related hypotheses, concepts, and constructs, based on facts and observations, that attempts to explain a particular phenomenon.

therapeutic community   See *milieu therapy.*

therapeutic foster care (TFC)   An intervention for serious and chronic offending delinquents in

which young clients live with carefully selected adults in the adults' homes, typically for six to seven months.

therapeutic foster home   A foster home for children who have significant emotional or behavioral problems in which the foster parents have received specialized training to enable them to provide homes for youngsters with such special needs. These are also known as "treatment foster homes."

therapist   One who helps individuals to overcome or abate disease, disability, or problems. Usually, a therapist has had extensive training and supervised experience and often uses specialized techniques, tools, medications, and resources to accomplish goals. Social workers often use this term as a synonym for *psychotherapist* and are more specific when discussing other kinds of therapists, such as physical therapists, marital therapists, and occupational therapists.

therapy   A systematic process and activity designed to remedy, cure, or abate some disease, disability, or problem. Social workers often use this term as a synonym for *psychotherapy, psychosocial therapy,* or *group therapy.* When social workers discuss other types of therapy, such as *occupational therapy,* physical therapy, recreational therapy, medication therapy, or *chemotherapy,* they use these more specific terms.

think tanks   Organizations funded largely by federal government and foundation moneys to conduct research and systematic inquiries, primarily into existing sociopolitical and environmental conditions and future trends.

third party   A government funding agency or private insurance company that reimburses a social worker or other service provider (first party) for helping a client (second party). See also *fourth party* and *managed health care program.*

third-party evaluations   A professional determination about some aspect of a client, such as mental or emotional state; pre-existing health condition; or capacity to undertake some new status such as marriage, a job, or a clearance. The information is obtained from interviews and tests with the client and provided to a third party. This could be an insurance company, a potential employer, a prospective spouse, an attorney, or others. The information is given only with the client's *informed consent.*

third-party payment Financial reimbursement made to the client's service provider by an insurance company or government funding agency. See also *fiscal intermediaries* and *fourth party*.

third-sector organizations See *nongovernment organizations (NGOs)*.

Third World The nations of the world that are economically underdeveloped but growing. The term derives from these nations' expressed nonalignment with the Western and Eastern-bloc nations (First and Second Worlds). Third World countries are distinguished from *Fourth World* countries (which have few resources and little hope of development) by regular increases in literacy rates, per capita income, financial reserves, and use of natural resources. Examples of Third World countries are India, Nigeria, and Egypt. See also *developing countries* and *underdeveloped nations*.

Thomas, Jesse O. (1883–1972) A leader in the *National Urban League* and social work educator. He led the movement to encourage more black people to enter social work and helped found various training programs for black social workers, including the Atlanta University School of Social Work.

thought disorders Disturbances in the process and content of one's thinking, including patterns such as *hallucination, delusion, loose association, paranoid ideation, flight of ideas,* and *ideas of reference*. Thought disorders may be symptomatic of *organic mental disorders* or of *schizophrenia*.

thought insertion The *delusion* sometimes found in certain forms of *schizophrenia* and other mental conditions that others are placing alien thoughts in one's mind.

thought stopping A technique used in *behavior therapy* in which obsessive thoughts are ended when the therapist or others say the word "stop."

thought switching A procedure commonly used in *behavior therapy* and *cognitive therapy* designed to eliminate fear-inducing anticipatory thoughts, such as speaking before large groups. The client is taught to stop the fearful thought, sometimes by saying "stop" and then concentrating on achieving relaxation, or by replacing the negative thoughts with positive ones until the positive ones predomi-

nate. Behavioral therapists also call the technique *thought stopping*.

thought withdrawal The *delusion* sometimes found in certain forms of *schizophrenia* and other mental conditions that one's mental processes and ideas are being extracted by outside forces.

three-strikes laws *Mandatory sentencing* requirements on habitual offenders (that is, people convicted for the same class of crime three different times). Sentences progressively increase until the third conviction, at which time the length of imprisonment is far beyond what is normally prescribed for the crime, including life sentences.

"three welfare systems" The conceptualization of public welfare as a three-tiered program to redistribute income through social, fiscal, and corporate welfare. According to Mimi Abramovitz ("Everyone is Still on Welfare," *Social Work*, October 2001), who refined and developed concepts originated by *Richard M. Titmuss*, welfare programs serve and benefit middle-class people, wealthy people, and large corporations as well as poor people. Some social welfare programs benefit individuals and families in financial need through programs such as *TANF, SSI, food stamps,* and *EITC*. However, fiscal welfare programs, primarily in the form of tax exemptions and deductions, provide fewer benefits to poor people than they do to wealthy and middle-class people. Corporate, occupational, and fiscal welfare programs benefit workers and executives through welfare incentives such as education and training reimbursements, tax-deducted health insurance, private pensions, bonuses, cost-of-living adjustments, and various other perks. In corporate welfare programs, sometimes called "aid to dependent corporations," government funding helps businesses through tax breaks, grants, support for research and development, and discounted user fees for public resources. See also *social welfare, fiscal welfare, occupational welfare,* and *corporate welfare*.

Thrifty Food Plan (TFP) A system devised by the *U.S. Department of Agriculture (USDA)* and used to determine the amount of *Food Stamp program* benefits each family can receive. The TFP for a four-person family is based on the recommended dietary allowances of two adults and two preadolescent children. The plan is often criticized as being too meager and not taking into account different family needs such as hungry teenagers or people with special health problems.

thrombosis Clogging of a blood vessel as a result of a blood clot. In a coronary thrombosis, the coronary arteries that supply blood to the heart are clogged, resulting in damage to the heart muscle.

thrownaway children Children who no longer live in the homes of their parents or legal guardians, or usually any other suitable residential facility, because of the wishes or indifference of the parents or guardians. Otherwise, the circumstances of these children are similar to or identical with those of *runaways.*

Thursz, Daniel (1929–2000) A social work educator, gerontologist, and advocate for the aging population who was a leader in the *Volunteers in Service to America (VISTA)* program, a founder and leader of the B'nai B'rith Youth Organization, president of the *National Council on Aging,* longtime social work dean at the University of Baltimore, and O'Boyle Professor at Catholic University.

tic A recurrent, uncontrollable, and inappropriate muscle movement of a part of the body.

tic disorder A disorder characterized by involuntary rapid muscle movements or vocalizations. This disorder includes the *transient tic disorder, chronic motor or vocal tic disorder,* and *Tourette syndrome.*

Ticket to Work Act The 1999 U.S. law (P.L. 106-170) making it possible for Americans with disabilities to join the workforce while retaining *Medicaid* and *Medicare* eligibility. Formally labeled "The Ticket to Work and Work Incentives Improvement Act," the program grants a "ticket" to *social security* and *Supplemental Security Income (SSI)* disability beneficiaries that they may use to obtain vocational rehabilitation and employment support services of their choice.

time-limited eligibility In *public assistance* programs, the discontinuance of benefits after a certain point, regardless of whether the client needs further assistance or not.

time-limited hot line A *hot line* or *help line* system set up to exist for only a short duration, during which intense, focused community attention can be given. For example, they can be set up for a few days after television specials or telethons dealing with certain problems, for political events that

seek new supporters, and for holiday season programs to attract year-round volunteers.

time-limited service A relatively short-term intervention model in which the date of termination or number of meetings is specified in advance. See also *open-ended service* and *open-ended service versus time-limited service.*

time-out procedure A technique often used by parents, group psychotherapists, and educators in which a child, client, or student is removed from an activity or discussion and required to sit, calmly detached from others, until able to participate with the group more appropriately.

tinnitus A condition of hearing persistent noises. Causes sometimes include infections of the middle ear, eardrum perforations, wax or dirt in the outer ear, neurological disorders, and exposure to loud noises. Causes do not include psychosomatic or psychological disorders such as *auditory hallucination.*

tiospaye The Lakota tribe's name for "family," which includes all those connected by biological ties and a wide variety of people in a social network.

Title III services A special range of services for older persons (60 and above) funded under Title III of the *Older Americans Act.* These services include home-delivered and congregate meals, transportation, information and referral, legal assistance, homemaker services, personal care, chore services, health promotion and disease prevention services, health screenings, exercise programs, and more.

Title IV Foster Care Various U.S. federal laws to fund *foster care* programs. The first of these was Title IV-A of the *Social Security Act* of 1935, which required states to provide federally funded foster care to receive *Aid to Dependent Children (ADC)* and *Aid to Families with Dependent Children (AFDC)* funds. In the late 1960s and early 1970s, Title IV-B provided for social services for foster care. IV-B was amended (P.L. 96-272) to limit foster care maintenance and increase preventive and reunification services. The 1985 Title IV-E foster care provision emphasizes efforts to achieve more stability for foster children, rather than moving them from home to home, and to facilitate the transition of children in foster homes to independent living. Title IV-E also has a similar provision to help financially those individuals and families in need with adoptive placements.

Title VII The section of the *Civil Rights Act of 1964* that guarantees equal employment opportunity and created the *Equal Employment Opportunity Commission (EEOC)* to prevent employment discrimination because of race, color, religion, gender, and, in some cases, sexual orientation. See also *706 agencies*.

Title IX Part of the Education Amendments Act of 1972 (P.L. 92-318) that prohibits most forms of *sex discrimination* in educational programs that receive federal funds. The legislation has influenced school systems to increase their athletic programs for girls and women, although it has not resulted in equal expenditures for athletics for both sexes.

Titmuss, Richard M. (1907–1973) British scholar, administrator, and developer of many *social welfare* programs and *social work education* programs. He had international influence on the development of social welfare theory and practice and wrote many of the field's most important works, including *Problems of Social Policy* (1950) and *Income Distribution and Social Change* (1962).

toddler A young child, about one to three years old, who is just developing walking and other *gross motor skills*.

TOEFL Test of English as a Foreign Language, the examination developed by university educators and the Educational Testing Service for international students seeking admission to study in American colleges and universities. Most institutions of higher education use this or similar tests to determine if the student's English-language skills are sufficient for the required academic work.

token economy The therapeutic procedure, used in *behavior modification, milieu therapy,* and various institutional settings, in which the clients are given tokens, slips of paper, or coupons whenever they fulfill specified tasks or behave according to some specified standard. These tokens may then be redeemed for the client's choice of certain goods or privileges.

tokenism Pretending to meet public pressure or legal requirements for nondiscrimination by hiring, promoting, or including for membership one or a few people of various racial and ethnic groups or women.

tolerance An individual's capacity to endure or resist the effects of certain drugs. Because drug response tends to decrease with repeated doses, the user increases the amount taken to get the same effect.

torpor A state of sluggishness, inattentiveness, or diminished responsiveness. This is usually a symptom of some physical or emotional disorder.

tort A wrongful act that harms someone and for which the injured party has the right to sue for damages in civil courts. Examples include *malpractice, libel,* and *slander. Crime* and breach of contract are not considered torts.

torture An extreme form of deliberate and strategic violence inflicted on victims to extract information or compliance, to intimidate the victim's supporters, or to gratify the individual perpetrators. Torture is practiced by the governments of at least 110 nations and by countless subnational political groups and individuals. Most survivors must cope with the physical injury as well as recurring symptoms of *posttraumatic stress disorder (PTSD)*.

total disability As used in *workers' compensation* and insurance contracts, an individual's inability—usually caused by work-related injury or health problems—to perform the occupational requirements of the job category once held.

total quality management (TQM) An orientation to management of organizations, including social services agencies, in which quality, as defined by clients and consumers, is the overriding goal and client satisfaction, employee empowerment, and long-term relationships determine procedures. TQM change is continuous and accomplished by teamwork; organizational communication goes in all directions; and long-term relationships with providers are developed (rather than encouraging them to compete with one another solely on the basis of price).

Totten trust A bank account with a named death beneficiary. Upon the death of the named holder of the account, the money transfers automatically to the beneficiary. Also referred to as payable on death (POD) accounts.

tough-love parenting   The parenting style based on the premise that some children and adolescents need firm discipline as well as love and forgiveness. Tough-love programs help parents establish minimum acceptable standards for their children's behavior and show them techniques for enforcing those standards. Tough-love emphasizes controls on children by providing and depriving them of privileges based on their conformity with explicit rules. Many communities have tough-love *self-help groups* made up of parents who provide mutual support to reinforce their goals and techniques with their children.

Tourette syndrome   An inherited, lifelong neurological disorder, characterized by involuntary movements (*tics*) accompanied by utterances of sounds, words, and sometimes phrases (vocalizations) that persist for more than a year. Also known as "Gilles de la Tourette's disease," the severity of symptoms varies greatly from person to person. The symptom *coprolalia* (involuntary use of socially inappropriate language) affects only 10 percent to 15 percent of people with the disorder. The age of onset is between 2 and 18, with most exhibiting their first symptoms between 6 and 8 years old. Typically, symptoms worsen in childhood but reduce in frequency and severity in young adults. High frequencies of comorbid obsessive–compulsive disorder (OCD), attentional and learning problems, and poor impulse control have been reported in this population. According to the Tourette Syndrome Association (Web site address: http://www.tsa-usa.org), the vast majority of people have mild cases, and a variety of medications are effective for those whose symptoms may interfere with daily living.

Towle, Charlotte (1896–1966)   Social work educator and scholar who created an influential generic casework curriculum used in many schools of social work and developed concepts for integrating *public assistance* programs with human behavior and needs. She wrote the classic social work text *Common Human Needs* in 1945 (Silver Spring, MD: National Association of Social Workers, revised 1987).

Townsend Plan   A proposal, made by Francis Townsend in the early 1930s, advocating federal payments of $200 monthly to all people older than age 60 who agree to retire from work and spend the money within a month. The plan spurred a strong *social movement,* especially among older

people in the United States, and contributed in part to the development of the *Social Security Act* of 1935.

toxic shock syndrome (TSS)   An acute and sometimes fatal disease with symptoms including high fever, vomiting, diarrhea, and a sharp drop in blood pressure. The symptoms are caused by bacterial infection, often stimulated by the use of vaginal tampons.

Toxic Substances and Disease Registry, Agency for (ATSDR)   The organization within *HHS* to prevent exposure to and adverse human health effects caused by exposure to hazardous substances from waste sites and other sources of pollution in the environment.

toxic waste disposal   Elimination of the poisonous chemicals that had been the residue of manufactured products. The enormous costs of cleaning up *toxic waste sites* have led environmentalists and scientists to seek better alternatives. So far the alternatives are to build better dumps, break down the poisons to eliminate their toxicity, and find manufacturing procedures that do not produce the toxins. Building better dumps (by developing landfills with secure liners or systems that recapture any leaked liquids or gasses) is the most economical response in the short term, but it only postpones the problem. Breaking down the poisons, mostly by neutralizing them with heat or other chemicals, is another alternative, but it is proving to be expensive and still wasteful. The best solution—changing the manufacturing process—is under way in many industries, but it is costly and meets with resistance from many groups.

toxic waste sites   Disposal grounds and dumps in which hazardous materials such as nuclear and chemical pollutants have been placed. Often, these materials are poorly contained and escape into the atmosphere, soil, or water table and contaminate the environment. See also *Superfund.*

toxin   A poison.

TOXNET   A *database* maintained by the National Library of Medicine, *National Institutes of Health (NIH),* to provide access to information about environmental pollutants, adverse drug reactions, and toxicity.

toxoids   The poisonous waste products of disease-causing microorganisms that are used to make certain vaccines to protect against specific diseases.

Toynbee Hall The British settlement house that was established in 1884 by *Samuel A. Barnett* and became the prototype for the 400 American *settlement houses* that developed during the next 20 years. It was located in a poor section of London and served as something of a "missionary outpost," bringing the ideas, values, and social skills of affluent people to those who were less fortunate.

trabajadores sociales "Social workers" in Spanish. The expression for social work is "trabajo social."

trafficking in persons The use of coercion, debt bondage, kidnapping, or fraud to bring people, especially girls and women, into one nation from another, often for the purpose of commercial sex or exploitative labor.

Trafficking Victims Protection Act The U.S. law (P.L. 106-386) established in 2000 to combat *trafficking in persons* through enforcing laws, apprehending traffickers, increasing punishments, educating and protecting victims, and influencing nations where trafficking originates.

tranquilizer A *psychotropic drug* used by physicians in the treatment of mental disorders and emotional discomfort. Major tranquilizers such as Thorazine, Stelazine, and Mellaril are frequently used to help with *psychotic* symptoms. Minor tranquilizers such as Valium, Librium, and Tranxene are frequently used to help with symptoms of *anxiety.*

transactional analysis (TA) A form of group and individual *psychotherapy* that explores the way clients tend to interact with others; play games; perform roles as though scripted to do so; and are influenced by the three parts of the mental–cultural apparatus known as the "parent," "adult," and "child." The International Transactional Analysis Association, based in San Francisco, was founded in 1958 by Eric Berne.

transactions Reciprocal exchanges between two entities, influencing or changing both. See also *circular causality.*

transcendent character The ability to rise above an environment that lacks nurturing and denies

legal and civil rights and still maintain one's sense of self-worth and integrity. The *deprecated character* refers to those who encounter this environment and cannot rise above its effects.

transegoic model A conceptual framework used in *transpersonal social work* to help clients confront the reality of their personal mortality. The intervention generally follows four stages: (1) recognizing and accepting the normality of death and resolving prior grief and fear; (2) developing faith in the existential self by discovering one's meaning in life and identifying the Will or the I, instead of one's roles; (3) discovering that there is meaning in death; and (4) acknowledging the transpersonal self and discovering the transpersonal mission. The model is used primarily with clients with terminal illness in one-to-one or structured group settings.

transfer payments Cash benefits, theoretically taken from one population group and redirected to another. Typically, this is done indirectly with money withheld from one group and placed into the government treasury, which then disburses funds to the eligible other party. For example, money is transferred from younger to older people in *social security,* from employed to unemployed people in *unemployment compensation,* and from more affluent people to poor people in *Temporary Assistance to Needy Families (TANF).* In the United States, some of the other major income transfer programs are *Supplemental Security Income (SSI), Medicare,* and *Medicaid.* In other countries, including most European nations, a major income transfer program is the family allowance.

transfer summary The social worker's final notes made about a client and placed in the relevant *case record* before the case is turned over to another professional. Included in this summary are the following (not necessarily in this order): the client's *prognosis;* probable service needs in the near future; a description of any anticipated or possible special health, emotional, or situational crises; unfinished tasks, goals, or commitments; an overall description of the entire intervention process; and a summary of the worker's final impressions, concerns, and recommendations.

transference A concept, originating in *psychoanalytic theory,* that refers to emotional reactions that are assigned to current relationships but originated in earlier, often unresolved and *unconscious* experiences. For example, a client who as a child felt extremely hostile to a parent and never resolved the feeling develops extremely hostile feelings toward the social worker even though no overt reason exists for such feelings. Transference is used by psychodynamically oriented social workers and other therapists as a tool for understanding and *working through* past conflicts. The transfer of affectionate feelings to the worker is known as *positive transference* and that of hostile feelings as *negative transference*. See also *countertransference*.

transgenerational poor   Families that remain poor from generation to generation (that is, the *poverty cycle*).

transient ischemic attack (TIA)   A strokelike episode that occurs when the blood supply to part of the brain is interrupted. TIA symptoms occur suddenly and are similar to a stroke but do not last as long (usually from 1 to 24 hours). For many, TIA is a warning sign for future stroke.

transient tic disorder   A disorder characterized by rapid repetitive muscle movements that have existed with varying intensity for less than one year. These movements are basically involuntary but can be suppressed for several minutes at a time, usually for no longer than a few hours. The movements tend to increase under stress and diminish during sleep or relaxed times. In diagnosing this disorder, it is necessary to specify whether the symptoms are recurrent or are a single episode. See also *tic disorder*.

transients   People who change places of residence frequently or maintain no fixed address. Although such people are often the most in need of health and social services and financial assistance, because they have no permanent homes they are frequently not eligible for existing welfare assistance, which tends to be contingent on fulfillment of certain residency requirements.

transinstitutionalizing   The practice of placing clients into different institutions from the ones to which they legally belong because of the belief that the legal placement is inappropriate. For example, youths held as status offenders are placed in mental hospitals rather than jails, or juvenile offenders are placed in youth detention centers to avoid incarceration in prisons.

transitional benefits   Social welfare transfer payments to provide continued support for a limited time after the assistance entitlement has ended. For example, some families who leave TANF may be eligible to continue in state medical insurance programs, or foster children who age out of care may continue with some benefits from ages 18 to 21.

transitional foster home   A program to help older adolescents (usually ages 16 to 20) learn independent living skills prior to graduating from the foster care system. The program is primarily for young people at risk of leaving their foster placements before developing essential adult living skills such as financial management, the ability to access community resources, proper nutrition and hygiene, and employment skills. They are placed in special homes in which the foster parent assumes the role of a mentor, resource person, teacher, and monitor rather than the parent.

transitional group   1. People brought together in a living situation or as a support group for mutual support while they move from one life stage or life crisis to another. 2. Residents of a *transitional living facility*. 3. A form of *group psychotherapy* or *social group work* involving preadolescent and pubescent children (latency-age children) who do not need the intensive experience of group treatment but benefit from mutual support that they cannot get in home situations or with peers.

transitional living facility   A residential program for people returning from some form of institutional living to relatively independent homes in communities. Typically, these are short-term group facilities that provide some guidance to and monitoring of the residents. See also *halfway houses* and *quarterway houses*.

transpersonal psychology   An orientation in the philosophies and therapies related to psychology that emphasizes *spirituality, moral development,* and human connectedness with the cosmos. Its focus is on the next level beyond *self-actualization* to the relationship between humans and all the natural and spiritual components of the universe. The transpersonal orientation draws on Eastern philosophies that recognize intuitive and mystical experiences and other sources of "transrational" wisdom. This orientation is considered the *fourth force* in psychology after the psychoanalytic, behavioral, and humanistic orientations. See also *transegoic model*.

transpersonal social work   A holistic and multidimensional approach to providing social services that emphasizes *spirituality, moral development,* and other aspects of *transpersonal psychology.* See also *transegoic model.*

transpersonal therapist A *psychotherapist* or *pastoral counselor* who provides a full range of *holistic* mental health services but who emphasizes issues of *spirituality, moral development,* and access to one's higher levels of consciousness, including the soul. The therapist does not focus exclusively on pathology or social problems and goes beyond *self-actualization* toward higher states of consciousness and a cosmic connection between humanity and the universe.

transplantation The medical procedure of moving organs, tissues, or cells from one part of the body to another or from one organism to another. The types of transplantation are autologous (transplanting an organism's own cells or tissues), allogeneic (transplanting from other organisms with as similar a genetic makeup as possible), and xenogeneic (transplantation of tissues or organs from other species—that is, animals to humans).

transport-disabled person An individual with certain physical or psychological incapacities that make it difficult or impossible to get to needed sources of health care and social or other services. Many such individuals have sensory deficits, orthopedic problems, or cognitive dysfunctions that are detrimental to their mobility and *wayfinding* ability.

Transportation Security Administration (TSA) An organization within the U.S. Department of Homeland Security, created in 2003, to help secure the nation's transportation infrastructure, especially its airports and seaports. This includes screening, educating, and inspecting airline passengers and monitoring safe movement of cargo.

transracial adoption *Adoption* of a child of one racial background by a family of another racial background (for example, a black child and white adoptive parents). This is the opposite of *inracial adoption.* See also *Multiethnic Placement Act.*

transsexualism 1. The changing of one's sex through surgery, hormone injections, *psychotherapy,* and special training. 2. A *gender identity disorder* in which an individual has a strong and persistent desire to be a member of the opposite sex.

transvestic fetishism See *transvestism.*

transvestism The *sexual disorder* in which erotic pleasure is derived from wearing clothing designed for members of the opposite sex. Mental health professionals refer to this disorder as "transvestic fetishism." See also *cisvestism.*

trauma An injury to the body or *psyche* by some type of *shock,* violence, or unanticipated situation. Symptoms of psychological trauma include numbness of feeling, withdrawal, helplessness, *depression, anxiety,* and *fear.* See also *posttraumatic stress disorder (PTSD).*

traumatic event debriefing (TED) An advanced level of *crisis intervention* in which groups of people who have recently (within 24 to 72 hours) experienced a catastrophic event are brought together with professional debriefers to share their perspectives and to relieve stress catharticly. The process moves them from a cognitive level to an emotional level and back again to a cognitive level. The seven phases of the process are (1) making introductions and rules, (2) establishing the facts, (3) describing initial thoughts at the time of the event, (4) individually identifying the worst part of the event, (5) discussing symptoms, (6) providing education, and (7) providing concluding thoughts and socializing. See also *multiple stressor debriefing (MSD)* and *critical-incident stress debriefing (CISD).*

travailleur sociaux "Social worker" in French.

Traveler's Aid Services and programs, located especially in airports, train stations, and bus terminals, to help people who are traveling. Services emphasize helping people find needed facilities in strange cities and locate emergency accommodations and health care as well as providing counseling with people who have developed emotional problems related to the stress of travel.

treatment Correcting or alleviating a disorder, disease, or problem. This term was once commonly used, in addition to "study" and "diagnosis," in social work; however, the preferred term now is *intervention,* because it does not have the medical connotation and implies an orientation toward resolving a wider range of problems. See also *therapy* and *typology of casework treatment.*

treatment matrix In *family group therapy* or *marital therapy,* the specific worker–client combination used—for example, one therapist for each family member, one therapist of the same gender for each marital partner, one therapist seeing both spouses either together or individually, or any other possible combination.

treatment modality   The specific intervention or combination of interventions used to help the client reach his or her goals. For example, the treatment modality for a particular child with acting-out behavior problems might include *play therapy* and behavior management.

tremor   Shaking or trembling, a symptom often seen in *anxiety, palsy, delirium tremens (DTs),* and some *organic mental disorders.*

triage   A *crisis intervention* technique for prioritizing the help that will be available to disaster victims. Triage originated as a military battlefield procedure of dividing casualties into three categories—those who will die regardless of help, those who will live whether they get help or not, and those who will live only if they receive immediate care. Help is given to this last group first.

trial balloon   A politician's or activist's declaration, issued in some covert fashion, to determine whether the public might be supportive. If the public disapproves of the declaration, the person can deny having made it, thus avoiding the appearance of indecisiveness or backing an unpopular cause.

triangulation   The process in which one individual who feels pressured, distressed, or powerless in relating to another individual brings into the relationship a third person to act as an ally or a distracter. For example, a mother who feels she has too little control over her children brings the father or a grandparent onto the scene.

TriCare   The managed health care financing program for retired and some active duty military personnel and their dependents. Whereas the U.S. uniformed services still maintain their own hospitals and other health care facilities for their personnel, TriCare helps pay for the health care in the civilian community of those who do not have access to military hospitals. TriCare replaced most of the *CHAMPUS* program in 2001.

trichotillomania   An *impulse control disorder* involving the obsessive pulling of one's hair, often seen in anxious toddlers and children and sometimes in adults with *anxiety,* masochistic tendencies, or another *mental disorder.* The pattern results in noticeable hair loss in those sites where it occurs (mostly the scalp, eyebrows, and eyelashes).

trickle-down theory   The view that federal funds flowing into corporations and private sectors of the economy will stimulate more job opportunities and economic growth than would direct federal payments and programs for unemployed and poor people.

trimester   A three-month period during *pregnancy,* usually identified as first, second, and third trimesters.

truancy   Failure to fulfill one's duty. This term especially applies to a child who stays away from school without permission.

trust versus mistrust   The basic conflict found in the first stage of human development, according to the *psychosocial development theory* of Erik Erikson (1902–1994), occurring from birth to about age two. The infant may develop feelings of security and confidence in those who provide care or, possibly, because of inconsistent nurturing, may come to doubt that others are reliable.

Truth and Reconciliation Commission   An organization established by a nation or international body to help determine responsibility for atrocities committed by the various sides of a conflict. Such commissions are set up usually after a civil war, rebellion, or change in government power to achieve social stability rather than class or cultural retribution. Typically, such commissions forgo punishing those found at fault in exchange for full disclosures and apologies for atrocities committed.

Truth in Lending Act   The 1968 federal law (P.L. 90-321) requiring full and clear disclosure of the terms of loans for which individuals apply. Commercial lenders, including banks, credit card companies, and retailers, are required to reveal the amount of interest charged, both as an annual percentage and a dollar amount. See also *usury.*

tubal ligation   A surgical method of *birth control* in which the fallopian tubes are severed and tied off. See also *sterilization.*

tuberculosis   An *infectious disease* that most commonly affects the lungs and is caused by the tubercle bacillus, which may enter the human body through contact with infected people, through inhalation, or through ingestion (contaminated food or dishes). The incidence of tuberculosis has been reduced by better sanitary conditions, pasteurization of milk, early case findings through sputum examinations and skin tests, and vaccines.

Tuckerman, Joseph (1778–1840) A minister who organized the Boston Society for the Prevention of Pauperism in 1835 using many of *Thomas Chalmers'* principles of individualized work with poor families, volunteer visitors, coordinated fundraising, and *social action*. His work influenced the subsequent development of the *Charity Organization Societies (COSs)*.

Tufts Report A 1923 study by James H. Tufts delineating the components of social work education. The report influenced the social work education system toward social cause and macro perspectives. See also *social work education, Hollis–Taylor Report*, and *Social Work Curriculum Study*.

"turf issues" Conflicts, usually between members of an organization or between different professional groups, about the allocation of responsibilities and benefits. For example, social workers are sometimes involved in such conflicts with psychologists, psychiatrists, or pastoral counselors in deciding who should be authorized to provide psychotherapy.

tutoring Providing individualized instruction and guidance outside the classroom, primarily to enhance the students' academic development.

12-step programs The central activity of many *self-help organizations,* such as *Alcoholics Anonymous (AA), Gamblers Anonymous (GA),* and *Batterers Anonymous (BA),* that asks members to proceed through 12 incremental activities. Although each organization modifies the steps slightly to suit its needs, the basic activities are (1) acknowledge powerlessness with the problem; (2) recognize the need for help from a higher power; (3) decide to turn one's life over to God as God is understood; (4) take a searching self-inventory; (5) admit to God, oneself, and one other person the exact nature of the wrongs done; (6) be ready to have God remove character defects; (7) humbly ask God to remove shortcomings; (8) list all people harmed and be willing to make amends; (9) make direct amends whenever possible; (10) continue to take personal inventory and admit one's wrongs; (11) seek improvements through prayer and meditation in contact with God; and (12) carry this message to others with the same problem.

Twining, Louisa (1820–1912) English social reformer for women's rights and improving standards in workhouses. She wrote influential books on women in workhouses, pauperism, and poor-law reform.

two-provider family A family in which both parents are wage earners, usually in such a way that there is little time to meet all the family demands and needs.

Type A personality A pattern of thinking and behaving characterized by impatience, competitiveness, and excessive concern about time.

Type B personality A pattern of thinking and behaving characterized by patience, noncompetitiveness, and a relaxed attitude about time.

typhoid fever An *infectious disease,* spread primarily through contaminated water or food. Symptoms include high fever, diarrhea or constipation, red spots on the body, enlargement of the spleen, and damage to various organs. Its incidence has been reduced dramatically through vaccination, sanitary laws pertaining especially to food handlers, and laws promoting a cleaner and safer environment.

typhus An acute *infectious disease* with symptoms of high fever, dark red spots on the skin, delirium, and extreme weakness. The disease is transmitted by fleas, ticks, mites, and lice.

typologies Classification systems used by social workers and others to delineate the components of an entity under scrutiny.

typology of casework treatment The classification of techniques used by social workers in direct work with individual clients, formulated by Florence Hollis in the 1960s. The techniques consist of *sustaining procedures, direct influence, ventilation,* reflective consideration of the person–situation configuration, reflection about the dynamics of patterns or tendencies, and thoughts about the historical development of those patterns. The typology permits examination of environmental as well as internal influences.

tzedakah Hebrew term for justice, including philanthropy and service. In the Jewish tradition, one of the highest forms of tzedakah is to provide poor people with the wherewithal to become productive and self-sufficient. See also *kupah* and *tamhuy.*

ulcer An open sore in the wall of the stomach or intestine or other internal organs, in the mucous membrane, or on the skin.

ultrasound The diagnostic procedure using high-frequency sound waves and computers to create a moving picture of internal body systems on a video monitor.

UN Convention on the Rights of the Child An agreement by all signatory nations binding them to uphold children's rights. Ratified in 1991, the convention asserts the right to a family and the right to certain supports from the state. It mandates against child labor exploitation, discrimination, and inadequate nutrition and for social and educational opportunities and the right to live with one's own family. The United States is one of the few developed nations that has not signed the agreement. The document may be read at the Web site address http://www.unicef.org/crc

unaccompanied refugee/entrant minor (UR/EM) A designation established in 1978 by the U.S. Department of State, the *U.S. Immigration and Naturalization Service (INS)* (now the *Bureau of Citizenship and Immigration Services*), and the *U.S. Department of Health and Human Services (HHS)* to develop a category of rights and protections for *refugee* children who come to the United States without parents or guardians. To qualify for the benefits that accompany this status, the individual must be younger than age 18, have no immediate relative in the United States, have legally entered the United States, and otherwise meet the criteria of being a refugee.

unbiased writing The use of language in the professional literature that avoids the promotion of stereotyped or discriminatory attitudes or assumptions about people. This includes using plural pronouns to avoid specific gender references; using nongender designations for occupations (police officer instead of policeman); and, when referring to an ethnic group, using the name that group itself prefers. Editors of virtually all social work publications maintain explicit policies against biased writing.

"Uncle Tom" A term of contempt, based on the character in Harriet Beecher Stowe's antislavery novel *Uncle Tom's Cabin* (New York: National Era, 1851), referring to a black person whose behavior toward white people is considered servile or whose behavior is seen as antithetical to the interests of *African Americans* as a group.

unconditional positive regard An element in the social work ethical principles of *acceptance* and *nonjudgmentality* in which the professional considers the client to be a person of worth whose rights and dignity are to be respected without reservation if the effective working relationship is to be viable. This position is maintained by the ethical professional even if the social worker personally does not approve of or condone the client's actions.

unconditioned response (UR) A response that occurs without the necessity of prior conditioning. In Ivan Pavlov's (1849–1936) experiments, the dog's salivation when given food was the UR. Then food was presented after a bell was rung, and eventually the dog began to salivate at the sound of the bell, whether or not food was given. Salivation at the sound of the bell was the *conditioned response (CR)*.

unconditioned stimulus (US) A *stimulus* that elicits a response without the necessity of conditioning or learning. For example, in Ivan Pavlov's (1849–1936) experiments, the food was the US because it elicited salivation with no prior conditioning. When a bell was rung before the presentation of food, the bell became the *conditioned stimulus (CS)* when it began to elicit salivation from the dog even when no food was near.

unconscious In *psychoanalytic theory,* that region of the mind or psychic structure that is not subject to an individual's immediate awareness and is the seat of all forgotten memories and thoughts, *primary process thinking,* repressed impulses, biological drives, and the *id.*

unconscious motivation A compelling wish or drive that is out of an individual's immediate awareness but that influences him or her to act in a way that would seem contrary to his or her rational objectives. For example, a client who has had a difficult session with a social worker "forgets" to attend the next scheduled session.

uncontested divorce   Dissolution of marriage granted automatically by a court when one person files for divorce and the other fails to offer a formal and legal response.

underachiever   One whose overt performance is not as accomplished as would be expected on the basis of the person's past activities, school or work record, or scores on aptitude tests.

underclass   A term used by some journalists and economists in referring to people and families who have been long-term poor, unemployed, and lacking in the resources or opportunities to improve their situations in the future. See also *culture of poverty* and *social exclusion.*

underdeveloped nations   Those countries of the world that have extremely low rates of literacy and income and few natural resources. They are also called *Fourth World* countries to distinguish them from *Third World* or *developing countries* that have resources and socioeconomic growth. The U.N. designation for these nations is *least developing countries.*

underemployment   1. For individuals, the condition of working fewer than full-time hours or working in jobs that are beneath their levels of education or previous salary, usually because more suitable jobs are not available. 2. For societies, the economic condition in which workers have to limit their work hours or incomes so that others can also work and have some income. See also *seasonal unemployment.*

underground economy   The unregulated system of financial transactions, exchange of goods and services outside regular accounting procedures, and bartering, especially to avoid taxes. See also *informal sector.*

underground railroad   Part of the *abolition movement* to eliminate slavery in the United States by facilitating the escape of slaves and helping them migrate to northern regions, where slavery was illegal.

underprivileged   A term pertaining to people who are deprived of the social, cultural, and economic benefits that are available to most others in their society.

undersocialized conduct disorder   An outdated term referring to a type of *conduct disorder* in which a person has not been able or willing to establish relationships with others that include affection, empathy, or bonding. This person seeks to harm or manipulate others for personal advantage but has no feelings of remorse or guilt.

understimulating environment   The condition in which an individual is confined physically, intellectually, socially, or emotionally in such a way that precludes sufficient access to the resources needed for healthy development. Examples include classrooms in which intelligent children are not challenged, drab mental hospitals devoid of opportunities for interaction, and high-rise slums in which most residents feel compelled to stay inside.

underutilization   See *utilization review.*

underworld   Organized *crime,* or the criminal element of society.

undifferentiated ego mass   A *family therapy* concept describing the members of a family as lacking much separate identity or differentiation of self and being "stuck together."

undifferentiated schizophrenia   A diagnostic category for *schizophrenia* in which the patient has *hallucinations, delusions,* incoherence, and disorganized behavior but does not meet the specific criteria for the other types of schizophrenia. See *catatonic schizophrenia, disorganized schizophrenia,* and *paranoid schizophrenia.*

undifferentiated somatoform disorder   One of the *somatoform disorders* in which the individual experiences only one or a few symptoms longer than six months. It is differentiated from *somatization disorder,* which has many symptoms over several years and begins before age 30.

undocumented alien   1. In the United States, an individual from another nation who has entered the country without legal status and is subject to deportation. 2. In certain circumstances, a person who enters the country legally but who remains after expiration of his or her visa.

undoing   A *defense mechanism* in which an individual engages in a repetitive ritual to abolish the results of an action previously taken and found to be unacceptable. For example, an individual who injures a youngster through reckless driving begins driving slowly and carefully everyday through the area where the accident occurred.

unearned income   Money received from sources unrelated to employment, such as interest on savings, dividends on investments, and capital gains.

unemployable   Being considered unable to work because of disability, age, insufficient education, or lack of job openings. This term often is used to describe people who are not in the potential workforce and thus are not counted as part of the *unemployment rate.*

unemployment   The condition of being without a job and the resulting income that is necessary to meet economic needs independently. The term is usually applied by economists and government statisticians only to those people without jobs who want to and are able to work. See also *cyclical unemployment, seasonal unemployment, frictional unemployment,* and *structural unemployment.*

unemployment compensation   Financial assistance for eligible persons who have temporary loss of income as a result of *unemployment.* In the United States, this assistance is provided primarily through the *Unemployment Insurance* program.

Unemployment Insurance   The program established as part of the *Social Security Act* to protect workers temporarily from economic hardship caused by involuntary job loss. The federal government levies a payroll tax on nearly all employers and credits most of these funds to each state's unemployment insurance fund. When an eligible worker becomes unemployed, compensation is paid for a specified time. Applications, eligibility determination, and processing of funds are, for the most part, handled through the states' public employment offices. The amount and duration of benefits vary from state to state.

unemployment rate   The economic and statistical measure of the proportion of people without jobs who are willing and able to work, relative to the number of people in the labor force. The figure is often used by social and economic planners to help determine actual and potential economic circumstances of specific population groups, such as teenagers, African Americans, college graduates, people older than age 50, women, and blue-collar workers. The measure may also

be manipulated by governments for political ends to reduce the apparent number of people without the opportunity for work.

unfreezing   An element in *psychotherapy,* especially *group therapy* and *social group work,* in which clients are helped to re-examine rigidly held assumptions about themselves and others (that is, status symbols and familiar social conventions) to achieve motivation for change.

Uniform Anatomical Gift Laws   Legislation adopted by all jurisdictions in the United States spelling out procedures for donating all or part of a deceased human body for organ transplants, medical education, or research.

Uniform Child Custody Jurisdiction Act (UCCJA)   A binding agreement between the U.S. states to honor and enforce the child custody decisions made by the divorcing family's original court. This nonfederal law was achieved mostly in the 1970s to prevent parents who were unhappy with a judge's ruling in one state from going to another state for a new lawsuit. The law also indicates that as long as one parent lives in the home state where the original decision was made, only that state has the power to change the order. See also *Hague Convention on Child Abduction.*

Uniform Crime Reports (UCR)   The FBI program that collects and publishes information about eight types of crimes reported to local law enforcement authorities. The crimes are homicide, forcible rape, robbery, aggravated assault, burglary, larceny-theft, motor vehicle theft, and arson. Established in 1929, the UCR also provides limited information about some other crime offenses, victims, and offenders. The UCR is being incorporated within the more comprehensive and inclusive *National Incidence-Based Reporting System (NIBRS).*

Uniform Reciprocal Enforcement of Support Act (URESA)   A law in all 50 states and the District of Columbia to establish and enforce child support obligations when the noncustodial parent lives in one state and the custodial parent lives in another jurisdiction.

Uniformed Services Social Workers (USSW)   The professional association made up of active duty and reserve uniformed, civilian, and contract social workers who provide professional services to members of the uniformed services, including personnel in the U.S. Army, Navy, Air Force, and Public Health Service Commissioned Corps. The social workers serve military personnel and their dependents, retired military personnel, and Public Health Service commissioned officers and their dependent family members. See also *military social work* and *Public Health Service.*

unilateral family therapy Psychosocial treatment of a family even though only one family member is present or directly involved in the therapeutic intervention. This is sometimes necessary when *pathology* exists within the family, affecting all its members, but key participants in the pathology refuse therapeutic intervention. A basic premise of family therapy is that a change in one member will result in a change in all members, so it is possible to help the whole family without seeing each member.

unintended consequences Outcomes and effects that follow actions planned for other purposes.

unipolar disorder A *mood disorder* in which only one side of the emotional continuum is present. Because that side is usually depression, which has its own name, the term "unipolar disorder" is rarely used. See also *affective disorder* and *bipolar disorder.*

unit of attention The focal point of intervention to which the social worker or other professional directs efforts to provide help or effect change. For example, the unit of attention for the clinical social worker with a psychoanalytic orientation would be the intrapsychic processes of the individual, and that of a community organizer would be the interacting social forces that exist in a given community. Units of attention for group workers are the group process, and for psychosocially oriented workers, the person–situation configuration. Specific behaviors may be considered the unit of attention for behaviorally oriented workers, and a proposed bill in Congress could be the unit of attention for a social activist. See also *target behavior, target segments of society,* and *target system.*

United Nations Children's Fund (UNICEF) An agency of the United Nations established in 1946 as the U.N. International Children's Emergency Fund. Its primary goal is to provide health, education, and social services to children, especially in *underdeveloped nations.* It is financed by voluntary

contributions from nations and individuals. Their Web site address is http://www.unicef.org

United Nations Development Program (UNDP) Established by the United Nations in 1965 to help nations maximize their natural and other resources by providing expertise and resources, the UNDP also works with other U.N. organizations to provide emergency relief services; upgrade educational levels of population groups; and, in cooperation with the *World Bank,* provide funding for development projects. Their Web site address is http://www.undp.org

United Nations Disaster Relief Organization (UNDRO) An office established in 1971 by the United Nations to coordinate the efforts of nations, groups, volunteers, and individuals in assisting populations experiencing disasters. UNDRO classifies disasters according to three general types: (1) sudden disasters, such as floods, hurricanes, earthquakes, and volcanic eruptions; (2) slow-developing disasters, such as droughts and epidemics; and (3) human-caused disasters, such as international wars and genocide. UNDRO does not participate in relief for human-caused disasters. Their Web site address is http://www.undro.org

United Nations Economic and Social Council (ECOSOC) The primary U.N. body for promoting the member nations' social and human services policies and economic and social development. ECOSOC's major goals are to promote higher standards of living, full employment, social health, human rights and freedoms, and cultural and educational development. Their Web site address is http://www.un.org/esa/coordination/ecosoc

United Nations Educational, Scientific, and Cultural Organization (UNESCO) An agency of the United Nations established in 1945 with headquarters in Paris. Its primary objectives include promoting the free interchange of ideas and cultural and scientific accomplishments, providing fundamental education for all people, and preserving the cultural heritage of humanity. Their Web site address is http://www.unesco.org

United Nations Environment Program (UNEP) An agency founded in 1972 with headquarters in Nairobi, Kenya, to coordinate intergovernmental measures to protect the environment. UNEP monitors environmental trends and brings together world leaders and organizations to make decisions about environmental protection. Their Web site address is http://www.unep.org

United Nations Fund for Population Activities
A U.N. agency that helps plan and finance countries gathering population statistics, providing reproductive education information, and developing *family planning* services.

United Nations High Commissioner for Refugees (UNHCR) The organization formed in 1951 by the U.N. General Assembly to provide economic assistance for refugees, including social services, international protection, voluntary repatriation, and resettlement in other countries. Their Web site address is http://www.unhcr.org

United Nations Relief and Rehabilitation Agency (UNRRA) One of the earliest U.N. organizations, UNRRA was staffed largely by professional social workers who focused on helping countries (especially those devastated in World War II) establish social welfare legislation and programs for assisting those who were needy. UNRRA was discontinued in 1949 and its functions were transferred to other U.N. agencies, including the *United Nations Children's Fund (UNICEF)* and the *Food and Agriculture Organization (FAO)*.

United Nations Relief and Works Agency for Palestine Refugees in the Near East (UNRWA) A program of the United Nations that was formed in 1950 primarily to help Palestinians who lived in what became Israel. It is funded by voluntary contributions from individuals and countries. Their Web site address is http://www.un.org/unrwa/palestine

United Nations Research Institute for Social Development The Geneva-based U.N. organization established in 1963 to conduct research about the conditions in which humans live and especially to study the effects of development policies in developing nations.

United Neighborhood Centers of America (UNCA) An affiliation of more than 200 U.S. *settlement houses,* headquartered in Cleveland, Ohio, to help settlements and neighborhood centers coordinate their activities. Founded in 1911 by *Jane Addams* and others as the National Federation of Settlements and Neighborhood Centers, it took its present name in 1979. Their Web site address is http://www.unca.org

United Network for Organ Sharing (UNOS)
The U.S. national organization to coordinate the procurement, maintenance, distribution, and transplantations of human organs. The UNOS Organ Center maintains and tracks all organ transplants and matches organ donors to waiting recipients at all times of the day and year. UNOS members include all the nation's organ procurement, tissue typing, and transplant labs and programs in the United States. UNOS seeks to give all patients an equal chance at receiving the needed organ, regardless of the patient's age, gender, race, lifestyle, religion, or economic circumstance. Their Web site address is http://www.unos.org

United Service Organizations (USO) The program established in 1941 to coordinate the recreational, social, and welfare services provided by six private voluntary agencies (*Young Men's Christian Association [YMCA], Young Women's Christian Association [YWCA], Traveler's Aid,* the *Salvation Army, Catholic Charities USA,* and *Jewish social agencies*) to members of the U.S. armed services. Their Web site address is http://www.uso.org

United States Conference of City Human Services Officials (USCCHSO) The professional association of administrators who manage city social services, public day care, income assistance, and employment programs. The organization was established in 1980 and is affiliated with the U.S. Conference of Mayors.

United Way The national federation of local organizations established to systematize and coordinate voluntary fundraising efforts. The money raised through the United Way is used to fund social agencies; nonprofit human services organizations; and some health, education, and recreation programs in local communities. The organization was established in 1918 as the Community Chest and Councils of America, modeled after the program developed in Denver by *Frances W. Jacobs.* In 1956, it was renamed United Community Funds and Councils of America. It acquired its present name in 1970. Their Web site address is http://www.unitedway.org

Universal Declaration of Human Rights The authoritative U.N. definition of *human rights* endorsed unanimously by its General Assembly on December 10, 1948. The declaration, which has increasingly gained the force of law in many nations, elaborates on four basic rights: (1) human dignity; (2) civil and political rights; (3) economic, social, and cultural rights; and (4) solidarity rights (intergovernmental cooperation to distribute food and deal with global problems). Many nations, including the United States, have not signed this declaration. The declaration may be read at the Web site address http://www.un.org/overview/rights.html

universal eligibility A *social services* policy in which services or benefits are provided at the same rate to all citizens or residents of a nation without regard to their specific needs, economic status, or circumstances. When applied, this policy can take the form of *universal programs* such as the family allowance system in some nations. This concept is contrasted with the policy of *selective eligibility*. See also *demogrant*.

universal programs Social welfare programs that are open to everyone in a nation who falls into a certain category. These programs do not subject people to individualized tests of income or need. *Social security* and *Medicare* are examples of universal programs in the United States (*public assistance* and *Medicaid* are *selective programs*).

universality 1. That which applies to everyone or everything. 2. In *social group work* and *group psychotherapy,* the exposure of people to others in the group who have similar problems, followed by the growing realization that the problems are not unique or incomprehensible to others and that they need not be faced alone.

universe A term used in research to designate a group of people or objects that are identified as the whole from which a *sample* is taken. In voter preference polls, for example, the universe consists of all potential voters. See also *population*.

unlawful entry The *crime* of using force or fraud to come into the home or office of people without their permission. This crime is similar to *burglary* except that it need not entail breaking in or the intention to steal property.

unprofessional A term applied to behavior engaged in by a *professional* during the course of practice that does not measure up to the standards of the *profession*. Usually, it is conduct in violation of the profession's *code of ethics* or misuse of knowledge or the laws pertaining to the licensing of the

profession in the relevant jurisdiction. The term is not to be confused with *nonprofessional*.

unreasonable searches and seizures A law authority or government official entering one's home, car, office, or personal space to look for evidence of wrongdoing and removing articles that may appear incriminating. In the United States, these searches and seizures are unconstitutional, a violation of the Fourth Amendment. A "reasonable" search and seizure may occur if a law official indicates to a judge what specific evidence is being sought and why it is thought to be in the suspect's possession, and a search warrant is thereby issued.

unsocialized delinquent A youngster whose periodic trouble with the authorities and *antisocial behavior* stem from insufficient guidance, inadequate role models, or lack of exposure to people who have more acceptable standards of behavior.

unstable Not firmly fixed or secure. Social workers often apply this term to phenomena in their clients' personalities, health, environment, or social relationships to indicate that the existing situation is likely to change.

"unworthy poor" A pejorative term applied to poor people who were considered too lazy to work or too dishonest to be acceptable in polite society. This designation was used primarily before the 20th century to distinguish people who "deserved" public assistance (such as widows and people with disabilities) from those who did not (such as able-bodied young men without jobs). The term is no longer used officially, but its underlying philosophy is still held by many. See also *victim blaming*.

unwritten law 1. Social *norms, mores,* and customs, rather than written statutes and formal laws, that regulate the conduct of people. 2. An erroneous belief that certain crimes can be committed and the law authorities will not prosecute or will be lenient. Such crimes are thought to include killing or beating a person who raped a family member, attacking the man who engaged in coitus with one's wife, or taking revenge on a person who has disgraced the family honor. In fact, such laws are written and do not indicate special leniency.

upper-class welfare Government policies, grants, tax advantages, and direct payments from the government treasury made to affluent people and those not in economic need. For example, in the United States, these benefits include *social security* and *Medicare* benefits in excess of contributions, tax deductions on home ownership, write-offs for meals for work-related travel, and reduced or no taxes on estates. See also *corporate welfare.*

"uppers" Slang for *amphetamines,* the *controlled substances* that have been used to control weight and to keep people awake and alert. When abused, they are psychologically and physiologically addictive.

Upstream Head Start program An educational program within the *Head Start* program for children of migrants, especially those in farm labor. Local programs over a vast geographic area are linked and coordinated so that children are not deprived of Head Start benefits even though they must move frequently.

Upward Bound The *War on Poverty* program, established in 1964, designed to provide special education and incentives to encourage students not to drop out of school. It is now part of the U.S. Department of Education. Their Web site address is http://www.ed.gov/offices/OPE/HEP/trio/upbound

upward mobility Socioeconomic advances by individuals, groups, or nations. In nations, this is due to good and productive economic conditions that result in high employment and increased wages, stable prices, better use of natural resources, political changes, and enhanced opportunities for education and cultural development. In individuals, it is also a common result of getting better education and jobs as well as exploiting opportunities. See also *downward mobility.*

urban homesteading The process of occupying a formerly empty house, usually in a run-down city neighborhood, and living in it while restoring it. Often, this is made possible by government laws, grants, and tax incentives to encourage community improvements. See also *gentrification.*

Urban Institute The independent Washington-based think tank and research organization founded in 1968 to facilitate, coordinate, and interpret research on social and economic problems and to propose understandable solutions to these problems. Their Web site address is http://www.urban.org

Urban League, National The community service and *civil rights group* established in 1910 by social workers *George E. Haynes* (1880–1960) and Ruth Standish Baldwin to help end racial *discrimination* and help socially disadvantaged people. Largely staffed by social workers and professionals from related fields, the Urban League provides direct services in areas such as unemployment, housing, education, social welfare, family counseling and planning, legal affairs, and business development. Their Web site address is http://www.nul.org

urban legends Anecdotes passed between people that purport to tell true incidents experienced by "a friend of a friend." Many stories tend to reinforce undocumented but strongly held biases about people and ridicule them or the culture of which they are a part. A common example is the story of seeing a woman pay for her groceries with food stamps before driving off in her limousine.

urban renewal A social philosophy and a set of programs designed to prevent urban blight in those areas where satisfactory housing exists, to tear down slums and replace them with new buildings where suitable housing no longer exists, and to rehabilitate neighborhoods that are beginning to decay. Most federal urban renewal funding now comes through *block grants.* See also *gentrification.*

urbanization 1. A social trend in which people adopt the lifestyles, residential patterns, and cultural values of those who live in or near cities. 2. The physical development of a rural area so that it includes features found in cities.

urbanology The scientific study of cities and their problems.

urinalysis Chemical testing of the urine to help determine the existence of certain diseases, potential diseases, or drug use. Urinalysis is the most convenient and common method of *drug testing.*

user charges The social services policy of requiring the client or recipient of a service to pay for part or all of the cost of providing the service. This policy is in contrast to programs that are provided at no cost or low cost to the recipient, with the funds coming from general government revenues, through public or privately supported agencies, or from private insurance payments.

usual, customary, or reasonable (UCR)   A method of reimbursing health care providers. Generally, the third party paying the fees develops a profile of prevailing fees in a geographic area and uses it to determine what the company will pay for any service. One method is to average fees and set the UCR at 80 percent or 90 percent of the average.

usury   The act of charging excessive or unlawfully high rates of interest on loaned money. See also *Truth in Lending Act*.

utilitarianism   The ethical philosophy that holds that the rightness or wrongness of an action is determined by whether its consequences are useful or not.

utility programs   In the use of computers, the programs that help in the general running of the system for things such as transferring data from one storage site to another, making copies of files, locating and eliminating viruses, and saving data.

utility theory   In economics, the concept that a person obtains satisfaction (utility) through the consumption of goods and that the individual will attempt to establish priorities of consumption to achieve the highest possible level of satisfaction. The theory suggests that the higher the level of satisfaction for a given cost and unit of time, the more desirable a particular item.

utilization review   A formal process of evaluating the type and amount of service offered and delivered to organizations to determine if those services are justified. Organizations that receive funds from government bodies or other third-party groups are most likely to be subject to such evaluations, because the funders want to know if they are getting proper value for their costs. The review might determine the existence of overutilization (too many services delivered or too many demands made on available services) or underutilization (insufficient demand or delivery to justify the costs spent on services). The reviews may be *retrospective utilization reviews, concurrent utilization reviews,* or *prospective utilization reviews.* See also *quality assurance.*

utopia   An idealization of a perfect society.

V Codes A list of conditions that are not specific mental disorders but are included in the American Psychiatric Association's *Diagnostic and Statistical Manual (DSM)* because they are frequent reasons for which individuals seek the services of mental health professionals. The V Code conditions and their numbers include the following: relational problems, including those with siblings (V61.8), partners (V61.1), parent–child (V61.20), and problems related to a *mental disorder* or *general medical condition* (V61.9); problems related to *abuse* or *neglect,* including physical or *sexual abuse* or neglect of a child (V61.21) or physical or sexual abuse of an adult (V61.1); noncompliance with treatment (V15.81); *malingering* (V65.2); adult *antisocial behavior* (V71.01); child or adolescent antisocial behavior (V71.02); *borderline intellectual functioning* (V62.89); *age-related cognitive decline* (V780.9); *bereavement* (V62.82); academic problem (V62.3); occupational problem (V62.2); identity problem (V313.82); religious or spiritual problem (V62.89); *acculturation* problem (V62.4); and *phase-of-life problem* (V62.89). Organizations that make a *third-party payment* tend to reject treatment reimbursement claims if these are the sole reasons for treatment.

vaccine A preparation used to increase the body's resistance to a specific disease.

vaccine-preventable diseases A range of illnesses that usually can be avoided when children are vaccinated at the appropriate age, including diphtheria, tetanus, rubella, measles, hepatitis A and B, mumps, pertussis, polio, and some forms of influenza.

vaginismus A *sexual disorder* in women in which continuing involuntary spasms of the musculature of the outer third of the vaginal wall interfere with satisfactory coitus. See also *dyspareunia.*

vaginitis An inflammation of the vagina, caused primarily by the presence of an excessive number of otherwise harmless microorganisms.

vagrancy Wandering from place to place with no permanent home or job.

validator role One of the major functions of social work intervention with clients—that of confirming and legitimizing the client's own ideas, values, and emotions. When the social worker provides validation for the client's thoughts and feelings, the client is empowered to work more effectively toward problem resolution.

validity In *social research,* the concept concerned with the extent to which a procedure is able to measure the quality it is intended to measure.

value-added tax (VAT) An indirect sales tax that is levied on products at each stage of production in proportion to their increase in worth. These add-ons are finally passed on to the consumer. VAT is a *regressive tax* rather than a *progressive tax.* This form of taxation is common in many European nations.

value judgment An assumption made about the worth of some person, group, place, or event.

value orientation The characteristic way individuals or groups look at their own and others' standards of conduct, moral principles, and social customs.

values The customs, beliefs, standards of conduct, and principles considered desirable by a culture, a group of people, or an individual. Social workers, as one group, ascribe to a set of core values on which social work's mission is based. These core values, as specified in the *NASW Code of Ethics,* are service, social justice, dignity and worth of the person, importance of human relationships, integrity, and competence.

values clarification A method of education in morality and ethical principles that occurs by bringing people together to share their opinions and value perspectives. This exposes the participants to different ideals and permits them to appreciate the relative nature of values.

vandalism Intentional and illegal destruction of public or private property.

variable In *social research,* a characteristic that may vary or assume different quantified values. For example, the number of applicants for welfare benefits varies when more jobs are available. See also *dependent variable* and *independent variable.*

variable interval schedule   In *behavior modification,* a planned procedure for reinforcing behaviors at varying times after they occur. Often, the times are varied around some average.

variable ratio schedule   In *behavior modification,* a planned procedure of *intermittent reinforcement* in which the *reinforcement* is given on a varying basis around some average. The reinforcement is given only after several of the behaviors occur on one occasion and then given after a different number of behaviors occur on a different occasion.

variance   1. In *research,* a measure of dispersion within the distribution of events. 2. In statistics, the square of the *standard deviation (SD).* 3. In social administration, the difference between budgeted expectations and actual results. 4. In urban development, a legal exemption from *zoning* and building codes.

varicella   An acute contagious disease caused by the herpes varicella zoster virus. Known more commonly as "chicken pox," varicella is seen most commonly among young children, with symptoms of fever, discomfort, and skin rash on the face and body. A vaccine has been available since 1990.

vascular dementia   Multiple cognitive deficits, including memory impairment, that persist over several months, causing significant impairment in social or occupational functioning. This dementia results from cerebrovascular disturbances such as strokes. The disorder was formerly known as *multi-infarct dementia.*

Vasey, Wayne (1910–1992)   A social work educator and author who was an effective advocate for the profession's continuing interest in *macro practice.* He is author of the influential 1958 text *Government and Social Welfare.*

vegetative signs   Behavior in which there is little indication of mental activity. The person is passive, mute, unresponsive to the environment, and not inclined to move. This behavior is often symptomatic of *organic mental disorders* and some types of *schizophrenia.*

vendetta   A feud between two families or groups, perpetuated by the wish to avenge a perceived

wrong done to a member of the group. The vendetta is illegal in all nations but persists, especially in remote areas or in areas where the government is distrusted.

vendor   One who sells a product or service. Because they are paid to provide social services, social workers and their agencies are referred to as vendors by insurance companies and other third-party funding organizations.

vendor payments   Money a government agency or insurance company pays to a social agency, institution, or independent professional to provide services. The U.S. government uses the term primarily to apply to payments made to professionals or agencies on behalf of people who cannot afford to pay for the services themselves. The largest vendor payment system of this type in the United States is *Medicaid.*

vendorship   1. The practice of providing goods and services for specific fees that are charged either to the consumer or to a *third party.* 2. In social work, the vendorship model is practiced primarily by private social work practitioners, proprietary workers, and even traditional social agencies selling specific professional services to individuals and groups and being reimbursed for each unit of service by the consumer or by third parties such as health insurance companies, government agencies, or business organizations.

venereal diseases   Infections acquired through sexual contact and the exchange of bodily fluids. These may include *gonorrhea, syphilis,* genital *herpes,* and *acquired immune deficiency syndrome (AIDS).* See also *sexually transmitted diseases (STDs).*

ventilation   In the social worker–client therapeutic relationship, the process of permitting the client to express feelings during the description of the problem situation. According to psychosocial theorists, this releases or discharges emotions that have built up and caused the individual to have internal *stress* and conflict. It is also referred to as *catharsis.* See also *purposeful expression of feelings.*

verbal following responses   See *following responses.*

verbatim recording   In the social work *case record,* the process of writing down every word said in the *interview* and, to the extent possible, every gesture, expression, and tonal inflection so that the meaning is accurately conveyed. This process is used primarily for social worker training purposes or for legal issues in the interview and generally only in a single session or parts of sessions. It has become rarely used because it is distracting to the interview process and has been supplanted by the use of audio or video recording.

verbigeration   A series of verbalizations that are continuous, repetitive, and pressured and that extend over a significant period or frequently recur. This is often seen in certain types of *schizophrenia.*

Verein für Socialpolitik   The Association for Social Policy, a German professional organization of economists, lawyers, educators, and social scientists established in 1872. One of its first acts was to organize a conference on old-age and disability pensions. Although the Verein was primarily oriented to plans to organize industry and workers, many of its welfare proposals became adopted in the nation's first social insurance plans of 1881.

vernepleier   In Norway and other Scandinavian areas, a professional social worker who specializes in the special education and treatment of children and adults who have mental retardation.

vertical career move   Taking a new job in which the pay, benefits, responsibilities, and prestige are higher or, less typically, lower. See also *horizontal career move.*

vertical disclosure   The revelation by a member of a *social group work* or therapy group of some significant information and the group's analysis of that information and how it will affect the one who disclosed it. This is the opposite of *horizontal disclosure.*

vested interest   A special concern an individual, group, or culture has about some cause, property, commitment, or institution. It is perceived that if the object of concern is lost or changed it will be considered personally harmful. For example, social workers in private practice have vested interests in third-party recognition of their capabilities.

vesting   The right to pension benefits upon retirement for employees who obtain different jobs before retirement age. Such benefits are usually based on accrued funds set aside by or on behalf of the employee.

Veterans Affairs, U.S. Department of   The federal organization, formerly known as the U.S. Veterans Administration, responsible for providing health, education, and welfare services for former military service personnel in need. The Department of Veterans Affairs was established in 1920 as the U.S. Veterans Bureau and renamed in 1930 as the Veterans Administration. The department administers hospitals for patients with physical and mental illnesses, maintains programs of financial assistance and personal social services, establishes loans and insurance services, and offers training and rehabilitation programs and many other services. Social workers are a large and integral part of the department's professional staffs. Their Web site address is http://www.va.gov

Veterans Health Administration (VHA)   A major unit of the *U.S. Department of Veterans Affairs* that provides for the health care needs of Americans who served in the military. The VHA provides acute medical, surgical, and psychiatric inpatient and outpatient care; nursing homes; professional outpatient services; and other health care through its 171 medical centers accredited by the *Joint Commission on Accreditation of Healthcare Organizations (JCAHO)* and 340 outpatient clinics. Their Web site address is http://www.va.gov/health_benefits

veto   Rejection of laws or resolutions (already passed by the legislature) by the president or another leader with the authority to do so. In the U.S. federal system, the president may veto any legislation that comes before him, thus preventing it from becoming law. It is a "pocket veto" if he chooses not to sign the legislation within 10 days. "Veto-proof legislation" refers to those bills that passed by vote margins wide enough to override any veto. The U.S. Constitution requires a two-thirds vote by both legislative bodies to overturn presidential vetoes, meaning that it takes 67 U.S. senators and 290 representatives to enact a law without the president's signature.

vicarious   The feelings derived from sharing the experiences of another person. This phenomenon is often observed in *family therapy,* when a parent experiences the child's achievements or pains, and in *codependency* situations.

vicarious learning   In *behavior modification,* the premise that a client's desired behavior is strengthened through observing someone else being rewarded for that behavior; a form of imitation or *modeling.*

vicarious liability   The legal principle that civil liability may not necessarily be limited to the defendant but may extend to the defendant's employer, supervisors, instructors, and relevant others. For example, in social work, an aggrieved client may include the worker's agency and supervisors as codefendants. See also *respondeat superior.*

vicarious trauma   The experience of *burnout,* anxiety, guilt, and stress as a result of close contact with a trauma victim, often felt by the victim's therapist, family members, or bystanders during the traumatic event. It is also known as "secondary trauma" and "compassion fatigue."

vice   Criminal activity including *prostitution, pornography,* gambling, sales of illegal drugs or contraband, and other behaviors that are made illegal because they offend the community's moral standards.

victim blaming   A philosophy or orientation that attributes complicity to the person who is harmed by some social circumstance. For example, a woman who is raped or sexually harassed is accused of seducing the attacker, an abused spouse is accused of being masochistic and encouraging the abusive action, or a poor person is accused of being too lazy to work.

victim compensation   Public payment in cash or services to people who are judged to have been harmed as a result of another person's negligence or criminal activity.

victim impact statement   A written document used in some courts to help judges determine appropriate sentences for the offender. These statements are written by, or on behalf of, the crime victim, those close to the victim, or the survivors of the victim to describe the loss, suffering, and trauma experienced as a result of the crime.

victim–offender mediation   A form of community-based corrections in which issues between lawbreakers and those they have harmed are dealt with in face-to-face confrontation. The goal is for material and emotional losses to be restored to the extent possible and to confront offenders with the consequences of their action. Mediators usually help propose and monitor agreed-on *restitution,* which often includes making repayment, working for the victim, or working for a charity of the victim's choice.

victim precipitation   Violent acts on a person who originated the situation that resulted in a crime. The term is most often used in situations in which wives kill or injure their husbands after being assaulted or abused.

"victimless" crime   A law violation in which, supposedly, no one is harmed. Prostitution, gambling, and pornography are examples. Many argue that harm does occur to those involved in such activities.

victimology   The study of people who are harmed, usually by sociocultural phenomena, and the conditions in which the harm occurs.

Victims of Crime, Office for (OVC)   The organization within the *U.S. Department of Justice* established in 1984 to assist the victims of crime. The office helps states and localities with victim compensation programs and helps train professionals about the rights and needs of crime victims. Their Web site address is http://www.ojp.usdoj.gov/ovc

video feedback   An intervention procedure social workers and other professionals use to show clients how they appear to others by showing videotape replays of the client's past behavior and systematically analyzing the results. The procedure has been effective with clients who have substance abuse problems, emotional self-control problems, communications problems with family members or peers, or other behavioral problems. See also *audio feedback.*

Vietnam veterans   Military personnel who served during the Vietnam conflict, which ended in 1975. Many American veterans of this war have experienced difficulties trying to readjust to civilian life and have needed help from social workers, vocational counselors, physicians, and other professionals. These difficulties are related to factors such as the lack of popular support for the war and its participants; "losing" the war; poor postwar economic conditions supposedly resulting in reduced veterans' services; the widespread use of drugs; and the use of defoliants such as *Agent Orange,* which may be *carcinogenic.* See also *posttraumatic stress disorder (PTSD).*

vigilante   One who engages in crime fighting and carries out judicial rulings without legal authority because of the perception that the duly constituted legal system is inadequate.

violence Severe and intense exercise of force and power, usually resulting in injury or destruction. The term "crimes of violence" pertains to those crimes in which physical harm occurs or is threatened, such as *homicide, rape, aggravated assault,* and *battery.*

violentologist A professional with training, experience, and expertise in the study of violence, its causes, and its progression and consequences and who advises individuals, communities, and social structures on how to deal with it.

violentology The scientific study of violence, violent behavior, terrorism, civil and military disorder, and the victims and perpetrators of these events.

viruses Tiny, simple, spherical or rod-shaped organisms (or bits of nucleic acid wrapped in coats of protein) that cause mild and serious diseases in plants, animals, and humans. Such diseases include *acquired immune deficiency syndrome (AIDS),* some forms of *cancer,* colds, flu, *poliomyelitis,* and *hepatitis.* Viruses reproduce only within the cells of other organisms. Antibiotics that are effective in fighting bacterial diseases have little use in the fight against viral diseases.

visa An official authorization permitting entry within a nation, or area within that nation, usually for a specified purpose and length of time.

visitation rights A court-ordered legal right of parents or other relatives who no longer have *custody of children* to be in contact with them during the times agreed to and specified. See also *shared custody.*

visiting teacher service Programs within the educational system in which professionals in *school social work* provide personal social services to students and their families and help acquaint the schools with the special needs of these families. Originally, these services were provided by educators, but eventually professional social workers assumed these duties in many school districts. The National Association of Visiting Teachers, which was established in 1916, was absorbed into the *American Association of Social Workers (AASW)* as the School Social Work Section in 1921.

visual hallucination An imagined perception of seeing something that does not exist outside subjective experience.

vital records Documents on each individual that must be filed and maintained in the office of the register of deeds or records for the county or local jurisdiction. Copies of these documents, which include birth and death certificates, marriage and divorce or annulment documents, and information on fetal deaths, may be made available to the family.

vital signs Indicators (such as pulse, respiration, temperature, and movement) that the body is alive and functioning.

vital statistics Official demographic data pertaining to the incidence of marriages, divorces, births, deaths, health statuses, diseases, causes of death, and so on.

vitiligo White patches on the skin, a condition resulting from the loss of melanocyte cells that produce melanin, the pigment that gives skin its color.

Vivas, Juan Luis (1492–1540) Spanish humanist who advocated for poor people and in 1525 published the influential treatise on poor relief, *De Subventione Pauperum.* He recommended the centralization of relief funds, forced labor, schools for poor children, and the prohibition of begging.

vivisection Experimentation on living animals to study biological and behavioral responses to various conditions.

vocational education A program of studies, often including supervised hands-on experiences, designed to prepare students for employment in one or more technical, semiskilled, or skilled occupations.

vocational guidance Assisting people in the systematic process of locating suitable *employment.* The activities inherent in such assistance include delineating qualifications and possible job opportunities and helping individuals determine if they have the aptitude and qualifications for a specific job, helping them find the training necessary to do a job, and counseling them on how to apply for a position.

vocational rehabilitation Training people with physical or mental disabilities so they can do useful work, become more self-sufficient, and be less reliant on public financial assistance. *Block grants* and other funding through the *U.S. Department of*

Health and Human Services (HHS) go to states to facilitate specific vocational rehabilitation programs. The *U.S. Department of Veterans Affairs* also works with state agencies in the training of veterans with disabilities.

Vocational Rehabilitation, Office of   Federally mandated, locally administered programs in every state to provide free vocational counseling and referral to training programs or job placement services for people with disabilities. In some states, the programs are administered by the Department of Social Services, whereas in other states, the Department of Labor is in charge.

"volags"   Slang for voluntary agencies.

volition   Free will; the act of deciding or choosing without being compelled to do so. Problems of volition are often seen in *schizophrenia, organic mental disorders,* and *drug intoxication.*

voluntary associations   Organizations in which funding comes from private contributions and in which the goals are to provide health, social, and other services to those who are disadvantaged and outside government auspices. Voluntary associations tend to specialize in particular needs and services. These include health and hospital support (for example, the American Cancer Society, the American Heart Association, and the National Kidney Foundation), help for specific groups (for example, *Big Brothers/Big Sisters of America* and the National Shut-in Society), church-related organizations (for example, *Catholic Charities USA* and *Lutheran Social Services*), and community fundraising groups (for example, the *United Way*).

volunteer   One who offers to serve, usually without financial compensation. See also *volunteerism.*

volunteer support organizations   Professional associations in which memberships are made up of professionals who help administer and advise volunteer groups. Among the largest of these organizations are the Association of Volunteer Administrators, the American Society of Directors of Volunteers, the Directors of Volunteers in Agencies, the National Council on Corporate Volunteerism, and the Directors of Volunteers in Hospitals.

volunteerism   The mobilization and use of unpaid individuals and groups to provide human services outside the auspices of government agencies. This term, or "voluntarism," also pertains to the ideologies of *self-help groups, mutual-aid groups, self-help organizations,* and *philanthropy.* The U.S. government maintains the *Corporation for National and Community Service* (which includes the *Senior Corps, AmeriCorps,* and *Volunteers in Service to America [VISTA]*) to help coordinate some of these efforts throughout the nation. Other organizations that serve the same purpose include the National Self-Help Clearinghouse, the National Self-Help Resource Center, and the National Center for Voluntary Action, which promotes the national network of local Voluntary Action Centers.

Volunteers in Police Service (VIPS)   A *U.S. Department of Justice* program to organize volunteers in every community to assist police officers. Volunteers help in performing clerical and administrative tasks, assisting with crowd and parking control, making follow-up calls to victims, and taking police reports. Their Web site address is http://www.policevolunteers.org

Volunteers in Service to America (VISTA)   The program established in 1964 to bring volunteers into urban and rural areas of the United States that face economic and cultural deprivation. In 1995, VISTA, as part of *AmeriCorps,* became part of the *Corporation for National and Community Service.* Often called the "Domestic Peace Corps," the workers are assigned to antipoverty (capacity-building) activities in disadvantaged communities. *AmeriCorps*VISTA* volunteers serve full-time for 12 months in these communities and receive a living allowance and health and child care (or a cash stipend at the end of service). Their Web site address is http://www.americorps.org/vista

Volunteers in Technical Assistance (VITA)   A volunteer organization composed primarily of engineers, architects, scientists, computer experts, and others who provide technical assistance, advice, and information to businesses and organizations in developing countries through the use of mail, computer interfaces, telephone, and e-mail. Their Web site address is http://www.vita.org

voter registration drives   A strategy used by social activists, community organizers, and other social workers to strengthen the power and influence of a community or segment of the population by encouraging and facilitating the enrollment of eligible citizens to permit them to vote in subsequent elections. See also *Human SERVE* and *National Voter Registration Act.*

voucher system A method of subsidizing a person's social services, health care, and other needs on the open market. Typically, in this system a poor person is given vouchers, often in the form of redeemable stamps or coupons, worth a certain amount of money as long as they are spent on a specified service or product. Among the most common of these systems are food stamps, tuition grants, and housing subsidy checks.

voyeurism A *sexual disorder* characterized by repetitive looking at unsuspecting people who are undressed or engaged in sexual activity. Popularly referred to as "Peeping Tomism," this activity is the preferred source of sexual excitement for voyeurs.

People who enjoy watching or observing others in everyday situations are sometimes informally referred to as voyeurs.

vulnerability factors Conditions in people's bodies, groups, or environments that make them open to harm or disease. These factors are not by themselves the cause of the harm or disease, but they increase the chances when they occur in conjunction with other risk factors.

vulnerable population Those individuals or groups who have a greater probability of being harmed by specific social, environmental, or health problems than the population as a whole. For example, African American men are a vulnerable population at risk for *hypertension,* and citizens of *underdeveloped nations* are more vulnerable to *malnutrition.* This is a synonym for *at-risk population.*

wage controls Government regulations that limit the amount of increase or decrease in money that employers can pay to their workers. The stated purpose is usually to control *inflation* and increase *employment*. This policy is often accompanied by *price controls*. See also *monetarism*.

wage earner's plan In bankruptcy proceedings, a written and enforceable pledge to pay a percentage of one's debts out of future earnings. The wage earner's plan is also referred to as "Chapter 13" (the relevant chapter in the Bankruptcy Code).

WAIS test See *intelligence quotient (IQ)*.

Wald, Lillian (1867–1940) An advocate for *public health* and *child welfare* programs. She founded one of the most influential of the *settlement houses,* the Henry Street Settlement in New York, and with *Florence Kelley* founded the U.S. *Children's Bureau.* In 1970, she became the second social worker, after *Jane Addams,* to be included in the Hall of Fame for Great Americans.

WAN Wide-area network; a connection of mainframe and personal computers located across the world. See also *LAN.*

war-affected children Adolescent boys and girls and younger children who live in current or former war zones. Some children are forced into combat roles as soldiers; others are forced into labor. Others live among land mines, bombed-out areas, and areas still under siege. Malnutrition, exploitation, family separations, lack of opportunities for educational or social development, and incessant stress are among the problems encountered.

War on Poverty President Lyndon B. Johnson's plans and programs established during his administration to encourage economic well-being, promote equal opportunity for all, and realize the *Great Society.* The "war" was to be fought primarily through the programs of the *Economic Opportunity Act of 1964* (P.L. 88-452). This included a major revision of the *Social Security Act* of 1935, including greatly extended coverage. The Economic Opportunity Act established *Volunteers in Service to America (VISTA),* the *Job Corps, Head Start,* the *Legal Services Corporation,* and the *Community Action Program (CAP).*

ward 1. A person, usually a child or mentally limited adult, who has a guardian or caregiver. If the custody of that person has been removed from the parents or other guardian through legal means, then the person usually becomes a "ward of the court" or "ward of the state." 2. A political district of certain cities.

warism The orientation that military conflict is morally justified and promises unique advantages for the nation declaring war that cannot be achieved in any other way. See also *militarism* and *pacifism.*

Warner, Amos G. (1861–1900) A social planner and welfare administrator. He wrote the influential text *American Charities* in 1894, the first attempt to find a scientific approach to the problems of *poverty.*

Washington, Forrester B. (1887–1963) A proponent of the scientific method for professional training of social workers. He was the longtime dean at the Atlanta University School of Social Work and an organizer–leader of the *National Urban League.*

"WASP" A term used sometimes disparagingly in referring to white Anglo-Saxon Protestants, virtually the only population group in which male members are not considered "minorities" or socially disadvantaged. Actually, the term also is frequently applied to white people who are Catholics and to people of non-English European ancestry— that is, white nonethnic persons. The "WASP" label often is used to imply that there is a single lifestyle (bland and comfortably affluent), political orientation (*conservatism*), and economic value orientation (*social Darwinism*) among these people, even though they are highly disparate in these characteristics. See also *ethnic group* and *white ethnic groups.*

watchdog group An ad hoc or formal *coalition* established to scrutinize the actions of political leaders, government officials, or institutions that influence the public. Watchdog groups usually consist of concerned citizens, paid or volunteer lobbyists, professional and trade associations, and business groups whose interests might be affected by the actions of those being observed.

waxy flexibility   A symptom seen especially in *catatonia* in which the person's facial expressions, limbs, and body posture remain relatively fixed or move only gradually. The formal term is "cerea flexibilitas."

wayfinding   The cognitive and physical ability to travel to a specific destination. This ability is facilitated by designs in the environment such as signs, directional arrows, traffic authorities, transit counselors, and pathways that can be used. *Transport-disabled persons* may need specially designed wayfinding services to give them access to needed health and social services.

WCTU   Women's Christian Temperance Union. See *temperance movements.*

Webb, Bernice (1858–1943) and **Webb, Sidney (1859–1947)**   British social reformers, leaders of the *Fabian Society,* advocates for better conditions for laborers and poor people, and founders of the London School of Economics. While Bernice worked to change existing poor laws and advocated for guaranteed minimum standards of living, Sidney engaged in politics and helped develop the Labour Party. They worked toward improved education and wrote influential books about the trade union movement.

Weber, Helene (1881–1962)   A German social worker and reformer who helped develop German social welfare policy; campaigned for equal rights for women; organized German schools of social work; and, as a member of the German parliament after World War II, helped create the nation's new constitution.

welfare   1. A condition of physical health, emotional comfort, and economic security. 2. The efforts of a society to help its citizens achieve that condition. The term is also used popularly as a synonym for *public assistance* or other programs that provide for the economic and social services needs of poor people.

welfare backlash   Resistance and opposition by some citizens and groups to public expenditures for poor people, often manifested in social movements such as "taxpayer revolts" and in political pressure to eliminate funding for some welfare programs.

Welfare Law Center   The professional organization of lawyers and others interested in advocating for and working to ensure adequate income supports for all. The organization monitors the development and effect of welfare laws and proposed laws and participates in legal actions against government organizations on behalf of low-income people. Their Web site address is http://www.welfarelaw.org

welfare magnet issue   A controversy about whether people seeking welfare benefits move to those states or regions where payments and services seem better. Objective research has not clearly affirmed that people move to states to obtain better welfare benefits. Even though legislation and court decisions have made certain residency requirements illegal, conflicts about the issue continue to be disputed in courtrooms.

"welfare queen"   A pejorative term applied to people, especially mothers, receiving *Temporary Assistance to Needy Families (TANF)* payments who apparently defraud the public assistance and social security systems. The fraud is accomplished by using many aliases and different addresses and by exaggerating the need to obtain more money, goods, and services. The term may be based on one of the *urban legends* that suggests that many recipients would live in luxury if not rigorously constrained.

welfare reform   Various efforts to change the way social welfare programs are administered, funded, and used. Some reformers seek more stringent rules to discourage people from obtaining assistance. Others advocate elimination of bureaucratic obstacles and any *means tests.* Some advocate replacing the entire welfare system with a *guaranteed annual income* for all people that would meet each person's minimal requirements. The most significant recent attempt to reform U.S. "welfare as we know it" occurred during the Clinton administration with the *Personal Responsibility and Work Opportunity Reconciliation Act* of 1996 (P.L. 104-193). Many welfare experts say the act needs to be reformed. Other welfare reform proposals identified in this dictionary include the *Family Assistance Plan (FAP),* the *guaranteed annual income,* the *negative income tax,* the *Newburgh welfare plan,* and *Workfare.*

welfare rights The view that public assistance and other social services are entitlements available to any of a nation's citizens. Welfare rights organizations say that included among the rights of welfare recipients are confidentiality of personal information from welfare investigators, greater availability of information about the benefits for people who are eligible, increased accessibility of welfare offices (nearer to transportation routes, open longer hours, and shorter waiting lines), and more equitable distribution of services and funds.

welfare state A nation or society that considers itself responsible for meeting the basic educational, health care, economic, and social security needs of its people.

Welfare-to-Work Partnership A nonprofit project established in 1997 by a consortium of American corporations to help people get off public assistance and into employment. Employers, known as Business Partners, are committed to hiring welfare recipients using information, technical assistance, and support from businesses representing all sizes, industries, and locations. Their Web site address is http://www.welfaretowork.org

Welfare-to-Work (WtW) Programs A variety of initiatives that originated in the various U.S welfare reform laws of 1996 and subsequent years to help hard-to-employ people get meaningful jobs in the public and private sectors.

wellness A dynamic state of physical, mental, spiritual, and social well-being; a way of life that equips the individual to realize the full potential of his or her capabilities and to overcome and compensate for weaknesses; a lifestyle that recognizes the importance of nutrition, physical and mental fitness, stress reduction, self-responsibility, and civic responsibility.

welt A reddish bump, swelling, or streak in the unbroken skin. These signs may indicate that a child or other client may have suffered beatings, whippings, or other abuse. Welts may also be the result of allergic reactions to certain foods or drugs or insect bites.

whiplash An injury to the neck, sometimes including torn or overextended muscles and ligaments. The injury usually occurs as a result of being struck from behind (for example, in a fast-moving car accident).

whistle-blowing Informing those people in positions of influence or authority outside an organization about the existence of an organization's practices that are illegal, wasteful, dangerous, or otherwise contrary to its stated policies. The informant is compelled to notify outsiders (investigative commissions, the media, *ombudspersons,* congresspersons, and others) because authorities within the organization ignore complaints. Some organizations, such as the U.S. government, encourage whistle-blowing by maintaining toll-free *hot lines* for anonymous tipsters and by trying to protect employees from subsequent retribution from their employers.

white-collar crime Nonviolent illegal acts typically committed by corporations or individuals, usually in the course of the offender's occupation. Such offenses include *embezzlement, fraud, forgery,* tax evasion, fraudulent use of credit cards, stock manipulation, *bribery,* and computer crime.

white ethnic groups White people who, because of their orientation toward a shared national origin, religion, or language other than that of the *"WASP"* mainstream, have as much or more in common with other racial and cultural groups. Such people include first- or second-generation Italian Americans, Greek Americans, and Jews. When comparing these groups with people of color, it is important to take into account the variability and cultural variations of different groups of white people.

"white flight" A lay term used to describe demographic patterns of racial resegregation in residential neighborhoods. The pattern is said to begin in some neighborhoods when one or more black families establish residence. Some white families who fear the possibility of negative economic or social conditions or who are racist move away precipitously. Many homes thus become vacant and then become occupied by more black families. The pattern continues as more white families "flee."

White House conferences Formal meetings, convened by the U.S. president, of the nation's leaders in various social welfare and health fields to discuss specified social problems and potential solutions. President Theodore Roosevelt convened the first conference (on child welfare) in 1909. Subsequent conferences have focused on problems of older Americans, health care, and families, and most have culminated in new laws and programs designed to resolve some of the problems addressed.

white paper   A document in which a specific issue, problem, or need is described, followed by summaries of the available research and problem statements and concluding with proposals for the most appropriate responses and actions to be taken. White papers often follow *green papers,* which introduce the problem and recommend procedures for dealing with it. White papers often lead to new policy decisions or action programs.

white supremacist groups   Organizations in the United States in which members seek to suppress people of racial and ethnic groups, religions other than Christianity, or the speaking of languages other than English, often through *ethnoviolence* and *hate crimes, propaganda,* and intimidation. The groups maintain *Ku Klux Klan (KKK)* or *neo-Nazism* ideologies and methods and include organizations such as Aryan Nations, Posse Comitatus, the National Alliance, the White Aryan Resistance, The Order, and the *skinheads.*

Whitton, Charlotte (1896–1975)   An influential advocate of professionalizing the administration of charity programs in Canada. She initiated the social survey method to identify Canada's social problems and needs. She advocated restricting welfare programs and opposed development of Canada's social and health care programs.

whole-family foster care   An intervention system in which social workers provide therapy and other social services not only to children removed from their homes into foster placements, but also to the children's family members to prepare all of them for their eventual reunion and improved family relationship.

whooping cough   See *pertussis.*

WIC program   The Special Supplemental Food Program for Women, Infants, and Children, established in 1972 to provide assistance services under the auspices of the *U.S. Department of Agriculture (USDA).* The program is designed to protect women, infants, and children who are identified as being at risk of nutritional deficiency as a result of inadequate income, primarily by subsidizing certain food purchases. Their Web site address is http://www.fns.usda.gov

Wickenden, Elizabeth (1910–2001)   Social work administrator who worked with *Harry Hopkins* in developing the *Federal Emergency Relief Administration* and helped design the *social security* system. Later, she advised President Lyndon B. Johnson in the development of *Medicare* and the *War on Poverty.*

widowhood   The stage of life following the death of one's spouse.

Wilberforce, William (1759–1833)   British humanitarian and political leader who led the fight for prison reform and especially for the abolition of slavery, which he achieved in Great Britain in 1807 and in the entire British Empire in 1833.

"wild analysis"   The expression used primarily by psychotherapists with a Freudian orientation to describe a therapist's poorly planned verbalizations and idiosyncratic approaches to *therapy.*

"wilding"   A slang term referring to spontaneous, violent activity by youth gangs.

Wiley, George (1931–1973)   A community organizer and advocate who led the *National Welfare Rights Organization (NWRO)* to organize poor people as a political force.

willful misconduct   Intentional, premeditated, and conscious violation of the laws, rules, or norms of the organization, group, or society to which one belongs, generally resulting in sanctions, disciplinary actions, or both.

willfulness   Determination, stubbornness, or purposeful intention. This quality is seen as having good and bad characteristics, depending on its use. It exists in various degrees in leaders of social causes, activists, rebellious adolescents, obsessive–compulsive people, people with personality disorders, and other people said to have "strong personalities."

Wilson, Gertrude (1895–1984)   Conceptualizer of social group work theories and the integration of group work methods with social casework methods.

"window period"   A term used by researchers of *acquired immune deficiency syndrome (AIDS)* for the time just after infection with the *human immuno-*

deficiency virus (HIV), during which the individual is infectious but antibody tests do not detect the virus. See also *incubation.*

Winnicott, Clare (1900–1984) A leader in the United Kingdom's postwar child welfare field who developed Great Britain's first social work training program for child welfare workers and integrated psychodynamic understanding of children's personalities with social and political realities. She was awarded the Order of the British Empire in 1971 for her work in child welfare.

witch-hunt The identification and persecution of people suspected of some activity thought to be detrimental to the existing political or social order. The term derives from the efforts to protect society in the 1600s by attempting to locate and kill those suspected of being witches.

withdrawal A pattern of removing oneself physically or psychologically from other people or circumstances that are disturbing. See also *withdrawal symptoms.*

withdrawal delirium A state of consciousness that is manifested by cloudy and unfocused thought, unclear awareness of the environment, and inconsistent attention to sensory stimuli, all associated with the cessation of alcohol or drug use. See *delirium tremens (DTs).*

withdrawal symptoms Physical and emotional reactions of people who have discontinued the use of certain drugs or alcohol to which they have become dependent, addicted, or habituated. The individual may experience reactions such as *tremor,* pain in the digestive system, *delirium tremens (DTs),* convulsions, *fear* and *panic disorder,* acute *anxiety,* and *mood swings.*

Wittman, Milton (1916–1994) A social work administrator who headed the social work training branch of the *National Institute of Mental Health (NIMH),* through which he forged a link between social work and mental health. He was also a leader in various social work organizations as well as a leader in the development of *military social work.*

"Wobblies" Slang for supporters of the Industrial Workers of the World (IWW), a federation of labor unions prominent before World War I that sought to improve working conditions and unite workers from all nations.

wolfahrtsverbände Welfare organizations in Germany.

Wollstonecraft, Mary (1759–1797) An English writer and reformer and one of the earliest feminists. She advocated especially for the opportunity for girls to receive educations.

Women in Community Service (WICS) The national voluntary organization established in 1964 to help young people move from poverty to full social participation by helping to provide life skills development, job readiness, and social supports. WICS began as a coalition of women's church and civil rights organizations, mostly to help recruit, screen, and mentor Job Corps applicants, and now provides a full range of mentoring and human services activities. Their Web site address is http://www.wics.org

Women's Bureau, U.S. The organization within the *U.S. Department of Labor* in which the primary concern is the working conditions of women. It administers a variety of programs to see that these conditions are favorable. Other programs of the Women's Bureau include helping *displaced homemakers,* teenage mothers, and women of racial and ethnic groups and providing child care services. Their Web site address is http://www.dol.gov/wb

Women's Christian Temperance Union (WCTU) See *temperance movements.*

Women's Health and Cancer Rights Act (WHCRA) The 1998 federal law to mandate that third-party health insurers provide coverage for women diagnosed with breast cancer who undergo mastectomy and reconstructive surgery.

Women's International Peace Congress The 1915 gathering of women from around the world who were leaders in their respective countries on behalf of the antiwar movement. American delegates *Jane Addams* and *Emily Greene Balch* (the only two social work leaders to receive Nobel Peace Prizes) were joined by delegates from neutral and belligerent nations on the eve of World War I. The later work of this group greatly influenced President Woodrow Wilson's Fourteen-Point Program for International Peace and the League of Nations.

The organization evolved through several names and currently exists as the *International League for Peace and Freedom.*

women's liberation movement The organized efforts of disparate people and groups to eliminate *sex role stereotyping* and *sex discrimination* against women, achieve equality of opportunity with men, and widen the range of acceptable behaviors identified with female roles and femininity. See also *men's liberation movement.*

women's suffrage movement The organized political and social campaign to establish civil and social rights for women, especially the right to vote. In the United States, this movement was strongest from the time of the *Seneca Falls Convention* in 1848, which outlined the equal rights for women goals, to the passage in 1920 of the 19th Amendment to the Constitution, which gave women the right to vote. The movement continues in several nations where the rights of women to participate in the political process are limited.

work activities center A facility in which people with physical or emotional impairments are paid to produce services or products. The U.S. *Fair Labor Standards Act (FLSA)* authorizes lower than *minimum wage* payments for some of those engaged in such activity.

work ethic An ideology and a behavior found in many individuals and sociocultural groups that emphasize purposeful activity, productivity, and accomplishment. People so oriented are considered to be socially responsible and deserving of the advancements they tend to receive. However, they often are considered by those who do not share this ideology to be dull, unimaginative, and spiritless.

work experience programs Social services and labor programs designed to help clients become more employable by placing them in subsidized jobs in *nonprofit agencies,* usually for short periods. The goal gives less emphasis to training for specific marketable skills and more to improving workplace *coping skills.* This includes enhancing clients' self-confidence, sense of responsibility, and self-discipline; stressing the importance of timely reporting for work; and teaching clients to relate cooperatively with coworkers. See also *Community Work Experience Program (CWEP).*

work-in A planned and coordinated activity by groups of employees who report to their jobs as usual but do not fulfill their usual responsibilities. Usually, the goal is to protest some workplace grievance while reducing the risk of being replaced by other workers.

Work Incentive (WIN) program The 1967 revisions to the *Aid to Families with Dependent Children (AFDC)* program that permitted and encouraged mothers receiving AFDC payments to work. The program was eliminated, but many of its goals were incorporated into the *Personal Responsibility and Work Opportunity Reconciliation Act* of 1996.

work incentives Benefits, requirements, or special aid to encourage people to seek and retain suitable *employment* and to encourage employer organizations to hire and keep people on the job. Work incentives for individuals include programs such as *day care,* higher wages (made possible by government subsidy), reduction or termination of welfare payments for those who refuse to work, and improvements in the work environment. Work incentives for employer organizations include tax breaks for hiring and retaining specified numbers or categories of people (as in *experience ratings*), direct payments to subsidize wages paid, and stimulation of the general economy to allow the organization to employ more workers.

work-oriented antipoverty programs Federal, state, and private efforts to raise the income of poor people by facilitating their access to jobs, creating more jobs, and providing incentives to work such as awarding tax credits and retaining Medicaid. These programs attempt to replace welfare entitlement programs.

work permit A proof of eligibility for employment, showing that a person from a monitored group is eligible for certain types of employment without violating U.S. labor laws. The *U.S. Department of Labor* issues such papers to immigrants and foreign nationals seeking to work in the United States and may control the employment of minors by requiring them to apply for such permits.

work release A criminal justice procedure that permits convicted law violators to leave temporarily their *carceral organization,* such as a jail, to go to their jobs and return to the facility immediately after work.

work release program A system whereby an inmate of a correctional or other institution is permitted to leave the facility regularly to maintain his or her paid employment. Often, this program is used in conjunction with a *halfway house* so that the inmate has greater local access to the job and greater opportunity to re-enter society when the required period of *incarceration* is concluded. See also *community service sentence.*

"workaholic"   One whose excessive involvement in work adversely affects healthy social functioning. In extreme examples, the condition is symptomatic of an *obsessive–compulsive disorder* or other compulsive trait.

worker performance   The productivity, efficiency, effectiveness, and quality of service with which an employee fulfills the requirements of the job.

worker satisfaction   The degree to which an employee has a positive attitude about the employer, the working conditions, relationships with other workers and those served, and future opportunities. The traditional view among social welfare administrators that increased job satisfaction leads to better work performance may not always be valid. Some evidence indicates that the two are not correlated.

workers' compensation   Programs—funded by employers, insurance companies, and government—to pay employees for some part of the cost of occupational diseases and injury. Most industrial countries have uniform national programs for such reimbursement. However, in the United States, the programs are established primarily under state law and thus vary widely as to the amount of compensation and the conditions under which compensation is to be awarded. In most states, the benefits are underwritten through private insurance companies in which premiums are paid by employers. The specific awards are usually under the scrutiny of state boards and *U.S. Department of Labor* supervision.

Workfare   The proposal by various economists, social planners, and politicians to discourage able-bodied people from receiving welfare benefits. It would establish programs and facilities in the public and private sectors so that these people could earn some of their benefits through work. It is a generic term rather than any specific program. See also *workhouse.*

workforce   1. Those individuals who are employed in a given organization or industry. 2. All individuals who are working or looking for jobs.

Workforce Investment Act (WIA)   The 1998 federal law (P.L. 105-220) to consolidate and coordinate the nation's job training and employment development programs and establish in every community in the nation one-stop centers where adults, dislocated workers, and youths can get information about available training programs, jobs, summer work experience, *Welfare-to-Work Programs,* and adult education. The program is administered by the *U.S. Department of Labor* through local Workforce Investment Boards, which work closely with employers, government agencies, planning organizations, and neighborhood citizens' groups. The WIA replaces the *Job Training Partnership Act* and other programs.

workhouse   An *indoor relief* form of "assistance," common in various countries in the 18th century, in which poor people who received help had to live and work in special facilities. The government contracted with private individuals to feed and house these people in exchange for the work they could do. The programs, which housed infants, children, older and disabled people, and diseased as well as able-bodied adults, were phased out in the late 18th century in favor of slightly more humane *almshouses* and *outdoor relief* programs.

working class   The *socioeconomic class,* according to many sociologists, in which family members tend to hold steady *employment* in industry and blue-collar jobs and have relatively modest incomes, limited education, and aspirations and values that tend to be oriented toward maintaining security and preserving their existing lifestyles.

Working Families Tax Credit (WFTC)   The United Kingdom's welfare benefit that supplements the income of low-wage working parents by reducing their taxes or giving them additional funds in their paychecks. The WFTC replaced the Family Credit system in 1999. The benefit includes a basic tax credit, an additional credit for those working more than 30 hours weekly, a tax credit for each child, and a child care tax credit. Their Web site address is http://www.inlandrevenue.gov/uk/wftc

working poor   Employed people whose assets and incomes from their jobs are so low that they fall below the *poverty line.* Although working poor people may be eligible for *food stamps* and some other means-tested programs, they often have limited access to housing, health care, or other necessities.

working through 1. In the social worker–client relationship, the process of mutually exploring a problem until there is agreement about the solution and the means to achieve it. 2. In *psychoanalytic theory,* those processes that enable infantile and repressed *unconscious* material to be made *conscious* so it can be analyzed in therapy.

workplace The setting in which one's employment or other work activity occurs.

Works Progress Administration (WPA) A *New Deal* employment program established in 1935 under the leadership of social worker *Harry Hopkins* (1890–1946). WPA provided jobs for more than 8 million people during its existence. Federal funds were used to build parks, bridges, roads, and airports and to sponsor the work of artists, musicians, writers, and scholars. The program was renamed the Work Projects Administration in 1939; it was disbanded in 1943 when employment conditions changed as a result of World War II.

World Bank The informal name for the International Bank for Reconstruction and Development, headquartered in Washington, DC, with offices in every part of the world. The bank lends money and provides economic advice to *developing countries.* The World Bank was founded in 1944 to help the economies of war-torn nations. Their Web site address is http://www.worldbank.org

World Food Programme A subsidiary of the United Nations *Food and Agriculture Organization (FAO)* that obtains and provides emergency supplies of food for populations suffering from famine or disaster. It also helps nations in which such populations exist to receive and distribute food. Their Web site address is http://www.wfp.org

World Health Organization (WHO) The United Nations agency established in its present form in 1948, with headquarters in Geneva, the purpose of which is the "attainment by all peoples of the highest possible level of health." WHO sponsors medical research, health education, and disease prevention programs and works toward the standardization of health and mental health statistics throughout the world. Their Web site address is http://www.who.int

World Neighbors A private, nonprofit organization located in 20 countries in Asia, Africa, and Latin America designed to help eliminate poverty, hunger, and disease through self-help and education programs, family planning, community-based health, sanitation, conservation, and the establishment of small business. Their Web site address is http://www.wn.org

World Resource Institute A private, nonprofit, Washington-based organization that provides technical support and services to governments and *nongovernment organizations (NGOs)* trying to manage sustainable natural resources. Their Web site address is http://www.wri.org

worldview The way a person tends to understand his or her relationship with social institutions, nature, objects, other people, and spirituality.

"worthy poor" The term once used to describe people who were poor because they were widowed, disabled, or had experienced unexpected economic reversals. They were considered to be honest, motivated to contribute to society, and basically hardworking. This term was used, mostly before the 20th century, to distinguish those people who "deserved" assistance from those who did not (the *"unworthy poor"*). Although the term is no longer officially used, many people still believe the concept. See also *victim blaming.*

Wright, Frances (Fanny) (1795–1852) A social reformer who came to the United States from Scotland and spent her life working for *human rights,* the gradual abolition of slavery, free public education, and *birth control.* A movement known as the "Fanny Wrighters" worked for these principles and gained political influence in the 1840s and 1850s.

Wyatt v. Stickney The 1971 legal ruling in Alabama declaring that patients with mental illness who are committed on civil grounds have the constitutional right to receive such individual treatment as will give them a realistic opportunity to be cured or to improve their mental condition. See also *right to treatment* and *deinstitutionalization.*

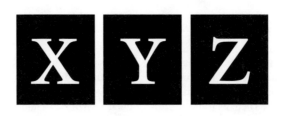

X chromosome One of the two human sex chromosomes, the pairing of which (XX for females, XY for males) determines an individual's sex. See also *Y chromosome*.

xanthines A group of drugs, related to *amphetamines* and *cocaine*, that act as *central nervous system (CNS)* stimulants. Caffeine is a common example.

xenodochium An institution established during the reign of Roman Emperor Constantine (288–337) to provide temporary food and shelter for those who were destitute or infirm.

xenophobia Persistent, intense, and unreasonable *fear* of strangers or foreign people.

xiao Chinese term for filial piety, or loyalty to one's kin, a central value among Chinese families. Xiao is manifested most notably in caring for one's elderly or infirm relatives.

XXY male A man or boy with an extra sex chromosome that results in an XXY chromosome arrangement instead of the usual XY arrangement. Also called Klinefelter's syndrome, this fairly common genetic abnormality remains undetected throughout many men's lives. In many others, there is occasional breast enlargement, lack of facial and body hair, a more rounded body type, and some self-esteem and other psychological problems. Treatment may include surgery to reduce breast size and regular injections of the male hormone testosterone beginning at puberty.

Y chromosome One of the two human sex chromosomes, the pairing of which (XX for females, XY for males) determines one's sex. See also *X chromosome*.

"YAVIS client" An acronym for "young, attractive, verbal, intelligent, and sexy," which refers to the type of person some psychotherapists seem to prefer treating, even though other clients may be in greater need.

yaws An infectious disease that commonly affects children who live in tropical climates in which bumps form on the skin; multiply; and may become ulcerated, filled with pus, or both. The disease is caused by the spirochete organism, which enters the skin where cuts or scrapes occur. It is easily treated with antibiotics but often occurs in countries or areas too poor to provide such treatments.

yellow fever An *infectious disease* caused by a virus transmitted by the bites of infected mosquitoes, found mostly in warm, damp climates. Symptoms include high fever, chills, jaundice, and often hemorrhaging and death. Prevention occurs through the control of mosquito habitats and through inoculations.

young carers In the United Kingdom and other nations, the designation for children and young people who have some responsibilities in caring for their parents because of some illness or incapacity. See also *carers*.

Young Men's and Young Women's Hebrew Associations (YM–YWHA) Organizations in communities with significant Jewish populations designed to provide young people with education, recreation, and social and spiritual opportunities. See also *Jewish communal agencies*.

Young Men's Christian Association (YMCA) The worldwide group of organizations devoted to the physical, intellectual, social, and spiritual well-being of young men. No longer limited to young people, Christians, or even men in some localities, the YMCA was first established in London in 1844 and in the United States in 1851. Their Web site address is http://www.ymca.net

"young Turks" A popular designation for ambitious, newer members of a political or industrial organization who seek to change the status quo.

Young, Whitney M. (1921–1971) Social worker and *civil rights* leader who led the *National Urban League* through the civil rights movement in the early 1960s while serving as president of several social work organizations.

Young Women's Christian Associations (YWCA) The worldwide group of organizations devoted to educating young women spiritually, socially, and physically. These organizations originated in boarding houses for young women in London in 1855. The first YWCA in the United States was formed in Boston in 1866. Their Web site address is http://www.ywca.org

Youngdahl, Benjamin (1897–1970) Social work educator who delineated the principles of social activism for the profession. He helped implement many *New Deal* programs, integrated social work into schools, facilitated doctoral education, and wrote the influential 1966 text *Social Action and Social Work*.

Younghusband, Eileen (1902–1981) A major organizer of British social work. Younghusband helped establish Great Britain's *citizen's advice bureaus (CABs)* during World War II and the modern British juvenile court system and helped redevelop the *International Association of Schools of Social Work (IASSW)*. Her classic social work texts include *Social Work and Social Change* (1964) and *Casework with Families and Children* (1965).

youth services organizations Privately funded and administered federated organizations, usually with chapters or recreational facilities in most communities in the United States, in which the purpose is to help young people achieve their developmental potentials. They focus on educationally oriented recreation, handicrafts, and sports activities designed to help youngsters keep physically fit and emotionally healthy while learning social skills, practical coping strategies, and moral conduct. Among the many groups of this type are the *Boy Scouts, Girl Scouts/Girl Guides,* the *Boys and Girls Clubs of America,* the *Young Men's Christian Association (YMCA),* the *Young Women's Christian Association (YWCA),* the *Young Men's and Young Women's Hebrew Associations (YM–YWHA),* and the *4-H Clubs.*

Youthbuild A *HUD* program to help school dropouts obtain meaningful employment skills and on-the-job work experience in a construction trade. HUD awards grant funds to contractors that employ and train qualified young applicants. Their Web site address is http://www.hud.gov/progdesc/youthb.cfm

"yuppies" Slang term for young urban professionals. The expression has given rise to similar terms such as "buppies" (black urban professionals), "suppies" (senior citizens), "guppies" (gay men

and lesbians), "luppies" (Latinos), and "puppies" (poor urban professionals).

zakat Giving charitable donations, a requirement of those faithful to Islam; that portion of a Muslim's income that must be allocated for *alms* to poor people. See also *tzedakah.*

zar A *culture-bound syndrome,* found more commonly in North African and Middle Eastern nations, in which an individual seems to experience possession by spirits and engages in behavior such as detachment, refusal to carry out daily tasks and functions, shouting, singing, laughing, and crying.

zeitgeist From the German for "spirit of the time," the characteristic feelings or thoughts of a people in a given period.

zero-based budgeting In social administration, the process of evaluating the entire future plan for the financial operation of the organization without reference to past expenditures. Each new financial plan starts from zero. Thus, the organization does not simply study whether to increase or decrease funds for each of its units but considers the objectives of the organization and means of achieving them.

zero population growth A state of stability in the population in which the number of births and deaths are equal. Advocates suggest that this is to be achieved through improved *sex education, contraception, family planning,* and sometimes tax penalties for those who have more children than prescribed. Population stability is a policy goal for some nations and an international movement supported by those concerned about the social, economic, and environmental costs of the expanding world population. A formal organization, also known as Zero Population Growth, was established in 1968 to promote these goals; its Web site address is http://www.zpg.org

zero-sum orientation In *social planning,* budgeting, and management, the perspective that the available resources are relatively fixed so that an increased expenditure of funds or resources in one sector must be accompanied by a commensurate decrease of funds or resources in another.

zero tolerance policies An organization's or government's explicit ruling that a specified intentional act will result in some sanction, including expulsion. For example, a school district's zero tolerance for the possession of drugs can result in the offending student being temporarily or permanently expelled.

zidovudine (ZVD) treatment   A medical treatment administered to HIV-positive pregnant women to reduce the risk of perinatal HIV transmission.

Zionism   The worldwide social movement in which the goal is to help maintain and develop the nation of Israel, primarily through fundraising, political advocacy in nations having relations with Israel, the facilitation of immigration to Israel, and public relations campaigns. The movement officially started in 1897. The World Zionist Congress, the principal organization, has no official connection with the government of Israel.

zone of transition   An urban area that is in the process of decline of its infrastructure, land value, and general living conditions for the inhabitants. This term is usually reserved for downward transition, although it could mean upward movement as well. See also *gentrification*.

zoning   Municipal rules about the use of land and the types of structures permitted on the land.

zoonoses   An infectious disease that can spread from animals to humans.

zoophobia   Pathological *fear* of animals.

Zwingli, Huldreich (1484–1531)   Reformation clergyman who developed a public welfare plan for the poor people of Zurich and later the rest of Switzerland. The model was emulated by many other cities and states. The system provided work, education, and nutrition; some protections for children, older people, and people with disabilities; and a system of fundraising to pay for the program.

zygote   A fertilized cell; the cell that forms when an ovum and a spermatozoon are united.

Milestones in the Development of Social Work and Social Welfare

B.C.E. 2500　In Egypt, papyrus scrolls, called "The Books of the Dead," are placed in many pyramids, spelling out the acts of mercy that are a king's duty, including caring for sick and hungry people and providing relief for homeless people.

B.C.E. 1750　In Babylonia, King Hammurabi issues his code of justice, which includes a requirement that the people help one another during times of hardship.

B.C.E. 1200　In Israel, the Jewish people are told that God expects them to help poor and disadvantaged people, widows, orphans, and elderly people.

B.C.E. 530　Siddhartha Gautama, the Buddha, begins teaching that the path to enlightenment includes love and charity for others.

B.C.E. 500　Philanthropy, from the Greek word for "acts of love for humanity," is institutionalized in the Greek city–states. Citizens are encouraged to donate money, which is used for the public good. Parks are built; and food, clothing, and other goods are kept in public facilities to be used for people in need.

B.C.E. 300　In China, the *Analects* of Confucius declare humans to be social beings bound to one another by *Jen*, a form of sympathy that is often expressed through helping those in need.

B.C.E. 100　In Rome, the *annona civica* tradition—in which patrician families distribute free or low-cost grain to all Roman citizens in need—is well established.

C.E. 30　Jesus Christ teaches that people's love for one another is God's will. He emphasizes the importance of giving to those who are less fortunate ("Inasmuch as ye have done it unto one of the least of these my brethren, ye have done it unto me").

313　Christianity is legalized by the Roman emperor Constantine. The more affluent converts can donate funds openly, and the church is able to use these funds to care for poor people.

400　"Hospitals" are developed and extended throughout India. These facilities provide shelter for poor and disabled homeless people and resemble almshouses rather than modern hospitals.

542　Hospitals similar to those in India have spread to China and the Middle East and now make their first appearance in Europe. The first of these, the Hôtel Dieu ("house of God") is established in Lyons, France, and is staffed primarily by religious workers and volunteers.

600　With the fall of the Roman Empire, Pope Gregory organizes programs to help poor people; the church replaces the state as the "safety net."

650　The followers of the Prophet Muhammad are told that they have an obligation to poor people and that paying a *zakat* ("purification tax") to care for poor people is one of the Five Pillars (obligatory duties) of Islam.

787　Clergy establish the first modern foundling hospital (orphanage) for abandoned children in Milan, Italy.

1084　Almshouses for poor and disabled people, similar to the hospitals in France, are established in Canterbury, England.

1100　The Roman Church issues the *Decretum*, a compilation of its canon law, which includes an elaborate discussion of the theory and practice of charity. It states that rich people have a legal and moral obligation to support poor people.

1140　Norman King Roger II decrees that only physicians with licenses issued by the government may practice medicine.

1200　Maimonides (Rabbi Moses ben Maimon), the Jewish philosopher from Spain, writes his "laws of charity," which assert that the most effective way to help poor people is to discourage dependency and promote self-reliance through education and opportunity.

1215 King John of England signs the *Magna Carta*, which establishes some human rights (for the nobility). It is considered a forerunner of modern civil rights law.

1348 The social system of feudalism begins to break down, partly because of bubonic plague, which kills nearly one-third of the population of Europe. Without the protection of the barons and lords, the serfs and peasants are at the mercy of economic and military threats.

1349 The Statute of Labourers is issued in England, requiring people to remain on their home manors and work for whatever the lords want to pay. Begging and almsgiving are outlawed except for older people and those unable to work. For the first time, a distinction is made between the "worthy poor" (older people, disabled people, widows, and dependent children) and the "unworthy poor" (able-bodied but unemployed adults).

1452 The first "professional association" is formed in Regensburg, Germany, for midwives.

1525 Swiss Reformation clergyman Huldreich Zwingli develops a system of public welfare for the poor of Zurich, a model emulated in many other European cities.

1526 Juan Luis Vives, a Spaniard living in northern Europe, develops a plan for organized relief. The plan includes registering poor people, raising private funds to help them, and creating employment for able-bodied poor people. Many of his ideas were later used in European cities and influenced the Poor Laws in England and colonial America in the next century.

1529 The city–state of Venice enacts a poor law requiring licensing for people seeking alms and some public service work in order to get the license.

1531 England's first statute dealing with poor relief is issued. The statute empowers local justices to license certain people (older and disabled people) to beg in their own neighborhoods and to give harsh punishment to any unlicensed beggars. To implement this law, the justices develop criteria and procedures for deciding which persons to license. Thus, each applicant is evaluated by representatives of the justices.

1536 The Henrician Poor Law, also known as the Act for the Punishment of Sturdy Vagabonds and Beggars, is established. The government of Henry VIII classifies types of poor people and establishes procedures for collecting voluntary donations and disbursing funds. The law requires that these procedures be carried out at the local rather than the national level. It also acknowledges that the state rather than the church or volunteers must play some role in caring for poor people.

1572 England can no longer depend on voluntary contributions to care for its poor people. A national tax, the Parish Poor Rate, is levied to cover these costs. This is accompanied by the registration of people needing relief. Funds left over from poor relief are used to create jobs for able-bodied people.

1601 The Elizabethan Poor Law is established. Built on the experiments of the earlier Henrician Poor Law (1536) and the Parish Poor Rate (1572), this legislation becomes the major codification of dealing with poor and disadvantaged people for more than 200 years. It also becomes the basis for dealing with poor people in colonial America. The Poor Law keeps the administration of poor relief at the local level, taxes people in each parish to pay for their own poor parishioners, establishes apprentice programs for poor children, develops workhouses for dependent people, and deals harshly and punitively with able-bodied poor people.

1624 Virginia Colony enacts legislation to provide for the needs of disabled soldiers and sailors.

1625 Father Vincent de Paul (canonized as St. Vincent de Paul in 1737) establishes seminaries, religious orders, and charitable organizations to care for the poor people of France and is the founder of organized charity in Europe. In many of those nations that do not become Protestant during the Reformation, the church rather than the state retains more responsibility for the care of poor people.

1642 Plymouth Colony enacts the first poor law in the New World, based on the Elizabethan Poor Law of 1601.

1647 Rhode Island Colony establishes a law to appoint an overseer to coordinate efforts to relieve the poor and find work for the able-bodied unemployed.

1650 The influence of Martin Luther, John Calvin, and others has become established and manifested as the Protestant ethic, a philosophy that becomes influential in England, parts of Europe, and the American colonies. It emphasizes self-discipline, frugality, and hard work and leads many of its adherents to frown on those who are dependent or unemployed.

1657 The first private welfare organization in America, the Scots' Charitable Society, is established in Boston.

The first almshouse in colonial America is established in Rensselaerswyck, New York; soon almshouses are developed in many other cities.

1662 The Law of Settlement and Removal is established in England as one of the world's first "residency requirements" in determining eligibility to receive help. Municipal authorities are authorized to help only poor local citizens and to expel from their jurisdictions anyone else who might become dependent for assistance. This law causes authorities to evaluate people as to the likelihood of their becoming poor. Thus, although the law is basically harsh and punitive, some efforts to look at the causes of poverty are codified.

1679 Writ of habeas corpus is instituted in England.

1692 Indentured servitude begins in Massachusetts. The law establishes "binding out," a system in which homeless children can be placed with other families and work for them for a specified time to compensate for their care. This model becomes a norm in many other jurisdictions in colonial America.

1697 The workhouse system is developed in Bristol and soon spreads throughout England and parts of Europe. The system is designed to keep down poor taxes by denying aid to anyone who refuses to enter a workhouse. These institutions are usually managed by private entrepreneurs who contract with the legal authorities to care for the residents in exchange for using their work. Residents—including very young children, disabled people, and very old people—are often given minimal care and are worked long hours as virtual slaves.

1711 David Hume's *Treatise of Human Nature* uses the experimental method in problems of mental functioning and human nature.

1729 Ursuline Sisters of New Orleans establishes America's first residential institution for orphaned children. The private facility provides a home for children and some mothers who survived epidemics and Indian massacres.

1773 The Colonies' first hospital for mentally ill people is established in Williamsburg, Virginia.

1776 The U.S. Declaration of Independence is signed; it argues for freedom, but not for the freedom of slaves.

1777 Prison reform efforts begin in England and the United States after John Howard's study reveals inhumane treatment of prisoners.

1782 The Gilbert Act is passed in England, enabling humanitarians, appalled by the exploitation of workhouse residents, to institute reforms in many English jurisdictions. Many workhouses are closed, assistance to poor people in their own homes is established, and children younger than six are placed with families. Many private entrepreneurs are replaced by municipal employees as managers of the remaining workhouses.

1787 The U.S. Constitution is adopted. Its preamble includes the phrase "promote the general welfare," which places social welfare at the mainstream of political concern. However, the Constitution does not outlaw slavery and permits each slave to be counted for census purposes as three-fifths of a person.

Richard Allen and Absolom Jones begin the nation's first formal social welfare agency, the Free African Society, in Philadelphia.

1790 The first publicly funded orphanage in the United States is established in Charleston, South Carolina.

1791 The Bill of Rights becomes part of the U.S. Constitution as its first ten amendments.

1793 Former slave Katy Ferguson establishes a school for children of all races who live in New York almshouses. The school, later known as the Murray Street Sabbatical School, helps educate hundreds of children and provides an extensive range of child welfare services.

1795 The Speenhamland system is inaugurated. In the English district of Speenhamland, a "poverty line" is developed, and some workers are made eligible for subsidization whenever their wages are below this amount. The amount is based on the price of bread and the worker's number of dependents. As prices increase or wages decline, the public treasury makes up the difference.

1797 Massachusetts enacts legislation on behalf of mentally ill persons, declaring them to comprise a special class of dependents.

1798 The U.S. Public Health Service is established.

Thomas Malthus publishes his *Essay on the Principle of Population As It Affects the Improvement of Society.*

1807 The slave trade (but not slavery) is abolished in England.

1808 Congress outlaws importing African slaves into the United States.

1812 Dr. Benjamin Rush publishes the first American psychiatric textbook, *Medical Inquiries and Observations upon Diseases of the Mind.*

1813 Child labor legislation is passed in Connecticut, requiring factory owners employing children to teach them reading, writing, and arithmetic.

1817 Gallaudet School for the deaf is established in Hartford, Connecticut.

1818 Societies for the Prevention of Pauperism are established in larger American cities to help organize relief efforts for the poor.

1819 Scottish preacher and mathematician Thomas Chalmers assumes responsibility for Glasgow's poor. He develops private philanthropies to help meet the economic needs of poor people and organizes a system of volunteers to meet individually and regularly with disadvantaged people to give them encouragement and training.

1824 The Bureau of Indian Affairs (BIA) is established in the United States. It is the first federal organization to attempt to provide direct assistance in the welfare of some Americans.

New York establishes the first public institution for juvenile delinquents.

1830 The National Negro Conventions begin in Philadelphia and thereafter meet periodically in various cities to provide a regular forum for discussion about the civil rights and health and welfare of people of color and women.

1833 Antoine Frédéric Ozanum establishes the St. Vincent de Paul Society in Paris, using lay volunteers to provide emergency economic and spiritual assistance to poor people.

1834 The new Poor Law is established in England to reform the Elizabethan Poor Law (1601). The underlying emphasis of the new law is on self-reliance. Public assistance is not considered a right, and government is not seen as responsible for unemployed people. The principle of "less eligibility" (a recipient of aid can never receive as much as does the lowest paid worker) is enforced.

1835 The Reverend Joseph Tuckerman, a Unitarian minister who is influenced by the reports of Thomas Chalmers' work in Scotland, organizes the Boston Society for the Prevention of Pauperism. This organization uses many of Chalmers's principles of individualized work with poor families, volunteer visitors, coordinated fundraising, and social action. Tuckerman's organization is influential in the subsequent development of the Charity Organization Societies (COSs).

1836 Laws offering some protection for child laborers are enacted in Boston.

1837 Ohio becomes the first state to establish an institution for blind people.

1841 Dorothea Dix's campaigns for the mentally ill lead many states in the United States to build public mental hospitals.

1843 Robert Hartley, using the teachings of Thomas Chalmers, Joseph Tuckerman, and French philanthropist Baron de Gerando, establishes the New York Association for Improving the Condition of the Poor. Soon imitated in many other American cities, the association stresses character building as a way to end poverty. Volunteers, usually middle-class Protestant laypersons, work to get poor people to abstain from alcohol, become more self-disciplined, and acquire the work ethic.

1844 The Young Men's Christian Association (YMCA) is founded in London.

Parisian nuns establish the first "day care" facility for infants of mothers working away from home.

1845 As a result of the social movement led by Dorothea Dix, the first state asylum for mentally ill people is established in Trenton, New Jersey.

1847 The British Factory Act restricts the working day for women and children to 10 hours, down from 13 to 18 hours a day.

1848 Feminists establish women's rights goals at Seneca Falls, New York; these include women's suffrage, legal rights, and equal opportunities in education and jobs.

The nation's first minimum wage law is passed in Pennsylvania.

Karl Marx and Friedrich Engels publish *The Communist Manifesto*.

1850 Old Age Insurance is established in France.

Massachusetts establishes a school for "idiotic" and "feeble-minded" youths.

1851 Mary Carpenter establishes reformatory schools for juvenile offenders.

The Young Men's Christian Association (YMCA) is founded in North America.

Traveler's Aid is founded in St. Louis.

1853 The Reverend Charles Loring Brace, concerned about the plight of New York's poor children, organizes the Children's Aid Society. The society transports thousands of children every year to the West to live with rural families.

1854 President Franklin Pierce vetoes legislation to provide national programs of charity and help

for mentally ill people, claiming these are the province of the states and localities. This policy remains in the United States until 1935.

1855 The first Young Men's Hebrew Association (YMHA) is founded in Baltimore.

The Young Women's Christian Association (YWCA) is founded in England.

1860 The Food and Drug Act is established in Great Britain.

1861 The U.S. Sanitary Commission is established; its original mission was to organize women volunteers to help care for infirm Civil War combatants.

1862 Congress establishes the U.S. Department of Agriculture (USDA).

The Homestead Act (Ch. 75, 12 Stat. 392) is passed, giving 160 acres of unoccupied public land to any American citizen who agrees to live on it for five years. Much of this land has become available by displacing Indian groups.

The Port Royal Experiment, a federally authorized but voluntarily funded relief organization, is established to help destitute abandoned slaves in border and southern states.

Freedmen's Aid Societies are established in the northern states to assist former slaves with education and supplies.

1863 President Abraham Lincoln issues the Emancipation Proclamation declaring freedom for slaves in all areas of the Confederacy still in rebellion against the United States.

Massachusetts establishes a State Board of Charities to investigate and supervise its almshouses, prisons, and mental institutions. Other states soon follow suit.

The Red Cross is established in Switzerland by writer Jean Henri Dunant, and soon there are Red Cross and Red Crescent organizations in many other nations.

1864 French sociologist and engineer P. G. Frédéric Le Play completes the first scientific study of poverty—its extent, causes, consequences, and possible solutions.

1865 The U.S. Constitution adds the 13th Amendment, which abolishes slavery in all parts of the United States.

At the end of the Civil War, the United States establishes its first federal welfare agency, the Freedmen's Bureau, as part of the War Department, to provide temporary relief, education, employment, and health care for the newly released slaves.

Octavia Hill begins London tenement dwelling reforms.

1866 The Young Women's Christian Association (YWCA) establishes its first group in Boston. YWCAs soon develop in many major cities and establish programs for helping women and their children, including child care facilities, boarding houses, and community organizing.

1867 Mary Prout establishes the Independent Order of Saint Luke, an African American women's organization to provide mutual self-help and advocacy; the order was considered the beginning of the Womanist movement.

1868 Orphans are boarded in private family homes in Massachusetts with the use of public funds.

1869 In London, the first Charity Organization Society (COS) is established. Formally named the "Society for Organising Charitable Relief and Repressing Mendicity," the society works to coordinate efforts at fundraising and to disburse funds in a systematic fashion. Volunteers get to know the applicants on an individual basis, assess the reasons for their poverty, and help them find ways to improve their circumstances.

1870 Social Darwinism gains influence. Herbert Spencer's thesis is that "survival of the fittest" should apply to human society and that poverty is merely an aspect of natural selection. Helping poor people, it is believed, can make them lazy and nonindustrious.

The 15th Amendment to the U.S. Constitution is ratified, guaranteeing each citizen (not including women) the right to vote, regardless of race, color, or previous condition of servitude.

The Board of Charities in Massachusetts designates agents to oversee children placed in foster homes.

1872 The Freedmen's Bureau is abolished.

Charles Loring Brace publishes *The Dangerous Classes of New York and Twenty Years' Work Among Them*, which raises U.S. consciousness about the plight of urban poor people.

The American Public Health Association (APHA) is established.

1873 Octavia Hill establishes training activities for voluntary charity workers in her London Society for the Prevention of Pauperism.

1874 The National Conference of Charities and Corrections (which evolves into the National Council on Social Welfare) is established.

The Women's Christian Temperance Union (WCTU) is established. Under the presidency of Frances Willard (1878–1896), the WCTU fights not only against drinking, but for many social reforms, including child labor, public health, and women's suffrage.

1877 The Society for Prevention of Cruelty to Children is formed in New York by E. T. Gerry.

Using the London organization as his model, the Reverend S. Humphreys Gurteen establishes America's first Charity Organization Society (COS) in Buffalo, New York. Volunteer workers dispense advice rather than money to poor people and information about them to philanthropists and private relief agencies. A sign at the doorway of the Buffalo COS reads "No relief here!" Within a decade, COSs are established in most larger cities, and many are giving direct financial relief to needy people.

1878 The Reverend William Booth reorganizes his East London Revival Society as the Salvation Army.

Susan B. Anthony drafts the women's suffrage amendment, which is introduced in the U.S. Senate. (After years of consideration, the Senate defeats the proposal in 1887.)

1881 Clara Barton establishes the American Red Cross.

Booker T. Washington establishes the Tuskegee Institute to help African Americans become economically and socially independent through academic and vocational education.

1883   In newly united Germany, Chancellor Otto von Bismarck establishes a national health insurance system and, shortly thereafter, accident insurance and old age and invalid insurance programs. This system becomes a model for social security programs in many other nations, excluding Great Britain and the United States.

1884   Toynbee Hall, the first settlement house, is established in London by Vicar Samuel A. Barnett. The settlement movement spreads quickly, and facilities are developed in most larger British and American cities. Their philosophy is to eliminate the distance between socioeconomic classes by locating settlements in working-class neighborhoods where ideas and information can be exchanged.

1885   Harvard professor Francis Peabody begins teaching courses in social problems and social reform.

1886   Stanton Coit, who had resided in Toynbee Hall, opens America's first settlement house, the Neighborhood Guild, in New York. Eventually, more than 400 houses are established. Their residents are involved in social advocacy, group work, and community development.

1889   In Chicago, Jane Addams and Ellen Gates Starr open Hull-House, which becomes one of the most influential social settlement houses in the United States.

1890   In England, activists establish the Consumer League to fight for better conditions in the work environment and safer products for the public.

Jacob A. Riis publishes *How the Other Half Lives,* which reveals the squalid conditions of New York's poor through photos and text. The book encourages public consciousness and legislation for public housing and other benefits for poor people.

1891   *Neighborhood Guilds,* the first text to conceptualize the settlement house movement, is published by Stanton Coit.

1892   Journalist Ida B. Wells publishes the first comprehensive survey of lynchings of African Americans and begins the antilynching campaign.

1893   Lillian Wald and Mary Brewster found the Nurses Settlement in New York, one of the beginnings of public health nursing. The Nurses Settlement later becomes the Henry Street Settlement.

1894   Amos G. Warner publishes *American Charities,* a text that formulates principles of poor relief and programs to assist those in need.

Japan's first social welfare law, the Indigent Person Relief Regulation, is enacted, requiring families to care for disabled, ill, and frail elderly people and children.

1895   Chicago's School of Social Economics at Chicago Commons is established by Graham Taylor and others and begins offering lectures for volunteer poverty workers, friendly visitors, and settlement house workers. Many consider this program to mark the founding of modern social work. By 1903, the school is known as the Chicago School of Civics and Philanthropy and offers a yearlong program.

The first systematic investigation of immigrant communities in the United States is published by Hull-House researchers, including Jane Addams, Florence Kelley, and others. The document, *Hull-House Maps and Papers,* demonstrates the value of settlements as research sites and sociological laboratories.

1896   In *Plessy v. Ferguson,* the U.S. Supreme Court upholds the "separate but equal" doctrine, which gives legal sanction to segregated schools and other facilities.

A training program for London's volunteer and paid charity workers begins. Organized by the British Women's University Settlement, the National Union of Women Workers, and the London Charity Organization Society (COS), the 18-month program was given concurrently with field work in COS district offices.

The National Association of Colored Women is founded by Josephine Ruffin, Mary Church Terrell, and others to organize mutual self-help efforts in the African American community and to campaign for improved conditions, rights, and opportunities.

1898   The New York School of Philanthropy (later to become the Columbia University School of Social Work) begins a series of summer workshops and training programs for volunteers and friendly visitors. Later, a one-year educational program is established.

1899 Charity Organization Society administrator Mary E. Richmond, who also served on the faculty of the New York School of Philanthropy, publishes *Friendly Visiting Among the Poor* (originally titled *A Handbook of Charity Workers*).

The National Consumers League (NCL) is founded by social worker–lawyer Florence Kelley and Josephine Shaw Lowell, who became its first president. The NCL, formed from many community leagues, leads successful campaigns to abolish child labor practices and to achieve minimum wages and shorter working hours as well as safe and effective consumer products.

The Institute for Social Welfare Training, a two-year full-time course in "methodical, theoretical and practical training" in social services, is established in Amsterdam, The Netherlands. Many consider this to be the first true school of social welfare in the world.

The American Hospital Association (AHA) is established to develop and maintain standards in the nation's health care facilities.

Chicago establishes the nation's first juvenile court.

1900 Educator Simon N. Patten coins the term "social workers" and applies it to friendly visitors and settlement house residents. He and Mary E. Richmond dispute whether the major role of social workers should be advocacy or delivering individualized social services.

The National Negro Business League is founded.

1901 U.S. citizenship is granted to some Indians residing on reservations. Citizenship for all Indians born in the United States is not granted until the 1924 Indian Citizen Act.

1902 Homer Folks, founder and head of the New York State Charities Aid Association, publishes *Care of Destitute, Neglected and Delinquent Children*. His philosophy becomes influential in subsequent child welfare goals and methods.

1903 Graham Taylor and others reorganize the Chicago School of Social Economics to establish the Chicago School of Civics and Philanthropy, with the first full-year educational program for those engaged in social service. (In 1908, this school becomes the University of Chicago School of Social Service Administration.)

The U.S. Department of Commerce and Labor is established; it is divided in 1913.

American farm workers of Mexican and Japanese descent organize the first successful farm-labor union; the American Federation of Labor refuses to recognize it.

1904 Robert Hunter publishes the classic text *Poverty*, which delineates the extent of, causes of, consequences of, and possible solutions to the problem of poverty.

1905 A social services department is established in Massachusetts General Hospital in Boston to help patients deal with the social problems of their illnesses. Hospital director Richard L. Cabot, MD, hires Garnet I. Pelton to establish this department. Within the next decade, more than 100 hospitals hire hospital social workers.

1906 School social work programs are introduced in New York and other cities.

Upton Sinclair's novel *The Jungle* leads to the U.S. Pure Food and Drugs Act (Ch. 3915, 34 Stat. 768).

1907 Psychiatric social work begins at Massachusetts General Hospital when social workers M. Antoinette Cannon and Edith Burleigh are hired to work with mentally ill patients.

The United States passes laws governing immigration.

Margaret Slocum Sage establishes the Russell Sage Foundation, named for her late husband. The foundation helps fund the early organizations, research, and publications that become the knowledge base of the new field of social work.

Paul Underwood Kellogg, editor of the early social work journal *Charities and the Commons*, heads the "Pittsburgh Survey" research team, which systematically investigates the conditions of the working people of that city; his grim findings and recommendations about working conditions, occupational safety, child exploitation, and excessive work hours lead to major reforms. Other social workers emulate this social survey technique in other communities. Later, in 1909, Kellogg changes the name of his journal to *Survey* (an important social work research journal).

1908   Congress enacts workers' compensation laws, the first public social insurance program in the United States.

Pittsburgh Associated Charities is founded as the first community welfare council in the nation.

The mental hygiene movement begins with publication of Clifford Beer's book *A Mind That Found Itself.*

1909   The National Association for the Advancement of Colored People (NAACP) is founded. Social workers Mary White Ovington and Henry Moskowitz and others help establish this voluntary organization, oriented toward the protection of the legal and social rights of African American people and other groups.

President Theodore Roosevelt convenes the first White House Conference, bringing together social workers and other leaders to discuss the problems of America's children.

1910   Several states pass "workmen's compensation laws" to supplement the 1908 federal legislation. These laws offer protection to wage earners from the economic risks of injury or unemployment. By 1920, all but six states have some form of workers' compensation program.

Dr. George E. Haynes and others found the National Urban League (originally the National League on Urban Conditions Among Negroes). Haynes also establishes the first social work training program for black people at Fisk University in Nashville.

Boy Scouts of America, Camp Fire Girls, and Catholic Charities are founded.

1911   Great Britain passes the National Insurance Act, which organizes a health and compensation program paid for by contributions from workers, employers, and the public.

States begin passing widows' and mothers' pension programs, the first forms of public assistance to mothers of dependent children. More than 40 states pass some form of mothers' pension programs between 1911 and 1920.

The National Federation of Settlements (later known as the United Neighborhood Centers of America) is established.

The Charity Organization Societies (COSs) become oriented increasingly toward helping families. Many local societies change their names to Family Welfare Agency.

The National Alliance for Organizing Charity is renamed the American Association for Organizing Family Social Work. By 1946, this organization is known as the Family Service Association of America, then Family Service America (FSA) in 1983, and in 1995 Families International, Inc.

1912   The U.S. Children's Bureau is created, headed by social worker and former Hull-House resident Julia Lathrop. She is the first woman to head a U.S. government bureau.

Girl Scouts of America is founded as part of the Girl Guides/Girl Scouts movement.

1913   The U.S. Department of Commerce and Labor is divided. The U.S. Department of Labor is formed primarily to promote the welfare of American workers. The U.S. Department of Commerce is primarily for the welfare of American business.

The Board of Education of Rochester, New York, Public Schools initiates a "visiting teacher" (school social worker) program. Other social work services in schools have been established earlier in New York, Boston, and Hartford, but have been funded through private organizations.

1914   The Harrison Narcotics Acts (Ch. 1, 38 Stat. 785) becomes U.S. law, establishing the government organization later known as the Bureau of Narcotics; the act makes the sale and use of certain drugs a criminal offense.

The Boston Psychopathic Hospital establishes a social services department and uses the title "psychiatric social worker" for the first time.

1915   In an address to the National Conference of Charities and Corrections (NCCC), Abraham Flexner declares that social work has not yet qualified as a profession, especially because its members do not have a great deal of individual responsibility and because it still lacks a written body of knowledge and educationally communicable techniques.

Margaret Sanger publishes *Family Limitation*, the first book on birth control.

1916 The U.S. Child Labor Act (Ch. 676, 520 Stat. 1060) becomes law, forbidding interstate commerce of goods manufactured by child labor. In 1918, the U.S. Supreme Court declares the law unconstitutional.

The American Birth Control League (renamed "Planned Parenthood Federation of America in 1939) is founded. Its principal founder, Margaret Sanger, also opens the first birth control clinic in Brooklyn, New York.

Social worker and suffrage activist Jeannette Rankin is the first woman elected to serve in the U.S. Congress.

1917 Mary E. Richmond publishes *Social Diagnosis* (New York: Russell Sage Foundation). Social workers use her book as a primary text and as an answer to Abraham Flexner's 1915 report.

The first organization for social workers is established. The National Social Workers Exchange exists primarily to process applicants for social work jobs. Later the group becomes the American Association of Social Workers (AASW) and eventually, with other organizations, becomes the National Association of Social Workers.

The National Jewish Welfare Board is created to coordinate the work and fundraising of Jewish social agencies. The board is renamed the Jewish Community Centers Association of North America in 1990.

U.S. citizenship is granted to Puerto Ricans.

1918 The American Association of Hospital Social Workers (AAHSW) is formed as the first specialty within the new field. The organization is renamed the American Association of Medical Social Workers (AAMSW) in 1934.

Ida M. Cannon, director of medical social work at Massachusetts General Hospital, delineates the principles of medical social work.

Smith College, Northampton, Massachusetts, establishes the first training program for psychiatric social workers.

The Community Chests and Councils of America (renamed the United Way in 1970) are organized. Local organizations with "Community Chest" and other names have started earlier in Denver, Cleveland, and other cities.

The Vocational Rehabilitation Act (Ch. 107, 40 Stat. 617) becomes law, providing occupational training and prostheses for handicapped veterans of World War I. The program expands in 1920 to cover some nonveterans.

The U.S. Women's Bureau within the U.S. Department of Labor is established. Led by Mary Anderson, the bureau conducts research about women's lives and labor and develops protective labor legislation for women.

1919 The 17 schools of social work that exist in the United States and Canada form the Association of Training Schools for Professional Social Work to develop uniform standards of training and professional education. This group is later renamed the American Association of Schools of Social Work (AASSW), which later merges with the National Association of Schools of Social Administration (NASSA) to become the Council on Social Work Education (CSWE).

Social workers employed in schools organize as the National Association of Visiting Teachers.

1920 The Child Welfare League of America (CWLA) and the National Conference of Catholic Charities are established.

The 19th Amendment to the U.S. Constitution gives women the right to vote.

The League of Women Voters is founded.

Unemployment insurance is established in Great Britain and Austria.

1921 The American Association of Social Workers (AASW) is formed out of the National Social Workers Exchange. AASW is the first social work professional association and merges into the National Association of Social Workers in 1956.

The U.S. Sheppard–Towner Act (Maternity Act, Ch. 135, 42 Stat. 224) goes into effect. Federal funds are granted to state health departments to provide for the pre- and postnatal health care of needy mothers and infants. Nearly 3,000 child and maternal health centers are established nationwide, and the nation's infant and maternal mortality rates drop significantly. Nevertheless, the program is dropped in 1929.

Social work educator Eduard C. Lindeman publishes *The Community* (New York: Republic Press), in which the basic concepts of community organization are delineated.

Japan's Women's College establishes that nation's first school of social welfare.

1923 Grace Coyle begins teaching the first social work course in social group work at Western Reserve University in Cleveland.

The Tufts Report on social work education is completed (*Education and Training for Social Work*, by James H. Tufts), formally delineating the components necessary to provide adequate education for social workers. The report recommends training students in bringing about improvements in society as well as in individuals.

The National Social Work Council is formed. In 1945, it was renamed the National Social Welfare Assembly and eventually becomes known as the National Voluntary Health and Social Welfare Organization.

1924 The Atlanta School of Social Work is established as the first professional social work school primarily for African Americans.

The University of Chicago's School of Social Service Administration appoints the first woman dean, Edith Abbott.

Ida M. Cannon, a founder of the American Association of Hospital Social Workers and director of medical social work at Massachusetts General Hospital, publishes the first book on the subject, *Social Work in Hospitals.*

New U.S. immigration laws drastically reduce the number of immigrants permitted and establish the "national-origins system," which permits far more immigration from Northern Europe and virtually none from Asia and Africa. The national origins quota system is modified but is retained until after the 1965 McCarran–Walter Act amendments.

The Snyder Act establishes that all Native Americans are full U.S. citizens with all the rights and responsibilities of all other citizens.

1926 The American Association of Psychiatric Social Workers (AAPSW) is founded, as social work increasingly includes caseworkers and clinical practitioners.

The first union for social workers, the American Federation Workers (AFW), is organized in New York by workers in Jewish philanthropies.

The American Association of Schools of Social Work begins certifying professional schools of social work.

The U.S. Veterans Bureau (now U.S. Department of Veterans Affairs) begins employing social workers in its hospitals.

The Canadian Association of Social Workers (CASW) is founded.

1927 Edith Abbott and Sophonisba Breckinridge of the University of Chicago School of Social Service Administration begin publishing the *Social Service Review,* the first research-based social work journal.

1928 The Milford Conference convenes to discuss whether social work is a disparate group of technical specialties or a unified profession with integrated knowledge and skills. The conclusion is that social work is one profession with more similarities than differences among its specialties. In 1929, the report of the conference is published as *Social Case Work: Generic and Specific* (New York: American Association of Social Workers).

The International Council of Social Work (ICSW) is founded in Paris.

1929 The stock market crashes, heralding the Great Depression.

The International Association of Schools of Social Work (IASSW) is founded.

The Russell Sage Foundation begins publishing the *Social Work Yearbook.* In 1951, publication is taken over by the American Association of Social Workers. In 1965, it is renamed the *Encyclopedia of Social Work,* published by the National Association of Social Workers.

1930 The American Public Welfare Association (APWA) is established.

Virginia Robinson, who with Julia Jessie Taft developed the "functional school" in social casework, publishes the first comprehensive text to integrate social and psychodynamic concepts, *A Changing Psychology in Social Casework* (Chapel Hill: University of North Carolina Press).

Grace Coyle publishes the first comprehensive text on social group work, *Social Process in Organized Groups* (New York: Richard R. Smith).

1931 Social worker Jane Addams becomes corecipient of the Nobel Peace Prize.

The "rank and file" movement, made up mostly of public assistance workers, begins its campaign to unionize social work and reform society. By 1934, it begins publishing the influential journal *Social Work Today*.

1932 The Emergency Relief and Construction Act (Ch. 520, 47 Stat. 709) becomes law, bringing the U.S. federal government into public welfare funding for the first time.

The American Association of Schools of Social Work establishes the minimum requirement for accrediting its schools as one academic year of professional education, including classroom and field instruction.

1933 President Franklin D. Roosevelt proclaims a "New Deal" for Americans and establishes major social welfare programs to combat poverty and unemployment. Programs include the Civilian Conservation Corps (CCC), the Civil Works Administration (CWA), the Federal Emergency Relief Administration (FERA), and later the Works Progress Administration (WPA). Social workers Harry Hopkins and Frances Perkins are appointed to the highest relevant positions, Hopkins as head of FERA and Perkins as U.S. Secretary of Labor (the first woman to head a cabinet department).

Through FERA, Harry Hopkins begins a federal grant program establishing public assistance offices in the states. Each office has to have at least one trained social worker on its staff. FERA awards training stipends for this purpose to schools of social work.

Der Kreis, the world's oldest known "homophile" organization is founded in Zurich, Switzerland; it is disbanded in 1968.

1934 Puerto Rico passes a law regulating social work practice. This is the first time social work is legally regulated in any U.S. state or territory.

The National Housing Act (Ch. 847, 48 Stat. 1246) becomes law to promote home construction for federal employees.

The Wheeler–Howard Indian Reorganization Act becomes law, emphasizing greater self-determination for Indian tribes on reservations; the provisions of the law are largely ignored by the federal government until the early 1970s when Indian civil rights groups protest to the Bureau of Indian Affairs.

1935 The U.S. Social Security Act (Ch. 531, 49 Stat. 620) is signed into law. It includes a workers' retirement insurance program and coverage for dependent survivors and disabled workers. The act also establishes a federal welfare program that helps states pay for and administer programs in Old Age Assistance (OAA), Aid to the Blind (AB), Aid to Dependent Children, and General Assistance (GA) for needy people who do not qualify for other forms of help.

The Works Progress Administration (WPA) is established to provide jobs for able-bodied but destitute workers.

The National Conference on Social Work recognizes social group work as a major function of social work.

Social worker Jane Hoey is appointed head of the U.S. Bureau of Public Assistance. She influences the state departments of public assistance so that qualified applicants for help receive counseling as well as income maintenance. She sees to it that professional social work education is a requirement for public assistance administrators.

Alcoholics Anonymous (AA), the nation's first self-help organization, is established in Akron, Ohio, and becomes the prototype for many other self-help groups such as Gamblers Anonymous, Narcotics Anonymous, and Parents Anonymous (for those who abuse their children).

1936 Group workers begin regular meetings and form the American Association for the Study of Group Work, an association that in 1946 becomes the American Association of Group Workers (AAGW).

1937 The American Association of Schools of Social Work (AASSW) declares that beginning in 1939 the requirement for social work accreditation will be a two-year master's degree program. The master of social work (MSW) degree becomes a requirement to be considered a professional social worker.

1938 The Federal Housing Administration (FHA) begins its home-loan guarantee program to encourage home ownership.

Japan establishes its Ministry of Health and Welfare.

1939 The Lane Report (*The Field of Community Organization*, by Robert P. Lane) presents a systematic and comprehensive description of the roles, activities, and methods in the field of community organization. The work builds on previous studies by Eduard C. Lindeman's 1921 book, *The Community*, and Jesse F. Steiner's 1930 book, *Community Organization*.

President Franklin D. Roosevelt launches the first Food Stamp Plan to help families hurt by the Great Depression. The program ends during the postwar economic upturn and is reauthorized permanently in 1964.

1940 Mary Parker Follett's posthumous book *Dynamic Administration* is published; it becomes an influence in the field of social welfare administration.

1941 The Fair Employment Practices Committee (FEPC) is established to monitor and correct discrimination practices in the U.S. labor market. FEPC is abolished in 1945.

The United Services Organization (USO) is formed by several national social service organizations, including the Salvation Army, the Jewish Welfare Board, Catholic Community Service, Traveler's Aid, YMCA, and YWCA. USO coordinates and provides services to armed forces and related personnel.

1942 The *Beveridge Report* is issued in Great Britain, recommending an integrated social security system that attempts to ensure cradle-to-grave economic protections for its citizens. Many of the report's recommendations go into effect after World War II.

The Lanham Act (Ch. 14, 56 Stat. 11) is passed in the United States for the first federal funding for day care for children of working mothers.

The National Association of Schools of Social Administration is organized by colleges with undergraduate social work programs. In 1952, it merges with the American Association of Schools of Social Work (AASSW) to become the Council on Social Work Education (CWSE).

Wartime labor shortages lead to the Bracero Program, in which workers from Mexico and other nations are employed on American farms. The program is reinstated after the war in 1951 and is criticized for exploiting these workers and keeping American farm workers underpaid and underemployed.

The Congress of Racial Equality is established.

1943 Social agencies begin charging modest fees for clients who can afford them.

The Marsh Report is issued in Canada. Based partly on Britain's Beveridge Report, it establishes the guidelines for the Canadian social welfare system.

1944 The G.I. Bill, formally known as the Servicemen's Readjustment Act (Ch. 268, 58 Stat. 284), is enacted to provide educational and vocational training opportunities for returning veterans of World War II. It also provides for loans for purchase of homes, farms, or business properties; job counseling and placement; and one year's adjustment allowance.

Native American tribes from 27 states form the National Congress of American Indians (NCAI).

1945 World War II ends. On October 24, the United Nations is established, with many agencies for dealing with world social welfare problems, including the United Nations Children's Fund (UNICEF); the World Health Organization (WHO); the United Nations Educational, Scientific, and

Cultural Organization (UNESCO); and the United Nations High Commission for Refugees (UNHCR).

The U.S. Federal Security Administration publishes social worker Charlotte Towle's book *Common Human Needs*. (The federal government stops publication in 1951 and burns its remaining copies because of complaints by medical associations that it advocates government-funded health care. The American Association of Social Workers begins publishing and distributing the book later in 1951.)

California becomes the first state to pass a social work regulatory act, a registration law.

1946　Great Britain establishes its National Health Service.

After meeting in special study groups since 1936, group workers formally organize as the American Association of Group Workers (AAGW).

The Association for the Study of Community Organization (ASCO) is established.

The National Mental Health Act (Ch. 538, 60 Stat. 423) is passed, establishing the National Institute of Mental Health (NIMH) and encouraging states, through grants, to develop and upgrade community and institutional mental health services.

The Hill–Burton Act (Hospital Survey and Construction Act, Ch. 958, 60 Stat. 1040) is passed, providing federal funds to develop new hospital facilities.

The School Lunch program is established. Cash and commodities are supplied to the states, municipalities, and schools to ensure that poor children have adequate midday nutrition.

Emily Green Balch, social reformer and social work educator, receives the Nobel Peace Prize.

1947　More than 1 million war veterans enroll in colleges under the G.I. Bill.

1948　Member nations in the United Nations ratify the Universal Declaration of Human Rights, which asserts social and political rights, including freedom from discrimination on the basis of race, color, sex, language, religion, political opinion,

property, or other status; freedom of religion; security for children and the aged; and rights to employment, shelter, food, and education.

1949　The Social Work Research Group (SWRG) is formally established.

1950　The Social Security Act is amended to broaden coverage for children and those relatives with whom needy children are living and to aid people who are permanently and totally disabled.

The first licensing for independent social work practice goes into effect in San Diego, California.

The Mattachine Society and One, Inc., gay rights organizations (then called "homophile" groups), are established.

The Evangelical Social Work Conference (now known as the North American Association of Christians in Social Work) is established.

U.S. federal programs begin to relocate Native Americans from reservations to urban areas.

1951　The Hollis–Taylor Report is published as *Social Work Education in the United States* (New York: Council on Social Work Education) and recommends a more generic orientation. Many of its recommendations are adopted.

1952　The Council on Social Work Education (CSWE) is formed through a merger of the American Association of Schools of Social Work (AASSW) and the National Association of Schools of Social Administration (NASSA)—the two competing organizations that had been setting standards for schools of social work. CSWE is soon granted the authority to accredit graduate (master of social work) schools of social work.

The McCarran–Walter Act (Immigration and Nationality Act, Ch. 477, 66 Stat. 163) is enacted to codify the requirements for immigration and naturalization into the United States. The law retains a quota system that permits many more people from Northern European nations to come to the United States than people from Asia, Africa, or Latin America. The national origins quota system remains in effect until 1968.

1953　The U.S. Department of Health, Education, and Welfare (HEW) is established.

1954 The U.S. Housing Act of 1954 (Ch. 649, 68 Stat. 590) becomes law, establishing a massive urban renewal program in most American communities.

In social casework, the so-called "diagnostic" and "functional" schools begin to merge and lose their separate identities. The functional school has followed a highly focused, goal-oriented approach to casework intervention. The diagnostic school has been influenced by Freudian theory, but adherents of this approach develop more of a psychosocial orientation in the 1950s.

In *Brown* v. *Board of Education of Topeka, Kansas,* the U.S. Supreme Court rules that racial segregation in public schools is unconstitutional.

1955 On October 1, the National Association of Social Workers (NASW) is created through the merger of seven organizations—the American Association of Social Workers (AASW), the American Association of Medical Social Workers (AAMSW), the American Association of Psychiatric Social Workers (AAPSW), the National Association of School Social Workers (NASSW), the American Association of Group Workers (AAGW), the Association for the Study of Community Organization (ASCO), and the Social Work Research Group (SWRG). Membership is limited to members of the seven associations and to master's degree–level workers graduating from accredited schools of social work.

The National Association of Puerto Rican Hispanic Social Workers is created.

Rosa Parks refuses to move to the back of a public bus in Montgomery, Alabama, precipitating the bus boycott led by Dr. Martin Luther King, Jr. This action begins the modern civil rights movement.

Daughters of Bilitis, America's first major lesbian organization, is established.

1956 The International Federation of Social Workers (IFSW) is established and includes national social work professional associations.

The Council of International Programs (CIP) is founded in Cleveland to facilitate an exchange program in social work education between the United States and 110 other nations.

The profession's major journal, *Social Work,* begins publication.

1957 The U.S. Commission on Civil Rights is created by federal law (P.L. 85-315) to enforce civil rights laws, including school desegregation.

Martin Luther King, Jr., and others establish the Southern Christian Leadership Conference (SCLC).

1958 The National Defense Education Act of 1958 (P.L. 85-864) is passed, providing federal aid to all levels of public and private education in the United States. The act stresses education in mathematics, sciences, and foreign languages and gives extensive funding for low-interest student loans.

The National Commission on Social Work Practice, chaired by Harriett Bartlett, completes the NASW-published book, *A Working Definition of Social Work Practice,* which delineates the profession's values, purposes, and methods.

1959 The first professional school of social work to focus exclusively on social policy and planning is established in Waltham, Massachusetts. It is the Florence Heller Graduate School for Advanced Studies in Social Welfare at Brandeis University.

Social Work Curriculum Study, a 13-volume evaluation and recommendation for improved social work education, edited by Werner Boehm, is published (New York: Council on Social Work Education).

1960 The Delegate Assembly of the National Association of Social Workers adopts the first *NASW Code of Ethics.*

1961 The federal government allows states to include unemployed parents in Aid to Families with Dependent Children (AFDC) payments if they elect to do so.

The White House Conference on Aging develops plans for effective care for the nation's older people. Its work leads to the Older Americans Act of 1965 (P.L. 89-73).

The National Association of Social Workers (NASW) organizes the Academy of Certified Social Workers (ACSW), restricted to NASW members with accredited master of social work (MSW) degrees, two years' agency experience under certified social work supervision, and adherence to the *NASW Code of Ethics*. ACSW membership requirements are subsequently revised to include testing and professional recommendations.

1962 The Council on Social Work Education (CSWE) recognizes community organization as a legitimate specialization for social work education. CSWE adopts an accreditation standard specifically banning discrimination for race, ethnicity, and religion. (A ban on gender discrimination is added in 1977.)

Michael Harrington's book, *The Other America*, is published.

President John F. Kennedy signs into law the social security amendments, which provide greatly increased federal support for states to employ social workers and others. The workers would provide counseling and training to help people get off the welfare rolls.

Cesar Chavez organizes the United Farmworkers of America.

The Manpower Development and Training Act (P.L. 87-415) becomes U.S. law to help train unemployed workers.

1963 In *Gideon v. Wainwright*, the U.S. Supreme Court rules that all needy defendants in criminal cases have the right to free legal counsel.

The Joint Commission on Mental Illness and Health issues its findings. President John F. Kennedy signs into law the Community Mental Health Centers Act (P.L. 88-164), which funds development of mental health centers, training programs, and outpatient treatment programs.

The civil rights "March on Washington" convenes at the Lincoln Memorial to hear Martin Luther King, Jr., Whitney M. Young, and others.

1964 President Lyndon B. Johnson's Great Society programs, established through the Economic Opportunity Act of 1964 (P.L. 88-452), create the Job Corps, Operation Head Start, Volunteers in Service to America (VISTA), the Neighborhood Youth Corps, the Community Action program, and many other programs and expansions of existing programs. Federal funding is also used to train

thousands of social workers and end social work personnel shortages.

The Civil Rights Act (P.L. 88-352) makes racial discrimination in public places illegal in the United States.

Social work student Michael Schwerner and two other young "freedom riders" are murdered by a Mississippi segregationist.

The Food Stamp program (Food Stamp Act of 1964, P.L. 88-525) is enacted. Recipients are required to purchase coupons that are redeemable in food stores. A family of four with a monthly income of $140 could buy $166 worth of coupons for $37.

1965 More Great Society programs and organizations are established and implemented, including Medicare, Medicaid, the Older Americans Act of 1965 (P.L. 89-73), and the Elementary and Secondary Education Act of 1965 (P.L. 89-10).

The U.S. Department of Housing and Urban Development (HUD) is established.

The Voting Rights Act of 1965 (P.L. 89-110) becomes law.

Wilbur Cohen, a social worker and economist who helped found the National Association of Social Workers (NASW) and served on the committee to create the Social Security Act, is appointed Secretary of the U.S. Department of Health, Education and Welfare (HEW), which is to administer most of the Great Society programs.

The U.S. Department of Health, Education and Welfare (HEW) publishes *Closing the Gap in Social Work Manpower*, a study of how to staff social service programs; the work specifies work classifications for various levels of social work and suggests that bachelor's level social workers be included in the profession.

1966 The U.S. Supreme Court issues the *Miranda* decision, requiring that police inform a suspect of his or her constitutional rights before questioning.

The Society for Hospital Social Work Directors is formed. (In 1993, the organization changes its name to the Society for Social Work Administrators in Health Care; in 1997, the name becomes the Society for Social Work Leadership in Health Care.)

1967 The Social Security Act is amended to include a Work Incentive (WIN) program designed to encourage recipients of Aid to Families with Dependent Children (AFDC) to work without losing most of their benefits.

Amendments (P.L. 90-36) to the Social Security Act separate the welfare system's income maintenance features from personal social services. Clerks can replace professionals in administering the income maintenance program. Social workers are needed only to provide personal social services; thus, their role in public welfare is greatly diminished. A federal administrative rule change permits states to use federal matching funds to contract out social services to private providers.

The National Welfare Rights Organization is established to advocate for and organize the people who receive public assistance.

The *In re Gault* decision by the U.S. Supreme Court determines that juveniles have the same constitutional rights as adults. The juvenile court system, which had minimized the adversary process and used social workers as advocates and probation officers, is greatly curtailed.

1968 The Kerner Commission (National Advisory Commission on Civil Disorders) issues its report, blaming white racism and limited opportunities for African Americans as major causes of the strife and rioting in urban ghettos.

The Omnibus Crime Control and Safe Streets Act of 1968 (P.L. 90-351) is passed and establishes the Law Enforcement Assistance Administration (LEAA) to help state and municipal governments control crime, rehabilitate offenders, recruit and train corrections officers and police, and improve correctional facilities.

The Office of Economic Opportunity (OEO) and War on Poverty programs start to dismantle. Within the next three years, many programs are abolished, while others are downgraded and placed within other federal agencies, especially the Community Service Administration.

In the "Poor People's March" on Washington, D.C., thousands of America's poor set up "Resurrection City," a camp on the Mall, to call world attention to the plight of the disadvantaged. Social workers

and other professionals volunteer their skills to help the residents achieve their goals.

The National Association of Black Social Workers (NABSW) and the National Association of Puerto Rican Social Service Workers (NAPRSSW) are founded.

The American Indian Movement (AIM) is established.

1969 Membership in the National Association of Social Workers (NASW), once restricted to people with master of social work (MSW) degrees, is opened to social workers with qualified bachelor's degrees. The NASW Delegate Assembly approves the resolution to pursue licensing of social work practice within each state.

The Association of American Indian Social Workers (now called the National Indian Social Workers Association) and the Asian American Social Workers organizations are established.

The Nixon administration proposes the Family Assistance Plan (FAP) to reorganize the nation's welfare program. The plan, which authorizes a minimum guaranteed annual income and incentives to encourage people to work, is not enacted.

The Stonewall gay rights movement begins. Riots break out in Greenwich Village, New York, at the Stonewall Inn, where gay patrons resisted efforts by police to arrest them for "indecency." The action provokes gay men and lesbians across the world to show support by resisting government efforts to discriminate against people on the basis of sexual orientation.

1970 The environmental movement leads the first annual celebration of Earth Day.

1971 The federal ACTION agency is formed to centralize government-sponsored volunteer agencies such as the Peace Corps and VISTA.

The National Federation of Societies for Clinical Social Work (NFSCSW) is established. (In 1977, its name becomes the Clinical Social Work Federation.)

The National Association of Social Workers (NASW) establishes the Educational Legislative Action Network (ELAN). Its political action functions are later assumed by local NASW chapters and by other NASW bodies at the national level. NASW's Academy of Certified Social Workers establishes a national examination, which must be passed to qualify for ACSW certification.

1972 The Supplemental Security Income program (P.L. 92-603) is enacted, which combines and federalizes public assistance for adult poor, aged, blind, and disabled people. The State and Local Fiscal Act (P.L. 95-512 permits federal revenue sharing with states for local administration of specified social services and other programs.

The National Institute on Drug Abuse is created (P.L. 92-255) to coordinate the national effort to prevent, control, and treat substance abuse problems.

The Equal Employment Opportunity Commission (EEOC) is created (P.L. 92-261) to implement and enforce national policy of nondiscrimination in the workplace for reasons of race, color, gender, religion, or national origin.

Title IX, a part of the Education Amendments Act (P.L. 92-318) abolishes sex discrimination in any educational program, including athletics, that receives federal funding.

Wyatt v. Stickney establishes the legal principle that patients are entitled to treatment, care, and habilitation when involuntarily confined to public mental hospitals.

The Asian American Mental Health Federation is established.

1973 The *Roe* v. *Wade* decision determines that state laws prohibiting abortion are unconstitutional.

Public Health Service social worker Peter Buxton, MSW, exposes the government's Tuskegee Syphilis Experiment conducted by the Public Health Service in 1930–1972 in which African American males were unknowing subjects of dangerous experimentation.

The American Psychiatric Association (APA) removes "homosexuality" from its list of mental disorders.

1974 CETA (the Comprehensive Employment and Training Act, P.L. 93-203) provides job opportunities and education for disadvantaged people.

Section 8 of the Housing and Community Development Act of 1974 (P.L. 93-383) helps low-income people live in housing provided by the private sector at fair market value.

The Equal Credit Opportunity Act (P.L. 93-495) prohibits discrimination in credit based on gender or marital status, among other criteria.

The Council on Social Work Education (CSWE) accredits educational programs that offer bachelor's degrees in social work. NASW recognizes undergraduate education as the first professional level of practice. NASW's six levels of practice are defined as social work fellow (doctorate or equivalent), certified social worker (ACSW), graduate social worker (MSW), social worker (bachelor's degree with a social work major), social service technician, and social service aide.

The Child Abuse Prevention and Treatment Act (P.L. 93-247) becomes law, establishing the National Center on Child Abuse and Neglect (NCCAN). (In 1978, this law is expanded to cover improvements in the nation's adoption system.)

The U.S. Supreme Court rules that public schools must provide bilingual programs for students who speak little or no English.

The International Association of Schools of Social Work publishes its *World Guide to Social Work Education*. The publication discusses professional social work education in each country where it has been established, including the Netherlands (established in 1899); Germany (1904); Canada (1914); France and South Africa (1916); United Kingdom and Switzerland (1918); Norway and Belgium (1920); Sweden and Austria (1921); Kenya (1924); Chile and Finland (1925); Ireland and Australia (1933); Portugal (1935); India (1936); Denmark, Egypt, and Uruguay (1937); Brazil and Columbia (1945); Panama (1946); Korea (1937); Jamaica, Greece, and Lebanon (1948); New Zealand, Japan, and the Philippines (1950); Singapore (1952); Pakistan, Sri Lanka, and Thailand (1954); Ghana and Indonesia (1956); Italy (1957); Israel, Venezuela, and Bangladesh (1958); Turkey (1961); and Uganda (1963).

1975 Personal social services, work training, housing and community development, and juvenile justice and delinquency programs become law. The amendment to the Social Security Act known as Title XX (P.L. 93-647) becomes the major source of funds for personal social services. Each state is reimbursed by the federal government for helping individuals achieve economic self-support and independence, preventing and remedying neglect and abuse, and reducing and preventing improper institutional care.

The Education for All Handicapped Children Act of 1975 (P.L. 94-142) becomes law, requiring that the nation's public schools provide equal educational opportunities for children with handicaps and learning disabilities.

The professional journal *Health & Social Work* begins publishing.

1976 The National Association of Social Workers (NASW) establishes Political Action for Candidate Election (PACE).

The Rural Social Work Caucus is formed (at the first National Institute on Social Work in Rural Areas) to coordinate the activities of social workers who serve nonmetropolitan people.

1977 President Jimmy Carter's "Jobs and Income Security Program" (to revise the nation's welfare system) fails to win congressional approval.

The Group for the Advancement of Doctoral Education in Social Work (GADE) is formed.

Big Brothers of America and Big Sisters merge to become Big Brothers/Big Sisters of America.

The journal *Social Work Research & Abstracts* begins publishing.

1979 The U.S. Supreme Court rules that welfare benefits must be paid to families left needy by the mother's loss of her job, just as to families in which the father becomes unemployed.

The American Association of State Social Work Boards (AASSWB) is incorporated to coordinate the procedures and activities of state licensing for social workers. The organization is now known as the Association of Social Work Boards (ASWB).

1980 The U.S. Department of Health and Human Services (HHS) is established when the Department of Health, Education and Welfare is divided. The U.S. Department of Education is established as an independent cabinet-level department.

The British government's *Barclay Report* is completed, defining the roles and tasks of social workers in public assistance and personal social services. It states that social workers should be more involved in social care planning and counseling, promoting community networks, negotiating, and social advocacy.

The Adoption Assistance and Child Welfare Act of 1980 (P.L. 96-272), which provides programs for children, including subsidized adoptions, changes in foster home care, and day care facilities, is passed.

The Parental Kidnapping Prevention Act of 1980 (P.L. 96-611) clarifies laws pertaining to parental custody rights and obligations and helps state and local law enforcement agencies coordinate their efforts to reunite children with their custodial parents.

The National Association of Perinatal Social Workers is incorporated.

1981 The Omnibus Budget Reconciliation Act of 1981 (P.L. 97-35) and the social services block grants are established to fund social services programs at the state level with reduced federal scrutiny and funding and to decentralize social services programs to states.

Computers in Social Services Network is founded to link people, resources, and ideas about the use of computers in human services.

1982 The proposed Equal Rights Amendment (ERA) for sexual equality fails to be ratified by two-thirds of the states by the deadline required by law.

The Job Training Partnership Act (P.L. 97-300) and the Emergency Job Bill (P.L. 97-404) are enacted. This legislation replaces many CETA public service job training programs and seeks to encourage state governments and private industry to train needy people for suitable employment.

The Tax Equity and Fiscal Responsibility Act of 1982 (P.L. 97-248) is enacted, cutting back social services funding as well as Medicare, Medicaid, Aid to Families with Dependent Children (AFDC), Supplemental Security Income (SSI), and unemployment compensation.

The Association for the Advancement of Social Work with Groups (AASWG) is formally established, after several years of preparation. It publishes the journal Social Work With Groups.

1983 The National Association of Social Workers (NASW) establishes the National Peer Review Advisory Committee and trains social workers to evaluate the work of other social workers to promote accountability and to meet quality control requirements of government and third-party funding organizations.

1985 The Canadian Health Act is established to provide universal comprehensive health care.

The National Network for Social Work Managers is established as an independent professional association for social service administrators and managers.

The Academy of Forensic Social Work (AFSW) is established by the National Organization of Forensic Social Work to develop, promote, and revise standards of certification for those who practice forensic social work.

The academic journal *Computers in Human Services* begins publication.

1986 The Family Services Administration (FSA) is created as a unit within the U.S. Department of Health and Human Services (HHS). It consolidates the six major federal low-income programs (Aid to Families with Dependent Children [AFDC], Work Incentive [WIN] program, Community Services Block Grants, Low-Income Home Energy Assistance, Refugee Assistance, and the Child Support Enforcement program).

The Immigration Reform and Control Act of 1986 (P.L. 99-603) establishes new criteria for immigration and opportunities for U.S. residents of illegal alien status to become citizens.

1987 The National Association of Social Workers (NASW) establishes the Center for Social Policy and Practice to coordinate the exchange of information, education, and policy formulation pertaining to social work and social welfare in the United States.

The first compilation of terms related to social work, *The Social Work Dictionary,* by Robert L. Barker, is published by NASW.

The International Conference on Human Services Information Technology Applications (HUSITA) is established; thereafter, annual meetings are held throughout the world.

The McKinney Homeless Assistance Act (P.L. 100-77) is established to coordinate national efforts to assist homeless people.

ACT UP (AIDS Coalition to Unleash Power) is formed as an international militant organization to advocate for gay rights and improved efforts to deal with the AIDS epidemic.

1988 The U.S. government formally apologizes and makes some financial reparations to Japanese Americans who were interned during World War II.

1990 The Americans with Disabilities Act of 1990 (P.L. 101-336) makes it illegal to discriminate against disabled people in terms of employment opportunity in businesses with more than 15 employees.

Ryan White Comprehensive AIDS Resources Emergency Act (P.L. 101-381) is established to provide funding for the prevention, early intervention, and treatment of HIV infection and for planning for communities affected by HIV disease and the AIDS epidemic.

NASW's School Social Work Specialist credential is created.

1991 The Academy of Certified Baccalaureate Social Workers (ACBSW) is established.

1993 The Family and Medical Leave Act of 1993 (P.L. 103-3) becomes law, requiring larger U.S. companies to permit employees job-protected unpaid leave to care for family members.

The Family Preservation and Support Services part of the Omnibus Budget Reconciliation Act (P.L. 103-66) provides funds for child welfare programs.

The Brady Bill (Brady Handgun Violence Prevention Act, P.L. 103-159) is passed to limit access to handguns in the United States.

1994 AmeriCorps is established to facilitate volunteer human services efforts in American communities.

The International Convention on the Elimination of All Forms of Racial Discrimination is ratified by the United States and many other nations.

The *Person-in-Environment System* is published by the NASW Press to enable social workers to classify and code problems of psychosocial, health, and environmental functioning.

1995 The U.S. National Voter Registration Act goes into effect, giving U.S. citizens easier access to voter registration while applying for government services.

The U.S. government signs the International Convention on the Rights of the Child treaty.

1996 President Bill Clinton signs into law the Personal Responsibility and Work Opportunity Reconciliation Act, a reform program to "end welfare as we know it." The program restricts or eliminates many entitlement programs for the poor, including Aid to Families with Dependent Children (AFDC), to be replaced by the Temporary Assistance to Needy Families (TANF) programs, and severely restricts many other programs such as Supplemental Security Income (SSI) and nutrition programs.

The *NASW Code of Ethics,* which originated in 1960, is revised.

In *Jaffee v. Redmond,* the U.S. Supreme Court decides social workers, in federal courts, have rights of privileged communication with clients.

1997 The Omnibus Consolidation Appropriations Act of 1997 (P.L. 104-208) restores some of the social service funding eliminated by the Personal Responsibility and Work Opportunity Reconciliation Act of the previous year.

1998 Social work in the United States celebrates the centennial of professional social work education, recognizing more than 100 years of social work's contribution to the well-being of individuals, families, communities, society, and the natural environment.

1999 The "Ticket to Work Act" (P.L. 106-170) makes it possible for Americans with disabilities to join the workforce without losing Medicaid and Medicare eligibility.

2000 The Human Genome Project announces and publishes the first complete sequencing of the genetic blueprint for human beings.

2001 Education reform is attempted through the "No Child Left Behind Act" (P.L. 107-110), requiring annual state tests in basic subjects to children in grades three through eight. Schools in which students do not improve to the specified standard can be restaffed, and poor students in those schools can receive extra tutoring or transportation to other schools.

2002 The U.S. Department of Homeland Security is created (P.L. 107-296), primarily to prevent terrorist attacks within the United States and to minimize the damage from potential attacks and natural disasters. The department incorporates many existing federal agencies.

2003 The Immigration and Naturalization Service (INS) is dissolved and replaced by two distinct agencies, the Bureau of Citizenship and Immigration Services (CIS) and the Border and Transportation Security Directorate (BTS). Both agencies are part of the U.S. Department of Homeland Security.

MORE RESOURCES FROM NASW PRESS!

The Social Work Dictionary, *5th Edition,* *Robert L. Barker.* The dynamic vocabulary of social work, like the profession itself, continues to grow and become more complex. Since the first edition of *The Social Work Dictionary* in 1987, this essential reference work has been recognized as the definitive lexicon of social work. Now in its fifth edition, the *Dictionary* captures more than 9,000 terms, cataloging and cross-referencing the nomenclature, concepts, organizations, historical figures, and values that define the profession. It is used extensively in schools of social work, social service agency libraries, licensing exam preparation centers, and social work offices worldwide. Every social worker—from professor to student, from novice to experienced professional—should own this unparalleled resource for understanding the language of social work and related disciplines!

ISBN: 0-87101-355-X. July 2003. Item #355X. $49.99.

Encyclopedia of Social Work, *19th Edition, 2003 Supplement,* *Richard L. English, Editor-in-Chief.* The *2003 Supplement* is an essential addition to the three-volume *Encyclopedia of Social Work, 19th Edition* and the *1997 Supplement,* widely accepted as the profession's most comprehensive reference work. The *2003 Supplement* features new articles on timely topics, including conservatism and social welfare, issues of multiculturalism and cultural diversity, strengths-based practice, hate crimes, and a variety of economic issues.

ISBN: 0-87101-353-3. June 2003. Item #3533. $42.99.

Encyclopedia of Social Work, *19th Edition, 1997 Supplement,* *Richard L. Edwards, Editor-in-Chief.* The *Supplement* updates the *Encyclopedia* with current concerns in social work and over 400 pages of information, including 30 new entries and 15 new biographies.

ISBN: 0-87101-277-4. 1997. Item #2774. $37.95.

Encyclopedia of Social Work, *19th Edition, Richard L. Edwards, Editor-in-Chief.* Three volumes provide nearly 3,000 pages of information on virtually every aspect of social work. Expanded content areas include new technologies, research, global changes, U.S. policy developments, and evolving roles for social workers.

ISBN: 0-87101-256-1. 1995. Item #2561s. $129.00.

Social Work Speaks, 6th Edition, *NASW Policy Statements 2003–2006.* A comprehensive and unabridged collection of policy statements adopted by the NASW Delegate Assembly in August 2002. More than 60 policy statements, ranging from foster care and adoption to disasters, capital punishment, cultural competence, women's issues, HIV and AIDS, technology, substance abuse, and others are arranged alphabetically and topically for easy reference. For professional value, *Social Work Speaks, 6th Edition* is an unrivaled reference tool that can assist in developing organizational responses to policy issues, conducting policy analysis and study, and working in political action coalitions.

ISBN: 0-87101-354-1. February 2003. Item #3541. $42.99.

(Order form and information on reverse side)

ORDER FORM

Qty.	Title	Item #	Price	Total
___	The Social Work Dictionary	355X	$49.99	_____
___	Encyclopedia of Social Work, 2003 Supplement	3533	$42.99	_____
___	Encyclopedia of Social Work, 1997 Supplement	2774	$37.95	_____
	Encyclopedia of Social Work			
___	Casebound version	2553s	$159.00	_____
___	Softcover version	2561s	$129.00	_____
___	Social Work Speaks	3541	$42.99	_____

POSTAGE AND HANDLING
Minimum postage and handling fee is $4.95. Orders that do not include appropriate postage and handling will be returned.

DOMESTIC: Please add 12% to orders under $100 for postage and handling. For orders over $100 add 7% of order.

CANADA: Please add 17% postage and handling.

OTHER INTERNATIONAL: Please add 22% postage and handling.

Subtotal	_____
Postage and Handling	_____
DC residents add 6% sales tax	_____
MD residents add 5% sales tax	_____
Total	_____

❏ **Check or money order** (payable to NASW Press) for $ _____.

❏ **Credit card**
    ❏ NASW Visa* I ❏ Visa I ❏ NASW MasterCard* I ❏ MasterCard I ❏ Amex

Credit Card Number   Expiration Date

Signature _____

Use of these cards generates funds in support of the social work profession.

Name _____

Address _____

City _____ State/Province _____

Country _____ Zip _____

Phone _____ E-mail _____

NASW Member # (if applicable) _____

(Please make checks payable to NASW Press. Prices are subject to change.)

NASW PRESS
P. O. Box 431
Annapolis JCT, MD 20701
USA

Credit card orders call
1-800-227-3590
(In the Metro Wash., DC, area, call 301-317-8688)
Or fax your order to 301-206-7989
Or order online at http://www.naswpress.org

Visit our Web site at http://www.naswpress.org.   CPDI03